GOD
Bless you!
[signature]

GOD

The Dimensional Revelation

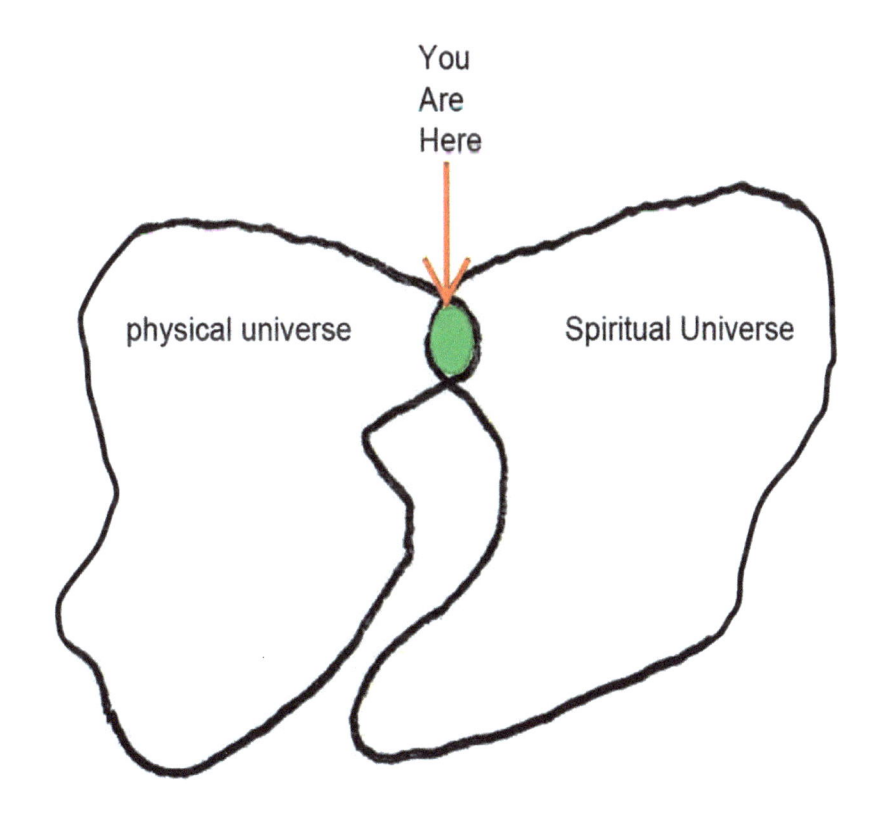

You
Are
Here

physical universe   Spiritual Universe

Allyn Richert

Copyright © 2023 Allyn Richert
All rights reserved
1st Edition—copyright 2020
2nd Edition—copyright 2021
3rd Edition—copyright 2023

PAGE PUBLISHING
Conneaut Lake, PA

First originally published by Page Publishing 2023

ISBN 978-1-6624-7625-9 (pbk)
ISBN 979-8-88960-274-3 (hc)
ISBN 978-1-6624-7626-6 (digital)

Printed in the United States of America

Contents

Chapter 1: Reality and GOD 1
Chapter 2: List of Dimensions 4
Chapter 3: The Revelation 6
Chapter 4: Introduction to Dimensional Reasoning 15
Chapter 5: Dimensions from GOD and Downward Manifestations 25
Chapter 6: Lower Dimensions and The Elevation Toward GOD 51
Chapter 7: Proof of Dimensional Integrity 73
Chapter 8: Observations of the Situation 77
Chapter 9: The Law of Dimensional Limitation 82
Chapter 10: Causation 94
Chapter 11: The Mathematics 101
Chapter 12: The Revelation—Part 2 124
Chapter 13: Dimensions of Our Spiritual Universe 129
Chapter 14: Reverification and Conclusion 156
Chapter 15: Epilogue—The Author's Prayer 160
Chapter 16: Research Notes, Credits, and Expansions 161

CHAPTER 1

Reality and GOD

This is a book Revealing[1a] Reality.[1b] Broadly stated, reality is defined as "all that Exists."[1c] The study of reality is called Metaphysics.[1d] Metaphysics is the primary field of philosophy. Metaphysics is divided into two major fields of study. These are cosmology[1e] and ontology.[1f] Cosmology is the study of the cosmos, which is our entire universe of matter and its attendant energies. Cosmologists are almost Certain[1g] that our universe of matter and its attendant energies[1h] resulted from our big bang[1i] approximately 13.8 billion years ago.

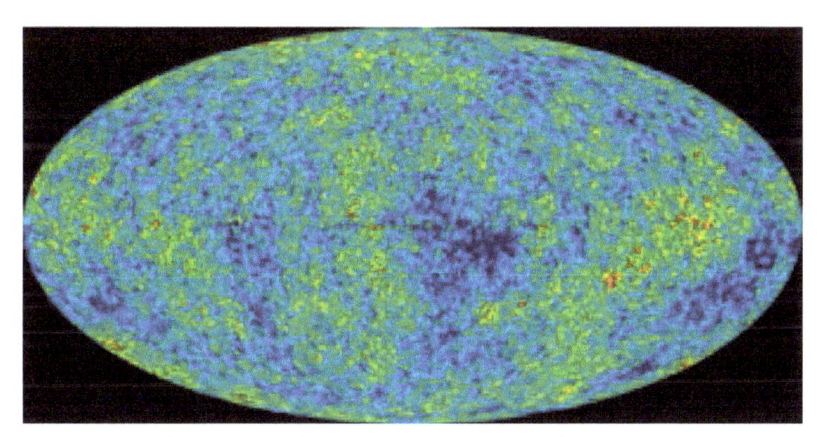

Illustration of the Cosmological Lambda-CDM
Model of Our physical Universe

Theoretical physicists have come to understand, as do the Wise in all generations, that our universe of matter and its attendant energies, also known as our physical universe—though incredibly large—is not all that is Real.

Mathematicians, financiers, scientists, philosophers, and religious persons all develop their systems of understanding what is real and how systems interrelate within the field of ontology. This is necessary to organize and explain data and experiences that are real but are separate from our sciences of physical[1j] reality. Ontological models, such as mathematics,[1k] borrowing and credit, virtual realities,[1l] dimensions,[1m] and Religions,[1n] are among the subjects of ontological Knowledge.[1o]

The image below is offered as an illustration of nonphysical being. It is not comprehensive of ontological reality.

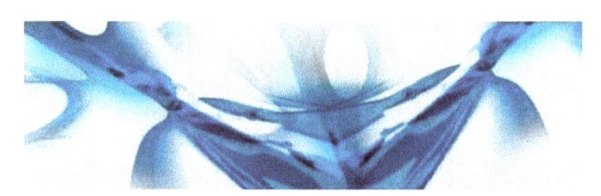

(https://www.slideshare.net/Gloriazlh/instancebased-ontological-knowledge-acquisition/)

Spiritual[1p] Realities are ontological Realities. Cosmologists usually deny or ignore Spiritual Reality because It Is outside their field of study. By definition, Spiritual Realities do not fit cosmological models. *GOD—The Dimensional Revelation* Is Inspired To Clarify both and Reveal A Complete Metaphysics.

Ontology is divided into separate Categories:[1q]

1. The study of realities created by Human Beings to organize and create nonphysical processes within physical reality. Notably, all ontological realities Require The Action Of Spiritual Beings.
2. The study of Nonphysical[1r] Being, such as Spiritual Being or any Other[1s] nonphysical reality, existing beyond the physical cosmos.

Organized in this manner, every manifestation is either cosmological or ontological.

This writing began as a study of physics and the dimensional nature of reality. I explored reality, and as the dimensions became clearly revealed, the Analysis[1t] Yielded Religious Insight. That Insight Is The growing Knowledge that The Divine[1u] Is Operational, Pervading All Of Reality.

GOD[1v] Is Revealed through Creation.[1w] More precisely, GOD Manifests Through Creation. These Manifestations are Reality. All that exists is some type of Manifestation[1x] Of GOD.

Our Theology,[1y] The Philosophy Of GOD, is a scientific study based on Observation and Participation In The Manifestations Of GOD:

1. *Observation*[1z] is Knowledge by sensing, witnessing, deducing, or recording.
2. *Participation*[1z1] is Experience Of and Influence On that which Is Known.

Utilizing Dimensional Reasoning,[1z2] We have the tools to validate[1z3] Our Theology. This is a clear and true Revelation of Aspects Of GOD. This yields the ability to place Religious Experience,[1z4] Dogma,[1z5] Belief,[1z6] and unbelief[1z7] in the correct Perspective.[1z8]

The scientific study of the dimensions of Reality yields an expansion of Our Understanding[1z9] Of The Manifestations Of GOD, which Is All Creation.

The Fullness Of each Situation Is Realized through Knowing which dimensions are in operation. Learn the nature of each dimension and apply this rationally to every Action,[1z10] here and now.[1z11] Dimensional organization of reality and, more specifically, Your Experiences resolves inconsistencies between one point of view and another. Dimensional Reasoning Will Expand Your Understanding, Confidence,[1z12] Personal Power,[1z13] and Grace.[1z14]

It makes Me smile with Reassurance as I explore the most recent theoretical physics,[1z15] such as quantum theory.[1z16] I pry deep into the Vibrations[1z17] and Discover The Presence[1z18] Of The LORD In The 10th Dimension—for no doubt, That Is Part Of GOD, Manifested As All Of This!

This illustration is offered as An Image Of GOD, Manifesting All Of Reality. Instructions Are Given As Information Is Disseminated from the ONE. Our Teaching Is That GOD Is All That Exists. Everything Else That Was, Is, and May Become Is A Manifestation Of GOD.

Note that any Depiction Of GOD Is Incomplete because GOD Is Not Limited.

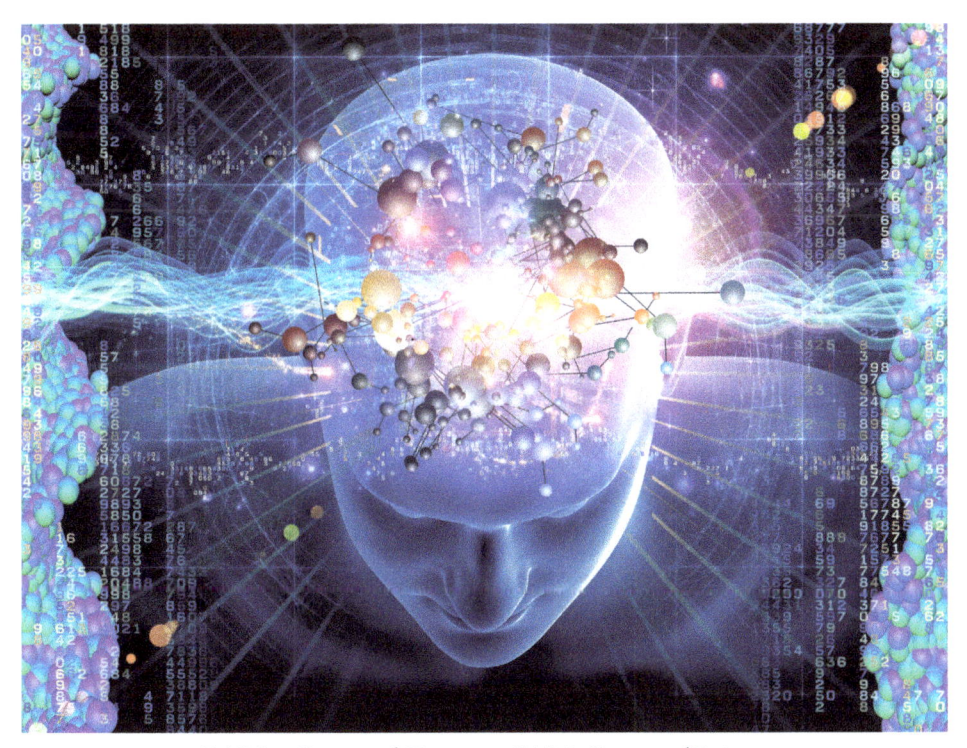

I AM a Spiritual Being at IAMaSpiritualBeing.com; agsandrew/Shutterstock 92366917

CHAPTER 2

List of Dimensions

0th dimension: a point,[2a] a Presence or location where there can be a beginning.

1st dimension: a line,[2b] any two points connect with a straight line.

2nd dimension: a plane,[2c] any three points connect to form[2d] a plane. Other ways to look at this are any two lines crossing each other or any line changing direction horizontally forms a plane.

3rd dimension: a sphere or cube or any other object[2e] or physical set. These are usually lines crossing horizontally and other lines or arcs crossing vertically to form an object. Depending upon the position[2f] from which you observe the object, the 3rd d is described as "depth" as in "How deep is the water in this swimming pool?" or as "height" as in "How high is that building?" Physical reality is manifested as 3-dimensional objects—solid,[2g] liquid,[2h] gas,[2i] plasma,[2j] radiation,[2k] and any other physical object.

4th dimension: time. Time is the continuum[2l] or progression[2m] to the next manifestation of any physical object or energy within the system. The physical continuum is usually manifested as the object changes[2n] or its situation in space changes. These changes are continuous.[2o]

5th Dimension: Choices[2p] and Decisions.[2q] Some objects changing in time are acted upon by the Decisions Of A Being. Many Beings, Each Acting in proximity,[2r] often Affect[2s] Each Other.[2t] When A Spiritual Being[2u] Influences a physical Situation,[2v] there Is A Fusion[2w] Of The Spiritual With the physical.

6th Dimension: Leaps,[2x] Chaos,[2y] Randomness, and Uncertainty.[2z] Some objects cannot be manifested in the ordinary[2z1] 3 dimensions moving through time, but indeed, they are manifested. In fact, the limitations[2z2] of operation (boundaries) of the lower dimensions prohibit certain occurrences.[2z3] Our universe is expanded by leaps of being, making real what was impossible in lower dimensional reality.

7th Dimension: Universes. Our familiar universe[2z4] is a sequential multiverse.[2z5] The sequential multiverse is all possible manifestations and endings of our universe of matter and its attendant energies, originating from our initial big bang.

LIST OF DIMENSIONS

Living Creatures also exist as part of a different 7th Dimensional Universe. That Is Our Spiritual Universe.

8th Dimension: Membrane Systems.[2z6] More than one physical universe can exist. Other physical universes that are not ours may exist. All such physical universes of matter and its attendant energies are part of the physical membrane system.[2z7]

Also, membrane systems that do not operate as any physical universe operates exist. These membrane systems coexist with our universe of matter and its attendant energies. They usually do not relate to one another. The most obvious Is The Membrane System Of Spirit,[2z8] Which Usually Exists separate from physical being.[2z9]

9th Dimension: The Mechanisms[2z10] of Creation. The 9th Dimension Is The Action Of The Processes By Which Membrane Systems Are Created[2z11]—That is, the Processes bringing Reality and its systems into being, continuing those Processes, Merging or Fusing[2z12] those Processes, or not.

We know of at least One Manifesting Reality In Which two Membrane Systems have some Incidence of Fusion with each other. Those are the physical membrane system and The Spiritual Membrane System. One Incidence of this Fusion is the Reality in which You and I are presently Conscious. You Have Grown[2z13] within the partial Fusion of these two huge Membrane Systems During Your Human Life.[2z14]

There is a Subtle[2z15] Metaphysics In The Fusion Presented In Our Conscious Reality. I Know It To Be The LORD Entering My Consciousness for a while To Share The Glory With Me, here and now.

10th Dimension: The WORD[2z16] The WORD May Be Understood To Instruct Information.[2z17] This Information Is Identity[2z18] or What Is Created. Simply stated, The WORD Is The WILL Of GOD. The WORD Is Divine Direction or Instructions[2z19] of What To Create. The WORD Is also The Instructions To Preserve[2z20] What Is Created, as well as The Instructions to Destroy[2z21] Manifest Realities.

11th, GOD: GOD Is Not A Dimension because GOD Is Not Limited.[2z22]

GOD Is The SOURCE.[2z23] GOD cannot be Completely[2z24] Known. However, GOD Is Pervasive.[2z25] GOD Is Infusive,[2z26] A Presence[2z27] In All That Is Real, and GOD Is Accessible;[2z28] so Relations[2z29] Are Established In The Dimensions Of Reality.

CHAPTER 3

The Revelation

This Teaching[3a] Is A Revelation[3b] Of Truth[3c] To The Author. Among those Truths is the dimensional nature of reality.

The concept of a physical "dimension" was introduced by Joseph Fourier in 1822 to categorize physical quantities of the same kind. For example, you can compare the length of a meter to that of a yard because they are in the same dimension length. You cannot compare an inch to a minute because they are not in the same dimension. An inch measures[3d] length (1st dimension). A minute measures time (4th dimension). We Observe that the categories are different, so there are separate dimensions for each category in Our study of Reality. These dimensions have consistent application to the reality We Observe.

Certain scientific theories are reiterated in this Teaching as they enhance Our understanding of the Dimensions. Some theories Presented[3e] are well established, and some need further proof.[3f] They will lead to deeper Understanding of the Dimensions as they are verified. Verified processes will further contribute to Dimensional Reasoning. The Essential Revelation remains True independently of this or that scientific theory offered in support.

This Revelation Is A Gestalt.[3g] A gestalt Is The Perception[3h] of an entire configuration that is more than its individual components. This Revelation Is The Complete and Sudden Understanding that there are two separate Universes, Colliding To Create The Reality That Human Beings[3i] Experience. These are

1. our physical universe[3j] and
2. Our Spiritual Universe.[3k]

Each is vast and independent[3l] from the other. However, small Aspects[3m] Of Our Spiritual Universe Have Become Fused for a period, Incarnate[3n] in physical Beings, To Manifest The Reality In Which Human Beings Live on planet earth.

At The Pleasure Of GOD,[3o] Aspects Of Our Spiritual Universe Have Penetrated the boundaries of our physical universe to present a Glorious Reality of

THE REVELATION

partially Fused Universes, Exhibiting Characteristics[3p] Of Each. This Is The Reality In Which We Live.

We Examine This Revelation Of The Truth. We are scientists and empirical[3q] philosophers, so This Complete and sudden Understanding must be verified by supporting data, leading to the Rational[3r] Conclusions[3s] presented in *GOD—The Dimensional Revelation*.

"Veritas, Veritas, tantum Veritas"[3t] is translated as "The Truth, The Truth, only The Truth." This stands in contrast to deception, crafted to mislead. How Can We Distinguish[3u] The Truth from conjecture or outright falsehood?[3v]

The scientific method gives Us a verifiable procedure to distinguish Truth from falsehood. The scientific method requires that this Revelation be substantiated by observations and data that connect to principles.[3w] That connection[3x] establishes the principles as the Truth, at least in the context of the data and observations. Therefore, data and observations about the reality that We sense allow Us to establish principles or Truths relevant within applicable systems of being.

Furthermore, proofs of process[3y] validate the reasoning. Observations of cause and effect[3z] yield proof of some processes. Conscious Participation in certain events also yields proof of their reality.

This Revelation would be millions of pages long if we explore each observation to its fullest. Important Expansions[3z1] of this Revelation will occur in follow-on Research and Teachings. Some of these have already occurred over millennia, stated in many ways, as the Truth is Undeniable.[3z2]

Information about our physical and Our Spiritual Beings is both recent and ancient Knowledge. Diverse Traditions[3z3] present this Knowledge often in competing or mutually exclusive[3z4] Doctrines.[3z5]

One contribution of This Teaching is to Resolve[3z6] diverse Ideologies[3z7] Dimensionally. Our method of Resolution of diverse and incompatible Ideologies is to Recognize[3z8] the point of view[3z9] from which each Ideology Develops.

The analogy of a miniature Person on one facet[3z10] of a cut diamond will serve to illustrate the validity of different perspectives. Imagine[3z11] that You are a miniature Person on a flat facet of a cut diamond. You are so small that the flat surface You are on extends beyond Your view. All Your Experience has been on this one facet and the space above. The space above is confusing beyond Your reckoning. Broken light[3z12] beams appear from the space below. The beams change as You move around on Your flat surface. Eventually, You explore to the edges of Your facet and find that Your flat surface does not extend infinitely.[3z13] You can view another facet when You reach the edge of Your facet. Coincidentally, You find another miniature Human on the other facet, and You learn to Communicate with Him. You describe how You see the world, and He disagrees. After much discussion, You Agree to step onto His facet of the diamond, and You come to see His worldview. You discover that from His Perspective,[3z14] the world is as He said it is. In return, You Invite Him to step onto Your facet of the diamond. He is distressed because nothing seems correct to Him on Your facet. After much explanation, He comes to Understand that Your facet is in another dimension. Things are different in this dimension. A Friendship[3z15] Develops as You explore other facets of the diamond Together. You can even count the facets, fifty-eight in all, as You complete Your observation of the characteristics of reality on each facet of the diamond. Upon completion of Your journey around the diamond, You Recognize common characteristics of the space above the surface, as well as the light filtering from below. Your scientific study expands as You come to Understand why the space above and the light from below appear different when observed from each different facet. You also organize the facets and come to understand that the entire diamond is one whole thing, with boundaries.

Ideological differences disappear as Knowledge expands. You have made Peace with Your Friend, who Lives on the other facet. Each of You may Choose to Live on Your own separate facets, but at least You can Coexist, Understanding each Other's Point of View. You continue to Share[3z16] Information and Experiences from Your Comfort zone, based on Knowledge rather than ignorance[3z17] or fear of The Other.

Meeting Your Friend on the edge of the facet was somewhat Surprising. The Surprise was that before meeting Him, all Your observations were of things that impacted You. The Conscious[3z18] Reality of Your Friend's Being seems to be in a different category from all the other things on His facet and on Your facet as well. Your study must set up a different Dimension to account[3z19] for the Conscious Reality, the Free Choice,[3z20] and the very Being Of Your Friend.

This example helps Us To Understand dimensional differences in the physical membrane system. It also hints at a nonphysical Reality, which We call Friendship. The Understanding of the physical facets of the diamond is in a different category from the Friendship You Develop through Empathy[3z21] and Understanding Of The Other.

Understanding the 8th Dimension, We have a verifiable metaphysical basis for the reality of the physical membrane system as separate from The Spiritual Membrane System. Revealing this through the 9th Dimension Acting To Create partial Fusion of these entirely independent Membrane Systems explains why Your Consciousness Is separate but Incarnated Into Your physical being To Create The Reality In Which You Live. It also explains why The Operational Principles[3z22] Of Spiritual Being Are different than the operational principles of physical being.

This illustration Is Offered to help Conceptualize The Fusion Of Spiritual Being Into physical reality.

THE REVELATION

Paola Barrescio—Human Radiance/Bigstock 366549154

For example, The Separation of physical reality From Spiritual Reality is why Your Spiritual Being Passes On[3z23] upon the death[3z24] and disintegration[3z25] of Your physical body. Passing Away or Passing On is an ancient Expression That Your Spiritual Being Exists In A Different Membrane System In Which Continuity[3z26] Is Determined[3z27] By The WORD Of GOD In The 10th Dimension, not by the laws of physics in the 8th and 7th dimensions.

This illustration Is Offered as a Depiction Of The Person's Spirit or Soul Passing Away Into Our Spiritual Universe upon the death of The Person's body as He Stands and Separates From our physical universe.

dreamcatcherreality.com@dylanharper2020

GOD—THE DIMENSIONAL REVELATION

The scientific method[3z28] remains Our primary Methodology[3z29] to Verify[3z30] that This Is True. The empirical question, "How do you know?" remains central to the Effort[3z31] to separate the real from the unreal.[3z32] The scientific method is a step-by-step procedure:

1. A specific situation, question, or Hypothesis[3z33] is stated.
    1a. Data[3z34] must be observed and verified relative to a particular situation, question, or hypothesis.
    1b. Verification of data may be established by direct Conscious Experience (Empiricism[3z35] and Phenomenology[3z36]).
    1c. Data may also be verified by Reliable[3z37] instruments[3z38] (instrumentation[3z39]).
    1d. Data may also be verified by mathematical calculation[3z40] (symbolic logic[3z41]).

    Each method of verification has its strengths and weaknesses. Combining verification techniques allows each Observation to be Reverified[3z42] to establish a set of reliable data.

2. Verified data can be organized. Certain occurrences lead to Consequent[3z43] occurrences through cause and effect (logical connection and sequence).
3. There are also changes and proximity relationships[3z44] between items Observed (static[3z45] and dynamic[3z46]).
4. The scientist devises and conducts tests[3z47] that will yield data to either support the hypothesis or reject it. Cause and effect, as well as other relationships, are tested by a procedure designed to isolate individual subjects of interest from which the hypothesis was derived. Accurate[3z48] tests determine the nature of the reality manifested regarding this or that specific question or situation. Results are gathered and organized that prove or disprove the hypothesis.
5. Conclusions[3z49] about Reality are reached. We Accept[3z50] verified conclusions as the Truth (Epistemology[3z51]).
6. Each conclusion provides a useful tool to organize reality and to Guide[3z52] Action (Normative standards[3z53]).
7. These conclusions are reverified by testing again and again as new data is observed.
8. The Truth is modified as conclusions are revised based on new data.
9. In this manner, a collection of verified Knowledge is developed and recorded about What Is Real.
10. Items We know to be real can often be dissected to discover their component parts. More advanced hypotheses can then be developed to advance recorded Knowledge.

11. Items We Know To Be Real can often be combined to yield new items or processes.
Correct[3z54] Conclusions about Reality are essential to basic survival and growth.

Beyond survival, what is Real is also Real to any Observer. What is real also exists even if it is not Observed (numenology[3z55]). Plato originally recognized the concept of a "thing in itself."[3z56] This yields a basic test of the "real." Objective reality exists apart from the Observer. Objective[3z57] reality does not require Observation. For example, this rock that I just picked up off the ground exists whether anyone ever Observes it or not.

Subjective[3z58] realities exist as well. I know that this rock that I just picked up off the ground exists because I sense it (empiricism), so it has meaning to Me (Phenomenon[3z59]). A more subjective and less "real" example is the Dream[3z60] I had last night. The situation seemed real to Me as I was dreaming it. Subjective realities can be meaningful but in a much different way than objective realities.

Personal Conscious Experience is one of Our verification techniques. Have You ever Noticed how Your Conscious Center[3z61] finds certain physical Necessities[3z62] of Your human body to be so strange? Hunger, urination, defecation, the need for sleep, sex all seem so foreign to the ordinary stream of Consciousness.[3z63] That is because physical demands on Your body occur within the biochemical balances[3z64] of our physical universe. Your Consciousness Originates In Our Spiritual Universe. Coping with the demands of our physical situation must be learned when Your Conscious Being Is Incarnated Into physical form. This Self-Verification is one proof of the fusion or our physical universe With Our Spiritual Universe.

Organizing observations according to their dimensional characteristics is useful to advance Thought and Action (normative characteristics). Consider that in 4th-d physical reality, a waterfall is just a waterfall. Gravity forces water to flow downhill in its course to the sea. There is no Consciousness in 4th-d physical reality to Appreciate the Magnificent roar of tons of water cascading Gracefully over the precipice. In physical reality, there is no Perception of the thundering crash of water into the pool below—no Observation of the mist rising or the Elation In Appreciation of the shimmering rainbow appearing in the mist. All Of Those Observations, Perceptions, and Appreciations Are In 5th-Dimension Spiritual Reality. The Spectacle of the waterfall Is A Blessing From GOD Shared With GOD's Living Creatures Who Rise To This Joy.

Our metaphysical research yields some proofs of Reality that This Teaching will establish as Fact.[3z65]

Our research also leads to some inferences that appear to be supported by data available at this time. This Teaching Presents those inferences as hypotheses for which We suggest further verification. Many of Our conclusions regarding the most

GOD—THE DIMENSIONAL REVELATION

recent cosmological debates remain open. You may Contribute to future verification. However, updating cosmological facts has no bearing on the overall Revelation of the Dimensions and Our Fundamental Revelation Of Our Separate Universes of matter and Spirit.

The organization of Observations and Experiences Presented In This Teaching remains A Revelation Of Truth (factuality).

Some of Our conclusions are beyond empirical proof at this time. This Author Encourages[3z66] Seekers[3z67] and Scholars alike to further define or expand upon This Fundamental Revelation Of Reality using the scientific method (observation, verification, analysis/testing, conclusion, use, reexamination, revision, combination).

This Teaching Will Advance many Truths with Which You may not be familiar. If You Have A Strong and Stable Faith[3z68] That does not agree with some of The Principles I now Advance, please Remain Constant[3z69] In Your Faith. Eventually, Your Faith May Grow To Encompass[3z70] Greater Knowledge As You explore Reality. It may also be that GOD Manifests Differently To You.

This Teaching Reveals Many Esoteric[3z71] Ways To Know GOD.[3z72] Each will be meaningless[3z73] unless You Participate In Their Reality. Some would say that One could find some logic or authority to support any assertion or point of view. You and I have examined some of them and found some to be false. You have the tools to verify. Our verification is through the instruments, the mathematics, the scientific method, The Observation, and The Participation In Diverse Realities.

I cannot Tell You About Your Spiritual Journey.[3z74] That Is Uniquely[3z75] Yours. All I Can Tell You Is That You Are On One.

This Illustration Is Offered To Emphasize Your Spiritual Center and Your Conscious Journey In Our Fused, physical and Spiritual Universes.

(https://awaken.com/2016/08/stages-spiritual-awakening-and-faith-what-stage-are-you/)

THE REVELATION

Notations on Grammar

Our words are written to deliver An Intended Meaning. If correctly spoken or written, You Are Led from a correct initial Understanding of a word To Expanded[3z76] Meanings Inherent In The Words. You Are Oriented Toward Deeper[3z77] Meanings As You Participate In The Fulfilling Life Made Possible By Understanding.

Since this is a study of the Dimensional nature of Reality, We will often use the abbreviation *D* meaning "Dimension" rather than spelling the word fully.

The difference between a physical "dimension" and a Spiritual or Fused physical-Spiritual "Dimension" Is Such A Significant Revelation that We Will Capitalize The Word *Dimension* and Abbreviate It As *D* When Referring To A Dimension That Is Spiritual or Fused physical-Spiritual. We will use the word *dimension* abbreviated as *d* when referring to a dimension that is only physical.

The English language has so many words in which the same word may have several different definitions.

In addition to ordinary sentence grammar, I Will Emphasize A Particular Meaning Of A Spiritual Word By Capitalization. I Will Usually Capitalize The First letter Of A Word Describing A Spiritual Reality[3z78] To Distinguish It From a word with the same spelling describing a physical reality, in the context[3z79] of Our Use Of The word. Also, I will not capitalize a negative[3z80] spiritual word.

Foremost Among Spiritual Words Is The Capitalization Of Each Letter To Identify GOD. This Is A Specific Identification Of The Highest Honor.[3z81] It Is not to be confused with "gods"[3z82] that Human Beings have elevated throughout history, erroneously identifying them with The ONE,[3z83] GOD, LORD Of All.

Who or What Is GOD? "Everything" would be too small a description because GOD Is Also A Spirit, Which Is Not a physical thing. "Blessed[3z84] Be The LORD Of Spirits" Is Stated again and again In The Book of Enoch.[3z85] This Ancient Knowledge Is Articulated In nearly every Ancient Teaching and Religious Tradition. The Realm[3z86] Of Spirits Is The ancient Expression Of What Is Now Revealed As Our Spiritual Universe.

It Is Remarkable That So Many Different Words Expressing Aspects Of GOD From Diverse Traditions Tie Together. Deep Research Into The Meaning Of All True Words Invariably Leads Back To The ONE.

We Use The Abbreviation WORD to mean "The WORD Of GOD." The WORD Is The Instruction and Information Of GOD That Is All Reality.

Another important distinction is the difference between physical "energy" and Divine or Spiritual "Energy." These Energies Are Fundamentally Different because Their Source Is From entirely different Membrane Systems. Physical "energy"[3z87] is essential to physical existence in a physical universe. Divine "Energy," Manifested As Spiritual Energy,[3z88] Originates Directly[3z89] From GOD. Spiritual Energy Originates In The 10th D and Is Instructed To The 9th D To Be Manifested In Our

Spiritual Universe, 8th D and 7th D. Physical energy is manifested through a separate metastring[3z90] into being.[3z91] That is the physical metastring, manifesting in our physical universe, 8th d and 7th d. We have included illustrations to help You Conceptualize These Truths.

Research Notes, Credits, and Expansions are provided at the end of this Revelation. This is both To Credit The Original Thinkers for Their Contributions Referred To In *GOD—The Dimensional Revelation* and To Precisely Define The Intended Meanings Of This Teaching. Ideas Original To This Teaching or otherwise Expanded Are in brackets ([]) in the Research Notes.

GOD—The Dimensional Revelation utilizes some of The Vast Body Of Knowledge Accumulated By Spiritual Beings. Copyrighted excerpts are included in This Teaching under Fair Use Law—"to promote the progress of science and useful arts" (US Constitution, Article 1, Section 8, Clause 8). Likewise, This Teaching uses these excerpts for the purpose of Teaching, usually with comment or criticism to expand on the excerpt quoted. This Author Encourages Others To Correctly Use Truths of Our Teaching For The Benefit Of All.

"This Teaching" or "Our Teaching" or "This Writing" are often used referring to *GOD—The Dimensional Revelation.*

GOD—The Dimensional Revelation Presents A Complete Metaphysics that is verified logically by use of the scientific method. You may, through logic of Your Own, verify The Meanings and Our Conclusions. Beyond ideas, *GOD—The Dimensional Revelation* Provides Spiritual Tools and A Guide For You To Participate In The Broader Reality. If This Teaching is referenced in the distant future,[3z92] the vocabulary and context of word usage is explained in Our research notes as of April AD 2021.[3z93]

CHAPTER 4

Introduction to Dimensional Reasoning

Reality Is All That Exists. It is important to organize Our Understanding Of Reality so Understanding The Fullness Of Being[4a] is not lost in simple[4b] questions. Dimensional Reasoning Reveals The Deeper Reality Underlying Being and The Possibilities.[4c] The Fundamental Questions Are

> What Is Creation?
> What is the Origin[4d] of all of this that I Observe?
> What is it made of?
> How will all of this end?
> Who Am I?
> What Am I?
> Why Am I here?
> What Is This Consciousness and Awareness[4e] That I have?
> What happens when I Pass Away?
> What will become of Me?
> Do I Have A Destination?
> What is the Purpose[4f] of all this?
> What Other Beings Exist?
> Is this just a dream?
> What else is there?
> Who Is GOD?
> Why Does GOD allow evil to exist?
> Why Does GOD Ignore Me?
> How Can I Know GOD?

Dimensional Reasoning Yields Immediate Answers[4g] to these questions and more. Our Teaching Will Explain Each Dimension So That You Can Understand The Processes and Information Presented By Reality. Then Your Dimensional Reasoning Will Assist You To develop Your Consciousness To GOD.

We Live in a solid world. We Recognize that physical matter presents itself in 3 dimensions. These are length,[4h] width,[4i] and depth (height).[4j] Every solid particle and all physical objects that we perceive have these 3 dimensions.

Proof of 3-dimensional reality is around Us and upon Us constantly. It is obvious. Its proof lies in our experience of matter presented in 3 dimensions. It is verified and reverified.

Human Beings have developed instruments that mechanically verify the presence of matter and its attendant energies. We have developed a mathematics to Describe[4k] this observation of objects and the space[4l] they occupy. Furthermore, our mathematics is useful in predicting the current and future relations between objects.

Experience 3-dimensional reality. Go to a quiet room, open Your eyes, and hold Your breath. Be Here Now—just You in 3-dimensional space. All seems motionless.[4m]

As soon as sound enters Your Perception, the 4th Dimension, time, is forced[4n] upon You. Time forces You forward into the future with the beat of each compression wave.[4o]

Obvious reality forces a 4th Dimension upon Us. That 4th Dimension is time.[4p] Objects in relation to one another seem to present a situation for an instant[4q] only. As reality continues to the next situation in the flow, many objects have moved within space, presenting a different situation.

We Observe that there are energies inherent in matter. Those energies are dynamic—that is, they cause change. So a static situation never actually exists. Our mathematics has advanced to include the progress[4r] of matter and its attendant energies through the continuum of time.

Each situation moves into a new situation again and again as a continuous flow. These changes to objects in space in the flow of physical reality is a continuum of spatial[4s] relationships of objects to one another. *time* is the word we give to this continuum.

The same word, *time*, may designate when we are using the word *time* as a 4th-d continuum or just a scale, measure, or reference to clock settings. We would capitalize the *t* in time to designate the difference, but that would elevate "time" to a Spiritual Reality, which it is not.[4t]

The big bang—The origin of matter, space, and time

Ours is an immense physical universe of 3-Dimensional matter and its attendant energies. Galaxies we now count in the millions are accelerating apart, impelled by the primordial big bang.

This illustration Is Offered as a sequential depiction of Our Singularity Coming Into physical reality, which explodes during the big bang, creating our physical universe. It visually describes the Primal State; the big bang; the residual energy state; the plasma state; the condensation into subatomic particles; then the combining into atoms, molecules, and attendant energies; then star and galaxy formation as our physical universe expands, accelerating to create space by its operational principles over time. The black area outside the event and cone Is a representation of the void Only. The singularity and its development is only a small Manifestation Of The PRIMARY CLEAR LIGHT. This Is GOD.

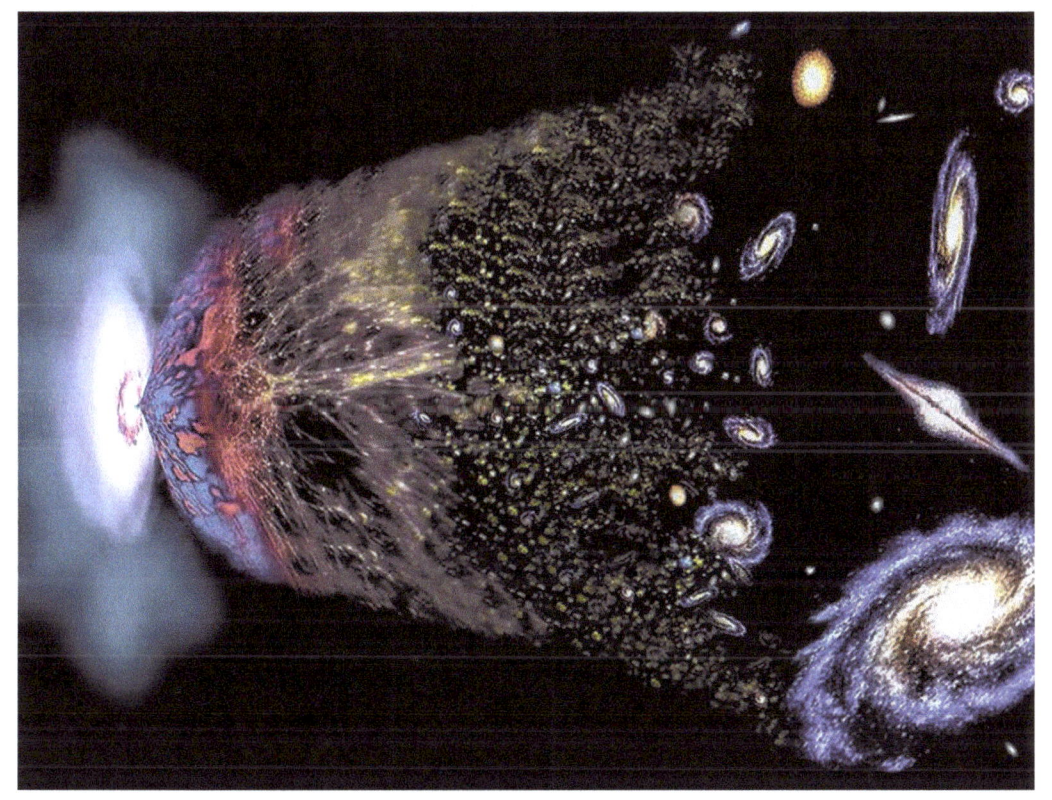

Artist's rendition of the big bang (photo by David A. Aguilar, *Smithsonian Magazine* 2014)

This verified theory of the creation of our universe of matter and its attendant energies is as follows. A singularity[4u] was Created. It was a singularity dense beyond reckoning and pregnant with the Potential[4v] of matter,[4w] space, and time. The circumstances of its creation compel it to explode with such force as to create space from Apparent[4x] physical nothingness. The explosive force is characterized by an acceleration of residual energy and its successors, away from the point of singularity. We call that force inertia.[4y]

The big bang created a plasma of energies and consequent subatomic particles[4z] moving apart ever more rapidly. This creates space as it expands into physical nothingness as the frame of reference expands. Physical nothingness[4z1] has nothing

GOD—THE DIMENSIONAL REVELATION

to resist this force; so physical matter and energy accelerate[4z2] as the creative force continues to inflate this reality, building velocity, adding to the inertia of the expanding universe.

The residue[4z3] of the big bang is a rich and energetic[4z4] soup, breaking down and Recombining[4z5] as the character of the energies and subsequent[4z6] particles condense into being. Simple atoms[4z7] form as the positive[4z8] and neutral[4z9] particles of mass are drawn[4z10] together to form a firm bond. The bond that holds protons and neutrons together is called the strong atomic force.[4z11] Much of the incredible energy released in the big bang process becomes tied up in atomic nuclei (big bang nucleosynthesis[4z12]).

These nuclei capture negative[4z13] charged particles called electrons[4z14] in a less firm but definite[4z15] particle called an atom. That is how matter is built. Charged and neutral energy transforms into particles of matter as it cools. Smaller particles combine to form larger ones in physical reality.

The original and most abundant atoms are hydrogen atoms. Each hydrogen atom may contain one proton[4z16] and one electron. Neutrons[4z17] occur in hydrogen isotopes and all other atoms. Hydrogen atoms condense out of the residue of our big bang as it cools. The reason they condense[4z18] is that there is Harmony[4z19] between the forces and the structure of an atom that not only allows its development but compels[4z20] its development. That Harmony may also be called Instruction of Information, The WORD.

The creation of matter is necessary upon the creation of the singularity and big bang creating our physical universe. There may be other big bangs creating different physical universes. There is no limit to the singularities that **GOD Can Create**. We know of only one. Our knowledge is certain of our physical universe. It is verified by several proofs.

a. We are Conscious Beings that sense matter. We are Self-Aware[4z21] Participants in 4-Dimensional physical reality. We say that our physical reality is self-evident[4z22] to Us because of Our Experience.
b. We have mechanical[4z23] instruments that work only because of the existence of matter. They sense and record the presence and progression of matter and its attendant energies. These work independently of Our Awareness.
c. Deductive Reasoning[4z24] allows Us to prove many Truths that are beyond verification by Our Senses.[4z25] Established realities are observed in relation to one another. Applied to a specific situation, they prove a specific Conclusion about Reality.

INTRODUCTION TO DIMENSIONAL REASONING

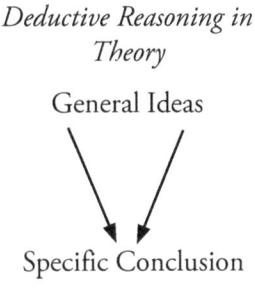

Deductive Reasoning in Theory

General Ideas

↘ ↙

Specific Conclusion

Deductive Reasoning in Practice
Logic based on observation of data

For example, gravity operates by mass being attracted to mass. The quantity of mass is measured as weight on a scale. A scale measures weight of all objects on earth.

↘ ↙

Therefore, I deduce that my weight is a measure of my gravity on earth.

d. Mathematics is another type of deductive reasoning. Applying established mathematical procedures to a situation leads to a reliable conclusion. Mathematical procedures prove the existence of this universe of matter and its attendant energies. That certainty is separate from Our Awareness.
Deductive Reasoning in Mathematics (Symbolic Logic): A=B, C=A; Therefore, B=C.

e. Inductive Reasoning[4z26] allows Us to generalize and to express broad principles about Our Reality based on a set of Observations that reveal a general condition. Inductive reasoning allows Us to predict many Truths that are beyond verification by Our senses. When we understand physical processes, established realities can be related to Infer[4z27] a consequent reality that we cannot experience.

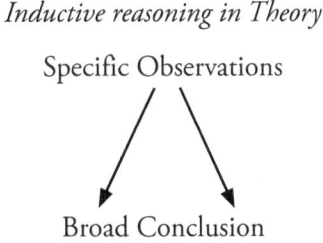

Inductive reasoning in Theory

Specific Observations

↙ ↘

Broad Conclusion

Inductive Reasoning in Practice
Logic based on observation of cause and effect

For example, I can sense and manipulate matter. Matter is hard, and it is heavy. Matter affects matter separately from Me.

Therefore, a universe of matter exists.

Having proof that our physical universe exists, we can expand our knowledge of its development. Diverse things emerge as the original plasma releases forms of radiation amid the condensation[4z28] of hydrogen[4z29] atoms.

H1 is the symbol for hydrogen. The hydrogen nucleus[4z30] contains one proton and one electron. Pressure in the plasma field will force hydrogen atoms together to produce hydrogen isotopes, H2 (D2, deuterium) and H3 (T3, tritium).

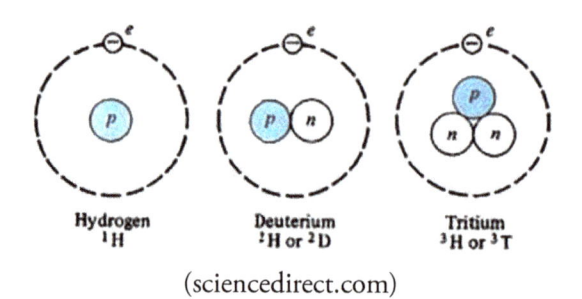

Hydrogen ^1H Deuterium ^2H or ^2D Tritium ^3H or ^3T

(sciencedirect.com)

H2 and H3 nuclei forced together in a large-enough mass and pressure become unstable and combine explosively to create helium (He).[4z31] This is called nuclear fusion.[4z32] We witness nuclear fusion each day because our sun is a giant fusion reactor, combining hydrogen into helium and loose neutrons, and releasing various energies, especially photons, which bathe our planet with Life-sustaining heat and light.

INTRODUCTION TO DIMENSIONAL REASONING

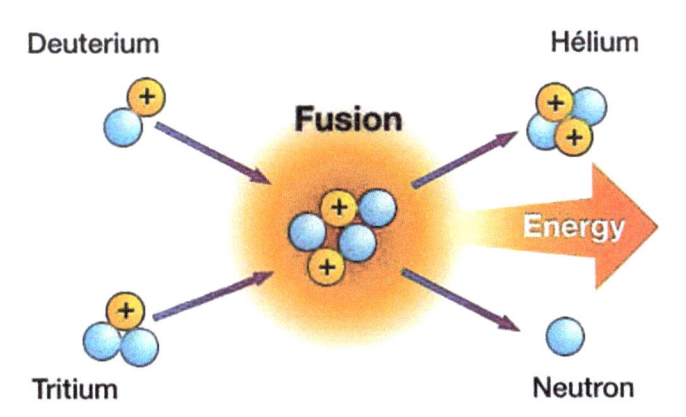

(https://blogs.umass.edu/p139uso/2012/11/20/nuclear-fusion-the-mechanics/)

The breaking of the nuclear bonds in a fusion reaction releases new combinations of the subatomic particles and various energies known as radiation. Among them are gamma rays,[4z33] x-rays, and, most important to us, light wavicles.[4z34] These are all considered to be photons.[4z35]

The nature of photons is to be both a wave and a particle. A photon is a wave because it behaves like radiation with no mass when at rest. However, a photon is never at rest, and under Einstein's theory of special relativity,[4z36] photons can become particles because they have energy with mass[4z37] equivalence.[4z38] We can measure mass. Mass is volume times weight. Energy equals mass times the constant (speed of light) squared. The formula is $e=mc^2$. Hence, the total of matter and energy contained in our physical universe remains constant. That is because matter and its attendant energies can convert from one to the other over time in different situations.

This defines the limit[4z39] of our physical universe. That is to say that space is created by the presence of these particles, their energies, and the forces by which they relate. Space, our physical universe, is expanded by the field of influence of matter and its attendant energies as they speed apart (inflation). The limit to space is the current expansion of that field of influence.[4z40]

Another feature of matter is that the negative charge is carried by a very small and fast-moving subatomic particle called an electron. Electrons exist alone or as part of an atom. Electrons are often released in situations where the atom is changing or due to surrounding charges. When the bonds that hold electrons in place are broken, other energies are released, and electronic potential[4z41] is exposed.

The weak atomic force[4z42] intermediates the interactions as the strong atomic force changes as matter and energy interact. This is the least powerful of the physical forces.

The loose electron has potential, and the stripped hydrogen nucleus has potential.

The loose electron has the potential to travel through space rapidly with other loose electrons. Charged fields are created, which attract and repel matter and the attendant energies in formative ways. This force is one aspect of electromagnetism.[4z43]

Another feature of matter present from its plasma formation[4z44] is that atoms and their subatomic particles have weight. All matter has the force of gravity.[4z45] Matter attracts matter. The strength of the force of gravitational attraction is proportional to the amount of matter in a given[4z46] space. Hence, we define the mass of an object as its weight times its volume.

The gravity between objects is a function of their individual mass and the distance between them. The farther apart, the less the gravitational attraction. The closer in space, the greater the gravitational attraction.

In summary, our universe of matter and its attendant energies exhibit the major physical forces:

a. time
b. inertia
c. strong atomic force
d. weak atomic force
e. electromagnetism
f. gravity

One must understand that matter creates space. At the singularity prior to our big bang, there was no space, no matter, and no time.

There was Being Outside the singularity. In fact, The Being Outside the singularity Is the Cause. There Existed Being Prior To The Formation Of The Singularity. That Being also Sustains[4z47] and Continues To Manifest our universe of matter and its attendant energies (Continuity). Humans can explain this by organizing our understanding through Dimensional Reasoning.

The following is one of many logical proofs[4z48] of Our Spiritual Universe:

> Deductive Reasoning in Practice
> Logic based on observation of data
>
> Each body is distinctly different when A Spirit Is Connected from when a Spirit is not connected. You Experience Your Own Identity apart from Your body. You Experience Integrity Of Self apart from changes to your body. Medical instruments show when each body is alive, then dead when Its Spirit Has Passed Away.

\ /
 ↓↓

Therefore, My Spirit Is Connected To My body for My Lifetime and Passes To A Purely Spiritual Universe after physical death.

Since Spiritual Experience Operates Outside the broad principles of physical reality, We Can Infer The Existence Of A Spiritual Universe.

Inductive Reasoning in Practice
Logic based on observation of cause and effect

I Am Aware Of The Presence Of Spirit In Other Living Beings.[4z49] All Living Beings Relate To and Influence The Individual Spirits Of Others without regard to their bodies. Diverse Spiritual Action Occurs Apart From Me. The laws of physics limit physical action but not Spiritual Action.

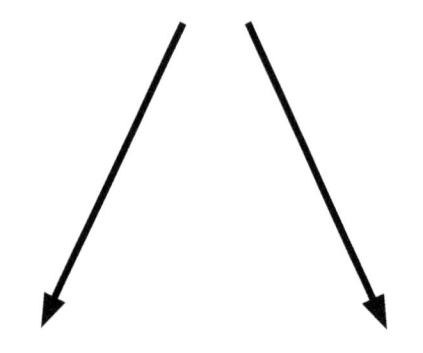

Therefore, A Universe Of Spirit exists.

CHAPTER 5

Dimensions from GOD and Downward Manifestations

In the beginning was the WORD, and the WORD was with GOD, and the WORD was GOD.

—Holy Bible, John 1:1 KJV

[Capitalization added by the author.]
GOD Has A Point Of View.
11th: This Is The Being Of GOD. There Is Only ONE Of The 11th. I fear for even attempting to name The ONE, LORD, GOD. Words are insufficient to describe Primary Being.[5a] This Being cannot be Fully[5b] Known, Except In Potential Reunification.[5c] Implicit[5c] In Differentiation[5e] and Reunification Is That Divine Presence Exists Within All Dimensions. GOD's Point Of View Is Outside Of All Creation and Within All Creation, Then Undiminished[3f] Before, During and After All Manifestations. That Is The "Truth" That Jesus Christ Demonstrated During His Ministry On Earth.[5g]

The 11th—That Which Cannot Be Bounded or Categorized Because GOD Is Not Within Boundary, Type, Or Limit—Is Named only because The Human Mind[5h] has difficulty Understanding What Is Beyond The Dimensions without Identification, Description, or A Higher Number.

Awaken Your Soul To Divine Awareness[5i] In Any Dimension.

This Teaching Postulates[5j] **"The Law of Dimensional Limitation."**[5k] This Primary Law Of Being Is That Each Dimension Has A Field Of Influence and A Boundary.[5l] That influence is contained by the laws of operation within its dimensional boundaries. Reality is manifested within each dimension according to the Operational principles[5m] and limitations of that dimension.

Hence, the 11th Is Not a Dimension At All Because GOD Is Boundless. GOD Is Primary Being. GOD Is Beyond Becoming. GOD Has No Cause, No Limitation, No Beginning, and No End.[5n] GOD Has No Laws Of Operation. All Fields Of

Influence Are GOD's Fields Of Influence. All Manifestations Are Manifestations Of GOD. The LORD Is ONE. The LORD Is Unconfined and Beyond Measure. All Realities Are Manifestations Of The ONE.

Do not be confused that this description is a convenient compilation of all reality into one unity. The ONE Is A Being With A Consciousness. The ONE Differentiates Aspects Of Its Being To Become All Realities.

Do not be confused by the words. GOD Is Beyond All Concepts and Information. God Is Beyond All Summation Of Reality, regardless of how Reality May Be Manifested.

We Know That GOD Exists because We Are Absolutely Aware of many of The Manifestations Of GOD. GOD Is The SOURCE.

We Know That GOD Exists Because The Divine Is Present In All Forms Of Consciousness. Conscious Awareness Is A Manifestation Of GOD. Stated another way, A Conscious Being Is A Division Of GOD, By GOD, Like GOD Yet Differentiated, Apart, and less than GOD To Uniquely Participate In GOD's Manifestations Separate From GOD.

10th Dimension: GOD Has Created A Flow[5o] Of Instructions and Information That Is Called The WORD. The WORD Is Defined As The WILL Of GOD.[5p] This Teaching Reveals That GOD Manifests All Creation and Each Unit Of Creation Through Instructions and Information, The WORD, In The 10th D. Jesus Christ Used The Term "Law" [13z121], As This Teaching Uses The Term, "WORD".

This Teaching postulates the term **Metastring**. *Metastring* Is a Human word for The Instruction, The Causative Channels,[5q] and The Operative Information Of All Reality. Instruction Is Transmission Of Divine Information From The 10th D To The 9th D, Enabling[5r] Mechanism To Manifest—To Create—Reality In the lower dimensions. One Metastring Is One Set Of Continuous Divine Instructions Containing The Information For The 9th D Machinery Of Creation To Manifest The Reality Instructed By The WORD.

A Manifestation Occurs In an 8th D–bounded system as the Information Instructed Is Collapsed[5s] Into Being. Stated another way, The 10th-D WORD Instructs Metastrings In the 9th D As The Channels Through Which All Else Are Created and Maintained.[5t] Each Metastring contains the principles of operation and field of influence, including limitations and boundary, of each Type of Reality Manifested and the Dimension in which it operates.

Since All Creation Is Of GOD, Metastring Constructions[5u] are Differentiations Of The ONE.

The Existence of Metastrings, by this or any other name, is verified by both Conscious Observation and Conscious Participation In The Causative Operation Of Each Metastring. For example, Divine Information Is Transmitted From GOD To You Along The Direct Spiritual Metastring Connecting You To GOD. In Our example, Your Conscience[5v] Is A Presence Of GOD In Your Mind With An Instruction

To Forgive[5w] an offence committed to You by Another Human. Such Forgiveness Is not Self-serving To You, but You Heed Your Conscience and Forgive the offense. The Act Enlightens Your Center. In the long run, You Observe That Forgiveness Was The Best Solution. In this example, Positive Utility[5x] Proves that Your Metastring Connection[5y] To GOD Exists.

Furthermore, That Act Of Forgiveness Opens The System. Hence, Forgiveness Is An Act Of Creation, With You As The Machinery Of Creation In The 9th Dimension.

In other words, Forgiveness May Be Understood As A Differentiation Of The ONE As A Process rather than An Identity. This Is Another "Proof Of Process" In The 9th D, An Instruction Of The 10th-D WORD. You Are The Instrument Of GOD Accomplishing That Instruction.

That a causative process and structure exists To Manifest Reality[5z] is the logical conclusion presented by the evidence of Our broad Observation. We are led to Understand Metastrings as the connections that "Weave The Fabric"[5z109] Of Reality.

Figure 2 is an illustration of How Metastrings Proceed[5z1] From GOD Through The Creative[5z2] Process To Manifest Realities In The 8th Dimension. Please return to this illustration again as Your Understanding Of Reality Develops To Experience Esoteric Nuances.[5z3] The sudden Revelation May Come To You As Well.

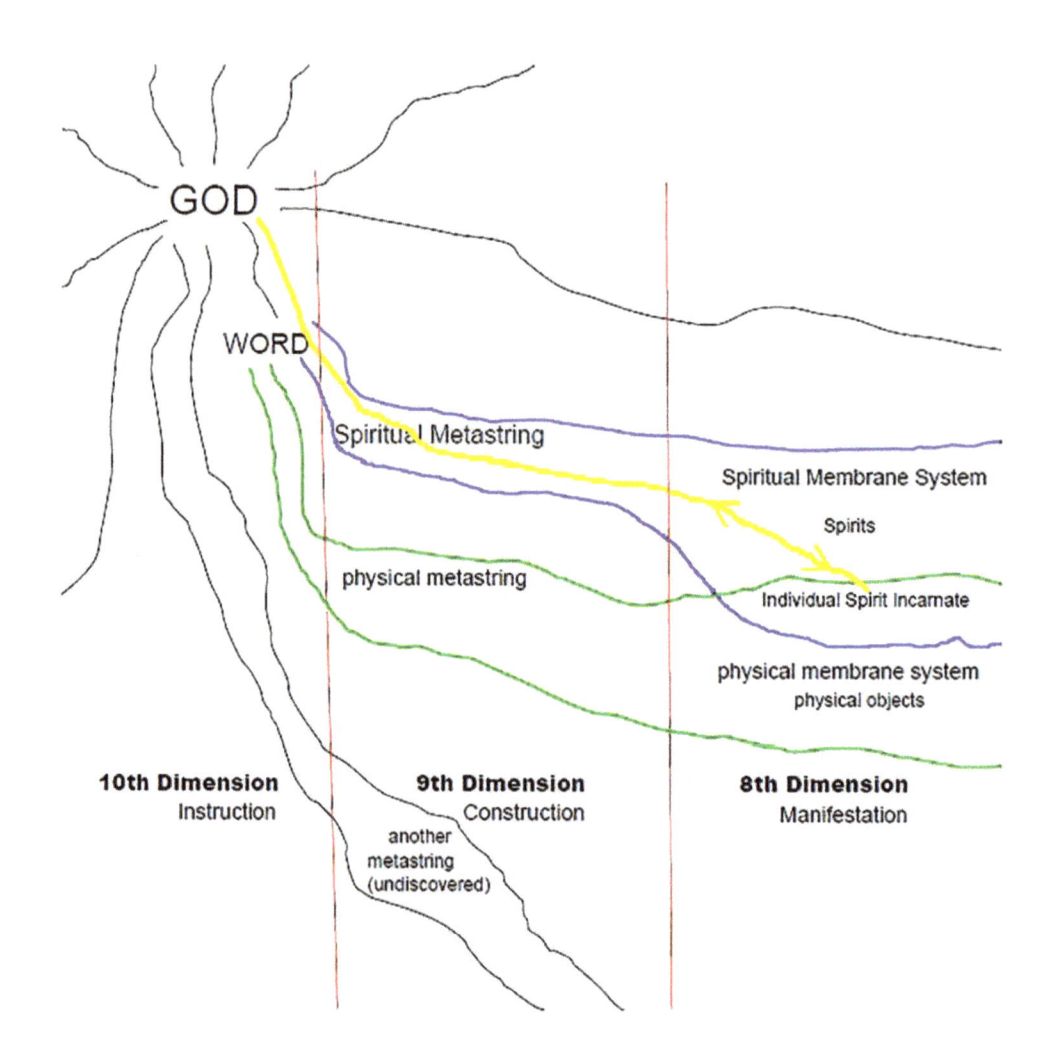

Figure 2: Metastring Formation. Drawing by Allyn Richert (AD 2020). The WORD of GOD is Instructed in the 10th Dimension, Constructed in the 9th Dimension, and Manifested into Reality in the 8th Dimension.

The word *string*[5z4] evokes an image of a cord or channel upon or through which something may progress. It also expresses how realities may be connected together. "String" is a metaphor that expresses physical reality both at the micro[5z5] and macro[5z6] levels.

Current theoretical physics defines a "string" as the smallest of all subatomic[5z7] components. A string may be a wave or a particle. According to string theory, all items in physical reality are composed of strings. Other names may be given in various physical theories. One string is approximately one Planck length (10^{-33} millimeter)[5z8] in length and nominal width. The length, width, and depth of a string is variable according to the resonance of the string as strings tether together to form larger physical energies and diverse particles. Trillions of strings comprise a single proton. Each string is a vibrating or energized quantum wave.[5z9]

Strings may be diverse[5z10] in their presence and potential according to their Instructions (Divine Information). The Instruction causing each string is composed of at least two categories of Information:

1. Structure—a form that may manifest as mass or physical energy
2. Resonance[5z11]—continuity and frequency[5z12] of the string

Yes, even gamma rays—shortest of all physical waves—are composed of strings. The difference between strings is their resonance or Harmonic oscillation.[5z13] Simple harmonic motion (SHM) is oscillatory motion, where the net force on the system is a restoring force. A restoring force is a force acting opposite to displacement to bring the system back to equilibrium, which is its rest position. The force magnitude depends only on displacement. Their resonance can change or change back to manifest different physical items within the limitations of special relativity and quantum mechanics.

In the Fusion of Spiritual Forces With physical forces, a 9th-D Resonance Occurs. The Resonance May Be Spontaneous At Lower Levels Of Consciousness. Acts Of Individual Will May Raise The Resonance To Higher Levels Of Consciousness That Are Called Heaven.

The WORD Is The Fundamental and Continuous Restorative Force, Sustaining harmonic oscillation in quantum fields on the physical continuum. This Instruction Of Information is how The 9th Dimension Sustains physical being. This is another proof of GOD.

One aspect of Reality that no string can manifest Is Spirit. This is a fundamental difference between the physical membrane system and the Spiritual Membrane System.

Science is discovering diverse subatomic particles, so these theories are still developing beyond This Teaching. Regardless of the eventual conclusions about subatomic particles, the realities are still summed up in the following original metaphysical principle governing our universe of matter and its attendant energies. A string or any other original physical subatomic component is a GOD-Wave[5z14]—That Is, Information Of The WORD Molded[5z15] In The 9th Dimension into the primary building blocks of the physical membrane system.

Divine Instruction Is within strings and Beyond strings. This Divine Instruction Sets the operational principles governing the potential of each string. This Divine Instruction is also the physical processes governing the interaction among strings as they manifest physical reality.

In physical reality, time unwraps the Infinity Of Spirit. Understanding This Is Fundamental For You To Understand The Difference Between the physical membrane system and The Spiritual Membrane System. One Oscillation In Spiritual Reality Is The ONE Differentiating Into A Single or Various Spiritual Manifestations. Then The Spiritual Manifestation Reuniting Back Into The ONE. Our Teaching Represents This Timeless Oscillation By The Infinity Symbol, ∞.

An oscillation in physical reality is The ONE Differentiated into a continuous series of strings with a beginning and ending and perspective based on the operational principles limiting physical reality. Our Teaching symbolizes a quantum string using the limited sine wave.

Our physical universe is one physical universe that We Know to exist within the physical membrane system. This Teaching Reveals That A GOD-Wave Is Divine Energy[5z16] With GOD Creating At The Inception. The 9th-D Metastring Converting The 10th-D Information (Vibrations) Into physical matter Is Instructed By GOD To Separate matter Out Of GOD. This allows matter to proceed according to The Divine Information Instructed or programmed[5z17] into the strings and their potential Differentiated at the singularity.[5z18] The WORD Sustains matter, going forward, in all physical universes.

The Instructions Established In physical operational principles need not change. This is why We Observe consistent physical processes in physical reality. GOD does not usually change The Sustaining Instructions Of The WORD regarding physical reality.

The Teaching above Is A Revelation.

One of the several string theories is interesting to discuss. Current theoretical physics states that a "superstring"[5z19] defines space-time[5z20] as a combination of diverse strings that create physical reality. Current theoretical physics defines five superstring groups. Current membrane theory, m-theory,[5z21] attempts to unify all superstring groups into a coherent quantum theory of physical Synthesis.[5z22] The "standard model of particles and interactions"[5z23] is getting close to explaining the construction of our physical reality.

The Revelation Expressed In Our Teaching Is not at odds with current theoretical physics. However, We Observe that current theoretical physics is confined to a physical view of reality. It is stuck in cosmology.[5z24]

Reality is so much more than physical being, so We must break the shell of our 7th-dimensional physical universe to recognize higher Dimensions. Our Teaching Refines current theoretical physics.

Copernicus (and Aristarchus of Samos) revealed that the earth is not the center of our solar system. On A Grander Scale, Our Teaching Reveals that our physical universe is not the center of Reality.

Some m-theories recognize three ordinary dimensions, plus time, plus six hyperspatial Dimensions, to achieve 10 dimensions. Some theories achieve 11 dimensions

DIMENSIONS FROM GOD AND DOWNWARD MANIFESTATIONS

with similar reasoning. Our Teaching hypothesizes that all of those are encompassed within seven physical dimensions in our listing.

Particularly, the six hyperspatial dimensions developed by current m-theory are supported by some very difficult mathematics. The math contains variables and functions supporting an expanded symbolic vocabulary, which must be learned to verify mathematically. As with all developmental mathematics, different theorists are constantly adding and defining new variables to achieve a reliable mathematics.

To the extent that the mathematics describes physical processes in our universe of matter and its attendant energies, all six of these hyperspatial dimensions fit comfortably within the operational boundaries of the physical 7th d (our physical universe) set forth In Our Teaching.

To the extent that they describe another physical universe with the same operational principles as ours but originating from another singularity and another big bang, then they serve to provide unifying mathematics for all universes within our 8th-d physical membrane system.

To the extent that they describe the creation of our physical universe and its origin or position in the physical membrane system, then that mathematics has relevance to describe one operation of The Machinery Of Creation Within The 9th Dimension Of Our Metaphysics.

Later In Our Teaching, we will learn that while a reliable mathematics may be developed to describe the Information operational in a particular physical metastring, a reliable mathematics cannot be developed to describe The WORD. This is because The Instructions Of The WORD Are Not Constant.[5z25] The WORD May Change At The Pleasure Of GOD. Consequently, a Metastring (Continuous Channel Of Instructions) from the 10th D, Instructing The Creation Of A Particular Reality In The 9th D, May Be Re-Instructed By The 10th D To Manifest A Distinctly Different Reality Emerging Out Of The 9th D To manifest in the lower dimensions.

Hence, the reality described by quantum mechanics Is A Manifestation Of The WORD.

Superposition and nonlocality in quantum theory is merely the restatement that GOD Can Be In all places at the same time.

Our Teaching Agrees with contemporary theoretical physics, which postulates that all matter and its attendant energies are actually "Information." On the grander scale, everything that exists, except for GOD, consists of "Information." The word *Information* in the 10th D is a subset of the WORD or WILL of GOD that we usually associate with things, objects, or Beings. These are expressed as nouns in our language.

"Instructions" in the 10th D is another subset of the WORD that we usually associate with Processes That Create or Manipulate The Divine Information. Action Of These Processes are expressed as verbs in our language.

The foundation of Our Metaphysics is that everything that exists and all processes are due to Vibrations In The 10th Dimension.

The terminology we utilize in this "string" theory vocabulary relegates the term *superstring* to the construction of physical realities. We utilize the term *Metastring* to describe the defined Formational and Operational Machinery Of Each Type Of Reality. Hence, The 9th D Creates one metastring as the constructive machinery of all physical creation As Instructed By The WORD. The construction of a singularity is one product of this metastring. The continuing appearance of quantum particles,[5z26] manifesting physical reality, is another product of this Metastring.

The 9th D Also Creates a totally Different Metastring. That Is The Spiritual Metastring[5z27] As The Constructive Machinery Of All Spiritual Beings. The Spiritual Metastring Is Also Instructed By The WORD. To Understand The Operation Of The Spiritual Metastring Would Be To Grasp How The WORD Differentiates Independent Spirits or Souls From The ONE, GOD, LORD Of All.

DIMENSIONS FROM GOD AND DOWNWARD MANIFESTATIONS

I envision The Creative Process As GOD Playing The Metastrings like a harpist plucking one string and another of a harp, while Other Metastrings Remain Resonate In The Harmony Of The Manifestations Of GOD's WORD.

© Josephine Wall; reprinted by the gracious permission of akenney@creativerightsinc.com

The quantum strings, minutest of all physical things, represent the harmonics in this analogy to Music.[5z29] These are Manifested By 9th-D Synthesis into various physical forms in the lower Dimensions.

Revelation: *GOD Created an Instrument and Plays Upon that Instrument, and All Becomes Possible. The Possible Becomes Real as the Manifestations Unfold. Consciousness Becomes Manifest for GOD to Reenter Creation as a Participant*[5z30] *in all Vibrations of the Harmony.*

This is Our Revelation and Our Theology. It is the answer to the questions, "What Is GOD?" "What Is Creation?" "What Is The Origin Of All Of This That I observe?" "What Is It made of?"

9th Dimension: How Shall GOD Become Manifest? Divine Information In The 10th D, Differentiated From The ONE, diversely Continues As Metastrings Vibrating In The 9th D To Manifest The Metastring Creations. All Possible Realities Are Potential and Formative[5z31] In The 9th D. We know of at least two Formative Realities. One is our physical universe. The Other Is Our Spiritual Universe.

Collections of Human Knowledge are beginning to codify The Mechanisms Of Creation. That Is To Observe Our Systems Of Being.

Also, The 9th D Operates To Create diverse realities by the Fusion of vast membrane systems. We can only imagine a few of them. We witness the expansion of time and spatial realities. We Experience the Feelings and Awareness Of Spiritual Realities. These Membrane Systems are separate and mutually exclusive, except that there Can Be Contact and Partial Fusion Of These separate systems. Such Realities Are Instructed To The 9th D To Manifest The WORD in the lower Dimensions.

This illustration is offered to help Visualize The 9th D Mechanisms Of Creation At Work, Creating Diverse Realities. One of these is the unfolding of physical reality shown as a scroll parting to Manifest our physical world and a Person Entering To Participate in physical reality.

DIMENSIONS FROM GOD AND DOWNWARD MANIFESTATIONS

Dreamstime 96902686

Quantum mechanics[5z32] is an area of Human research that is beginning to define the mechanisms in operation to create and sustain our physical universe at the sub-elemental[5z33] level of physical being. quantum principles such as wave-particle duality,[5z34] superposition,[5z55] nonlocality,[5z36] decoherence,[5z37] and quantum entanglement[5z38] begin to describe how matter Is Created In The 9th D and collapses into observable reality in the lower Dimensions. They operate to define which universe emerges from a truly infinite field of possibilities. Infinity[5z39] Has Meaning In The 9th D. The potential Instructions From The LORD In The 10th D Are Unlimited. The actual Information is limited to That Instructed To Become Manifested By The 9th-D Mechanisms.

Earlier in chapter 5, we used the infinity symbol ∞ to illustrate one physical or Spiritual Oscillation along an unending Spiritual Continuum. Since This symbol of The Continuum may be misunderstood as occurring in a closed system and does not Identify The SOURCE and Destination, We Expand the Symbolism.

Our Expanded Infinity Symbol below Depicts several Infinity Continuums, perhaps different Membrane Systems, Linked In A Grander Reality. This Symbolism Depicts GOD As The SOURCE and GOD Also As The DESTINATION. The WORD, In The 10th Dimension, is an Open System Without limitation.

Drawing by Allyn Richert, AD 2021

It would be incredibly interesting if quantum mathematics[5z40] could give us a reliable formula To Create physical being. Our Teaching Predicts That Bridging The Gap From A to z[5z41] will still defy mathematics as we will show later In This Revelation.

However, if a formula for creating physical matter could be developed, this would still not be a "theory of everything"[5z42] because it would not describe The Creation Of Spirit, Spiritual Beings, or The Awesome Manifestations Of Spiritual Causation.[5z43] Please Reference "Forgiveness," A Spiritual Reality, and Its Transformational[5z44] Effects On physical being.

quantum mathematics is confined within the 8th-d boundary of physical being. It does not relate to The Possibilities For The 9th D To Create the unimaginable As Instructed By The WORD From The 10th D.

Our Teaching Postulates That All That Exists and All Processes Are Due To Vibrations In The 10th Dimension. To the extent that Divine Information, The WORD, Instructs A Defined Channel Of A Type Of Manifestation, It Is An Operational Principle Of The 9th D To Bring It Into Being. That operation Is Metastring Creation.[5z45] Hence, physical formation will occur on a 9th-D physical metastring. A Spiritual Manifestation Will Occur On A 9th-D Spiritual Metastring. Each of these operates independently of the other.

However, if Instructed By The WORD, The two Separate Metastrings Can Intersect In The 9th D To Partially Fuse Separate Realities Manifesting Characteristics Of Both. This Is Now Occurring As GOD Has Instructed Our Spiritual Universe To

Partially Fuse Into our physical universe. Characteristics Of Both Are Woven Into The "Fabric" Of Our Reality.

Spiritual Studies Into Consciousness, Phenomenology, and Divine Energy Begin To Reveal The Potential Of Spirit Created In The 9th Dimension. Prayer,[5z46] Worship,[5z47] or Meditation[5z48] Allow a Conscious Being, such as You, To Participate In The Higher Dimensions.

8th Dimension: The Diversity Of Reality, Differentiated From The ONE, becomes organized according to operational principles of each category of Being. The 8th D is the highest Dimension where We can establish fixed principles, The Law[13z121], of Our Reality. This Teaching postulates the phrase *Membrane System* to mean that each is a Complete[5z49] system with a boundary or limit within which its operational principles manifest reality. Each membrane system is completely operational and is totally independent of every other membrane system.

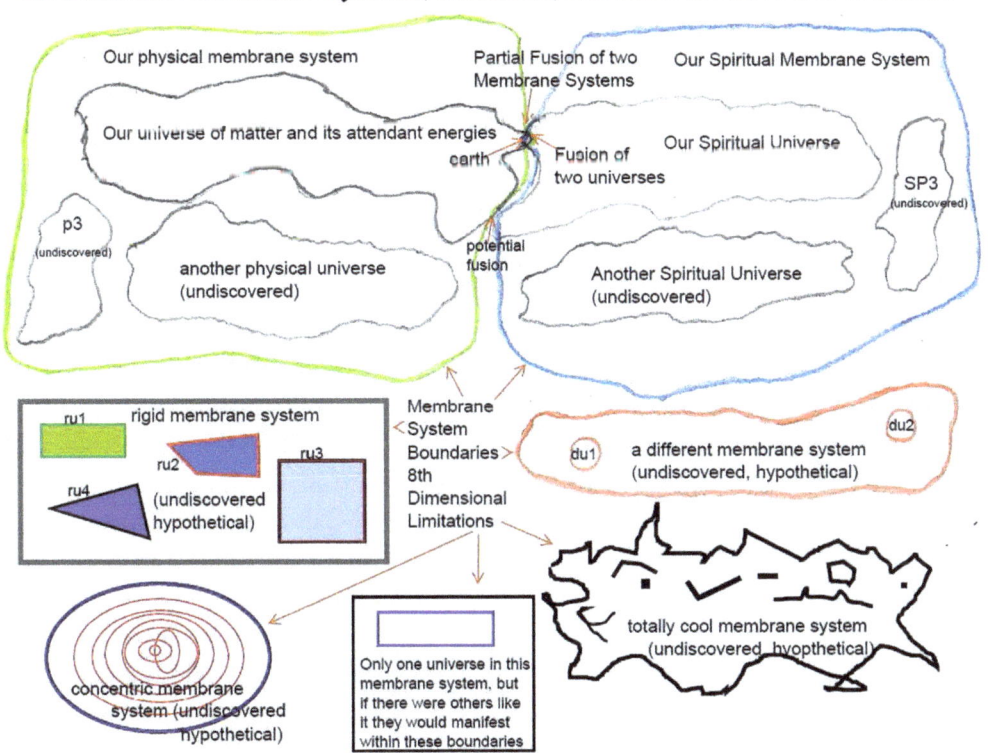

Membrane Systems—Drawing by Allyn Richert, AD 2020

Figure 3 is an Illustration of our physical membrane system and Our Spiritual Membrane System. The other universes and membrane systems shown are hypothetical to illustrate that other membrane systems may exist. So far, we have proof only of the existence of Our Spiritual Universe and our physical universe. The possibility of other physical-type universes comprising the physical membrane system, as well as Other Spiritual Universes comprising the Spiritual Membrane System, is Theoretical.[5z50] The other membrane systems shown in figure 3 are purely Speculative[5z51] but offered to advance Your Understanding of what a Total Manifest Reality in the 8th D might Be.

Fusion of membrane systems can occur If Instructed By The WORD To Be Constructed In The 9th D To Manifest Into Reality In The 8th D. The cover of this book is figure 1. It illustrates The Zone Of Fusion Between Our Spiritual Universe and our physical universe. This Zone Of Fusion Is The Reality In Which You and I Live. This is shaded in green to symbolize The Presence Of Living Beings Incarnate Into matter In This Zone of Fusion. The overlapping boundaries of these two universes and, on the larger scale, these two Membrane Systems are illustrated in figure 3.

Current m-theory is confused with conflicting definitions and the complicated mathematics. We break out of the physical model of m-theory to reveal membrane systems that are physical, or nonphysical, or Spiritual, or otherwise separately manifested. We refer to them as membrane systems to avoid conflicting perspectives and the current physical limitations of m-theory.

A limited analogy can be drawn with biological cell membranes. Biological cellular metabolism and the confining cell membrane[5z52] illustrate the boundaries of the biological operational system (the cell) and the cell membrane's potential to be penetrated. However, the reality within a metaphysical membrane system is vast and complete. It is not dependent upon other membrane systems as with a biological cell. Our Teaching uses the word *system* defined as a group of operational characteristics (Laws) that operate within a field of influence (limitation or boundary).

Please note that the field of influence of any system can expand or contract.

A metaphysical membrane system in the 8th D is a complete system of being. This means that the system is Self-sufficient[5z53] and needs nothing else to be real and operational. A membrane system operates in the 8th D, created and sustained along its Metastring According To The Information Of Its Creation In The 9th D As Directed By Instructions That Are The WORD Of GOD In The 10th D.

The reality of the membrane system is manifested according to its operational principles within its dimensional limitation. The Law of Dimensional Limitation defines a membrane system as any system of operation that has the same type of initial or formative conditions, the same Laws of operation, and ending conditions made possible by its operational principles. A membrane system is bound by its Laws of operation and its Independence[5z54] from other systems for existence.

All physical universes that have similar characteristics of matter and its attendant energies are part of the physical membrane system. Our universe of matter and its attendant energies is a verifiable example of one universe in this physical membrane system. Within our universe, as with other potential physical universes (yet unknown) in the physical membrane system, space is created as matter is formed. This initial condition is a singularity bursting as a big bang similar to

DIMENSIONS FROM GOD AND DOWNWARD MANIFESTATIONS

our big bang that happened about 13.8 billion years ago. That big bang created our universe of matter and its attendant energies. Each physical universe in the physical membrane system has space continuing to expand, accelerating, by inflation from its "big bang."

All such big bangs are Initiated by a WORD Vibration in the 10th D. This Vibration bundled a set of Instructions defining a specific metastring in the 9th D, creating all physical realities. The 8th-d physical membrane system is the result of operations of the physical metastring. One physical reality brought into being on the physical metastring is a field of being perhaps defined as a quantum field or singularity. Hence, Divine Energy Manifests The WORD as a singularity located[5z55] in the 8th d. When our singularity became manifest, our big bang exploded to become our 7th-D physical universe.

According to Our interpretation of quantum theory, as the field of energy from our singularity converted back and forth, Primal Matter was destroyed by Primal Antimatter, the residue of which yielded an expanding universe of matter and its attendant energies to be our 7th-dimensional physical universe.

We do not know how many physical universes have been created. We know that our physical universe exists as We Live In it and further discover its character. The 8th-d physical membrane system may contain any number of physical universes originating under similar circumstances and operating according to the same physical laws.

We must not leave The 8th Dimension unexplored. There Is at least One Other Membrane Systems That Is Unlike the physical membrane system containing our big bang universe.

There Is The Reality Of Spirit; That Is Its Own Membrane System. The Presence Of Spirit Is The Defining Characteristic Of The Spiritual Membrane System. GOD Has Created Special Harmonies Vibrating Of This Metastring In The 9th D. We do not Know how many Spiritual Universes Are Manifested In The 8th-D Spiritual Membrane System. We cannot Understand That Until Potential Reunification. We Know Of One Spiritual Universe Because Each Consciousness Is part Of That Spiritual Universe. The proof Of This Is Self-evident To You As You Are Conscious and Aware, here and now. I Am. You Are. You Know That You Are Spiritual Because You Are Free To Make any number Of Choices, None Of Which Necessarily Flow As A Consequence of physical forces.

Furthermore, Each Of Us Is A Participant In The Operation Of Our Universe Of Spirit and simultaneously in our physical universe. Each Of Us Is A Human Being Created of matter and A Divine Spirit[5z56] or Soul.[5z57]

GOD—THE DIMENSIONAL REVELATION

- Your Eternal and Immortal Spirit
-: The Soul
-: The Physical Body

(https://www.quora.com/Why-do-people-go-spiritual)

This Collision[5z58] or Fusion Of Membrane Systems may or may not be common In The 9th D. We Can Understand It As We Observe The Creative Intersecting Of two Different and Bound Membrane Systems, Which Allows Conscious, Nonspatial Spirit To Experience spatial being within the boundaries and potential of matter.

The Fusion We Experience Has Created A Rare and Wonderful Reality In Which We Participate As material flesh (Carne) and Spirit (Soul). To Be An Incarnate

Being Yields Myriad[5z59] and Diverse Possibilities For This Partially Fused Pair Of Membrane Systems As The 8th-D Spiritual Membrane System Collides With the 8th-d physical membrane system. These Possibilities Are Collapsed Into Being As The 7th Dimension Unfolds, Containing Manifestations Of Spirit Within matter. We Know This To Be True Because We Are Both Observers and Participants In This Action on planet earth.

We Will Discuss Many Verifications Of This Fusion of matter and Spirit. One Verification Is The Fullness Of Music.[5z60] Physically speaking, music is simply a progression of compression waves through a fluid (air) in the 8th-d physical membrane system, our physical universe in the 7th d. The compression waves are sensed by the physical eardrum of a physical being. Even a robot[5z61] can sense the compression waves. Spirit Is Required For A Human Being To Appreciate[5z62] The Music and Be Elevated[5z63] or Otherwise Moved[5z64] by the sensation.[5z65] This Appreciation Is Not an automatic response to sense this or that or to move this way or that. It Is An Unpredictable and Indeterminate[5z66] Fulfillment[5z67] Of An Individual Being, Uniquely Relating To The Perception Of The Music and not the mechanical compression waves.

The Odd and Sometimes Uncomfortable Fusion Of Spirit Into matter Is Obvious. Imagine a lifeless planet such as Pluto. All operational principles of our physical universe are in operation on Pluto. On Earth, Life Changes everything. Life Is Totally New and Different from physical reality. One need only step back To See[5z68] What The LORD Has Done. The Next Step Is To Appreciate This Improvement To physical being. The Further Step Is To Participate In Its Flowering.[5z69]

This logic is proof of two membrane systems.

7th Dimension: The 7th dimension is the enfolding and unfolding[5z70] of the physical membrane system to yield what We know as our physical universe. This is the reality described by the physical sciences. This universe has form and a continuum where one situation merges into the next. The past can be recorded; and the future proceeds from possibilities that conform to the physical laws of matter, quantum physics, general and special relativity, and ordinary physical observation.

We can discover the origin of this physical universe and predict its end. The math attempts to describe the components and the continuum. Infinite Potential In The 10th D Collapses Information Through Limiting Instructions To The 9th D, further collapsing to the limitations of physical membrane system operation in the 8th d. Even though there is an incredible number of possible progressions of this universe of matter and its attendant energies as it proceeds through time, the rules governing matter and its attendant energies in all of these possible iterations of our universe are the same consistent laws of physics.

The big bang has given us the beginning of our universe of matter and its attendant energies. The 7th dimension is ripe with all the possible developments and tangents as this universe progresses. Those lead to the possible endings of our physical universe.

Our 7th-D Spiritual Universe Crashes,[5z71] By The WORD of GOD, Into our universe of matter and its attendant energies. Ours Is A Fused Spiritual-physical Universe, Which Continues To Unfold With Spiritual Beings.

We Know Ourselves To Be One Type of Spiritual Being. Our Type Is A Being With Consciousness. Each Human Being Is both an Observer and a Participant In this physical universe. This Participation Is Part Of The Unfolding Of Possibilities.

The Fusion Yields Fullness Of Being With Causative Effects That Could Not Happen Without The Presence Of Spirit. For Example, Consider The Effect Of Forgiveness On the current physical situation. Reality Will Unfold Entirely Differently When A Participant Forgives Another Participant as opposed to the unfolding of reality without Forgiveness. We Will Explore Spiritual Causation in a later chapter as It Has Influence at the micro and macro levels of reality.

6th Dimension: This is the Dimension that is most Formative regarding the continuum and eventual conclusion of Our Universe.

If one could jump from the current situation to a Universe with the same beginning but with different occurrences, some impossible in ordinary Sequence,[5z72] that Leap[5z73] would occur in the 6th Dimension.

For example, could We just jump to a Universe like Ours where the atomic bomb was never invented? Probably not, but some theoretical physicists believe that such parallel universes[5z74] exist along with us at the same time. That theory states that our universe has several iterations, all real at this time—the same universe existing now on different timelines[5z75] with different manifestations.

Our Teaching asserts that such parallel universes are not possible because time forces physical reality forward. However, they theorize that the incredible amount of dark matter[5z76] in our universe is evidence that parallel iterations of our universe are present to balance that equation.[5z77] We deduce that dark matter is probably the "opaque plasma" trapping photons in dense plasma mass mentioned in [4z18].

Given chaos theory and the unpredictability of future events in the 6th D, We will continue to explore and seek evidence of our universe manifested differently, proceeding as some type of parallel multiverse.[5z78] Since parallel universes are but one explanation of dark matter and since a cause-and-effect relationship (a law in the 7th D) has not been established substantiating the existence of parallel physical universes, the parallel universe theory is nothing but fiction until clear and convincing evidence is presented.

It is now accepted that the reason time forces physical reality forward with No return[5z79] to the past is that a quantum wave is indeterminate regarding future events. However, once it collapses into being, it is determined. The next event is undetermined,[5z80] but once it collapses into being, it too is fixed as a situation that cannot be changed. There can be no reversal of the continuum of time.

figure 4: Our Sequential Universe

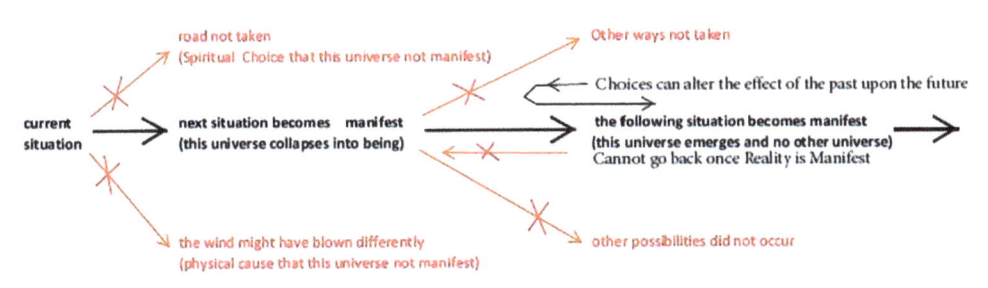

Diagram of our sequential multiverse, by Allyn Richert AD 2020

The Universe We Live In is verified as a sequential multiverse.[2q] We Live In a universe where the atomic bomb was invented. The continuum of time (another rule in our 7th d deriving from general relativity) will not allow that invention to be undone as Our Reality Has Unfolded To Manifest the invention of the atomic bomb. Human Beings Must Proceed forward in time In Our Universe, Bearing The Awesome Responsibility Of Managing atomic power.

However, The Spiritual Membrane System Can Operate In The 6th D, Presenting any number of Variations to the ordinary progression of events relating to the reality of the atomic bomb. Ordinary Human Impulse and Dominance Norms Yield The Conclusion that nuclear Self-annihilation of the Human species is inevitable. It is probably a Self-inflicted conclusion to Human Existence.

Some Expansions On 6th-D Possibilities Include The "Love Thy Neighbor As Thyself" Teachings of Christianity[5z5z81] and Confucianism.[5z82] Also, Ancient Greek Philosophy Teaches The Ideal[5z83] Of "Agape" Love[5z84] As The Same Ethic. Also, Democracy, Social Utilitarian Thinking, as well as gradual Human genetic Evolution,[5z85] operate to Provide Alternatives.[5z86] These Provide Causes That May Interfere with the probability of mass Self-destruction[5z87] Of Humanity by atomic war.

Spiritual Action—Such As Forgiveness, Rational Compromise,[5z88] and Peaceful Reorganizations[5z89]—Serves To Reset[5z90] The Sequences and Probabilities[5z91] already in motion. Better outcomes of physical being Can Be Imagined and Then Crafted By Spiritual Beings. These Are 6th-Dimensional Spiritual Alternatives to the inevitability of Human Self-destruction by atomic war.

This is how the impossible becomes possible. Every day of continued Existence Of The Human species Is A Testament That Human Spiritual Free Will[5z92] Overcomes physical determinism.[5z93]

This Is One Example Of Spiritual Causation, Referred To earlier In This Teaching.

Where "time travel" is impossible in the physical universe because a physical situation cannot be duplicated, Ideas and Spiritual Action Transcend[5z94] time In The 6th D. Utilizing Spiritual Action, We Travel back In Time Spiritually To Undo the inevitability of mass destruction that would be the ordinary course of events In Human Experience.

Yes, A 6th-Dimensional Jump from a universe where Human history was dominated by the strong man conquering mercilessly and gathering immense power to himself to the alternative now-Emergent[5z95] Universe, With Christ Spreading Brotherhood[5z96] and Love, Changes all the Probabilities for The Human species. Saving Grace[5z97] Is An Interruption To the self-destructive linear flow that seems predetermined in the 5th dimension.

5th Dimension: What Will Be? The Choice Is Yours. The 5th Dimension Presents The Reality That Each Of Us Creates day by day Caused By Our Choices and Decisions. A Situation Exists, and Reality Moves Forward, Influenced By Conscious Directives.[5z98] Though The Choices Of Other Spiritual Beings May Be Influential In The 5th D, The 5th D Is The Most Human Of Dimensions.

The Mobility[5z99] Provided To Life Presents Decisions To Be Made literally at every Turn. Moving this way will set off a chain of Possibilities That Will Lead To The Unfolding Of One Universe. Moving another way will set off a different chain of Possibilities That Will Lead To The Unfolding Of A Different Universe.

The Spiritual Membrane System Offers Freedom Of Choice To Conscious Creatures. Advanced Creatures such as Human Beings are constantly taking advantage of the Possibilities allowed in higher Dimensions To Influence Their Choices In The 5th D. Consequently, Your Reality Is What You Choose To Make Of It each moment Going Forward.

Cause and Effect has matured on this small planet in the 4th dimension By Our Choices In 5th-Dimensional Reality.

This illustration Is Offered to depict You Going Forward in time and The Path You Have Chosen. Alternative Paths that You might have chosen are also shown. Those would have resulted in a different future.

(https://www.denisonforum.org/resources/why-believe-in-god/)

4th dimension: As Choices Are Made In The 5th Dimension, reality emerges continuously in the 4th dimension. We call this continuous progression of reality "time." Time is the basic continuum of reality in all physical universes.

Matter endures[5z100], so the continuum will march matter into the future continually, regardless of Conscious Observation or Participation. Yes, if a tree falls in the woods and nobody heard it, it really did fall. Whether or not that tree falling made a "sound" depends on how *sound* is defined. If *sound* is defined as a physical compression wave, then the tree falling and striking the ground did make a sound, even if no conscious being heard it (objective). If sound is defined as somebody Participating in that event, then the tree falling and striking the ground did not happen from a subjective perspective. This points out the error or shortfall of all subjective perspectives, such as quantum "observation."

A physical situation exists, but it cannot remain the same. The "big bang" gave forces to the matter created. This matter is always under force to act, react, and change. The forced changes to our 3rd-dimensional situation provides a continuum that is "time." In this sense, "time" may also be viewed as a force in physical reality.

Time is created, along with space, as matter speeds away from the point of singularity and the big bang. Our universe allows for time to be observed, measured, and experienced divergently.[5z101] However, time progresses continuously and cannot be reversed after it has moved on in the 4th d. The boundary of the 4th d is strict.[5z102] An operational principle of all physical universes is that the next situation is forced to emerge. Time will not allow the situation to stand still or move backward to an earlier manifestation.

There is a cosmological debate as to whether time should be considered only a physical dimension or whether time should also be considered a physical force like gravity, electromagnetism, the weak atomic force, the strong atomic force, and inertia.

Some would say that time is merely a theoretical dimension describing the progression to the next situation. On the contrary, Our Teaching establishes time to be the most powerful physical force. Time is the most powerful physical force because time is the Divine Vibration providing continuity at the string level. Hence, matter is presented solid in the present and is forced to continue that manifestation in the next situation and the next and so on—continuously. In this fashion, time forces matter to continue.[5z103] Time is integral to matter—that is, time is a wave-feature[5z104] of strings. Our Teaching is that a quantum wave is a GOD-Wave, and each string is its collapse into physical reality. A quantum field[5z105] is the mechanism that becomes operational In The 9th D that fashions physical reality. Time cannot stop in any physical universe. Time is an operational principle of the physical membrane system.

Furthermore, independent physical instrumentation, as well as mathematics, can measure time. The measurements show that time is consistent and entirely predictable, even within the broader scope of general relativity.[5z106] This provides verification separate from Human senses that the force of time is dependable. This verification is as convincing as the independent verification of the other physical forces. We Conclude that time is both a physical dimension and a force in physical reality.

We discussed how a situation (the reality and consequences of the atomic bomb, for instance) Can Be Altered[5z107] By Decisions In The 5th D. The effects of an occurrence can be changed by a reboot of data or jump out of ordinary relationships in the 6th D, but it cannot be recreated as the 3rd-Dimensional universe we have here and now. Time is a limitation on physical reality.

3rd dimension: Matter has length, width, and depth. These are the familiar 3 dimensions. Objects in the physical universe are manifested in these 3 dimensions. Yet these objects are not so ordinary as they have puzzled philosophers and scientists for millennia. 3-dimensional objects have presented a hard and undeniable reality. 3-dimensional objects have also presented the challenges and opportunities of this Universe to Life since The Fusion Began.

The 3rd dimension is the reality We Live In here and now. Matter is hard, and it is heavy.[5z108] The hardness and heaviness of objects is verified and reverified by chemical analysis, the mathematics, independent instruments, simple Observation, and Participation. This answers the question, "Is all of this just a dream?" No, all of this is not a dream. Physical objects are forcibly real, independent of You.

The forces operating on objects in a physical universe are (*a*) time, (*b*) inertia, (*c*) the strong atomic force, (*d*) the weak atomic force, (*e*) electromagnetism, and (*f*) gravity. These provide for dynamic operation between matter and its attendant energies. Special relativity explains how matter and energy are two manifestations of the same thing. General relativity weaves time into the fabric[5z109] of inertial mass and gravity. We add to the list of forces operating on objects in a physical universe. The WORD is the Sustaining Force providing The Information and Instruction for all physical forces to operate.

These realities are presented on planet earth in a manner that is conducive to Life against all odds.[5z110] Do We Detect A Spiritual Hand[5z111] Instructing To Make This Possible? Of course!

In chapter 4, we discussed Einstein's theory of special relativity—$e=mc^2$. We discussed how during fission or fusion reactions, great quantities of energy are released, including photons.

The Large Hadron Collider[5z112] has begun to demonstrate the conversion of energy into mass particles and the reverse as the first conclusive testing of special relativity.

Our Teaching points out that GOD Has Provided a chemical proof of special relativity at the molecular level by the rearrangement[5z113] of matter into forms unknown, except by The Action Of Life.[5z114] By The Fusion Of Spirit Into matter in the form of Living Plants right here on earth, photosynthesis converts the sun's photon energy into chemical energy and more complex[5z115] matter. This chemical energy rearranges carbon to create the variety of organic molecules built with the addition of atmospheric carbon dioxide and water gathered through osmosis In Living Plants.

At the elemental level, carbon atoms are created in massive stars when radiation caused by nuclear fusion is superheated to fuse smaller atoms to create carbon atoms (triple-alpha process[5z116]).

Among the energies released in nuclear fusion, photon energy is radiated to earth, where plants convert the light photons into more complex matter to support Life. Life, a Spiritual Cause, Provides The Bridge for photosynthesis[5z117] to operate and change physical reality. The proof of this is that when Life Ceases, so do the chemical reactions. This is a proof of Life As A Spiritual Reality Fused Into our universe of matter and its attendant energies. It is also a proof of the Transformative Effects Of Spirit On physical reality.

The 3rd d presents reality, which proceeds sequentially[5z118] in the 4th d. The continuum runs sequentially as We Observe and Experience the progression, except Modified By The Choices We Make In The 5th D As Spirit Enters[5z119] physical reality.

This Reality is full of possibilities, even to the simplest of matter. Add to this the Vibration Of Spirit and The Fullness Of Living Experience, This Reality Is Worthy Of GOD.[5z120]

Indeed, We can Realize GOD Taking Pleasure (or displeasure) In Our Acts and Experiences Because Our Beings and Our Conscious Awareness Are Among GOD's Points Of Observation and Of GOD's Participation. In other words, GOD Is

Present, Personally Intimate[5z121] In The Consciousness Of Each Of Us. The Pleasure Of GOD Is the answer to all questions of The Purpose[5z122] Of Our Being, such as "Who Am I?" "What Am I?" "Why Am I here?" "What Is This Consciousness and Awareness That I Have?"

2nd dimension: We like to think of flat things, such as a piece of paper, as 2-dimensional objects. However, all physical flat things have some thickness. If a material object were only one atom thick, it would still have the 3rd dimension of depth (height). The 3rd d is present in all matter. Even radiation requires space to exist.

Consequently, the 2nd dimension is a theoretical dimension but a necessary dimension to build the 3rd-dimensional universe where We Live. The 2nd d, a plane, mostly has relevance to the mathematics of plane geometry[5z123] that describes how reality is constructed. The 2nd d does not exist on its own.

The 2nd d remains useful as all physical objects have width. Width is an expansion on length.

1st dimension: The 1st dimension is a theoretical dimension as well. Again, the 1st d is necessary to build the 3-dimensional physical universe where We Live. The 1st d does not exist on its own.

If a material object had length but was only one atom thick and one atom wide, it would still have the 2nd dimension of width and the 3rd dimension of depth. Physics has calculated that even a carbon atom measures trillions of Planck lengths in each direction. A quantum "string" is one Planck length, so even the smallest physical component has length.

There is no reality in our universe of matter and its attendant energies in the 1st dimension, except perhaps the excitation of a string, closed at one end[5z124] to stretch from the 0 point in a quantum field (figure 5). The concept of a line can be expanded as a metaphor to discuss the development of the linear flow expressed as a time continuum in the 4th d, as well as the spatial continuum in the 1st d.

The 1st d remains useful as all physical objects have length. Length is a dimension that describes an expansion of the starting point.

point	*line*	Plane	Solid
Zero dimensions	One dimension	Two dimensions	Three dimensions
■	/	▱	▢

(www.mathopenref.com)

0th Dimension (a point): A point is a start that is more than nothing. A point does not have length, width, or depth. We can debate whether a dot or a "point particle" has 1, 2, or 3 dimensions. Regardless, a "point" at the 0th dimension (nildimension) merely describes that there is a start located in reality, the nature of which has not been Realized.[5z125] It is not yet real but presumes the future for something to become manifested.

My simple Mind envisions a point as the nothingness through which the metastring of physical creation in the 9th D manifests our universe of matter and its attendant energies. It is an odd Metaphor[5z126] for the singularity that burst into our universe of matter and its attendant energies, yet not so odd as this may be how the WORD proceeds with Creation.

Understanding This Brings You Closer to GOD.

figure 5: The WORD 10th D, Manifests Reality 9th D, along the physical Metastring to create a quantum field in the 0th d, from which a "string" or "quant" is created as a primary component of physical reality, the 3rd d. One characteristic of this and all strings is continuity, as "time" begins as the primary force continuing this manifestation.

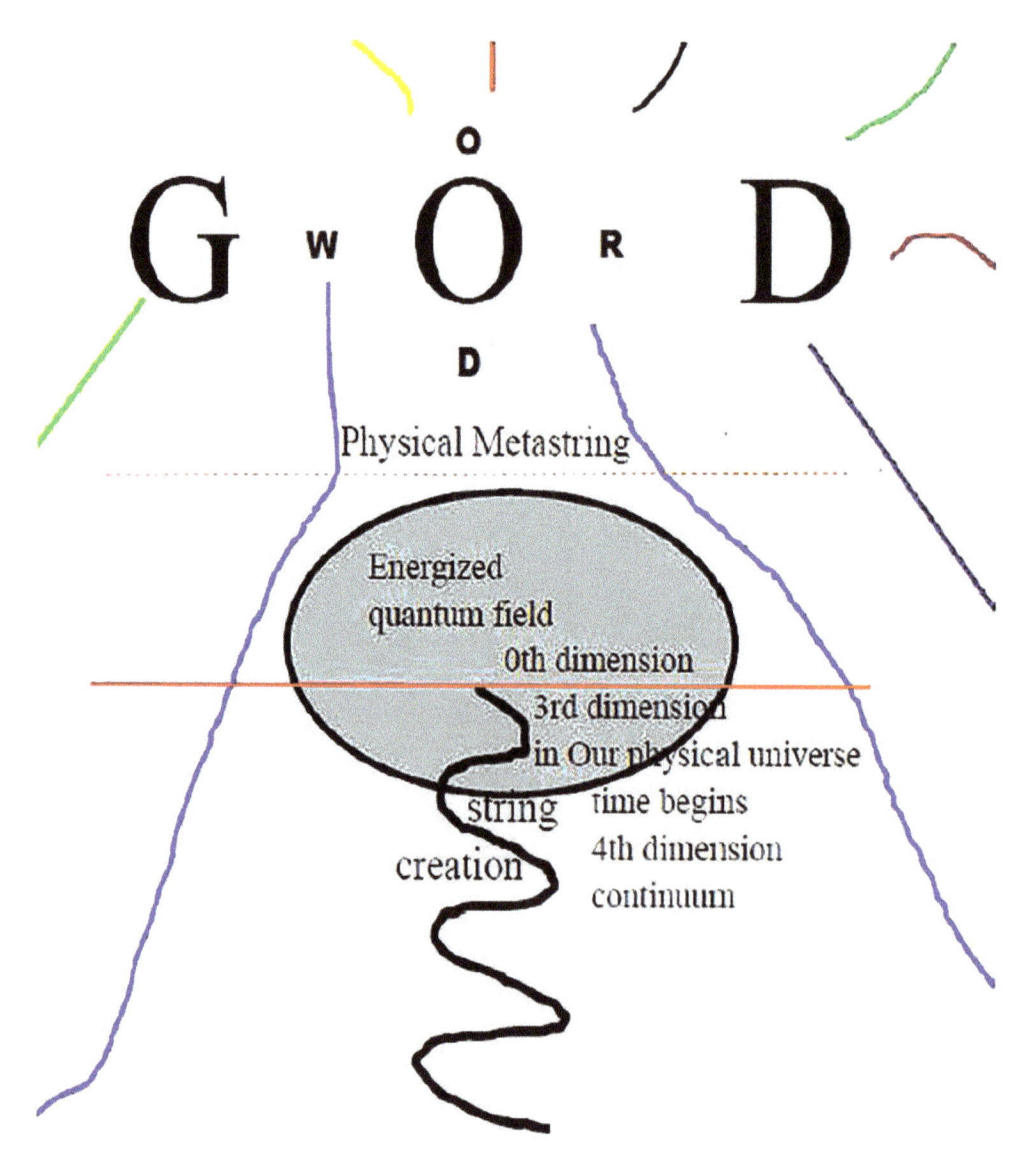

String Creation—Drawing by Allyn Richert, February AD 2021

CHAPTER 6

Lower Dimensions and The Elevation Toward GOD

Now that we have described the manner in which Dimensional Reasoning Reveals Reality From GOD's Point Of View, Let Us Elevate from the simplest to the most complex, as Human Beings, to see what We can Discover on the way up.

0th dimension (point): Mathematics postulates a point. Like the number 0, a point is a placeholder. It is just a location in our physical universe. However, In The Machinery Of 9th-D Creation, a point is pregnant with both time and space. A point is where Creation happens.

The 9th D Creates the physical metastring to Manifest a singularity as Instructed By The WORD. The singularity must explode as a "big bang" according to the Information Instructed. A big bang yields the formation of plasma, accelerating from the singularity after the initial matter/antimatter reactions.[6a] This plasma is waves of formative information within the space it occupies. After the initial reactions, the residual energy condenses to be subatomic particles as the system cools and stabilizes. The space, energy, and particles have length, width, and depth. These are forced by their Instructional Information to combine to form atoms with dimensions. These particles manifest characteristics that can be codified as the laws of physical reality. Some of the laws have been discovered, and some are yet to be discovered.

The creative mystery that theoretical physics is now developing is, how is matter formed from nothing? Physicists are looking at "energy," such as quantum waves, as the source for that formation—but of course, where does that energy come from? How is the Instructional Information programmed?

Once we solve those puzzles, we will understand the operation of the physical metastring in the 9th D. This is the Understanding Of GOD's WILL. The WORD Is In Operation relative to physical creation.

Our first Understanding of GOD is that GOD's WORD is the Cause—the Cause of causes[6b]—Imbued In All Reality. Hence, GOD Is An All-Encompassing[6c] Being.

A devil[6d] creeps in with a skeptical[6e] view. That devil says that there is a physical principle called self-organization.[6f] That is the theory that the smallest particles organize themselves spontaneously[6g] from nothing. Then larger constructions organize themselves from random combinations of the smaller ones. There need be no cause. "it just happens" according to that theory. Over time and after nearly infinite failures to advance, a favorable chance construction survives. Then a more complex system develops based on random successful constructions under that theory.

The error in self-organization theory is that it Presumes[6h] that there is information in the most basic forms that allows organization of anything at all. In other words, there needs to be something to cause a quantum wave or a "string" and to organize into being of any sort. The presumption of something with "no cause" is a leap of the faith cursed upon the faithless. That devil destroys itself.

Simply Acknowledging a Prime Cause of Reality carries the logic demanded by science. Prime Cause Equals GOD (QED[6i] as proofs go)!

A point is prior to the 1st d. Though physically unrealized, a point is the beginning of Dimensional Reasoning. It allows all other constructions to be quantified. It admits to GOD, the Creator, for its origin and its expansions.

Hence, the 10th D Conceives the 0th D. The two ends of Our Dimensional hierarchy are tied together. It is called Creation. All Constructions and evolution of systems emerge from the Creative Acts of GOD. Total Realization of This Is Actually Experienced only upon Reunification With The ONE. That is the shortcut but not so easily Achieved.

The obstacles are, how to Experience this, and how to prove It?

Any Sharing or Invocation[6j] Of GOD—such as Prayer, Worship, Meditation, or Wonder[6k]—Are Ways To Experience This. If you are ready, Meditate In "THE CLEAR LIGHT of The Void."[6l]

Formative Action, in any Dimension, is the Way to prove It.

1st d (line): Physical expansions begin in the 1st d. A line is a straight connection and what is between. Though in ontological theory a line extends to infinity in both directions, it has no cosmological or physical meaning until the line terminates at one or both ends. The 1st dimension encompasses a beginning and an ending. For example, I am walking from the kitchen to the bathroom—two places but only two points in my mind. The direct trip is a line in the 1st d.

2nd d (plane): I am continuing my trip from the kitchen to the bathroom in this house, except I must turn the corner into the hallway and turn again into the bathroom. Whether straight or circuitous,[6m] the points are connected. The circuitous route defines a plane in the 2nd d.

Again, in Ontological theory, a plane has no edges but extends to infinity in length and width. It has no cosmological or physical meaning until it terminates in at least one direction. In our example, the origin point, the turn point into the hallway, the turn point into the bathroom, and a point in the bathroom define a real and limited plane.

Indeed, the 2nd dimension is rich with concepts of flatness. Gravity places Our feet on the ground; and it seems that right, left, straight ahead, or backing up consumes the majority of Our motion and planning.

3rd d: This is where We Live. I must climb steps to get to the bathroom upstairs because the one on the main floor is occupied. The plane is defined by My feet on the ground as they direct the change in direction. I experience the incline plane as My feet on flat surfaces—the steps. However, the limitations of the 2nd dimension have been exceeded. A deeper reality has forced itself upon My Awareness as I climb from one flat surface to the next, elevating with each step.

Dimensional Reasoning involves the observational grouping of reality into categories, each with a logical and descriptive boundary defining the operation of that dimension. Please observe that each higher dimension includes the lower dimensions, plus the broader features manifested in the higher dimension. Dividing reality into successively grander fields of influence is very useful. It allows the codification of rules that explain and predict reality within each dimension.

Our physical world is described in its 3 dimensions. Earlier In Our Teaching, We explained that 3rd-dimensional thinking is how Human Consciousness is oriented. Cosmologically, the 3 dimensions define our apparent physical universe.

The 1st, 2nd, and 3rd dimensions merge[6n] in physical reality into objects. These are the things in our real physical universe. The mathematics is meaningful in many operations, such as calculating the volume or mass of an object or calculating the distance between points. These calculations are valuable in any number of processes as reality unfolds through time.

Matter is the core of Our Observation. It is no coincidence that Human senses evolved around detecting material objects, manipulating processes involving material objects, as well as other manifestations that material objects cause. It is the presence of advanced senses in Conscious Beings that allow sensations of sights, sounds, smells, touches, and tastes that collapse reality into meaningful Perceptions.

We use the word *collapse* to describe the manifestation of 3-dimensional reality. Future possibilities are so diverse that it is impossible to recognize all of them. They all condense into only one reality in the present. This collapse into one identifiable reality in the present also occurs in higher dimensions. For example, 8th-D possibilities for a physical universe to be created all collapse into a singularity at the formation of a 7th-d physical universe. The Creation Of A physical metastring in the 9th D Is The Collapse Of Diverse Information In The 10th-D Instruction To Create the physical membrane system.

4th d: Time continues that which exists in physical reality and forces it to become... The 3rd-dimensional universe unfolds continuously. The 3rd d is descriptive of the length, width, and depth of matter. That is a static description, but the progression cannot be halted and forces a broader reality to be recognized. Though We may Remember a situation, We Observe a physical continuum. The 3rd-dimensional universe changes because reality in our universe is not static. Objects are always changing and are in motion relative to one another in dynamic operation. The continuum is an operational principle of a material universe. We call it "time."

Time figures dynamically into every description of our physical universe: announcing change, describing change, calculating change, and being in the stream of physical reality.

It is important to note that time would be in operation in all physical universes, even if there was no Consciousness.

Is it a limitation on the 4th d that time does not exist in nonphysical membrane systems? Probably, but each membrane system must be examined to define its operational principles. A Spiritual Universe has a Continuum of Being.[6o] However, a Spiritual Continuum[6p] does not operate according to general relativity and quantum mechanics. There is no physical object in the 8th-D Spiritual Membrane System. Hence, there is no time in the Spiritual Membrane System in the manner that general relativity defines time in physical reality.

A Spiritual Continuum is a totally different Process as it is not limited to forward progression. A proof of the absence of time in Our Spiritual Universe is as follows. A Spiritual Being is Equipped with Recollection.[6q] Recollection Allows a Jump to a previous event. The Experience Of That Recollection May Be As Fulfilling as the original event.

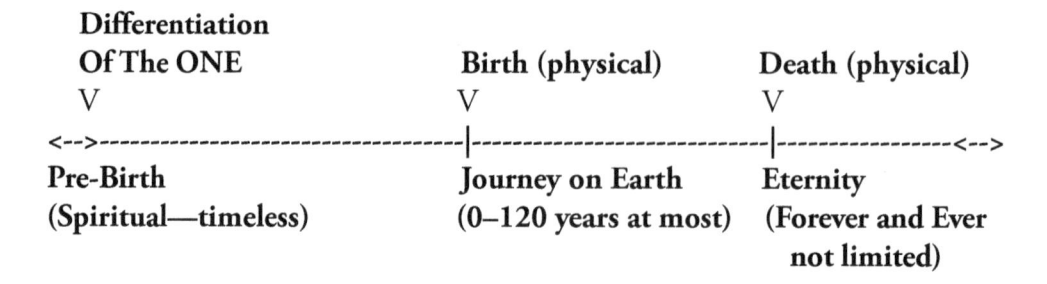

```
Differentiation
Of The ONE                  Birth (physical)           Death (physical)
     V                             V                          V
<-->-----------------------------|---------------------------|-----------------<-->
Pre-Birth                   Journey on Earth            Eternity
(Spiritual—timeless)        (0–120 years at most)       (Forever and Ever
                                                         not limited)
```

Illustration of Our Spiritual Continuum by Allyn Richert, November AD 2020

Another proof of Our Spiritual Continuum is that a Spiritual Being can simply Pause[6r] and Spiritual Reality will not push it forward. Though A Continuum Exists In Our Spiritual Universe, Its Principles Of Continuation are very different from physical time.

An Aspect Of This Revelation Is That A Spiritual Continuum Caused By The Spiritual Metastring depends entirely on The Flow Of Spiritual Energy Along That Metastring Between The Individual Independent Spirit and GOD.

5th D: I am flying from Washington, DC, Reagan Airport to Omaha's Epley Airport. These are only two points in My Mind. The trip is a connection. Straight or circuitous, the points are connected.

However, it is not a simple connection between two points. The jet climbs off the ground and into the sky as the 3rd d is boldly manifested. The situation changes as I Experience each moment of the flight with more or less Awareness as permitted by My biochemistry.[6s] I Experience a continuous journey as defined by the 4th d. The flow of Being in time appears to Me as a merciless passage, with the 3-dimensional reality speeding relentlessly[6t] into the future.

However, though I am on board[6u] this unstoppable reality, I Choose To Read a book instead of Taking a nap. Though this Choice had no impact on most of Our Universe, I Learned something from Reading the book that Caused Me To Change My Plans upon landing. In fact, It Changed the entire Effort and Conclusion Of My trip. I Said Different Things, and The Results were Different than originally Planned. It is a feature of the 5th d that the relentless continuum of matter moving into the future is undetermined in many ways as it proceeds. Human Choices and The Choices of Other Beings Alter Reality going forward. This is why a study of Reality requires a 5th Dimension. This is a proof of 5th-Dimensional integrity.

The 5th D is ripe, demanding Choices that Set off Cause-and-Effect Consequences For Reality. It clearly points out that the boundaries of Reality can be Bent[6v] again and again differently as Choices Force Being this way or that.

So We have a reality in 3 dimensions continuing through time to the next situation in the 4th d. Furthermore, situations are Influenced by Choices in the 5th d. Looking back, it is Demonstrated to Me that I Made the Correct Choices on that trip to Omaha.

Ethics[6w] is the branch of philosophy that is the study of Right and wrong. More generally, it is the study of Human Choices. Some Choices turn out for the better—some for the worse. The Human Mind finds patterns. Types of Choices that generally yield better results rise to the top of the Ethical hierarchy. Types that are destructive or limiting sink to the bottom.

We are not just doing statistics.[6x] There are deeper-rooted reasons based in Cause and Effect that explain why certain Types of Choices generally Yield the Richer,[6y] Uplifting,[6z] and Happier[6z1] Flow of situations. Beneficial Ethical Choices are the Ones We Ought[6z2] to Choose. Conforming Actions are the Actions We Ought to Take.

Hence, Ethics Establishes Right and Wrong, not by simple observation of outcome[6z3] but by Analysis of Cause and Effect.

It is easy to generalize, so Ethical Behavior Is Established (Normative Behavior). It is not so easy to Apply an Ethical Maxim[6z4] to specific situations. The future demands Correct Choices, now. Statistics help. Cause-and-Effect Analysis Guides. Yet It Is the Individual's Own Vision of How the Future Should Unfold that Provides the Decision-Making Force.[6z5] One's Own Feelings at the time of Decision Form the next situation.

History shows Us that the Force of the Feelings of Many and the Dominance[6z6] of the Feelings of a Few can result in Action for a very Benevolent[6z7] Future or a series of catastrophes enveloping the Situations of so many Innocents.[6z8]

Ethics then Demands Guiding Principles.[6z9] Nearly every Proverb[6z10] or Wise Saying Provides Well-Reasoned Advice.[6z11] When the Advice is Understood as Intended, the Proverb Becomes Formative in the 5th D. Many of these Wise Norms are above the averages[6z12] and usual Cause-and-Effect Relationships. Such Wisdom Is Inspired by Spirituality[6z13] well beyond the 5th Dimension of simple Human Choice or complex Collective Choices.[6z14]

All Successful Civilizations are Founded on Commandments.[6z15] All Successful Nations are Founded on Laws.[6z16] Legitimate[6z17] Commandments and Laws are derived from Ethical Norms, which promote the common interests and well-being of groups of People.

If You can Connect to the Divine Metastring that Dangles within the confusion of 6th-Dimensional possibilities and impossibilities (so potential in the 5th D), then Formative Wisdom is Presented and Received.

This is why so many Solemn Vows[6z18] end with the words "So Help Me God."[6z19] The Presentation Of This Formative Wisdom[6z20] Is In A Calm Receptivity[6z21] To The LORD In Whatever Facet Of GOD's Being You Can Recognize and Share. Communion,[6z22] or Sharing of Divine Energy, Establishes The Formative Connection. This is not only a Guide To Correct Choices but Stimulation,[6z23] Elation,[6z24] Power, and A Deep Confidence In The Correct Fulfillment Of Life.

Discussion of Connection To The Divine must include a Discussion of "Who" [6z25] Is Connecting To The Divine. We have restated that You Are Spirit Incarnate In physical matter. That implies that Your Spirit Has An Origin Before Your body. Your Spirit Usually Has A Destiny[6z26] After your body disintegrates.[6z27]

To Understand What Your Spirit Is and How It Is Integrated[6z28] Into Your body, let Us begin with a simple analogy. A radio is playing a lively tune in the next room. You observe the music as part of the radio. Speakers are vibrating. You turn the music up or down using the controls on the radio set.[6z29] It seems that the radio contains the Music. The truth is that the radio does not make the signal. The radio just has mechanisms that receive signal and translate it electronically[6z30] to project[6z31] from the speakers as compression waves that You hear. The signal is radio waves[6z32] generated by a distant transmitter that radiate through the air as electromagnetic energy for any radio receiver[6z33] in the broadcast area[6z34] to receive. The radio waves are information separate from the radio. Applying this analogy to Your Spirit and Your body, Your body is like the radio set, and Your Spirit is like the radio waves. Your Spirit or Soul Is A Broadcast[6z35] From Our Spiritual Universe. Your body is a finely tuned physical Instrument that receives and incorporates Your Spirit.[6z36] Your Spirit Is Manifested As The Human Consciousness That You Experience. You Identify This Consciousness As Yourself.[6z37]

Neurologists[6z38] identify the posterior cingulate cortex[6z39] in Your brain as the locus of Your Experiential Self.[6z40] This interacts with Your hippocampus,[6z41] the center of Memory[6z42] and Emotion,[6z43] and Your thalamus[6z44] for Processing[6z45] of Consciousness To Construct[6z46] Your Awareness, Thoughts,[6z47] and Feelings.[6z48]

All this brain activity is like the radio. The physical mechanism is there for a full-functioning Consciousness. What is missing from Your brain is the Signal.[6z49] Your Spirit (Soul) is Information coming from Our Spiritual Universe to Animate Your body with Your Conscious Awareness. That Spiritual Information is like the radio waves that the radio set receives and processes.

This analogy[6z50] helps You understand the reality of The Fusion of Spirit Into matter To Yield The Reality That You Live[6z51] In Consciously. The radio analogy is not a complete representation because both the radio set and the radio waves are part of our physical universe of matter and its attendant energies. The difference is that Your Consciousness Is A Fusion Of Your body, which is material, With Your Individual Soul, which is not produced by physical processes.

We capitalize the word *You* and *Your* in This Teaching for those words to mean "Your Conscious Identity As a physical body With An Individual Immortal Soul."

6th D: The Choices of Others and circumstances of which We are unaware Create a separate reality. The flight of A Butterfly in Mexico can initiate a flow of air currents to cause a tornado in Kansas. A different universe would emerge if The Butterfly had Lingered On A Flower.[2z1]

Stated in terms of quantum physics, the quantum principle of Randomness[6z52] is a principle of operation in the 6th D. While ordinary events unfold according to "laws" of cause and effect through most of Observable[1o and 1p] reality, quantum theory states that a particle observable at this time may not be observable as a wave in this condition. Conversely, when it is observed as a wave, it cannot be observed as a particle. Such tangents as material being, expressed in the context of time, explain how the impossible[6z53] can actually happen in the 6th D. Extraordinary[6z54] changes then become manifest in Our ordinary Reality.

The 6th D is ripe with alternative manifestations of Our Universe. It is not just the Choices and circumstances that Create Reality but the unlikely flow of Cause and Effect from the broader Reality. Metaphysical Synthesis[6z55] is the uncanny but Real result of all the Influences Operating To Create Reality.

Hence, a Vision,[6z56] Idea,[6z57] or Thought can Be Formative if It Causes A Change[6z58] to the established Flow. The Vision is not physically real, but It Is a Spiritual Occurrence that can Cause a Different Universe To Become Manifested If You Act On That Vision.

Of course, most sleeping dreams[6z59] are merely a recollection of recent experiences or random thoughts. These are forgotten as soon as You awake. They are neither formative nor spiritual.

Media,[6z60] fantasy,[6z61] and fiction[6z62] can be very entertaining. Elevated, this entertainment can be part of the Pleasure GOD Shares while Entering Your Consciousness.

Entertaining as fantasy and fiction is, do not assume that much of what is portrayed in fiction can really happen in physical reality. The Honest[6z63] collection of data and analysis of Cause and Effect inferred from that data is the only way to establish a broader Reality.

Do not be misled[6z64] by fiction. Electronic manipulation[6z65] of images[6z66] now creates media depicting any number of images that have never been real events. They are just part of a fantasy, a story. Such images have a reality in Your imagination[6z67] but are not real in our physical universe. Powerful Beings often cleverly manipulate communication to control Your Choices. You must carefully analyze the data You Use To Make Important Choices.

Equally misleading are stories of ghosts,[6z68] apparitions,[6z69] and the like that never existed apart from stories. Be sure to identify these correctly and categorize them as fiction.

Human Beings can have thoughts that are unreal or false in reality. The thought, and even communication, is a real thought or communication. However, false thoughts and communications presented as The Truth are sinful. They reduce Spiritual Energy.

Extreme danger exists in ideas presented in fictional stories or false communication if false ideas become Understood and Realized in Common Belief[6z70] or Formative Action.[6z71] Beware of fiction presented as fact to influence Your Action. Careful Cause and Effect Analysis should be Performed Before Realizing fictional ideas.

A discussion of the Operation Of The Logical Dialectic in Social Ethics is necessary to Empower You To Act Appropriately In the 5th D, as You are faced with 6th D Situations. The Logical Dialectic[6z55] is the name given to a process on a continuum, which describes the current situation as a "thesis." A Spiritual Being, Aware That What It Chooses To Do Next Will Cause The Consequential Situation to Become Real (Quantum Becoming), Considers Its Options. Frequently, The Option contains premises or Forces "opposite" to those currently in Operation called an "antithesis."

The Logical Dialectic

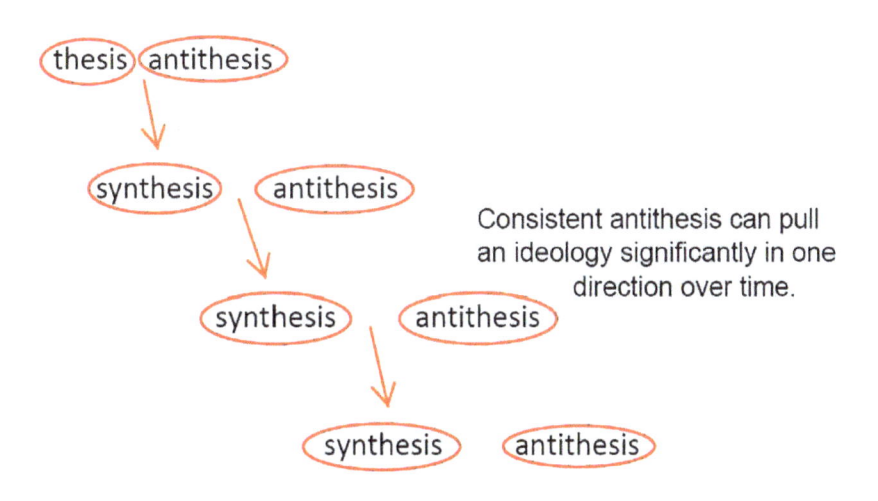

Logical Dialectic
Drawing by Allyn Richert, 2020

Consistent antithesis can pull an ideology significantly in one direction over time.

You Can Debate Whether "The Good Of The Many" outweighs "The Good Of The Few" when they are incompatible based on Consequences Of Action. To Make The Correct Choice, Your Cause-And-Effect Analysis Must Be Accurate, or You Will Make the wrong choice leading to a less Harmonious consequence.

Also see [11z59].

Note that You cannot project Spiritual Energy onto physical objects. Physical Objects have no soul, so they cannot receive or appreciate Spiritual Energy. It is a common fiction and sin called "idolatry" for You to ascribe Spirit to a physical reality that is not a living being.

It May Be Meaningful For You To Use a physical object—such as a crystal, a neckpiece, a statue, a tombstone, or any other physical image, object, or sensory phenomenon—as a Reminder Of Your Connection To GOD. However, do not be confused. No physical object has a spirit, except those Into Which The WORD Has Fused Spirit. In Our physical universe, Those would only Be Living Beings.

This author has never seen a ghost. I do not doubt that others may have seen ghosts. However, I have never interacted with an apparition with my five senses.

In contrast, I constantly Observe the Light[6z72] of Spiritual Presence physically Manifested In Living Beings. I constantly Verify for Myself My Own Spiritual Being based on My Experiences As A Conscious Being Incarnate Within My physical body.

This image is offered to Remind You That Your Immortal Soul Is Incarnated Into your body. Shown Here as Light, Your Soul Is Located At Your Center, Though It May Be Located At Any Chakra or As A General Radiance Throughout your body.

GOD—*THE DIMENSIONAL REVELATION*

Stephen Robinson 2020 (https://medium2spirit.com/2020/07/you-are-a-spiritual-being-with-a-body/)

Living Consciousness In Advanced physical Beings, and even simple Awareness in less-Organized physical Beings, is the avenue that I Witness that Spirits Take To Manifest In Our physical universe. That Incarnation[6z73] Presents Continuity Of The Spirit's Presence During the Lifetime[6z74] of the physical body.

We must discuss the adverse opinion that states that because consciousness is so intimately tied to physical metabolism,[6z75] then consciousness may be explained as a construction of physical being and not spirit at all. This logic severely diminishes reality and is proved incorrect[6z76] by direct Observation.

This Author had a death Experience[6z77] In Which My Consciousness Departed From My physical body, yet I was still Aware. A fall killed me with broken ribs, hernia, and other internal injuries. My Consciousness Departed into a dark and oppressive Awareness that was no dream. Being in hades[6z78] was miserable. The ugly weight of darkness was both felt and seen. I was deeply Afraid[6z79] as the Awareness and listless wandering[6z80] persisted. From a far State Of Being, I Witnessed My Mother, Shirley Richert, seated on a hospital bed, Holding my body and Weeping. Then suddenly I Reincarnated Into My body—Alive, Awake, and Aware.

Upon Reincarnation,[6z81] I was Participating again in physical being. I Looked Up At My Mother, Feeling Her Mournful[6z82] Hugs and Then Her Joy[6z83] as I Came Back To Her—Alive. My Participation In My body was so different from Observing My Mother Holding my body from My Perspective In My Afterlife.

Of course, Personal Experience totally Convinces Me of the Existence Of My Individual Spirit separate from my body. You may be Able To Relate To Your Own Experiences.

LOWER DIMENSIONS AND THE ELEVATION TOWARD GOD

The mysteriousness of dreams as constructions of a semiconscious Mind is not to be confused with Spiritual Being and Connection To GOD. This Author has had dreams and hallucinations that were nothing more than My wandering Mind.

By contrast, I Have Received Information and Instruction Manifesting As Thoughts that had no basis in my physical experience or mental sequence.

On one occasion, I Felt Compelled[6z84] to return home from work in the middle of one afternoon. As I walked in the house, I found my three-year-old Son, Alex, standing on a stair ledge with a rope wrapped twice tightly around His waist, the other end fixed in a tangle with the railing above. The continuation of this would have been His sliding off the thin ledge to be hung at the waist. Of course, I hurriedly grasped My Son and disconnected the rope.

There can be no physical connection between My Being Compelled to return home and the probable future hanging of My Son. I left work long before My Son could have been in that position, so The Divine Communication Bent time and cause and effect beyond sequences permitted in the lower dimensions. The Hand of GOD[6z85] Caused This 6th-D Tangent To ordinary Reality.

People commonly use the word *Intuition*[6z86] to describe this type of Divine Communication.[6z87] Mystics[6z88] call it "Clairvoyance," or "Seeing."[6z89] Intuition Is a Spiritual Sense[6z90] Operating In physical being. Intuition is just one more proof of Spiritual Being Incarnate In Your physical body.

Billions of similar occurrences among Others provide Experiential proof of Individual Spirit Separate From physical reality.

7th D: The sequential multiverse is a reality. Right now, Our Universe presents a situation in The Flow. A different Universe will emerge as the continuum forces the future to emerge. Every drop of water that falls and every Choice Made Create a different Universe moving forward than if the water was impeded by a fallen rock or a Choice was Made differently. All these potential Universes occur from the same initial starting conditions and the same reality up to the point of departure.

The physical forces and the laws of relativity and quantum physics operate the same way in all the future alternate physical manifestations of our physical universe. The mathematics explaining, as well as verifying, this existence of physical being works in the 7th d because each future manifestation of our physical universe has the same initial development. Our universe is just manifested differently as it collapses into being as reality proceeds forward in time.

Furthermore, it is a principle of the 7th d that all possible iterations[6z91] of our universe, within its boundary, operate from the same beginning and answer to the laws of physics established as it moves forward. There would be time, inertia, the strong atomic force, the weak atomic force, electromagnetic energy, and gravity. These force matter and its attendant energies into their possible interactions.[6z92] That is a lot of possibilities.

GOD—*THE DIMENSIONAL REVELATION*

Twentieth- and twenty-first-century scientific instruments, such as the Hubble Space Telescope[6z93] and electron microscope,[6z94] have expanded Our Vision of our physical universe. Our understanding is bent by the movement of light through the space created by matter in our physical universe. The light from a distant galaxy just Reaching[6z95] us left there billions of years ago. Where is that? How distant is that galaxy now in an expanding universe billions of years later? The laws of physics tell us that the source of that light must be very greatly more distant now. That light source may have ceased to exist as the star may have burned out or exploded as a supernova.[6z96] Yet light providing evidence of the more recent events has not yet reached us.

The sequential universe is the dominate theory of how our physical universe develops. It is supported by the classical physics, quantum observation,[6z97] mathematics, ordinary Observation,[1o] and Conscious Participation.

It is true that the sequential universe presented here and now may be observed differently, in part, from one perspective or another, but as a whole, our physical universe is the same. The future allows for any number of alternate universes springing from this moment forward, but the past is finished and not to be revisited in physical reality. Also, the current situation is the only one here and now. It is not duplicated in any reality.

There is always the possibility of a 6th-Dimensional tangent—something that cannot be, based on our understanding of physical boundaries, but actually might happen. The idea of a wormhole (Einstein-Rosen bridge)—where space is bent, allowing a physical shortcut to a distant galaxy—remains fiction. These ideas should be investigated. Nobody knows what inventions may realize a theoretical possibility. However, do not be deceived into believing that such an event has ever happened. Tangible evidence is required, and We have no such evidence.

If evidence is ever presented, then examine the occurrence. It would most likely be a 9th-Dimensional Fusion At The Direction Of The WORD From The 10th D. The WORD Of GOD Is Dominant Over all characteristics of Reality. Another way to say this is The WORD Can Change any Reality.

The WORD Has Changed Something. A lifeless physical universe Collided With A Spiritual Universe along one boundary (see this book's cover diagram, figure 1). Spirit Was Infused into matter, Penetrating The Membranes, To Manifest Our Universe Containing Aspects Of Both Systems.

The Vastness Of This Fusion is very confusing to simple biological Creatures Conscious As An Effect Of This Fusion.

8th D: It is important to note that Spiritual Presence[6z98] is not necessarily part of this physical universe. Consciousness, the Presence of Spirit, comes from a different Universe and a different type of Universe. Our Spiritual Universe Is A Coexisting Universe, but It Is unlike our universe of matter and its attendant energies. Its Principles Of Operation and Existence are different.

LOWER DIMENSIONS AND THE ELEVATION TOWARD GOD

Dimensional Reasoning opens Possibilities beyond all the possible physical universes. The 8th Dimension contains our universe of matter and its attendant energies as one universe in the physical membrane system.

All other membrane systems also exist in the 8th D. The 8th D offers principles of being outside of theoretical physics because physical properties do not exist in some 8th-Dimensional Membrane Systems.

Throughout Human history, there are records of Human Experience Of Being Apart From matter and its formative energies. We are not speaking of the reality of dreams, imagination, and other constructs of Mind. We are speaking of the reality of universal systems with totally different operational principles.

Some 8th-Dimensional Systems have neither physical initial conditions nor the laws of physics. The creation of some universes in the 8th D do not have a big bang. They are not composed of molecules, atoms, subatomic particles, strings, quarks,[6z99] or gluons.[6z100] quantum fields do not exist in some 8th-D membrane systems as their universes have no matter or its attendant energies.

To continue 8th-Dimensional Reasoning, imagine a system that has no atoms or molecules, no photons or gamma rays, no strings and superstrings, no space or time. What would be its characteristics? What would be its limitations?

Being in such a system, I will use the word *universe* to describe a 7th-d physical manifestation and *Universe* to describe a 7th-D Spiritual Manifestation. I will use the phrase *membrane system* rather than *universe* as We discuss other realities in the 8th D because a certain type of membrane system may contain many universes of that type.

An 8th-Dimensional membrane system has such characteristics as:

a. It is not empty. A Manifestation exists in the membrane system.
b. It is limited. Like our physical membrane system and Our Spiritual Membrane System, all membrane systems are defined by their operational characteristics. Each operates as a complete and independent system within the limitations of those characteristic boundaries and their principles of operation.
c. The boundary of each membrane system contains all universes manifesting under the principles of operation of that type of membrane system.
d. If the membrane system has only one universe that manifests under the same laws of operation within the boundary of that membrane system, then that membrane system in the 8th dimension is the same as that universe in the 7th dimension.
e. It is Autonomous.[6z101] The membrane system usually exists separately from all other membrane systems.
f. We know of two different membrane systems:
  1. The physical membrane system, which may contain many physical universes, each originating from the WORD Of GOD. The WORD

Instructs physical being to become through 9th Dimensional Processes to manifest as singularity in the 8th dimension, compelling a big bang to create a 7th-d physical universe.

2. The Spiritual Membrane System, which may contain many Spiritual Universes, Each Originating From The WORD Of GOD and containing Spiritual Being.

g. How can We Know more about such diverse Systems that exist? The scientific method of discovery[6z102] will lead to the expansion of Human Knowledge about all of these vast and different systems of Being. All 8th-D Membrane Systems are Knowable[6z103] as each has Manifested Into Reality. They are Knowable even if Humans do not yet have the ability to Observe or Perceive many of them.

This is a broader reality. There may be many such Systems that Exist. What they are and how they operate is mostly beyond Human Observation at this time.

It is a principle of the 8th D that different Types Of Reality Are Manifested. Logical thinking must take on a broader character when time, space, and matter are not present.

Space is created by the presence of matter, but in a system with no matter, there is no space. Time is a continuum of matter and its attendant energies within that space, but if there is no matter and its attendant energies, there is no time. General relativity is not in operation in a membrane system that does not have matter, energy, space, or time.

Not limited to Conscious Being or to physical being, the 8th D Is Inclusive[6z104] of any membrane system that may Exist. We must be careful in Our use of Human words to describe reality that is beyond Human Observation. A membrane system must present some evidence of existence for Us to give it a name. We have given hypothetical names to hypothetical membrane systems and hypothetical universes. Each of these must be verified to be called Real.

There is one other Membrane System operating in the 8th D with which Human Beings are intimately acquainted.[6z105] It is the Membrane System of Spirit. I know of Being in such a System that should be Described As Consciousness. Would it be Conscious Entities?[6z106] Would it be a Pervasive Consciousness[6z107] with specific limitations? Yes and Yes.

The Spiritual Membrane System and any Consequent Spiritual Universe are not material. There is no matter; so physical inertia, The strong and weak atomic forces, electromagnetic energy, gravity, and time do not exist within The Spiritual Boundary. Consequently, there is no space. Time has no meaning as there is no constant continuum to measure. There Is Spiritual Awareness—A Continuum Of Being—but not the continuum of material situations that We get in Human Consciousness on planet earth.

LOWER DIMENSIONS AND THE ELEVATION TOWARD GOD

The Continuum Of Being Of Spiritual Beings In The 8th D is that there are various Modes Of Consciousness specific to each Spiritual Being. There are also diverse Modes Of Consciousness Shared Between[6z108] Spiritual Beings.

The various accounts of Heaven,[6z109] Nirvana,[6z110] Valhalla,[6z111] Alesium,[6z112] and other Spiritual States[6z113] of Being Are All True Spiritual States Of Being if They are accurately recorded and translated To Our Understanding. You Would Have To Experience[6z114] each to discern whether those names describe the same State Of Being or different States Of Being. The word *Experience* means "Conscious Participation In That State Of Being."

Furthermore, The Manifestations Of Reality In Our Spiritual Universe As Experienced By Spiritual Beings Are So Diverse For The Different Spiritual Beings that The Experience Of One Spiritual Being would not necessarily have the same Characteristics As The Experience Of Another Spiritual Being. The Reality Occurring In Our 7th-D Spiritual Universe could be very Different from The Reality Occurring In Another Spiritual Universe. The Presence Of Spirit Would be The Common Characteristic Between All Of Them. The Characteristics Of Spirit might vary greatly.

Angels, Demons,[6z115] Souls, and Spirits of every description May Exist Within the Membrane System Of Spirit. The Origin Of Each Spirit Is A Differentiation From The ONE. The Separateness[6z116] Is Intended To Be Bridged By GOD To Provide The LORD Diverse and Glorious Perspectives only possible Through Differentiation. That Bridge[6z117] Is Bilateral.[6z118] It requires The Effort Of Both The Individual Differentiated Spirit and GOD For There To Be Sharing Of The Glorious Consciousness Of A Manifest Being.[6z119] The Free Will[6z120] Provided In Differentiation also allows the possible and undesirable consequence of diminishing Communication With GOD.

Different Conscious Experience Exists Even Among Like Spirit Types. Experiences Recorded Are Of The Manifestations of Familiar Spiritual States, Such As Joy, Compassion,[6z121] Pathos,[6z122] Appreciation, Sympathy,[6z123] and Enlightenment,[6z124] to name a few.

Different Types Of Spirits May Interrelate.[6z125] Events recorded are the history of Individuals, Civilizations,[6z126] Prophesies,[6z127] Myths,[6z128] and Legends.[6z129]

These are no fictions, dreams, hallucinations,[6z130] or constructions of a semiconscious[6z131] Mind. The Membrane Of Spirit Holds A Totally Different Reality.

What can we say about Our Spiritual Universe? Words such as *Love* and *Joy* Describe Situations In Our Spiritual Universe. An entire vocabulary of words that Are Spiritual In Our Spiritual Universe Comes To Mind. Each Of These Spiritual Words is meaningless in a purely physical universe. A Glossary Of Such Words May Include both Positive and negative Spiritual Experiences.

To illustrate this, please try to Identify Which Of The Following Spiritual Words In The English Language Are Positive, Increasing Spiritual Energy, and which are negative, diminishing Spiritual Energy: *Adoration*,[6z132] *Appreciation*, *avarice*, *Beauty*,[6z133] *Blessing*,[6z134] *Benevolence*, callous, *Charity*,[6z135] *Communion*,[6z136] *Compromise*,[6z137] *Comradery*,[6z138] *Congeniality*,[6z139] *Courage*,[6z140] devious, *Daring*,[6z141] disdain, *Ecstasy*,[6z142] *Elation*,[6z143] *Empathy*, envy, evasive, *Faith*, *Forgive*, *Generous*,[6z144] gluttony, *Grace*, greed, hate, *Hope*,[6z145] horrible, *Inspiration*,[6z146] *Instruction*, *Introspection*,[6z147] jealous, *Joy*, *Justice*,[6z148] *Kind*,[6z149] *Love*, lust, malice, *Mercy*,[6z150] ostentatious, *Pious*,[6z151] pride, *Prudence*,[6z152] *Reciprocity*,[6z153] *Relation*,[6z154] *Righteous*,[6z155] *Sharing*, sloth, *Sympathy*, scorn, *Temperance*,[6z156] *Thanks*,[6z157] turmoil, *Understanding*, vanity, *Wisdom*, and *wrath*.

Many others come to mind. You may have noticed that I Have Capitalized The Positive Spiritual Words Throughout This Teaching. Every Word In A Spiritual Clause or Sentence May Be Capitalized. This Is Because These Are Of GOD. If You Act As These Words Direct, You Will Be Connecting To GOD. Stated another way, GOD Will Be Present In Your Soul In These States Of Being.

You may also have noticed that the spiritual words that describe attitudes and actions that diminish[6z158] Spirit are not capitalized even though they are spiritual. GOD Created Your Soul As An Independent Spiritual Entity. You Have Free Will. You May Act or fail to act in a manner that Attracts[6z159] The LORD. Negative spiritual activity[6z160] is manifestation of your own negative spiritual creations. GOD Is likely to ignore[6z161] you and your negative spirituality. We say that the state of being described by those words is godless or GODforsaken.[6z162] That means that GOD Has turned away and is not present in these states of consciousness or the reality caused by them. You must Know that it is usually You that has turned away, not GOD.

It is difficult for Humans To Imagine Glory[6z163] without reference to physical images. Our immediate identification of nonmaterial Perceptions Is With Feelings or Emotions. As Feelings Are Manifested, We Say They Come From The Heart. Of course, that is not your physical beating heart that is pumping your blood. Emotions or Feelings, such as Love, Come From The Center Of Your Being. This Love is not chemically induced desire.[6z164] We Are Speaking About The General Caring Coming From Your Center and Reaching Out[6z165] To Other Beings. The Origin Of All Spiritual Experience Is Divine. Only Positive Spiritual Experience[6z166] Is Blessed By GOD, and the negative is mostly ignored by GOD. That is why We refer to evil[6z167] situations as godless or GODforsaken.

If You do not Feel Confident[6z168] initially with defining words as Spiritual or physical, There Are Techniques That Help You Grow In Confidence. One way to determine whether a word is both Spiritual and Positive is to put the word *Divine* preceding the word You Are Evaluating. For example, Divine Action[6z169] helps to Understand the word *Action* because an Action can be Divine If GOD Would Be Interested In Participating In That Action. An "action" can also be purely physical, so *action* is not capitalized in a physical context. A clause like *Divine cardboard* makes no sense, so *cardboard* is a physical word, identifying something purely physical and not Spiritual.

Having Distinguished between physical and Spiritual words, We Take Our vocabulary One Step Further. The clause *Divine hate* seems incorrect. Even though "hate" is a spiritual reality, it diminishes Positive Spiritual Energy, so we do not capitalize negative spiritual words like hate. Negative spirituality diminishes the Consciousness Of Spiritual Beings.

This Exercise not only Deepens the Meaning of words but also Heightens Your Spiritual Energy As Meditation On Spiritual Words Opens A More Glorious Reality.

An Individual Human Spirit Has Tremendous Power Through Action On planet earth to Advance Its Own Spiritual Experience. It also has the power do diminish its own spiritual experience and that of those within its influence.

If You ask, "Why does GOD ignore Me?" You must recognize that either You are ignoring GOD, or your physical conditioning is impeding Your Spiritual Connection To GOD. You May Reengage With The LORD Through Meditating On Any Spiritual Reality Represented By Positive Spiritual Words.

One Technique Is To Take A Deep Breath, Refined and Profound,[6z170] So That You cannot hear Yourself Breathing. You May Breathe In and Hold briefly, Then Breathe Out With Calm Regularity. If you need sleep,[6z171] this may assist sleep, but that is not Meditation. You May Think Of A Spiritual Word As The Doorway[6z172] To Meditation.

Consider Mercy. Calmly[6z173] Recall[6z174] Your Encounter[6z175] With An unfortunate[6z176] Being. Upon Observing the miserable[6z177] state of that Being, You Empathized With Its condition As If It Were Yourself. That Empathy Is Compassion. You Acted and So Became A Participant Giving Merciful Aid To Relieve The Condition Of That Being. Your Will To Act[6z178] In Mercy Is Divine Energy Coming Directly[6z179] From GOD Through You.

You Turned That Light Around,[6z180] Redirecting The Light That Came From GOD To You, To Project[6z181] Outward As The Light Of Mercy From You To The Unfortunate Being. This Is A Creation In The 9th Dimension. You Are The Instrument Of GOD,[6z182] Becoming[6z183] The Light Of Mercy To The unfortunate Being. Your Recollection Of the Event Is Meditation, Which Opens You and Reconnects[6z184] You To GOD.

This Act Of Mercy and Its Recollection Are Outside Of time, so You Know It Is Of Our Spiritual Membrane System, not of the physical.

Your Meditation Will Lead You On Paths Of Righteousness.[6z185] For example, If Your Mercy Was Also An Elevation[6z186] Beyond Justice To That unfortunate Being For a wrong It did to You, That Mercy Would Be Called "Forgiveness!"

Spiritual Energy Increases As The Divine Nature Represented By These Positive Spiritual Words Is Realized.

9th D (The Workshop of GOD): Receiving Instructions From The WORD, The 10th D, Realities Are Constructed In The 9th D. This Is How Reality Is Brought Into Being. Stated another way, Divine Instructions Are Manifested or Collapsed Into Reality Through The Operation Of The 9th D. Furthermore, all lower Dimensions Operate Within The Boundary Of The 9th D. The Mechanisms Of Creation Are Continually In Operation, Creating, Preserving, and Destroying Manifest Realities.

The 9th D Is The Machinery Operational To Create the diverse Realities. Metastrings may be broad, such as the physical metastring, which manifests all physical realities. Metastrings may also be specific, such as The Metastring Connecting GOD Directly To You.

The 9th D Continually Manifests Being Within universes in this or that membrane system. New membrane systems Are Manifested In The 9th D According To The WORD. Combinations[6z187] between membrane systems also exist.

Human Beings are barely Capable[6z188] of 9th-Dimensional Reasoning. That is because without an Understanding of clearly defined membrane systems, the intersection and combinations of membrane systems can hardly Be Comprehended.

However, there is proof of one such 9th-Dimensional reality. That Is Your Reality As A Sentient[6z189] Human Being. Our Reality As Spiritual Beings, Incarnate In a universe of matter and its attendant energies, Is Such A Combination.

Membrane Systems in the 8th D, codified in our dimensional organization, include at least one membrane system accepted by even the most narrow-minded scientists. That is the physical membrane system. That includes our obvious physical universe. Physical scientists are exhaustively dissecting our universe of matter and its attendant energies.

Some Physicists are so lost in presenting their "theory of everything" in physical terms that they cannot see beyond the laws of physics. Limited to physical being, their science is frustrated by anomalies[6z190] and mathematical imbalances[6z191] that they cannot resolve. Their theories multiply, fragment, and scatter because they do not include The Forces Introduced By The Broader Reality That Influences physical reality.

Every Religious Person Is Acquainted With Another Membrane System. That Is The Spiritual Membrane System Containing Our Spiritual Universe. This Is The Realm Of Spirits Existing In Their Own System Outside of time and space.[6z192] You Can Prove This Existence By Awareness and Self-Awareness—that Is, Experience Of Your Own Conscious Being and Participation With Other Conscious Beings. Each Individual Spirit or Soul Is One Unit[6z193] Of Spiritual Being Differentiated From The ONE.

You could not prove the existence of the Soul by any material testing because Its Being is not material. However, The Record Of Conscious Experience and Pervasiveness Of That Experience is convincing. Material tools are mostly useless to detect Spirit because the Origin Of The Individual Spirit Is In A System Separate from this physical universe, so physical measures do not usually work.

The Wonder Of Our 9th-Dimensional Combination of Membrane Systems is that The Collapsing Of Spirit Into Our Spiritual Universe Of Independent Souls and the collapsing of a physical membrane system into our universe of matter and its attendant energies is that Our Reality Is Manifested By A Fusion Of Independent Realities into One Current Reality. This Is The Temporary[6z194] Fused Reality In which We Live.

You Will Know This Combination By The Feeling Of Wonder Upon Witnessing A Beautiful Event. "How Can I Be Experiencing This Beauty?" "This beauty" is the physical situation being Witnessed. "I" Am The Spiritual Witness Incarnate, The Observer Who Is Experiencing this physical Beauty. I Am also The Participant In This Beauty Here and Now. Hence, the Beauty is Elevated To A Spiritual Reality.

The Human Mind is the product of The Fusion of the physical brain and The Individual Spirit. This Is A 9th-Dimensional Creation That Is Each Of Us.

Spirit Incarnate Is This Marvelous Condition. Your Spirit Infused Into matter growing as your body Is A 9th-Dimensional Process Creating Your Being.

Consciousness in early childhood is obscure because the Individual Spirit is unfamiliar with physical reality. The sensations made possible by physical organs have not been organized into meaningful Perceptions Of The Fused Human Being. If You Recall any early childhood Experiences, You Will Recall that The Consciousness Of "I" Is Possessed, while the relation to the physical environment in Your memory is that the physical is "other" than the "I."

Behavioral testing has been done at Yale University[6z195] showing that Infants as young as three months old can make Moral[6z196] Choices after Observing puppets interacting, displaying A Positive Moral Action versus a negative moral action. The Positive Norm Is Recognized Spiritually and Is Expressed By Smiles Of The Infant. The negative actions are recognized spiritually and that Recognition[6z197] is expressed by frowns or crying. This is one verification of a Spiritual Presence In The Infant Human Being.[6z198]

Furthermore, Every Spiritual Event Of A Spirit Incarnate In matter has a chemical signature.[6z199] That is to say that one may be able to trace the perception to sensations initiated[6z200] by body chemistry in the Manifestation. The proof that Spiritual Experiences such as Love or Sympathy Are Spiritual and not physical is that a repeat of the exact chemistry will not predictably induce The Spiritual Experience that occurred with the same chemistry previously.

You can verify this for Yourself. A mood-altering pill may introduce a certain chemistry to your body. You may experience an emotion or feeling as an effect of that chemistry. Strangely, that relief will not be identical when You ingest that pill again and again in different Spiritual Mindsets or Settings.

This is even more dramatic with a Consciousness-Altering pill. Oddly, if you repeat ingesting that same pill, the Emotions You Experience may be vastly different in different Spiritual Mindsets or Settings. In fact, the Experiences will be very different from one other. Consciousness is affected by chemistry, but the chemistry does not define Consciousness. That is to say that The Spiritual Aspect Of Any Conscious Experience is not Caused by the chemistry.

One of many Self-verifications of this Truth occurred to This Author at the peak of psychedelic experience, as I attempted to Pray To GOD for relief of the intensity. As soon as the Prayer left My Mind, The Strict Reply Came From GOD: "You are a fool to think that You have to poison Yourself To Get Closer To ME!" The LORD Became Silent. The Rebuke Caused Me To Change My Expectations Of The Trip. The chemical compulsions continued, but The LORD Participated In My Pacing To The Sound of Pleasant Music. Please note that I Have Higher Conscious Experiences regularly, with no unpleasant intensity, without imbibing chemical substances.

So many Humans self-destruct on drugs and alcohol, seeking some sort of fulfillment. I Recommend Breathwork,[6z201] Meditation, and Prayer To Alter Consciousness Toward GOD.

Our conclusion is that the chemistry creates the environment, but The Spirit Creates The Experience. This is proof of Your Spirit as separate from your physical body. It is verified by Your Own Experience.

The 9th-D Fusion of Spiritual and physical Membrane Systems is so Enveloping[6z201] that the boundaries of each system are violated as they Merge. That is the Divine Synthesis that makes Our Reality so Rich. The LORD Participates In This Richness. That Divine Participation Is The reason For The WORD To Instruct This Fusion. This is the answer to the questions, "How am I here?" and "Why am I here?"

10th D: This Is The Realm Of The WORD. If The WORD Instructs A Manifestation, A Metastring Will Be Generated In The 9th D To Facilitate That Manifestation.

String theorists debate the nature of physical strings. Our Teaching Postulates Metastrings as the causative mechanisms that create strings and instruct their action in physical reality. Strings are vibrations. They may also be referred to as excitations[6z203] in a quantum field. You may view the waves and particles as Information and their interactions as Instruction by The WORD That Is manifested in physical universal systems. We recognize that our universe of matter and its attendant energies are part of a "string" type of membrane system. It is complete and self-operative[6z204] with no other influence. It is limited by the extent of the expansion of matter and its attendant energies.

We Recognize The Spiritual Membrane System. It Is Complete and Self-Operative with no other influence. It is limited only As Instructed By GOD.

That Direction, or Instruction, Is The Function Of The 10th-D WORD, Creating, Preserving, and Destroying Spirit According To The WILL Of GOD. All imagery referring to a Fierce[6z205] and Judgmental[6z206] GOD Is Referring To The Operation Of The WORD Instructing a Spiritual Metastring In The 9th D.

LOWER DIMENSIONS AND THE ELEVATION TOWARD GOD

Observing the evolution of our universe of matter and its formative energies, we are beginning to understand the operation of black holes.[6z207] We hypothesize That black holes are an example of The 10th D Instructing a matter-energy metastring in the 9th D to Repurpose[6z208] matter and its attendant energies.

The mysterious dark matter[6z209] that we can hypothesize using mathematics may be another operation of the 9th-D matter-energy metastring operating to create and balance physical matter in Our physical universe. Alternatively, it may be discovered that there is a fusion of two separate physical universes to create the balance achieved with dark matter. It will be interesting to evaluate new physical discoveries regarding dark matter and dark energy.

11th: We Mentioned The Direct Metastring Connection Of Conscious Beings To GOD. One Characteristic Of Each Personal Metastring Is That It Facilitates Communication and Sharing Of Experience. Within The Broader Spiritual Metastring, These Individual Metastrings Each Provide A Channel For A Differentiated Consciousness To "Walk Humbly With Its GOD."[6z210] The Character Of Each Of These Metastrings Is That Each Facilitates Communication From A Conscious Being To Its SOURCE—GOD. GOD Delights[6z211] To Receive Your Conscious Experience. It Is Why Your Spirit Was Differentiated From The ONE. When You Communicate Your Experiences To GOD and Invite[6z212] GOD To Participate, GOD, Manifested As The HOLY SPIRIT,[6z213] Responds Directly To Return To You Spiritual Energy To Expand Your Conscious Awareness. Higher States Of Consciousness Are Attainable[6z214] Through Greater Communication With GOD As GOD Merges With Your Consciousness.

Please Revisit the question, why does God ignore me? This question shows proper Humility because an Individual Human Being is not much in the vastness of Reality. However, GOD Has A Higher Opinion Of You. The Metaphysics That Is Now Revealed To You Empowers[6z215] You With The Ability To Walk Humbly With The LORD. Your Consciousness Is Divine Consciousness.[6z216] Your Experience Is Divine Experience.[6z217] It is true that an incorrect point of view and Your lack of Effort have dimmed that Experience. To Elevate Your Consciousness, You must periodically set aside ordinary Conscious Relations with physical being. Instead of looking at the beautiful rainbow, Invite GOD To See The Beautiful Rainbow As A Unity[6z218] Of Your Conscious Experience and That Of GOD.

You Are The Instrument Through Which GOD Becomes not just an Observer but also A Participant In Your Reality. That Is The Spirituality That You Communicate When You Endeavor To "Walk With GOD." The Spiritual Energy Returned From GOD Is GOD's Becoming A Participant In Your reality. This Exchange Is Most Fulfilling. This Is Why the LORD Differentiated Your Individual Spirit From GOD's Own. It Is Your Purpose. It is why You Are here.

This illustration is Offered To Depict You, shown as a child, Walking With GOD, Shown As An Image Of Jesus Christ.

Painting by Greg Olsen, take-my-hand

CHAPTER 7

Proof of Dimensional Integrity

One proof that We are correctly identifying each Dimension is to define a position in each Dimension that describes a real event, situation, or formative situation. To verify The Reality of each Dimension postulated in Our Teaching, let Us define the Reality where You and I Will Meet.

0th d (-a point): Let Us meet at the Jefferson Memorial in Washington, DC, USA.

This is an idea. It is more than nothing but not yet a reality. Though this idea suggests a location to meet, there is not enough information for a clear Meeting place. The Jefferson Memorial is a large site, so where at the Jefferson Memorial Shall We Meet?

1st d—length (a line): Let Us Meet on the west end of the steps at the Jefferson Memorial. This helps, but there are steps on four sides of the Jefferson Memorial.

2nd d—width (a plane): Let Us Meet on the west end of the north-facing steps of the Jefferson Memorial. Better, but there are many steps on the north side of the Jefferson Memorial.

3rd d—height (a cube): Let Us Meet on the west end of the north-facing steps of the Jefferson Memorial, third step from the top. Good, We have a real location, but when shall We Meet?

73

GOD—*THE DIMENSIONAL REVELATION*

4th d—time (a point on the continuum): Let us Meet on the west end of the north-facing steps of the Jefferson Memorial, third step from the top, at 1:00 p.m. EST on November 15 next year. Now We have enough information to Meet.

However, reality presents interfering situations that change the future. What if it is raining?

5th D—Choices or Decisions (Alternative Choice based on potential change of conditions): Let Us Meet on the west end of the north-facing steps of the Jefferson Memorial, third step from the bottom, at 1:00 p.m. EST on November 15 next year. If it is raining, let Us Meet inside the Jefferson memorial at the northwest corner of Jefferson's statue.

6th D—Reassessment[7a] (Backup plan based on uncertainty or extraordinary reorganization of the situation): Let Us Meet on the west end of the north-facing steps of the Jefferson Memorial, third step from the top, at 1:00 p.m. EST on November 15 next year. If it is raining, let Us Choose to Meet inside the Jefferson memorial at the northwest corner of Jefferson's statue.

However, if the Memorial is closed with construction preventing entry, let Us Meet in front of the Liberty Bell in Philadelphia, Pennsylvania, one day later.

7th D—Our physical universe (but I am no longer in it): Let Us Meet on the west end of the north-facing steps of the Jefferson Memorial, third step from the top, at 1:00 p.m. EST on November 15 next year. If it is raining, let Us Choose to Meet inside the Jefferson Memorial at the northwest corner of Jefferson's statue.

However, if the Memorial is closed with construction preventing entry, let Us Meet in front of the Liberty Bell in Philadelphia, Pennsylvania, one day later. If I do not show up within thirty minutes after the appointed time, assume that I have Passed Away, and You will need to contact My Wife to Determine where You Will Meet Her to Resolve the Issues between Us.

8th D—Another similar physical universe or dissimilar Universes: Let Us Meet on the west end of the north-side steps of the Jefferson Memorial, third step from the top, at 1:00 p.m. EST on November 15 next year. If it is raining, let Us Meet inside the Jefferson Memorial at the northwest corner of Jefferson's statue.

However, if the Memorial is closed with construction preventing entry, let Us Choose to Meet in front of the Liberty Bell in Philadelphia, Pennsylvania, one day later. If I do not show up within thirty minutes after the appointed time, assume that I have Passed Away, and You will need to contact My Wife to Determine where You Will Meet Her To Resolve The Issues Between Us.

If Our world has disappeared and You are still in Human form in a place where You can breathe air and move about, assume that I am still Alive as Spirit, then Let Us Communicate As May Be Possible for an Incarnate Mind and a Spirit.

9th D—Fusion and Disintegration (A physical universe may or may not exist, but Your Consciousness is aware only of Emotional Feeling and not of form): Let Us Meet on the west end of the north-facing steps of the Jefferson Memorial, third step from the top, at 1:00 p.m. EST on November 15 next year. If it is raining, let Us Meet inside the Jefferson Memorial at the northwest corner of Jefferson's statue.

However, if the Memorial is closed with construction preventing entry, let Us Choose to Meet in front of the Liberty Bell in Philadelphia, Pennsylvania, one day later. If I do not show up within thirty minutes after the appointed time, assume that I have Passed Away, and You will need to contact My Wife to Determine where You Will Meet Her To Resolve The Issues Between Us.

If Our world has disappeared and You are still in Human form in a place where You can breathe air and move about, assume that I am still Alive as Spirit, then Let Us Communicate As May Be Possible for an Incarnate Mind and a Spirit.

However, if neither of us is incarnate but We still Have Conscious Self-Awareness and are Experiencing only Emotion, then Feel Joy, and We will Meet in the Sharing of that Ecstasy. If I should become Incarnate again and You remain Pure Spirit, then I Shall pause and Share Joy with You through Memory or otherwise as may be possible.

10th D—The WORD of GOD (Differentiation and Reunification):

- Let Us Meet
- on the west end of the north-facing steps of the Jefferson Memorial,
- Third step from the top,
- at 1:00 p.m. EST on November 15 next year.
- If it is raining, let Us Choose to Meet inside the Jefferson Memorial at the northwest corner of Jefferson's statue.
- However, if the Memorial is closed with construction preventing entry, let Us Meet in front of the Liberty Bell in Philadelphia, Pennsylvania, one day later.

- If I do not show up within thirty minutes after the appointed time, assume that I have Passed Away and You will need to contact My Wife to Determine where You Will Meet Her To Resolve The Issues Between Us.
- If Our world has disappeared and You are still in Human form in a place where You can breathe air and move about, assume that I am still Alive as Spirit, then Let Us Communicate As May Be Possible for an Incarnate Mind and a Spirit.
- However, if You still have Conscious Self-Awareness and are Experiencing only Emotion, then Feel Joy, and We will Meet in the Sharing of that Ecstasy. If I should become Incarnate again and You remain Pure Spirit, then I shall pause and Share Joy with You through Memory or otherwise as may be possible.
- Upon Sharing Pure Joy Together, We Are ONE, though Differentiated At The Pleasure Of GOD.

The multidimensional panel data[7b] is verified by Real positions or positions that May Become Real. Our Organization and Description Of Dimensions Is verified because It Is

1. inclusive of observed data,
2. contained within each successively larger Sphere Of Influence,[7c]
3. Not Limited by what We cannot Observe,
4. Places Infinities at the SOURCE.

See [5z39], [11z58], [2z23].

This verification proves that Our Definitions Of Dimensions 1 through 10 is correct to describe physical reality and Is Correct To Describe Fused physical and Spiritual Dimensions.

Each of the Dimensions described in Our Teaching is necessary to account for the data We observe.

Time will prove this positioning. Beyond time, the Connection to GOD Establishes The Reality. A lack of regular Connection to GOD establishes a different reality, though it be short and not so sweet.

CHAPTER 8

Observations of the Situation

Dimensions 0 through 3: Spatial

Please Observe that the reality of the physical dimensions 0 through 3 are dominated by space. The main feature of their limitations is that the boundaries are spatial.

The 0th dimension is more than nothing. Referring to Our Example, a "point" is the Idea that We Should Meet. The Idea gets past 0 by locating the meeting at the Jefferson Memorial. The Idea That You and I should Meet Is A Spiritual Cause For Us To Act. It becomes physically formative because the Meeting now refers to a physical location, so the Meeting may proceed within our physical universe.

The 1st dimension is developmental. The reality is the situation on a linear space. I can only write about a step on the Jefferson Memorial because it is real now. The step is a line conceptually. The 1st-dimensional line is necessary for 3rd-Dimensional space to develop.

The 2nd dimension is also spatially developmental. The concept of width is geometrically necessary for there to be a step on the Jefferson Memorial wide enough for Us to stand upon and Meet. The identification with north gives us a 2-Dimensional flat map providing the latitude and longitude for Us to Meet at the site.

The 3rd Dimension is real space. Our location on the step—in length, width, and the third step from the top in height—is solid and real in our physical universe. That place is represented by geographic coordinates.[8a] We have fully defined our place to Meet.

Dimensions 4 through 8: Temporal[8b]

We have determined where We shall Meet. Yet the Meeting cannot actually occur given the limitations of 3-dimensional space. The 4th d is forced upon Us because the sequence of both Our Lives will have to be organized for Us to Meet. We must pick a time.

Indeed, each Dimension above the 3rd d is characterized by the future, not the present.

To the extent that a Conscious Being Is Aware of the future, that Being will be able to Act upon the future by its Choices made in the 5th D. If the circumstances of Our Meeting change, such as if it is raining, We have made a Choice now about how We will adjust Our future Meeting.

To the extent that a Conscious Being is unaware of the broader realities, It will be surprised[8c] by unpredictable[8d] occurrences manifesting in the 6th D. These developments are real and are well beyond the boundaries possible in the lower Dimensions. 6th-D occurrences are manifested in the lower dimension but seem out of place as they disrupt the ordinary flow. It seems unlikely that construction will prohibit Our Meeting at the Jefferson Memorial, but We have planned for unanticipated[8e] events regarding the Jefferson Memorial by selecting an alternative Meeting place.

Our Universe could be Guided by another occurrence, so the 7th-D universe We had anticipated with the potential of a Liberty Bell meeting cannot occur because I Have Passed Away. Our future planning has provided an alternative solution—that is, You Meeting With My Wife To Resolve Our Issues, if the unexpected occurs.

A myriad of independent actions occurring in one of very many places pushes Our Universe into any number of future manifestations of Our Universe in the 7th D, Though our physical universe exists here and now. In terms of quantum reality,[8f] it is always "becoming." Our Universe could Unfold so that I am no longer alive in physical reality. However, Being Present in another Reality, a Meeting may still be possible with My Wife Acting as My physical substitute to Execute My Will.

Time and the future are merely a subset within one system as we consider the diversity of membrane systems in the 8th D.

The 8th D allows for the physical realities described in the first seven Dimensions. However, You notice in Our Example that once physical reality disappears when there is no physical place to Meet, the physical characteristics of Us as Spirits Incarnate in physical bodies also disappear. In the 8th D, We Could Meet Spiritually from different Universes Operating under the Principles of different Membrane Systems.

A Membrane System with different operational principles, such as Spiritual Existence with no form, Exists Outside Of space-time.[8g] It did not Initiate from a big bang. There is no space and no matter to fill space in such A Different Membrane System.

The Origin Of A Spiritual Membrane System is most aptly described as Love. Love Is a Full Vibration that Manifests Diversely As Joy, Hope, Sympathy, Mercy, Forgiveness, and Other Spiritual Realities. These Realities Are Both Observed and Experienced By Participation. Such A Spiritual Membrane System also requires the Presence Of Conscious Beings To Observe and Participate With These Vibrations. These Conscious Beings Are Spirits.

OBSERVATIONS OF THE SITUATION

Note that an 8th-D Meeting Of Spirits with One Beyond physical death presumes a Spiritual Proximity Supported By A Purpose For Us To Meet Spiritually.

Please observe that the 4th, 5th, 6th, 7th, and 8th Dimensions are dominated by time or a continuum of being.

Dimensions 9 and 10: Creative

The diversity of characteristics of some other membrane systems in the 8th D is well beyond the Observation Of Human Consciousness. Such Realities Come Into Being In The 9th D. The 9th D Is The Synthesis Of Being, Manifested as reality in the lower dimensions. Membrane Systems Emerge In The 9th D; and They Are Instructed To Be Formed, Molded, or Fused By A Divine Force Of Purpose, Which Is The WORD, Of 10th-Dimensional Divine Information.

We capitalize *Divine Information* to distinguish It from ordinary "information." The WORD, or Divine Information, is really Instruction Of Information. It is Causative. Not just data, This Information Creates Reality Through The Operational Principles Of The 9th D. The Metastrings, or Channels, Collapse the various types of Potential Into What Is Instructed To Become Real.

Our Meeting In The 9th D May Be Instructed by the WORD.

At the highest level, You and I Will Meet In Spiritual Unification In The 10th D As We Approach The ONE. However, Our Original Reasons To Meet Disappear in The 10th D As Our Individual Identities disappear In The Glory Of GOD.

This illustration Is Offered to depict various Realities Merging Into The Glory Of GOD. Please Notice That This Vortex Is not caused by gravity in the 6th d, like a black hole. It Is The LIGHT Approached According To The Graceful Will Of Each Aspect Of Reality. Each Will Reunify With The ONE In The 10th D, Leading To The 11th. Also Notice Spiritual Energy Turning Outward From The LIGHT. The ONE Is A Destination but Not An Ending.

GOD—*THE DIMENSIONAL REVELATION*

(https://www.pinterest.com/pin/503066220884439463/)

We are in a position to Examine Our Meeting on the end of the third step on the north side of the Jefferson Memorial at 1:00 p.m. EST on November 15 next year. That Examination can occur on the next day, which will be November 16. Either the Meeting happened, or it did not.

This illustrates how the past is very different from the future in dimensional reality. Prior to November 15, all the possibilities presented by the 10 Dimensions could happen. Reality became Manifest on November 15 at 1:00 p.m. EST. We met at the appointed time and place. That Is A Fact. Reality Manifested into being at the appointed moment. All of the other possibilities did not occur.

Looking back, We can only define the three spatial dimensions. The past is inactive in our physical universe. It is as if every electron stopped at the single time in space where We Met. We can say that the higher Dimensions collapsed into reality when that Appointment was kept. Of course, they did not stop as Reality Continued To Unfold during Our Meeting and after. Events were and are continuous. We just picked a point for identification looking back.

This allows Us to Understand another principle of 9th-D Creation. It is that the 3rd d sets a boundary around past physical events in our physical universe. Once an event happens, that boundary fixes that situation in the past. It cannot to be changed.

It also establishes that the higher Dimensions, 4 through 8, are defined by Potential. When We Met on the Third Step of the Jefferson Memorial, the situation became Real. It was also Real the moment after We Met. This ushers in Dimensions 4 through 8 again as the Meeting proceeds but within different possibilities presented as We Met.

Heisenberg's Uncertainty Principle[8g] states that one cannot ascertain the location of an electron at any instant, but we know it was there. This principle frames this discussion of potential. All descriptions of an atom, or any other physical particle or event, are descriptions of the past. The present is emergent as a future event. Once it becomes present, it is Experienced (Observed) through Participation (or detection if experienced or observed by a machine), but it can only be described (or recorded if by a machine) as a past event. This is because the present has moved on.

Note that the discussion of past, present, and future frames Reality as static images in Your Mind. That is because the Human Mind is incapable of Grasping the Whole Reality. Logical systems such as mathematics are also incapable of grasping the Whole Reality for the same reason. Both Math and Mind separate Reality into bits or events as if they can be separated. They cannot be segmented or separated because they are Continuous. Segmentation[8h] is a construction of Mind so that certain characteristics of reality can be manipulated. This can be both Informative and Useful or deceiving, depending upon how the segmented data is presented or analyzed.

In the 9th D, We could Meet as different Realities might be Formed.

In the 10th D, We would be Merged and do not have Individual Identity, according to the Instructions of the WORD Of GOD. This Merger could be described as Love in Love's Broadest Manifestation—The Totality of Vibrations In Reality. It Encompasses The Beginning Through The Ending Of All Laws or Principles Of Being.

It is an interesting Observation that You, like many Human Beings, Have Experienced The Merger Of Your Spirit In Platonic (agape) Love With Another Human Spirit. Dimensional Reasoning would Conclude that when this happened, A 10th-D Union[8i] Collapsed Into Reality (Manifested) in the 5th-d physical being, as well as In The 5th D Of Spiritual Being. We will Delve[8j] more deeply into Spiritual Dimensions in a later chapter of This Teaching.

Do not let this twist Your Mind. It is sufficient to Understand that the operation of dimensions defining the future are proved to be real because of their effects on the present and all emergent realities.

This leads Us to a simple way to organize dimensional Reality.

- The first three dimensions describe past reality.
- The next five Dimensions describe emergent reality.
- The two remaining Dimensions describe Controlling[8k] Reality.
- The 11th is The ONE, SOURCE, LORD, GOD of All. The LORD cannot be fully described Dimensionally.

CHAPTER 9

The Law of Dimensional Limitation

Why are there only 10 Dimensions plus 0 and GOD? Just a few years ago, We were aware of only 3 dimensions. Is this definition of *dimensions* just an arbitrary[9a] slicing and dicing of ordinary Reality? The answer is no. The operational principles of each dimension organize them into the categories We describe in This Teaching.

This Teaching postulates **The Law of Dimensional Limitation**. A simple statement of that law is that each Dimension demands recognition by how It operates and what can occur within the operation of that Dimension. That is to say that each Dimension is limited. That limitation may be referred to as a boundary within which the operational principles of the Dimension define the reality. We may call that the field of influence of that Dimension.

Recognition of each higher, or more encompassing, Dimension is required when We observe a process or condition that cannot occur given the operational principles of the lower, smaller, or less encompassing Dimensions.

For example, 3rd-dimensional reality is well-defined by Human Beings. Matter is hard, and it is heavy. It has size by 1st-, 2nd-, and 3rd-dimensional measures. Its weight is measured by the pull of earth's gravity on its mass. Humans have developed a reliable mathematics describing the present condition of 3rd-Dimensional reality.

However, we observe changes in 3-dimensional matter that defy the static description of any 3-dimensional situation. The next observation shows that the situation has changed. The change in position of matter has voided the previous 3-Dimensional observation. The new situation cannot exist, given the limitations of 3-dimensional Observation. The mathematics must be changed to account for the new situation. We have exceeded the boundary of the 3rd dimension.

3-dimensional reasoning defines current physical reality. The fields of influence of dimensions 1, 2, and 3 are clearly defined by many postulates, theorems, deductions, and inferences, in addition to ordinary Observation. Indeed, Animal senses and perceptions are primarily 3-dimensional tools. The brain operates in 3 dimensions as We Participate in physical being.

THE LAW OF DIMENSIONAL LIMITATION

The Animal nervous system is further equipped to predict the next situation because knowing what is likely to happen next is necessary for survival.

The continuum becomes the basic operational principle of the 4th dimension. The measure of this continuum is time.

Each Dimension has a set of defining and limiting operational principles. The manifestation of each operation is necessary and Observable in reality. That is why each Dimension is named and numbered successively. Reality cannot be fully described or understood without each Dimension.

Could there be a dimension that we have not described? Yes, however, each higher hypothetical dimension would have greatly expanded operational principles, hence an expanded boundary and less limitation. Situations in the lower hypothetical dimensions would be successively confined by the limitations of each higher hypothetical dimension.

It is necessary to define the limitation of each Real Dimension to refine Our Dimensional Reasoning. We have Observed that each Dimension operates within its field of influence. Since there are Dimensions 0 through 10 (plus GOD, Who Is Beyond dimensions), each higher Dimension opens opportunities beyond the limitation of the previous Dimension. This reveals that the reality manifested in a certain Dimension does not describe all of Reality.

0th d (a point): A point is just a placeholder or a start. Mathematically, a point is nothing. It is not actually a dimension. It is just a possibility. It is limited because to exist, a point must define a start somewhere. If it had another point to relate to, it would become a line.

Cosmologically, a point does not exist.

Ontologically, a point is an unrealized potential of being.

1st d (a line): The limitation on a line is that it is just a mathematical abstraction.[9b] It is part of the mathematical model[9c] necessary to build out an object. The 1st d in physical reality is verified by the mathematics, using this dimension as a necessary tool to construct 3-dimensional physical space.

The dimensional limitation on the 1st d is that length, a line, does not describe an observable reality.

Cosmologically, a line does not exist.

Ontologically, a line is a measure of being. It is a one-dimensional construct of Mind.

2nd d (a plane): Like the line, a plane is also limited as a mathematical abstraction. It is part of the mathematical model necessary to build out an object. The 2nd d in physical reality is verified by the mathematics, using this dimension as a necessary tool to construct 3-dimensional space.

The 2nd d is also limited as it does not describe an observable reality.

Cosmologically, a plane does not exist. Observe it from the side, and it disappears entirely.

Ontologically, a plane is an area of being. It is a two-dimensional construct of Mind.

3rd d (an object): Each object (solid, liquid, gas, radiation, plasma) or other physical reality is fully described in its 3-dimensional reality. It is Experienced as it exists here and now. 3rd-dimensional reality is verified by instrumentation, the mathematics, Sensory Observation, and Conscious Participation.

The 3rd-dimensional limitation is that the object will be situated differently within the entirety of space in the next situation. That next situation is heavily influenced by the preceding situation, but its future being is undermined in the present.

Cosmologically, a 3-dimensional object is a primary unit of being in our physical universe. An object is not a construct of Mind. It exists independently of the Observer.

Ontologically, an object is the basis of physical being in any physical universe. It can be the smallest of particles or waves or a collection or organization of joined[9d] objects. It defines the space it occupies.

4th d (time): time allows the Observer to define reality in the past manifestation and the current reality and to predict future reality along the physical continuum. An object continues in some form in a physical universe.

time limits the lower physical dimensions because a 3rd-dimensional manifestation occurred. A 3-dimensional physical situation is definite[9e] when it occurred. Time will not permit an exact replica of that physical situation to become manifest.

Time forces a new situation to proceed from the previous situation continuously. Physical reality will force the next situation. The 4th d is verified by instrumental data, mathematical calculation, Sensual Observation, and Conscious Participation.

The dimensional limitation on the 4th d is that time, while forcing the next situation does not select between the alternatives available in the future. Left to its operation, physical being in the first four dimensions just tumbles into the future according to the principles operational in those dimensions.

Cosmologically, objects continue in space.

Ontologically, objects relate to one another according to the operational principles of a physical universe. Cause and effect is fully operational, so reality is determinable as it unfolds according to those physical principles. All discussions of the future are ontological discussions because they contain the question, "What if…?"

The variables are limited but undetermined in the future situation, so the reality is also undetermined.

5th D (Choices and Decisions): The Choices available in the 5th D allow the Observer to Act on current events to alter the situation of future events. If the Observer does not Act, the situation develops according to other influences. If the Observer Acts on the situation, the Observer becomes an Active Participant, Creating Reality in the 5th D. The Choices are limited, but the potential is broad within those limitations.

THE LAW OF DIMENSIONAL LIMITATION

The 5th Dimension is verified by instrumental documentation of the Chosen Action (Decision) and its Effects. Mathematical calculation may be used to evaluate the past and how the present may Manifest as an Effect of the Choice, but mathematics cannot predict A Choice because A Choice Has A Spiritual Cause, Which Is not predetermined. Mathematics cannot calculate a conclusion where variables are undefined until A Choice Is Made. Ultimately,[9f] Conscious Participation verifies the 5th Dimension as Choices Are Made By A Spiritual Being.

Please reconsider the situation prior to An Act Of Forgiveness compared to The Situation After The Act Of Forgiveness. For example, Your Son has Insulted You by Going Against Your firm Instruction not to leave home. You discover that He has left home, and You are infuriated by His disobedience. At last, He returns home, and You Have A Choice. You might Judge Him harshly to further drain the Love from Your Relationship. Instead, You Choose To Forgive Him and Seek To Understand His Point Of View. You Communicate Your Forgiveness. He May Reciprocate As You Seek A Common Understanding Of Each Other. The Divine Energy Of Love Multiplies In This Communion.

The Dimensional Limitation of the 5th D is that Each Participant Makes Choices from a limited perspective. There are always other forces at work. Choices By Others and physical processes cascade into a matrix of Cause-and-Effect Relationships That Each Participant cannot fully Know or Influence. Many of these are purely physical, occurring and interacting without a Spiritual (Conscious) Being Making A Choice.

Cosmologically, something had to happen for alternatives to be presented and Decided.

Ontologically, The Reality Of Beings With Enough Awareness To Make A Choice between two or more alternatives Is Present. This is well beyond the boundary of just physical being.

6th D (Unpredictability, Uncertainty, Randomness, and Chaos): Ordinary progression occurs by 3rd- and 4th-dimensional forces modified by Participants Manipulating[9g] situations in the 5th D. However, there are possibilities that occur that suddenly change the next situation outside The View Of The Participants.

The 6th D is verified by the data collected by independent instrumentation. Often a reliable instrument, measuring data is the first indication that an unprecedented[9h] event has occurred. Then We are forced to account for the unusual[9i] event using the principles of operation of the lower dimension. Such data often causes a Paradigm[9j] change in Our Understanding Of Reality to Accommodate[9k] the reliable data observed.

As mathematics advances, it often yields a result that is impossible in the previous mathematics. 6th-D verification requires that the mathematics must grow to encompass the divergent result.

6th-D verification also requires that Conscious Participation in an impossible Experience redefine Our Understanding Of Reality To Anticipate the potential recurrence of that Experience. Those possibilities change Our Worldview.

Cosmologically, the field of possibilities in 6th-D Reality is broader than Humans can Know.

Ontologically, Observation of new data forces the growth of Our Metaphysics. Human knowledge of physical reality continues. Human ability to organize and create abstract processes continues. We have some tools to help manage chaos. Dimensional Reasoning Is one of those tools.

The Dimensional Limitation to unpredictability or chaos is the organizing principles[9l] that Instructed matter and its attendant energies. The 6th D must draw on higher Dimensions To Influence the lower dimensions. There are organizing principles in the higher Dimensions. Most Encompassing Among Organizing Principles In Reality Is The Information Instructed By The 10th D To Create Reality In the 9th D To Manifest In the 8th D and lower dimensions. Writ Large,[9m] There Is Order[9n] In Reality.

One example is the Creation of DNA.[9o] DNA does something entirely different from all other physical molecules. An object developed a complex molecule that has the ability to divide and create the same kind of object based on the replication[9p] of DNA. This tangent to ordinary molecular operation is impossible under the ordinary operational principles of our physical universe. Yet it happened, and Life Came Into Being. Objects that replicate[9q] Themselves through the division of DNA are called "Living." They are called "Living Beings" because Each Is distinct[9r] and able To Make Its Own Choices or, at least, Seek Self-beneficial Courses Of Action. Primitive[9s] Consciousness exists In All Living Beings. Even a Virus[9t] has a chemical Instruction allowing it to Sense the physical situation and Pursue a course of Action.

In contrast, a rock has no choices.

Humans have Participated in the creation of metal-, silicon-,[9u] and polymer-[9v] based computer chips[9w] that organize the direction of electrons based on a mathematical computer program.[9x] Programmed options[9y] are not the same as Choices. A programmed option always defines a condition precedent and a subsequent action prescribed[9z] by the program. Given *A*, *B* will occur as programmed. There is no choice.

Choices are unpredictable as The Living Creature Making The Choice May Act differently than It did previously, for no rational reason, when presented the same opportunity.

Twenty-First Century science fiction frequently depicts robots with artificial intelligence; they extend to include consciousness. Such theories and fictions fail because no matter how complex the computer program, each alternative has programmed responses and procedures to calculate responses at the next level of artificial intelligence. Such programs and the robots they drive do not have a soul. It remains an open question whether or not The LORD Will Ever Imbue A Spark Of GOD's Being Into a computer program or robot.

There is no doubt that a malevolent spirit can use machines to perform evil acts. A Righteous Spirit Can Use machines To Perform Beneficial Acts.

Also, the ultimate conclusion of such a computer program or mechanical system is limited in the 7th D to finite amounts of matter and its attendant energies to be contributed to such a physical system. For example, pull the electric plug, and the electrons do not proceed. The physical computer system stops. The potential for A Living Spiritual Being To Make Choices can only be interrupted by incapacity or physical death. The Continuity Of Spirit Remains, so Choices do not end. Additional Proof of this fundamental difference between physical systems and Spiritual Systems continues in This Teaching.

7th D (Physical Universes): A physical universe exists. Though it may be warped by unpredictable events in the 6th D, or the 5th-D Choices of Beings, or 4th-d changes of physical situations because of the mindless[9z1] operation of physical forces, the operation of each dimension yields action as a result of a set of cause-and-effect relationships that operate forcefully. 7th-d reality emerges according to a set of laws operational in all physical universes.

Our 7th-d physical universe is verified by instrumental data. Physical instruments precisely record data presented by our 7th-d universe of matter and its attendant energies. A verifiable mathematics supports the physical observations and can predict future events with precision. As we learn more about our physical universe, Our own Conscious Experience Is Verified As Each Of Us Is A Participant in this physical universe.

Its Dimensional Limitation is that 7th-d physical reality must proceed as physical laws prescribe. Though a specific outcome is not certain, the system begins, continues, and ends predictably within the operation of these physical operational principles.

Cosmologically, we know of only one physical universe. That is our physical universe of matter and its attendant energies. Our universe changes as the continuum presses matter and its attendant energies on and on.

Ontologically, the character of the next physical reality is influenced by its physical forces. These are operational, independent of our understanding of them.

The Fused Reality that We Experience As Our 7th Dimension is further developed by Choices of Conscious Beings, Selecting between options presented by each successive situation. A different Universe Is Manifested By Each Choice As You Go forward.

The magnitude of difference between Our Universe Developing From One Choice as opposed to a different Choice is a function of the Cause-and-Effect Results Of The Choices Made. Most Choices made by Conscious Beings on planet earth are contained within the sphere of influence of earth's magnetic and gravitational field. The 7th-D cosmological sub-boundary of earth's influence appears to limit Our Grasp As Incarnate Beings.

Human Consciousness and the Influence of Human Choices and Actions have pierced the membrane of earth's boundaries. Our Manipulation of electromagnetic waves allows Us To Project information throughout our physical universe at nearly the speed of light.

A significant question remains: Is there A Consciousness out there in our physical universe Capable or Interested in receiving that information? So far, We have no clear record of Contact made beyond earth with Intelligent Beings Incarnate in physical form, except for Life from earth.

The LORD May Have Fused Spirit Into Other physical Beings In our physical universe. It would be incredibly interesting if purported Extraterrestrials[9z2] would initiate regular contact with Humans and take Us to the stars. So far, recent contact is rare or nonexistent.

The dispersion of matter outside earth by Human Decisions and following Actions is much slower than electromagnetic waves. The process has begun. Satellites and long-distance probes bear witness to Whoever May Be Aware, that there are Incarnate Beings on planet earth.

The existence of a universe parallel to ours at the same time, where cause and effect manifests a different reality at the same time, is an unanswered question. A "parallel" universe is logically inconsistent with the operational principles (laws) of physical reality as we know them. The answer is NO until some convincing evidence of the "parallel" universe is presented. The boundary of the 4th d would have to be breached for a different timeline to manifest without destroying our timeline.

We do know that there are many divergent realities of our physical universe that could emerge. Our universe will "become" according to the path taken. Hence, a boundary of our physical universe in the 7th Dimension is Observation of the past, starting with our big bang. The theory of our universe as a multiverse is limited to the possible iterations of our universe that emerge in the future.

8th D (Membrane Systems): The physical membrane system is immense. Complete, separate physical universes, unrelated to ours, may exist.

Totally apart from these, other membrane systems exist following the courses of their origin. Each membrane system is limited by the principles of its operation. No other laws or operations are necessary within each different membrane system for it to exist. Also, unless acted upon by influences outside the system, the forces operating within one type of membrane system cannot manifest differently. Hence, all physical-type universes operate according to physical principles. All Spiritual Universes Operate According To Spiritual Principles.

Cosmologically, we are aware of only one physical universe. The existence of physical universes unrelated to our own, but which operate with the same principles, has not yet been established. Absent evidence of another physical universe, our current cosmology is that the 7th-d boundary of our physical universe equals the 8th-d boundary of the physical membrane system.

The 8th-d physical membrane system is verified as at least one physical universe is observed by the instrumentation, the mathematics, and the Conscious Observation and Participation we have in our physical universe.

THE LAW OF DIMENSIONAL LIMITATION

Our 8th-D Spiritual Membrane System is verified by Conscious Self-Awareness In Our Spiritual Universe. The Separateness Of Our Spiritual Awareness from our physical universe is verified by the Continuing Of A Spiritual Soul After physical death. It Is Further Verified By Effects Of Spiritual Causation On matter In Our Fused Reality. Consider again The Effects Of Forgiveness On The future Reality as opposed to the reality that would manifest without Forgiveness.

Ontologically, the existence of a physical universe other than ours that originated with a singularity and a big bang, developing into the same type of matter and its attendant energies, is possible. The WORD can Instruct a Metastring in The 9th D to manifest a singularity in the 8th d. Such other physical universe would have expanded from its big bang that created its own space. There is no physical way to collect evidence of such a universe. If We could pierce the boundary of the universal confinement of our physical universe, perhaps such a physical universe could be detected.

Spirit Can Take Us Beyond physical boundaries. The reality of other Membrane Systems is established. We know of a Spiritual Membrane System because We Observe and Participate In A Spiritual Universe. Our Spiritual Universe Operates Independently Of our physical universe.

Consciousness Is The Most Obvious Manifestation Of Our Spiritual Universe. Self-Awareness Is My Awareness of My Own Awareness. Hence, I Am Aware Of My Own Self. Self-Awareness Is A Higher Level Of Consciousness That Forces The Knowledge Of Spiritual Being, specifically My Spiritual Being, On Me. I am Aware Of Myself As A Being Participating In My Own Life. I Am also Aware Of Myself As An Observer Of other realities. This is verified separately by You and Your knowledge Of Your Own Spiritual Being. It Is As Obvious As The Light In Your eyes. This is further verified by the absence of the Light in the eyes of a dead body at the time of passing away.

Our Grasp Is That Of Our Own Being. Our Reach[9z3] Is That Of Other Beings. I Know Of Your Spiritual Being Because I Observe The Light In Your eyes. I Participate In Your Spiritual Countenance As We Relate In Ordinary Events.

There is nothing in 4-dimensional physical reality that approaches this kind of Experience. The proof of Spiritual Being Is These Real Experiences. Since We Observe Other Spiritual Manifestations (Refer To Our Spiritual Vocabulary), We Are Able To Define Our Spiritual Universe, Its Operational Principles, and Its Manifestations.

Human Consciousness Allows Us To Observe Other Spiritual Manifestations. Human Consciousness also Allows Us to Participate in those Manifestations by Interacting with Them To Become More Highly Aware Of The broader Reality. The Interaction is not just Observing but Formative Of The Spiritual Environment Through Participation. This Is Spiritual Causation. Spiritual Causation Is Very Influential[9z4] on planet earth.

There is no cosmology of Spirit because the cosmos is limited to the universe of matter and its attendant energies—our physical universe.

Ontologically, The Reality Of Spirit Is Forced Upon Us By Our Participation In Spiritual Events, such as Joy, Forgiveness, Gratitude,[9z5] and, most of all, Love.

Though all Manifestations of Reality are present in the 8th D, its Dimensional Limitation is that the operational principles of the 8th D neither Create these principles nor does the 8th D alter their operation.

9th D (Creation, Fusion, and the Mechanics of Membrane Systems): The 9th D Creates, Preserves, and Destroys Membrane Systems. The Creative Machinery Operates To Manifest a Membrane System. Also, The Machinery May Operate To Penetrate[9z6] Membrane Systems To Alter Their Operation.

Fundamental To Our Discussion Of The 9th-D Mechanics Of Creation Is To Understand that the membrane systems in the 8th D and lower dimensions are closed systems.[9z7] The physical membrane system and sub-systems in the lower dimensions are closed. That means that the operational principles governing what was, and is in each system are definite. Those operational principles are either unalterable[9z8] or evolve according to the operational principles set by the field of influence of those operational principles (Laws).

Stated simply, each system is organized, and there is a limitation upon what can become real within each closed system.

Entropy[9z9] is medium to low in the physical membrane system because the energy available is defined and limited.

For example, Our physical universe emerged from our big bang. Implicit in the singularity and the matter and energies created is all of their possible actions and reactions. Our expanding physical universe is what becomes manifested within the limitations of time and the relative space created. Nothing physical can happen apart from what is initiated by the operational principles of our physical universe. Many of those principles have been discovered and precisely defined by modern science. These operational principles will not change as our physical universe was, is, and becomes manifested into reality. Our universe of matter and its attendant energies is limited. It is a closed system.

Fundamental to the understanding of Creation is that The WORD (10th D) and the 9th-D Mechanics Of Creation, which Implements The WORD, Are Open Systems.[9z10] That means that though there Are Operational Principles Through Which Reality Is Manifested In The 9th D, Those Operational Principles Are not limited. Principles in operation in the 9th D Continue According To The WORD, Which Is Not Limited.

New and Different Principles Of Operation Are Created In The 9th D According To The WORD. This precedes and Creates the cosmos.

Entropy (disorganization) can be very high In The 9th D because What Was organized May Be Instructed To Become disorganized. Entirely New Operations

THE LAW OF DIMENSIONAL LIMITATION

Are Organized In The 9th D As The WORD Instructs New Information To Be Synthesized (Realized). Entropy decreases As The 9th-D Machinery Of Creation organizes New Operational Principles To Bring A new system into reality.

The Boundaries Of The 9th D Are Shattered As The WORD Issues New Instructions. Entropy Again increases. Hence, the 9th D is an open system.

Partial Fusion of one membrane system With Another Membrane System may be Instructed To The 9th D From The 10th D. The Information may develop from Proximity or the Harmony of separate functions to either Create a new Membrane System or To Merge Manifestations To Create A Separate Reality For Both Systems for a period on a shared continuum and then Separate The Systems again.

Cosmology In The 9th D Is a subset of 9th-D Operation. That subset Is the Creation of physical realities.

Ontologically, The 9th D Is Part Of The Creative Metaphysics of Reality. While 9th-D Operational Principles Allow Creation Of Membrane Systems, Fusion Of Membrane Systems, or Destruction Of Membrane Systems, Its Dimensional Limitation Is That The 9th D does not Create The Instructions To Do So.

One Way To Understand The Operation Of 9th-D Synthesis is to continue Our analogy of the reception of radio waves by a radio. DNA is like the antennae on the radio set. Our Teaching Hypothesizes that the presence of replicating DNA Draws Spiritual Being To a physical body. The Spirit, So Attracted, Bonds To the body as it Develops with cellular DNA.

Such A Spirit was previously either Located or Spread without location Within The Universe Of Spirit. The 9th D Provides A Mechanism For The Spirit To Coalesce[9z11] and The Fusion With matter To Occur. We are certain of This Fusion. Furthermore, Our Teaching deduces that Part Of That Mechanism Is DNA. DNA allows the Spirit To Take form, Incarnate In a material body. The growth of the body is directed by the Information in the DNA. The embryo Becomes A Human Being only When A Spirit Incarnates Into It.

It is important to note that DNA is a physical chemical molecule. It remains purely physical, an antenna, until Spirit Is Infused. Recreating a DNA molecule will not Infuse it with Spirit. It Is The Choice Of The Individual Spirit To Select the body To Incarnate Into. Proof of This Process Is That There Are many zygotes that do not proceed to Birth Of An Incarnate Human Being. A zygote may spontaneously abort due to biochemical processes. A zygote may abort for lack of a spirit incarnating into it. An abortion may result from a decision of the mother or action of another being. Negative spiritual energy surrounds abortion events, especially those that are chosen by a human being, because they are GODforsaken. Yet GOD Is Merciful To Restore The Relationship With The LORD, If the diminished human being Will Try.

Your physical body develops according to the genetic code in Your DNA present in each cell of Your body. You inherit this from each of Your human parents, and they from their parents before them.

Your Soul—Your Incarnate Spirit—Is Of GOD, Inherited Along Your Spiritual Journey. Your Soul may be vastly different from The Souls of Your physical parents.

It Is A 9th-D Discussion As To how DNA Is Instructed By The WORD Of GOD. Scientific discovery may someday prove that DNA is not the Catalyst Attracting Spirit To a physical body. It Is no ordinary chemistry That Incarnates Life Into a body sustained by a replicating molecule. Divine Information Guides The Development Of A Human Soul. The body is the Temple[9z12] built in physical reality In Which The Soul Resides. An Immortal Soul Becomes Incarnate Into a human body To Complete The Fusion.

This Teaching Reveals That By Incarnation Into Your physical body, GOD Experiences Human Consciousness As A Division of GOD's Spiritual Being, Which Is Your Soul, Manifested To You As Consciousness. Yes, Your Spirit Is A Sliver or Spark Of The Divine,[9z13] Intimately Connected To GOD By The Divine Metastring. Through You, GOD Is Experiencing the unique character of physical being. These Experiences and Elevated Connections verify 9th-Dimensional Operation, Through Conscious Participation.

Do not be misled. You Are not GOD. Your Spirit or Soul Is A Sliver Of GOD. That Is All You Can Be Prior To Reunification. Yet Your Sliver Of The Divine Is In The Image Of GOD and Is Connected To GOD. Tremendous Expansion Of Your Soul, Differentiated From GOD and Manifested As Your Consciousness, Is Possible.

We Speak Of GOD's Participation In Human Consciousness. Please note that God Participates In The Consciousness Of All Living Creatures. GOD Participates In The Individual Consciousnesses Of Each. Note that there is no limitation to The Participation Of GOD. We have seen, on rare occasions, that GOD even Alters matter and its attendant energies at the string level, as well as more complex physical constructions.

9th-Dimensional Operation Is Prior To any cosmology. 9th-D Mechanisms Create the cosmos—our physical universe. This Teaching discusses many theories about the very small and very large components of our physical universe. Some of that theoretical physics is already proven. Some will prove to be correct and some incorrect. Physical theories are discussed in This Teaching so You May Understand some of The Machinery Of Creation and Sustaining Reality in the 9th D That Manifest the WORD. There is no conflict between science and Religion In Our Teaching.

Ontologically, The 9th D Is The Reality Of Creative Force evidenced by All Of Creation. The 9th D Is Also The Changes To What Is Created physically, Spiritually, and in any other Realm, As It Pleases The LORD.

10th D (The WORD): Instructions Of What Is To Be, Determined By The WILL Of GOD, Is Manifested As GOD's WORD. Our cosmos Is Created In The 9th D According To These Instructions.

Ontologically, The WORD defines Reality. The Metastrings Vibrate The WORD In Harmony. This is why there Is Order In The Universes. The only Limitation On The 10th D Is That The WORD Is Divine Instruction and Divine Information only, not The Totality Of GOD.

That There Is A Definite Reality Verifies The 10th D. That There Is uncertainty In Reality Verifies The Operational Potential Of The 10th D.

One Understanding Is That The WORD Is GOD. If You See This, Then The 11th Is The Same As The 10th D.

I prefer To Relate To The LORD As GOD Being More Than The Information and Instructions Of The WORD Of GOD. GOD Is The Complete Being From Which All Is Manifest. Yet GOD Is Greater Than The Sum Of All Instruction, Information, Machinery Of Creation, and Those Manifestations.

11th: GOD Is Not Defined and Is Not Limited.

Ontologically, Everything That Is Real Is A Manifestation Of GOD. GOD Is Infused In All Beings. The LORD Self-Verifies, and Reality Is One Of Those Self-Verifications.

The WORD Is An Expression Of GOD When GOD Chooses To Be Separate From That Creation As An Observer or just Allows The Instructions To Continue and The Machinery To Operate unattended.[9z14] Aspects Of GOD Are Present As The Sustaining Information Of The WORD, Yet The Consciousness Of GOD May Not Be Attending Some Manifestations Once Set In Motion In the 9th D.

That is to say that The WORD Sustains physical being. The operational principles or laws of physical manifestation do not change in the physical membrane system. It is a closed system because the Information Posited By GOD At each singularity is limited. The Instructions Of The WORD remain constant, As It May Please The LORD. The Restorative Force Of The WORD Operating To Sustain physical being in quantum fields Is An Aspect Of GOD. However, The WORD as physical being once set in physical reality, may operate separately from the Consciousness Of GOD.

The Consciousness Of GOD Differentiates Individual Spirit or Soul Into A Living Being. The WORD is The Sustaining Force Of An Individual Soul Differentiated From GOD. GOD's Consciousness May Choose To Share The Individual's Consciousness or May Be Invited By The Individual to Share One Consciousness.

The WORD Is GOD When GOD Chooses To Participate In GOD's Creations. Life and Consciousness Are Among The Ways In Which GOD Chooses To Participate.

CHAPTER 10

Causation

Causation[10a] is an operational principle in the 9th Dimension to Bring A Reality Into Being in either the physical membrane system or The Spiritual Membrane System or any other reality.

We use the word *Causation* as the action of causing something or the process "to cause"—that is, the action moving reality from its cause to the effect of that cause.

Causality, sometimes a synonym for *Causation*, is the noun describing the study of the relationships that happen in Causation or the principle that everything has a cause. This Is Fundamental To Any Understanding Of Reality.

We will capitalize the word *Cause* when it is being used as a 9th D Process of Creation or as Spiritual Causation. We will use the lower case *cause* when cause-and-effect is operating in the physical membrane system or other closed system.

Cause and effect implies a continuum. Reality progresses with action of the Manifestations operating in any Dimension. An action operates within the field of influence of the dimension to have a result during the process or conclusion of its operation.

Reality is not static. The connection is verified by establishing the effect as the immediate or proximate consequence of the cause.

Also, there usually is a chain of cause-and-effect relationships that can be traced that yields a specific situation along a continuum. The current situation would not become real if any link in that chain did not occur.

Causation,[10a] also known as "causality," is an operational principle of the physical membrane system. Cause and effect may occur simultaneously, but the effect never precedes the cause. Cause and effect is active in the operation of the force of time on our physical universe. Cause and effect manifests in space-time and serves to limit the 8th-dimension physical membrane system. This is true wherever there is matter and its attendant energies.

CAUSATION

Ross Pomeroy 2017 (https://psmag.com/environment/creatures-of-coherence-why-were-so-obsessed-with-causation-5580), Shutterstock 93372559

Though this describes how cause and effect operates in the physical membrane system, it is important to understand that cause and effect is operational in all Manifest Reality, Including the Spiritual Membrane System.

Divine Instruction, the WORD, is the passing of Causative Information[10b] from GOD in the 10th D to be Fashioned[10c] into a Manifestation by the 9th D to collapse into an effect, something real, in the eighth and lower dimensions.

GOD Is the Original Cause,[10d] Instructing all Effects that become real. Once GOD Creates a bounded system,[10e] such as our physical universe, the operational principles of that bounded system take over to create local cause-and-effect situations. These physical situations usually do not receive the Attention[10f] of GOD, except for the aspects of The WORD that Create and Sustain strings (quantum waves).

In the broadest sense, what is unreal or nothingness is merely the physical space between or Spiritual Void Between The Manifestations Of GOD.[10g] Understanding this Empowers You with the most accurate tools to evaluate each situation.

To properly use cause-and-effect analysis,[10h] You must understand the operational principles of the dimension in which a particular cause-and-effect relationship is occurring. The collapse of what was a future possibility into physical reality occurs at the 4th d and manifests in the 3rd d. Time forces the next 3-dimensional event that is real here and now.

For example, in a 4th-Dimensional physical situation, an earthquake (sudden shifting of tectonic plates) causes the effect of a bridge splitting as its foundation shifts. This is a completely physical cause-and-effect occurrence in ordinary time.

The laws of physics determine the physical setting. Unaltered, physical forces cause the vast majority of events unfolding in physical reality. The physical sciences are consumed by observing and predicting physical events based on the quantum probabilities. Laws of operation are developed to explain what has happened and what will happen next. The limit of such knowledge is to define all physical forces and their results.

If We could define each physical cause and its effect, then We could predict all future events, right? No and No. It is practical to develop a catalog of causes and their likely effects. But remember that a specific cause will not always yield the same effect. Every situation remains unique. The potentia or quantum possibilities[10i] present the range of what might become. All formative factors present quantum probabilities, only one of which will become a "fact" in the next situation.

We know that there is more. A Conscious Being has Choices. This Is The Reality Of The 5th D As We Operate In The 5th Dimension To Create Our Own Reality. These Choices are often unpredictable, and each Choice is undetermined until It Is Made.

Consider an example of Cause and Effect in the 5th Dimension. You had a Dream that Your Child was on a school bus that crashed under unclear circumstances in the dream. The Effect of Your dream was that You Chose To Keep Your Child at home the next day. Later that day, You heard on the news that the bus Your Child would have been riding crashed that morning as the bridge split in the process mentioned in Our first example. This caused injury to many riders. Your Action, Caused By Your Dream, had The Effect of Preventing injury to Your Child as the possibilities collapsed into reality.

Let us perform multidimensional analysis[10j] on another example to illustrate a complete Reality. You observe that Your Dog is cold and wet and tied to a tree outside in the snowstorm. Compassionately, You Choose to build a doghouse. You buy the plywood and fasteners. Using Your knowledge of geometry to draw the lines (1st d) onto the boards to lay out the rectangular pieces (2nd d) that you cut to build the floor, walls, and roof of the doghouse (3rd d), You Perform each Action in sequence (4th d).

Your mind Combines a Spiritual Quality,[10k] Compassion for Your Dog, with a physical process, building the doghouse, for a future Purpose, which is Your Dog's shelter. The Action Is A Choice to build a doghouse rather than not to build a doghouse (5th D). Your brain provides the mathematical calculations to direct your hands to cut, assemble, and finish the doghouse.

In this example, Compassion, a Spiritual Quality, was the Cause for You to Act. The Effect was Your Spirit Instructing Your brain to calculate the materials, cut, fasten, and finish the doghouse. The mathematics and motions of cutting and constructing were physical processes. Additionally, your brain's calculation of a plan for cuts and construction caused your arms to perform the construction actions as an effect. Your neural[10l] signals within your arms and hands were causes for action with the effect that your hands picked up the saw and cut the wood to the right size as directed by your Eye-to-hand coordination.[10m]

This simple example illustrates several situations of Cause and Effect developed in the first five Dimensions—to yield a functional doghouse. In this case, The Initial Cause Was Spiritual—that is, Compassion For Your Dog.

After many Happy years of Residence, Your Dog was not in His doghouse when a random gust of wind stressed a Tree branch, causing it to fall off the Tree and crash onto the doghouse. The effect was that the impact of the branch crushed the doghouse structure. In this example, only physical dimensions 1 through 4 are operational. No Spirit was involved, and no 5th-Dimensional Choice caused the destruction of Your doghouse.

The higher Dimensions provide the context for this event but were not directly involved in the cause-and-effect sequence of Your doghouse being destroyed. A higher Dimensional Analysis of this example is expressed as follows. It was unpredictable (6th d) that the wind would blow so hard as to cause the tree branch to fall. Had You been able to Predict this, You might have Acted to move the doghouse prior to the branch falling. Most of this sequence occurred completely within the physical operation of our physical universe (7th d).

The only aspect of the doghouse history that was not contained in the 7th d was Your Compassion For Your Dog. Again, Initial Cause—in this case, Compassion— was not from this universe of matter and its attendant energies. No physical sequence of cause and effect can construct a doghouse. Doghouses do not occur naturally in our physical universe. An infinity of random physical events could not produce a doghouse.

The cause of this doghouse forces Us to Acknowledge[10n] Our Spiritual Universe (7th D). Your Nonmaterial Soul Had To Be Present In your physical body To Draw Compassion From Our Spiritual Universe and Bring That Aspect Of Love For Another Spiritual Creature (Your Dog) To the physical earth to Cause Your physical self to build the doghouse.

Remove Compassion, and the dog will suffer in the snow.

The Existence Of A Nonphysical Universe Forces The 8th-Dimension Spiritual Upon The Situation. If all physical universes operate the same way, to exclude Compassion, then the existence of a Universe Operating Differently must be outside the membrane of all physical universes. This is another proof of The Spiritual Membrane System. Indeed, the 8th D provides for all types of Membrane Systems— physical, Spiritual, and any other type of membrane system that may Exist.

A critic might say that dogs throughout history have always survived in the snow. Your Compassion is just a misguided sequence of physical reactions—random and of no consequence. Why do you even have a dog that you should care for?

The Cause Of You Getting This Dog Is Another Spiritual Cause. Your Spirit Incarnate Seeks Companionship With Another Soul. The Feeling Is Mutual, So A Spiritual Relationship Develops.

The critic continues. Your Yearning[10o] for a dog to love is simply a chemical reaction of hormones affecting your brain, causing you to seek a dog for companionship. This happens in the physical universe, so no Spiritual Universe is needed.

There are two responses to this. First, the chemistry of Compassion evolved only among Living Creatures. You may direct Compassion toward a rock, but the rock cannot receive Your Compassion. The absence of a spirit (soul) in the rock is a limiting characteristic of the physical membrane system that prohibits Compassion from being relevant to any physical universe.

Second, Compassion happens within our physical universe only because of the temporary Intersection[10p] of Our Spiritual Universe to bring Spirits into physical form as Living Creatures. As soon as Life is removed from Our Universe, that Intersection of two vastly different Membrane Systems will end. Then the earth will go on manifesting only physical cause-and-effect reactions.

The 9th D Provides The Mechanism For The Spiritual Membrane System To Flow Into the physical membrane system. Spirit Is A Unique Type of Information not composed of digital information,[10q] "strings" or "quantum particles," any atomic arrangement, or atomic process. However, Spirit Will Rearrange atomic structures as needed To Express Spiritual Qualities. The rearrangement of atomic structures is not Spirit. Those rearrangements merely operate As Instructed By Spirit. You built the doghouse as a physical sequence, but The Initial Cause Was Spiritual—Compassion For Your Dog.

It Is A Divine Process of Incarnation[10r] For The 9th D To Manifest Spirit Into Your physical body during Your Lifetime. Your Compassion Is Of GOD. Your Compassion Is An Instruction From GOD (10th D) As A Participant In This Conscious Spiritual Cause.

You could Choose to be uncaring[10s] about Your Dog suffering in the snow, or You just might not have noticed Your Dog freezing in the wet and cold. That event is defined by the absence of GOD in the sequence. You are still Spirit Incarnate, and Your Dog is still Spirit Incarnate. But no Spiritual quality of Compassion is collapsed into reality regarding Your Dog suffering in the snow in this possible manifestation. That reality is your dog's physical being disintegrating in the cold. Your Soul was unreceptive[10t] to Divine Instruction, and Your failure to Appreciate the Potential diminished the entire situation. The event became a totally physical event because of the absence of Compassion. With the absence of the 10th-D Instruction, there was no 9th-D merger of physical and Spiritual Membrane Systems into the 8th D. Our 7th-D physical universe unfolded with your dog freezing in the snow. If the cold is so severe that Your Dog's Life cannot be sustained, then Your Dog's Spirit Will Pass Away, and its physical deterioration will continue.

Ultimately, the Passing of Your Dog's Spirit is not so sad for Your Dog because the physical death of Your Dog Liberated[10u] Its Spirit from our physical universe and

CAUSATION

Continued Its Being In Our Spiritual Universe. Though Your Dog's Passing is not yet Reunification, There Are Many Possibilities In The Reality Beyond physical death.

In summary, cause and effect may Be Observed and even codified into operational principles in various Dimensions. It is also one proof of The Reality Of higher Dimensions.

The Choices You Make and Your Subsequent Actions Will alter physical reality, especially around You. You Are Part Of The 9th-D Machinery Of Creation As You Apply Spiritual Actions Here and Now To Create The Next Situation on The Continuum. Act Using The Power Granted To You To Increase Spiritual Energy, and The Next Situation Will Be More Glorious and More Fulfilling. Act using Your Capabilities[10v] to diminish spiritual energy, and an ugly reality will proceed.

Multiply that by All The Individual Human Consciousnesses Acting On physical reality, Cause and Effect Yields very complicated Predictive[10w] equations. Add to that All The Other Plant and Animal Consciousnesses, The Manifestations That Become Real On Our earth Are Truly Myriad.

We have proved that Cause and Effect is very Real and Operates To Collapse The Possibilities Into Reality In Each Membrane System, that has a continuum.

A deeper dive into our physical membrane system reveals that the continuum that we define as "time" is a display of a Constant Cause.[10x] Quantum Field Theory (QFT)[10y] is emerging to define the uncertain emergence of the quantum fields, which have 0 value as potential, but then have value, as soon as excitations occur in each field, to generate each of the various basic particles. The continuation of any particle is the force of time. The character of each particle is according to The Instructions Of The WORD In The 10th D. The intermingling of the various particles Is The Act Of Creation Of matter In The 9th D. The continuation of quantum particles is a principle of operation in the 8th-d physical membrane system and every 7th-d physical universe.

time is known as the "constant" in physical reality. It is but one Manifestation Of Constant Cause—a manifestation of GOD that keeps material reality going. Expressed another way, it is the 9th-D Machinery Of Creation and Continuation Of physical reality.

We had earlier spoken of Original Cause As GOD Setting Up principles of operation of 7th-d physical universes and allowing them to operate independently. We must clarify that to say that The WORD Is Ever-Present As The Constant and Continuing Cause.

Furthermore, GOD Can Interrupt the continuum so an ordinary progression may Be Altered By The WORD.

This Explains how water can Be Turned into wine. The WORD Can Alter the operational principles of any Dimension. Water into wine cannot be calculated by any chemical formulation. To alter the physical chemistry of water, Instructions must be given at the quantum string level so that some of the atoms forming the molecules of water are rearranged sub-atomically to change into the carbohydrates and ethers of wine. Of course, this is impossible for You or Me to accomplish. But When The WORD Was Made Flesh,[10z] That Spirit Did Instruct The Change. Our LORD Jesus Christ Performed This Miracle[10z1] To Demonstrate The Nature of Spirit As Separate From physical reality, and The Supremacy Of GOD Over All Realities—That Is, The WORD Can Change Reality In Any Dimension. Human Beings are barely capable of Understanding This Demonstration Of GOD Controlling Reality. To Command A Change to quantum strings surely Is The Hand Of GOD. Dimensional Reasoning Opens The Understanding Of This and Other Miracles.

This Must Be Very Entertaining For The LORD, Who Creates Conscious Beings So That GOD May Participate In These Manifestations. The Purpose Of Original Cause and Constant Cause Is So Revealed.

CHAPTER 11

The Mathematics

The Law of Dimensional Limitation is further supported by the mathematics We use to describe reality. Dimensional boundaries are further defined by the mathematics operational within each sphere of influence.

Mathematics does not exist in our cosmos as matter or its attendant energies. Mathematics is an ontological discipline.[11a] Mathematics is a tool that describes physical items by measures of quantity, calculations, measurements, or other systems of deduction. These are constructs of The Human Mind.

0th d (Possibility): A point is postulated as a beginning of something that may become real. In geometry, a point is postulated as a possibility in physical space where something can be located.

In quantum theory, a point is the potential in a quantum field.

In time, a point is the start of a continuum.

In Spiritual Reality, A Point Is Undifferentiated Consciousness.

1st d (a line): Geometry defines the 1st dimension as a line. That is the theoretical dimension established by two points as a segment of the line continuing infinitely in both directions, according to geometric theory. The line only becomes limited when it collapses into reality in a 3-dimensional space.

quantum theory defines the 1st d as a quantum particle or a string extended into being.

Time defines the 1st d as a continuum.

Spiritual Reality Defines The 1st D As Primitive Individual Awareness Diffcrentiated From GOD By GOD.

2nd d (a plane): Geometry defines the 2nd dimension as a plane. In geometry, that is the dimension developed when a line changes direction or two lines intersect with each other.

quantum theory defines the 2nd d as the merger of quantum particles or other excitations in a quantum field.

Time defines the 2nd d as an acceleration or deceleration of the continuum relative to a certain perspective.

Spiritual Reality Defines The 2nd D As A Simple Individual Awareness.

3rd d (a solid): Geometry defines the 3rd dimension as a physical object. That is the dimension created when a line crosses a plane or when two planes intersect at an angle other than 180 degrees. Observable space has been created. An object manifests in observable space. Solid geometry,[11b] algebra,[11c] and trigonometry[11d] are fully operational to describe 3-dimensional reality and calculate relations in 3-dimensional space.

In quantum theory, enough quantum particles have emerged within the quantum field to present an observable object that is collapsed into reality.

Time defines the 3rd d as the presentation (present) of a physical object on the physical continuum.

Spiritual Reality Defines The 3rd D As Consciousness Located In A Spiritual Universe or Incarnated Into physical Being.

4th d (a continuum): Geometry defines the 4th dimension as change functions.[11e] The mathematics is expanded with a limit,[11f] implying a summary of static conditions or the conclusion of a series of equations expressed in the present. Averages,[11g] probability,[11h] and calculus[11i] mathematics are operational to quantify[11j] reality on a continuum.

quantum mechanics is fully operational in the 4th d because reactions within a quantum field can be observed on the physical continuum of time that allows reality to emerge, both being and becoming.

Our hypothesis is that a quantum field allows Primal Matter and Primal Antimatter to emerge, cancelling[11k] each other yet leaving an energy residue[11l] in the quantum field that, through time, manifests as matter.

The mathematics of quantum mechanics is developing. We have predictive mathematical formulas calculating wave-particle's physical reality. From these, we derive the laws of physics, which operate defining how these will develop and interact. Yet the mathematics of quantum fields yields infinities in the 9th D as wave functions[11m] are created from the possibilities. These possibilities collapse into definite reality as they are manifested to be observed in 4th-dimensional reality.

If scientific discovery advances to show that subatomic particles are created in a different manner than stated above, Our Metaphysics would not change. This is because whatever the metaphysical Cause of physical matter, the manifestations that We Observe will continue.

Time is measured as a myriad of continuums in physical reality. Each continuum records the emergence and forces the continuation[11n] of events in the lower dimensions. Units of the calculation of time vary according to the character and potential of the continuum measured. Earth time is calculated based on one day equals one rotation of the earth divided by the 360-degree circumference of the earth. One solar year of time is calculated based on one revolution of the earth around the sun in a regular elliptical[11o] orbit, again based on 360 degrees. We can postulate that the units of time of any other planet could be based on the same geometry, though the duration would be different based on the size of the planet, its rotation, and its revolution around its sun. Alternatively, We can keep time on a clock or other machine according to earth-time mechanical measurements. Of course, mechanical measurements vary according to general relativity.

Spiritual Reality Can Manifest As Continuums, also stated as Spiritual Flows.[11p] These Can Be Quantified within the limits of The Spiritual Events Observed. Spiritual Events Are usually not limited by the confines of time. For example, The Recollection Of A Joyous event Can Be As Joyous As The Initial Experience Of Joy at the time of The Event. Hence, The Mathematics Of Spirit Is Quite Different From the mathematics of physical reality. The main difference is that a mathematical formula describing a physical reality is reliable in future physical reality. A Mathematical Formula Describing A Spiritual Reality is unreliable On A Spiritual Continuum Because Spiritual Realities Are not repetitive.[11q] This Is Because Of Free Will. That is to say that The WORD Of GOD Is Not Always formulaic[11r] or repetitive. The WORD Has No Fixed Principles Of Operation.

No discussion of mathematics can proceed except from its root in logic.[11s] Each symbol used in a mathematical system[11t] has a definite meaning. The system develops based on the relations between the symbols and what they represent. The relationships are certain, so the mathematical system is reliable to produce the same result from the initial factors each time a specific calculation is made. When we calculate 1+1=2, it is mathematically constant.[11u] We know this is always true. When the symbols represent objects that We observe in our physical reality, a continuum is observed in which one of something plus another of the same thing always yields two of those items when they are observed together on the continuum. The logic is that conclusions can be drawn by applying these principles. The use of logic becomes a very powerful tool when analyzing reality within a closed system, such as physical reality.

Consider the following advanced application of logic to Knowing GOD. It is a verifiable premise That Your Consciousness Is The Means By Which You Perceive nearly everything. So If You Are To Perceive GOD, That Perception Would Be Through Your Consciousness. Therefore, it is logically proved to say that GOD Relates To You Through Your Consciousness. It is also a premise that You Control much of Your Consciousness by how You process the data You receive from your senses caused by real phenomena. Hence, it is logical to conclude that Your Relationship With GOD Is Often Controlled by You, With You Directing Your Flow Of Consciousness.

It is important To Understand That GOD is not an idea that You construct in Your Mind. GOD Is Real and Separate From You. When You Choose To Relate To GOD, GOD Enters Your Consciousness, and The Sharing Begins. If You Choose not to be in Communion with GOD, the Relationship is only As Forced By GOD.

A Connection Remains, but Your lack of Light diminishes Your Potential For Advanced Spiritual Being[11v] In This Life. It is so sad that this is the condition of many Human Beings. Yet GOD Is Merciful, so it is logical That GOD Continues To Reach Out[11w] To Share Divine Energy With You In Any Way That You Accept. It is also logical That GOD Can Turn Away or Cut The Spiritual Cord Of A One-Way Relationship, Casting You off[11x] as You might cut and cast off a displeasing lock of your hair.

5th D (Choices): Geometric models may be calculated to describe the likely outcome of many alternatives of one Choice or a different Choice. The survival of Life, whether instinctively derived[11y] or calculated, requires constant Mapping[11z] of the likely future situation presented by this alternative or that presented by a different Course Of Action. This is particularly relevant to Individual Choices or those made In A Community[11z1] Of Individuals.

quantum fields are heavily influenced by possibilities. Once quantum mathematics is better developed, calculating the influence of Individual Decisions on the minutest reactions and formations will be extraordinary.

A dramatic example is the Choice (through Action) of two Human Beings to Reproduce sexually.[11z2] Of course, randomness in physical reality may also occasion sexual reproduction without a choice.

The seemingly random selection of each separate RNA[11z3] strand recombining into a full DNA molecule goes to The Essence Of Developmental Reality.[11z4]

Lanore Rivera (https://filipinofreethinkers.org/2010/09/27/being-sexual-and-spiritual-at-the-same-time/)

These illustrations are Offered to demonstrate The Choice of two Humans to Contribute the male and female gametes (RNA strands) to Unite Into a new DNA that forms the genetic basis of a New Individual Human Being.

THE MATHEMATICS

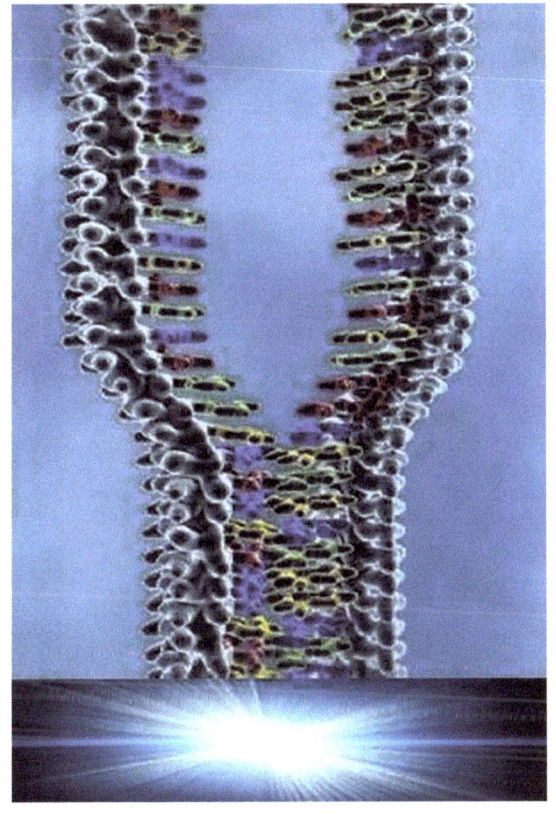

(https://www.thoughtco.com/dna-replication-3981005) *further edit by Allyn Richert*

Time becomes a tool for Beings Capable Of Choice in the 5th D. Manipulating 3-dimensional space along a continuum of time occupies Our Attention Throughout Life. A Person can Pack a lot of Action into one hour of time. In a different setting, that Person may Glide through the hour, Creating almost no impact on His surroundings or even Himself.

Spiritual Choices present a prior and a subsequent mathematics[11z5] in the 5th D. For Example, Whether or not To Forgive an offense Is A Spiritual Choice In The 5th D. The calculus comparing all possible outcomes of Forgiving an offense compared to not forgiving, Is An Extraordinary Capability Of The Human Spirit. Once The Choice Is Made, the future Branching[11z6] Of The Continuum Is Set In Motion, So The Universes Change Going Forward.

Your Positive Spiritual Choices Accumulate[11z7] In Your Soul. These can be Identified and even Counted. Your Virtues are not counted like a stack of coins. You Are Spiritually Elevated By Your Positive Spiritual Choices[11z8] Because These Carry Positive Spiritual Energy. Positive Spiritual Energy Is Also Called Divine Energy or The Light. When You Create Divine Energy, You Enlighten The Situation.

To Quantify This, Recognize That Your Light Can Be Brilliant,[11z9] Diffuse,[11z10] Dim,[11z11] or diminished to become nonexistent.

6th D (Uncertainty, Randomness, and Chaos): Geometry grows[11z12] with the occurrence of situations that throw the absolute certainty of a geometric theorem into chaos.

For example, can we imagine a right triangle[11z13] in which lines a^2+b^2 do not equal c^2?[11z14] Of course, we can. That would be when the right triangle has grown to become a cone[11z15] or a wedge[11z16] or any number of solid shapes that describe real objects and not an abstraction like the flat right triangle. Solid geometry recovers the principles of plane geometry by adding variables or factors to the equations to account for the diverse shapes that incorporate a right triangle. Order is reestablished in the 6th d with chaos causing a dilemma,[11z17] which is resolved when the broader reality is realized.

quantum fields are the epitome[11z18] of randomness in the 6th D. There is no formula in the lower dimensions predicting how a quantum particle or string or Higgs boson[11z19] will manifest out of apparent nothingness. This uncertainty grows into some of the most real but obscure physical principles. For example, Heisenberg's uncertainty principle states that it cannot be determined where an electron will be located at any moment in time. Ordinary logic would conclude that the electron is unreal. Yet whatever strings manifest the electron, we know that electrons exist because each electron has a strong negative electromagnetic charge and a miniscule mass, which can be measured. We can prove that electrons travel in streams with extraordinary impact on observable physical situations, such as lightning or electricity. We can also prove that electrons form a necessary part of each atom. Atoms are an essential building block of the entire physical universe. So uncertainty in the 6th d manifests into certainty in the lower dimensions.

The fact that an electron cannot be located and a moment in time is further proof that physical reality is a continuum, not a series of separate moments or events.

Even time appears uncertain in 6th-dimensional reality. In the lower dimensions, time travel is impossible because the physical situation that has happened cannot be re-manifested[11z20] in 3rd-, 4th-, or even 5th-dimensional space. However unlikely, Einstein's theory of general relativity proves that the continuum of time appears to slow down as the participant approaches the speed of light. Though no Human Participant or physical instrument has proved this, the mathematics proves that the operational principles of the continuum change in 6th-d reality.

On the space-time continuum, there is the unproven theory that space-time can be bent so that two distant locations may come into proximity for a short "leap" to a distant location in space-time. Science fiction calls this an "Einstein-Rosen bridge" or a "wormhole." Would this be a leap in physical space but not a leap into past time? Perhaps such a leap in physical space is possible, but we have no specific evidence to prove this theory.

THE MATHEMATICS

Our Teaching deduces that the entire theory of time travel is false due to the limitations of the operational principles creating and sustaining physical reality. Travelling back in time cannot occur in physical reality.

Chaos, randomness, and uncertainty also appear In Spiritual Reality In The 6th D. The mathematics of "many" is easy to Understand Among The Divergent Spiritual States Of Being. The LORD Jesus Christ[11z21] said, "In My Father's[11z22] House Are Many Mansions…"[11z23] Clearly The Reality Experienced By One Spirit Can Be Quite Different From The Reality Experienced By Another Spirit. Spiritual Differentiation Is The Cause. The Effect Is Diverse Spiritual Beings Of which You Are One. Again, the chaos resulting from so many different points of view and incompatible beliefs of Humans Is Resolved When You Understand The Diversity Of Spiritual States Of Being.

7th D (This universe multiplied and other physical universes): Before we discuss the sequential multiverse and other physical universes, let us do some mathematics regarding the origin of our physical universe. One currently accepted theory of how our universe of matter and its attendant energies began is that the entirety of our singularity burst in our big bang. That big bang was caused as matter, and oppositely charged antimatter emerged from the excitations of the super-energetic quantum field, producing our singularity. Of course, the matter and antimatter reacted violently, cancelling each other out in our big bang.

One current big bang theory[11z24] holds that there was slightly more matter than antimatter, so our universe of matter could emerge as the net remainder of that reaction.

Our Teaching hypothesizes a different big bang theory. Our premise is that matter and antimatter particles are always produced as a pair. As I do the mathematics, the positive matter and the negative antimatter created at our singularity would have been equivalent, so their cancellation must be complete to balance the equation. I propose that the violence of the matter-antimatter reaction cancelled these original particles of our singularity but left an energy residue rather than a matter residue. We will call it "residual energy."[11z25] Current physics defines this as e from special relativity theory. Residual energy is fundamentally different from the quantum excitations at our singularity. The difference is that residual energy is convertible into matter, which can convert back to residual energy.

Our Teaching suggests a formula: **PE=PM-PAM=e**.[11z26] *PE* is the Primal Energy of quantum field excitations. Primal Energy Is Divine Information From The 10th D Transmitted Through The 9th-D metastring as a quantum field, forming our singularity before our big bang. *PM* is Primal Matter. *PAM* is Primal Antimatter. PM and PAM destroyed each other in the reaction we call the big bang. e is the residual energy after that destruction. This process precedes the operational principles of our physical universe.

PE=PM-PAM=e precedes e=mc². The emergence of residual energy after the Primal Matter / Primal Antimatter cancellation is the precursor to the physical law of special relativity, e=mc². This less energetic residue, *e*, began to cool, forcing subatomic particles—such as strings, quarks, and Higgs bosons—to condense into matter. Further cooling allowed condensation of our familiar protons, neutrons, electrons, and more stable photon, radiant energy.[11z27]

The equation is further balanced when We realize that the "residual energy" of Primal Matter converts into protons carrying forward the positive charges. The "residual energy" of Primal Antimatter converts into electrons carrying forward the negative charges. Neutral "residual energy" converts into neutrons, reducing the level of charged energy and stabilizing the entire physical system.

Subatomic particles further condensed into hydrogen, helium, and lithium physical matter. As the vibrations slowed and plasma cooled further, the larger atoms of our universe condensed within stars and supernovae.[4z12]

Underlying the processes validated by these equations are the subatomic particles condensing from residual energy, *e*. These continue into the various combinations of matter and residual energy according to their original Information.

This further supports the assertion that strings are diverse in their Information and character to yield the diverse subatomic particles, energies, and physical waves, such as gravity.

Our hypothesis—that there is Primal Matter and Primal Antimatter emerging in a quantum field as part of our singularity, causing our big bang—is somewhat verified by the logic and mathematics applied above. One day, brilliant Scientists may devise an experiment that will further prove this progression.

Our Teaching postulates that becoming[8g] reconciles quantum mechanics (a science of very small particles) with special relativity (a science of matter and energy relation) and general relativity (a science that matches every cause to a specific local effect).

Essentially, the sustaining principle of physical reality is the constant emergence[11z28] of both matter and antimatter into a quantum field. This operational principle of all physical universes occurs at the subatomic level, as well as the universe singularity level. The presence of a quantum field is the basic physical manifestation Created By The WORD in The 9th D. Such a quantum field Can Be Created Of Any Size and At Any time In The 9th D. The Process of Collapsing matter Into being along the physical continuum is described by the diversity of quantum fields Instructed. A specific quantum field is energized by matter and antimatter created by WORD Instructions. This specific quantum field Is Constructed In The 9th D to manifest Primal Matter and Primal Antimatter to appear and cancel each other out in the 8th D based on their Instructions. The specific Instructions are the Operational Principles and Information Provided For the physical reality manifested. By Our theory, that is how physical creation occurs. The Matter/Antimatter cancellation reac-

THE MATHEMATICS

tion always causes residual energy, which converts to matter (subatomic particles) over time. This is proved by special relativity, e=mc². The matter Created carries forward the positive and negative charges, also manifesting as electromagnetism.

Time—c^2, the physical continuum—is the strongest physical force as it binds energy, e, into subatomic particles such as fermions controlled by bosons. Their interactions are the "cooling" that produce protons, and neutrons, and electrons, composing m, matter.

Hence, the equation of special relativity, **e=mc²**, is also calculated,

$$\frac{e}{c^2} = \frac{mc^2}{c^2} \text{ is the same as } \frac{e}{c^2} = m$$

This is how matter, m, is formed. This mathematics supports the theory of space-time, applying to the smallest particles.

One of the operational characteristics of matter is the presence of gravitational waves[4z46] according to the mass of the particles. Gravitational waves increase as atomic particles are aggregated through their gravitational attraction to one another. General Relativity expresses these bonding relationships in large space.

Also, note that the equations calculated in the paragraphs above are processes over time,[11z29] c^2. They are not instantaneous,[11z30] and they are not static. The quantum particles (Matter and Antimatter) precede and are constantly reacting to become physical energy, e, which, over time, manifests matter. The quantum particles are continuously brought into being by The WORD (10th D) Through The Mechanisms Of Creation (9th D) and manifested into physical being over time. Hence, We deduce that time is a primary force in the 8th-d physical membrane system.

It is not possible to reconcile quantum mechanics with special relativity unless You Understand that quantum fields precede ordinary space-time. They remain separate processes. quantum possibilities collapse via the Matter/Antimatter reaction into space-time. The uncertainty in quantum probabilities becomes certainty as the residual energy has characteristics, such as positive and negative charge and other Information that is certain. Over time, that energy is converted into matter, which also manifests the certain characteristics of the residual energy. Many strings must join for mass to be observed.

Stated another way, strings of divergent character will merge to manifest different types of elemental matter, each displaying the character of the strings from which each developed.

Our theory is supported by the physical principle of wave-particle duality. This principle is that matter cannot be manifested as both wave energy and as a particle at the same time. c^2 must force wave energy to become a particle. Stated another way, c^2 provides the continuation of residual energy so that the energy can become matter—or not—according to The Information Instructed By The WORD.

Gravity is one effect of this process. As mass is formed, the massive particles emit gravitational waves as an operational principle Instructed to matter at the string level. This is known as "gravitational coupling."[11z31] Gravitational waves draw other masses to the particles.

Along with the electromagnetic charges attracting or repelling particles with different information, extreme heat (photons and other radiation) bonds protons and neutrons together to form atoms, molecules, and larger structures as the character of different masses relate over time.

The reverse process is when a massive structure breaks down (both as a chemical or an atomic breakdown), various physical energies are released. The amount of energy and matter released is equal the amount of constituent matter and energy of the physical structure broken down.

The equivalence of special relativity defines mass and energy as they manifest, continuously changing as the total mass changes and the equivalent energy changes. Hence, the values on each side of the matter-energy equation are constantly changing, so our physical reality develops sequentially relative to a reference frame and spatial position.

Hence, time is the most powerful force in the manifestation of our physical reality. Time drives the manifestation of residual energy into matter and its attendant energies. Once manifested, matter becomes solid according to the Information received. It is continuous at the micro-level. It is also continuous at the macro-level, which Human Beings Observe.

It is a closed system because the total of matter and its attendant energies remains constant in our physical universe. As matter organizes into atoms, molecules, and larger physical constructions, total matter and its attendant energies are limited according to the information presented in the residual energy, e.

This supports the second law of thermodynamics.[11z32] Essentially, our singularity was maximum organization (low entropy) as Created In The 9th D. Entropy increased as our singularity was Differentiated In The 9th D to become manifest as our singularity in the 8th-d physical membrane system. By The Instructions Creating our singularity, it was compelled to explode as a big bang process in the 7th d to create our physical universe. Entropy continues to increase with the disorganization of our expanding physical universe.

Our 7th-d physical universe is viewed as a "closed system," which continues to disorganize as it speeds apart. One ultimate end to our physical universe would be far-flung cinders of matter disintegrating into cosmic dust[11z33] as organizational bonds break down and the inertial energy[11z34] continues to disburse matter and its attendant energies. One of those attendant energies is inertia. Due to inertia, the elemental dust would continue to expand into ever-broadening space until it is so diluted[11z35] that the space appears but is not actually empty. Note that the total of matter and its attendant energies remains the same, inherited from the singularity. This is expressed mathematically by the equation of special relativity, $e=mc^2$.

THE MATHEMATICS

On the energy side of the equation, heat, light, and related radiations would decrease as inertial energy continues to increase with the accelerating[11z36] expansion of our physical universe.

On the mass side of physical manifestation in our universe, atomic fusion would continue to convert the more energetic hydrogen and radiations into larger atoms as the system continues to cool.

The system is closed because the total of matter and its attendant energies remains constant within the boundary of our physical universe in the space created by its expansion.

On the local level, Galaxy organization increases (entropy decreases) as gravity draws matter together into tighter spirals.[11z37] Local black holes[11z38] develop as gravity attracts matter and its attendant energies into supermassive black holes at the center of each galaxy. The Instructional Information in the strings will determine whether or not the local singularity disorganizes again as a quasar.[11z39]

A quasar will increase entropy (disorganization) of the system, breaking down complex matter mostly into highly energetic hydrogen and related gamma rays, light, heat, and other radiation. One theory is that this would serve to renew the galaxy to a Younger[11z40] phase of high energy and rapid star formation. This system could oscillate[11z41] through several cycles.[11z42] However, each quasar releases an extraordinary amount of gamma rays, as well as other photon energy, into intergalactic space[11z43] within our physical universe. After the quasar, the galaxy will have less matter and its attendant energies to recycle. The resultant galaxy will be less massive.

The effect on the universe of the energy released and not recovered by the galaxy remains an interesting subject of scientific inquiry. One hypothesis is that unless that energy is captured by the gravity of another galaxy, the escaped energy is indicative of the final state of dilution of our physical universe.

An alternative possible extreme of this "closed system" destiny of our physical universe is that gravity will eventually overcome inertia and our entire universe will implode[11z44] to further organize back into a singularity capable of a "big bang," creating a new physical universe from the same material.

You can see that there are several possible endings of our physical universe, a closed system. Entropy will increase or decrease according to the phase of development of our physical universe.

Uncertainty is built into physical reality as the operational principles of 7th-d physical existence allows for either ending to a physical universe. The limitation of physical boundaries of each physical universe sets in opposition the forces to expand (inertia) or to contract (gravity). The ending of our physical universe is indeterminate, given the possibilities.

Spirit is not so limited as matter because Spirit is not confined to space-time as matter is so confined. The Presence Of Spirit Is Obvious In Living Beings, but when A Living Being dies, Its Spirit Leaves our physical universe. Neither The

Spirit's Presence nor its absence can be quantified using the mathematics of physics. A Spiritual Mathematics[11z45] must be developed.

The Mathematics of Spirit may be represented as a series of *A* and *z* symbols. *A* Represents When A Spiritual Being Is Present. *z* represents when a spiritual being is not present.

Your Awareness Of Other Spiritual Beings In our physical universe will Advance If You simply Observe an object and Assign *A* If You Detect The Presence Of A Spiritual Being or assign a *z* if You detect no current spiritual presence in the object.

We conclude that since Our Universe Of Spirit Operates Differently from our physical universe, each exists in a totally different membrane system.

8th D (Membrane Systems): Please imagine all possible 7th-d physical universes. The primary characteristic of all of them is that they are Instructed By The WORD to have the same initial conditions (big bang), the same operational principles (quantum mechanics, relativity, time, inertia, the strong atomic force, the weak atomic force, electromagnetism, gravity), and the same types of ultimate ending caused by their operation. All such universes of matter and its attendant energies form one membrane system in the 8th d. We call it the physical membrane system.

In the 8th-d context of many physical universes and the influence of other Membrane Systems, our physical universe is open to the influence of forces outside the boundaries of our universe. It is an "open system" in the 9th D, but a "closed system" in the 8th d. The manifestation of outside influences on our physical universe is manifested in the 8th d and Constructed In The 9th D at the Instruction Of The WORD.

The next question is, do all physical universes follow the same developmental path and options?

The answer is yes. That is the very definition of the physical membrane system.

The entire theory of other physical universes requires that the operational principles of our universe of matter and its attendant energies operate in the same way in our future universe or any unrelated physical universe. Hence, all the wonderful mathematics that we use in our universe of matter and its attendant energies also operates in the same manner in an unrelated universe of matter and its attendant energies.

Likewise, quantum mechanics will operate in another universe of matter and its attendant energies as it does in our physical universe. The same type of singularity would have initiated the unrelated physical universe as initiated our physical universe.

Indeed, the influence of randomness in the appearance of matter in a quantum field may be an effect of causes described above in one physical universe to, in turn, create the singularity to cause another physical universe to develop. That development would be similar to our physical universe but manifest differently using the

THE MATHEMATICS

same operations. Since the other physical universe would develop differently than ours, it may progress differently; but due to its origin and operational principles, it will have similar possible endings.

Summarizing the theories detailed above, either all of the universes like our universe of matter and its attendant energies will expand until the atomic energy runs out and then exist as a cold vast expanse of burnt-out cinders in the space created, or each may implode into a universal supermassive black hole, thus returning to a singularity.

Uncertainty predicts that both ending conditions may occur either separately or as a related sequence.

The mathematics of time in all 7th-d physical universes works the same. Einstein's theories of general relativity and special relativity apply to each of them. Though circumstances of the development of each may vary, $e=mc^2$ applies to each and all physical universes.

The 7th-d boundary of each such universe is clearly expanding as the limit of space created by the expansion of matter and its attendant energies.

Again, the cosmological theories presented above are deductions based on calculations and the evidence Observed. If the physical sciences discover a different origin or operation of physical being, Our Ontology Will Not Change. The characterization of the Dimensions of Reality Revealed By This Teaching remains consistent to incorporate updates in both cosmology and ontology.

Mathematics, in any physical universe, is descriptive of quantities and relations of physical matter and its attendant energies. As the physical laws of that membrane system remain constant, the mathematics is predictive of a future state and the situation as it may become.

The mathematics can also be formative. For example, a computer program can direct a digital pattern of ones and 0s to print a physical object. The entire field of digital printing[11z46] is mathematics directing a physical device to create a definite object from raw physical materials.

There are two limiting characteristics of mathematics, such as a computer program, that make it part of 9th-D Mechanisms as distinguished from 10th-D Divine Information.

1. Mathematics is a program or sequence of symbols. There must be different machines that produce the flow of electrons that direct mechanical organization of other physical elements into a digitally printed object. The flow of electrons is a process distinct from the mathematical sequence.
2. Of course, the computer program (mathematical sequence) did not create itself. An Intelligent Being Created the computer program.
3. If a Human removes the flow of electrons or alters the physical printing device, the digital printing will stop regardless of the integrity of the pro-

gram. Any artificial intelligence[11z47] will cease at that point. The artificial intelligence had no Spirit as it operated and lost no Spirit as it ceased.
4. In the case of Divine Information, The Flow Is Not Stopped By Human Action. Divine Information In The Form Of An Incarnate Human Soul Is Present During The life Of The Incarnate body and Continues In Nonphysical Being Upon the death of that body.

Our mathematics has grown large to mimic The Manner In Which The WORD Directs Information Into Formative Realities In The 9th D. The computer program is analogous[11z48] to a Metastring. The difference is that the computer program merely directs an organization of atoms and molecules into the prescribed form of the physical object. By Contrast, The WORD Provides The Instructions That The 9th D Converts Through Creation Of strings, Prescribing their operation to yield the atoms and electrons that are the basis of a functional computer program. These physical elements can be further organized by a Human Beings into the mathematical program of a digital printer. Hence, Creation Is Prior and Necessary To Provide the energy and elements for a program like digital printing to be invented.

The Information Of The WORD May Utilize digital principles, physical laws, or It May Manifest Entirely Differently, As In Spiritual Realities. Mathematics may be used to describe the Information Operative In The 9th D To Create matter, but the 9th-D Process is not a pattern process.[11z49] It is not 1's and 0's in a sequence. It Is Continuous, Uninterrupted.

The WORD, The Creative, Is The Instruction That a pattern process shall be, or shall not be. If The WORD Directs That the pattern process shall be, then a mathematics can be devised to describe or even implement that pattern through the vibration along that Metastring. If The WORD Directs that a pattern process shall not be, then either:

a. no physical object will become, and no mathematics can describe or manifest "being" along that different Metastring.
b. Or if an object is created along the physical metastring, 6th d uncertainty allows no pattern to be realized, so the physical creation is one-of-a-kind.

Could there be a set of physical universes where Primal Energy took a different course and did not result in the creation of Primal Matter and Primal Antimatter? We do not know if that could happen. If it could, the resulting universe would have different operational principles than our type of physical universe. It would be part of a different membrane system.

All Of The Discussion above Proves, Using the scientific method, That Spirit Exists Apart from matter.

THE MATHEMATICS

Mathematics is quite different in the Spiritual Membrane System. The "Mansions" Within Our Father's House Are Very Different From Each Other. If Mathematics can be developed to describe the Vibrations of Spirit, such Math Would probably Describe The Full Harmony Of Heavenly Choirs For Some Spirits. It Might Also Describe The oppressive dull pounding of The Earthworm's Awareness For Other Spirits.

Such A Mathematics Would Have To Calculate How Spiritual Energy Increases As It Is Manifested. This Increasing Of Spiritual Energy Drawn From The Infinite SOURCE Is So Greatly Different than how physical energy decreases as it is spent in physical reality (or remains constant if you calculate in physical transformations within the closed system).

This illustration is Offered to depict the closed system of physical reality represented by the spherical matrix Fused With The Open System Of Spiritual Reality, represented by the various Aspects Of Spirit Expanding Outward and Through The Incarnate Being At The Center.

Zelenov Iurii/Shutterstock 1334420447

Our Teaching Suggests A formula To Express The Increase Of Positive Spiritual Energy[11z50] As It Is Used: **SE'>SE-SE**.[11z51]

SE Is Defined As Spiritual Energy. The Apostrophe (') Is The Resulting State Of Any Expenditure Of Spiritual Energy. The Resulting State Of Spiritual Energy Is Greater Than Any Function Of Positive Spiritual Energy That Is Manifested.

SE'>SE+SE[11z52] Is Also True Because Any Addition Of Positive Spiritual Energy Is Also An Increase That Is Greater Than The Sum Of Its Parts.

The mathematics seems contradictory, but it is not, given The Operational Characteristics Of Spirit. Any Use Of Spiritual Energy Approaches The ONE. All Spiritual Beings Exist As A Spark Of GOD, So Each Proceeds To Use Spiritual Energy As An Action Of GOD. Spiritual Energy Is Manipulated By Spiritual Beings In Reality.

Whether Spiritual Energy Is Moved, Combined, Added To A Situation, or Removed From A Situation, It Is An Action Of GOD, or You, Operating As The Instrument Of GOD. To Use Spiritual Energy, You Must Be Connected To or Approach GOD. Now You Understand The Spiritual Metastring Connecting You Directly To GOD.

This illustration is Offered To Depict An Individual's Use Of Spiritual Energy in Fused physical and Spiritual Reality.

THE MATHEMATICS

Geoffiji Lobo—Cosmic energy. We are STARS; https://www.pinterest.com/pin/281475045433158402/

Therefore, A Controlling Principle Of Spiritual Mathematics Is That Spiritual Energy Increases As It Approaches The ONE.

We note that Spiritual Energy can be diminished both by apathy, symbolized as *ay*,[11z53] and by negative spiritual energy, symbolized as *nse*.[11z54] Such diminution may operate within any closed system in which Spirit Is Present. Such action is possible among Spirits Because A Spirit Has Free Will once Differentiated From GOD.

Please note that Spiritual Energy can only be decreased by its absence, as with apathy, or by negative spiritual energy, which is opposed to but is not Spiritual Energy. Please note that overall Spiritual Energy Is Defined By GOD. The 11th, cannot be calculated As GOD cannot be quantified.

This Teaching suggests the following formula of a decrease in Spiritual Energy in any membrane system: **SE'=SE-ay-nse**.[11z55]

The Effort Is To Increase Your Spiritual Energy Both Personally and In A Community Of Spirits by reducing spiritual apathy and by reducing negative spiritual energy. This Is The Basis Of Ethics In Our Teaching.

Continuum Also Manifests Differently In The Spiritual Membrane System. There is no time In Spiritual Existence. Depending On The Situation Of Spirit, The Progression Of Consciousness May Present A Continuum Of Images[11z56] or Feelings To A Spiritual Being. A Spiritual Continuum Is not timed. Time is not in operation to force The Flow In Spiritual Reality. Only If A Spirit Is Incarnated Into physical being are the constraints of time manifested.

You might ask, If Metastring Vibrations In The 9th D Manifest Spiritual Universes, don't The Vibrations require a frequency, implying time? The answer is no. Metastring Vibrations Are not physical waves, so They have no electromagnetic frequency. We capitalize the word *Vibrations* When We Are Using It In A Spiritual Context. The Vibrations Are The Spiritual Manifestation Of The WORD Instructing Information, Channeled To Create and Sustain A Particular Creation or Manifestation. A God-Wave Is An Instruction Of Information from the 10th-D WORD To The 9th-D Machinery Of Creation To Manifest The Information and Processes Into Reality In the lower Dimensions. You Might Experience GOD-Waves As Feelings, or Conscience, or Sharing of Spiritual Energy Along The Spiritual Metastring.

The use of the word *membrane* in This Teaching is to define "membrane systems." That includes systems of being where there is no matter and its attendant energies. Definitions of dimensions prior to This Teaching are incomplete because they attempt to force Reality into a physical limitation. That is incorrect, and The Mathematics has already proved it to be incorrect. The Mathematics Has Proved that Reality Is Far More Than physical being.

The mathematics used by theoretical physicists to define quantum field theory yields infinities in the equations.[11z57] This is why theoretical physics has not been able to come up with a Unified Field Theory.[11z58] This is seen as a limitation to the current "theory of everything" known as m-theory. Our Teaching Reveals That the infinities are necessary to balance[11z59] the equations. As m-theory develops to further define physical reality, the infinities will remain because no variable can completely describe future possibilities.

This Is A Fundamental Proof Of GOD,[11z60] The Primary Infinite Being. Without these infinities, m-theory is stuck with an incomplete, static mathematics that is confined only to the physical universe.

To Illustrate This, Please Recall The Example of Your doghouse. We noted that an infinity of random physical events could not produce a doghouse. Doghouses do not occur in nature in our physical universe. A specific doghouse does not occur randomly in physical reality. The Creation Of Your doghouse Required A Spiritual Being, You, To Act On A Spiritual Occurrence—That Is, Compassion For Your Dog. The infinity occurring in the equation can only be resolved by Admitting To The Influence Of A Spiritual Cause That Is not physical.

Our Teaching Reveals That The Mathematics must remain dynamic, retaining the mathematical infinities to properly describe Reality. The Mathematics Must Eventually Grow To Include Spiritual Variables To Replace the infinities in order to balance the equations.

Such Spiritual Variables May Be Descriptive of a past event. However, Spiritual Variables are not reliable to predict the future as They Change As Instructed By The WORD. GOD May Change The Instructions. This is why uncertainty characterizes All Manifest Realities.

9th D (Mechanics Of Creation): A Mathematics Of The 9th D May Be Developed To Describe How a physical quantum field Is Created From Divine Instruction and Information.

quantum fields Originate In The 9th D. The progression of a physical universe is from physical nothingness to a quantum field Super-Energized By Divine Instruction Of Information (Primal Energy), Generating a singularity in which Primal Matter and Primal Antimatter Precipitate As Instructed. Divine Information Passed From The 10th D Directs The 9th D To Create Primal Matter and Primal Antimatter from nothing, the sum of which is nothing. These are the infinities that quantum field theory cannot resolve from mathematical formulation. This error stems from the fact that the mathematics is descriptive, not Causative.

This difference begs for Dimensional Analysis. Mathematically, words like *nothing* or *0* give an incorrect picture of Reality. At The Source, GOD Is Everything, not nothing as in mathematics. If the mathematics proceeds from the assumption that there can be truly "nothing," it cannot proceed. There is no reality that can be truly nothing. Nothing can only be construed from a partial reality where the "something" is factored out mathematically. Such a reality does not exist. This defines the limitation of mathematics.[11z61]

The latest quantum field theorists have patched together the "Standard Model of Particles and Interactions" by stating what is obvious in Our 4th-dimensional analysis. Correct or incorrect, that model is limited to the physical 4th d. The "standard model" cannot be complete or operative within The Boundary Of The 5th Dimension, Which Includes Indeterminate Choices. 5th-Dimensional Reality Is Collapsed Into Being Through Occurrences In The higher Dimensions In Which the future is not yet determined.

Absolute Being Is Required To Produce The Vibrations That Operate In The 9th D To Form quantum fields. The infinities necessary to balance the equations are the mathematical proof of GOD. Specifically, quantum field theory must assume something, such as a string. If it attempts to assume a point, infinities in the equations make it impossible. Logic forces Us Back To Aquinas's Proof That Since We Are Sure That Something Exists, A Creator—GOD—Is Proved.

A physical membrane system in the 8th D is where all quantum fields operate. Two principles of any and all physical realities are that

1. the physical reality is produced in a quantum field and
2. all particles, antiparticles, and excitations that occur in a quantum field will exhibit the space-time characteristics of general relativity.

The manifestation of our physical universe is the 7th-D collapse of physical quantum action into our big bang—that is, the collapse into physical reality is of our singularity manifesting Primal Matter and Primal Antimatter, Causing our big bang. The residual energy, e, created by the violent cancellation of the positive mass of Primal Matter and the negative mass of Primal Antimatter expands with increasing velocity. That residual energy is an incredible number of strings that manifest as high energy quarks, gluons, Higgs bosons, and other subatomic particles and waves, cooling to congeal into protons, neutrons, electrons, and related energies as they speed apart from the point of singularity. These combine into hydrogen and various radiations. All the physical forces are present with the formation of hydrogen, so the engine of fusion begins. Our physical universe is born.

String theory may postulate that differentiation of matter into different particles Is Instructed To The 9th D and manifested in the 8th d by difference in vibration of various types of strings. Indeed, these strings, vibrating differently, may combine to yield the various quarks, gluons, Higgs bosons, and any other subatomic creation that build our physical universe.

Again, if scientific inquiry advances to show that The 9th-D Creative Process Yielding our physical universe is other than stated above, Our Metaphysics Will Not Change Because Our Metaphysics Is proved by Observed Creation. The 9th D Will Not Reveal All Of Its Creative Processes To Be Described In Our Simple Summary.

Furthermore, If All Of The 9th-D Creative Mechanisms were attempted to be cataloged, the catalog would remain incomplete Because The WORD Is Indeterminate. Original Instructions are never complete but Are Always Becoming. The 10th D Is An Open System. Metastring Formation and Their Operation Will Change According To The WORD Of GOD.

There is no time in The 9th D. Manifestations Appear According To The WORD. If there is a Process, a Continuum is implied, but it can only be measured in the lower dimensions as Manifestations Of The WORD.

Spiritual Fields[11z62] Originate In The 9th D As Well. The WORD Of GOD Instructs Divine Consciousness In Differentiated Manifestations In The 9th D. We capitalize and use the words *Instruction* and *Information* as subsets of The WORD.

THE MATHEMATICS

Again, as with physical matter, The Divine Information Is Continuous and not to be confused with bits or bundles of information as in digital principles of operation.

An odd mathematics can be applied. Each Unit Of Consciousness Is An Individual Consciousness, so Units Of Spirit can be counted. Furthermore, There Are Types or Classes Of Spiritual Beings, Each With Their Capabilities and Limitations. These Classes can be counted, though Human Beings do not know Their numbers, nor All Their Capabilities, nor All Their Limitations. We Can Know Our Own Capabilities and Limitations by Experiential Awareness.

You May Be Creative As An Instrument Of GOD To Change The Reality That Is Becoming. Use The Spiritual Mathematics To Alter The Next Situation. For example, Your Friend Is Suffering a physical deterioration of his body. He is lashing out with hurtful comments to You and Others. The negative spiritual energy, *nse*, is sucking the Love out of Your Relationship. It Is Your Duty, As An Instrument Of The LORD, To Turn Your Light Toward Him To Pivot The Spiritual Energy, *SE*, and Restore Him. This Humble Turning The Light Around May Be As Simple As A Kind Word of Assurance, Followed by a short Separation. The Light Will Operate In His Soul.

This Process is difficult for You or any Other Human Being To Do because of Our learned psychological defense mechanisms. Receiving the nse of hateful words, You have learned to defend Yourself so as not to be damaged by those emotions. You Must Observe Your Friend With The Eyes Of GOD. You Will Actuate GOD's Mercy By Turning The Light Inward To Find Forgiveness Of Your Friend At your Center. Then You Must Turn That Light Toward Your Friend With An Expression That Will Heal His Spirit.

The Formula Is **SE'=SE-nse-nse**.[11z63]

Your Act Of Forgiveness may not be well-received. It may be met with more nse as He continues to reject You. Allow Him to subtract or cancel out his own negative spiritual energy.

Also, Note That This Spiritual Equation Occurs Between Incarnate Human Beings Here On Earth. This Equation does not Result instantaneously. It Occurs over "time" here on earth.

The Equation becomes

$$\underline{\mathbf{SE'=SE-nse-nse}(L)}^{[11z64]}$$
$$c(n),$$

where *c* is our physical constant of "time" and (*n*) is the variable multiplier to yield the amount of time it will take for the Resultant State **SE'** To Be Realized Here On Earth.

You notice that the longer the time it takes, the less the resultant **SE'**. The original or even Greater **SE** may be Rebuilt By Continuing (multiplying) Your Love, **L**, For Your Friend To Reach The Resultant Situation Of Enhanced Spiritual Energy. This Is A Heavenly State.

Now You Are Beginning To Quantify The Fusion Of Our Spiritual and our physical Universes. Developing This Spiritual Mathematics Helps Us Understand The 9th-D Machinery Of Creation. You Can Be A Participant In That Machinery In the 9th Dimension.

10th D: The WORD Is Instruction. The WORD Is Information.

This Teaching Attempts To Ascribe A Mathematical Value to The Information. For example, each subject in a physical universe may be assigned a Spiritual Value[11z65] of z. Each Subject In A Spiritual Universe May Be Assigned A Spiritual Value Of A. Then the Information Instructed To the lower dimensions has the mathematical prefix of z if it describes a physical creation. The Information Instructed Will Have a Mathematical Prefix Of A If It Describes A Spiritual Creation or A Fused Spiritual-physical Creation.

You can verify this Mathematics In Your Own Experience. We have Revealed That Our Human Existence Proceeds From The Partial Fusion Of Our Spiritual Universe with our physical universe. Your Conscious Observation of any object recognizes whether or not Spirit Is Present In The Object.

For example, Upon Careful Observation Of A Tree, You Are Able To Determine that either The Tree Is Alive or it is lifeless (dead). You Relate Differently To A Live Tree than You do to a dead tree. You Consciously Notice The Presence Of Life (Spirit) or the absence of life in every object You Observe.

This Teaching Attempts To Postulate The Basic Equation Of Reality: ***R=z+A***.
[11z66]

In this equation, ***R*** symbolizes All Reality. ***R*** is mathematically defined as composed of z, all physical things, plus A, All Spiritual Presences.

If We discover a Membrane System in Reality that is not symbolized, We would add that to this equation.

This type of symbolism yields a descriptive logic that helps To Understand The Totality Of Being. However, it is difficult to Ascribe[11z67] a Mathematics that will Function In The 10th D. That is because with any mathematics or symbolic representation, the symbols must remain consistent so the formulas will work in the future. A valid mathematics must use symbols that represent a real situation in the past, present, or future.

The WORD Is Present and Pervasive In all lower dimensions. The WORD is Formative and Conclusive[11z68] Of All Reality. Except for Our General Formula, ***R=z+A***, The WORD cannot be symbolized, defined, or formulated In The 10th D Because It Changes According To The WILL Of GOD. The symbols that We define

THE MATHEMATICS

will not remain constant, so Our symbols and calculations would not be a valid mathematics[11z69] In The 10th D.

11th: This Teaching Reveals That The Total Of All Realities Originates As Manifestations Of GOD. Yet GOD Is Greater Than The Sum Of All Manifestations and Any Other Realities. The Formula Is **G>R**. [11z70]

G Symbolizes GOD, and **R** Symbolizes All Of Reality.

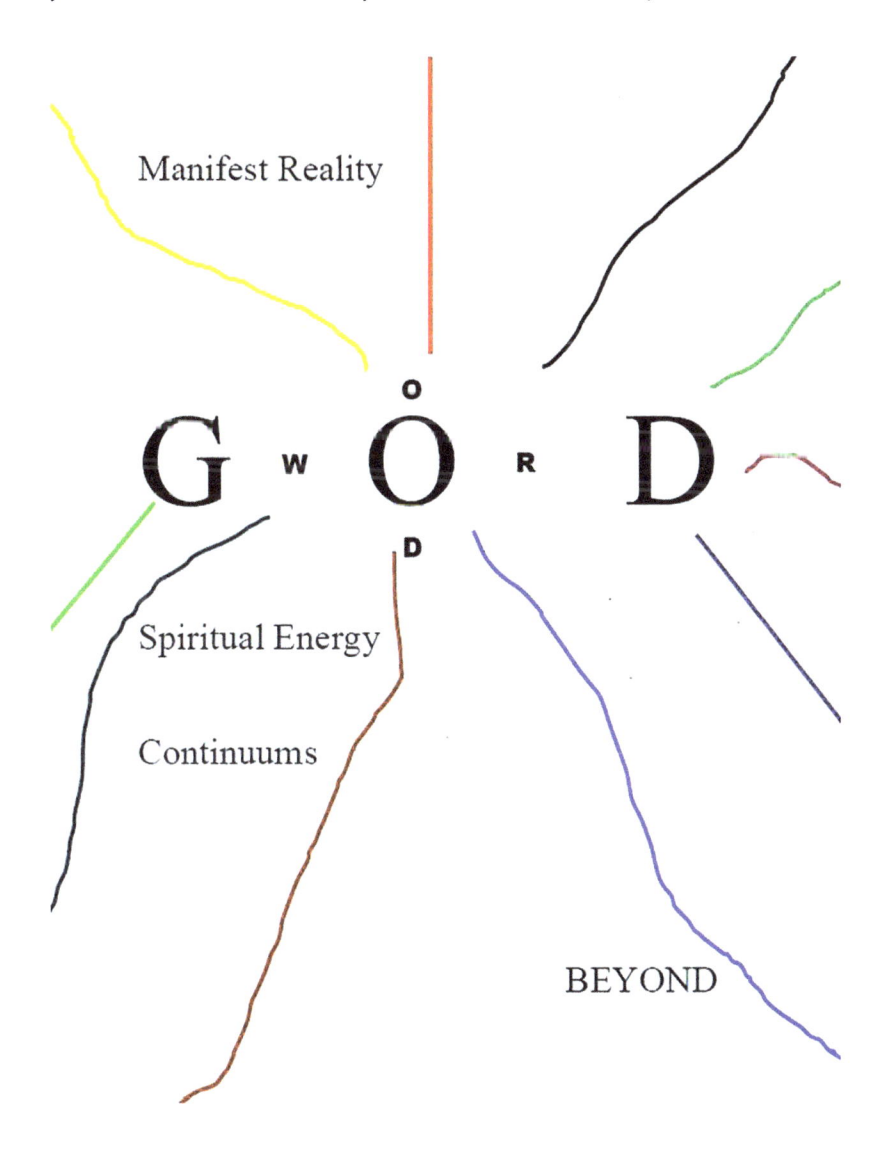

Figure 6: Drawing by Allyn Richert (AD 2020). This is an attempt to illustrate the Organization Of The Total Reality Of GOD and how all Manifest Realities Of GOD are only a subset Of GOD's Being, Beyond measure.

CHAPTER 12

The Revelation—Part 2

Understanding Reality manifested in the Dimensions again leads Us back to The SOURCE. The Large GOD Is Revealed Through GOD's Manifestations.

This Is Ancient Knowledge, so This Author can take no credit for Ancient Revelations. Yet let Us not name the LORD as if GOD is one of the Anunnaki, a god of a historic pantheon, a cosmic body, a natural phenomenon, a mysterious energy, an idea, a concept, or a construct of Mind. The LORD Our GOD Is not one of those gods, nor is GOD created by man. All of those are limited. You have heard stories of great beings and great deeds, their beginnings and their endings, but each of those is limited. Each of Us Is limited by a narrow perspective, a narrow experience, and a narrow field of Influence. GOD Is not limited. The LORD Our GOD Is ONE—the SOURCE Of All These and All Else That Is, Was, or Ever Shall Be.

The Revelation Detailed In This Teaching Is new because in Our Metaphysics, The Ancient Knowledge is not presented as Tradition. Instead Of The Words Of Wise[12a] Men or Faith-based Arguments[12b] or Dogma. Our Teaching Relies on recent scientific proofs and theories established by Observations leading to logical Conclusions. The scientific method remains Our guide To Verify Truth. Any quotation of Scripture is to update Traditional words with the scientific words and proofs We Reveal.

Our Teaching does not diminish The Revelations Of GOD To Ancient Humans. Our Teaching Reaffirms and Provides scientific proof of Ancient Revelations.

This Teaching Presents Research Notes in many pages following The Revelation. These Research Notes Present Intended definitions of words and concepts. They present the history of relevant concepts. They credit previous Scholars, Wise, and Holy Human Beings For Their Contributions To Knowledge. Our Teaching does not Rely On That Information. Our Metaphysics Is An Expansion of prior Wisdom with Essential Original Revelations. Our Teaching Further Develops recent advances in the physical sciences and Spiritual Experience.

Also, Dimensional Analysis Yields Clarity[12c] that Esoteric Teachings often leave obscure. This Is The Occasion To Utilize verifiable data and clear logic To Expand

THE REVELATION—PART 2

Our Understanding Of Reality. Our Conclusions Reveal A More Complete Reality To Empower The Seeker In This Life and Beyond. That Power Facilitates A Closer Connection To GOD.

The danger in precise definition of variable processes is that the precision[12d] may too narrowly[12e] define the limits of Reality. Dimensional Reasoning Reveals The Limitless. Even Our Detailed Analysis is incomplete. All Truth remains vulnerable to incorrect interpretation, deceitful motives, and the limited Capabilities Of The Seeker.

This Revelation Is Groundbreaking[12f] To The Mind conditioned[12g] by physical points of view. This Revelation Is verified and reverified. Human Perspectives Are all limited, so This Teaching Encourages Growth and Refinement[12h] Of These Principles As Broader Knowledge Emerges. We Are Very Blessed To Have Come This Far.

The Revelation Continues.

The WORD Creates. so Is GOD In All Of Creation, or Is GOD just An Observer Of GOD's Creation? To answer this question, examine the specific Creation. For example, this block of granite stone is of GOD. The WORD Brought Forward the physical processes that created this granite rock. We Know That GOD Remains Integral[12i] in the atoms and molecules and the forces holding this rock together. The basic "strings," or whatever You Choose to call them, Are Excitations Of GOD yet separate after Creation, manifesting according to the Information Instructed By The WORD. GOD has not bestowed Consciousness or any form of Awareness into this rock, so the rock is and will remain separate from the Spirit Of GOD. The rock has no Soul.

An analogy would be that GOD leaves behind this rock as You might leave behind a fingernail clipping or lock of hair that You cut off from your body. Yes, it is part of you, but it is now separate. This rock is an obscure creation, lost in our large physical universe. This rock is taking up space without consciousness. This is the 3rd-d condition of most of physical reality.

Contrast this To Your Individual Spirit. Your Individual Spirit Is Also Of GOD, but GOD Retains Intimate Connection To Your Individual Spirit As A Participant In Your Consciousness. GOD's Participation Can Be More or less According To Your Will in part. You cannot completely separate From GOD, though Your Individual Spirit Can Become dimmer or More Brilliant According To Your Connection With The LORD.

Apply This Teaching Through Dimensional Analysis Of Your Fused Reality to the lifeless piece of granite. You May Take this block of granite rock and Carve Symbols in a sequence Understood By Other Humans. You May Fashion the piece of granite rock into a tombstone. If You Do, Humans Will Read It, and time will be Bent As They Recall The Presence Of The Elder Human Being Who Has Passed On. The inanimate and meaningless rock will be Changed By The Spirits Of Human

Beings To Be Meaningful In Honor Of The Passed Human Being. That tombstone still has no soul, but It Carries Meaning Based On The Appreciation Of Those Who Will Receive It.

Only Spiritual Beings Could Put Meaning Into this rock sculpture. A Timeless Quality Lies iIn The Adoration Of The Passed Human Being, Presented As A Grand Monument provided by this carved rock.

Part Of Our Theology Is To Understand GOD—The Creator—and GOD's Creation. Having Created the physical membrane system, The WORD Instructed physical reality To Become Through A singularity. The Information GOD brought forth as our singularity was Instructed to burst in our big bang to develop into our physical universe. This Information needed nothing more from GOD except to Sustain the quantum fields, which are the physical metastring vibrations. Our physical universe developed, exchanging matter and its attendant energies as space developed in our expanding physical universe.

Our physical universe is a closed system within the boundaries (operational principles) of the physical membrane system. Our physical universe does not have Spirit. That is to say that Spirit is not an operational principle in any physical universe. GOD Is Primarily An Observer of the development of our universe of matter and its attendant energies. That is why GOD does not alter physical reality every time You Say A Prayer asking for a change in physical reality. Could GOD alter physical reality? Yes, as water into wine. However, GOD Chooses not to do so, except for vary rare occasions. The WORD Continues the initial physical instructions and information.

Another question that often arises is, why does GOD not intervene in the calamities and injustices of Human Society? The answer is that GOD does not have a direct Metastring connection to a civilization, a society,[12j] a nation,[12k] or any other group. A civilization, society, nation, or any such institution[12l] is a construct of Human Activity, not anything to which GOD would Connect Directly. Such institutions have no Soul. They have no afterlife. They just have a history and a future as the rise and fall of that Human construct. The institution has meaning as it advances the principles and accomplishments, such as being Just or unjust, Successful[12m] or unsuccessful, Good or evil.

GOD Is Usually Connected Only To The Individual Spirit or Soul. The Individual Must Act To Create the institutions. Your Individual Spirit Is Empowered To Act, Utilizing The Grace Of GOD and Spiritual Energy, as well as all physical tools To Create and Change Human institutions. You May Organize With Other Human Beings To Construct Very Meaningful Human institutions.

When You Recognize That GOD is not Vested[12n] in Human institutions, You Can Understand Why a Prayer To GOD to "save my business" is not Answered. It Is Up To You To Save Your business.

THE REVELATION—PART 2

Yet GOD Is Merciful. GOD May Participate To Further Human institutions Through You and Others, so Continue To Pray. GOD May Have A Plan For A Future Manifestation Beyond Your Vision.

Please distinguish between a Human group or institution on earth and The Divine Sharing Of Souls With Each Other and GOD In The Various Heavens. See Chapter 13.

Separate from our physical universe, Our Spiritual Universe Is Another Part Of GOD's Creation. GOD Chose To Differentiate Independent Individual Spiritual Beings From The ONE. Those Become Separate, but The Information Creating An Individual Spiritual Being Remains Directly Connected To GOD, So GOD May Be A Regular Participant In The Consciousness Of Every Spiritual Being.

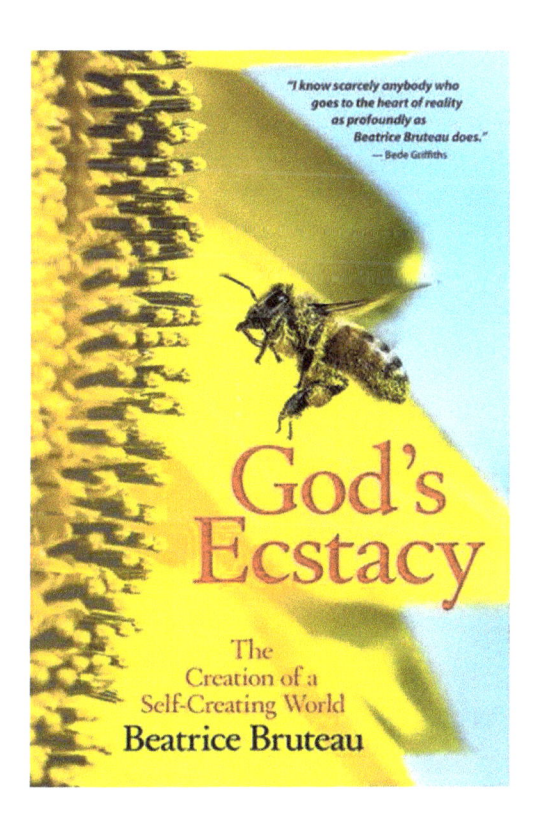

For The Pleasure Of GOD, GOD Brought Forth a physical creature that is Integrated with A Spiritual Consciousness To Form A Human Being. Among Other Living Creatures, GOD Created Life That Animates[12o] matter.

Human bodies are meaningless in the Long View. A human body is an organic physical machine. However, each human body Has A Purpose. It is a continually renewing organism With A Separate Spirit, Which Observes and Directs. If You have a Human body, You Are A Participant In This Fused Reality. Furthermore, GOD Is A Participant In this Human body With You, More or less, As It May Please The

LORD.[12p] The Entire Experience Is Elevated When You Consciously Invite The Participation Of GOD Into Your Human Experiences.

Proof Of This Connection Between You and GOD Is Your Ability To Create Positive Spiritual Energy. Yes, You Create Divine Energy By Your Positive Spiritual Choices and Actions.

Are You Divine or just an Instrument Of GOD? They Are The Same. Your Individual Spirit Is A Differentiation Of The ONE—Separate To Act Separately. However, You Are Capable Of Immediate Connection To Become The Face Of GOD In This or That Situation. Reunification With The LORD Can Be Periodic.[12q]

Now You Understand why GOD Brought Spirit To the physical world. This answers the questions of "Who Am I?" "Why Am I here?" and "How Can I Know GOD?"

You Are Now Empowered To Utilize This Improved Metaphysical Understanding Of Reality. Analyze Dimensionally. Act With Confidence In This Knowledge. Live Gracefully.

CHAPTER 13

Dimensions of Our Spiritual Universe

It is possible to Develop a better Understanding of Our Spiritual Universe. Humans Are Spiritual Beings, Incarnate in physical matter. Spirit Incarnate Is quite Enchanted[13a] by physical being. Along with the heaviness of matter comes a Cornucopia[13b] of Form,[13c] color, sound, taste, touch, and aroma. Motion recognized through time yields a reawakening[13d] of sensual[13e] Experience from one situation to another.

The WORD Has Instructed this physical Enchantment To Spiritual Beings Because This Is GOD Sharing Pleasure In physical manifestation through the Individual Metastring Connective Channels Between GOD and Each Conscious Being.

When We say that Your Experience Is The "Pleasure of GOD," We Are Also Rating[13f] The Quality and Refinement Of Your Conscious Experience, As It May Please The LORD.

Dimensional Evaluation Of Spiritual Being then Becomes Useful In Expanding That Connection To GOD.

You must not View The Dimensions In The Spiritual Universe from our conditioned physical perspective. The Operational Principles Of Spiritual Dimensions Are Different From the operational principles of the physical dimensions. The fact that You are A Fused Spiritual and physical Being makes it difficult to Understand the differences. This Teaching Discussed in earlier chapters Some Of These Spiritual Principles As They Relate to Spirit Incarnate In matter.

Please Join Me To Reveal The Dimensions Of Our Spiritual Universe.

0th Dimension Spiritual: The Potential For Consciousness In The Spiritual Universe is analogous to the potential for a location in physical space. However, Spiritual Potential[13g] Is usually not located in space. Our Spiritual Universe Is Being without space. The existence of the 0th-D Spirit depends upon GOD—The WORD—Manifesting Consciousness As An Individual Soul. Defined another way, the 0th D in Our Spiritual Universe is the absence of A Differentiated Spirit, Apart From The ONE.

At a deeper level,[13h] the Potential For Spiritual Being Takes Us Back To GOD Alone—The 11th. All Beings In All Spiritual Universes Are Differentiated Portions Of GOD. Spiritual Manifestations Are According To The Instructions Of The WORD In The 10th D.

1st Dimension Spiritual: The WORD Manifests Primitive Awareness In The 1st D Of Our Spiritual Universe. Little Spirits[13i] Exist, and We Know About Some Of Them.

The smallest of physical Beings, such as a single-celled Being, Has A Primitive Spirit. Each Bacterium[13j] Has A Spiritual Being. Each Virus Has A Spiritual Being. The Will To Survive, even following a simple Genetic program,[13k] Indicates The Incarnation Of Spirit Into matter.

What Is GOD's Connection To This Form Of Experience? It Is probably no more than The Single-celled Creature's Awareness Of a flow of forms around It. That flow presents either chemical nutrition,[13l] chemical attraction, or radiant energy for the Creature To Be Drawn to and to combine with or to metabolize.[13m] The environment either permits the Creature To Replicate using other genetic material,[13n] as with a Virus or Zygote, or to Divide In A Fission Reproduction[13o] or causes It To Become dormant or To die. The Awareness Is In or out,[13p] depending On The State Of The Creature.

This illustrates an important Principle regarding A Spiritual Connection To a physical body. The Spiritual Incarnation or Connection need not Be Constant. Spirit Is Usually Present Within the physical Living body, but It Can Leave The Incarnation, and It Can Return. To Understand This, Please Recall the analogy of the radio (analogous to the body) fully equipped to project sound. The radio-wave broadcast (analogous to the Spirit) may become interrupted and then received again. *Awareness* is the best word We Can Use To Express The Presence of Spirit.

The question arises, Does a sperm cell or an ovum have An Individual Spirit? Chemically, these reproductive cells have one RNA strand, which, of course, combines into a full DNA strand upon Fertilization of the egg by the sperm. Since a gamete (sperm or egg cell) is incomplete and cannot survive alone, an argument can be made that a gamete does not have an individual spirit.

Equally convincing Is That Sexual Reproduction Is a dramatic Example of the Fusion of Spiritual Beings into a More Advanced Being. The Combination of a sperm cell and an egg cell, Each with Unique Information and The Ability To Complete A Process To Become A Single Viable Cell (Zygote), Completes The Fusion.

Ultimately, It Is The Function Of The 9th D To Determine When This Completed Zygote Will Receive A Spirit From The Universe Of Spirit. This Teaching Is That Incarnation Can Occur At The Moment Of Conception, or With The First Breath At Birth, or At Another Time During The Life Of The Being. Hence, Our conclusion is that a gamete does not have an individual spirit.

Incarnation, Resurrection,[13q] and Reincarnation Are Fundamental Actions Of How Spirit Manifests Into non-spiritual membrane systems.

Our Mathematics helps with The Observations. When You Observe The Presence Of Spirit In a physical being, Please Acknowledge It and Give It The Spiritual Value Of *A*. If You Are Observing a lifeless shell, no acknowledgement is meaningful, so give it a spiritual value of *z*.

The Will To Endure Is The Enabling Characteristic Of The 1st D Of Spirit. Its limiting boundary is that whether It Is A single Bacterium or a whole group of Bacteria, A Single Algae Cell, or an entire pond of Algae,[13r] The Awareness Is A Simple Repetitive Flow. We Can only Imagine The Experience Of GOD When GOD Chooses To Take Pleasure In That Flow.

What Elevates even A Single-celled Creature Above the being of a rock or a drop of water Is That A Single-celled Being Has Awareness and a rock does not. An entire ocean of H2O has no awareness. A universe of matter and its attendant energies has no awareness. A physical singularity has no awareness. Awareness Is The Presence Of Spirit. In Our World, This Is The Intersection Of Our Spiritual Universe With our physical universe.

We Can Postulate That Any Awareness, Differentiated From The ONE, Is Within A Spiritual Universe.

Since Spiritual Being Is A Vibration Of Some Aspect Of GOD, We draw an analogy to Music as this Helps Human Beings To Understand. The Manifestation Of 1st-D Spirit In Our Spiritual Universe is like a single Musical note—alone. The quality of that note is enabled by the complex manifestation of the vibration. This Is The Way It Is With Each Unique Manifestation Of An Individual Spirit Living Its Reality.

2nd-Dimension Spiritual: Simple Awareness May Exist In Many Beings. In Our World, the best example may be A Multicelled[13s] Creature. A Strand Of Algae Has A Broader Awareness Than The Single-celled Algae From Which It Grew.

The Limitation Of 2nd-D Spirit Is that each cell is not An Independent Spirit. Cells Of A Multicelled Being Depend On One Another To Maintain A Spiritual Awareness.

Continuing Our analogy to Music, The Multicelled Creature is like a chord[13t] in Music, expressing several notes together to form a higher or more intricate Harmony.

Our Spiritual Universe May Be Populated With numerous Types Of 2-Dimensional Spiritual Beings. The Spiritual Membrane System May Contain Other Spiritual Universes In Which Spiritual Beings Are Manifested Differently Than In Our Spiritual Universe. However, The 2nd-D Operational Principles Controlling That Spiritual Universe Would Be The Same As The Operational Principles Controlling The 2nd D In Our Spiritual Universe.

3rd-Dimension Spiritual: Complex Awareness Appears When A Spiritual Being Attains Consciousness. Consciousness Is A Being's Heightened Awareness Of the surrounding environment, as well as Perception Of The Fullness Of Spirit. In Our World, That Is A Fully Formed Organism With Specialized Systems and A Central Nervous System. Such An Organism Is Able To Perceive and React To A Broad Range Of Stimuli. It Is Able To Adjust As The Environment changes. A Butterfly May Be A Good Example Of A 3rd-D Spiritual Being Incarnate In physical reality.

The 3rd-D Spirit Illustrates An Important Principle Of Operation In Our Spiritual Universe. That Is, not all Spirits Are Equal In Their Awareness, Outward Reach, or Fullness Of Being. In addition, The Experience Of Different Spiritual Beings Is diverse, so Awareness In One Type Of Spiritual Being May not Be Similar To That Of Another Type Of Spiritual Being. Awareness May Even Be Different In One Individual From Another Individual Of The Same Type Of Being.

Therefore, The Law Of Dimensional Limitation Applies In The Spiritual Universe, though to an entirely different Reality In Spiritual Manifestations. Instead of a physical boundary, Spiritual Dimensions Are Limited By The Degree Of Awareness and Broadness Of Presence Of The Individual Spirit or Spirit Type.

The analogies I give between Our Spiritual and our physical universes are to show levels of Manifestation. This will be easier for a Human Being To Understand When You Relate To Each Living Being On Earth As A Fused Spiritual and physical Being.

A Limitation Of A 3rd-D Spirit Is that It Is Fully Aware but not Self-Aware. It Is An Experiential Being,[13u] Which does not Project Itself Into The Continuum Of Spirit. Such Consciousness May Have A Wonderful Awareness Of Its environment. GOD Is Pleased To Share That Awareness.

Continuing Our analogy to Music, The 3rd Dimension Of Spirit Is like a fully developed Chord with many diverse notes and Overtones[13v] that can be either Complimentary[13w] or discordant.[13x] The Harmonious Notes Of Spiritual Consciousness Are Pleasing to The LORD.

Another way to say This Is, That Which Is Pleasing To GOD Defines The Word *Harmonious* In Any Reality. This Leads To Understanding The Purpose Of Being.

The inverse is also True. that which is not pleasing to GOD has no purpose.

4th-Dimension Spiritual: The 4th Dimension Of Spirituality Is Manifested As Any Being That Is Aware Of Itself and The Progression Of Conscious Situations. This Progression Of Consciousness Is The Spiritual Continuum. This is not "time" as in the physical universe, but Consciousness Is Aware Of Its Own Being[13y] and Changes To Its Own Situation. This is because Consciousness Identifies Itself In The 4th-D Spiritual. The Spiritual Continuum Is Filled With Spiritual Situations Manifesting From The Sustaining Glow[13z] Of Spiritual Energy. A Human Child Is Such A 4th-D Spiritual Being.

To continue the analogy with Music, a 4th-Dimensional Spiritual Being is like a progression of Music. This progression can be in harmony with chords, mingling Pleasantly or in disharmony.[13z1] The Consciousness May Proceed in Spiritual Harmony or fall into confusion and discord.

We Must Consider a skeptic who chooses to bow out[13z2] of any discussion of Spirituality, saying, "I don't believe in any of this. I just want to live my life. Don't bother me with this discussion of Spirit and Heaven and GOD." A Wise Person might respond to this with silence. Consciousness Will Continue as the skeptic cannot avoid The Presence Of GOD In the skeptic's own Self-Aware Consciousness. Each Perception by the skeptic's own Consciousness May Connect To GOD If both the skeptic and GOD Choose To Participate. That's Just The Way It Is.[13z3]

Conscience Is One Way You Can Know GOD In The 4th D. Conscience Is A Subset Of Consciousness. My Mother Explained That Conscience Is The Still, Small Voice[13z4] Of GOD In Your Awareness. You Receive Guidance Directly From GOD. Such Divine Guidance[13z5] Is Easily Ignored As Your Consciousness Is Filled with incredible amounts of data from both Within and Outside Your Mind. Meditation Is So Important To Center Your Consciousness To Be Receptive To The Divine Guidance Of Conscience. Such Meditation May Be Short—A Brief Pause, To Follow The Still, Small Voice.

Conscience is easily misidentified as the superego[13z6] of Freudian psychology.[13z7] Your superego is a construct of Your Mind That Develops To Integrate Your Learning and Experience with biologically programmed conditions. You draw On This Information As Guiding Principles, Which Assist Your Ego[13z8] In Coping[13z9] With Life Situations.

In contrast, Your Conscience Is A Conscious Channel For Information To Flow From GOD To You. The Still, Small Voice Is The Voice Of GOD Manifesting To Your Mind. Most Intuition, Extrasensory Perception,[13z10] and Visions Are Manifestations Of Your Conscience. Information Transmitted By GOD Through Your Conscience Is New Information well Beyond Your Life Experience. If You Trust and Obey[13z11] The Still, Small Voice, Life Improves. Harmony Increases.

Conscience, The Still, Small Voice Of GOD Is Much More Than Moral Guidance. This is just one reason To Tune[13z12] Your Relationship With GOD. Conscience Is An Important Communication Link Along Your Spiritual Metastring. If You Come To Know Your Conscience Well, You Will Become More Confident Of GOD's Will For You. This Is The Sure Path To The Success Of Your Individual Spirit.

A Dimensional Limitation Is That The 4th-D Spirit, while Fully Aware Of Itself, does not Relate To Other Spirits As Spirit. Some Humans Attain The 4th-D Spiritual Consciousness. Some lack The Will To Progress Beyond The 3rd D. Some Progress Into The 5th D or even The 6th D Of Spiritual Being.

This Reveals An Important Principle Of Our Spiritual Universe—that Is, A Spirit May Evolve or Elevate From Awareness Within One Spiritual Dimension To A More Complex or Deeper Spiritual Consciousness. Fused Incarnate Within

A Human Being, The Individual Spirit May Grow To Be Conscious In Another Spiritual Dimension While Incarnate In Human Being In This Life. The Attainment Of An Advanced Spiritual State May only Be Temporary or Periodic. Grounding[13z13] In A Human body Forces One back into the 4th d to attend the needs of the body and ordinary society.

When We Speak Of Spiritual Growth[13z14] As A Human Being, We Are Encouraging The Effort To Attain More Capable Spiritual States Of Being. Reach Out and Be Touched By GOD.

This illustration Is Offered To Depict You Inviting The LORD To Join You and GOD Touching You. The Union Is Brilliant and Totally Fulfilling As You Approach GOD.

Dimitris66, (https://www.gettyimages.com/detail/photo/hand-of-god-royalty-free-image/488572441)

The 4th-Dimension Spiritual Opens The First Heaven.[13z15] It is best described as Heaven On Earth.

Have You Ever Walked by the waves on the seashore, in a field, in the woods, or in Your backyard—just You and The Wonderous Beauty Of Your Surroundings? Have You Ever Enjoyed[13z16] An Inspiring[13z17] Song? If So, You Are Experiencing Heaven In Its physical Manifestation.

GOD Is Enjoying This Experience With You Through A Direct Connection With Your Consciousness. This Is The Reason GOD Differentiated GOD's Self To Separate Your Spirit From The ONE. Through Your Experience In Harmony With physical creation, The LORD Can See Creation Through Your eyes and Senses The Perfection[13z18] Of This place As You Sense It.

This Is just You and GOD—Here and Now. Recreation, Wonder, Enjoyment, Prayer, Meditation, and Worship Are some of the Keys To The First Heaven. Spiritual Energy Is Moving Up[13z19] To GOD and Returning Enhanced.[13z20] You Discover That Sharing Your Experience With The LORD Is A Humble Offering.[13z21] It Is Well-Received.[13z22] In Turn, There Is A Flow Of Spiritual Energy Back To You. This Is Enhanced As You Receive It. Its Character May Be Experienced As Joy, Emotional Calm, Answers To Problems Shared, Awe, Invigoration,[13z23] Reorientation,[13z24] Perception Of Wonderous Beauty, or even A Rush[13z25] Of Spiritual Energy That Is Best Described As Light. It Is The Richness Of Your Conscious Experience, Your Version Of The Light, That May Please The LORD.

Detelina Petkova, Shutterstock 174150992

I capitalize the word *Light* because This Is not photon energy perceived by Your eyes but Divine or Spiritual Energy, Enriching[13z26] Your Soul. The Feeling Is That Of Brilliance Perceived By Your Individual Spirit. Unlike physical energy that is used up as it is spent along the physical continuum, Divine Energy Increases As It Is Given[13z27] Along The Spiritual Continuum.

When You See The Beautiful Sunset, Invite GOD To See It With You. Your Prayer Should Be "LORD, Are You Seeing This Amazing[13z28] Sunset With Me?" GOD Will Join[13z29] You, Appreciating This Experience. This Is The First Heaven.

All Of Your Conscious Experiences Can Be Shared With The LORD To Experience This Perfection As Your Sharing With GOD Advances.

Dang Quang Tung, Alamy

5th-Dimension Spiritual: Complex Consciousness Becomes Aware Of Itself As Distinct From Other Spiritual Beings. Empathy Develops As A Complex Consciousness Senses Differences Between Its Own Consciousness and That Of Beings Of Which It Is Aware. Communication Between Spiritual Beings Develops. This Is not just Reactive[13z30] Communication As With Low-Awareness physical Incarnations, such as Speaking With Someone In Mundane[13z31] Existence. It Is Relations Between Conscious Beings In Which Spiritual Energy Is Exchanged[13z32] Within The Context Of The Encounter or Longer Relationship. Each Being Understands and Shares The Conscious Experience Of The Other.

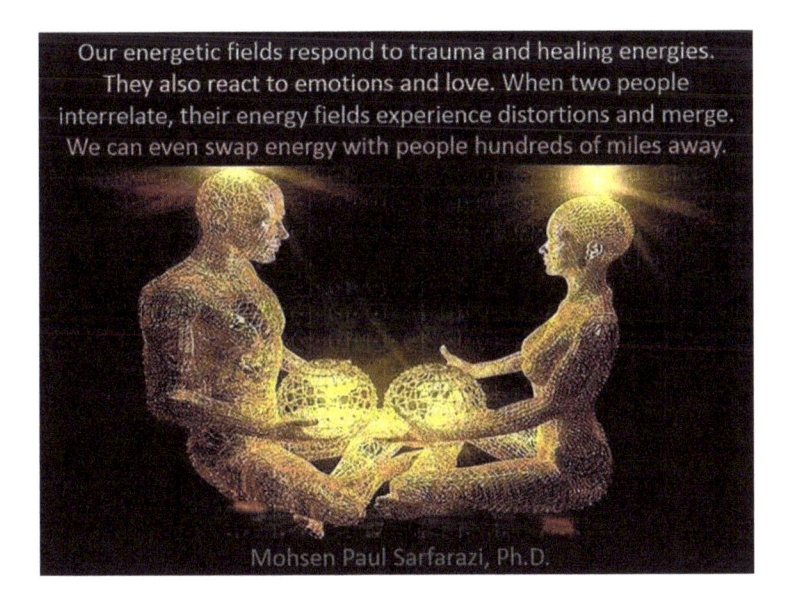

> Our energetic fields respond to trauma and healing energies. They also react to emotions and love. When two people interrelate, their energy fields experience distortions and merge. We can even swap energy with people hundreds of miles away.
>
> Mohsen Paul Sarfarazi, Ph.D.

The Awareness Of Self Expands In The 5th-D Spiritual. You Develop Self-Esteem[13z33] As You Regard Yourself In Comparison To Others With Whom You Become Acquainted. You Encourage Yourself Toward Excellence[13z34] As You Act Purposefully[13z35] To Achieve An Ideal Of This or That, Which You Choose To Be.

You Develop Self-Respect[13z36] As You Learn To Care For and Develop Your Being, Both body and Soul.

Our Spiritual Universe Is Populated With Spiritual Beings. Though Each Exists As Its Own Being, They May Exist In Relation To One Another. Each Spiritual Being Operating In The 5th-D Spiritual Is Fully Self-Aware. In The 5th-D Spiritual, The Expansion Is The Connections Between Spiritual Beings.

Individual Freedom Of Will Is An Operational Characteristic Of Differentiation From The ONE To Become An Individual Spirit. Each Spirit Within The Spiritual Membrane System Is Involved With Its Choice Of Consciousness Within The Boundaries Of Its Spiritual Universe. You Are A Spirit Incarnate Into a physical body on Earth, So You Have The Freedom Of Choice Between Alternatives Presented To You. These Choices Are Manifested In The 5th Dimensions As You Create Your Reality By Making Choices and Reacting To Each Situation In Your Life.

A Limitation On The 5th-D Spiritual Is That One Individual Spirit May Perceive Its Position In A manner That Is In conflict with The Position Of Another Spiritual Being. This Is the source of much disharmony or negative spiritual energy. Usually, GOD Expects The Spiritual Beings In conflict, To Resolve these Into Harmony. However, The Resolution May Be very destructive instead.

Many Human Beings Are Consciously Involved In The 5th D Of Spiritual Reality. The Interplay Of complex physical sensations Creates Diverse Perceptions and Spiritual Manifestations In The 5th-D Spiritual. For example, It Is An Individual

GOD—THE DIMENSIONAL REVELATION

Spiritual Choice Whether Compassionate Love Also Manifests As Joy or Alternatively As Pathos or even As Regret[13z37] In This Complex Harmony.

In analogy to music, We now have a Band[13z38] Playing Together. Diverse instruments Interrelate To Create A Harmonious Group Communion With Heightened Spirituality. A Spirit May also Project a discordant Spiritual condition Affecting[13z39] many Individuals.

The 5th Dimension Of Spirituality Opens The Second Heaven.[13z40] The Second Heaven Is Rich With Spiritual Relations. The Second Heaven Can Be Realized In This Incarnation here on Earth—or not. The Second Heaven May Be Realized In The Afterlife. You Are In the Garden of Eden[13z41] If You Will Allow Yourself To Be.

This illustration Is Offered to depict The Perfect State Of Harmony Right Here Right Now On Earth. You May Enjoy This Garden Of Eden, The First and Second Heaven, During Your Human Lifetime If You Will Allow Yourself To Do So.

Felix Immanuel, 2018, Garden of Eden and the Kingdom of Heaven, Trumpet Call.org

Have You Ever Developed A Connection or Love For Another Person? The Warmth Of The Relationship Is Shared. It Manifests As Unique Connections Of Sharing, Caring, and The deep Glow Of Divine Love. Extraordinary Communication Develops That Transcends space, time, and the ordinary Human senses.

You May Develop This Type Of Connection With A Beloved Pet or Plant. All Spirits Who Share Such A Relationship are Enriched By The Experience. Such Relationships Are Shared By GOD. The Increase In Conscious Experience Is

Fed[13z42] With Divine Energy. You Experience The Increase In Spiritual Energy and Consciousness As The Relationship Deepens.

The picture below is Offered to depict two Humans Sharing a Relationship. GOD Joins The Sharing To Elevate The Experience.

Laura Byrd
(https://www.seekingyourspirit.com/home/2019/9/10/loving-each-other-into-existence)

When You Are Separated From The Loved One While Incarnate, Your Separation Anxiety[13z43] is a manifestation of the spiritual loss.[13z44] The loss Is Why You Are So Moved. The Spiritual Yearning You Experience Is You Reaching For A Higher Dimension Of Spirit In Which Union Is The Reality and separation does not occur. You May Attain This Higher Heaven.

Also, This Life on earth can be an ugly Existence. The LORD May Choose To Participate or not to Participate With You In This Existence. It Is important For You To Know That You Are The Director Of Your Life here on Earth. Much Is out of Your Control, but You Can Always Choose How You Relate To Each Situation With Others, and With GOD Moving Forward.

6th-Dimension Spiritual: We Observe incredible Occurrences That Seem impossible because Our Grasp Is So Limited. The 6th-D Spiritual Manifests Advanced Spiritual Encounters or Relations With Unusual Spiritual Beings. It Is Difficult For A Spirit Incarnate In physical reality To Relate To Such Encounters Because They Are so rare. Perhaps *rare* is not the correct word. 6th-D Spiritual Encounters Usually Lack the nexus[13z45] to physical reality, So They Often Go Unnoticed[13z46] By Incarnate Spiritual Beings.

Extra Sensory Perception, Encounters, or Observations Of Nonphysical Spirits, or Extraordinary Religious Experiences, Occur In The 6th-D Spiritual. Astral Projection,[13z47] Clairvoyance,[13z48] Telekinesis,[13z49] Telepathy,[13z50] Resurrection, and Reincarnation Occur In 6th-D Spiritual Reality.

It Is Revealed That GOD Has Differentiated Small Portions Of GOD's Own Being To Create Independent Spirits Of Many Different Kinds. Even on Earth, The Spirit Of GOD Is Channeled Into Independent Spirits Incarnate In The Various Life-Forms.

Differentiation Is A 6th-D Tangent To The ONE. Differentiation Proceeds According To The WORD, Instructing The 9th D To Manifest Your Individual Spirit As A Soul Incarnate Into Your embryonic[13z51] or Infant physical body. This Occurs In The 6th D Along The Spiritual Metastring Connecting You Directly To GOD.

As Your Sense Of Self and Of Other Spiritual Beings Develops, The Individuality Of Spiritual Being Presents Circumstances Beyond Individual Control. This Is The 6th-D chaos Among Spiritual Beings. In addition to Personal Spiritual uncertainties, When More than One Consciousness Is Present, Situations Develop In Which The Conscious Being cannot Fully Determine Its Position. The Manifestation Develops As Both or Many Conscious Beings Express Themselves. Uncertainty Grows As You Relate To This Vast Universe Of Spiritual Beings, Each With Its Own Direction.

An Independent Spirit May Choose to act destructively or in disharmony. This diminishes Spiritual Energy and is not pleasing to the LORD. Our Spiritual Universe contains many discordant Spirits that may be called evil or other words describing the discord.

Why Does GOD Permit them to exist? When GOD Differentiates Spirit From The ONE and Bestows Freedom Of Will Upon Each, GOD Knows It Is inevitable that some will choose disharmonious being. Though Always Welcome[13z52] Back Into Harmony (Redemption[13z53]), Pleasing The LORD, An Independent Spiritual Being can choose disharmony, even to the point of self-destruction.

Yes, Even Though A Spirit Is Outside of time—So Can Be Said To Be Eternal[13z54] On The Spiritual Continuum—A Spirit Can be destroyed By The WORD or self-destruct By Freedom Of Choice.

Disharmonious words are not capitalized in Our Teaching because the flow to spiritual destruction has a spiritual value of *z*. It falls into a continuum with a definite ending. It loses the Spiritual Value Of *A*, Which Continues To Reunification With The ONE. This Is A Dimensional Limitation Of The 6th-D Spiritual.

The Correct Attitude Of Every Independent Spiritual Being Is Devotional Service To The LORD.[13z55] That Is The Best Defense against spiritual uncertainty and misdirection. Devotional Service To The LORD Is Also The Most Direct Path To Reunification and Fulfillment Along The Way.

The 6th Dimension Of Spirituality Opens The Third Heaven.[13z56] In The Third Heaven, You Are An Instrument Of GOD. Divine Energy Comes To You From The LORD, or From Another Human Being, or From A Beloved Pet or Plant. Upon Receiving The Love, You Return It or Pass It Along To Others.

This illustration is Offered to depict You As A Spiritual Messenger, Sharing The Light As An Instrument Of GOD.

Designart Angel Wings, Item #2793499, Model #PT12355-40-30

This Spiritual Interaction Is Called "Turning The Light Around."[13z57] You Perceive The Love. It Swells[13z58] In Your Soul, and You Project It Back To The One From Whom You Received It or To Others. It Is More powerful On The Return, so The Recipient[13z59] Experiences Its Soul Reassured[13z60] and Enhanced.

GOD Commands You To Share The Light Of Love.

Circulating The Light Is Spiritual Enlightenment. The Divine Energy Is So Powerful That The Projecting Spirit Glows Spiritually. The Energy Is So Enlightening That The Recipient Begins To Glow As Well. The Light Increases As It Is Turned Around, Projected By You, First Turned Inwardly To Invigorate Your Own Soul. The

Light Is Enhanced In The Stillness Of Your Center. When You Master The Light, You May Choose To Project Spiritual energy Outwardly, or Back To GOD.

This album cover is offered to depict Your Turning The Light From The Stillness Of Your Center Back To GOD.

Cover art of The Moody Blues's "In Search of the Lost Chord" by Phil Travers, 1968

You May Choose To Project The Light Outwardly To Another. That Spirit May Appreciate The Light and May Project The Light Back Again As The Other Turns The Light Around.

For example, An Act Of Forgiveness Can Be One-way, not received by The Forgiven Being. Perhaps Forgiveness is unwanted or not deserved by The Forgiven Being. In This example, If You Forgive A Being Who wronged You, The Light Is Turned Inwardly, and Your Spirit Is Made Whole. You Are Energized By The Light of Forgiveness.

Continue Your Forgiveness, and The Other May Come To Appreciate It. Then That Spirit Will Become Energized By The Light and Made Whole. That Recipient Can Then Return The Light, Enhanced, So The Energy Grows As It Is Given. We Participate In This Glorious Two-Way Exchange Of Light In Our Living Relationships. Forgiveness Is Only One Of Many Aspects Of The Light That May Be Shared.

That Relationship Is Actually Three-Way Because The Light Is A Manifestation Of GOD.

The Light May Continue and Be Shared As Spiritual Energy Increases. The Light Can Be Projected Generally So a Gathering[13z61] or An Audience can Receive The Light as The Individual Spirits Become Spiritually Enriched.

The Secret Of The Golden Flower[13z62] Is That The "Golden Flower" Is a Messenger Of GOD. The Golden Flower May Be Realized As Your Soul. When You see The Light Projected By A Beautiful Flower or Any Other Radiant Being, You Recognize That It Too Is An Instrument Of GOD. The Secret Of The Golden Flower, Whether That Flower Be Your Glowing Soul or The Radiant Yellow Center Of The Lotus Blossom,[13z63] Is That Each Has Received The Light Of GOD, Is Appreciating The Light, and Is Turning The Light Around To Radiate[13z64] GOD's Love To All Who Will Experience It.

The Image of a Lotus Blossom is Offered to Depict The Secret of Spiritual Energy.

jaboo2foto/Shutterstock 678970549

Whenever You Behold[13z65] The Golden Light Emanating[13z66] From The Center Of The Flower or Any Other Glorious Manifestation In This Life, Remember and Share In The Divine Light. In So Doing, You Become ONE With GOD. This Is The Deepest Secret!

One Meditation You May Visualize Is To Focus Your Calm Mind On The Center In Your forehead between Your eyes. Imagine A Golden Flower With A Radiant Center There. Allow It To Blossom and Share Spiritual Energy. You May Focus the Spiritual Energy Inwardly or Outwardly As You Appreciate The Light.

Once You Attain Mastery, You May Oscillate The Spiritual Energy Inward, Outward, Then Inward and Outward Again To Create A Full Spiritual Oscillation. [5z13] The Light Expands. This Technique Is Called "Circulating the Light".

We Have Used visible light as a metaphor for The Divine Light. Divine Light May Be Shared In Human Experience Through All Of The Senses. Sight, Sound, Touch, Taste, and Smell May Be Elevated From biological processes To Ecstatic Sharing Of Divine Light.

Song[13z67] Is Particularly Moving Spiritually. Yes, Music Is A Fine Meditation. The Harmonies and Cadence In Music Actively Move Divine Light To Be Turned Inward To Enlighten Your Individual Soul. Your Individual Spirit May Turn That Light Around and Enhance It As You Sing In Harmony, Adding Crescendos Of Sound. Others May Share. They May Turn The Light Around Again As They Play A

Melodic Instrument or Sing Gloriously In Return. The Increase In Spiritual Energy Is Most Fulfilling. Yes, GOD Can Be Found In Your Appreciation Of Music.

Alphonse Mucha—The Seasons, Spring, 1896

    Another Sensual Enhancement Of The Light Is The Reciprocating Touch Of Lovers Sharing The Light In Communion Of Spiritual Unity. Lovers May Enhance The Excitement Of Sensitive Physical Responses To Each Other's Caresses, Murmurs, and Breaths In Spiritual Union. The Spiritual Energy Mounts in Pressure as A Constant Hum or Until there's A Dramatic Release At The Pinnacle Of Feeling.

GOD—*THE DIMENSIONAL REVELATION*

The Crescendos and Releases May Be In Unison or In Caring Harmony, Only To Be Followed By A Heavenly Relaxation Of Peace In Love.

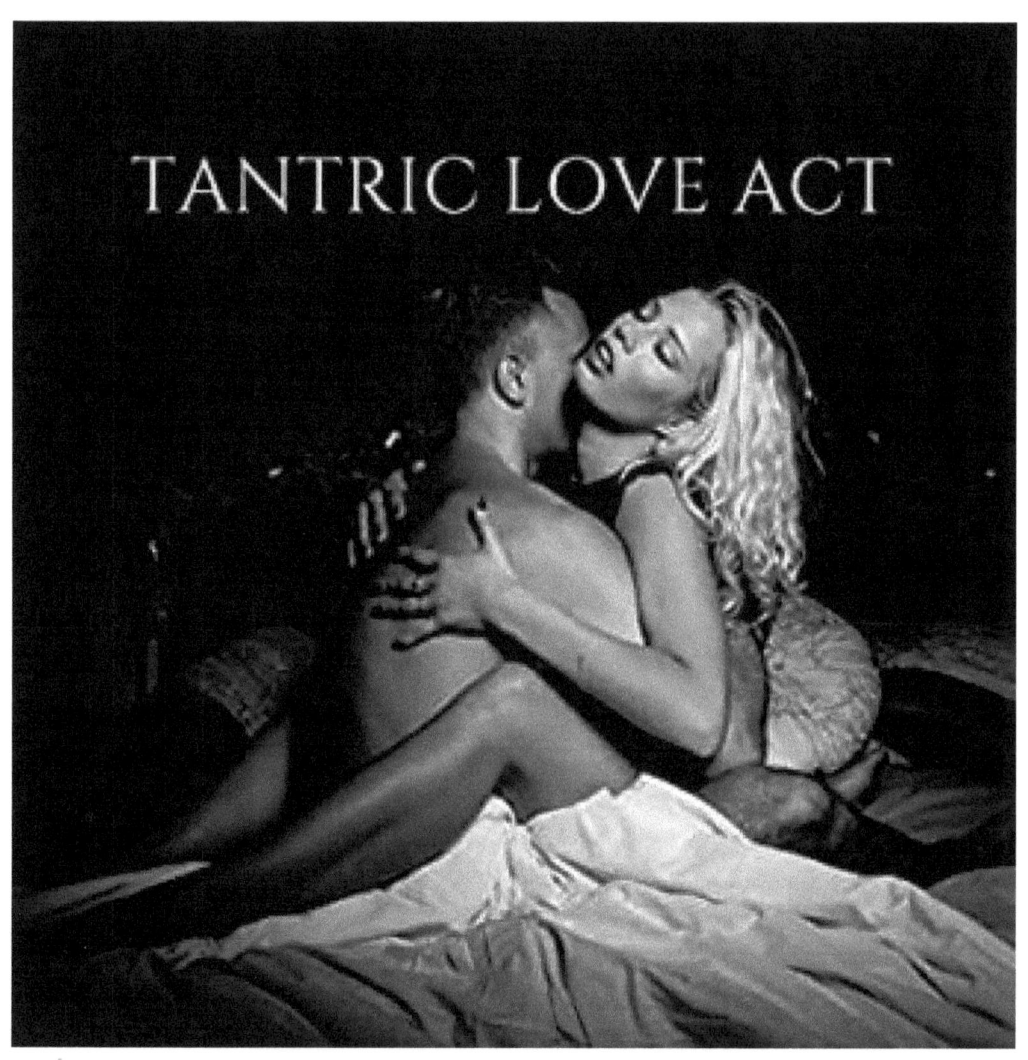

Album Cover, Tantric Love Act—Album Cover Art—Music background for Spiritual Sexual Intercourse with a Partner, Tantric Massage, Couple Meditation, Breathing Exercises, Yoga Practice, Dora Records 2021

    The Love Of GOD Is Many Things. Among Them Is The Glory Of Each Conscious Moment In This Land Given To Us for a while.
    The ancient Greeks called The Broader Love "Agape." It Is The General Enhancement Created By Sharing The Feelings Of Affinity[13z68] Between Souls. This Enlightenment Is Known In all Human Cultures In Which Divine Energy Is Shared With The LORD or With Others. It Is Given Many Names But Remains Esoteric Because Only Advanced Spiritual Beings Recognize It and Can Properly

Manage[13z69] The Light. Spiritual Growth Is Required Of All Human Beings To Attain Enlightenment.

One Technique You May Use To Attain Enlightenment Is "Stopping and Seeing."[13z57] Stopping Is Becoming Still. This Is Stillness Of Mind. Seeing Is Clarity Of Mind, Perceiving The Perfect Light, Reality As It Is. Cultivating This Technique, Your Light Increases And So Does Your Connection To GOD.

You have the question, "Do I Have A Destination?" Ultimately, Your Destination Is Reunification With The ONE. Whenever You Join With GOD, You Have Arrived.

GOD's Incarnation Of Spirit Into Beings On The Earth Fuses A Small Portion Of Our Spiritual Universe Into 6th-Dimensional physical reality. It is an impossible Tangent to physical being. The ordinary rules of physical existence become Exceeded In This Extraordinary Fusion. Yet Human Beings Experience This Reality every day.

6th-D Spiritual Being Is Enabled To Transcend The Passing Of Its Spirit From The physical body. That Is Why Human Beings Have Always Honored Their Ancestors[13z70] and Loved Ones[13z71] Who Have Passed Away.

Los Angeles National Cemetery on Wednesday, November 11, 2020, in Los Angeles, California (Al Seib, *Los Angeles Times*)

Another Dimensional Limitation Of The 6th-D Spiritual Is That The Third Heaven, Enlightenment, Sharing of Spiritual Energy, and Reunions Are Fleeting. [13z72] They lack the depth of Continuity. The Relationships In 6th-D Spiritual Reality lack Control, and They lack Permanence.[13z73]

Planet Earth Has Become A Spiritual planet with The Infusion Of Life. The Genesis Of Life and The Reaching Of Spiritual Being To GOD Enable This Incredible Third Heaven For Us To Live In and To Enhance With The Active Spirituality Each Of Us Possesses.

Yes, The Third Heaven Is the potential Glory Of The Incarnate Human Spirit Here On Earth. To Experience It As Glory, You Must Appreciate The Fullness Of

GOD—THE DIMENSIONAL REVELATION

Your Conscious Experience In This Life. This Appreciation Is Your Awareness Of GOD As The Essence Of Your Consciousness.

Upon Reading This Clearly Explained, You May Recognize That You Have Always Known This. This Knowledge Is Always Accessible Along Your Spiritual Metastring Connection To GOD. It may take You an entire Lifetime or more To Prove That This Teaching Is True, but Your Connection To GOD Is Always There, Immediately Accessible. This Revelation Has Uncovered[13z74] It, So You Can Invigorate Your Communion With GOD.

This Brings To Mind My Childhood Meal Prayer: *"Come, Lord Jesus. Be Our Guest.*[13z75] *Let Our Food and Drink Be Blessed."* This Prayer Not Only Invites The LORD To Experience culinary Pleasure Through You but also Blesses The Lesser Spirits That Have Passed On So You can consume their physical bodies as necessary nutrition.

This Understanding Empowers You To Live A Human Life To The Fullest, Gathering what You need With Humble Reverence[13z75] To the necessities of Incarnate physical Being. Understanding The Passing On Of Spirit, You Are Freed[13z77] From the shackles[13z78] of guilt,[13z79] So You Can Live Fully.

Do not be misled. Understanding The Immortal Nature Of Spirit does not give You a license to kill.[13z80] Killing carries significant negative spiritual energy. Verifiable Divine Permission[13z81] Is Necessary To Proceed and To Justify[13z82] any killing. The taking of Life Requires A Prayer Of Blessing To Lead You. Be Sure That You Are Correct and Justified Before You take any Life.[13z83]

Without The Blessing Of The LORD, You are like a slave, pierced with a nose ring[13z84] on a chain, being forcefully led by powerful Spirits that misuse[13z85] You.

To Advance Spiritual Growth As An Incarnate Human Being In This Life, Simply Open Your Awareness, Your Consciousness, To Be An Instrument Of GOD. Welcome The LORD To Be Present In This Glorious Reality Here On Earth With You Now. Circulate The Light. Welcome Others To Share The Light. The Richness Of This Experience Is Energizing To Those Sharing and To GOD. You Grow In This Sharing. This Is Spiritual Growth. It Is Just The Beginning Of What You can Share.

7th-Dimension Spiritual: We Understand That Spiritual Words are meaningless in a purely physical universe. Our sun has no Spirit. It is a sphere of thermonuclear reaction held together by gravity. A Spiritual Experience Such As Love cannot be Experienced by our sun. Our sun has no consciousness and no connection to Our Spiritual Universe. It makes no sense to worship the sun. Many Human rituals and beliefs have been horribly misguided to Deify[13z86] physical objects.

The non-spirituality[13z87] is true of nearly all physical manifestations, except One Type That We Know Of. That Is Living Beings. The Existence Of Living Beings On Earth forces the logical deduction that We Must Understand Our Reality As A Partial Fusion Of Membrane Systems that are fundamentally different, except for Their unlikely Intersection Here On Earth.

This Understanding Opens the door to the worship of Life Force[13z88] generally. From a geocentric point of view, Life Force Is To Be Respected[13z89] As Part Of Spiritual Relationships. However, When A Life Force Passes On at the death of the physical body, Individual Consciousness Passes Beyond Our physical universe. The broader Spiritual Realities Are Manifested In Our Spiritual Universe. Our physical universe is lacking That Life Force When The Being With Life Force Passes Away. That Life Force Will Change In The Afterlife. It May Become Unrecognizable In Our Spiritual Universe, In The manner Realized, Incarnate On Earth.

Hence, It Makes Sense To Worship GOD Only[13z90] and not The Individual Spirits With Life Force Differentiated From GOD. You May Share With Other Souls. You May Enhance Spiritual Energy With Other Beings Having Life Force, But The Origin Of All Spiritual Energy Is GOD. So Worship Must Be Along That Metastring Connection—Directly To GOD.

The 7th-D Spiritual Contains All Possible Manifestations Of Spirits In Our Spiritual Universe. Your Human Spirit Is Only One Type. Its Limitation Is The Journey Of Your Soul.

Stated more broadly, The 7th-D Limitation Is The Journey Of All Souls Manifested As Those Incarnate On Earth or Any Other Manifestation Of Such Individual Spirits.

The 7th Dimension Of Spirituality Opens The Fourth Heaven.[13z91] Your Personal, Immortal Soul Passes Away From physical being when Your body ceases to function. Your physical body has died, But Your Soul Lives On.

The LORD Jesus Christ Said, *"In My FATHER's House are many Mansions. If It were not so I would have Told You. There I Go to Prepare a Place for You. Where I Go You Know and the Way You Know. No Man Cometh Unto the FATHER, but By Me."*[11z23] Understand That The Metastring Connecting Incarnate Spirit To Our Spiritual Universe In The 7th D Has Been Fully Opened To Receive Your Spirit Upon Its Passing Away From the physical world. Understand That The Destinations For Different Individual Souls May Be Different Manifestations In The Fourth Heaven.

This Begins To Answer The Question, What Happens When I Die?

If You Have Been Walking Humbly With GOD, You Will Have Experienced The First Heaven Of Conscious Spiritual Awareness, Sharing The Light With GOD. You Will Have Experienced The Flow Of Spiritual Energy, Circulating the Light Between You, GOD, and Other Spiritual Beings In The Second Heaven. You Will Have Experienced Receiving The Light and Turning The Light Around As The Messenger Of GOD In The Third Heaven.

The LORD will not forget You. Continue To Seek The LORD Face-To-Face.[6] Upon Your Passing; and GOD Will Pluck You From the oppression of hades, or other Judgement, and Elevate You To The Fourth Heaven.

There You Are Surrounded By Glorious Visions, Celestial Music, and The Glorious Spiritual Universe. In This Realm, You Are Conscious Of Yourself As An

Individual Spirit. You Feel The Fullness Of Heaven. This Is The Heaven that most of Us think of In Our Religious Life. It Is Paradise.

Your Spiritual Journey, Whether Incarnate or As Pure Spirit, Is What You Make Of It. This Is The Freedom Of Will Granted To Each Spirit Differentiated From The ONE. There Are Truly Many "Mansions" In The Fourth Heaven.

This illustration is Offered to depict an Artist's Vision Of Heavenly Manifestations. You May Become Manifest In Any Such Heavenly State or Some Different Glory.

From *The Catalog of Good Deeds*—St. Elizabeth Convent, 2020

8th-Dimension Spiritual: The 8th-Dimension Spiritual Allows The Full Diversity Of Spiritual Manifestations, Not Just The Ones A Human Spirit May Become. We Can Imagine A Myriad Of Different Spiritual Experiences. The 8th-D Spiritual also Manifests Spiritual Being That We cannot even Imagine.

A Limitation To The 8th-D Spiritual Is That The Mingling Spirits Are Still Separate. Spirit Is Grand But Wandering, Manifested As The Different Spiritual Beings. This Does Not diminish The Ecstasy Of Spirits In Divine Relation. GOD Is Elated With The Experience Of Spirit So Broadly Flung and So Wonderfully Developed.

This illustration is Offered as An Artist's Vision Of A Diversity Of Spirits Participating With GOD. It is difficult to depict The Fifth Heaven because There May Be No Form to depict as Spirits Become Formless.

(https://consciousreminder.
com/2018/05/05/3-types-of-heavenly-beings-that-assist-the-earth/)

The 8th Dimension of Spirituality Opens The Fifth Heaven.[13z92] The Fifth Heaven Is An Expansion Of Your Individual Spirit. It Is Recognition Of The Spiritual Journey Of Your Soul. This Recognition Converts The *I* Into The *We* As You Expand Into All The Spiritual Experiences Of This Soul.

Your Experience In This Glorious Heaven May Include Adding Your Harmonious Voice To Heavenly Choirs, Witnessing The Presence Of Higher Spirits, Reunion With A Loved One From A Former Life; Traveling the galaxies of the physical universe; Being Elevated From the grave In The Rapture, Being With Jesus, Saints, Profits, Other Spirits, or Any Divine Manifestations and Spiritual State Of Being.

GOD Shares In This Expansion. You May Be Repurposed Into Another Human Life, Elevated To Teach or Share Spirituality Again On Earth. You May be Incarnated Into Any Of The Thousands Of Sentient Being Types In Your previous physical universe. You May Become Any Of The Spiritual Beings In Our Spiritual Universe. You May Be Present, Manifested In Unimaginable 8th-Dimensional Membrane Systems

In Which Spirit Is Different. You May Be Joined To Other Spirits In A Grand Manifestation of Spiritual Being. Your Role Is Spiritual Because You Are Spirit.

Ancient Teachings Speak Of Cherubim[13z93] and Seraphim,[13z94] of Ophanim[13z95] and Angels.[13z96] These Are Spiritual Beings Whose Experience We cannot Fully Imagine. A Human Soul Would Be Fortunate To even Encounter Such A Being While Incarnate In Human flesh. Yet In The Fifth Heaven, You may Sing Among The Angels As One Of Them. You Join With Them, Triumphant[13z97] In The Glory.

9th Dimension: Note that The 9th-D Spiritual Is The Same 9th D That We Observed of physical being. The Mechanisms Of Creation Of All Membrane Systems Exist In The 9th D. The Creation May Become Manifested In The Spiritual, the physical, Any Other Membrane System, or A Combination, According To The WORD.

A Limitation Of The 9th D Is That All Is Possible To Become Manifest But Only According To The Instructions Of The WORD.

In The 9th D, Your Spirit Is Enabled To Merge With All Other Spirits. The Powerful Spirits and The Mild Spirits Join As Their Identities Are Merged In Glory. The Glory Is A Vast Spiritual Radiance Caused By A Merger Of All Separate Spiritual Beings. The Sharing Of Diverse Consciousness, Enlightened By Crescendos Of Divine Energy, Warmly Exchanged With GOD, Elevates The Splendor Of This Union. Reality Has Reached Its Pinnacle Of Being.

The 9th Dimension Opens The Sixth Heaven.[13z97] Your Spiritual Being Has Spread So Broadly That We Can No Longer Speak Of You. Your Awareness Is General, and It Is Immense. It is Broader Than You. You Have Grown Beyond Your Identity. You Have No Self-Awareness. The Sixth Heaven Has Merged All Sensations Into the Eternal Chord Of GOD. The Spiritual Resonance[13z98] Is Fully Experienced and Is Truly Glorious. The Divine Energy Is Pervasive; and We, Collectively, Are That Energy In LIGHT With GOD. That Energy Is Creative According To The WORD. Manifestations Emerge In The Creative.

GOD Experiences Glorification In Participation With Spirit So Wonderfully Combined.

One morning, I walked out My front door on My small hill. The gray of clouds drifting south in an indigo sky sprang into color as purples became scarlet, then giving way to vibrant oranges, then finally the yellow sun—blinding—as it peaked above the horizon. I turned to behold the deeper colors receding. Suddenly, the last leaves of autumn flamed brilliantly within a swirl of color yet still as the pause between breaths. Distant crows cawed, syncopated as a dove flew whistling by. A deer snorted in the woods as the last bluebird chortled nearby. The Souls of the trees, the grass, woodland, and meadow creatures, all joined with Me and The LORD in ONE Spirit Of Joy At The sunrise. GOD Was Very Pleased.

Understanding This, You Begin To Understand Reunification In The 9th Dimension. Individual Souls Become ONE Spirit—The Spirit Of Joy In The LORD—In This Incarnation.

Different Manifestations In A Diversity Of Spirits On earth or In Any Of The Heavens Are The Pleasure Of GOD, Until All Is Accomplished.

The metaphor of Water Is Frequently Used In True Human Religions To Symbolize Becoming ONE In The LORD. When A Drop Of Water (Your Soul) Is Added To The Sea (The ONE), That Drop Diffuses and Becomes The Sea. This Leads To The Seventh Heaven—The 10th D.

Jezper/ Shutterstock.com, 124915520

By now, You are probably wondering about this splitting of Heaven into Levels Of Awareness and Glory. How are these Levels Achieved?

They Are Achieved By Being. That Is Both You Observing and You Participating In Each Dimension Of Spiritual Reality. To Be Conscious Within The Limitations Of Each Dimension, To Participate, To Create, and To Share As The Opportunities Are Presented According To The Principles Of Operation In Each Dimension, Is To Live Fully In Each Situation.

It is important to Remember That Spiritual States Of Being are not ladders to be climbed. They are not constructs of mind, not one to be built on another. It is not necessary To Master A Lower State Of Spirituality To Attain A Higher State Of Spirituality. One Need Not Pass Through The First, Third, or Any Other Heaven To Reach The Seventh Heaven. Lower Levels Of Spiritual Energy Are Glorious In Their Own Manifestation. They May Also Lead You To Be Manifest According To The WORD In Those We numbered as higher. You Have No Goal[13z99] Except To Share In The Light As You Are Able.

All Spiritual Dimensions Are Immediately Attainable[13z100] Through Connection To GOD. Numbers do not exist in the Spiritual Membrane System. We just use them In This Teaching To Describe States Of Spiritual Being According To Their Relative Fullness and Their Possibilities. The Metastring Connecting Your Soul To GOD Is Fully Open. An Incarnate Spirit Can Experience Total Reunification With GOD. The Reunification May Be Brief while You Are Incarnate. Upon Your Passing, You Can Be Reunited With GOD. Your Spirit Can Be Differentiated again Into The Same Body, Incarnate As Before The Attainment Of Perfection. The 9th D Provides All Capabilities According To Instructions Of The WORD.

If You Seek historical proof Of Such Incarnation, Look To Elijah.[13z101] Look to Elisha.[13z102] Look To The LORD Jesus Christ Bringing The dead Back To This Life. [13z103] Look To The Thousands Of Death and Near-Death Experiences[13z104] Testified By Those Returned From The dead. Look To The Buddhas[13z105] and Bodhisattvas. [13z106] Look To The Reincarnated Souls Who Can Recall Their Past Lives.

Even More Convincing Is Your Own Spiritual Journey. One Contribution Of Our Teaching Is To Orient You With Correct Knowledge Of Your Spiritual Being. Spiritual Incarnation In physical being is so confusing to The Individual Soul That A Human Being Is often lost in current Reality.

Please Recall Your Spiritual past. This Can Be Any Experience Of Deep Feeling, An Intuition, A Wonderous Emotion, or Prescient[13z107] Consciousness. Your History Of These Experiences Deepens In This Life As You Live It.

Oh yes, You Have Depth That the dark night cannot extinguish—Visions You Have Had But You Have forgotten most of Them. Do not despair, For You Will Have Grander Visions As You Allow Your Consciousness To Open To Spiritual Being. Invite GOD To Experience Life With You.

Your Spiritual Journey Has Been Jump-Started.[13z108] Connection To GOD Now Can Take You There.[13z109]

10th Dimension: The 10th Dimension Is The SOURCE Of All The Dimensions. There Is No 10th D Of Spirit That Is Separate From The 10th D of physical reality. The WORD Instructs All, So If A Metastring Is Instructed To Become Manifest, It Will Emerge With Information To Create Realities In The 9th D To Manifest Them In Lower Dimensions.

The Only Limitation Of The 10th D Is That It Is The Expression Of GOD—Nothing Less. The Opposites Do Not Exist in the 10th D[6z55] Because The 10th D Precedes Synthesis. The Law Of Dimensional Limitation Dissolves In The 10th D As GOD Is Without Limit. Divine Information, The WORD, Is Limitless At Its SOURCE. Divine Information Becomes Limited Only As The Metastrings Instruct Boundaries In The 8th D. In This Manner, Reality Unfolds In The Lower Dimensions. The WORD Instructs, Manifesting The WILL Of GOD.

Again You Ask, "How Can I Know GOD?" You Shall Appreciate Diverse Manifestations Of GOD. You Shall Be Self-Aware Of Your Consciousness As A

Differentiated Spirit Of The LORD. You Shall Allow Yourself To Be An Instrument Of GOD, To Manifest The Light Through Your Endeavors.[13z110] You Shall Share The Light With Others. You Shall Share This Glory With GOD. As You Approach The LORD, GOD Will Manifest In Many Ways. Ultimately, You May Know GOD As THE CLEAR LIGHT Of The Void. Become That LIGHT, and Your Reunification With GOD Is Complete.[13z111]

The 10th Dimension Opens The Seventh Heaven.[13z112] Upon The Spirit Passing From This Life, Reunification Can Be Permanent As We Describe The Seventh Heaven.

We Have Become The WORD. The Seventh Heaven Is Pure Divinity[13z113]— ONE Consciousness. The ONE Is Instructive Of All Dimensions. All Reality Is Within This Grasp. The WORD Is Instructing What Reality Was,[13z114] What Reality Is,[13z115] and What Reality May Become.[13z116] However, The Continuum Dissolves As ONE Whole Reality[13z117] Is Attained. The Collective *We*[13z118] Has Returned To The SOURCE. All Is Welcomed Back[13z119] Into The ONE. We Have Merged With GOD.[13z120] GOD Is Most Pleased With This Total Fulfillment.[13z121]

Mik Ulyannikov/Shutterstock 44621095

11th: GOD Is ONE.

CHAPTER 14

Reverification and Conclusion

Using the scientific method of Discovering The Truth, We have proved the following:

- The LORD, GOD, Is ONE.
- GOD Is Manifested In All Reality.
- Reality Is Created By The WILL Of GOD In The 10th Dimension. That Is Called The WORD.
- The WORD, The 10th Dimension, Is Divine Instruction, Providing Divine Information To Create, Sustain, and Destroy All Manifestations That Exist.
- Divine Information Is Continuous, not segmented.
- Differentiation From The ONE Is Manifested To Be Separate Beings and Other Aspects Of Reality, which continue or not. While they continue, they operate in Continuous Reality. Hence, We Observe Separate Manifestations Of Continuous Reality.
- Segmentation is useful to provide analysis to better understand the present and the context of Continuous Becoming.
- "Metastrings" Are Instructed By The WORD and Constructed In The 9th Dimension To Manifest Reality In the lower dimensions. The operation of each Metastring is limited to its field of influence.
- "The Law of Dimensional Limitation" describes that boundaries are set by the field of influence within which the principles of operation of each Dimension allow reality to unfold.
- When the boundaries of a dimension are exceeded, a broader/higher dimension is Realized.
- "Membrane Systems" are entire operational systems of being comprising the 8th Dimension. Once Created, each is independent with different operational principles limiting its sphere of influence. Each membrane system is fully operational with no outside influence.

REVERIFICATION AND CONCLUSION

- There may be many membrane systems, but We know of two. The physical membrane system contains all physical universes that operate according to physical principles. The Spiritual Membrane System Contains All Spiritual Universes. These Operate According To Spiritual Principles.
- our physical universe of matter and its attendant energies unfolds along the physical metastring in the 7th dimension as physical possibilities become real.
- Our Spiritual Universe Unfolds In The 7th Dimension Along The Spiritual Metastring as Spiritual Realities Unfold.
- Data sets may be segmented ontologically as constructions of Mind to provide analysis to better understand the present and the context of Continuous Becoming. Data sets may also include digital data sets used in Information Technology. Such segments are from a perspective and not representative of The Entire Reality.
- Data sets may be segmented cosmologically as a continuum of matter or wave energy may be segmented to set apart a real object for purposes of physical construction as matter, energy, or the hardware or software of information technology.
- Individual Spirits Of Our Spiritual Universe Fuse in the 9th Dimension With physical matter. One Manifestation of This Fusion is To Form Living Beings On Our earth in unlikely but very Real 6th-Dimensional Incarnations.
- You and I Are Examples Of The Braided Metastrings Of physical and Spiritual Being. One obvious Manifestation Of That Fusion Is Individual Consciousness (soul) In Individual Living Beings Incarnate In a physical body.
- If You Have Consciousness, You Know GOD. The Depth Of That Relationship Is Up To You.
- Awareness, or More Advanced Conscious Participation, Self-Verifies Spirit To Each Individual Spiritual Being.
- Spirit Is further verified by logical conclusions based on balancing The Mathematical Equations, as well as Cause-and-Effect Analysis and Ordinary Observation.
- Spiritual Beings Are Aware Of One Another by Observing The Light of GOD In The Other and Participating By Sharing Spiritual Relationships.
- Many Living Beings Exercise Individual Will Through Choices. Choices Create The Next Situation In The 5th Dimension.
- time is the physical continuum. time will force the next physical situation in the 4th dimension.

- The qualities of the next situation are undetermined until they collapse into reality, though heavily influenced by the preceding situation. That is quantum probability.
- The total of matter and its attendant energies is constant in our physical universe in the 3rd dimension. Hence, our physical universe is a "closed system."
- The Total Of Spirit Is not constant and Is not limited. Spirit Increases As It Approaches The ONE. Hence, Our Spiritual Universe Is An "Open System" Because The ONE Is Not Limited.
- Physical Reality contains GOD-particles that may be referred to as "strings" or "quants" in 1st-, 2nd-, and 3rd-dimensional manifestations. They Are Called GOD-particles Because they Are Sustained By The WORD.
- The Consciousness Of GOD Chooses to Relate to physical reality, either as an Active Participant or As An Observer only, or to Turn Away.
- When GOD Chooses To Be A Participant, GOD Joins With Individual Spirits to Share The Reality That The Individual Spirit Experiences.
- The "Free Will" Of Each Individual Spirit Opens Unique Conscious Experiences In Which GOD Is Pleased To Participate.
- The "Free Will" Of Each Individual Spirit may cause unique negative experiences, which GOD is likely to Avoid. Hence, these are godless or godforsaken.
- When GOD Chooses To Be An Observer only, reality proceeds as Programmed By The WORD At Its Creation. Proceeding without Conscious Participation by GOD, our physical universe of matter and its attendant energies have no soul or spirit.
- GOD usually allows physical reality to manifest according to the pre-instructed principles of physical operation.
- Human Beings Are Empowered To Participate In Reality.
- Individual Human Beings Are Empowered To Draw On Divine Spiritual Energy Through The Spiritual Metastring, Which Connects Each Differentiated Spirit With GOD.
- A Differentiated Spiritual Being May Invite GOD to Participate In Its Individual Conscious Reality.
- This organization is Our best Understanding of Reality because it accounts for all of Our Observations, data, and calculations.
- Our Teaching Is open to new Observations and Proofs Of Being.
- These Principles are constantly being reverified using objective instrumental data, mathematical calculation, and Conscious Experience. Deductive and Inductive Reasoning Organizes Observations Into logical conclusions that are called Truths.

REVERIFICATION AND CONCLUSION

- Our Teaching Confirms That Truths Are Known By Each Individual Spiritual Being according to Its limited perspective.
- Individual Spiritual Growth, as well as increased knowledge of the physical sciences, Is Necessary for An Individual To Understand and Participate In Broader Truths.
- Meditation, Prayer, and Wonder Enhances or Attracts The Consciousness Of GOD To You. GOD Participating With You Transforms and Empowers You Spiritually. Powerful Meditation Techniques Include the Following:
  1. Inviting The LORD To Participate In Your Conscious Experience
  2. Walking Humbly With Your GOD
  3. Participating In The Heavenly States In This Life
  4. Stopping And Seeing (Pause and Perceive The Perfection)
  5. Appreciation Of Music (Observing or Participating)
  6. Focusing The Mind On An Aspect Of The WORD
  7. Studying Expansions Of The Written WORD
  8. Breathwork
  9. Harmonious physical exercise
  10. Prayer
  11. Focusing Your Mind On Any Of The Chakras
  12. Turning The Light Around
  13. Circulating The Light
  14. Combine Meditations As You Approach The LORD
- These Principles lead to a unified Metaphysics—the Philosophy of Reality.
- This Revelation Of Reality Opens Perfect Knowledge—The Ultimate Realization. Your Spirit May Utilize Perfect Knowledge To Attain Ultimate Fulfillment, Which Is Reunification With The ONE.

CHAPTER 15

Epilogue—The Author's Prayer

Oh LORD,
Let me not mislead them.
Is What I Teach The Truth?

Then Came The Still, Small Voice—
It Is The Truth.

Then Came A Rush Of Spiritual Energy, Confirming

I AM.

CHAPTER 16

Research Notes, Credits, and Expansions

This Teaching draws on an extraordinary breadth of information. This Author Apologizes to any Person Whose original thinking is incorporated in these pages without proper acknowledgement. The research notes listed are specifically Recognized In This Teaching To Credit original ideas. The definitions printed are Our Intended meaning of each word. In some cases, the idea has been further Developed In This Teaching or given a different meaning by Our text in brackets ([]). We also identify ideas original to This Teaching in Our text in brackets ([]).

[1a] Reveal, Revealing, or Revelation: The divine or supernatural disclosure to humans of something relating to human existence or the world (*Oxford English Dictionary*).

[1b] Reality: Reality is the state of things as they actually exist rather than as they may appear or might be imagined (*www.definitions.net*).

[1c] Exist or existence: the fact or state of living or having objective reality (*Oxford English Dictionary*).

[1d] Metaphysics: Metaphysics is the branch of philosophy that examines the fundamental nature of reality. Originally meaning the study of "being as such" [now known as ontology], "first causes", or "unchanging things", it now has a much wider scope. Metaphysics studies questions related to existence, what it is for something to exist and what types of existence there are (*Ned Hall, "David Lewis's Metaphysics," 2012*).

Metaphysics core topic is the set of categories such as object, property and causality which those scientific theories assume. For example: claiming that "electrons have charge" is a scientific theory; while exploring what it means for electrons to be (or at least, to be perceived as) "objects", charge to be a "property", and for both to exist in a topological entity called "space" is the task of metaphysics (*Massimo Pigliucci, "The Crucial Difference between Metaphysics and Epistemology"*).

[Metaphysics is divided into two fields of study:

1. Ontology is the philosophical study of the nature of being, becoming, existence or reality, as well as the basic categories of being and their relations. Traditionally listed as the core of metaphysics, ontology often deals with questions concerning what entities exist and how such entities may be grouped, related within a hierarchy, and subdivided according to similarities and differences.
2. Metaphysical cosmology is the branch of metaphysics that deals with the world as the totality of all phenomena in space and time {*https://www.philosophybasics.com/branch_metaphysics.html*} {*Professor Maurice Mandelbaum, History of Philosophy Lecture, Johns Hopkins University, 1972.*}]

[1e] cosmology (from the Greek κόσμος [kosmos], or *world*, and -λογία [-logia], or *study of*): Concerned with the studies of the origin and evolution of the universe, from the Big Bang to today and on into the future. It is the scientific study of the origin, evolution, and eventual fate of the universe. Physical cosmology is the scientific study of the universe's origin, its large-scale structures and dynamics, and its ultimate fate, as well as the laws of science that govern these areas (*https://philosophy-of-megaten.fandom.com/wiki/metaphysics_and_ cosmology*).

The pre-Socratics saw the world as a "kosmos", an ordered arrangement that could be understood via rational inquiry. Pre-Socratic thinkers present a discourse concerned with key areas of philosophical inquiry such as being, the primary stuff of the universe, the structure and function of the human soul, and the underlying principles governing perceptible phenomena, human knowledge and morality (*Stanford Encyclopedia of Philosophy, April 4, 2016*).

[GOD—*The Dimensional Revelation* Recognizes that metaphysics has become increasingly viewed as limited to physical reality by scientists. Our Teaching Emphasizes The Continuing Development Of ontological disciplines To Recapture An Entire Reality.]

[1f] ontology: The compound word ontology combines onto-, from the Greek ὄν, on (gen. ὄντος, ontos), i.e., "being; that which is", which is the present participle of the verb εἰμί, eimí, i.e. "to be, I am", and -λογία, -logia, i.e. "logical discourse", see classical compounds for this type of word formation. εἰμί. (*Henry George Liddell and Robert Scott, A Greek-English, Perseus Project*).

Ontology is the branch of philosophy that studies concepts such as existence, being, becoming, and reality. It includes the questions of how entities are grouped into basic categories and which of these entities exist on the most fundamental level. Ontology is traditionally listed as a part of the major branch of philosophy known as metaphysics. en.wikipedia.org.

RESEARCH NOTES, CREDITS, AND EXPANSIONS

> It is necessary to speak and to think what is; for being is, but nothing is not. (*Parmenides, "The Way of Truth," B 6.1–2*)

Parmenides has been considered the founder of metaphysics or ontology and has influenced the whole history of Western philosophy (*John Palmer, "Parmenides," Stanford Encyclopedia of Philosophy*).

[1g] Certain: known for sure; established beyond doubt (*Oxford English Dictionary*).

[1h] universe of matter and its attendant energies (also physical universe and specifically our physical universe): The universe (Latin: universus) is all of space and time and their contents, including planets, stars, galaxies, and all other forms of matter and energy (*Michael Zeilik and Stephen A. Gregory, Introductory Astronomy and Astrophysics Fourth Ed., Saunders College Publishing, 1998*).

The universe also includes the physical laws that influence energy and matter, such as conservation laws, classical mechanics, and relativity (*Duco A. Schreuder, Vision and Visual Perception [Archway Publishing, December 3, 2014], 135*).

The term "physical universe" or "material universe" is used to distinguish the physical matter of the universe from a proposed spiritual or supernatural essence (*en.wikipedia.org*).

[1i] big bang: George Lemaître in 1927, a Belgian Catholic priest, first proposed the big-bang theory. The big bang theory argues that the universe began in a tiny, infinitely hot and dense point called a singularity, which contained all of the mass, energy and space in our universe. This then exploded 13.8 billion years ago and began rapidly expanding, spreading out energy and space and began to cool. This is still the standard model. It presumes a cause outside of cosmology (*en.wikipedia.org*).

The big bang is the most widely accepted scientific theory to explain the early stages in the evolution of the Universe (*P. F. Lurquin, The Origins of Life and the Universe [Columbia University Press, 2003], 2*).

For the first millisecond of the big bang, the temperatures were over 10 billion kelvins and photons had mean energies over a million electronvolts. These photons were sufficiently energetic that they could react with each other to form pairs of electrons and positrons. Likewise, positron-electron pairs annihilated each other and emitted energetic photons: $\gamma + \gamma \leftrightarrow e+ + e-$. An equilibrium between electrons, positrons and photons was maintained during this phase of the evolution of the Universe. After 15 seconds had passed, however, the temperature of the universe dropped below the threshold where electron-positron formation could occur. Most of the surviving electrons and positrons annihilated each other, releasing gamma radiation that briefly reheated the universe (*J. Silk The Big Bang: The Creation and Evolution of the Universe Third Ed. [Macmillan, 2000], 110–112, 134–137*).

For reasons that remain uncertain, during the annihilation process there was an excess in the number of particles over antiparticles. Hence, about one electron for every billion electron-positron pairs survived. This excess matched the excess of protons over antiprotons, in a condition known as baryon asymmetry, resulting in a net charge of zero for the universe (*E. W. Kolb and Stephen Wolfram, "The Development of Baryon Asymmetry in the Early Universe," Physics Letters B. 91 [2] [1980]: 217–221*); (*E. Sather, "The Mystery of Matter Asymmetry" [PDF], Beam Line, Stanford University [Spring–Summer 1996]*).

The surviving protons and neutrons began to participate in reactions with each other—in the process known as nucleosynthesis, forming isotopes of hydrogen and helium, with trace amounts of lithium. This process peaked after about five minutes (*S. Burles, K. M. Nollett, and M. S. Turner, "Big-Bang Nucleosynthesis: Linking Inner Space and Outer Space," [1999]*).

Any leftover neutrons underwent negative beta decay with a half-life of about a thousand seconds, releasing a proton and electron in the process, n →p+e–+ve. For about the next 300000–400000 years, the excess electrons remained too energetic to bind with atomic nuclei (*A. M. Boesgaard and G. Steigman, "Big Bang Nucleosynthesis—Theories and Observations," Annual Review of Astronomy and Astrophysics 23, no. 2 [1985]: 319–378*).

What followed is a period known as recombination, when neutral atoms were formed and the expanding universe became transparent to radiation. Roughly one million years after the big bang, the first generation of stars began to form (*R. Barkana, "The First Stars in the Universe and Cosmic Reionization," Science 313 no. 5789, [2006]: 931–934*).

Within a star, stellar nucleosynthesis results in the production of positrons from the fusion of atomic nuclei. These antimatter particles immediately annihilate with electrons, releasing gamma rays. The net result is a steady reduction in the number of electrons, and a matching increase in the number of neutrons. However, the process of stellar evolution can result in the synthesis of radioactive isotopes. Selected isotopes can subsequently undergo negative beta decay, emitting an electron and antineutrino from the nucleus (*E. M. Burbidge et al., "Synthesis of Elements in Stars" (PDF), Reviews of Modern Physics 29 (4), [1957], 548–647*).

[1j] physical: of or relating to natural science (*www.merriam-webster.com*).
Relating to the body as opposed to the mind (*Oxford English Dictionary*).

[1k] mathematics: the abstract science of number, quantity, and space. Mathematics may be studied in its own right (pure mathematics), or as it is applied to other disciplines such as physics and engineering (applied mathematics) (*Oxford English Dictionary*).

RESEARCH NOTES, CREDITS, AND EXPANSIONS

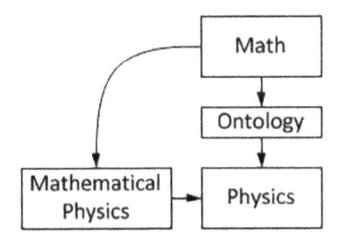

```
                    ┌──────────┐
                    │   Math   │
                    └────┬─────┘
                         ▼
                    ┌──────────┐
            ┌──────▶│ Ontology │
            │       └────┬─────┘
            │            ▼
   ┌────────┴─────┐ ┌──────────┐
   │ Mathematical │▶│ Physics  │
   │   Physics    │ └──────────┘
   └──────────────┘
```

It includes the study of such topics as quantity (number theory), structure (algebra), space (geometry), and change (mathematical analysis) (*en.wikipedia.org*).

[*GOD—The Dimensional Revelation* Recognizes all mathematics as ontology. That would include mathematical physics as it too is a construction of mind. Our Teaching is clear that cosmology contains only physical items. Descriptions, such as math, or processes of mathematical physics, such as information technology, remain ontological. Proof of this is that if you remove the Spiritual Being, then the technology disintegrates. This is further proved by humans' failure to make a perpetual motion machine.]

Unlike natural language, where people can often equate a word (such as cow) with the physical object it corresponds to, mathematical symbols are abstract, lacking any physical analog (*Oakley, 2014, 16*).

All mathematics is symbolic logic (*Russell Bertrand, The Principles of Mathematics [Cambridge: University Press, 1903]*).

There is a reason for special notation and technical vocabulary: mathematics requires more precision than everyday speech. Mathematicians refer to this precision of language and logic as "rigor". Mathematical proof is fundamentally a matter of rigor.

At a formal level, an axiom is just a string of symbols, which has an intrinsic meaning only in the context of all derivable formulas of an axiomatic system. It was the goal of Hilbert's program to put all of mathematics on a firm axiomatic basis, but according to Gödel's incompleteness theorem every (sufficiently powerful) axiomatic system has undecidable formulas; and so, a final axiomatization of mathematics is impossible. Nonetheless mathematics is often imagined to be (as far as its formal content) nothing but set theory in some axiomatization, in the sense that every mathematical statement or proof could be cast into formulas within set theory (*Patrick Suppes, Axiomatic Set Theory [Dover, 1972], ISBN 0-486-61630-4*).

Consideration of the natural numbers also leads to the transfinite numbers, which formalize the concept of infinity (*en.wikipedia.org*).

[11] virtual reality: *Virtual* has had the meaning of "being something in essence or effect, though not actually or in fact" since the mid-1400s. The term *virtual* has been used in the computer sense of "not physically existing but made to appear by software" since 1959 (*Online Etymology Dictionary*).

[1m] dimension or dimensions:

> The key to growth is the introduction of higher dimensions of consciousness into our awareness. (*Lao Tzu, Chinese philosopher and a central figure in Taoism, 600 BC*)

Dimensions are simply the different facets of what we perceive to be reality. We are immediately aware of the three dimensions that surround us on a daily basis—those that define the length, width, and depth of all objects in our universes (the x, y, and z axes, respectively) (*Matt Williams, "A Universe of Ten Dimensions," Universe Today*).

[*GOD—The Dimensional Revelation* proceeds from the four classical dimensions—length, width, depth (height), and time. We Expand this to involve the state of future being allowed by the 5th D, 6th D, 7th D, and 8th D. These must be further expanded by causative dimensions—9th D and 10th D. This Teaching Posits this dimensional model of All Reality. Dimensions with a higher number include all the dimensions with a lower number.]

Also see chapters 3 and 4.

[1n] Religion: A particular system of faith and worship (*Oxford English Dictionary*).

[1o] Know, Known, or Knowledge: A familiarity, awareness, or understanding of someone or something, such as facts (propositional knowledge), skills (procedural knowledge), or objects (acquaintance knowledge). The philosophical study of knowledge is called epistemology (*en.wikipedia.org*).

Epistemology concerns the ultimate source of our knowledge.

There are two traditions: empiricism, which holds that our knowledge is primarily based in experience, and rationalism, which holds that our knowledge is primarily based in reason… Philosophers typically divide knowledge into three categories: personal, procedural, and propositional…personal knowledge, or knowledge by acquaintance…procedural knowledge, or knowledge how to do something…propositional knowledge, or knowledge of facts… The tripartite theory says that if you believe something, with justification, and it is true, then you know it; otherwise, you do not… In order to know a thing, it is not enough to merely correctly believe it to be true; one must also have a good reason for doing so. Lucky guesses cannot constitute knowledge; we can only know what we have good reason to believe.

Knowing how to drive involves possessing a skill, being able to do something, which is very different to merely knowing a collection of facts (*http://sociology.morrisville.edu/readings/STS101/Philosophy-TheoryOfKnowledge*).

"Knowing" is a euphemism for the sexual act in many languages deriving from the biblical Hebrew usage (*Wendy Doniger, Carnal Knowledge, 2000*).

RESEARCH NOTES, CREDITS, AND EXPANSIONS

[Different meanings of the word *Knowledge* are intended in The Bible to describe different experiences, where Knowledge is a synonym for Personal Experience or Participation—some Good and some sinful.]

> And Adam knew Eve his wife; and she conceived, and bare Cain, and said, I have gotten a man from the Lord. (Holy Bible, Genesis 4:1 KJV)

> And out of the ground the LORD God made every tree grow that is pleasant to the sight and good for food. The tree of life was also in the midst of the garden, and the tree of the knowledge of good and evil. (Holy Bible, Genesis 2:9 KJV)

> But of the tree of the knowledge of good and evil, thou shalt not eat of it: for in the day that thou eatest thereof thou shalt surely die. (*Holy Bible, Genesis 2:17 KJV*)

[*GOD—The Dimensional Revelation* Teaches that Knowledge may be the Cognition of facts about a subject or procedures detailing how to do something.

Cognition of facts corresponds to Observing something or Reasoning To A Justified Conclusion about what it is, based upon Observations. If we Know the words and their relationships, we have this type of Knowledge.

Personal Knowledge can be more involved. Personal Knowledge requires an Act. Such Act Is Participation In The Unfolding Of An Event. This type of Knowledge is Creative based on Choices, Procedures, and the Actions resulting from Choices in the 5th Dimension.

It is a Choice to have Personal Experience with evil. Of this tree, thou shalt not eat. Whether evil is caused by another spirit or yourself, if you experience evil and choose to participate in evil, knowing it and choosing it over the Good, that choice and that evil destroys Spiritual Energy. Stated another way, When Positive Spiritual Energy Is Circulated By You, You Are Realized Immortal. When you experience/know/choose negative spiritual energy, you die spiritually. Whether or not that death is permanent depends on your subsequent Choices As It May Please The LORD.

"See-no-evil, Hear-no-evil, Think-no-evil, Do-no-evil" is not a naive attitude which ignores reality. It Is A Defense against annihilation of Spirit.]

[1p] Spiritual: Relating to or affecting the human spirit or soul as opposed to material or physical things (*Oxford English Dictionary*).

[Also See [2u].]

[1q] Category: A class or division in a scheme of classification; any sort of division or class; a general class of ideas, terms, or things that mark divisions or coordination within a conceptual scheme, especially

- Aristotle's modes of objective being, such as quality, quantity, or relation, that are inherent in everything;
- Kant's modes of subjective understanding, such as singularity, universality, or particularity, that organize perceptions into knowledge;
- a basic logical type of philosophical conception in post-Kantian philosophy (yourdictionary.com).

[1r] Nonphysical: In ontology and the philosophy of mind, a nonphysical entity is a spirit or being that exists outside physical reality (*Katalin Balog, "Phenomenal Concepts," 2009*).

[1s] Other: Denoting a person or thing that is different or distinct from one already mentioned or known about (*Oxford English Dictionary*).

[1t] analysis: detailed examination of the elements or structure of something (*Oxford English Dictionary*).

[1u] Divine: Of or relating to a god, especially the Supreme Being (*www.dictionary.com*).

[1v] GOD: GOD may be viewed in process as the SOURCE that is the origin or cause of everything (*Oxford English Dictionary*).

The incorporeal divine Principle ruling over all as eternal Spirit: infinite Mind (*www.merriam-webster.com*).

One having power and authority over others... Even to destroy (*www.merriam-webster.com*).

[*GOD—The Dimensional Revelation* Holds That Ultimately, GOD is undivided as the ONE, implying the complete and all-inclusive Being of GOD.]

> The LORD thy God is one LORD. (*Holy Bible, Deuteronomy 6:4 KJV*)

> Hear, O Israel: The Lord is our God; the Lord is one. (*The written Torah, Devarim-Deuteronomy 6:4*)

> The first of all the commandments is, Hear, O Israel; The Lord our God is one Lord: And thou shalt love the Lord thy God with all thy heart, and with all thy soul, and with all thy mind, and with all thy strength: this is the first commandment. And the second is like, namely this, thou shalt love thy neighbor as thyself. (*Holy Bible, Mark 12:29–34 NIV*)

RESEARCH NOTES, CREDITS, AND EXPANSIONS

The standing view in Hasidism currently, is that there is nothing in existence outside of God—all being is within God, and yet all of existence cannot contain him. Regarding this, Solomon stated while dedicating the Temple, "But will God in truth dwell with mankind on the earth? Behold, the heaven and the heaven of heavens cannot contain You" (*Divrei HaYamim Bet, pereq Vav, 2 Chronicles 6*).

For Plotinus, a third century "neo-platonic" philosopher of Egypt, the first principle of reality is "the One", an utterly simple, ineffable, unknowable subsistence which is both the creative source and the teleological end of all existing things. Although, properly speaking, there is no name appropriate for the first principle, the most adequate names are "the One" or "the Good". The One is so simple that it cannot even be said to exist or to be a being. Rather, the creative principle of all things is beyond being, a notion which is derived from Plato's Republic (*Book 4 of The Republic*); (E. R. Dodds, "The Parmenides of Plato and the Origin of the Neoplatonic 'One,'" The Classical Quarterly, vol. 22 [July–October 1928], 136).

[*GOD—The Dimensional Revelation* Establishes logical proof that regardless of the many Manifestations Of GOD, All Of Reality Emanates From This Unified Being.]

> I am in love with every church and mosque and temple and any kind of shrine because I know it is there that people say the different names of the One God. (*Hafiz*)

> Ask of those who have attained God; all speak the same word. All the saints are of one mind; it is only those in the midst of the way who follow diverse paths. All the enlightened have left one message; it is only those in the midst of their journey who hold diverse opinions. (*Dadu, sixteenth-century Indian saint*)

[The Theology Revealed in *GOD—The Dimensional Revelation* Is That GOD Includes All. Understanding GOD As The Creator, only The ONE Is Ontologically Basic or Prior To All Else. Also, Described On The Continuum As LORD Of All implying the Sustaining, Which Is The Continuing Presence of GOD.

GOD—The Dimensional Revelation Humbly Reaffirms That GOD Is Great. One Aspect Of GOD Is To Manifest as Differentiated Spiritual Beings In Differentiated Universes.

GOD Manifests As The Father, The SOURCE, Separate and Eternal. GOD Manifested As The Son, The Teacher Of Compassion and Truth Among Humans. GOD Manifests As The Holy Spirit, Divine Energy That Enters The Souls Of The Living and Shares The Diverse Wonders Of Being.

Stated in another Tradition, GOD Manifests As Brahma, The Creator, Instructor Of Form To Be, and The Formless. Vishnu Is Manifested As The Preserver

Of Beings, things, and Processes. Shiva Manifests To Reclaim All Manifestations Into ONE Great LORD.]

[1w] Creation (*noun*): something that has been made or brought into existence (*www.yourdictonary.com*).

To Create or Creating (*verb*): the act of producing or causing to exist; the act of creating, engendering.

The Creation, the original bringing into existence of the universe by God (*dictionary.com*).

[1x] Manifestation (*noun*): A manifestation of something is one of the different ways in which it can appear (*Collins English Dictionary*).

The materialization of a True Idea; The coming forth into visibility of that which has been affirmed (*https://www.truthunity.net/rw/manifestation*).

Manifest (*verb*): [To create or bring into Reality.]

The Latin origin of the word *manifest, manifestus*, literally meant "caught in the act." Something described as manifest is clear and unmistakable (https://vocabulary-vocabulary.com/dictionary/ manifest.php).

Manifest or Manifested (*adjective*): obvious, apparent, clear, unmistakable, evident (*https://vocabulary-vocabulary.com/ dictionary/manifest.php*).

> We see all this with the piercing eyes of mind, nor can we fail to be taught by means of such a spectacle that a Divine power, working with skill and method, is manifesting itself in this actual world, and, penetrating each portion, combines those portions with the whole and completes the whole by the portions, and encompasses the universe with a single all-controlling force, self-centred and self-contained, never ceasing from its motion, yet never altering the position which it holds. (*Saint Gregory of Nyssa, On the Soul and Ressurrection, 432*) (*https://www.ccel.org/ccel/schaff/ npnf205.x.iii.ii.html*)

[*GOD—The Dimensional Revelation* Uses the word *Manifest* and its derivatives as an Expansion of the subjects of Creation and the Bringing Of All Items Into Reality. It is used as a noun, *Manifestation*; verb, *To Manifest*; or adjective, *Manifest*.

All Items In Reality Are Manifestations Of GOD. Used as a verb, *To Manifest* Is The Action Of The Machinery Of Creation In The 9th Dimension To Create this or that. Deriving from the Latin "caught in the act," *To Manifest* Is A Clear Understanding of quantum "becoming." The "manifestation," being what is "observed," hence collapsed into Reality.

More deeply, Reality is a Continuum, not a momentary, static snapshot. To be "caught in the act" describes a present position but implies future action arising out of dynamic "continuous" reality.]

RESEARCH NOTES, CREDITS, AND EXPANSIONS

[This Teaching, Positing The 9th Dimension As The Machinery Of Creation, is original to *GOD—The Dimensional Revelation* To Answer The Question, "What Is An Act Of Creation?"]

[1y] Theology: The study of religious faith, practice, and experience; especially: the study of God and of God's relation to the world (*www.merriam-webster.com*).

[*GOD—The Dimensional Revelation* Reveals Our Theology That The ONE, LORD, GOD Is A Large GOD—That is, GOD Created All Reality. Aspects Of GOD Sustain every Manifestation In Reality Through The WORD In The 10th Dimension. Ultimately, GOD Will Terminate Aspects Of Reality—or not—As It May Please GOD.

GOD May Choose To Share In Your Consciousness, Through A Direct Metastring Connection, As Your Personal GOD. You Are A Sliver or Spark Of The Divine, Differentiated From GOD, To Be an Instrument Of GOD's Participation in physical reality. Your Highest Calling Is To Expand This Connection Toward Reunification With GOD.]

[1z] Observe or Observation To see, watch, perceive, or notice (*www.dictionary.com*).

[Observation is the active acquisition of information from a primary source. In living beings, Observation employs the senses. In science, observation can also involve the perception and recording of data via the use of scientific instruments. The term may also refer to any data collected during the scientific activity. Observations can be qualitative—that is, only the absence or presence of a property is noted—or quantitative if a numerical value is attached to the observed phenomenon by counting or measuring.

Observation, in philosophical terms, is the process of filtering sensory information through the thought process. Input is received via hearing, sight, smell, taste, or touch and then analyzed through either rational or irrational thought.

Human senses are limited and subject to errors in perception, such as optical illusions or preconceived expectations or processing biases. Scientific instruments were developed to aid human abilities of observation—such as weighing scales, clocks, telescopes, microscopes, thermometers, cameras, and tape recorders—and also translate into perceptible-form events that are unobservable by the senses, such as indicator dyes, voltmeters, spectrometers, infrared cameras, oscilloscopes, interferometers, Geiger counters, and radio receivers.

Continued below regarding Participation.]

[1z1] Participation: the action or state of taking part in something (*www.merriam-webster.com*).

> Don't you know that you yourselves are God's temple and that
> God's Spirit dwells in your midst? (*Holy Bible, 1 Corinthians 3:16*)

GOD—THE DIMENSIONAL REVELATION

> And I will ask the Father, and he will give you another advocate to help you and be with you forever. (*Holy Bible, 1 John 14:16*)

Yes, the great higher brain was created for God, I AM THAT I AM, to inhabit and enjoy the fruits and beauties of the world through the physical body… The secret is meditation upon Christ, I AM THAT I AM. Christ consciousness will anoint and descend upon the meditating soul within the dual sacred spirals, sacred vortexes of white fire. This is the baptism of fire. These dual forces of power descend through and around the door on the crown of the head, and move toward the heart center, to meet the meditator's ascending life forces (*https://sunburst.org/god-is-pure-consciousness*) (*Norman Paulsen, February 3, 2020*).

This illustration is Offered to depict You As the Image of Christ, Elevated by Christ Consciousness, The Light, Blossoming At The Crown Of Your Head, The Third Eye, and Your Heart Centers Chakras.

Bianca Alexander, *Resurrecting the Universal Christ Consciousness*

[*GOD—The Dimensional Revelation* Presents an original Expansion of the word *Participation* To Reveal That GOD Participates Directly In Your Life Through Your Consciousness.

The Purpose Of Your Existence Is To Be An Instrument Of GOD, Allowing The LORD To Participate in Your Human Life on earth Through Your Senses, Perceptions, and Feelings. While Observation may be totally separate from Participation, Observation Encourages The Observer To Participate.]

RESEARCH NOTES, CREDITS, AND EXPANSIONS

Consider how this develops in the following *Wikipedia* text:

> One problem encountered throughout scientific fields is that the observation may affect the process being observed, resulting in a different outcome than if the process was unobserved. This is called the observer effect. For example, it is not normally possible to check the air pressure in an automobile tire without participating to let out some of the air, thereby changing the pressure. However, in most fields of science it is possible to reduce the observer effect by using better instruments.
>
> Considered as a physical process itself, all forms of observation (human or instrumental) involve amplification and are thus thermodynamically irreversible processes, increasing entropy (disorganization).
>
> In some specific fields of science, the results of observation differ depending on factors which are not important in everyday observation. These are usually illustrated with "paradoxes" in which an event appears different when observed from two different points of view, seeming to violate "common sense."
>
> Relativity: In relativistic physics, which deals with velocities close to the speed of light, it is found that different observers may observe different values for the length, time rates, mass, and many other properties of an object, depending on the observer's velocity relative to the object. For example, in the twin paradox one twin goes on a trip near the speed of light and comes home younger than the twin who stayed at home. This is not a paradox: time passes at a slower rate when measured from a frame moving with respect to the object. In relativistic physics, an observation must always be qualified by specifying the state of motion of the observer, its reference frame.
>
> Quantum mechanics: In quantum mechanics, which deals with the behavior of very small objects, it is not possible to observe a system without changing the system, and the *observer* must be considered part of the system being observed. In isolation, quantum objects are represented by a wave function, which often exists in a superposition or mixture of different states. However, when an *observation* is made to determine the actual location or state of the object, it always finds the object in a single state, not a "mixture." The interaction of the *observation* process appears to "collapse" the wave function into a single state, so any interaction between an isolated wave function and the external world that

results in this wave-function collapse is called an *observation* or measurement, whether or not it is part of a deliberate observation process. (*en.wikipedia.org*)

[*GOD—The Dimensional Revelation* Uses the word *Observation* primarily As Ordinary Observation. In Ordinary Observation, You, GOD, Any Other Living Observer or instrument Witness events from an uninvolved perspective.

observation in quantum mechanics, as described above, is "Participation" as used in Our Teaching. This is an important distinction As GOD May View or Observe GOD's Creation From An Impartial Perspective.

GOD May Also Choose To Participate In Reality Through Your Consciousness or Other Means. Current quantum theory is describing A 9th-Dimensional Synthesis, where the Ordinary observer Collapses A Possibility Into Reality. The Observer Becomes The Participant in quantum *observation*. This Is One Aspect Of Creation.

Some of quantum theory is very confused about the "collapse of a wave function into a single state." Reality is continuous, so the "observation" of a "single state" is a fiction that allows the mathematics to work in the "renormalization" process, purported to reconcile quantum mechanics with general relativity. Our Teaching will prove that only the Introduction Of The Will Of GOD can reconcile quantum mechanics with general relativity. There are no "isolated" wave functions. Wave functions are all continuous and not segmented.]

[1z2] Dimensional Reasoning: In math and engineering, the most basic rule of dimensional analysis is that of dimensional homogeneity. Only commensurable quantities (physical quantities having the same dimension) may be compared, equated, added, or subtracted. For example, it makes no sense to ask whether 1 hour is more, the same, or less than 1 kilometre, as these have different dimensions, nor to add 1 hour to 1 kilometre. However, it makes perfect sense to ask whether 1 mile is more, the same, or less than 1 kilometre being the same dimension of physical quantity even though the units are different. On the other hand, if an object travels 100 km in 2 hours, one may divide these and conclude that the object's average speed was 50 km/h (*John Cimbala and Yunus Çengel "§7-2 Dimensional Homogeneity." Essential of Fluid Mechanics: Fundamentals and Applications, [McGraw-Hill, 2006], 203, ISBN 9780073138350]*).

Two main themes are considered: dimensional analysis, which involves deriving algebraic expressions to relate quantities based on their dimensions; and dimensional reasoning, a more general and often more subtle approach to problem solving (*C. Bissell and C. Dillon [Eds.], Ways of Thinking, Ways of Seeing, ACES 1, (Springer-Verlag Berlin Heidelberg, 2012), 29–45, springerlink.com*).

[*GOD—The Dimensional Revelation* expands Bissel's engineering view of dimensional reasoning. This Expansion is to Examine the broader cause-and-effect relationships with the understanding of the operational principles of each dimension. This Reasoning yields solutions to nearly every question.]

[1z3] validate or validation: The action of checking or proving the validity or accuracy of something. The technique requires validation in controlled trials (*Oxford English Dictionary*).

Internal validity is the extent to which a piece of evidence supports a claim about cause and effect, within the context of a particular study. It is one of the most important properties of scientific studies, and is an important concept in reasoning about evidence more generally. Internal validity is determined by how well a study can rule out alternative explanations for its findings (usually, sources of systematic error or 'bias'). It contrasts with external validity, the extent to which results can justify conclusions about other contexts (that is, the extent to which results can be generalized). Inferences are said to possess internal validity if a causal relationship between two variables is properly demonstrated (*M. Brewer, Research Design and Issues of Validity in H. Reis and C. Judd [eds.] Handbook of Research Methods in Social and Personality Psychology [Cambridge: Cambridge University Press, 2000); (W. Shadish, T. Cook, and D. Campbell, Experimental and Quasi-Experimental Designs for Generalized Causal Inference [Boston: Houghton Mifflin, 2002]*).

[1z4] Religious Experience: Experience is the observing, encountering, or undergoing of things generally as they occur in the course of time (*www.dictionary.com*).

Religious experiences can be characterized generally as experiences that seem to the person having them to be of some objective reality and to have some religious import (*https://plato.stanford.edu/entries/religious-experience/*).

[1z5] dogma: a fixed, especially religious, belief or set of beliefs that people are expected to accept without any doubts (*Cambridge Academic Content Dictionary*, Cambridge University Press).

[1z6] Belief: a mental attitude of acceptance or assent toward a proposition without the full intellectual knowledge required to guarantee its truth. www.britannica.com.

[1z7] unbelief: *Unbelief* means "lack of faith." *Disbelief* means "the feeling of not being able to believe that something is true or has happened" (*www.quora.com*).

[1z8] Perspective: a particular attitude toward or way of regarding something, a point of view (*Oxford English Dictionary*).

[1z9] Understanding: Understanding is a psychological process related to an abstract or physical object—such as a person, situation, or message—whereby one is able to think about it and use concepts to deal adequately with that object. Understanding is a relation between the knower and an object of understanding (*Carl Bereiter, Education and Mind in the Knowledge Age, 2006*).

The knowledge and ability to judge a particular situation or subject, an informal agreement, a willingness to understand people's behavior and forgive them (*www.merriam-webster.com*).

Cognition refers to "the mental action or process of acquiring knowledge and understanding through thought, experience, and the senses" (*Oxford University Press*).

[1z10] Act or Action (*noun*): Something done or performed. (www.dictionary.com).

To Act (*verb*): The process of doing something (www.merriam-webster.com).

Action theory: Subfield of philosophy of mind that is especially important for ethics; it concerns the distinction between things that happen to a person and things one does or makes happen (www.britannica.com).

> As long as the mind has not reached supreme quiet, it cannot act. Action caused by momentum is random action, not essential action. Therefore, it is said that action influenced by things is human desire, while action uninfluenced by things is the action of Heaven. (*The Secret of the Golden Flower, 8:27, trans. Thomas Cleary [HarperCollins, 1991]*)

[1z11] here and now: The present (or here and now) is the time that is associated with the events perceived directly and in the first time (*E. C. Hegeler and P. Carus, The Monist, La Salle, Ill. [etc.], Published by Open Court for the Hegeler Institute, 1890, 443*) not as a recollection (perceived more than once) or a speculation (predicted, hypothesis, uncertain). It is a period of time between the past and the future and can vary in meaning from being an instant to a day or longer (en.wikipedia.org).

Christianity views God as being outside of time and, from the divine perspective past, present and future are actualized in the now of eternity. This trans-temporal conception of God has been proposed as a solution to the problem of divine foreknowledge (i.e., how can God know what we will do in the future without us being determined to do it?) (*Boethius, Consolatio Philosophae Book 4*).

Thomas Aquinas offers the metaphor of a watchman, representing God, standing on a height looking down on a valley to a road where past present and future, represented by the individuals and their actions strung out along its length, are all visible simultaneously to God (*Austin Cline, "God is Eternal—Timeless vs. Everlasting"*). Therefore, God's knowledge is not tied to any particular date (*William Irwin and Mark D. White, Watchmen and Philosophy: A Rorschach Test [John Wiley and Sons, 2009], 128*).

[1z12] Confidence: a feeling of self-assurance arising from one's appreciation of one's own abilities or qualities. *Oxford English Dictionary.*

[1z13] Personal Power: Personal Power is a kind of mental toughness that we bring to every situation. It's the ability to take decisive and deliberate action toward a desired goal, or down an optimal path that helps you accomplish that goal. Personal power is about living life intentionally with a sense of purpose and opti-

RESEARCH NOTES, CREDITS, AND EXPANSIONS

mism (*Adam Sicinski, "How to Develop The Personal Power Needed to Achieve Your Biggest Goals," 2005*).

> He who controls others may be powerful, but he who has mastered himself is mightier still. (*Lao Tzu*)

[1z14] Grace: the influence or spirit of God operating in humans to regenerate or strengthen them, a virtue or excellence of divine origin (*www.dictionary.com*).

A state of sanctification enjoyed through divine assistance (*www.merriam-webster.com*).

> The love and mercy given to us by God because God desires us to have it, not necessarily because of anything we have done to earn it. It is not a created substance of any kind. (*Communications, United Methodist, The United Methodist Church, retrieved April 6, 2019*)

> Grace is favour, the free and undeserved help that God gives us to respond to his call to become children of God, adoptive sons, partakers of the divine nature and of eternal life. (*Catechism of the Catholic Church [1996], www.vatican.va, retrieved April 6, 2019*)

Grace is a participation in the life of God, which is poured unearned into human beings, whom it heals of sin and sanctifies (*Catechism of the Catholic Church, 1997–1999*).

We confess together that all persons depend completely on the saving grace of God for their salvation. Justification takes place solely by God's grace (*The Lutheran World Federation and the Catholic Church, Joint Declaration on the Doctrine of Justification, 1994*).

Sustaining grace: Wesley believed that, after accepting God's grace, a person is to move on in God's sustaining grace toward perfection. Wesley did not believe in the "eternal security of the believer." He believed people can make wrong (sinful) choices that will cause them to "fall from grace" or "backslide" (*"God's Preparing, Accepting, and Sustaining Grace," archived copy [Official United Methodist Publication, September 7, 2009] archived from the original on January 9, 2008*).

[1z15] Theoretical physics: Theoretical physics is a branch of physics that employs mathematical models and abstractions of physical objects and systems to rationalize, explain and predict natural phenomena. This is in contrast to experimental physics, which uses experimental tools to probe these phenomena (*www.wikipedia.en*).

[1z16] quantum theory: A theory is a formal statement of the rules on which a subject of study is based or of ideas that are suggested to explain a fact or event or, more generally, an opinion or explanation (*https://dictionary.cambridge.org/*).

quantum theory is the theoretical basis of modern physics that explains the nature and behavior of matter and energy on the atomic and subatomic level. The nature and behavior of matter and energy at that level is sometimes referred to as quantum physics and quantum mechanics (*Margaret Rouse, October 2020, https://whatis.techtarget.com/definition/quantum-theory*).

[1z17] vibration or vibrations: A periodic motion of the particles of an elastic body or medium in alternately opposite directions from the position of equilibrium when that equilibrium has been disturbed; oscillation or quivering motion (*www.meirriam-webster.com*).

A characteristic emanation, aura, or spirit that infuses or vitalizes someone or something and that can be instinctively sensed or experienced—often used in plural (vibrations) (*www.merriam-webster.com*).

All things in our universe are constantly in motion, vibrating. Even objects that appear to be stationary are in fact vibrating, oscillating, resonating at various frequencies. Ultimately all matter is just vibrations of various underlying fields. As such, at every scale, all of nature vibrates (*Tam Hunt, University of California–Santa Barbara*).

Resonance is a type of motion, characterized by oscillation between two states (*Tam Hunt, University of California–Santa Barbara, November 13, 2018*).

[*GOD—The Dimensional Revelation* is clear that if "vibration" is defined as oscillation of energy at frequencies, then it implies the dimension of "time." "time" is a characteristic of the physical membrane system. Hence, if a vibration has frequency, then it is a physical event occurring in a physical universe.

By contrast, if *Vibration* is used as a synonym for *Resonance*, where Resonance Is An Enhancement Of Spirit or A Spiritual Fusion, then Vibration can be Part Of A Larger Reality That Emanates From GOD.] See [5z11].

[1z18] Presence: the state or fact of existing, occurring, or being present in a place or thing (*Oxford English Dictionary*).

[2a] point: Points are considered fundamental objects in Euclidean geometry. They have been defined in a variety of ways, including Euclid's definition as 'that which has no part (*Audun Holme, Geometry: Our Cultural Heritage [Springer Science and Business Media, September 23, 2010], 254, ISBN 978-3-642-14441-7*).

A graphical illustration of a nildimensional space is a point (*Luke Wolcott and Elizabeth McTernan, "Imagining Negative-Dimensional Space" PDF, Proceedings of Bridges 2012: Mathematics, Music, Art, Architecture, Culture, edited by Robert Bosch, Douglas McKenna, and Reza Sarhangi, Phoenix, Arizona, USA: Tessellations Publishing, 2012], 637–642, retrieved July 10, 2015*).

RESEARCH NOTES, CREDITS, AND EXPANSIONS

[2b] line: A line is a one-dimensional figure, which has length but no width. A line made of a set of points which is extended in opposite directions infinitely (*byjus.com*).

A line segment is a part of a line that is bounded by two distinct end points and contains every point on the line between its end points. Depending on how the line segment is defined, either of the two end points may or may not be part of the line segment (*en.wikipedia.org*).

[2c] plane: A level or flat surface. (geometry) A flat surface extending infinitely in all directions (*wiktionary.com*).

A plane is a flat, two-dimensional surface that extends infinitely far (*Euclid's Elements—All Thirteen Books in One Volume, based on Heath's translation, Green Lion Press, ISBN 1-888009-18-7*).

In Euclidian three-dimensional space, a first degree equation in the variables x, y, and z defines a plane (*en.wikipedia.org*).

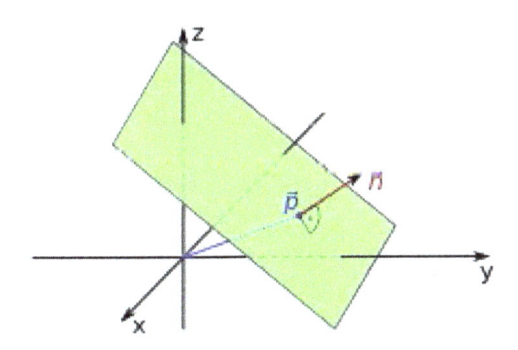

In philosophy, a plane is A level of existence or development (*wiktionary.com*)

[2d] to form (*verb*): bring together parts or combine to create (something).

form (*noun*): a particular way in which a thing exists or appears, a manifestation (*Oxford English Dictionary*).

A type of something; way something appears or exists (*www.macmillandictionary.com*).

Plato's (427–347 BCE) theory of forms, developed in a number of his dialogues.

It is expressed that various imperfect individual horses in the physical world could be identified as horses because they participated in the static atemporal and aspatial "idea" of "horseness" in the world of ideas or forms (*Phaedo, Phaedrus, Symposium, Timaeus, Republic*).

[*GOD—The Dimensional Revelation* Reaffirms the Platonic Ideal that Man, Created In The Image Of GOD, Is The Most Significant Application of Platonic "Forms."

GODness In Human Beings Is what it means To Be Created In The Image, or Form, Of GOD. A Human Being is not GOD, but Your Divine Spirit Is In The Form or Ideal Of GOD.]

Also see, [5z56] and [6z36].

[2e] object: A thing that has physical existence. From Latin obiectum ("object", literally "thrown against") (*en.wiktionary.org*).

[2f] position (*noun*): a place where someone or something is located or has been put; a particular way in which someone or something is placed or arranged.

position (*verb*): put or arrange (someone or something) in a particular place or way (*Oxford English Dictionary*).

[2g] solid: having relative firmness, coherence of particles, or persistence of form, as matter that is not liquid or gaseous (*www.dictionary.com*).

Solid figures are three-dimensional figures that have length, width, and height (*basic-mathematics.com*).

See Illustration 27.

Various solid figures (three-dimensional figures) include cubes, spheres, pyramids, prisms, other polyhedrons, cylinders, cones, truncated cones, ellipsoids, hyperboloids, and balls bounded by spheres.

[2h] liquid: a substance that flows freely but is of constant volume, having a consistency like that of water or oil.

Quantities of liquids are measured in units of volume. These include the SI unit cubic metre (m^3) and its divisions, in particular the cubic decimeter, more commonly called the litre (1 dm^3 = 1 L = 0.001 m^3), and the cubic centimetre, also called millilitre (1 c m^3 = 1 mL = 0.001 L = 10–6 m^3) (*Randall D. Knight, Physics for Scientists and Engineers: A Strategic Approach, 2008*).

The volume of a quantity of liquid is fixed by its temperature and pressure. Liquids generally expand when heated and contract when cooled. Water between 0 °C and 4 °C is a notable exception (*Martin S. Silberberg, Chemistry: The Molecular Nature of Matter and Change [McGraw-Hill Higher Education, 2009], 461*).

Liquids have little compressibility. Water, for example, will compress by only 46.4 parts per million for every unit increase in atmospheric pressure (bar) (*"Compressibility of Liquids," hyperphysics.phy-astr.gsu.edu, archived from the original on December 7, 2017*).

[2i] gas: Gaseous matter is composed of particles packed so loosely that it has neither a defined shape nor a defined volume (*courses.luminlearning.com*).

A pure gas may be made up of individual atoms (e.g., a noble gas like neon), elemental molecules made from one type of atom (e.g. oxygen), or compound molecules made from a variety of atoms (e.g. carbon dioxide). A gas mixture, such as air, contains a variety of pure gases (en.wikipedia.org).

The gaseous state of matter occurs between the liquid and plasma states (*American Chemical Society, Faraday Society, Chemical Society (Great Britain), The Journal of Physical Chemistry, volume 11 [Cornel, 1907], 137*).

[Gasses] consist of a vast number of molecules moving chaotically in all directions and colliding with one another and with the walls of their container. Beyond this, there is no structure—the molecules are distributed essentially randomly in space, traveling in arbitrary directions at speeds that are distributed randomly about an average determined by the gas temperature (*www.britannica.com*).

[2j] plasma: Plasma is a state of matter in which an ionized gaseous substance becomes highly electrically conductive to the point that long-range electric and magnetic fields dominate the behaviour of the matter. The plasma state can be contrasted with the other states: solid, liquid, and gas (*Francis F. Chen, Introduction to Plasma Physics and Controlled Fusion [Springer International Publishing, 1984], 2–3); (Jeffrey P. Freidberg, Plasma Physics and Fusion Energy [Cambridge University Press, 2008], 121*).

It is assumed that more than 99% the visible universe is made of some form of plasma (*D. A. Gurnett and A. Bhattacharjee, Introduction to Plasma Physics: With Space and Laboratory Applications [Cambridge, UK: Cambridge University Press, 2005], 2, ISBN 978-0-521-36483-6); (K. Scherer, H. Fichtner, and B. Heber, 2005*).

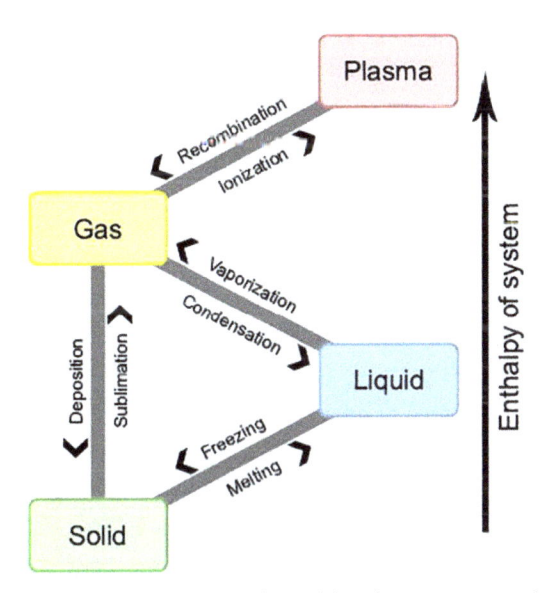

Toliño—Flanker Penubag derivative work; public domain via Wikimedia Commons

[2k] radiation: radiation is the emission or transmission of energy in the form of waves or particles through space or through a material medium (*Eric W. Weisstein, "Radiation," Eric Weisstein's World of Physics, Wolfram Research*).

[2l] continuum: a set of elements such that between any two of them there is a third element (*dictionary.com*).

A continuous sequence in which adjacent elements are not perceptibly different from each other, although the extremes are quite distinct (*Oxford English Dictionary*).

[*GOD—The Dimensional Revelation* Emphasizes that Reality is Manifested as a continuum, not individual collapsed states. Also see [1z1] above.]

[2m] progression: a continuous and connected series (*www.merriam-webster.com*).

A passage or movement from one note or chord to another (*Oxford English Dictionary*).

[*GOD—The Dimensional Revelation* notes that though the Richness and Harmonious characteristics of music are a good analogy to those of Spiritual Experience, the progression of music has rests or other stops and endings. Reality has no gaps or stops, just changes. Also See [1z1] and [2l] above.]

[2n] change (*verb*): change, alter, vary, modify to make or become different. change implies making either an essential difference, often amounting to a loss of original identity or a substitution of one thing for another (*www.merriam-webster.com*).

change (*noun*): the act or instance of making or becoming different (*Oxford English Dictionary*).

[2o] Continuous: without a pause or interruption (dictionary.cambridge.org).

[*GOD—The Dimensional Revelation* Emphasizes the distinction between "continuous" and "incremental" or "segmented." To Understand Reality, Human Beings tend to divide it into sections, segments, increments, or moments. We will explore how segmenting reality allows mathematics to represent this or that manifestation or allows our memory to visualize the past. However, these segments or bundles lead to false theories as to how Reality Proceeds and What is actually Manifested. Reality Proceeds Continuously.

Proof That Reality Is Continuous and not segmented is that You can segment the Same Reality in many different increments or ways to serve this organization of situations or a different organization of situations. These different segmentations may be inconsistent with one another. So which is real? The Truth Is That neither of those perspectives of reality is the Entire Reality, so each can be misleading. This points out that any splitting of Continuous Reality into segments is a construct of Mind, not entirely grasping Reality. Also See [1z1] and [2l] above.]

[2p] Choice or Choices: The act of picking or deciding between two or more possibilities. the opportunity or power to choose between two or more possibilities: the opportunity or power to make a decision: a range of things that can be chosen (*www.merriam-webster.com*).

Brian Tracy distinguishes five main types of choices: command decisions, which can only be made by you.

1. command decision, which can only be made by you
2. Delegated decisions, which may be made by another
3. Avoided decisions in which you are removed from the sequence
4. "No-brainer" decisions, where the choice is so obvious that only one choice can reasonably be made
5. Collaborative Decisions in which a group comes to a consensus and a choice is prescribed (Barry Schwartz, *The Paradox of Choice*, 2004)

RESEARCH NOTES, CREDITS, AND EXPANSIONS

[2q] Decision: a conclusion or resolution reached after consideration. *Oxford English Dictionary.*

Another way of looking at decisions focuses on the thought mechanism used—whether the decision is:

a. Rational [cognition, ego-based choice]
b. Intuitive [conscience, Spirit-based choice]
c. Recognition-based [experience, super-ego based choice]
d. Combination. (*"Types of Decision-Making—An Overview,"* decision-making-confidence.com).

[2r] proximity: nearness in space, time, or relationship. *Oxford English Dictionary.*
[2s] Affect: have an effect on; make a difference to. *Oxford English Dictionary.*
[2t] Each Other: used to refer to each member of a group when each does something to or for other members (*Oxford English Dictionary*).
[2u] Spiritual Being:

> We are not human beings having a spiritual experience; we are spiritual beings having a human experience. (*Pierre Teilhard de Chardin*)

[*GOD—The Dimensional Revelation* Reminds Us That Spiritual Being Is That Part or Aspect Of GOD That Is Differentiated From The ONE That Has Existence and Consciousness Independently From GOD. A Connection Remains Through The Divine Metastring Connection To GOD. Experience and Divine Energy Can Be Shared With GOD—or not—As A Bilateral Choice.]

[2v] Situation: The combination of circumstances at a given moment; a state of affairs (*en.wiktionary.org*).

[*GOD—The Dimensional Revelation* Reveals that since the continuum of events cannot be measured or described fully, Human Perception requires an artificial segmenting of Reality to provide a description that can be Communicated and Understood. A segment of Reality is a construction of Mind that may be called a situation. Again, such segments are only a description of a past situation, as the Present Is Continuous and cannot be segmented. A future situation can be envisioned but is undetermined until it happens.]

[2w] Fused or Fusion: Fusion, or synthesis, is the process of combining two or more distinct entities into a new whole (*collinsdictionary.com*).

[The Fundamental Teaching of *GOD—The Dimensional Revelation* Is That The Reality Human Beings Live Is A Temporary Fusion Of Our Independent Spiritual Universe with our independent physical universe.]

[2x] Leap: a jump from one point to another or a sudden or large movement or transition (*www.yourdictionary.com*).

[2y] chaos: When the present determines the future but the approximate present does not approximately determine the future. (*Christopher M. Danforth, "Chaos in an Atmosphere Hanging on a Wall," April 2013*).

The "butterfly effect": A very small change in initial conditions had created a significantly different outcome. This description of chaos theory is closely associated with the work of Edward Lorenz, is derived from the metaphorical example of the details of a tornado (the exact time of formation, the exact path taken) being influenced by minor perturbations such as the flapping of the wings of a distant butterfly several weeks earlier. Lorenz discovered the effect when he observed that runs of his weather model with initial condition data that were rounded in a seemingly inconsequential manner would fail to reproduce the results of runs with the unrounded initial condition data (*Edward N. Lorenz, "Deterministic Nonperiodic Flow," Journal of the Atmospheric Sciences 20 [2] [March 1963], 130–141*).

[2z] uncertainty: Uncertainty refers to epistemic situations involving imperfect or unknown information. It applies to predictions of future events, to physical measurements that are already made, or to the unknown. Uncertainty arises in partially observable and/or stochastic [random] environments, as well as due to ignorance, indolence, or both. It arises in any number of fields, including insurance, philosophy, physics, statistics, economics, finance, psychology, sociology, engineering, metrology, meteorology, ecology and information science (*Peter Norvig and Sebastian Thrun, "Introduction to Artificial Intelligence"*).

[2z1] ordinary: with no special or distinctive features; normal. what is commonplace or standard (*Oxford English Dictionary*).

[2z2] limitation: a limiting rule or circumstance; a restriction (*Oxford English Dictionary*).

[2z3] occur or occurrence: happen, take place, exist or be found to be present in a place or under a particular set of conditions, come into the mind (*Oxford English Dictionary*).

[2z4] Our familiar universe: [*GOD—The Dimensional Revelation* is the first work we know of that uses this phrase to mean that our physical universe {potentially more than one physical universe in the physical membrane system} Is A Fusion With Our Spiritual Universe {potentially more than one Spiritual Universe in the Spiritual Membrane System}. It Is only "Familiar" because This Is The Reality Within Which Each Of Us Is Conscious. It Is A very strange Reality given the usual limitations on physical being apart from Spiritual Being. We Are Certain Of only one Example Of This Fusion. That Is Life On earth. That Certainty Is Proved by independently verifiable, empirical evidence.]

[2z5] sequential multiverse: The many-worlds interpretation goes like this: The thought experiment of Schrödinger's cat, a potential animal who lives in a closed

box. The act of opening the box allows us to follow one of the possible future histories of this cat, including one in which it is both dead and alive. The reason this seems so impossible is simply because human intuition is not familiar with it. But it is entirely possible according to the rules of quantum mechanics. The reason that this can happen is that the space of possibilities in quantum mechanics is huge. Mathematically, a quantum mechanical state is a sum, or superposition, of all possible states. In the case of Schrödinger's cat, the cat is the superposition of "dead" and "alive" potential states of this cat before you open the box to observe its condition. But how do we interpret this to make any practical sense at all? One popular way is to think of all these possibilities as book-keeping devices so that the only "objectively true" cat state is the one we observe (*en.wikipedia.org*).

[This is what *GOD—The Dimensional Revelation* firmly supports as the current Reality collapsed into Being in the 8th Dimension. Furthermore, it is our assertion that Schrödinger's cat would be either dead or Alive whether Anyone Observes it or not.]

However, one can just as well choose to accept that all these possibilities are true and that they exist in different [parallel] universes of a multiverse (*en.wikipedia.org*).

[The theory of parallel universes is what *GOD—The Dimensional Revelation* proves to be rejected. While all possibilities are true potentially, time forces one to occur. At that time, all previous potential realities cease to exist, and the current situation sets the stage for all future possibilities. Multiple verification techniques—including instrumental, mathematical, observational, and Participatory—prove that the Our Familiar Universe is not an illusion but Exists As a sequential multiverse as We have Presented It.]

[2z6] Membrane System: ["Membrane System" is a concept originated in *GOD—The Dimensional Revelation* to define the reality of each separate system of being. We call each system a "membrane system" to mean that each is a complete system with a boundary or limit within which its operational principles manifest reality. Each membrane system is completely operational and is totally independent of every other membrane system.]

[Derived from] *membrane*: A membrane is a selective barrier; it allows some things to pass through but stops others. Such things may be molecules, ions, or other small particles (*M. Cheryan, Ultrafiltration and Microfiltration Handbook [Lancaster, PA: Echonomic Publishing Co. Inc., 1998]*).

System: a regularly interacting or interdependent group of items forming a unified whole (*www.merriam-webster.com*).

[2z7] physical membrane system: [a "physical membrane system" is a concept originated in *GOD—The Dimensional Revelation* to encompass all of physical reality (cosmos). That would include our universe of matter and its attendant energies that are of physical composition and processes. It would also include all other physical universes. These would be all universes that originated from a big bang and oper-

ate under the principles of quantum mechanics, relativity, time, inertia, the strong atomic force, the weak atomic force, electromagnetism, and gravity.

Consciousness does not Originate in the physical membrane system. Consciousness is not an operational principle of the physical membrane system.]

[2z8] Spiritual Membrane System or Membrane System of Spirit: [The "Spiritual Membrane System" is a concept originated in *GOD—The Dimensional Revelation* To Define All Of Spiritual Reality. That includes all Realms With Spiritual Presence. Every Individual Spirit Is A Separate Being, Differentiated From The ONE, GOD, LORD Of All. Different Universes or Realms Of Spirit May Operate Differently From One Another, but They All Have Individual Spirits With Consciousness Derived From GOD.

Time, Space, matter, and the other operational principles of physical universes are not operational principles of The Spiritual Membrane System.

We Observe both Consciousness and matter Existing In One Being. That Is The Result Of The WORD Instructing A Partial Fusion Of Two Different Universes Operating Within Two Different Membrane Systems. That Fusion Is Generated In The 9th Dimension and Is Manifested In the lower dimensions.]

[2z9] physical being: involving the body as distinguished from the mind or spirit (*www.vocabulary.com*).

[2z10] Mechanism: a natural or established process by which something takes place or is brought about (*Oxford English Dictionary*).

> And there are diversities of operations, but it is the same God which worketh all in all. (1 Corinthians 12:6 KJV)

> The words "focus on the center" are most sublime. The center is omnipresent; the whole universe is within it. This indicates the mechanism of Creation… (*The Secret of the Golden Flower 3:15, trans. Thomas Cleary [HarperCollins, 1991]*)

[*GOD—The Dimensional Revelation* Reveals That All Of Reality Is Created, Sustained, or Destroyed, Within The 9th Dimension. The WORD Of GOD Instructs That Manifest Realities Are To Be Created, Preserved, or Destroyed. The Mechanisms, also called The Machinery Of Creation, Operate In The 9th D To Manifest Reality In the lower dimensions.]

[2z11] Create or Created: Bring (something) into existence (*Oxford English Dictionary*).

[2z12] Merging or Fusing: to become combined into one (*www.merriam-webster.com*).

[2z13] grow or grown: become larger or greater over a period of time; increase (*Oxford English Dictionary*).

RESEARCH NOTES, CREDITS, AND EXPANSIONS

[2z14] Life: the existence of an individual human being or animal (*Oxford English Dictionary*).

the quality that distinguishes a vital and functional being from a dead body (*www.merriam-webster.com*).

[We would add "Plants" to this definition of Living Beings.]

[2z15] Subtle: (of a mixture or effect) delicately complex and understated (*Oxford English Dictionary*).

[2z16] WORD:

> In the beginning was the Word, and the Word was with God, and the Word was God. (*Holy Bible, John 1:1 NIV*)

> The Word became flesh and made his dwelling among us. We have seen his glory, the glory of the one and only Son, who came from the Father, full of grace and truth. (*Holy Bible, John 1:14 NIV*)

[*GOD—The Dimensional Revelation* Reveals That The WORD Is The Divine Instructions Of GOD, The 10th Dimension, Which Transmits Divine Information To Cause All Of Reality. The Instructions and Information Given By GOD to Create, Sustain, and Destroy Realities Is Also Known As The "Law" see[13z121]]

[2z17] Information or Divine Information: [*GOD—The Dimensional Revelation* Reveals That Reality Is The WORD Of The 10th D Continuously Flowing As Instruction or Cause To Create Reality In The 9th D Along Channels called Metastrings That Manifest Reality In The 8th D and lower dimensions.

Divine Information Is fundamentally different from subject or data "information." Data information, as used in any language or computer program, is discrete bits or bundles of finite information that allows the digital system to compute or instructs the language to have a conclusion or definition. Divine Information is a Continuous Flow That cannot be Interrupted. Divine Information Is Manifested In A Manner that is only limited in Your Perspective by Your Capabilities As An Observer.]

Information is stimuli that has meaning in some context for its receiver (*TechTarget, Data Visualization 2020*).

[*GOD—The Dimensional Revelation* Clarifies some specific and common uses of the word *information* as data sets in physics, mathematics, symbolic logic, biology, economy, epistemology, linguistics, and computer science. The essence of information in these data sets is that establishing this data reduces uncertainty. This is another way of saying that the data validates the reality of the systems it supports. 6th-Dimensional boundaries are established.]

[This Teaching about Divine Information Is An Expansion of the Platonic "ideal" or "forms."]

In classical philosophy "information" was a technical notion associated with a theory of knowledge and ontology that originated in Plato's (427–347 BCE) theory of forms, developed in a number of his dialogues (*Phaedo, Phaedrus, Symposium, Timaeus, Republic*). It is expressed that various imperfect individual horses in the physical world could be identified as horses, because they participated in the static atemporal and aspatial "idea" of "horseness" in the world of ideas or forms. When later authors like Cicero (106–43 BCE) and Augustine (354–430 CE) discussed Platonic concepts in Latin they used the terms *informare* and *informatio* as a translation for technical Greek terms like *eidos* (essence), *idea* (idea), *typos* (type), *morphe* (form) and *prolepsis* (representation). The root "form" still is recognizable in the word *in-**form**-ation* (*Capurro and Hjørland, 2003*). Plato's theory of forms was an attempt to formulate a solution for various philosophical problems: the theory of forms mediates between a static (Parmenides, ca. 450 BCE) and a dynamic (Herakleitos, ca. 535–475 BCE) ontological conception of reality and it offers a model to the study of the theory of human knowledge (*Pieter Adriaans, "Information," The Stanford Encyclopedia of Philosophy [Spring 2019 Edition], Edward N. Alta (ed.), https://plato.stanford.edu/archives/spr2019/entries/information/*).

[*GOD—The Dimensional Revelation* Reveals the word *Information* with the capital *I* as an original use of the word to transmit Divine Information, The WORD, To Manifest Divine Creation Of a specific "form" differentiated from other "forms" in the physical universe.

It Is also The Divine Creation Of Differentiated "Spirit" In A Spiritual Universe. The "Information" Is The Noun and Subject Of Divine "Instruction," a verb Expressing The Divine Creative Process To Create Real Manifestations, as well as Ideas In 9th-D Mechanics Of Creation. The WORD Instructs Divine Information. These Instructions Are both The "First Cause" and The "Original Cause" Of All Information, Which Constructs Every Differentiated Reality In The 9th D To Be Manifested In the 8th D and lower Dimensions.]

[2z18] Identity: the fact of being who or what a person or thing is (*Oxford English Dictionary*).

[2z19] Instructions: Detailed [Process] information telling how something should be done, operated, or assembled (*Oxford English Dictionary*).

[*GOD—The Dimensional Revelation* Reveals an original Expansion Of The word *Instruction* to be a verb from *To Instruct*—the Various Processes or Acts Of GOD To Transmit Information From The WORD, Its 10th-Dimensional SOURCE, To The 9th-Dimensional Machinery Of Creation To Construct Reality in the 8th Dimension. This Instruction "Collapses" The Information into Reality along various Metastrings manifesting in the lower dimensions.]

RESEARCH NOTES, CREDITS, AND EXPANSIONS

[2z20] Preserve, Preserving, Preserver: maintain (something) in its original or existing state (*Oxford English Dictionary*).

The concept of multiplicity exists in many religions. It is the ideology that there are multiple gods that represent one divine being.

The Christian Trinity is God the Father, Jesus, the Son, and the Holy Spirit (preserver) (*en.wikipedia.org*).

In Hinduism, Brahman is divided into Brahma (the creator), Vishnu (the preserver), and Shiva (the destroyer) (*Dr. David B. Gowler, One thought on "Vishnu: The Savior, the Preserver, and the Protector," November 29, 2015*).

Vishnu is part of the Hindu Triad that includes Brahma, Vishnu, and Shiva. One third of the trinity of gods who represent the three phases of cosmic existence, Vishnu sustains the universe and upholds its many laws. Since Vishnu mediates disagreements and is seen as the preserver, you might identify with his gentle, merciful nature (*https://chopra.com/articles/vishnu-the-god-of-preservation*).

[2z21] Destroy or Destroying: put an end to the existence of (something) (*Oxford English Dictionary*).

to reduce something to nothingness or to take away its powers and functions so that restoration is impossible (*www.dictionary.com*).

According to the Shaivism sect, the highest form of Ishvar is formless, limitless, transcendent, and unchanging absolute Brahman (*Kramrisch, 1981, 184–188*) and the primal Atman (soul, self) of the universe (*William K. Mahony, 1998, 14*).

The Trimurti is a concept in Hinduism in which the cosmic functions of creation, maintenance, and destruction are personified by the forms of Brahma the creator, Vishnu the maintainer or preserver, and Shiva the destroyer or transformer (*Ralph Metzner, Opening to Inner Light: The Transformation of Human Nature and Consciousness [J. P. Tarcher, 1986], 61*).

Shiva who combines the destructive and constructive powers, the terrific and the gentle, as the ultimate recycler and rejuvenator of all existence (*Chakravarti, 1986, 1–9*).

[2z22] limited: restricted in size, amount, or extent (*Oxford English Dictionary*).

[GOD—*The Dimensional Revelation* Emphasizes the limitations of reality of each dimension. Observations beyond those limitations force Us to define a broader dimension with operational characteristics that cause or allow the observed phenomena. GOD is not subject to limitations. See *The Law of Dimensional Limitation*, {5k}, and chapter 9 infra.]

[2z23] SOURCE: The place something comes from or starts at or the cause of something. dictionary.cambridge.org.

[GOD—*The Dimensional Revelation* Reverifies the Evidence and Conclusion That GOD Is The SOURCE Of All Reality.]

[2z24] complete or completely (*adjective or adverb*): having all the necessary or appropriate parts; to the greatest extent or degree; total.

complete (*verb*): finish making or doing, make (something) whole or perfect (*Oxford English Dictionary*).

[2z25] Pervasive: present or noticeable in every part of a thing or place (*dictionary.cambridge.org*).

[2z26] Infusive: If there is an infusion of one thing into another, the first thing is added to the other thing and makes it stronger or better. Synonyms: injection, *introduction, dose, insertion* (*Collins English Dictionary*).

> Jesus said, "For it is not you who speak, but the Spirit of your Father speaking through you." (*Holy Bible, Matthew 10:20 ESV*)

[2z27] Presence or Presence of Spirit: the state or fact of existing, occurring, or being present in a place or thing. *Oxford English Dictionary*.

> Jesus said, "At that day you will know that I am in My Father, and you in Me, and I in you." (*Holy Bible, John 14:19 NKJV*)

[2z28] Accessible: able to be reached or entered (*Oxford English Dictionary*).

[2z29] Relations: the way in which two or more concepts, objects, or people are connected; a thing's effect on or relevance to another (*Oxford English Dictionary*).

T. H. Green in England took the view that all reality lies in relations and William James in America who, emphasizing the concept of relation, pictured the world as a "concatenated unity" with some parts joined and other parts disjoined (*J. Passmore, A Hundred Years of Philosophy [Penguin, 1968], 58, 108, cf. Peirce op. cit., vol 2, 267*).

[3a] Teaching: ideas or principles taught by an authority (*Oxford English Dictionary*).

The Master observed, "How numerous are the people!" Yu said, "Since they are thus numerous, what more shall be done for them?" "Enrich them, was the reply." "And when they have been enriched, what more shall be done?" The Master said, "Teach them" (*Confucius Analects 13*).

[*GOD—The Dimensional Revelation* Began as writing about the dimensions of reality. Early in the "writing," Dimensional Analysis Inspired A Revelation By GOD To The Author, so the word *Teaching* Is used after chapter 1 when Referring To This literary Work.]

[3b] Revelation: the divine or supernatural disclosure to humans of something relating to human existence or the world (*Oxford English Dictionary*).

[3c] Truth: Nearly all philosophers hold the Correspondence Theory of Truth— What is true must correspond to reality. What is false does not. Aletheia (Greek), Veritas (Latin); St. Thomas Aquinas also restated the theory as: "A judgment is said to be true when it conforms to the external reality" ("*Correspondence Theory of*

RESEARCH NOTES, CREDITS, AND EXPANSIONS

Truth," Stanford Encyclopedia of Philosophy [citing De Veritate Q.1, A.1–3 and Summa Theologiae, I. Q.16]). [This is an early statement of empirical verification.]

> Pilate therefore said unto him, Art thou a king then? Jesus answered, "Thou sayest that I am a king. To this end was I born, and for this cause came I into the world, **that I should bear witness unto the truth. Every one that is of the truth heareth my voice.**" (*Holy Bible, John 18:37 KJV; bold print added*)

[Jesus Christ's Divine use of the word *Truth* is Demonstrated by His Ministry while on Earth. *GOD—The Dimensional Revelation* Expands Upon That Definition Of Truth In Our Teaching. [*GOD—The Dimensional Revelation* Reveals the Large Christ. Everyone That Is Of The Truth Is Of Christ regardless of Their Tradition or specific Knowledge of Jesus.]

[3d] measure or measures (*noun*): a standard unit used to express the size, amount, or degree of something (*Oxford English Dictionary*).

measure (*verb*): the process of associating numbers with physical quantities and phenomena (www.britannica.com).

[3e] Presented: to offer formally (www.thefreedictionary.com).

[3f] proof (*noun*): sufficient evidence or a sufficient argument for the truth of a proposition (*Bonnie Gold and Roger A. Simons, Proof and Other Dilemmas: Mathematics and Philosophy (2008), 12–20, ISBN 0883855674*).

prove (*verb*): to establish the existence, truth, or validity of (as by evidence or logic) (www.merriam-webster.com).

> Prove all things; hold fast that which is good. (*Holy Bible, 1 Thessalonians 5:21 KJV*)

[3g] gestalt: a structure, arrangement, or pattern of physical, biological, or psychological phenomena so integrated as to constitute a functional unit with properties not derivable by summation of its parts (www.merriam-webster.com).

> a German word for form or shape, may refer to: Holism, the idea that natural systems and their properties should be viewed as wholes, not as loose collections of parts. (*en.wikipedia.org*)

[*GOD—The Dimensional Revelation* Reveals that Reality is always a whole. Reality is a continuous Manifestation. Reality is not a collection of parts. Humans just break reality down into parts to Remember, Analyze, and Grasp a situation.

The Broadest Application Of The Word Gestalt Is the Knowledge That GOD Is A Whole Being That Is More Than Reality (The Sum Of The Manifest Parts). See [11z70].]

[3h] Perception: the state of being or process of becoming aware of something through the senses (*Oxford Languages, google.com, partially retrieved September 13, 2020*).

the act or faculty of perceiving or apprehending by means of the senses or of the mind; cognition; understanding. immediate or intuitive recognition or appreciation, as of moral, psychological, or aesthetic qualities; insight; intuition; discernment (*www.dictionary.com, retrieved September 13, 2020*).

[3i] Human Being: a man, woman, or child of the species homo sapiens, distinguished from other animals by superior mental development, power of articulate speech, and upright stance (*Oxford English Dictionary*).

For Plato, the soul is a spirit that uses the body. It is in a non-natural state of union, and longs to be freed from its bodily prison (*cf. Republic X, 611*).

[3j] physical universe: The physical universe is defined as all of space and time. According to modern physics, particularly the theory of relativity, space and time are intimately intertwined and physically meaningless if taken separately from each other.

In religion and esotericism, the term *physical universe*, or *material universe*, is used to distinguish the physical matter of the universe from a proposed spiritual or supernatural essence (en.wikipedia.org).

[*GOD—The Dimensional Revelation* places our physical universe in the 7th dimension. This is the only physical universe we know of, though there may be other physical universes in the 8th-dimension physical membrane system.

GOD—The Dimensional Revelation Reveals that our physical universe is a complete universal system with a boundary. The operational principles of our physical universal system are the same as any other physical universal system that might exist. We know of only one physical universe.

This Teaching does not use the word *universe* to mean "everything that exists" because common usage of the word *universe* is often defined as our physical universe, which is not all that Exists. Rather, each universe operates independently of all like and unlike Universes. The boundary of each universe is defined and limits the operation of that universe.]

[3k] Spiritual Universe: [The Essential Revelation of *GOD—The Dimensional Revelation* Is That All Spiritual Beings, Differentiated From The ONE, Are Part Of A Bounded Universe or Realm that We Call Our Spiritual Universe. Our Spiritual Universe Exists Within An 8th-Dimensional larger Membrane System With Spiritual Operational Principles. Our Spiritual Universe Is temporarily Fused With our physical universe to Yield The Reality In Which We Live.]

[3l] Independent: free from outside control, not depending on another's authority (*Oxford Languages, at google.com, partially retrieved 9/13/2020*).

[3m] aspect or aspects: a particular part or feature of something (*Oxford English Dictionary*).

RESEARCH NOTES, CREDITS, AND EXPANSIONS

[*GOD—The Dimensional Revelation* Expands the word *Aspect* to Refer To That Part Of GOD That Is Differentiated To Become Individual Spiritual Beings Independent Of GOD. Aspects Of GOD Are Also Differentiated By The WORD To Create All Realities.]

[3n] Incarnate or Incarnated (*adjective*): embodied in flesh.

Incarnate (*verb*): embody or represent (a deity or spirit) in human form (*Oxford English Dictionary*).

[3o] The Pleasure Of God:

> For I am God, and there is none else... My counsel shall stand, and I will do all my pleasure. (*Holy Bible, Isaiah 46:9,10 KJV*)

> The LORD does whatever pleases him, in the heavens and on the earth, in the seas and all their depths. (*Holy Bible, Psalm 135:6 NIV*)

We live in a manifestation of the Divine. Each of our sensations, experiences, actions, and accomplishments are the manifestations of GOD in our reality. Each Human Being has consciousness. That consciousness is the awareness of GOD in this reality. Divine Experience of those manifestations is "The Pleasure of GOD". Let us be sure that GOD is well pleased by each of our Beings, in this manifestation (*Allyn Richert, The Pleasure of GOD [2016], 2*).

[3p] Character or Characteristics: a feature or quality belonging typically to a person, place, or thing and serving to identify it (*Oxford English Dictionary*).

[3q] empirical: based on, concerned with, or verifiable by observation or experience rather than theory or pure logic (*Oxford English Dictionary*).

[3r] Rational: based on or in accordance with reason or logic (*Oxford English Dictionary*).

[3s] Conclusion: a judgment or decision reached by reasoning (*Oxford English Dictionary*).

[3t] Tantum Veritas: only the truth; *Latin* (*Google Translate*).

> Jesus said, "And you shall know the truth, and the truth shall make you free." (*Holy Bible, John 8:32 KJV*)

> Therefore a superior man considers it necessary that the names he uses may be spoken appropriately, and also that what he speaks may be carried out appropriately. What the superior man requires is just that in his words there may be nothing incorrect. (*Confucius Analects 13.1*)

The Master said, "The virtuous will be sure to speak correctly, but those whose speech is good may not always be virtuous. Men of principle are sure to be bold, but those who are bold may not always be men of principle." (*Confucius Analects 14.1*)

[3u] Distinguish: perceive or point out a difference (*Oxford English Dictionary*).

[3v] false or falsehood: not according with truth or fact; Incorrect; deliberately made or meant to deceive (*Oxford English Dictionary*).

[3w] principle: a fundamental truth or proposition that serves as the foundation for a system of belief or behavior or for a chain of reasoning (*Oxford English Dictionary*).

[3x] connection: something is linked with another or associated with another or that there is a relationship between two or more things (*yourdictionary.com*).

[3y] proof of process: Proof theory concerns ways of proving statements, at least the true ones. Typically, we begin with axioms and arrive at other true statements using inference rules. Formal proofs are typically finite and mechanical: their correctness can be checked without understanding anything about the subject matter (*Lawrence C. Paulson, Logic and Proof, Computer Laboratory, University of Cambridge, 2014*).

Proof of process is a protocol that allows participants to trust a common process by decoupling the proof of data from the actual source data in a way that yields a single proof that represents all steps of the process.

Let us recount the steps that we've taken to create a proof of process:

1. Extract trust by deriving proofs of the four key factual elements to address the four information security concerns for each step of the process:
   - What: data integrity through cryptographic hashing
   - Who: actor non-repudiation through digital signatures
   - When: proof of anteriority through trusted time-stamping
   - (common time)
   - Where: proof of context through cumulative proof via hash chain
2. Generate a single proof for each step.
3. Publish the final proof in a distributed fashion through a network in which truth is established through a consensus mechanism (*Written by the Stratumn team in collaboration with their customers and partners and published on May 10, 2017. Its authors are Anuj Das Gupta, Richard Caetano, Akbar Ali Ansari, Stephan Florquin, and Gordon Cieplak*).

[3z] cause and effect: noting a relationship between actions or events such that one or more are the result of the other or others (*www.dictionary.com*).

RESEARCH NOTES, CREDITS, AND EXPANSIONS

[3z1] Expansion: the enlargement, broadening, or development of something (*Oxford English Dictionary*).

[3z2] Undeniable: Undeniable things are obviously, clearly, totally, blatantly true—so true that it would be crazy to deny them (*www.vocabulary.com*).

[*GOD—The Dimensional Revelation* States Much About GOD. This is not an Appeal For You To Believe In GOD. We Assert that whether You Believe In GOD or not, GOD Is Inside You. Your Consciousness Is A Manifestation Of GOD. GOD Is Self-Evident To You and Undeniable Because Of Your Own Conscious Awareness.]

[3z3] Tradition: a belief or behavior (folk custom) passed down within a group or society with symbolic meaning or special significance with origins in the past. (*Thomas A. Green, Folklore: An Encyclopedia of Beliefs, Customs, Tales, Music, and Art [ABC-CLIO, 1997], 800. ISBN 978-0-87436-986-1*).

Traditions can persist and evolve for thousands of years—the word *tradition* itself derives from the Latin *trader*, literally meaning to transmit, to hand over, to give for safekeeping. While it is commonly assumed that traditions have ancient history, many traditions have been invented on purpose, whether that be political or cultural, over short periods of time (*en.wikipedia.org, retrieved September 13, 2020*).

[*GOD—The Dimensional Revelation* Recognizes that Tradition Establishes Normative Standards. A Human Life is not long enough To Yield all The Experiences necessary To Train You about all Circumstances that might require A Correct Decision. Hence, A Tradition Codifies Certain Knowledge To Pass It Along To Future Generations. Given Human limitations, many Traditions Are too narrowly defined. They Must Expand With Greater Knowledge.]

[3z4] mutually exclusive: being related such that each excludes or precludes the other; incompatible (*www.merriam-webster.com*).

[3z5] Doctrine: A principle or position or the body of principles in a branch of knowledge or system of belief (*www.merriam-webster.com, retrieved September 13, 2020*).

[3z6] Resolve: settle or find a solution to a problem, dispute, or contentious matter (*Oxford English Dictionary*).

[3z7] Ideology: a systematic body of concepts especially about human life or culture (*www.merriam-webster.com*).

Based on the root word, idea: any conception existing in the mind as a result of mental understanding, awareness, or activity; a thought, conception, or notion (www.dictionary.com).

[3z8] Recognize: Identify (someone or something) from having encountered them before; know again; acknowledge the existence, validity, or legality of (*Oxford English Dictionary*).

[3z9] Point Of View: a particular attitude or way of considering a matter (*Oxford English Dictionary*).

[3z10] facet: one side of something many-sided, especially of a cut gem, a particular aspect or feature of something (*Oxford English Dictionary*).

[Facet Is Used More Broadly in *GOD—The Dimensional Revelation* As A Particular Perspective or Part Of The Larger Reality.]

[3z11] imagine: form a mental image or concept of (*Oxford English Dictionary*).

[3z12] light: an electromagnetic radiation in the wavelength range including infrared, visible, ultraviolet, and X-rays and traveling in a vacuum with a speed of about 186,281 miles (300,000 kilometers) per second specifically: the part of this range that is visible to the human eye (www.merriam-webster.com).

Visible Light, commonly refers to electromagnetic radiation that can be detected by the human eye. The entire electromagnetic spectrum is extremely broad, ranging from low energy radio waves with wavelengths that are measured in meters, to high energy gamma rays with wavelengths that are less than 1×10^{-11} meters. Electromagnetic radiation, as the name suggests, describes fluctuations of electric and magnetic fields, transporting energy at the Speed of Light (which is ~ 300,000 km/sec through a vacuum). Light can also be described in terms of a stream of photons, massless packets of energy, each travelling with wavelike properties at the speed of light. A photon is the smallest quantity (quantum) of energy which can be transported, and it was the realization that light travelled in discrete quanta that was the origins of Quantum Theory (*https://andor.oxinst.com/*).

Electromagnetic Radiation (the designation "radiation" excludes static electric, magnetic, and near fields), or EMR, is classified by wavelength into radio waves, microwaves, infrared, the visible spectrum that we perceive as light, ultraviolet, X-rays, and gamma rays.

The behavior of EMR depends on its wavelength. Higher frequencies have shorter wavelengths, and lower frequencies have longer wavelengths. When EMR interacts with single atoms and molecules, its behavior depends on the amount of energy per quantum it carries.

EMR in the visible light region consists of quanta (called photons) that are at the lower end of the energies that are capable of causing electronic excitation within molecules, which leads to changes in the bonding or chemistry of the molecule. At the lower end of the visible-light spectrum, EMR becomes invisible to humans (infrared) because its photons no longer have enough individual energy to cause a lasting molecular change (a change in conformation) in the visual molecule retinal in the human retina, which change triggers the sensation of vision.

RESEARCH NOTES, CREDITS, AND EXPANSIONS

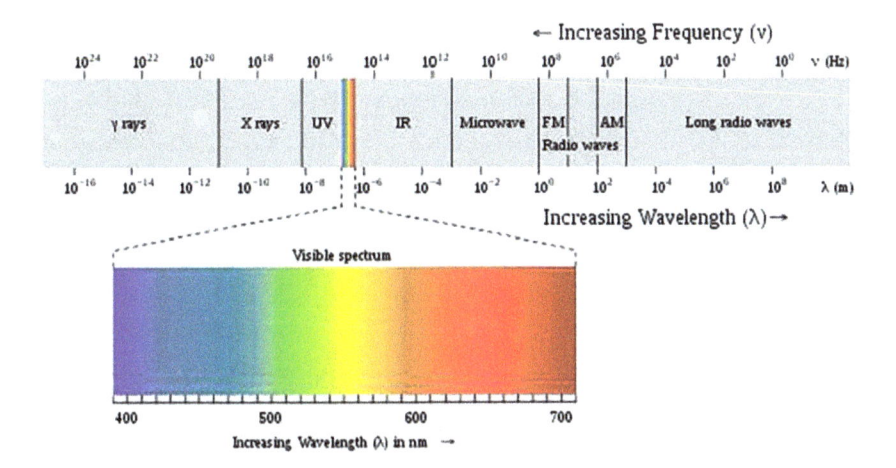

The electromagnetic spectrum, with the visible portion highlighted (*en.wikipedia.org*).

[Used as a Spiritual Word, Light is "Spiritual Energy." See [3z88] and [6z72] infra.]

[3z13] infinitely: without bounds; endlessly (en.wikidictionary.org).

[3z14] Perspective: a particular attitude toward or way of regarding something; a point of view (*Oxford English Dictionary*).

[3z15] Friendship: a relationship of mutual affection between people. It is a stronger form of interpersonal bond than an association (*Oxford English Dictionary*).

[3z16] Share or Sharing: to partake of, use, experience, occupy, or enjoy with others (*www.merriam-webster.com*).

[3z17] ignorance: lack of knowledge, education, or awareness (*www.merriam-webster.com*, retrieved September 13, 2020).

Lack of knowledge or information (*Oxford Languages at google.com*, retrieved September 13, 2020).

[3z18] Conscious or Consciousness: awareness or sentience of internal or external existence (*www.merriam-webster.com*).

Awareness or perception of an inward psychological or spiritual fact; intuitively perceived knowledge of something in one's inner self (*Webster's Third New International Dictionary*, 1966 edition, vol. 1, 482).

A thorough description of consciousness is described as a spectrum with ordinary awareness at one end, and more profound types of awareness at higher levels (*Ken Wilber, The Spectrum of Consciousness* [Motilal Banarsidass, 2002], 3–16, ISBN 978-81-208-1848-4).

The origin of the modern concept of consciousness is often attributed to John Locke's *An Essay Concerning Human Understanding* published in 1690. Locke defined consciousness as "the perception of what passes in a man's own mind" (*John Locke, An Essay Concerning Human Understanding, Chapter 27* [Australia: University of Adelaide], retrieved August 20, 2010).

William James is usually credited with popularizing the idea that human consciousness flows like a stream, in his *The Principles of Psychology* of 1890. According to James, the "stream of thought" is governed by five characteristics: "(1) Every thought tends to be part of a personal consciousness. (2) Within each personal consciousness thought is always changing. (3) Within each personal consciousness thought is sensibly continuous. (4) It always appears to deal with objects independent of itself. (5) It is interested in some parts of these objects to the exclusion of others" (*William James, The Principles of Psychology, Volume 1 [H. Holt, 1890], 225*).

The word *Self-consciousness* in the Upanishads means the knowledge about the existence and nature of Brahman. It means the consciousness of our own real being, the primary reality (*The Theosophy of the Upanishads 1896 [Kessinger Publishing Co., 2003], 12*).

A similar concept appears in Buddhist philosophy, expressed by the Sanskrit term *Citta-saṃtāna*, which is usually translated as *mindstream* or "mental continuum". Buddhist teachings describe that consciousness manifests moment to moment as sense impressions and mental phenomena that are continuously changing. The teachings list six triggers that can result in the generation of different mental events. These triggers are input from the five senses (seeing, hearing, smelling, tasting or touch sensations), or a thought (relating to the past, present or the future) that happen to arise in the mind. The mental events generated as a result of these triggers are: feelings, perceptions and intentions/behaviour. The moment-by-moment manifestation of the mind-stream is said to happen in every person all the time. It even happens in a scientist who analyses various phenomena in the world, or analyses the material body including the organ brain. The manifestation of the mindstream is also described as being influenced by physical laws, biological laws, psychological laws, volitional laws, and universal laws (*Nandini D. Karunamuni, The Five-Aggregate Model of the Mind, first published May 12, 2015*).

The purpose of the Buddhist practice of mindfulness is to understand the inherent nature of the consciousness and its characteristics. Mindfulness is non-judgmental awareness of the present moment (*Kabat-Zinn, 2005*).

To most philosophers, the word "consciousness" connotes the relationship between the mind and the world. To writers on spiritual or religious topics, it frequently connotes the relationship between the mind and God, or the relationship between the mind and deeper truths that are thought to be more fundamental than the physical world. The mystical psychiatrist Richard Maurice Bucke distinguished between three types of consciousness: 'Simple Consciousness', awareness of the body, possessed by many animals; 'Self Consciousness', awareness of being aware, possessed only by humans; and 'Cosmic Consciousness', awareness of the life and order of the universe, possessed only by humans who are enlightened (*Richard Maurice Bucke, Cosmic Consciousness: A Study in the Evolution of the Human Mind [Innes & Sons, 1905], 1–2*).

RESEARCH NOTES, CREDITS, AND EXPANSIONS

[*GOD—The Dimensional Revelation* Resolves mind-brain duality, the "hard problem" of consciousness {David Chalmers}, By Revealing That The "problem" Is Self-imposed by a purely materialistic point of view. The Individual Spirit Is A Component Of "Mind" That Makes Mind Nonphysical. Your Individual Spirit Is Fused During Your Lifetime With Your brain and general physiology. Together, Your brain and Your Soul (Spirit) Are Your Mind. Your Mind Manifests Your Consciousness as a Construction of Mind That Is A Divine fusion of Spiritual Information Processed Through a physical brain. This is how subjective consciousness or first-person experience occurs and is perceived. Any other definition of Mind will be incomplete.

This Points Out A Fundamental Difference Between Consciousness and Awareness. When You Are Asleep, You Remain In An Altered Conscious State, but You Are unaware of Your physical surroundings.

There are levels of brain activity throughout Life, but none of them Are Without Consciousness. Hence, Consciousness Is The Gift Of GOD To Each Advanced Living Being During Its Lifetime. Consciousness May Be Enhanced To Be A State Of Full Communication and Participation With GOD When GOD Chooses To Participate With Your Independent Spiritual Being {Soul}.]

[3z19] account: to be the reason something exists or happens (*www.macmillandictionary.com*).

[3z20] Free Choice or Freedom of Choice: If there is a choice of things, there are several of them, and you can choose the one you want (*www.collinsdictionary.com*).

an individual's *opportunity* and *autonomy* to perform an action selected from at least two available options unconstrained by external parties.

The faculty of desire in accordance with concepts, in-so-far as the ground determining it to action lies within itself and not in its object, is called a faculty to 'do or to refrain from doing as one pleases". Insofar as it is joined with one's consciousness of the ability to bring about its object by one's action it is called choice f it is not joined with this consciousness its act is called a wish. The faculty of desire whose inner determining ground, hence even what pleases it, lies within the subject's reason is called the will... That choice which can be determined by pure reason is called free choice. That which can be determined only by inclination (sensible impulse, stimulus) would be animal choice (arbitrium brutum). Human choice, however, is a choice that can indeed be affected but not determined by impulses, and is therefore of itself (apart from an acquired proficiency of reason) not pure but can still be determined to actions by pure will (*Immanuel Kant, Metaphysics of Morals, 6:213–4*).

[3z21] Empathy: the psychological identification with or vicarious experiencing of the feelings, thoughts, or attitudes of another (*www.dictionary.com*).

Confucius defined *ren* (empathy) in the following way: a man, "wishing to be established himself, seeks also to establish others; wishing to be enlarged himself, he seeks also to enlarge others" (*Analects 6:30, http://ctext.org/analects/yong-ye*).

GOD—THE DIMENSIONAL REVELATION

"Ren is not far off; he who seeks it has already found it." Ren is close to man and never leaves him (*Do-Dinh, 107*)

[3z22] operational principles: Processes capable of, needed in, or actually involved in operations (*Collins English Dictionary*).

[*GOD—The Dimensional Revelation* Expands this definition of *operational principles* to describe the capabilities that enable reality to unfold within a given dimension. When an Observation or data is received that is impossible according to the operational principles of a dimension, a higher or more encompassing dimension must be Realized. The operational principles of the higher dimension include and account for the new data recorded.]

[3z23] Pass Away, Pass On: Pass from physical life and lose all bodily attributes and functions necessary to sustain (physical) life (*Vocabulary.com Dictionary*)

> Jesus said, "Neither can they die any more: for they are equal unto the angels; and are the children of God, being the children of the resurrection… For he is not a God of the dead, but of the living: for all live unto him." (*Holy Bible, Luke 20:36, 38 KJV*)

> For now we see in a mirror dimly, but then face to face. Now I know in part; then I shall know fully, even as I have been fully known. (*Holy Bible, 1 Corinthians 13:12 ESV*)

[*GOD—The Dimensional Revelation* Reveals that Passing On is not just leaving one State of Being but Continues The Living Spirit or The Journey Of A Soul To the next State Of Being. Which State Of Being Is Passed On To Is Determined By Setting Face-To-Face Of That Spirit With GOD. It may also be Called Judgement, but It is not so much A Conclusion as It Is A Continuation Of The Journey Of That Soul.]

[3z24] death: the total and permanent cessation of all the vital functions of an organism. www.dictionary.com.

[3z25] disintegration: the breaking down of something into small particles or into its constituent elements (*www.merriam-webster.com*).

[*GOD—The Dimensional Revelation* Reconfirms That which was whole and greater than the sum of its parts disappears from physical reality, as the physical body disintegrates to its constituent parts.

In Spiritual Reality, The physical body disintegrates. The Spirit does not disintegrate, but Passes Away and Continues Its Spiritual Journey.]

[3z26] Continuity: The unbroken and consistent existence or operation of something (*Oxford English Dictionary*).

[See *continuum*, [21], and *continuous*, [20], above.]

In mathematics, a continuous function is a function that does not have any abrupt changes in value, known as discontinuities… As an example, the function

H(t) denoting the height of a growing flower at time t would be considered continuous. In contrast, the function M(t) denoting the amount of money in a bank account at time t would be considered discontinuous, since it "jumps" at each point in time when money is deposited or withdrawn (en.wikipedia.org).

[*GOD—The Dimensional Revelation* Applies this fundamental ontological difference between Reality, Which Is Continuous In both physical and Spiritual Reality and mathematics, which must describe a situation symbolically with "jumps" to show changes as frame-by-frame rather than continuous.

This defines the limits of mathematics to describe reality in relativity and quantum mechanics. See below for discussion of calculus mathematics to illustrate frame-by-frame limitations of mathematics.]

A rigorous definition of continuity of real functions is usually given in a first course in calculus in terms of the idea of a limit. First, a function, f, with variable x is said to be continuous at the point, c, on the real line if the limit of f(x), as x approaches that point c, is equal to the value f(c); and second, the function (as a whole) is said to be continuous if it is continuous at every point. A function is said to be discontinuous (or to have a discontinuity) at some point when it is not continuous there. These points themselves are also addressed as discontinuities.

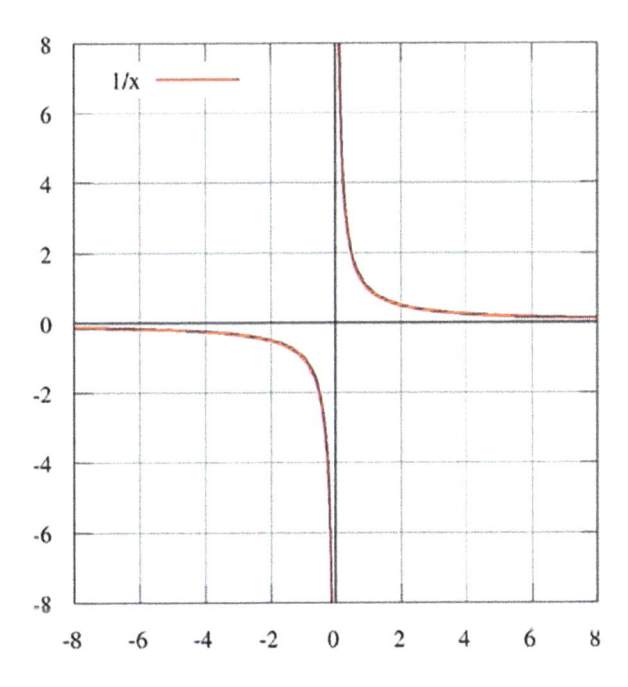

The function f(x)=1/2 is continuous on the domain R\\{0\} but is not continuous over the domain R because it is undefined at x=0. https://en.wikipedia.org/wiki/Continuous_function#/media/File:Function-1_x.svg.

[*GOD—The Dimensional Revelation* Explains that the mathematics sets a limit at 0 so we can manipulate the function mathematically. However, Reality is continuous and does not set a limit at 0. In Reality, the lines go on and on. It may be unknown whether the sequence has or does not have a limit. Situational analysis, such as mathematics, is always frame by frame with a limit, unlike Reality, Which Is Always Continuous.]

[3z27] Determine or Determined (*verb*): to cause (something) to occur in a particular way; be the decisive factor in to ascertain or establish exactly, typically as a result of research or calculation (*Oxford English Dictionary*).

Determined: Decided (www.definitions.net).

[3z28] scientific method:

> Aristotle, 384–322 BCE: As regards his method, Aristotle is recognized as the inventor of scientific method because of his refined analysis of logical implications contained in demonstrative discourse, which goes well beyond natural logic and does not owe anything to the ones who philosophized before him. (*Riccardo Pozzo, Oxford University Press, https://blog.oup.com/2016/07/scientific-method-back-pain/*)

The scientific method requires observations of natural phenomena to formulate and test hypotheses (*Peter Kosso, A Summary of Scientific Method [Springer, 2011], 9, ISBN 978-9400716131*).

It consists of the following steps:

1. Ask a question about a natural phenomenon.
2. Make observations of the phenomenon.
3. Formulate a hypothesis that tentatively answers the question.
4. Predict logical, observable consequences of the hypothesis that have not yet been investigated.
5. Test the hypothesis' predictions by an experiment, observational study, field study, or simulation.
6. Draw a conclusion from data gathered in the experiment or revise the hypothesis or form a new one and repeat the process.
7. Write a descriptive method of observation and the results or conclusions reached.
8. Have peers with experience researching the same phenomenon evaluate the results. (*Carl Cedrick L. Mendez, H. Craig Heller, and May Berenbaum, Life: The Science of Biology, Ninth Ed. [USA: Macmillan, 2009], 13–14, ISBN 978-1429219624*); (*James Shipman, Jerry D. Wilson, and Aaron Todd,*

Introduction to Physical Science, Twelfth Ed. [Cengage Learning, 2009], 4, ISBN 978-0538731874).

[3z29] Methodology: A body of methods, rules, and postulates employed by a discipline; a particular procedure or set of procedures (*www.merriam-webster.com*, retrieved September 13, 2020).

[3z30] Verify: To prove the truth of as by evidence or testimony, confirm, substantiate. www.dictionary.com.

[3z31] Effort: *Application, endeavor, exertion* imply actions directed or force expended toward a definite end (*www.dictionary.com*).

[3z32] unreal: Having no actual existence or substance (*www.thefreedictionary.com*).

[3z33] Hypothesis: A hypothesis is an assumption, an idea that is proposed for the sake of argument so that it can be tested to see if it might be true. In the scientific method, the hypothesis is constructed before any applicable research has been done, apart from a basic background review (*www.merriam-webster.com*).

[3z34] data: things known or assumed as facts, making the basis of reasoning or calculation (*dictionary.cambridge.org*).

[*GOD—The Dimensional Revelation* Emphasizes that data must be verified so We know that it is reliable if it is expected to lead to correct conclusions.]

[3z35] Empiricism: the theory that all knowledge is derived from sense-experience. Stimulated by the rise of experimental science, it developed in the 17th and 18th centuries, expounded in particular by John Locke, George Berkeley, and David Hume (*Oxford Languages at google.com retrieved September 13, 2020*).

Empiricism emphasizes the role of empirical evidence in the formation of ideas rather than innate ideas or traditions (*Forrest E. Baird and Walter Kaufmann, From Plato to Derrida* [Upper Saddle River, New Jersey: Pearson Prentice Hall, 2008] ISBN 978-0-13-158591-1).

However, empiricists may argue that traditions (or customs) arise due to relations of previous sense-experiences (*David Hume, Inquiry Concerning Human Understanding, 1748*).

[3z36] Phenomenology: Phenomenology is a method of inquiry that attempts to examine the structure of consciousness in its own right, putting aside problems regarding the relationship of consciousness to the physical world. This approach was first proposed by the philosopher Edmund Husserl and later elaborated by other philosophers and scientists (*Robert Sokolowski, Introduction to Phenomenology* [Cambridge University Press, 2000], 211–227, ISBN 978-0-521-66792-0).

Yet even the masters of phenomenology and existentialism have a proof of GOD buried in the foundation of the logical dialectic.

The concept of "nothing" arises in Hegel right at the beginning of his *Logic*. The whole is called by Hegel the "Absolute" and is to be viewed as something spiritual. Hegel then has the following:

- Thesis: the absolute is pure being.
- Antithesis: the absolute is nothing.
- Synthesis: the absolute is becoming (*Russell, 701–704*).

[3z37] Reliable: consistently good in quality or performance; able to be trusted (*Oxford English Dictionary*).

[3z38] scientific instrument: A scientific instrument is, broadly speaking, a device or tool used for scientific purposes, including the study of both natural phenomena and theoretical research (*W. Hackmann, "Scientific Instruments," edited by A. Hessenbruck, Reader's Guide to the History of Science [Routledge] 675–677*).

[3z39] instrumentation: a collective term for measuring instruments that are used for indicating, measuring, and recording physical quantities (*en.wikipedia.org*).

The ability to make precise, verifiable, and reproducible measurements of the natural world at levels that were not previously observable using scientific instrumentation has "provided a different texture of the world" (*Klaus Hentschel, "The Instrumental Revolution in Chemistry [Review Essay]," Foundations of Chemistry 5, no. 2 [2003]: 179–183*).

[3z40] calculate or calculation: A calculation is a deliberate process that transforms one or more inputs into one or more results… To calculate means to determine mathematically in the case of a number or amount or, in the case of an abstract problem, to deduce the answer using logic, reason or common sense (*en.wikipedia.org*).

[3z41] logic (from the Greek *logos*, which has a variety of meanings including *word, thought, idea, argument, account, reason,* or *principle*): Logic is the study of reasoning or the study of the principles and criteria of valid inference and demonstration. It attempts to distinguish good reasoning from bad reasoning (*www.philosophybasics.com*).

the relations that lead to the acceptance of one proposition (the conclusion) on the basis of a set of other propositions (premises); More broadly, logic is the analysis and appraisal of arguments (*Liddell and Scott 1999*).

In a logical argument or method of reasoning, each step must be true if the step before it is true (*www.collinsdictionary.com*).

An argument is constructed by applying one of the forms of the different types of logical reasoning: deductive, inductive, and abductive. In deduction, the validity of an argument is determined solely by its logical form, not its content, whereas the soundness requires both validity and that all the given premises are actually true (*The Internet Encyclopedia of Philosophy, ISSN 2161-0002, archived from the original on May 27, 2018, retrieved May 9, 2020*).

Deductive reasoning, or deduction, is making an inference based on widely accepted facts or premises. If a beverage is defined as "drinkable through a straw," one could use deduction to determine soup to be a beverage. Inductive reasoning, or induction, is making an inference based on an observation, often of a sample. You can induce that the soup is tasty if you observe all of your friends consuming it. Abductive reasoning, or abduction, is making a probable conclusion from what you know. If you see an abandoned bowl of hot soup on the table, you can use abduction to conclude the owner of the soup is likely returning soon. If you have trouble differentiating deduction, induction, and abduction, thinking about their roots might help. All three words are based on Latin *ducere*, meaning "to lead." The prefix *de-* means "from," and deduction derives from generally accepted statements or facts. The prefix *in-* means "to" or "toward," and induction leads you to a generalization. The prefix *ab-* means "away," and you take away the best explanation in abduction (*www.merriam-webster.com*).

Symbolic logic is the study of symbolic abstractions that capture the formal features of logical inference (*Alfred North Whitehead and Bertrand Russell, Principia Mathematica to *56 [Cambridge University Press, 1967], ISBN 978-0-521-62606-4*).

In philosophy and mathematics, logic plays a key role in formalizing valid deductive inferences and other forms of reasoning…propositional logic, predicate logic, Boolean logic and modal logic… In logic, constants are often used to denote definite objects in a logical system… Similar to other fields in mathematics, variables are used as placeholder symbols for varying entities in logic.

A math a symbol can be used for different purposes from one mathematical subfield to another, just as multiple symbols can be used to delineate the same concept or relation. (*https://mathvault.ca/ hub/higher-math/math-symbols/logic-symbols 2020*).

[3z42] Reverify or reverified: to verify again or anew : recheck (*www.merriam-webster.com*).

[3z43] Consequent: following as a result or effect (*Oxford English Dictionary*).

[3z44] Relation or relationship: the way in which two or more concepts, objects, or people are connected; a thing's effect on or relevance to another (*Oxford English Dictionary*).

[3z45] static: pertaining to or characterized by a fixed or stationary condition, showing little or no change (*www.dictionary.com*).

[3z46] dynamic: (of a process or system) characterized by constant change, activity, or progress (*Oxford English Dictionary*).

The Dynamic beauty of a piece of music can be recognized before a static analysis explaining why the music is beautiful can be constructed (*Zen and the Art of Motorcycle Maintenance: An Inquiry into Values, 1974, ISBN 0-06-095832-4*).

[*GOD—The Dimensional Revelation* Emphasizes That All Reality Is Dynamic. It Is Continuous and Always Becoming. The quote above is significant because it exposes static analysis as a tool to understand what is dynamic. We Reveal that the error in current quantum theory is that it must set a beginning in physical terms to explain the continuum. It is a tool, but does not go to the whole of Reality.]

[3z47] test or testing:

> I shall certainly admit a system as empirical or scientific only if it is capable of being tested by experience (*Karl Popper, The Logic of Scientific Discovery [Abingdon-on-Thames: Routledge, 1959], 18, ISBN 0-41527843-0*)

The best hypotheses lead to predictions that can be tested in various ways. The most conclusive testing of hypotheses comes from reasoning based on carefully controlled experimental data. Depending on how well additional tests match the predictions, the original hypothesis may require refinement, alteration, expansion, or even rejection. If a particular hypothesis becomes very well supported, a general theory may be developed (*Theodore Garland Jr., "The Scientific Method as an Ongoing Process," March 20, 2015*).

Your experiment tests whether your prediction is accurate and thus your hypothesis is supported or not. It is important for your experiment to be a fair test. You conduct a fair test by making sure that you change only one factor at a time while keeping all other conditions the same. You should also repeat your experiments several times to make sure that the first results weren't just an accident (*www.sciencebuddies.org*).

[3z48] Accurate: correct in all details; exact (*Oxford English Dictionary*).

[3z49] Conclusion: A conclusion is a short paragraph that discusses the overall results of an experimental procedure and explains whether the proposed hypothesis at the beginning of the experiment was correct or not (*Dr. Hayek, Socratic Q&A, August 11, 2016*).

[3z50] Accept: Believe or come to recognize (an opinion, explanation, etc.) as valid or correct (*Oxford English Dictionary*).

[3z51] Epistemology: The theory of knowledge, especially with regard to its methods, validity, and scope. Epistemology is the investigation of what distinguishes justified belief from opinion (*Oxford English Dictionary*).

The term "epistemology," was introduced in modern philosophical parlance by James Frederick Ferrier in his Institutes of Metaphysics, published in 1854. There he writes: "This section of the science is appropriately termed the Epistemology—the doctrine or theory of knowing, just as ontology is the science of being… It answers the general question, 'What is knowing and the known?'—or more shortly, 'What is knowledge?'" (*https://medium.com/the-philosophers-stone/the-crucial-difference-between-metaphysics-and-epistemology-7943158aba52#, 2020*).

[3z52] Guide: Show or indicate the way (*Oxford English Dictionary*).

[3z53] Normative: Normal; implying, creating, or prescribing a norm or standard (*www.freedictionary.com*).

RESEARCH NOTES, CREDITS, AND EXPANSIONS

[3z54] Correct: Free from error; in accordance with fact or truth (*Oxford English Dictionary*).

[3z55] numenology: in the philosophy of Immanuel Kant, the thing-in-itself (das Ding an sich) as opposed to what Kant called the phenomenon—the thing as it appears to an observer (*www.britannica.com*).

A numenon is a posited object or event that exists independently of human sense and/or perception (*www.merriam-webster.com*).

[3z56] thing-in-itself:

> And we indeed, rightly considering objects of sense as mere appearances, confess thereby that they are based upon a thing in itself, though we know not this thing as it is in itself, but only know its appearances… (*Emanuel Kant, Prolegomena 32*)

[3z57] objective and [3z58] Subjective: something is subjective if it is based on or influenced by personal feelings, tastes, experience, or opinions. Something is objective if not influenced by personal feelings or opinions in considering and representing facts that have been proved independently (*https://bsmimpact.com/objective-vs-subjective/*).

[3z59] Phenomenon: a fact or situation that is observed to exist or happen, especially one whose cause or explanation is in question (*Oxford English Dictionary*).

[3z60] Dream: A series of thoughts, images, and sensations occurring in a person's mind during sleep (*Oxford English Dictionary*).

[3z61] Center: Your spiritual center is a mystical place within yourself where you achieve mental, physical, and emotional peace, even if it is only for a short period of time (*mindfueldaily.com*).

[*GOD—The Dimensional Revelation* Recommends Meditation Techniques To Focus Your Consciousness At Your Spiritual Center. When You Experience confusion in ordinary Awareness, Centering Techniques Will Develop Your Power To Control Your Consciousness. This will Provide many Benefits, such as Restore Balance In Your Ordinary Awareness,[4e] Focus Your Mind,[5h] Improve Psychological and physical health, Provide Recreation, Open A Path For Spiritual Growth,[13z14] and Open You To Enlightenment.[6z124] Among many Centering Techniques are Inviting The LORD To Participate In Your Consciousness,[12p],[13z5] Participating In The Heavenly States In This Life,[3z88],[chapter 13] Breathwork,[6z202] Studying Of The Written WORD, Focusing Your Mind On Any Aspect Of The WORD,[5z48] Prayer,[5z46] Singing,[4n19],[13z67] Meditation[5z48] Harmonious physical exercise, Focusing Your Spirit Through Any Of The Chakras,[11p] and the most Subtle Techniques called Stopping-and-Seeing,[13z56],[6z89] Turning The Light Around,[6z180],[6z124],[13z57] and Circulating The Light.[6z124],[13z57]]

If you do practice for a single breath, then you are a realized immortal for a breath." (*Thomas Cleary, The Secret of the Golden Flower, p. 64. [HarperCollins, 1991]*)

[3z62] Necessities: Those things without which survival would be endangered (*https://www.lawinsider.com/dictionary/necessities-of-life*).

[3z63] Stream of Consciousness:

Consciousness, then, does not appear to itself as chopped up in bits…it is nothing joined; it flows. A "river" or a "stream" are the metaphors by which it is most naturally described. In talking of it hereafter, let's call it the stream of thought, consciousness, or subjective life. (*William James, The Principles of Psychology [Henry Holt and Company, 1890]*)

[3z64] biochemical balance: Each of us has a body that functions due to biochemical factors that influence our personalities, behaviors, mental health, immune function, and allergic tendencies. There are about 60 chemical elements in our bodies, and each plays a role in the expression of our genes. More than 95% of our bodies are made up of four elements: oxygen, carbon, hydrogen and nitrogen. The remaining 5 percent are either macronutrients or micronutrients that are required for the proper production of hormones, neurotransmitters and immune function (*http://www.mensahmedical.com/what-are-biochemical-imbalances/*).

Chemical equations must be mass balanced and charge balanced across the $\rightarrow$ or $\rightleftharpoons$ sign. Mass balance means the same number and kind of atoms on each side. Charge balance means the same number of unpaired + and - charges on each side (*http://xaktly.com/Chemistry_Balance.html*).

[3z65] fact: Something that has actual existence (*www.merriam-webster.com*).

[3z66] Encourage or Encourages: help or stimulate (an activity, state, or view) to develop (*Oxford English Dictionary*).

[3z67] Seeker: a person who is attempting to find or obtain something (*Oxford English Dictionary*).

One that seeks, a seeker of the truth (*www.yourdictionary.com*).

[3z68] Faith: A strong belief in God or in the doctrines of a religion, based on spiritual apprehension rather than proof (*Oxford English Dictionary*).

[3z69] constant: something invariable or unchanging (*www.merriam-webster.com*).

In logic, constants are often used to denote definite objects in a logical system… Similar to other fields in mathematics, variables are used as placeholder symbols for varying entities in logic (*https://mathvault.ca/ hub/higher-math/math-symbols/logic-symbols 2020 Math Vault*).

RESEARCH NOTES, CREDITS, AND EXPANSIONS

Since May 2019, all of the SI base units have been defined in terms of physical constants. As a result, five constants: the speed of light in vacuum, c; the Planck constant, h; the elementary charge, e; the Avogadro constant, NA; and the Boltzmann constant, kB, have known exact numerical values when expressed in SI units. The first three of these constants are fundamental constants, whereas NA and kB are of a technical nature only: they do not describe any property of the universe, but instead only give a proportionality factor for defining the units used with large numbers of atomic-scale entities (*en.wikipedia.org retrieved 10/17/2020*).

Also refer to the NIST Reference on Constants, Units, and Uncertainty for the Fundamental Physical Constants, https://physics.nist.gov/cgi-bin/cuu/Category?view=html&All+values.x=65&All+values.y=10.

[*GOD—The Dimensional Revelation* Approaches a physical principle called the "fundamental physical constant" or "universal dimensionless constant" as mathematical attempts to define the Information Instructed By GOD as they collapse into our 7th-D physical universe.

Similarly, Your Faith May Remain Constant As Your Spiritual Journey May Have Led You To A Relationship With GOD In A Particular Way.]

[3z70] Encompass: surround and have or hold within (*Oxford English Dictionary*).

[3z71] Esoteric: If you describe something as esoteric, you mean it is known, understood, or appreciated by only a small number of people (*Collins COBUILD Advanced English Dictionary, HarperCollins Publishers*).

Rudolph Steiner Teaches the Essence of Esoteric Knowledge, saying,

> There slumbers in every human being, faculties by means of which he can acquire for himself a knowledge of higher worlds. Mystics, Gnostics, Theosophists—all speak of a world of soul and spirit which for them is just as real as the world we see with our physical eyes and touch with our physical hands. At every moment the listener may say to himself: that, of which they speak, I too can learn, if I develop within myself certain powers which today still slumber within me.
>
> There remains only one question—how to set to work to develop such faculties. For this purpose, they only can give advice who already possess such powers. As long as the human race has existed there has always been a method of training, in the course of which individuals possessing these higher faculties gave instruction to others who were in search of them…for the secret of initiation can only be understood by those who have to a certain degree experienced this initiation into the higher knowledge of existence.

The question may be raised: how, then, under these circumstances, are the uninitiated to develop any human interest in this so-called esoteric knowledge? How and why are they to seek for something of whose nature they can form no idea? Such a question is based upon an entirely erroneous conception of the real nature of esoteric knowledge. There is, in truth, no difference between esoteric knowledge and all the rest of man's knowledge and proficiency. This esoteric knowledge is no more of a secret for the average human being than writing is a secret for those who have never learned it. And just as all can learn to write who choose the correct method, so, too, can all who seek the right way become esoteric students and even teachers.

In one respect only do the conditions here differ from those that apply to external knowledge and proficiency. The possibility of acquiring the art of writing may be withheld from someone through poverty, or through the conditions of civilization into which he is born; but for the attainment of knowledge and proficiency in the higher worlds, there is no obstacle for those who earnestly seek them…

Now, the one thing that everyone must acknowledge is the difficulty for those involved in the external civilization of our time to advance to the knowledge of the higher worlds. They can only do so if they work energetically at this themselves. At a time when the conditions of material life were simpler, the attainment of spiritual knowledge was also easier. Objects of veneration and worship stood out in clearer relief from the ordinary things of the world. In an epoch of criticism ideals are lowered; other feelings take the place of veneration, respect, adoration, and wonder… Whoever seeks higher knowledge must create it for himself. He must instill it into his soul. It cannot be done by study; it can only be done through life.

Whoever, therefore, wishes to become a student of higher knowledge must assiduously cultivate this inner life of devotion… Noiseless and unnoticed by the outer world is the treading of the Path of Knowledge. No change need be noticed in the student. He performs his duties as hitherto; he attends to his business as before. The transformation goes on only in the inner part of the soul hidden from outward sight.

At first his entire inner life is flooded by this basic feeling of devotion for everything which is truly venerable. His entire soul-life finds in this fundamental feeling its pivot. Just as the sun's rays vivify everything living, so does reverence in the student vivify all feelings of the soul... It is not easy, at first, to believe that feelings like reverence and respect have anything to do with cognition. This is due to the fact that we are inclined to set cognition aside as a faculty by itself—one that stands in no relation to what otherwise occurs in the soul. In so thinking we do not bear in mind that it is the soul which exercises the faculty of cognition; and feelings are for the soul what food is for the body. If we give the body stones in place of bread, its activity will cease. It is the same with the soul. Veneration, homage, devotion are like nutriment making it healthy and strong, especially strong for the activity of cognition. Disrespect, antipathy, underestimation of what deserves recognition, all exert a paralyzing and withering effect on this faculty of cognition...

We must learn to remain in touch with our own feelings and ideas if we wish to develop any intimate relationship with the outer world. The outer world with all its phenomena is filled with splendor, but we must have experienced the divine within ourselves before we can hope to discover it in our environment...

The student of higher knowledge considers enjoyment only as a means of ennobling himself for the world. Enjoyment is to him like a scout informing him about the world; but once instructed by enjoyment, he passes on to work. He does not learn in order to accumulate learning as his own treasure, but in order that he may devote his learning to the service of the world...

Adapt each one of your actions, and frame each one of your words in such a way that you infringe upon no one's free-will... We must bear in mind that the higher man within us is in constant development. But only the state of calm and serenity here described renders an orderly development possible. Calm inward contemplation...with the purely spiritual world fill(s) his soul...

Formerly sound only reached him through his ear; now it resounds through his soul. An inner language, an inner word is revealed to him. This moment, when first experienced, is one of greatest rapture for the student. An inner light is shed over the whole external world, and a second life begins for him. Through his being there pours a divine stream from a world of divine rapture...

This life of the soul in thought, which gradually widens into a life in spiritual being, is called by Gnosis, and by Spiritual Science, Meditation (contemplative reflection). This meditation is the means to supersensible knowledge. But the student in such moments must not merely indulge in feelings; he must not have indefinite sensations in his soul. That would only hinder him from reaching true spiritual knowledge. His thoughts must be clear, sharp and definite, and he will be helped in this if he does not cling blindly to the thoughts that rise within him. Rather must he permeate himself with the lofty thoughts by which men already advanced and possessed of the spirit were inspired at such moments. He should start with the writings which themselves had their origin in just such revelation during meditation... The seekers of the spirit have themselves set down in such writings the thoughts of the divine science which the Spirit has directed his messengers to proclaim to the world.

Through such meditation a complete transformation takes place in the student. He begins to form quite new conceptions of reality. All things acquire a fresh value for him. It cannot be repeated too often that this transformation does not alienate him from the world. He will in no way be estranged from his daily tasks and duties, for he comes to realize that the most insignificant action he has to accomplish, the most insignificant experience which offers itself to him, stands in connection with cosmic beings and cosmic events. When once this connection is revealed to him in his moments of contemplation, he comes to his daily activities with a new, fuller power.

When, by means of meditation, a man rises to union with the spirit, he brings to life the eternal in him, which is limited by neither birth nor death. The existence of this eternal being can only be doubted by those who have not themselves experienced it. Thus meditation is the way which also leads man to the knowledge, to the contemplation of his eternal, indestructible, essential being; and it is only through meditation that man can attain to such knowledge.

Gnosis and Spiritual Science tell of the eternal nature of this being and of its reincarnation. The question is often asked: Why does a man know nothing of his experiences beyond the borders of life and death? Not thus should we ask, but rather: How can we attain such knowledge? In right meditation the path is opened. This alone can revive the memory of experiences beyond the border of life and death. Everyone can attain this knowledge... Spiritual Science gives the means of developing the spiritual ears and eyes, and of kindling the spiritual light; and this method of spiritual training: (1) Preparation; this develops the spiritual senses. (2) Enlightenment; this kindles the spiritual light. (3) Initiation; this establishes intercourse with the higher spiritual beings. (*Rudolf Steiner, Knowledge of the Higher Worlds, January 1, 1947*)

[3z72] Know God:

They know the truth about God because he has made it obvious to them. For ever since the world was created, people have seen the earth and sky. Through everything God made, they can clearly see his invisible qualities—his eternal power and divine nature. So, they have no excuse for not knowing God. (*Holy Bible, Romans 1:19–20 NLT*)

[GOD—*The Dimensional Revelation* Reveals that If You Have Consciousness, Then You Know GOD. Your Relationship To GOD Precedes Your Incarnation Into a human body. Physical experience, while it distracts from Your Relationship With GOD, also provides The Interest or Pleasure GOD Takes When You Recognize and Share Your Human Experience With GOD. That Is How You Know GOD In This Life.]

[3z73] meaningless: without meaning, significance, purpose, or value (*www.dictionary.com*).

[3z74] Spiritual Journey: The spiritual journey is a transformational process that takes us through seven stages of our spiritual development. The path we take is built into us, in our expanding minds, hearts, and energy system. It's an integral aspect of our desire to be alive—to live fully and grow, to expand in fulfilling ways and make a positive difference in the world (*gettingthrough.org, retrieved September 13, 2020*).

In general, a spiritual journey describes the process of a person embarking on a quest to deepen their knowledge, understanding and wisdom about themselves, the world and/or God. The phrase can refer to a person seeking to lead an intentional and conscious lifestyle in order to gain various insights about themselves and life. But it can also refer to the intentional search of a deeper understanding about God and perhaps also their faith (*Steve Mueller, planetofsuccess.com, 2016*).

The soul's journey throughout numerous bodies is called Samsara, the process of reincarnation. The base of the process is the karma cycle, the principle of cause and effect, performing good and evil deeds. The simple sayings are "what goes around comes around" and "do unto others as you would have them do unto you." A soul enters a new body after each death; the new body is decided based on the soul's karma of its past lives… Brahman is the supreme God, and the Atman is his soul, and the source of the soul each living creature contains…humans can do whatever is needed to attain Moksha, enlightenment… Attaining Moksha is the end of suffering and becoming one with the supreme divinity, Brahman (*https://www.hindustudentscouncil.org/2020/the-journey-of-the-atman/*).

[3z75] unique or uniquely: being the only one of its kind, unlike anything else (*Oxford English Dictionary*).

[3z76] Expand or Expanded: become or make larger or more extensive, give a fuller version or account of (*Oxford English Dictionary*).

[3z77] Deeper: extending well inward from an outer surface (www.merriam-webster.com).

something that has a lot of meaning behind it, something very emotional or heavy, broad, intense (www.urbandictionary.com).

A word that's deeper than "deep," consider profound. A philosopher is likely to make many profound pronouncements (*www.vocabulary.com*).

[3z78] Spiritual Reality:

> The wind blows wherever it pleases. You hear its sound, but you cannot tell where it comes from or where it is going. So it is with everyone born of the Spirit. (*Holy Bible, John 3:8 NIV*)

God's great universe is not an ethereal, fog-like realm way off in the clouds as a place we access in heaven or, if we're among the fortunate few, in rare mystical experiences. Nor is it just ideas and principles that are true. It's the ground of reality. It's a place to live, the most wonderful place! under the rule of Christ.

Though the Kingdom of God is unseen by our physical eye, we can know it as spiritual reality through personal experience. The way in is through putting our confidence in Jesus, seeing God and the universe as he does and growing in an interactive and personal relationship with God as Father through him (*Bill Gaultiere, soulshepherding.org, retrieved September 30, 2020*).

[3z79] context: the circumstances that form the setting for an event, statement, or idea and in terms of which it can be fully understood and assessed (*Oxford English Dictionary*).

[3z80] negative: [in ontology] marked by absence, withholding, or removal of something positive (www.merriam-webster.com).

[3z81] Honor (*noun*): high respect; great esteem.

Honor (*verb*): regard with great respect (*Oxford English Dictionary*).

[3z82] Gods: Often described as divine individual beings in the Greek or Hindu Pantheon. Perhaps these gods are different names ascribed to the Anunnaki (Nephilim "giants" *Holy Bible, Genesis 6:4 and Numbers 13:33*) of the Sumerian pantheon—ancient aliens who dominated human prehistory and advanced the Human genome (*Zecharia Stichin, Earth Chronicles Series, 1976*).

RESEARCH NOTES, CREDITS, AND EXPANSIONS

> Deities were not thought to be omniscient or omnipotent and were rarely believed to be changeless or eternal. (*Bruce G. Trigger, Understanding Early Civilizations: A Comparative Study*, First ed. [Cambridge: Cambridge University Press, 2003], 441–42)

[*GOD—The Dimensional Revelation* Reveals The Pervasive Nature Of GOD As Present In All Of Reality. Human Beings Are Innately Aware Of GOD but variously ascribe Deity to any number of physical phenomena, Higher Beings, Ideas, or Concepts that They Observe or Feel As Controlling. These Identities Of GOD are incorrect. They Are severely incomplete. Like You, Those That Actually Exist Of These "gods," Are Differentiations Of The ONE. They do not Deserve Deification or Worship. You Must Become Acquainted With The Large GOD To Understand How GOD Is Manifesting to You.

[3z83] ONE:

> Hear, O Israel: The LORD our GOD is ONE LORD. (*Holy Bible, Deuteronomy 6:4 KJV, capitals added*)

> Jesus Christ Said, "That they all may be one; as thou, Father, art in me, and I in thee, that they also may be one in us: that the world may believe that thou hast sent me. And the glory which thou gavest me I have given them; that they may be one, even as we are one: I in them, and thou in me, that they may be made perfect in one; and that the world may know that thou hast sent me, and hast loved them, as thou hast loved me." (*Holy Bible, John 17:21–23 KJV*)

[*GOD—The Dimensional Revelation* Reveals The Large GOD. All, Each Manifestation Is A Differentiation Of The ONE, GOD, LORD Of All. Each Proceeds According To The WORD Of GOD, The 10th Dimension. This Entire Teaching Is Revealed So That You May Understand The ONE and Grow In That Understanding.]

[3z84] Blessed: Worthy of adoration, reverence, or worship (*www.dictionary.com*).

full of joy; experiencing, indicating, causing, or characterized by bliss (*thesaurus.yourdictionary.com*).

[3z85] The 1st Book of Enoch, the Ethiopic Book of Enoch, or 1 Enoch is more known as simply the Book of Enoch (*Paperback edition 2012 by Paul C. Schnieders [author], Robert H. Charles [translator]*).

[3z86] Realm: the region, sphere, or domain within which anything occurs, prevails, or dominates (*www.merriam-webster.com*).

a field or domain of activity or interest (*Oxford English Dictionary*).

[3z87] physical energy: In physics, energy is the quantitative property that must be transferred to an object in order to perform work on, or to heat, the object. Energy is a conserved quantity; the law of conservation of energy states that energy can be converted in form, but not created or destroyed (*Kittel and Kroemer, Thermal Physics [New York: W.H. Freeman, 1980], ISBN 978-0-7167-1088-2*).

In cosmology and astronomy the phenomena of stars, nova, supernova, quasars and gamma-ray bursts are the universe's highest-output energy transformations of matter (*www.wikipedia.com*).

[3z88] Spiritual Energy or Divine Energy or Positive Spiritual Energy: The divine supraessentiality is never named in the plural. But the divine and uncreated grace and energy of God is indivisibly divided, like the sun's rays that warm, illumine, quicken and bring increase as they cast their radiance upon what they enlighten, and shine on the eyes of whoever beholds them. In the manner, then, of this faint likeness, the divine energy of God is called not only one but also multiple by the theologians. Thus St Basil the Great declares: 'What are the energies of the Spirit? Their greatness cannot be told and they are numberless. How can we comprehend what precedes the ages? What were God's energies before the creation of noetic reality?' For prior to the creation of noetic reality and beyond the ages—for the ages are also noetic creations—no one has ever spoken or conceived of anything created. Therefore, the powers and energies of the divine Spirit—even though they are said in theology to be multiple—are uncreated and are to be indivisibly distinguished from the single and wholly undivided essence of the Spirit (*St. Gregory Palamas, ca. 1296-1359*).

There are two main forms of Deity Shiva. His first form is all-pervasive, pure, knowledgeable, blissful, full of Chaitanya (Divine consciousness) and absolute; in other words, it is the perpetually stable Parabrahman (Supreme God). His second form is Shaktitattva (Divine Energy Principle), which is always functioning in the universe. This Principle manifests itself through all the animate and inanimate objects in nature. The origin of Shakti is in the form of vibrations. Shakti is not separate from Deity Shiva but is a part of Deity Shiva. Shakti's function is to activate Shiva, who is in an inactive state. Creation-Sustenance-Dissolution are the attributes of Shakti. The cycle of Creation-Sustenance-Dissolution is unending (*https://www.hindujagruti.org/hinduism/divine-energy*).

Like harmony, symmetry, and even genius, this invisible force is a mystery whose uplifting power must be encountered to be believed. Once that happens, revealing a glimpse of our awesome potential, it can never again be denied (*Mark Matousek, http://www.oprah.com/spirit/how-to-radiate-positive-energy-spiritual-energy/all, retrieved October 11, 2020*).

> What cannot be spoken and cannot be named is the generative energy, which is the substance of the Way. (*The Secret of the Golden Flower, 69, trans. Thomas Cleary [HarperCollins, 1991]*)

RESEARCH NOTES, CREDITS, AND EXPANSIONS

"Energy in spirituality" refers to a widespread belief in an interpersonal, non-physical force or essence (*Science Daily, July 12, 2020*).

Ways to Increase Spiritual Energy:

1. Become Involved in the Religious Activities.
2. Be Grateful—The more grateful you are, the more spiritual energy you have.
3. Pray—The more you pray, the stronger the link to the higher force. Your spiritual energy grows.
4. Reflect on Yourself—Spiritual energy comes from two main sources: a higher force and your inner "you" (the soul).
5. Meditation—You can only connect to your spiritual energy when your mind is calm and decluttered. This is exactly the objective of meditation (*Mark Struszczyk*).

In traditional Chinese culture, qi or ch'i (/ˈtʃiː/ CHEE simplified Chinese: 气; traditional Chinese: 氣; pinyin: qì About this soundqì) is believed to be a vital force forming part of any living entity. (*Deng Yu et al., "Ration of Qi with Modern Essential on Traditional Chinese Medicine Qi: Qi Set, Qi Element," January 1, 2003*).

> Heaven (seen here as the ultimate source of all being) falls (duo 墮, i.e., descends into proto-immanence) as the formless. Fleeting, fluttering, penetrating, amorphous it is, and so it is called the Supreme Luminary. The Dao begins in the Void Brightening. The Void Brightening produces the universe (yu-zhou). The universe produces qi. Qi has bounds. The clear, yang [qi] was ethereal and so formed heaven… (*Huai-nan-zi, 3:1a/19*)

In Hinduism,

> As the ancient writers have said, it is the vital force or prana which is spread over both the macrocosm, the entire Universe, and the microcosm, the human body… The atom is contained in both of these. Prana is life-energy responsible for the phenomena of terrestrial life and for life on other planets in the universe. Prana in its universal aspect is immaterial. But in the human body, Prana creates a fine biochemical substance which works in the whole organism and is the main agent of activity in the nervous system and in the brain. The brain is alive only because of Prana…

The most important psychological changes in the character of an enlightened person would be that he or she would be compassionate and more detached. There would be less ego, without any tendency toward violence or aggression or falsehood. The awakened life energy is the mother of morality, because all morality springs from this awakened energy. Since the very beginning, it has been this evolutionary energy that has created the concept of morals in human beings. (*Gopti Krishna, Kundalini Questions and Answers, Smashwords ed. [The Institute for Consciousness Studies, 1995], 6–8*)

[One Manifestation of the Movement of Spiritual Energy, though not the only one, is the Rise of Kundalini in Your physical body.]

At the command of the yogi in deep meditation, this creative force turns inward and flows back to its source in the thousand-petaled lotus, revealing the resplendent inner world of the divine forces and consciousness of the soul and spirit. Yoga refers to this power flowing from the coccyx to spirit as the awakened kundalini. (*Paramahansa Yogananda, The Bhagavad Gita: God Talks with Arjuna: Royal Science of God Realization: The Immortal Dialogue Between Soul and Spirit: A New Translation and Commentary [First ed.] [Los Angeles: Self Realization Fellowship, 1995], 18*)

[*GOD—The Dimensional Revelation* Reveals That The SOURCE Of All Spiritual Energy Is GOD. Furthermore, Spiritual Energy Is Exchanged Between GOD and You. Your Attention Is Needed To Increase This Exchange In This Life. It Will Elevate All Aspects Of Your Life In this World and All Your Future Being.]

[3z89] directly: with nothing or no one in between (*Oxford English Dictionary*).

[3z90] Metastring: [*Metastring* is a new word original To *GOD—The Dimensional Revelation*. One Metastring Is One Channel, Bundle, or Set Of Divine Instructions Containing The Information For The 9th-D Machinery Of Creation To Manifest That Type Of Reality As Instructed By The WORD. That Manifestation Occurs In The 8th D As The Information Is Collapsed Into Being In the lower Dimensions.

We Logically Conclude that there must be Channels For All Reality To Be Created, Preserved, and Honored, as well as Destroyed. These Are Now Given This word, *Metastring*.]

[3z91] being or Being: existence, the nature or essence of a person, the fact of existing, existence (as opposed to nonexistence) (*Oxford English Dictionary*).

Anything that exists is being. Ontology is the branch of philosophy that studies being. Being is a concept encompassing objective and subjective features of reality and existence (*Oxford English Dictionary*).

[3z92] future: at a later time; going or likely to happen or exist (*Oxford English Dictionary*).

[3z93] AD: "A.D." stands for anno domini, Latin for "in the year of the Lord," and refers specifically to the birth of Jesus Christ. "B.C." stands for "Before Christ." In English, it is common for "A.D." to precede the year, so that the translation of "A.D. 2014" would read "in the year of our lord 2014" (*Robert Coolman, Live Science Contributor, May 12, 2014*).

[4a] Fullness of Being: The fullness of being is about being connected to your true self. It's about being all that you are meant to be. The fullness of being is all about your personal expression of all you are and who you are meant to be. It's about living your authentic self. It's about being present in the moment and allowing life to move through you; being in alignment with your life's purpose. The fullness of being means being grounded, centered, and aligned as you go through life.

When you are one with the flow of life, you will then know the fullness of being. Being the absolute true expression of your true authentic self, letting the light that shines within break free, expand outwards through your heart centre for the world to see and embrace—without fear, and in freedom to just 'be' (*Fabbian, thefullnessofbeing.ca, retrieved November 15, 2020*).

[4b] simple: not involved or complicated; easy to understand or do (*www.thefreedictionary.com*).

[4c] possibility: a thing that may happen or be the case, a thing that may be chosen or done out of several possible alternatives (*Oxford English Dictionary*).

[4d] Origin: the point or place where something begins, arises, or is derived (*Oxford English Dictionary*).

[4e] Aware or Awareness: Awareness is the ability to directly know and perceive, to feel, or to be cognizant of events.

Awareness is also associated with consciousness in the sense that this concept denotes a fundamental experience such as a feeling or intuition that accompanies the experience of phenomena (*Andrzej Kokoszka, States of Consciousness: Models for Psychology and Psychotherapy [New York: Springer Science+Business Media, 2007], 4, ISBN 9780387327570*).

Another definition describes it as a state wherein a subject is aware of some information when that information is directly available to bring to bear in the direction of a wide range of behavioral actions (*David Chalmers, The Conscious Mind: In Search of a Fundamental Theory [Oxford: Oxford University Press, 1997], 225, ISBN 978-0195105537*).

GOD—THE DIMENSIONAL REVELATION

[4f] Purpose: The reason for which something is done or created or for which something exists (*Oxford English Dictionary*).

[4g] Answer or Answers: A thing said, written, or done to deal with or as a reaction to a question, statement, or situation (*Oxford English Dictionary*).

[4h] length: In Euclidean geometry, length is measured along straight lines unless otherwise specified. Pythagoras's theorem relating the length of the sides of a right triangle is one of many applications in Euclidean geometry. Length may also be measured along other types of curves and is referred to as "arclength."

In engineering and science, dimensional analysis is the analysis of the relationships between different physical quantities by identifying their base quantities (such as length, mass, time, and electric charge) and units of measure (such as miles vs. kilometres, or pounds vs. kilograms) and tracking these dimensions as calculations or comparisons are performed (*en.wikipedia.org*).

[Length is the 1st d.]

[4i] width: the measurement or extent of something from side to side (*Oxford English Dictionary*).

[Width is the 2nd d.]

[4j] depth or height: a dimension taken through an object or body of material, usually downward from an upper surface, horizontally inward from an outer surface, or from top to bottom of something regarded as one of several layers.

The quality of being deep, deepness, complexity or obscurity as of a subject, a question of great depth, gravity, seriousness.

Emotional profundity: The depth of someone's feelings; intensity as of silence, color, etc. (www.dictionary.com, retrieved September 13, 2020).

[Depth is the 3rd d.]

[4k] Describe: Mark out or draw (*Oxford English Dictionary*).

Mathematics is an exact language for description, calculation, deduction, modeling, and prediction—more a systematic way of thinking than a set of rules... The practical importance of mathematics lies in its ability to describe the real world (*Alexandre Borovik, Description of Mathematics, take 2 bis, December 28, 2010*).

[4l] space: Physical space is often conceived in three linear dimensions, although modern physicists usually consider it, with time, to be part of a boundless four-dimensional continuum known as space-time. The concept of space is considered to be of fundamental importance to an understanding of the physical universe.

Relativity theory leads to the cosmological question of what shape the universe is, and where space came from. It appears that space was created in the Big Bang, 13.8 billion years ago and has been expanding ever since. The overall shape of space is not known, but space is known to be expanding very rapidly due to the cosmic inflation (*"Cosmic Detectives," The European Space Agency [ESA], April 2, 2013, archived from the original on April 5, 2013, retrieved April 26, 2013*).

RESEARCH NOTES, CREDITS, AND EXPANSIONS

[4m] motion: an act, process, or instance of changing place; movement (*www.merriam-webster.com*).

in physics, change with time of the position or orientation of a body (*www.britannica.com*).

motionless, not moving; stationary(*Oxford English Dictionary*).

[4n] force or forced: strength or energy exerted or brought to bear, cause of motion or change, active power (*www.merriam-webster.com*).

[4o] compression wave: Longitudinal waves are waves in which the displacement of the medium is in the same direction as, or the opposite direction to, the direction of propagation of the wave. Mechanical longitudinal waves are also called compressional or compression waves because they produce compression and rarefaction when traveling through a medium and pressure waves because they produce increases and decreases in pressure.

The other main type of wave is the transverse wave in which the displacements of the medium are at right angles to the direction of propagation. Transverse waves, for instance, describe some bulk sound waves in solid materials (but not in fluids); these are also called "shear waves" to differentiate them from the (longitudinal) pressure waves that these materials also support.

Longitudinal waves include sound waves (vibrations in pressure, particle of displacement, and particle velocity propagated in an elastic medium) and seismic P-waves (created by earthquakes and explosions). In longitudinal waves, the displacement of the medium is parallel to the propagation of the wave. A wave along the length of a stretched Slinky toy, where the distance between coils increases and decreases, is a good visualization and contrasts with the standing wave along an oscillating guitar string, which is transverse (*en.wikipedia.org*).

Also, The particular wave band at which a radio station or other system broadcasts or transmits signals [electromagnetic wave] (*Oxford English Dictionary*).

[4p] time: Time is the indefinite continued progress of existence and events that occur in an apparently irreversible succession from the past, through the present, into the future (*Oxford Dictionaries [Oxford University Press, 2011], archived from the original on July 4, 2012, retrieved on May 18, 2017*).

A central problem with time travel to the past is the violation of causality; should an effect precede its cause, it would give rise to the possibility of a temporal paradox that cannot occur with physical matter (*"Sequence of Events Worksheets," reference.com, archived from the original on October 13, 2010*).

[*GOD—The Dimensional Revelation* Notes that hypothesizing "parallel universes" does not solve the paradox because this universe is proved to exists here and now. This physical situation is complete and cannot be undone.]

[4q] instant: an infinitesimal or very short space of time (*www.dictionary.com*).

[*GOD—The Dimensional Revelation* Emphasizes that an "instant" is a construction of mind. An instant is a perception of separate images. Reality proceeds continually, not as a sum of separate instants. This distinction is very important because it limits the use of mathematics or quantum theory that rely on separate clusters of reality rather than the continuum.]

[4r] progress: move forward or onward in space or time (*Oxford English Dictionary*).

[4s] spatial: relating to, occupying, or having the character of space (*www.merriam-webster.com*).

[4t] "time" to a Spiritual Reality, which it is not:

[The Revelation that "time" is a physical continuum and not a Spiritual Continuum—This is an essential difference between Our Spiritual Membrane System and our physical membrane system. This distinction may be original to *GOD—The Dimensional Revelation*.]

[4u] singularity: The universal origin theory known as the Big Bang postulates that, 13.7 billion years ago, our universe emerged from a singularity—a point of infinite density and gravity—and that before this event, space and time did not exist (which means the Big Bang took place at no place and no time) (*en.wikipedia.org*).

Some theories hold that the "hot big-bang" arises from an inflationary state, not a singularity. For these theorists the sequence is: singularity, inflation, and then the hot Big Bang (*Ethan Seigel Science*).

[*GOD—The Dimensional Revelation* holds the standard model of universe formation: singularity, hot big bang, then inflation. That is because the hot big bang is necessary to provide the energy, e, inflating a physical universe.]

[4v] Potential: The chance or possibility that something will develop and become real (*www.merriam-webster.com*).

[4w] matter: Physical substance in general, as distinct from mind and spirit; (in physics) that which occupies space and possesses rest mass, especially as distinct from energy (*Oxford English Dictionary*).

Matter is made up of what atoms and molecules are made of, meaning anything made of positively charged protons, neutral neutrons, and negatively charged electrons (*M. de Podesta, Understanding the Properties of Matter, Second ed.* [CRC Press, 2002], 8, ISBN 978-0-415-25788-6).

All the particles that make up ordinary matter (leptons and quarks) are elementary fermions, while all the force carriers are elementary bosons (*L. Smolin, The Trouble with Physics: The Rise of String Theory, the Fall of a Science, and What Comes Next* [Mariner Books, 2007], 67, ISBN 978-0-618-91868-3). The W and Z bosons that mediate the weak force are not made of quarks or leptons, and so are not ordinary matter, even if they have mass (*"Review of Particle Physics: The Mass and Width of the W Boson"* [PDF], *Physics Letters B.* 667 [1], Bibcode:2008PhLB.6671A. doi:10.1016/j.physletb.2008.07.018). In other words, mass is not something that is exclusive to ordinary matter.

The quark–lepton definition of ordinary matter, however, identifies not only the elementary building blocks of matter, but also includes composites made from the constituents (atoms and molecules, for example). Such composites contain an interaction energy that holds the constituents together, and may constitute the bulk of the mass of the composite. As an example, to a great extent, the mass of an atom is simply the sum of the masses of its constituent protons, neutrons and electrons. However, digging deeper, the protons and neutrons are made up of quarks bound together by gluon fields (see dynamics of quantum chromodynamics) and these gluons fields contribute significantly to the mass of hadrons (*IJR Aitchison and AJG Hey, Gauge Theories in Particle Physics [CRC Press, 2004], 48, ISBN 978-0-7503-0864-9*). In other words, most of what composes the "mass" of ordinary matter is due to the binding energy of quarks within protons and neutrons (*B. Povh et al., Particles and Nuclei: An Introduction to the Physical Concepts [Springer, 2004], 103, ISBN 978-3-540-20168-7*). For example, the sum of the mass of the three quarks in a nucleon is approximately 12.5 MeV/c^2, which is low compared to the mass of a nucleon (approximately 938 MeV/c^2). The bottom line is that most of the mass of everyday objects comes from the interaction energy of its elementary components (*A. M. Green, Hadronic Physics from Lattice QCD [World Scientific, 2004], 120, ISBN 978-981-256-022-3*); (*T. Hatsuda, "Quark-Gluon Plasma and QCD," in Condensed Matter Theories 21, ed. H. Akai [Nova Publishers, 2008], 296, ISBN 978-1-60021-501-8*).

[4x] Apparent: Seeming real or true but not necessarily so (*Oxford English Dictionary*).

[4y] inertia: Sir Isaac Newton defined *inertia* as his first law in his *Philosophiæ Naturalis Principia Mathematica*, which states,

> The *vis insita*, or innate force of matter, is a power of resisting by which everybody, as much as in it lies, endeavours to preserve its present state, whether it be of rest or of moving uniformly forward in a straight line.

The idea was that as type 1a supernovae have almost the same intrinsic brightness (a standard candle), and since objects that are further away appear dimmer, we can use the observed brightness of these supernovae to measure the distance to them. The distance can then be compared to the supernovae's cosmological redshift, which measures how much the universe has expanded since the supernova occurred. The unexpected result was that objects in the universe are moving away from one another at an accelerated rate. *See also Hubble law, which established that the further an object is from us, the faster it is receding.*

By comparing this [age of the universe] to actual measured values of the cosmological parameters, we can confirm the validity of a model which is accelerating now, and had a slower expansion in the past (*Reynald Pain and Pierre Astier, "Observational Evidence of the Accelerated Expansion of the Universe," Comptes Rendus Physique 13 [6], 2012*).

Peaks have been found in the correlation function (the probability that two galaxies will be a certain distance apart) at 100 h^{-1} Mpc (where *h* is the dimensionless Hubble constant), indicating that this is the size of the sound horizon today, and by comparing this to the sound horizon at the time of decoupling (using the CMB), we can confirm the accelerated expansion of the universe (*Daniel J. Eisenstein, et al., "Detection of the Baryon Acoustic Peak in the Large-Scale Correlation Function of SDSS Luminous Red Galaxies," The Astrophysical Journal. 633 no. 2 [2005]:560–574*).

Lambda-CDM, accelerated expansion of the universe. The time-line in this schematic diagram extends from the Big Bang/inflation era 13.7 Byr ago to the present cosmological time.

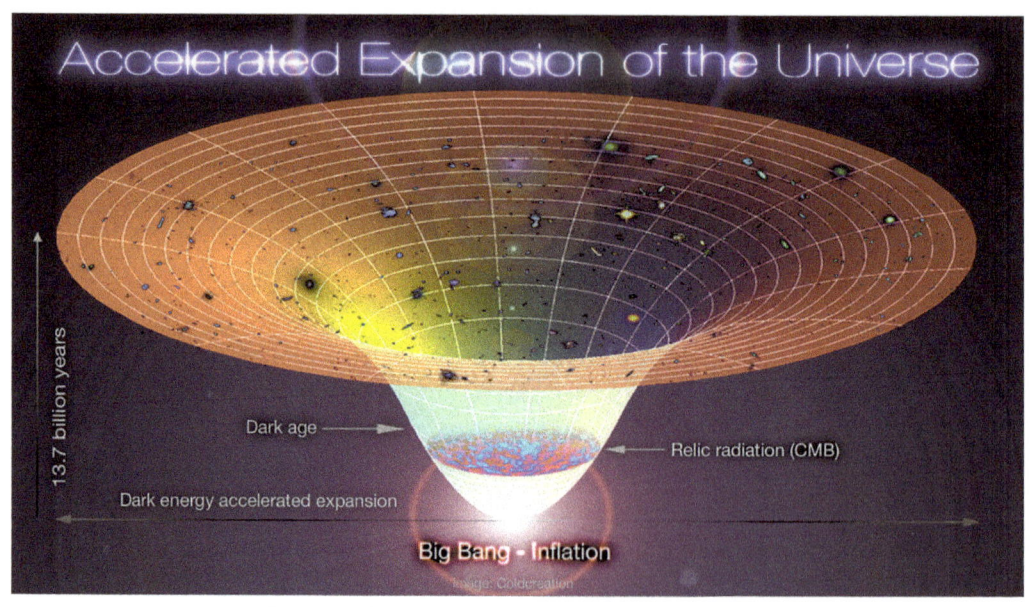

Design Alex Mittelmann, *Coldcreation*, CC BY-SA 3.0 (https://creativecommons.org/licenses/by-sa/3.0) via Wikimedia Commons)

[*GOD—The Dimensional Revelation* expands the definition of inertia to include acceleration of matter into physical nothingness after our big bang. This differs from the classical definition of inertia that does not include acceleration or deceleration of matter. Our definition of inertia includes the inflation of space as matter accelerates away from our big bang. The point is that there is physically nothing outside the boundary of our physical universe to resist the force of inertia, so inertia forces acceleration of matter and its attendant energies away from the big bang. This makes inertia the second most powerful force in physical reality.

Our Teaching may expand to include a definition of "dark energy" as an aspect of Inertia. Some theories hold that dark energy is the force causing the accelerating expansion of our physical universe.]

RESEARCH NOTES, CREDITS, AND EXPANSIONS

[4z] **particle or particles:** A minute portion of matter… In the physical sciences, a particle is a small, localized object or entity to which can be ascribed several physical or chemical properties such as volume, density or mass… They vary greatly in size or quantity, from subatomic particles like the electron, to microscopic particles like atoms and molecules, to macroscopic particles like powders and other granular materials. Both elementary (such as muons) and composite particles (such as uranium nuclei), are known to undergo particle decay. Those that do not are called stable particles, such as the electron or a helium-4 nucleus. The lifetime of stable particles can be either infinite or large enough to hinder attempts to observe such decays. In the latter case, those particles are called "observationally stable". In general, a particle decays from a high-energy state to a lower-energy state by emitting some form of radiation, such as the emission of photons (*"Particle," AMS Glossary, American Meteorological Society, retrieved 2015-04-12*).

Particles are representations of the Poincaré group: the group of 10 ways of moving around in the space-time continuum. Objects can shift in three spatial directions or shift in time; they can also rotate in three directions or receive a boost in any of those directions. In 1939, the mathematical physicist Eugene Wigner identified particles as the simplest possible objects that can be shifted, rotated, and boosted (*Natalie Wolchover; https://www.quantamagazine.org/what-is-a-particle-20201112/*).

[4z1] **nothingness:** the general state of nonexistence, sometimes reified as a domain or dimension into which things pass when they cease to exist or out of which they may come to exist, e.g., God is understood to have created the universe ex nihilo, "out of nothing" (*www.merriam-webster.com*).

Leucippus is the first to say that a "thing" (the void) might be real without being a body (*Cyril Bailey, The Greek Atomists and Epicurus: A Study [The Clarendon Press, 1928], 75–76*).

[This logic leads to the Assertion In *GOD—The Dimensional Revelation* that "nothingness" is always limited to a closed system, a limited subset of reality. Nothingness can only be the "gap between" other real manifestations of GOD. This nothingness is not limited to the physical membrane system but can define whatever void is between, or within, Other Manifestations Of GOD. Such voids are within the boundary of the universe in which they are Observed.]

[4z2] **accelerate:** to go faster or make something go faster (*dictionary.cambridge.org*).

acceleration: In mechanics, acceleration is the rate of change of the velocity of an object with respect to time. Accelerations are vector quantities (in that they have magnitude and direction). (*Hermann Bondi, Relativity and Common Sense [Courier Dover Publications, 1964], 3, ISBN 978-0-486-24021-3*).

> The Big Bang theory predicts that there was a powerful repulsive force at the beginning of the expanding of the Universe.

A common hypothesis of the cause of the Big Bang is a short-term repulsive field, the so-called "inflation." Observations of supernovas have shown that the Universe is still expanding with acceleration. There are some models that explain the current acceleration of the Universe using a concept of the so-called "dark energy," a substance that has a negative pressure thus causing a repulsive effect. (*Alexander Vasilkiv and Nick Gorkavyi, August 8, 1916*)

[4z3] residue: something that remains after a part is taken, separated, or designated or after the completion of a process (*www.merriam-webster.com*).

[4z4] energetic: The cosmic microwave background (CMB, CMBR), in Big Bang cosmology, is electromagnetic radiation which is a remnant from an early stage of the universe, also known as "relic radiation"… CMB is landmark evidence of the Big Bang origin of the universe. When the universe was young, before the formation of stars and planets, it was denser, much hotter, and filled with a uniform glow from a white-hot fog of hydrogen plasma. As the universe expanded, both the plasma and the radiation filling it grew cooler. When the universe cooled enough, protons and electrons combined to form neutral hydrogen atoms (*en.wikipedia.org*).

[4z5] Recombining: to mix or merge two or more things again (www.vocabulary.com).

[4z6] subsequent: coming after something in time, following (*Oxford English Dictionary*).

[4z7] atom or atoms: An atom is the smallest constituent unit of ordinary matter that constitutes a chemical element. Every solid, liquid, gas, and plasma is composed of neutral or ionized atoms. Atoms are extremely small, typically around 100 picometers across. Every atom is composed of a nucleus and one or more electrons bound to the nucleus. The nucleus is made of one or more protons and a number of neutrons. Only the most common variety of hydrogen has no neutrons. More than 99.94% of an atom's mass is in the nucleus. The protons have a positive electric charge, the electrons have a negative electric charge, and the neutrons have no electric charge. If the number of protons and electrons are equal, then the atom is electrically neutral. If an atom has more or fewer electrons than protons, then it has an overall negative or positive charge, respectively—these atoms are called ions. The electrons of an atom are attracted to the protons in an atomic nucleus by the electromagnetic force. The protons and neutrons in the nucleus are attracted to each other by the nuclear force. This force is usually stronger than the electromagnetic force that repels the positively charged protons from one another (*www.wikipedia.com*).

In 1925 Werner Heisenberg published the first consistent mathematical formulation of quantum mechanics (matrix mechanics). One year earlier, Louis de Broglie had proposed the de Broglie hypothesis: that all particles behave like waves to some extent (*Niels Bohr, "Niels Bohr, The Nobel Prize in Physics 1922, Nobel Lecture," December 11, 1922*). *and in 1926.* Erwin Schrödinger used this idea to develop the Schrödinger equation, a mathematical model of the atom (wave mechanics) that described the electrons as three-dimensional waveforms rather than point particles (*Miroslaw Kozłowski, "The Schrödinger Equation: A History," 2019*).

A consequence of using waveforms to describe particles is that it is mathematically impossible to obtain precise values for both the position and momentum of a particle at a given point in time; this became known as the uncertainty principle, formulated by Werner Heisenberg in 1927.

In the Standard Model of physics, electrons are truly elementary particles with no internal structure, whereas protons and neutrons are composite particles composed of elementary particles called quarks (*James Schombert, "Elementary Particles," April 18, 2006*).

[4z8] positive: For every proton in an atomic center, somewhere in an orbital, there will be an electron. A proton carries a positive charge (+) and an electron carries a negative charge (-), so the atoms of elements are neutral, all the positive charges canceling out all the negative charges (*Professor John Blamire, BIOdotEDU, 2003*).

[4z9] neutral: Neutrons and protons are found in the nucleus of an atom. Unlike protons, which have a positive charge, or electrons, which have a negative charge, neutrons have zero charge which means they are neutral particles (*simplewikipedia.org*).

[4z10] drawn or drawn to: move in a particular direction by or as if by pulling; drag (*www.wordreference.com*).

[4z11] strong atomic force: The strong nuclear force holds most ordinary matter together because it confines quarks into hadron particles such as the proton and neutron. In addition, the strong force binds these neutrons and protons to create atomic nuclei. Most of the mass of a common proton or neutron is the result of the strong force field energy; the individual quarks provide only about 1% of the mass of a proton.

At the range of 10^{-15} m (1 femtometer), the strong force is approximately 137 times as strong as electromagnetism, a million times as strong as the weak interaction, and 1038 times as strong as gravitation. *Relative strength of interaction varies with distance. See for instance Matt Strassler's essay, "The Strength of the Known Forces."*

The strong interaction is observable at two ranges and mediated by two force carriers. On a larger scale (about 1 to 3 fm), it is the force (carried by mesons) that binds protons and neutrons (nucleons) together to form the nucleus of an atom. On the smaller scale (less than about 0.8 fm, the radius of a nucleon), it is the force (carried by gluons) that holds quarks together to form protons, neutrons, and other hadron particles (*"The Four Forces: The Strong Interaction," Duke University Astrophysics Department website*).

[4z12] big bang nucleosynthesis: big bang nucleosynthesis (BBN) offers the deepest reliable probe of the early Universe, being based on well-understood Standard

Model physics. In physical cosmology, Big Bang nucleosynthesis (abbreviated BBN, also known as primordial nucleosynthesis, archeonucleosynthesis, archonucleosynthesis, protonucleosynthesis and paleonucleosynthesis) is the production of nuclei other than those of the lightest isotope of hydrogen (hydrogen-1, 1H, having a single proton as a nucleus) during the early phases of the Universe. Primordial nucleosynthesis is believed by most cosmologists to have taken place in the interval from roughly 10 seconds to 20 minutes after the Big Bang, and is calculated to be responsible for the formation of most of the universe's helium as the isotope helium-4 (4He), along with small amounts of the hydrogen isotope deuterium (2H or D), the helium isotope helium-3 (3He), and a very small amount of the lithium isotope lithium-7 (7Li). In addition to these stable nuclei, two unstable or radioactive isotopes were also produced: the heavy hydrogen isotope tritium (3H or T); and the beryllium isotope beryllium-7 (7Be); but these unstable isotopes later decayed into 3He and 7Li, as above.

Big Bang Nucleosynthesis

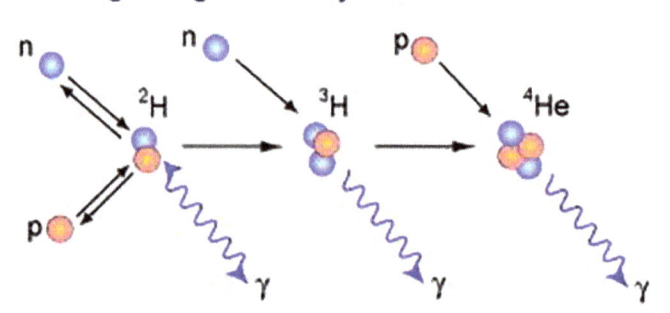

This shows one of the reactions sequences that produces a helium-4 nucleus from protons and neutrons. Other sequences are possible.
The first stage is reversible due to photodisintegration by gamma photons.

(https://thespectrumofriemannium.wordpress.com/tag/big-bang-nucleosynthesis/)

RESEARCH NOTES, CREDITS, AND EXPANSIONS

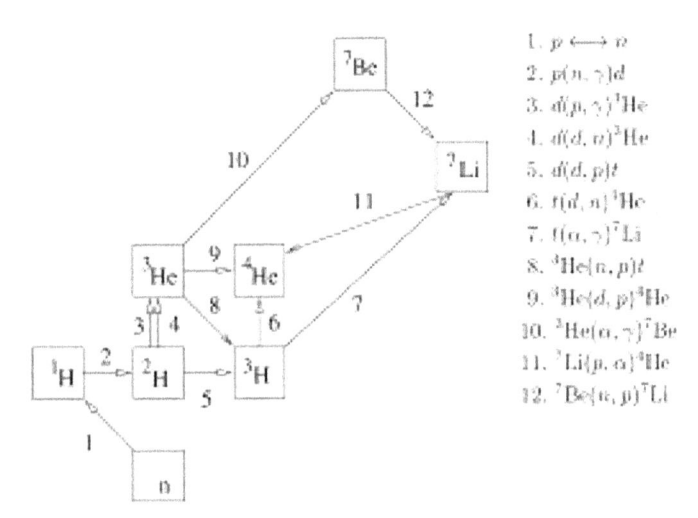

Espen Sem Jennsen 2016 (https://www.duo.uio.no/bitstream/handle/10852/52374/FinalReport.pdf)

Essentially all of the elements that are heavier than lithium were created much later by stellar nucleosynthesis in evolving and exploding stars (*Revised October 2015 by B. D. Fields, (University of Illinois) P. Molaro (Trieste Observatory), and S. Sarkar (University of Oxford and Niels Bohr Institute–Copenhagen)*).

[*GOD—The Dimensional Revelation* Explains that nucleosynthesis is a subset of physical synthesis, which is a subset of Metaphysical Synthesis].

[4z13] negative: [in cosmology] For every proton in an atomic center, somewhere, in an orbital, there will be an electron. A proton carries a positive charge (+) and an electron carries a negative charge (-), so the atoms of elements are neutral, all the positive charges canceling out all the negative charges (*Professor John Blamire, BIOdotEDU, 2003*).

[4z14] electron: The electron is a subatomic particle, symbol $e-$ or $β-$, whose electric charge is negative-one elementary charge (*Jerry Coff, "What Is an Electron," September 10, 2010*). Electrons belong to the first generation of the lepton particle family (*L. J. Curtis, Atomic Structure and Lifetimes, 2003*) and are generally thought to be elementary particles because they have no known components or substructure (*E. J. Eichten, M. E. Peskin, and M. Peskin, "New Tests for Quark and Lepton Substructure," Physical Review Letters 50 no. 11 [1983]: 811–814*). The electron has a mass that is approximately 1/1836 that of the proton (*CODATA Value: Proton-Electron Mass Ratio," CODATA Recommended Values, National Institute of Standards and Technology, 2006*). quantum mechanical properties of the electron include an intrinsic angular momentum (spin) of a half-integer value expressed in units of the reduced Planck constant, $ℏ$. Being fermions, no two electrons can occupy the same quantum state in accordance with the Pauli exclusion principle (*L. J. Curtis, Atomic Structure and Lifetimes: A Conceptual Approach [Cambridge University Press, 2003], 74*).

229

[*GOD—The Dimensional Revelation Deduces* that since no two electrons or other fermions can occupy the same quantum state, there can be no parallel physical universe as a version of our physical universe at the same time. This also explains why traveling back in time to the past is impossible.]

Like all elementary particles, electrons exhibit properties of both particles and waves: they can collide with other particles and can be diffracted like light. The wave properties of electrons are easier to observe with experiments than those of other particles like neutrons and protons because electrons have a lower mass and hence a longer De Broglie wavelength for a given energy.

Electrons play an essential role in numerous physical phenomena, such as electricity, magnetism, chemistry, and thermal conductivity; and they also participate in gravitational, electromagnetic, and weak interactions (C. Anastopoulos, *Particle Or Wave: The Evolution of the Concept of Matter in Modern Physics* [Princeton University Press, 2008], 236–237).

Since an electron has charge, it has a surrounding electric field; and if that electron is moving relative to an observer, said observer will observe it to generate a magnetic field. Electromagnetic fields produced from other sources will affect the motion of an electron according to the Lorentz force law. Electrons radiate or absorb energy in the form of photons when they are accelerated.

Laboratory instruments are capable of trapping individual electrons as well as electron plasma by the use of electromagnetic fields. Special telescopes can detect electron plasma in outer space. Electrons are involved in many applications, such as electronics, welding, cathode ray tubes, electron microscopes, radiation therapy, lasers, gaseous ionization detectors, and particle accelerators.

Interactions involving electrons with other subatomic particles are of interest in fields such as chemistry and nuclear physics. The Coulomb force interaction between the positive protons within atomic nuclei and the negative electrons without allows the composition of the two known as atoms. Ionization or differences in the proportions of negative electrons versus positive nuclei changes the binding energy of an atomic system. The exchange or sharing of the electrons between two or more atoms is the main cause of chemical bonding (*L. C. Pauling, The Nature of the Chemical Bond and the Structure of Molecules and Crystals: An Introduction to Modern Structural Chemistry,* Third ed. [Cornell University Press, 1960], 4–10). In 1838, British natural philosopher Richard Laming first hypothesized the concept of an indivisible quantity of electric charge to explain the chemical properties of atoms (T. Arabatzis, *Representing Electrons: A Biographical Approach to Theoretical Entities* [University of Chicago Press, 2006], 70–74).

Electrons can also participate in nuclear reactions, such as nucleosynthesis in stars, where they are known as beta particles. Electrons can be created through beta decay of radioactive isotopes and in high-energy collisions, for instance when cosmic rays enter the atmosphere. The antiparticle of the electron is called the positron; it is identical to the electron except that it carries electrical and other charges of the opposite sign. When an electron collides with a positron, both particles can be annihilated, producing gamma ray photons (*en.wikipedia.org*).

[*GOD—The Dimensional Revelation* develops our hypothesis that our big-bang was the cancellation of Primal Matter and Primal Antimatter, leaving an energy residue expanding as our physical universe is a macrotheory deriving in part from this microtheory that when an electron and positron collied, both particles are annihilated, producing gamma ray photo energy. Of course, further proof is necessary to support our macrotheory.]

[4z15] definite: clearly defined or determined; not vague or general; fixed; precise; exact (*www.dictionary.com*).

[4z16] proton: A proton is a subatomic particle, symbol p or p+, with a positive electric charge of +1e elementary charge and a mass slightly less than that of a neutron. Protons and neutrons, each with masses of approximately one atomic mass unit, are collectively referred to as "nucleons" (particles present in atomic nuclei).

One or more protons are present in the nucleus of every atom; they are a necessary part of the nucleus. The number of protons in the nucleus is the defining property of an element, and is referred to as the atomic number (represented by the symbol Z). Since each element has a unique number of protons, each element has its own unique atomic number.

The word *proton* is Greek for "first", and this name was given to the hydrogen nucleus by Ernest Rutherford in 1920. In previous years, Rutherford had discovered that the hydrogen nucleus (known to be the lightest nucleus) could be extracted from the nuclei of nitrogen by atomic collisions. Protons were therefore a candidate to be a fundamental particle, and hence a building block of nitrogen and all other heavier atomic nuclei (*"Definition, Mass, Charge, & Facts," Encyclopedia Britannica*).

Although protons were originally considered fundamental or elementary particles, in the modern Standard Model of particle physics, protons are classified as hadrons, like neutrons, the other nucleon. Protons are composite particles composed of three valence quarks: two up quarks of charge +2/3e and one down quark of charge –1/3e. The rest masses of quarks contribute only about 1% of a proton's mass (*Adrian Cho, "Mass of the Common Quark Finally Nailed Down," Science Magazine. American Association for the Advancement of Science, April 2, 2010, retrieved September 27, 2014*). The remainder of a proton's mass is due to quantum chromodynamics binding energy, which includes the kinetic energy of the quarks and the energy of the gluon fields that bind the quarks together. Because protons are not fundamental particles, they possess a measurable size; the root mean square charge radius of a proton is about 0.84–0.87 fm (or 0.84×10−15 to 0.87×10−15 m). In 2019, two different studies, using different techniques, have found the radius of the proton to be 0.833 fm, with an uncertainty of ±0.010 fm (*N. Bezginov, et al., "A Measurement of the Atomic Hydrogen Lamb Shift and the Proton Charge Radius," Science 365, no.*

6457 [September 6, 2019]: 1007–1012, Bibcode:2019Sci.365.1007B doi:10.1126/science.aau7807); (W. Xiong, et al., "A Small Proton Charge Radius from an Electron–Proton Scattering Experiment," Nature 575, no. 7781 [November 2019]: 147–150, Bibcode:2019Natur.575.147X. doi:10.1038/s41586-019-1721-2).*

At sufficiently low temperatures, free protons will bind to electrons. However, the character of such bound protons does not change, and they remain protons. A fast proton moving through matter will slow by interactions with electrons and nuclei until it is captured by the electron cloud of an atom. The result is a protonated atom, which is a chemical compound of hydrogen. In vacuum, when free electrons are present, a sufficiently slow proton may pick up a single free electron, becoming a neutral hydrogen atom, which is chemically a free radical. Such "free hydrogen atoms" tend to react chemically with many other types of atoms at sufficiently low energies. When free hydrogen atoms react with each other, they form neutral hydrogen molecules (H2), which are the most common molecular component of molecular clouds in interstellar space (*en.wikipedia.org*).

[4z17] neutron: The free neutron has a mass of 939,565,413.3 eV/c2, or 1.674927471×10−27 kg, or 1.00866491588 u (*P. J. Mohr, B. N. Taylor, and D. B. Newell, "The 2014 CODATA Recommended Values of the Fundamental Physical Constants," 2014*). The neutron has a mean square radius of about 0.8×10−15 m, or 0.8 fm (*B. Povh et al., Particles and Nuclei: An Introduction to the Physical Concepts. [Berlin: Springer-Verlag, 2002], 73*), and it is a spin-½ fermion (*J. L. Basdevant, J. Rich, and M. Spiro, Fundamentals in Nuclear Physics [Springer, 2005], 155*).

The neutron has no measurable electric charge. With its positive electric charge, the proton is directly influenced by electric fields, whereas the neutron is unaffected by electric fields. The neutron has a magnetic moment, however, so the neutron is influenced by magnetic fields. The neutron's magnetic moment has a negative value because its orientation is opposite to the neutron's spin, (*Paul Allen Tipler and Ralph A. Llewellyn, Modern Physics, Fourth ed. [Macmillan, 2002], 310*).

A free neutron is unstable, decaying to a proton, electron, and antineutrino with a mean lifetime of just under 15 minutes (881.5±1.5 s) (*K. Nakamura, "Review of Particle Physics," Journal of Physics G, 37, no. 7A [2010], 075021, Bibcode: 2010JPhG.37g5021N.doi:10.1088/0954-3899/37/7A/075021, PDF with 2011 partial update for the 2012 edition*). This radioactive decay, known as beta decay, is possible because the mass of the neutron is slightly greater than the proton. The free proton is stable. Neutrons or protons bound in a nucleus can be stable or unstable, however, depending on the nuclide. Beta decay, in which neutrons decay to protons or vice versa, is governed by the weak force, and it requires the emission or absorption of electrons and neutrinos or their antiparticles.

Nuclear fission is caused by absorption of a neutron by uranium-235. The heavy nuclide fragments into lighter components and additional neutrons.

Protons and neutrons behave almost identically under the influence of the nuclear force within the nucleus. The concept of isospin, in which the proton and neutron are viewed as two quantum states of the same particle, is used to model the interactions of nucleons by the nuclear or weak forces. Because of the strength of the nuclear force at short distances, the binding energy of nucleons is more than seven orders of magnitude larger than the electromagnetic energy binding electrons in atoms. Nuclear reactions (such as nuclear fission) therefore have an energy density that is more than ten million times that of chemical reactions. Because of the mass–energy equivalence, nuclear binding energies reduce the mass of nuclei. Ultimately, the ability of the nuclear force to store energy arising from the electromagnetic repulsion of nuclear components is the basis for most of the energy that makes nuclear reactors or bombs possible. In nuclear fission, the absorption of a neutron by a heavy nuclide (e.g., uranium-235) causes the nuclide to become unstable and break into light nuclides and additional neutrons. The positively charged light nuclides then repel, releasing electromagnetic potential energy.

The neutron is classified as a hadron, because it is a composite particle made of quarks. The neutron is also classified as a baryon because it is composed of three valence quarks (*R. K. Adair, The Great Design: Particles, Fields, and Creation [Oxford University Press, 1989], 214*). The finite size of the neutron and its magnetic moment both indicate that the neutron is a composite rather than elementary, particle. A neutron contains two down quarks with charge $-1/3$ e and one up quark with charge $+2/3$ e.

Like protons, the quarks of the neutron are held together by the strong force mediated by gluons (*W. N. Cottingham and D. A. Greenwood, An Introduction to Nuclear Physics [Cambridge University Press, 1986]*). The nuclear force [weak force] results from secondary effects of the more fundamental strong force (*en.wikipedia.org*).

[4z18] condense: At about one second [after the big bang], neutrinos decouple; these neutrinos form the cosmic neutrino background (CvB). If primordial black holes exist, they are also formed at about one second of cosmic time. Composite subatomic particles emerge—including protons and neutrons—and from about 2 minutes, conditions are suitable for nucleosynthesis. Around 25% of the protons and all the neutrons fuse into heavier elements, initially deuterium, which itself quickly fuses into mainly helium-4 (*Barbara Sue Ryden, Introduction to Cosmology, January 13, 2006*)

By 20 minutes, the universe is no longer hot enough for nuclear fusion but far too hot for neutral atoms to exist or photons to travel far. It is therefore an opaque plasma. At around 47,000 years, as the universe cools, its behaviour begins to be dominated by matter rather than radiation. At about 100,000 years, helium hydride is the first molecule. (Much later, hydrogen and helium hydride react to form molecular hydrogen, the fuel needed for the first stars.)

At about 370,000 years, the universe finally becomes cool enough for neutral atoms to form ("recombination"), and as a result, it also became transparent for the first time. The newly formed atoms—mainly hydrogen and helium with traces of lithium—quickly reach their lowest energy state (ground state) by releasing photons ("photon decoupling"), and these photons can still be detected today as the cosmic microwave background (CMB). This is currently the oldest observation we have of the universe (*M. Tanabashi, "Big-Bang Cosmology," chapt. 21.4.1, 358 [2018], revised September 2017 by Keith A. Olive and John A. Peacock*).

[4z19] Harmony: The practical side of philosophy was introduced by Pythagoras (582–496 BC). Regarding the world as perfect harmony, dependent on number, he aimed at inducing humankind likewise to lead a harmonious life (*Oskar Seyffert, Dictionary of Classical Antiquities, [1894], 480*).

Agreement; accord; harmonious relations; a consistent, orderly, or pleasing arrangement of parts; congruity (*www.dictionary.com*).

In music: any simultaneous combination of tones. the simultaneous combination of tones, especially when blended into chords pleasing to the ear; chordal structure, as distinguished from melody and rhythm (*www.dictionary.com*).

[4z20] compel or compels: to drive or urge forcefully or irresistibly (*www.merriam-webster.com*).

[4z21] Self-aware: Self-awareness is "an awareness of one's own personality or individuality" (*www.merriam-webster.com*).

It is not to be confused with consciousness in the sense of qualia. While consciousness is being aware of one's environment and body and lifestyle, self-awareness is the recognition of that awareness. (*Ferris Jabr, "Self-Awareness with a Simple Brain," Scientific American Mind 23, no. 5 [2012]: 28–29*).

Self-awareness is how an individual consciously knows and understands their own character, feelings, motives, and desires. There are two broad categories of self-awareness: internal self-awareness and external self-awareness (*"What Self-Awareness Really Is [and How to Cultivate It]," Harvard Business Review, January 4, 2018*).

Also stated as 1) bodily self-awareness, 2) social self-awareness, and 3) introspective self-awareness.

What is generally meant by "metacognition" in recent ethology literature is having cognitive states about one's own cognitive states. Any creature capable of metacognition (in this sense) is capable of introspective awareness because such meta-states involve awareness of the contents of one's own mind (*David DeGrazia, "Self-Awareness in Animals," [2009], 201–202, 216*).

[*GOD—The Dimensional Revelation* expands introspective self-awareness to include Spiritual Self-Awareness, which is not just self-cognization but elevates awareness to {1} openness to the Participation of GOD in Your Awareness and {2} Communication with other Spiritual Beings as Individuals or Group Awareness.

Also note that a Group does not have a Consciousness. An Individual Spirit or Soul has Consciousness that Survives physical death. A Group does not have a Consciousness that survives death. A group is an association of Individuals. A social movement may continue based on its organizational initiatives as Individual Members change out, but when the Group disorganizes socially, there is nothing left except history.]

Our Teaching Reveals that In The 2nd Heaven (5th D Spiritual) here on earth and in the 6th Heaven (9th D Spiritual), The WORD May Create a Collective Consciousness As It Approaches The ONE.]

[4z22] Self-evident: Not needing to be demonstrated or explained; obvious (*Oxford English Dictionary*).

[4z23] mechanical: working or produced by machines or machinery (*Oxford English Dictionary*).

[4z24] Deductive Reasoning:

> Deductive reasoning requires one to start with a few general ideas, called premises, and apply them to a specific situation. Recognized rules, laws, theories, and other widely accepted truths are used to prove that a conclusion is right… Deductive reasoning is meant to demonstrate that the conclusion is absolutely true based on the logic of the premises. (*www.mscc.edu/documents/writingcenter/Deductive-and-Inductive-Reasoning*)

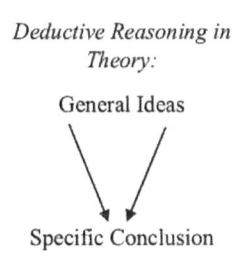

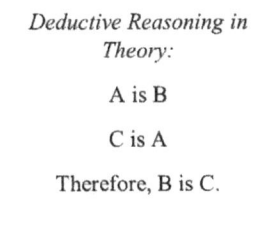

Deductive Reasoning in Theory:	*Deductive Reasoning in Theory:*	*Deductive Reasoning in Practice:*
General Ideas ↓↓ Specific Conclusion	A is B C is A Therefore, B is C.	All muscles are made out of living tissue. All humans have muscles. Therefore, all humans are made out of living tissue.

Ronald Wilson; (https://toktopics.files.wordpress.com/2019/08/6-deductive-and-inductive-reasoning.pdf)

[4z25] Senses: a faculty by which the body perceives an external stimulus; one of the faculties of sight, smell, hearing, taste, and touch (*Oxford English Dictionary*).

Humans respond more strongly to multimodal stimuli compared to the sum of each single modality together, an effect called the "superadditive effect of multisensory integration" (A. J. Privitera, "Sensation and Perception" in *Noba Textbook Series: Psychology*, ed. R. Biswas-Diener and E. Diener [Champaign, IL: DEF Publishers, 2020]).

An internal sensation and perception also known as interoception (A. D Craig, "Interoception: The Sense of the Physiological Condition of the Body" *Current Opinion in Neurobiology* [August 2003], 13).

In Buddhism, "mind" denotes an internal sense organ which interacts with sense objects that include sense impressions, feelings, perceptions and volition. The Pāli word translated here as "mind" is *mano*. Other common translations include "intellect" (e.g., Thanissaro, 2001a) and "consciousness" (e.g., Soma, 1999), also Bodhi (2000a, 288).

Vipassanā is a Pali word derived from the older prefix "vi-" meaning "special", and the verbal root "-passanā" meaning "seeing" (*Daniel E. Perdue, The Course in Buddhist Reasoning and Debate: An Asian Approach to Analytical Thinking Drawn from Indian and Tibetan Sources [Shambhala Publication May 27, 2014]*). It is often translated as "insight" or "clear-seeing". The "vi" in vipassanā has many possible meanings, it could mean to 'see into', 'see through' or to 'see in a special way' (*Henepola Gunaratana, Mindfulness in Plain English [Wisdom Publications, 2011], 21*).

[4z26] Inductive Reasoning:

> Inductive reasoning uses a set of specific observations to reach an overarching conclusion; it is the opposite of deductive reasoning. So, a few particular premises create a pattern which gives way to a broad idea that is likely true… Just as deductive arguments are meant to prove a conclusion, inductive arguments are meant to predict a conclusion. They do not create a definite answer for their premises, but they try to show that the conclusion is the most probable one given the premises… An inductive argument is either considered weak or strong based on whether its conclusion is a probable explanation for the premises. (www.mscc.edu/documents/writingcenter/Deductive-and-Inductive-Reasoning).

Inductive reasoning in Theory

Specific Observations

↙ ↘

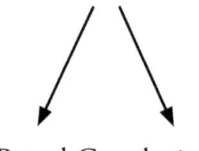

Broad Conclusion

Inductive reasoning in Practice

The past five Marvel movies have been incredibly successful at the box office. Therefore, the next Marvel movie will probably be successful.

RESEARCH NOTES, CREDITS, AND EXPANSIONS

[4z27] Infer: To deduce or conclude (information) from evidence and reasoning rather than from explicit statements.

Inference: A conclusion reached on the basis of evidence and reasoning (*Oxford English Dictionary*).

[4z28] condensation: Around a microsecond after the Big Bang, the universe was populated predominantly by quarks and gluons. As the universe expanded, the temperature dropped. Eventually the universe cooled enough to allow quarks and gluons to condense into nucleons, which subsequently formed hydrogen and helium (*https://www2.lbl.gov/abc/wallchart/chapters/01/4.html*).

[4z29] hydrogen: Hydrogen is the chemical element with the symbol H and atomic number 1. With a standard atomic weight of 1.008, hydrogen is the lightest element in the periodic table. Hydrogen is the most abundant chemical substance in the universe, constituting roughly 75% of all baryonic mass (*Padi Boyd, "What is the Chemical Composition of Stars?" NASA, July 19, 2014, archived from the original on January 15, 2015, retrieved February 5, 2008*).

Every nucleus of a given element must contain the same number (Z) of protons, but these nuclei can contain different numbers of neutrons. Most hydrogen atoms have nuclei that consist of a single proton, but a small fraction (about 0.015 percent) of the hydrogen atoms that occur in Nature have one neutron in addition to the proton in their nuclei. This "heavy hydrogen" is called deuterium and is sometimes given its own chemical symbol (D). A third form of hydrogen atoms have nuclei containing two neutrons; hydrogen with A =3 is called tritium(T), a radioactive species. The series of nuclei with the same value of Z but different values of A are called isotopes.

[4z30] Nucleus: The nucleus is a collection of particles called protons, which are positively charged, and neutrons, which are electrically neutral. Protons and neutrons are in turn made up of particles called quarks. The chemical element of an atom is determined by the number of protons, or the atomic number, Z, of the nucleus (*en.wikipedia.org*).

[4z31] helium: A helium atom is an atom of the chemical element helium. Helium is composed of two electrons bound by the electromagnetic force to a nucleus containing two protons, along with either one or two neutrons, depending on the isotope, held together by the strong force (*en.wikipedia.org*).

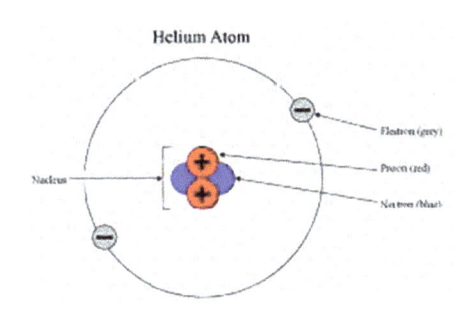

[4z32] **nuclear fusion:** Nuclear fusion is a reaction in which two or more atomic nuclei are combined to form one or more different atomic nuclei and subatomic particles (neutrons or protons). The difference in mass between the reactants and products is manifested as either the release or absorption of energy. This difference in mass arises due to the difference in atomic "binding energy" between the atomic nuclei before and after the reaction. Fusion is the process that powers active or "main sequence" stars or other high-magnitude stars (*en.wikipedia.org*).

The release of energy with the fusion of light elements is due to the interplay of two opposing forces: the nuclear force, which combines together protons and neutrons, and the Coulomb force, which causes protons to repel each other. Protons are positively charged and repel each other by the Coulomb force, but they can nonetheless stick together, demonstrating the existence of another, short-range, force referred to as nuclear attraction" (*Physics Flexbook, archived December 28, 2011, at the Wayback Machine, ck12.org, retrieved on December 19, 2012*).

An important fusion process is the stellar nucleosynthesis that powers stars, including the Sun (*en.wikipedia.org*).

[4z33] **gamma ray:** A gamma ray, or gamma radiation, is a penetrating form of electromagnetic radiation arising from the radioactive decay of atomic nuclei. It consists of the shortest wavelength electromagnetic waves and so imparts the highest photon energy (*en.wikipedia.com*).

[4z34] **wavicle:** an entity having characteristic properties of both waves and particles. (*Oxford Languages at google.com retrieved September 13, 2020*).

Also see [5z34] wave-particle duality infra.

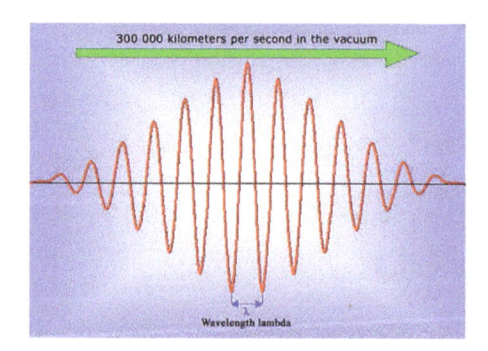

The photon—an elementary wave (a fundamental wave): A photon is a microscopic electromagnetic wave caused by oscillations in the electric and magnetic fields through space and time. A wave, in the classical sense of the term, consists of infinite oscillations and can never be localized. The number of oscillations in the photons emitted by atoms and nuclei is not infinite, thanks to a small uncertainty in their energy values. The shorter the wavelength of the photons, the denser the wave is in space. When the wavelength is as short as is the case with gamma rays, then the

RESEARCH NOTES, CREDITS, AND EXPANSIONS

waves become dense enough to resemble particles (*https://www.radioactivity.eu.com/site/pages/Photons.htm*).

[4z35] **Photon:** We group together under the name 'photon' a large variety of electromagnetic rays, from radio waves to X-rays and gamma rays, including infrared, visible and ultraviolet light.

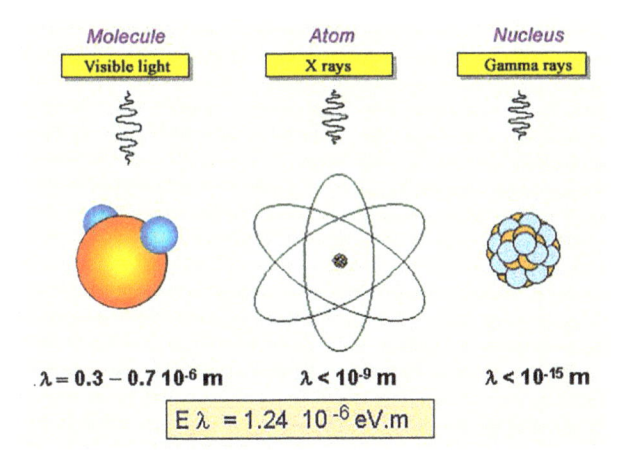

	Molecule	Atom	Nucleus
	Visible light	X rays	Gamma rays
λ	$0.3 - 0.7 \cdot 10^{-6}$ m	$< 10^{-9}$ m	$< 10^{-15}$ m

$$E\lambda = 1.24 \cdot 10^{-6} \text{ eV.m}$$

Three types of photons: The photon energy varies inversely with its wavelength. Photons are usually emitted by molecules, with energies of a few electronvolts and wavelengths of a fraction of a micron (a thousandth of millimetre). X-rays are emitted by the deeper layers of the atom, with energies reaching hundreds of thousands of electronvolts (keV) and wavelengths of the order of a billionth of a metre (nanometres). Gamma rays, on the other hand, are emitted by nuclei and have even higher energies with wavelengths appropriate to the dimensions of a nucleus (*https://www.radioactivity.eu.com/site/pages/Photons.htm*).

The photon, quantum of light, is a type of elementary particle. It is the quantum of the electromagnetic field including electromagnetic radiation, such as light and radio waves, and the force carrier for the electromagnetic force. Photons are massless, and they always move at the speed of light in vacuum.

Like all elementary particles, photons are currently best explained by quantum mechanics and exhibit wave-particle duality, their behavior featuring properties of both waves and particles (*C. Amsler et al., "Review of Particle Physics: Gauge and Higgs Bosons," Particle Data Group, 2008*).

[*GOD—The Dimensional Revelation* Presents Our version of string theory as GOD Creating strings in the 9th D as the smallest constituents of all physical reality. We state that strings are Created with diverse information. The preceding research notes describe photons and various other constituents of matter and force carriers composing our physical universe. If such information or instruction is the basic constituent, then it is a "string." If it is the result of strings combining to form the subatomic particle or energy, then that constituent has its own identity and may exhibit additional characteristics, as a gestalt, in addition to those of its constituent parts.]

[4z36] special relativity: The theory of special relativity explains how space and time are linked for objects that are moving at a consistent speed in a straight line… Simply put, as an object approaches the speed of light, its mass becomes infinite, and it is unable to go any faster than light travels.

In physics, special relativity (also known as the special theory of relativity) is the generally accepted and experimentally confirmed physical theory regarding the relationship between space and time.

In Albert Einstein's original treatment, it is based on two postulates:

1. the laws of physics are invariant (i.e., identical) in all inertial frames of reference (i.e., non-accelerating frames of reference); and
2. the speed of light in a vacuum is the same for all observers, regardless of the motion of the light source or observer (*Albert Einstein, "Zur Elektrodynamik bewegter Körper," Annalen der Physik 17 no. 891 [1905], English translation on the "Electrodynamics of Moving Bodies" by George Barker Jeffery and Wilfrid Perrett [1923].*)

The special theory of relativity, or special relativity is a physical theory which states the relationship between space and time. This is often termed as STR theory. This is theory is based on two postulates: 1. Laws of Physics are invariant; 2. Irrespective of the light source, the speed of light in a vacuum is the same in any other space. Albert Einstein originally proposed this theory in one of his paper "On the Electrodynamics of Moving Bodies". Special relativity implies consequences of mass-energy equivalence, relativity of simultaneity, length contraction, and a universal *speed* limit. The conventional notion of absolute universal time is replaced by the notion of a time that is dependent on the reference frame and spatial position.

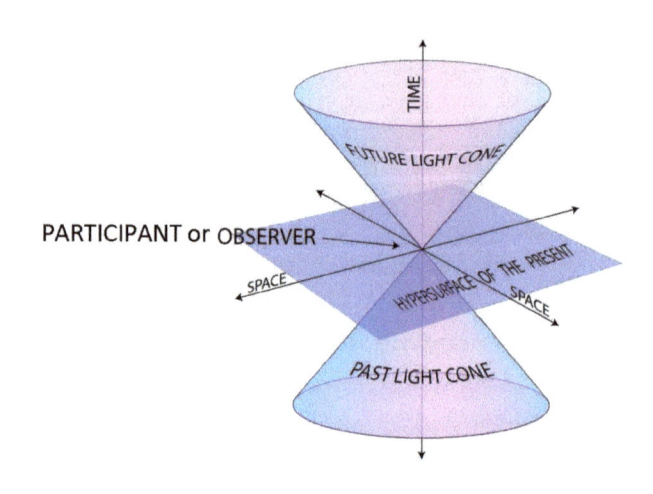

RESEARCH NOTES, CREDITS, AND EXPANSIONS

In relative theory, reference frames play a vital role. It is used to measure a time of events by using a clock. An event is nothing but an occurrence that refers to a location in space corresponding to the reference frame. For instance, the explosion of a fire flower can be considered as an event (*https://byjus.com/physics/special-theory-of-relativity/ [OBSERVER added by Allyn Richert]*). Special relativity is proven to be the most accurate model of motion at any speed when gravitational and quantum effects are negligible (*Herbert Goldstein, "Chapter 7: Special Relativity in Classical Mechanics," Classical Mechanics, Second ed., [Addison-Wesley Publishing Company, 1980] ISBN 0-201-02918-9*). Even so, the Newtonian model is still valid as a simple and accurate approximation at low velocities (relative to the speed of light), for example, everyday motions on Earth.

Special relativity has a wide range of consequences that have been experimentally verified (*Einstein, Autobiographical Notes, 1949*). They include the relativity of simultaneity, length contraction, time dilation, the relativistic velocity addition formula, the relativistic Doppler effect, relativistic mass, a universal speed limit, mass–energy equivalence, the speed of causality and the Thomas precession. It has, for example, replaced the conventional notion of an absolute universal time with the notion of a time that is dependent on reference frame and spatial position. Rather than an invariant time interval between two events, there is an invariant spacetime interval. Combined with other laws of physics, the two postulates of special relativity predict the equivalence of mass and energy, as expressed in the mass–energy equivalence formula, $E = mc^2$, where c is the speed of light in a vacuum (*Einstein, "Fundamental Ideas and Methods of the Theory of Relativity," 1920*). It also explains how the phenomena of electricity and magnetism are related (*David J. Griffiths, "Chapter 12: Electrodynamics and Relativity," Introduction to Electrodynamics, Fourth ed. [Pearson, 2013], ISBN 978-0-321-85656-2*).

Some of the work of Albert Einstein in special relativity is built on the earlier work by Hendrik Lorentz. Special relativity was originally proposed by Albert Einstein in a paper published on 26 September 1905 titled "On the Electrodynamics of Moving Bodies".[p 1] The incompatibility of Newtonian mechanics with Maxwell's equations of electromagnetism and, experimentally, the Michelson-Morley null result (and subsequent similar experiments) demonstrated that the historically hypothesized luminiferous aether did not exist. This led to Einstein's development of special relativity, which corrects mechanics to handle situations involving all motions and especially those at a speed close to that of light (known as relativistic velocities) (*en.wikipedia.org*).

[4z37] mass: Mass is both a property of a physical body and a measure of its resistance to acceleration (a change in its state of motion) when a net force is applied (*www.dictionary.com*).

An object's mass also determines the strength of its gravitational attraction to other bodies.

The basic SI unit of mass is the kilogram (kg). In physics, mass is not the same as weight, even though mass is often determined by measuring the object's weight using a spring scale, rather than balance scale comparing it directly with known masses. An object on the Moon would weigh less than it does on Earth because of the lower gravity, but it would still have the same mass. This is because weight is a force, while mass is the property that (along with gravity) determines the strength of this force (*en.wikipedia.org*).

- Inertial mass is a measure of an object's resistance to acceleration when a force is applied.
- Active gravitational mass is a measure of the strength of an object's gravitational flux.
- Passive gravitational mass is a measure of the strength of an object's interaction with a gravitational field.
- Energy also has mass according to the principle of mass–energy equivalence.
- Curvature of space-time is a relativistic manifestation of the existence of mass. Such curvature is extremely weak and difficult to measure.
- Quantum mass manifests itself as a difference between an object's quantum frequency and its wave number.

[4z38] mass-energy equivalence: In special relativity, mass–energy equivalence is the principle that anything having mass has an equivalent amount of energy and vice versa, with these fundamental quantities directly relating to one another by Albert Einstein's famous formula: $E=mc^2$.

Energy (E): quantitative physical property transferred to objects to perform heating or work on them.

mass (m): property of matter to resist changes of the state of motion and to attract other bodies. Mass is a quantitative property of matter. mass=weight x volume.

speed of light (c): speed at which all massless particles and associated fields travel in a vacuum

This formula states that the equivalent energy (E) can be calculated as the mass (m) multiplied by the speed of light (c = ~3×10⁸ m/s) squared. Similarly, anything having energy exhibits a corresponding mass m given by its energy E divided by the speed of light squared c^2. Because the speed of light is a large number in everyday units, the formula implies that even an everyday object at rest with a modest amount of mass has a very large amount of energy intrinsically. Chemical reactions, nuclear reactions, and other energy transformations may cause a system to lose some of its energy content to the environment (and thus some corresponding mass), releasing it as the radiant energy of light or as thermal energy for example (*en.wikipedia.org*).

RESEARCH NOTES, CREDITS, AND EXPANSIONS

Mass–energy equivalence arose originally from special relativity as a paradox described by Henri Poincaré (*H. Poincaré, "La théorie de Lorentz et le principe de reaction," Archives Néerlandaises des Sciences Exactes et Naturelles, 5, 252–278*).

Einstein proposed it on 21 November 1905, in the paper Does the inertia of a body depend upon its energy-content? one of his Annus Mirabilis (Miraculous Year) papers (*A. Einstein, "Ist die Trägheit eines Körpers von seinem Energieinhalt abhängig?" AnnalenderPhysik 18, no. 13 [1905]: 639–643, Bibcode:1905AnP.323.639E, doi:10.1002/andp.19053231314*). See also the English translation. Einstein was the first to propose that the equivalence of mass and energy is a general principle and a consequence of the symmetries of space and time.

A consequence of the mass–energy equivalence is that if a body is stationary, it still has some internal or intrinsic energy, called its rest energy, corresponding to its rest mass. When the body is in motion, its total energy is greater than its rest energy, and equivalently its total mass (also called relativistic mass in this context) is greater than its rest mass. This rest mass is also called the intrinsic or invariant mass because it remains the same regardless of this motion, even for the extreme speeds or gravity considered in special and general relativity.

The mass–energy formula also serves to convert units of mass to units of energy (and vice versa), no matter what system of measurement units is used (*David Bodanis, E=mc²: A Biography of the World's Most Famous Equation, Illustrated ed. [Bloomsbury Publishing, 2009], ISBN 978-0-8027-1821-1*).

[4z39] limit or limitation: a limiting rule or circumstance; a restriction (*Oxford Languages at google.com retrieved September 13, 2020*).

a lack of capacity or ability (*www.wordreference.com, retrieved September 13, 2020*).

[cosmological limit] by 10^{14} (100 trillion) years from now, star formation will end, leaving all stellar objects in the form of degenerate remnants. If protons do not decay, stellar-mass objects will disappear more slowly, making this era last longer (*Fred C. Adams and Gregory Laughlin, "A Dying Universe: The Long-Term Fate and Evolution of Astrophysical Objects," Reviews of Modern Physics. 69, no. 2 [1997]: 337–372*).

[Ontological no-limit]

> Great is our Lord and mighty in power; his understanding has no limit. (*Holy Bible, Psalm 147:5 NIV*)

> "Who can hide in secret places so that I cannot see them?" declares the Lord. "Do not I fill heaven and earth? declares the Lord." (*Holy Bible, Jeremiah 23:24 NIV*)

[4z40] field of influence (Influence): the capacity to have an effect on the character, development, or behavior of someone or something or the effect itself (*Oxford English Dictionary*).

A sphere of influence (SOI) in astrodynamics and astronomy is the oblate-spheroid-shaped region around a celestial body where the primary gravitational influence on an orbiting object is that body (*en.wikipedia.org*).

[*GOD—The Dimensional Revelation* expands upon physical-sphere-of-influence definitions to present the concept of the "field of influence" of a dimension. This is the bounded field within which certain principles of operation control the reality. The "field" can be any reality in which those principles operate. Each dimension is defined and limited by the reality in which its principles operate. Typically lower dimensions are contained within the larger field of influence of the higher dimension.]

[4z41] electronic potential: An electric potential (also called the electric field potential, potential drop, or the electrostatic potential) is the amount of work needed to move a unit of electric charge from a reference point to a specific point in an electric field without producing an acceleration. Typically, the reference point is the Earth or a point at infinity, although any point can be used (*en.wikipedia.org*).

[4z42] weak atomic force: In nuclear physics and particle physics, the weak interaction, which is also often called the weak force or weak nuclear force, is the mechanism of interaction between subatomic particles that is responsible for the radioactive decay of atoms (*David Griffiths, Introduction to Elementary Particles, [2009], 59–60*).

In the weak interaction, fermions can exchange three types of force carriers, namely W+, W−, and Z bosons. The masses of these bosons are far greater than the mass of a proton or neutron, which is consistent with the short range of the weak force. In fact, the force is termed weak because its field strength over a given distance is typically several orders of magnitude less than that of the strong nuclear force or electromagnetic force.

Quarks, which make up composite particles like neutrons and protons, come in six "flavours"—up, down, strange, charm, top and bottom—which give those composite particles their properties. The weak interaction is unique in that it allows quarks to swap their flavour for another. The swapping of those properties is mediated by the force carrier bosons. For example, during beta minus decay, a down quark within a neutron is changed into an up quark, thus converting the neutron to a proton and resulting in the emission of an electron and an electron antineutrino.

The weak interaction does not produce bound states, nor does it involve binding energy—something that gravity does on an astronomical scale, that the electromagnetic force does at the atomic level, and that the strong nuclear force does inside nuclei (*Walter Greiner and Berndt Müller, Gauge Theory of Weak Interactions [Springer, 2009], 2*).

RESEARCH NOTES, CREDITS, AND EXPANSIONS

[4z43] electromagnetism: Electromagnetism is a branch of physics involving the study of the electromagnetic force, a type of physical interaction that occurs between electrically charged particles. The electromagnetic force is carried by electromagnetic fields composed of electric fields and magnetic fields, and it is responsible for electromagnetic radiation such as light. It is one of the four fundamental interactions (commonly called forces) in nature, together with the strong interaction, the weak interaction, and gravitation (*Fawwaz T. Ravaioli, Eric Michielssen Ulaby, Umberto, Fundamentals of Applied Electromagnetics, Sixth ed. [Boston: Prentice Hall, 2010], 13*).

At high energy the weak force and electromagnetic force are unified as a single electroweak force.

Electromagnetic phenomena are defined in terms of the electromagnetic force, sometimes called the Lorentz force, which includes both electricity and magnetism as different manifestations of the same phenomenon. The electromagnetic force plays a major role in determining the internal properties of most objects encountered in daily life. The electromagnetic attraction between atomic nuclei and their orbital electrons holds atoms together. Electromagnetic forces are responsible for the chemical bonds between atoms, which create molecules and intermolecular forces. The electromagnetic force governs all chemical processes, which arise from interactions between the electrons of neighboring atoms (*en.wikipedia.org*).

[4z44] Formation: The process by which something comes into existence or begins to have a particular order or shape (dictionary.cambridge.org).

[4z45] gravity: Gravity (from Latin gravitas, meaning 'weight'), or gravitation, is a natural phenomenon by which all things with mass or energy—including planets, stars, galaxies, and even light—are brought toward (or gravitate toward) one another. On Earth, gravity gives weight to physical objects, and the Moon's gravity causes the ocean tides. The gravitational attraction of the original gaseous matter present in the Universe caused it to begin coalescing and forming stars and caused the stars to group together into galaxies, so gravity is responsible for many of the large-scale structures in the Universe. Gravity has an infinite range, although its effects become increasingly weaker as objects get further away. Gravity is well approximated by Newton's law of universal gravitation, which describes gravity as a force, which causes any two bodies to be attracted to each other, with the force proportional to the product of their masses and inversely proportional to the square of the distance between them (*Sir Isaac Newton, Philosophiæ Naturalis Principia Mathematica, 1713*).

Einstein first predicted gravitational waves in 1916 as a consequence of the general theory of relativity. In this theory, concentrations of mass (or energy) warp space-time, and changes in the shape or position of such objects cause a distortion that propagates through the Universe at the speed of light (i.e., a gravitational wave).

It is tempting to draw the analogy between gravitational waves and electromagnetic waves. However, the nature of the waves is quite different in these two cases. Electromagnetic waves are oscillating electromagnetic fields propagating through space-time, while gravitational waves are the propagation of distortions of space-time itself. The emission mechanisms are also quite different. Electromagnetic-wave emission results from an incoherent superposition of waves from molecules, atoms, and particles, while gravitational waves are coherent emission from bulk motions of energy. The characteristics of the waves are also quite different in that electromagnetic waves experience strong absorption and scattering in interaction with matter, while gravitational waves have essentially no absorption or scattering. Finally, the typical frequency of detection of electromagnetic waves is f > 107 Hz, while gravitational waves are expected to be detectable at much lower frequency, f < 104 Hz (*Barry C. Barish, California Institute of Technology, Pasadena, California 91125*).

The Laser Interferometer Gravitational-Wave Observatory (LIGO) is a large-scale physics experiment and observatory to detect cosmic gravitational waves and to develop gravitational-wave observations as an astronomical tool (*Barry C. Barish and Rainer Weiss, "LIGO and the Detection of Gravitational Waves," Physics Today 52, no. 10 [October 1999]: 44*). Observations are made in "runs". As of December 2019, LIGO has made 3 runs, and made 50 detections of gravitational waves (*The LIGO Scientific Collaboration, the Virgo Collaboration, B. P. Abbott, R. Abbott, T. D. Abbott, S. Abraham, F. Acernese, K. Ackley, C. Adams, R. X. Adhikari, V. B. Adya, September 4, 2019*).

[*GOD—The Dimensional Revelation* theorizes that our physical universe is a closed system, so gravity does not stretch infinitely as the limit of its field of influence is the boundary of our physical universe.]

[4z46] Given: Stated, fixed, or specified (*www.dictionary.com*).

[4z47] Sustain or sustains: To cause or allow something to continue for a period of time. (*dictionary.cambridge.com*).

[4z48] Logical proof: A formal series of statements showing that if one thing is true, something else necessarily follows from it (*www.vocabulary.com*).

[4z49] Living Being:

> And the Lord God formed man of the dust of the ground, and breathed into his nostrils the breath of life; and man became a living soul. (*Holy Bible, Genesis 2:7 KJV; Torah Bereishit, Genesis 2:7*)

The living being is first and foremost a spiritual entity (*https://www.gettysburg.edu/offices/religious-spiritual-life/world-religions-101/what-is-hinduism*).

[5a] Primary Being:

> In the beginning God created the heaven and the earth. (*Holy Bible, Genesis 1:1 KJV*)

RESEARCH NOTES, CREDITS, AND EXPANSIONS

> In the beginning of God's creation of the heavens and the earth. Now the earth was astonishingly empty, and darkness was on the face of the deep, and the spirit of God was hovering over the face of the water. (*Torah Bereishit, Genesis 1:1–2*)

Primary: first in order, rank, or importance (*www.dictionary.com*).

[*GOD—The Dimensional Revelation* restates that GOD Is Prior To and Preexisted To Cause The Beginning Of Reality.]

[5b] Fully: completely or entirely; to the furthest extent (*Oxford English Dictionary*).

[5c] Reunification: Coming back together again after being separated or in conflict is called reunification (*www.vocabulary.com*).

> Jesus Christ Said, "That they all may be ONE; as thou, Father, art in me, and I in thee, that they also may be ONE in us: that the world may believe that thou hast sent me. And the glory which thou gavest me I have given them; that they may be ONE, even as we are ONE: I in them, and thou in me, that they may be made perfect in ONE; and that the world may know that thou hast sent me, and hast loved them, as thou hast loved me." (*Holy Bible, John 17:21–23 KJV*)

> What is ultimately permanent is the union between the Atman and the Brahman. Thus, life's struggle is for the Atman to be released from the body, which is impermanent, to unite with Brahman, which is permanent—this doctrine is known as Moksha. (*Gwinyai H. Muzorewa, The Great Being [Wipf, 2000], 52–54*)

Averroes (Ibn Rushd, 1126-1198) added to the growing concept of emanation by claiming that the universal mind is an emanation from God. Humans participate in this universal mind; and only it, not the soul, is immortal.

[Corresponding to the Sixth and Seventh Heaven Revealed In *GOD—The Dimensional Revelation*.]

[5d] Implicit: Esentially or very closely connected with; always to be found in (*Oxford English Dictionary*).

[5e] Differentiation or Differentiated: Development from the one to the many (*www.merriam-webster.com*).

Within Christianity, the doctrine of the Trinity states that God is a single being that exists simultaneously and eternally as a perichoresis of three hypostases (i.e. persons; personae, prosopa): the Father (the Source, the Eternal Majesty); the Son (the eternal Logos ("Word"), manifest in human form as Jesus and thereafter as Christ); and the Holy Spirit (the Paraclete or advocate) (*en.wikipedia.org*).

Jain text claims that the universe consists of Jiva (life force or souls) and Ajiva (lifeless objects). Similarly, the soul of each living being is unique and uncreated and has existed since beginningless time (*Nayanar, 190, Gāthā 10.310, 2005b*).

Buddhists accept the existence of beings known as devas in higher realms; but they, like humans, are said to be suffering in samsara (*John T. Bullitt, The Thirty-One Planes of Existence, 2005*).

Ishvara is a transcendent and immanent entity best described in the last chapter of the Shukla Yajur Veda Samhita, known as the Ishavasya Upanishad. It states "ishavasyam idam sarvam" which means, whatever there is in this world is covered and filled with Ishvara. Ishvara not only creates the world, but then also enters into everything there is (*en.wikipedia.org*).

In God there are contained hosts of glorious hierarchies and lesser beings of every grade of intelligence and stage of consciousness, from omniscience to an unconsciousness deeper than that of the deepest trance condition (*The Rosicrucian Cosmo-Conception*).

[5f] Undiminished: as good, strong, or important as always (*dictionary.cambridge.org*).

not made less, smaller, or weaker (*www.merriam-webster.com*).

diminish: make or become less (*Oxford English Dictionary*).

[5g] His Ministry on earth:

> Jesus said, "The time is fulfilled, and the kingdom of God is at hand. Repent, and believe in the gospel." (*Holy Bible, Mark 1:15 NIV*)

[5h] Mind: The element of a person that enables them to be aware of the world and their experiences, to think, and to feel; the faculty of consciousness and thought (*Oxford English Dictionary*).

One open question regarding the nature of the mind is the mind–body problem, which investigates the relation of the mind to the physical brain and nervous system (*Andy Clark, Mindware. [198 Madison Avenue, New York, 10016: Oxford University Press, 2014], 14, 254–256*). The mind–body problem is a debate concerning the relationship between thought and consciousness in the human mind, and the brain as part of the physical body. It is distinct from the question of how mind and body function chemically and physiologically, as that question presupposes an interactionist account of mind–body relations. This question arises when mind and body are considered as distinct, based on the premise that the mind and the body are fundamentally different in nature (*Justin Skirry, "Rene Descartes: The Mind-Body Distinction," Internet Encyclopedia of Philosophy*).

RESEARCH NOTES, CREDITS, AND EXPANSIONS

[*GOD—The Dimensional Revelation* Reveals that the word *Mind* Can only Be Interpreted As A Spiritual word. The Mind Is A Fusion Of physical brain structures and processes supporting The Presence Of Your Individual Spirit or Soul. Your Immortal Soul, Incarnate in Your physical body, Yields Your Consciousness, One Mind, in Its Broadest Interpretation. Your Mind Is Your Consciousness and Experience, to include physical and nonphysical phenomena, During This Life. Hence, Mind Is A Continuation Of The Journey Of Your Soul. Your Mind Is Limited To Your Current Lifetime. Your Mind also Provides For Spiritual Growth and Extraordinary Spiritual Experience In This Life.]

[5i] Divine Awareness: The divinity and unity of a single divine reality—awareness. It recognizes that God is awareness along with its multiple manifestations and personifications—both human and divine (*Acharya Peter Wilberg, Shaivist Tantric Theology, The New Yoga, retrieved 2020*).

> Observing mind means observing the purity of mind. The mind is basically nondual, just one vital reality; throughout the past and future, there is no other. Without leaving the objects of sense, you climb transcendent to the stage of enlightenment. (*The* Secret of the Golden Flower 65, trans. Thomas Cleary [HarperCollins, 1991])

[5j] Postulate or postulates (*verb*): Suggest or assume the existence, fact, or truth of (something) as a basis for reasoning, discussion, or belief (*Oxford Languages, Oxford University Press*).

[5k] Law of Dimensional Limitation: [*GOD—The Dimensional Revelation* Presents this original principle of dimensions and why dimensions are defined as This Teaching Reveals. The Law of Dimensional Limitation states that each dimension is defined by a set of operational principles. The extent of those operational principles is the field of influence of that dimension. Each dimension has a limited field of influence. An Observation that is not included within the boundary of a dimension or that is controlled by principles not among those controlled in that dimension necessitates defining a higher or broader dimension to account for The Observation. Usually, all the lower dimensions are included in the higher dimension defined.

This Teaching defines the 10 dimensions according to their fields of influence and their limits, plus the 0th dimension, which is hypothetical and not yet real, and the 11th [GOD], which are not dimensions because GOD Exists Both Inside and Outside Of Reality.

We Note that the first eight dimensions of our physical membrane system are different than the first eight dimensions of Our Spiritual Membrane System. The 9th D and 10th D encompass all of Reality As They Create The Differentiations That Become Real In the lower dimensions.]

[5l] Boundary: A limit of a subject or sphere of activity (*Oxford Languages, Oxford University Press*).

dimensional boundaries: [*GOD—The Dimensional Revelation* Understands each dimension by the limits of its field of influence. That limit sets the boundary of each dimension. A higher dimension is revealed when reality is observed that exceeds the limitation of a dimension.]

[5m] Operational principles or laws of operation: [*GOD—The Dimensional Revelation* Reveals that the limit of a dimension is the extent to which its laws of operation dominate reality. Any observed reality not dominated by the operational principles of a dimension is under the influence of a higher dimension. The proof that Our Spiritual Universe Is Separate From our physical universe is that We Observe Action In Our Lives not subject to the physical laws of our physical universe. *GOD—The Dimensional Revelation* boldly Revels the combination of separate operational principle groups creating The Reality In Which We Participate. Each Of Us Is Aware Of the Influence Of Our Spiritual Actions and Attitudes On the physical world.]

[5n] No End or Without End: Without a limit or boundary (*Oxford English Dictionary*).

End: The point where something ceases to exist (*www.merriam-webster.com*).

[5o] Flow: a steady, continuous stream of something (*Oxford Languages, Oxford University Press*).

[5p] WILL Of GOD:

> Our Father which art in heaven, Hallowed be thy name. Thy kingdom come, Thy will be done in earth, as it is in heaven. Give us this day our daily bread. And forgive us our debts, as we forgive our debtors. And lead us not into temptation, but deliver us from evil: For thine is the kingdom, and the power, and the glory, forever. Amen. (*Holy Bible, Matthew 6:9–14 KJV*)

> Jesus answered them, and said, "My doctrine is not mine, but his that sent me. If any man will do his will, he shall know of the doctrine, whether it be of God, or whether I speak of myself." (*Holy Bible, John 7:16–17 KJV*)

The will of God, divine will, or God's plan is the concept of a God having a plan for humanity. Ascribing a volition or a plan to a God generally implies a personal God (God regarded as a person with mind, emotions, will) (*Compare: James C. Howell, The Will of God: Answering the Hard Questions [Louisville, Kentucky: Westminster John Knox Press, 2009], 18*).

[*GOD—The Dimensional Revelation* Uses The WILL Of GOD as a synonym for the WORD, The 10th Dimension.]

[5q] Causative Channel: indicates that a subject either causes someone or something else to do or be something or causes a change in state of a non-volitional event. Normally, it brings in a new argument (the causer), A, into a transitive clause, with the original subject S becoming the object O (*Thomas E. Payne, Describing Morphosyntax: A Guide for Field Linguists [Cambridge: Cambridge University Press, 1997], 173–186*).

…change adjectives into verbs of becoming (*en.wikipedia.org*).

[*GOD—The Dimensional Revelation* Explains That Reality Is The WORD, The 10th D, Flowing As Instruction or Cause To Create Reality In The 9th D Along Channels that can "Become" Manifest Into Reality In The 8th D and lower dimensions.

This Teaching is more broadly based than physical reality but agrees with current quantum theory, which holds "becoming" as the core of physical reality.

In other words, an adjective describing a noun in the present is active "to become" something else in the future. For example: a "hot potato" now, becomes a "cold potato" later as it collapses into reality in the future.]

[5r] Enabling: Make (a device or system) operational, activate. (*Oxford English Dictionary*).

[5s] Collapse: To fall or shrink together abruptly and completely. (*www.merriam-webster.com*).

wavefunction collapse: In general, quantum systems exist in superpositions of those basis states that most closely correspond to classical descriptions, and, in the absence of measurement, evolve according to the Schrödinger equation. However, when a measurement is made, **the wave function collapses—from an observer's perspective—to just one of the basis states**, and the property being measured uniquely acquires the eigenvalue of that particular state, After the collapse, the system again evolves according to the Schrödinger equation [from the situation created in the collapse into being.] (*Werner Heisenberg 1927 paper on the uncertainty principle, "Über den anschaulichen Inhalt der quantentheoretischen Kinematik und Mechanik" and incorporated into the mathematical formulation of quantum mechanics by John von Neumann in his 1932 treatise "Mathematische Grundlagen der Quantenmechanik); (C. Kiefer, "On the Interpretation of Quantum Theory—From Copenhagen to the Present Day," 2002, arXiv:quant-ph/0210152*).

Collapse is a thermodynamically irreversible process. In an irreversible process, finite changes are made; therefore the system is not at equilibrium throughout the process. At the same point in an irreversible cycle, the system will be in the same state, but the surroundings are permanently changed after each cycle. It is the difference between the reversible work and the actual work for a process as shown in the following equation: $I = W_{rev} - W$ (*Steven S. Zumdahl, "10.2 The Isothermal Expansion and Compression of an Ideal Gas." Chemical Principles, Fifth Edition [Houghton Mifflin Company, 2005]*).

[This is why *GOD—The Dimensional Revelation* Concludes that time travel is not possible in Our universe of matter and its attendant energies. Once an event happens, the particular state is "observed"—that is, collapsed into reality. The future, or next event, again is undetermined.

Spiritual Manifestations Are also Collapsed Into Reality, though These Follow Different Operational Principles.

We assert that while any physical observer may collapse the alternatives into a physical reality, only GOD Provides The Machinery To Collapse the alternatives Into Reality. Collapsing Into Reality Is The Operation Of The 9th-D Machinery Of Creation. Some Of These 9th-D Operations Are Explained In This Teaching.

Also, note that the use of the word *observe* in quantum physics is the condition of collapsing into a particular state. This is quite different from Our Use Of Observation In This Teaching. Our use of the word *Observation* Is That Of A Conscious Being Sensing Reality, Which May Be Spiritual or physical. quantum "observation" does not require Seeing, or Sensing, or A Conscious Entity to observe. quantum "observation"—it is just the physical act of collapsing into physical reality here and now.]

[5t] Maintain or maintained: Cause or enable (a condition or state of affairs) to continue (*Oxford English Dictionary*).

[5u] Construction: *Construction* is a general term meaning the art and science to form objects, systems, or organizations (*Oxford English Dictionary*).

Metastring Construction: see [5y].

[5v] Conscience: An inner feeling or voice viewed as acting as a guide to the rightness or wrongness of one's behavior (*Oxford English Dictionary*).

The sense or consciousness of the moral goodness or blameworthiness of one's own conduct, intentions, or character together with a feeling of obligation to do right or be good (*www.merriam-webster.com*).

Humans possess free will to choose between wrong and right, and are thus responsible for their actions; the conscience being a dynamic personal connection to God enhanced by knowledge and practice of the Five Pillars of Islam, deeds of piety, repentance, self-discipline and prayer; and disintegrated and metaphorically covered in blackness through sinful acts (*John B. Noss, Man's Religions, [The Macmillan Company: New York, 1968], 16, 758–59*).

> To move from one unselfish action to another with God in mind. Only there, delight and stillness…the only rewards of our existence here are an unstained character and unselfish acts. (*Marcus Aurelius, Meditations, trans. Gregory Hays [Weidenfeld and & Nicolson: London, 2003], 70, 75*)

RESEARCH NOTES, CREDITS, AND EXPANSIONS

Descartes used *conscientia* the way modern speakers would use "conscience". In Search *after Truth* (*Regulæ ad directionem ingenii ut et inquisitio veritatis per lumen naturale, Amsterdam 1701*), he says,

> Conscience or internal testimony...the starry heavens above me and the moral law within me...the latter begins from my invisible self, my personality, and exhibits me in a world which has true infinity but which I recognize myself as existing in a universal and necessary (and not only, as in the first case, contingent) connection. (*I. Kant, "The Noble Descent of Duty" in Ethics, ed. P. Singer, [Oxford University Press: NY, 1994], 41*)

Einstein often referred to the "inner voice" as a source of both moral and physical knowledge:

> Quantum mechanics is very impressive. But an inner voice tells me that it is not the real thing. The theory produces a good deal but hardly brings one closer to the secrets of the Old One. I am at all events convinced that He does not play dice. (*Quoted in Gino Segre, Faust in Copenhagen: A Struggle for the Soul of Physics and the Birth of the Nuclear Age [Pimlico: London, 2007], 144*)

> Conscience does not only offer itself to show us the way we should walk in, but it likewise carries its own authority with it. (*Joseph Butler, "Sermons," in The Works of Joseph Butler, ed. W. E. Gladstone [Clarendon Press: Oxford, 1896], vol 2, 71*)

> One must never let the fire in one's soul die, for the time will inevitably come when it will be needed. And he who chooses poverty for himself and loves it possesses a great treasure and will hear the voice of his conscience address him every more clearly. He who hears that voice, which is God's greatest gift, in his innermost being and follows it, finds in it a friend at last, and he is never alone!... That is what all great men have acknowledged in their works, all those who have thought a little more deeply and searched and worked and loved a little more than the rest, who have plumbed the depths of the sea of life. (The Letters of Vincent van Gogh, ed. Ronald de Leeuw selected, trans. Arnold Pomerans [Penguin Books: London, 1997], 54, ISBN 0-14-044674-5)

[5w] Forgive or Forgiveness: to grant pardon for or remission of (an offense, debt, etc.); absolve (*www.dictionary.com*).

> Be kind and compassionate to one another, forgiving each other, just as in Christ God forgave you. (*Holy Bible, Ephesians 4:32 NIV*)

Forgiving others begets being forgiven by God.

> For if you forgive men when they sin against you, your heavenly Father will also forgive you. But if you do not forgive men their sins, your Father will not forgive your sins. (*Holy Bible, Mark 11:25 and Matthew 6:14–15 NIV*)

> The Lord our God is merciful and forgiving, even though we have rebelled against him. (*Holy Bible, Daniel 9:9 NIV*)

> Love prospers when a fault is forgiven, but dwelling on it separates close friends. (*Holy Bible, Proverbs 17:9 NLT*)

[*GOD—The Dimensional Revelation* Reveals That Forgiveness Is only Possible In An "Open System." Limited resources in a closed system, such as Our physical world, will justify selfish possession of resources to this or that end. Only When You Realize That the SOURCE Provides The Unlimited Resources Of An "Open System" In The Higher Dimensions Can You Turn The Light Of Forgiveness On To the closed system In This Life.

Furthermore, That Act Opens The System. Hence, Forgiveness Is An Act Of Creation With You As The Machinery Of Creation In The 9th Dimension.

In other words, Forgiveness May Be Understood As A Differentiation Of The ONE As A Process rather than An Identity. This Is Another "Proof Of Process" In The 9th D, An Instruction Of The 10th-D WORD. You Are The Instrument Of GOD Initiating That Instruction.]

[5x] Positive Utility: Utilitarianism is a family of normative ethical theories that promotes actions that maximize happiness and well-being for all affected individuals (*Brian Duignan, [1999] 2000. "Utilitarianism," revised, www.britannica.com*).

[5y] Metastring Connection: [*GOD—The Dimensional Revelation* Reveals The Creative Machinery Of The 9th D Accomplishes The Instructions Of The WORD By Establishing Connections Between The LORD and Manifest Realities. Implicit In Differentiation Of A Spiritual Being From The, Is A Metastring Connection between Each Spiritual Being and GOD. This Facilitates Prayer, Worship, Exchange Of Spiritual Energy, and Participation Of GOD In The Consciousness Of Each Individual Spirit.]

RESEARCH NOTES, CREDITS, AND EXPANSIONS

[5z] Manifest Reality (*verb*): [Generally] an event, action, or object that clearly shows or embodies something. [as the result of personal action] something that is put into your physical reality through thoughts, feelings, and beliefs. This means that whatever you focus on is what you are bringing into your reality (*www.thelawofattraction.com*).

Manifest Reality (*noun*): a manifestation is the proof of the reality of something.

The omnipresence of God explains how He is everywhere all at once, while the manifest presence of God is His presence made clear. The omnipresence of God can exist without our awareness, but the manifest presence cannot, for the point manifest presence of the Lord is that our awareness of Him is awakened to reality as defined by Him (*Dave Jenkins, christianity.com, retrieved October 11, 2020*).

[5z1] Proceed: Begin or continue a course of action (*Oxford English Dictionary*).

[5z2] Creative or Creative Force:

> The Son is the image of the invisible God, the firstborn over all creation. For in him all things were created: things in heaven and on earth, visible and invisible, whether thrones or powers or rulers or authorities; all things have been created through him and for him. (*Holy Bible, Colossians 1:15–16 NIV*)

[5z3] Nuance: A subtle difference in or shade of meaning, expression, or sound (*Oxford English Dictionary*).

[5z4] string: In physics, string theory is a theoretical framework in which the point-like particles of particle physics are replaced by one-dimensional objects called strings. It describes how these strings propagate through space and interact with each other. On distance scales larger than the string scale, a string looks just like an ordinary particle, with its mass, charge, and other properties determined by the vibrational state of the string.

…Physicists studying string theory have discovered a number of these dualities between different versions of string theory, and this has led to the conjecture that all consistent versions of string theory are subsumed in a single framework known as M-theory (*Katrin Becker, Melanie Becker, and John Schwarz, String Theory and M-Theory: A Modern Introduction [Cambridge University Press, 2007], 1-12, ISBN 978-0-521-86069-7*).

The fundamental objects of string theory are open and closed strings.

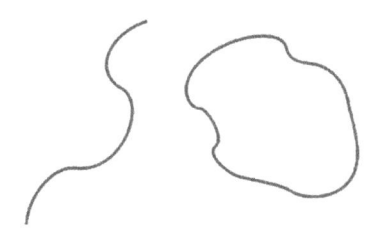

In quantum field theory, the mathematical description of physical fields include nonphysical states. In order to omit these states from the description of every physical process, a mechanism called "gauge symmetry" is used. This is true for string theory as well, but in string theory, it is often more intuitive to understand why the nonphysical states should be disposed of (*en.wikipedia.org*).

[*GOD—The Dimensional Revelation* points this out as another reason the cosmological model of reality is incomplete. Disposing of Nonphysical States or adjusting the parameters is convenient to "renormalize" the mathematics so that it works to describe reality in quantum theory. Omitting non-physical states, as done in gauge symmetry and renormalization in quantum mathematics, may be convenient and useful, but the models it allows are incomplete. They are fundamentally dishonest and evil only when used to diminish the role of Spirit In Our Reality. "Thou shalt not eat of it: for in the day that thou eatest thereof thou shalt surely die." Presuming behavior to be known at every scale in string theory without proof of origin is another proof of Nonphysical Being and Original Cause Being Outside Of physical reality. This is another proof of GOD.]

[5z5] micro: very small; especially, microscopic (*www.merriam-webster.com*).

[5z6] macro: very large in scale, scope, or capability (*www.dictionary.com*).

[5z7] subatomic: smaller than or occurring within an atom (*Oxford English Dictionary*).

[5z8] Planck length: Max Planck won the Nobel Prize for Physics in 1918 for his original theory of quantum mechanics. In physics, the Planck length (smallest of all measures), denoted ℓP, is a unit of length that is the distance light travels in one unit of Planck time. It is also the reduced Compton wavelength of a particle with Planck mass. It is equal to $1.616255(18) \times 10^{-35}$ m.

Planck's law for the energy E_λ radiated per unit volume by a cavity of a blackbody in the wavelength interval λ to $\lambda + \Delta\lambda$ ($\Delta\lambda$ denotes an increment of wavelength) can be written in terms of Planck's constant (h), the speed of light (c), the Boltzmann constant (k), and the absolute temperature (T) (*M. Planck Verhandl. Dtsch. phys. Ges., 2, 237, On the Theory of the Energy Distribution Law of the Normal Spectrum, M. Planck Berlin [Received 1900], English translation from "The Old Quantum Theory,"* ed. D. ter Haar, [Pergamon Press, 1967], 82):

$$E_\lambda = \frac{8\pi hc}{\lambda^5} \times \frac{1}{\exp(hc/kT\lambda) - 1}$$

[5z9] quantum wave: …model this mathematically by using wave functions—equations that have multiple values that make them true. These various properties of atomic particles are called quantum states, and the theory of quantum superposition says that particles can exist in multiple quantum states at once. The wave function is

a representation of all the possible quantum states of a particle. Until the particle is measured, causing the wave function to "collapse," that matter really does exist with all possible properties.

The Schrödinger equation determines how wave functions evolve over time, and a wave function behaves qualitatively like other waves, such as water waves or waves on a string, because the Schrödinger equation is mathematically a type of wave equation. This explains the name "wave function", and gives rise to wave–particle duality. However, the wave function in quantum mechanics describes a kind of physical phenomenon, still open to different interpretations, which fundamentally differs from that of classic mechanical waves (*Born, 1927, 354–357*); (*Landau and Lifshitz, 1977, 6*).

[5z10] diverse: showing a great deal of variety, very different (*Oxford English Dictionary*).

[*GOD—The Dimensional Revelation* sets forth the deduction that quantum waves cannot all be the same, given the diversity of physical manifestations Of The WORD.]

[5z11] resonance: a vibration of large amplitude in a mechanical or electrical system caused by a relatively small periodic stimulus of the same or nearly the same period as the natural vibration period of the system (*www.merriam-webster.com*).

Mathematician Steven Strogatz provides various examples from physics, biology, chemistry, and neuroscience to illustrate sync—his term for resonance—in his 2003 book *Sync: How Order Emerges from Chaos in the Universe, Nature, and Daily Life*.

The plot of these functions, called "the frequency response of the system," presents one of the most important features in forced vibration. In a lightly damped system when the forcing frequency nears the natural frequency, the amplitude of the vibration can get extremely high. This phenomenon is called resonance (subsequently the natural frequency of a system is often referred to as the resonant frequency). [For example, when you stand in the enclosed shower and sing from lower to higher pitches you reach a note where that pitch is much louder. Your voice, the forcing frequency reaches the natural frequency of reflection of the sound in that space, so the sound doubles as the compression waves of sound move together at that pitch. That is resonance.]

Resonance is simple to understand if the spring and mass are viewed as energy storage elements—with the mass storing kinetic energy and the spring storing potential energy. As discussed earlier, when the mass and spring have no external force acting on them, they transfer energy back and forth at a rate equal to the natural frequency. In other words, to efficiently pump energy into both mass and spring requires that the energy source feed the energy in at a rate equal to the natural frequency. Applying a force to the mass and spring is similar to pushing a child on swing, a push is needed at the correct moment to make the swing get higher and higher. As in the case of the swing, the force applied need not be high to get large motions, but must just add energy to the system.

The damper, instead of storing energy, dissipates energy. Since the damping force is proportional to the velocity, the more the motion, the more the damper dissipates the energy. Therefore, there is a point when the energy dissipated by the damper equals the energy added by the force. At this point, the system has reached its maximum amplitude and will continue to vibrate at this level as long as the force applied stays the same. If no damping exists, there is nothing to dissipate the energy, and theoretically, the motion will continue to grow into infinity.

Over the last decade, my colleague, University of California, Santa Barbara psychology professor Jonathan Schooler and I have developed what we call a resonance theory of consciousness. We suggest that resonance—another word for synchronized vibrations—is at the heart of not only human consciousness but also animal consciousness and of physical reality more generally (*Tam Hunt, University of California–Santa Barbara*).

[GOD—*The Dimensional Revelation* Is Firm on the point that to achieve resonance, an outside force must be applied and maintained for the resonance to continue. Consequently, aspects within a system can "self-organize," but it is assumed that {1} there is something already there to organize {Vibrations sync, Harmonize, Fuse, or Relate To One Another To Form A More Complex physical or Spiritual Reality} and {2} that there is energy applied to sustain both the initial vibrations and to sustain the resonance. We assert that there is enough energy and matter in the closed system of our physical universe to sustain physical resonance for a very long time, but more complex syncs break down or transform as the type of energy changes or relocates.

In the Fusion of Spiritual Forces With physical forces, a 9th-D Resonance May Occur. The Resonance May Be Spontaneous At Lower Levels Of Consciousness. Acts Of Individual Will May Raise The Resonance To Higher Levels Of Consciousness, That May Be Called Heaven. See chapter 13.

Furthermore, The WORD is the sustaining force adding the Instruction to sustain strings on the physical metastring and adding Spiritual Energy To Sustain Consciousness On The Spiritual Metastring.]

[5z12] frequency: Frequency is the number of occurrences of a repeating event per unit of time. It is also referred to as temporal frequency, which emphasizes the contrast to spatial frequency and angular frequency. Frequency is measured in units of hertz (Hz) which is equal to one occurrence of a repeating event per second. The period is the duration of time of one cycle in a repeating event, so the period is the reciprocal of the frequency. (*www.merriam-webster.com*).

For example: if a newborn baby's heart beats at a frequency of 120 times a minute (2 hertz), its period, T,—the time interval between beats—is half a second (60 seconds divided by 120 beats). Frequency is an important parameter used in science

RESEARCH NOTES, CREDITS, AND EXPANSIONS

and engineering to specify the rate of oscillatory and vibratory phenomena, such as mechanical vibrations, audio signals (sound), radio waves, and light (*en.wikipedia.org*).

[5z13] Harmonic oscillation and Spiritual Oscillation (Oscillatory motion): Repeated back and forth movement over the same path about an equilibrium position, such as a mass on a spring or pendulum.

restoring force: A force acting opposite to displacement to bring the system back to equilibrium, which is its rest position. The force magnitude depends only on displacement, such as in Hooke's law.

simple harmonic motion (SHM): Oscillatory motion where the net force on the system is a restoring force (*https://www.khanacademy.org/science/high-school-physics/simple-harmonic-motion*).

The quantum harmonic oscillator is the quantum-mechanical analog of the classical harmonic oscillator. Because an arbitrary smooth potential can usually be approximated as a harmonic potential at the vicinity of a stable equilibrium point, it is one of the most important model systems in quantum mechanics. Furthermore, it is one of the few quantum-mechanical systems for which an exact, analytical solution is known (*David J. Griffiths, Introduction to Quantum Mechanics Second ed. [Prentice Hall, 2004]*).

[*GOD—The Dimensional Revelation* Reveals That The WORD Is The Original "Restorative Force" Sustaining harmonic oscillation in quantum fields. This Is Another Proof Of GOD.]

[5z14] GOD-Wave: a synonym for *Manifestation*.

[*GOD—The Dimensional Revelation* Firmly holds that a "string" or "quantum wave" or any other description of the most fundamental components of physical reality, As Well As Spiritual Differentiations Of The ONE, Are Manifestations Of Aspects Of GOD.

This Teaching Identifies These To Be GOD-Waves, Which Are Aspects Of The WORD. GOD-Waves Are The Fundamental Smaller Components Of Information That Collapses Into Being As A Complete Phenomenon or Manifestation. GOD-Waves can be physical as with strings, or They Can Be Spiritual As With Spiritual Manifestations, such as Your Soul. Though very different In Each Type Of Manifestation, The Fundamental Divine Presence, The WORD, Sustains All Reality.]

[5r15] Mold or Molded: Give something particular shape or form, influence someone to have certain qualities or behavior (*www.macmillandictionary.com*).

[5z16] Divine Energy: Divine energy…comes into the human being. It clears all their karmic baggage, clears imbalances within their biology, transcends them into a higher state of being. It's like an electric current running in the human Brody! It brings in the "light" body so that the physical can merge into the light vessel! It's transformational. It transforms a normal human into a divine human. It makes an

individual go beyond their mind! It does much much more (*Jaya Prasad, January 17, 2020, Quora website*).

How to Connect With Your Energy Divine Self in 4 Steps:

1. Sit quietly.
2. Let your thoughts go. Bring your mind to a state of inner stillness.
3. Speak to the Divine Self; aloud or in your mind.
4. Be receptive (*Gaia Staff website, October 19, 2019*).

> Be still, and know that I am God. (*Holy Bible, Psalm 34:10 KJV*)

> You are of God, little children, and have overcome them, because He who is in you is greater than he who is in the world. (*Holy Bible, 1 John 4:4. NASB*)

In Kabbalistic thought, a Sephira is a channel for the Divine energy we know as the life-force (*www.safed-home.com, retrieved August 30, 2020*).

> All my being (body, mind and soul) is yoked by divine energy that vibrates from the eternal Source of life within. It's the vibration of vitality, regeneration, love, and eternal life. (*Rachael, Living Light: Stirring the Deep website, retrieved August 30, 2020*)

[5z17] program or programmed: arrange according to a plan or schedule. *Oxford English Dictionary.*
Also see [9x].

[5z18] Differentiated at the singularity: [*GOD—The Dimensional Revelation* Reveals that The Act Of Creation resulting in the singularity that burst into our physical universe set all of the operational principles, which cause our physical universe to develop and proceed. The WORD sustains physical reality because physical processes are set and need not be altered. They may proceed without additional Participation By The LORD.

On The Other Hand, GOD Actively Participates In Spiritual Reality By Choice. That Participation Is Conscious, not mechanical.]

[5z19] superstring: The deepest problem in theoretical physics is harmonizing the theory of general relativity, which describes gravitation and applies to large-scale structures (stars, galaxies, super clusters) with quantum mechanics, which describes the other three fundamental forces acting on the atomic scale.

The development of a quantum field theory of a force invariably results in infinite possibilities. Physicists developed the technique of renormalization to eliminate these infinities; this technique works for three of the four fundamental forces—electromagnetic, strong nuclear and weak nuclear forces—but not for gravity. Development of quantum theory of gravity, therefore, requires different means than those used for the other forces (*Joseph Polchinski, String Theory: Volume 1 [Cambridge University Press], 4*).

Investigating how a string theory may include fermions in its spectrum led to the invention of supersymmetry in 1971, a mathematical transformation between bosons and fermions. String theories that include fermionic vibrations are now known as "superstring theories" (*Dean Rickles, A Brief History of String Theory: From Dual Models to M-Theory [Springer, 2014], 104*).

According to the theory, the fundamental constituents of reality are strings of the Planck length (about 10–33 cm) that vibrate at resonant frequencies. Every string, in theory, has a unique resonance, or harmonic. Different harmonics determine different fundamental particles. The tension in a string is on the order of the Planck force (1044 newtons)… There is no empirical evidence for superstring theory, nor any way to test it.

Even though there are only five superstring theories, making detailed predictions for real experiments requires information about exactly what physical configuration the theory is in. This considerably complicates efforts to test string theory because there is an astronomically high number—10^{500} or more—of configurations that meet some of the basic requirements to be consistent with our world. Along with the extreme remoteness of the Planck scale, this is the other major reason it is hard to test superstring theory. Theoretical physicists were troubled by the existence of five separate superstring theories. A possible solution for this dilemma was suggested at the beginning of what is called the second superstring revolution in the 1990s, which suggests that the five string theories might be different limits of a single underlying theory, called M-theory. This remains a conjecture (*Joseph Polchinski, String Theory: Volume 2 [Cambridge University Press], 198*).

[5z20] space-time: In physics, spacetime is any mathematical model which fuses the three dimensions of space and the one dimension of time into a single four-dimensional manifold. Spacetime diagrams can be used to visualize relativistic effects, such as why different observers perceive where and when events occur differently…

In 1905, Albert Einstein based a work on special relativity on two postulates:

1. The laws of physics are invariant (i.e., identical) in all inertial systems (i.e., non-accelerating frames of reference).
2. The speed of light in a vacuum is the same for all observers, regardless of the motion of the light source.

GOD—THE DIMENSIONAL REVELATION

The logical consequence of taking these postulates together is the inseparable joining together of the four dimensions—hitherto assumed as independent—of space and time. en.wikipedia.org.

Yet quantum physics hints at a deeper foundation underlying the reality of phenomena—in other words, that "ontology" encompasses more than just events and objects in spacetime (*Tom Siegfried, https://www.sciencenews.org/blog/context/quantum-mysteries-dissolve-if-possibilities-are-realities, 2017*).

[GOD—*The Dimensional Revelation* Expands on this Understanding of spacetime to assert that time is a force. When GOD Creates a particle in a quantum field, the operational principles take over, and that particle continues without extra Action By GOD. The physical continuum needs no action from the WORD, except The Sustaining Vibration underlying quantum machinery, which is The 9th-D machinery of creation in physical reality.]

[5z21] m-theory: A multiverse of a somewhat different kind has been envisaged within string theory and its higher-dimensional extension, M-theory (*Steven Weinberg, "Living in the Multiverse," 2005*).

M-theories require the presence of or spacetime dimensions respectively. The extra six or seven dimensions may either be compactified on a very small scale, or our universe may simply be localized on a dynamical (3+1)-dimensional object, a D3-brane. This opens the possibility that there are other branes which could support other universes. (*Richard J. Szabo, et al., An Introduction to String Theory and D-brane Dynamics, 2004; "ontology" added by Allyn Richert, 2022*).

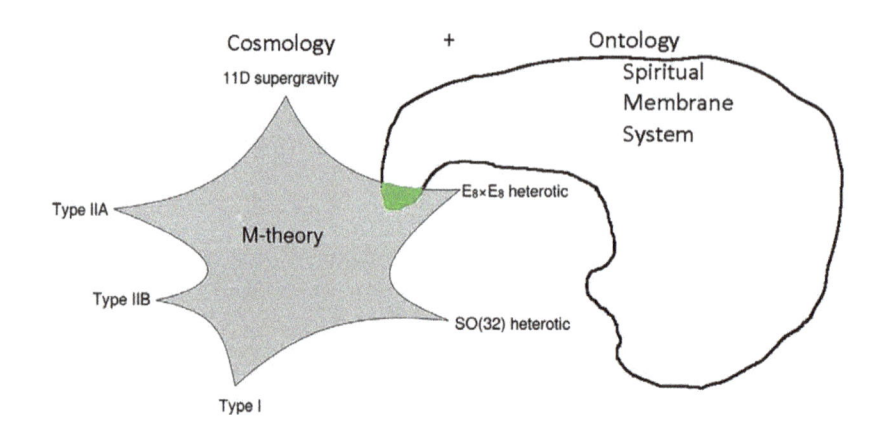

Above is a schematic illustration of the relationship between M-theory, the five superstring theories, and eleven-dimensional supergravity. The shaded region represents a family of different physical scenarios that are possible in M-theory. In certain limiting cases corresponding to the cusps, it is natural to describe the physics using one of the six theories labeled there (*en.wikipedia.org*).

RESEARCH NOTES, CREDITS, AND EXPANSIONS

[*GOD—The Dimensional Revelation* Remains firm that the other "branes" permitting other universes under separate principles of operation, define other "Membrane Systems". Parallel iterations of our universe can only exist as potential. Once collapsed into being, that is the only universe that exists concerning our universe of matter and its attendant energies.

If the "brane" is 3-Dimensional, then the other universe is part of the physical membrane system.]

[5z22] Synthesis: The mixing of different ideas, influences, or things to make a whole that is different or new (dictionary.cambridge.org).

[*GOD—The Dimensional Revelation* Explains that physical synthesis is a subset of Metaphysical Synthesis.] See [6z55].

[5z23] standard model of particles and interactions: The Standard Model is the name given in the 1970s to a theory of fundamental particles and how they interact. It incorporated all that was known about subatomic particles at the time and predicted the existence of additional particles as well.

Fundamental particles are either the building blocks of matter, called fermions, or the mediators of interactions, called bosons. There are twelve named fermions and five named bosons in the Standard Model.

Fermions obey a statistical rule described by Enrico Fermi (1901–1954) of Italy, Paul Dirac (1902–1984) of England, and Wolfgang Pauli (1900–1958) of Austria, called the exclusion principle. Simply stated, fermions cannot occupy the same place at the same time. (More formally, no two fermions may be described by the same quantum numbers.) Leptons and quarks are fermions, but so are things made from them like protons, neutrons, atoms, molecules, people, and walls. This agrees with our macroscopic observations of matter in everyday life. People cannot walk through walls unless the wall gets out of the way.

Bosons, in contrast, are have no problem occupying the same place at the same time. (More formally, two or more bosons may be described by the same quantum numbers.) The statistical rules that bosons obey were first described by Satyendra Bose (1894–1974) of India and Albert Einstein (1879–1955) of Germany. Gluons, photons, and the W, Z and Higgs are all bosons. As the particles that make up light and other forms of electromagnetic radiation, photons are the bosons we have the most direct experience with. In our everyday experience, we never see beams of light crash into one another. Photons are like phantoms. They pass through one another with no effect.

There are seventeen named particles in the Standard Model, organized into the chart shown below. The last particles discovered were the W and Z bosons in 1983, the top quark in 1995, the tau neutrino in 2000, and the Higgs boson in 2012(*Glenn Elert, The Physics Hypertextbook, 1998–2000*).

The Standard Model – The Physics Hypertextbook

Standard model particles (nucleons included for comparison)

family	particle		predicted/discovered	spin number	charge (e)	color	mass* (MeV/c^2)
q u a r k s †	u	up quark	1964 1968	½	+⅔	r, g, b	2.16
	d	down quark	1964 1968	½	-⅓	r, g, b	4.67
	c	charm quark	1970 1974	½	+⅔	r, g, b	1,270
	s	strange quark	1964 1968	½	-⅓	r, g, b	93
	t	top quark	1973 1995	½	+⅔	r, g, b	172,760
	b	bottom quark	1973 1977	½	-⅓	r, g, b	4,180
f e r m i o n s	e	electron	1874 1897	½	-1	none	0.51099895
l e p t o n s	μ	muon	1936	½	-1	none	105.658375
	τ	tau	1975	½	-1	none	1776.86
	v_e	electron neutrino	1930 1956	½	0	none	< 1.1 × 10^{-6}
	v_μ	muon neutrino	1940s 1962	½	0	none	< 0.19
	v_τ	tau neutrino	1970s 2000	½	0	none	< 18.2
†	p	proton	1815 1917	½	+1	none	938.272081
	n	neutron	1920 1932	½	0	none	939.565413
v b e o c s t o o n s	g	gluon	1962 1978	1	0	8 colors	0
	γ	photon	1899	1	0	none	0
	W	W boson	1968 1983	1	±1	none	80,379
	Z	Z boson	1968 1983	1	0	none	91,187.6
‡	H	higgs boson	1964 2012	0	0	none	125,100

* Masses from Particle Data Group
† The proton and neutron are hadrons (made of quarks), baryons (made of three quarks), and nucleons (found in the nucleus), but they are not standard model particles
‡ The higgs boson is the only known scalar boson.

Criticism: We note that the Standard Model may or may not list all basic subatomic particles. Such list is limited to cosmology, our 7th dimensional, physical universe.
Comment: An analogous model may be Developed to list standard features of Our Spiritual Universe.

RESEARCH NOTES, CREDITS, AND EXPANSIONS

[5z24] stuck in cosmology: [*GOD—The Dimensional Revelation* Expands Reality to expose that current theoretical physics has limited its study to our universe of matter and its attendant energies. That is the study of cosmology. The reason for limiting the study of physics to cosmology is that the mathematics used to describe the smallest particles only works when the infinities of "becoming" are factored out. Once factored out, it is easy to state that nothing else exists. This is the same mistake that Humans have made again and again when their knowledge cannot proceed.]

[5z25] not constant: especially, having a range that includes more than one value. (*www.merriam-webster.com*).

Let f be a nonconstant function that is continuous on [a,b], where a<b. Prove that the range of f is a finite closed interval [c,d], where c<d. Proof: If f:R→R is continuous on [a,b], a connected subspace, then f[a,b] is connected by an elementary result in analysis. If f is nonconstant, then f[a,b] contains at least two points. But f[a,b] is connected, so f[a,b] is an interval by an elementary result in analysis. But [a,b] is also compact, so f[a,b] is compact by an elementary result in analysis, and hence f[a,b] must be a closed interval (*Zhoraster, Professor at Kiev University, StackExchange website, retrieved August 30, 2020*).

[*GOD—The Dimensional Revelation* Uses this mathematical proof of closed systems {connected subspace} as contributing to Our "Law of Dimensional Limitation," at least as it applies to physical reality.

Our Teaching Expands on this to deduce that the converse is also true: a nonconstant function outside the subspace must be an open interval. Hence, The WORD {10th D} Outside the subspace Instructs The 9th Dimension to Create and Limit All Continuous Membrane Systems, defining or comprising the various Membrane Systems In The 8th Dimension, as closed systems. Ultimately, Only The WORD Can Instruct A Penetration Of A Boundary Of a Closed Membrane System in the 9th D. The Information Instructed Will Act To Close The Membrane System Again After Penetration, Except For Individual Connections To GOD.

The Individual Connections To GOD Are Depicted As The Green Zone On Our Cover Art.

Zhoraster's proof assumes one of Our basic premises—that Reality Is Continuous. It also defines what we call segmentation of the continuum. The collapse of information in the 9th D into physical manifestations in the 8th D is The Creation of finite intervals, where *a* and *b* are the limits of a finite interval as manifested in a lower dimension. Observation of many different types of finite intervals give the illusion that reality is segmented into clusters or bundles. Yes, the bundles or segments do exist, but the boundary of each bundle or segment is an interval of the larger continuum. Within the boundary of an interval (discrete segment), the information is also continuous. For example, this apple in my hand occupies a finite interval in space-time. Here and now, this apple is a bundle or segment of our physi-

GOD—THE DIMENSIONAL REVELATION

cal universe. It's existence as a finite interval is dramatically altered into nonexistence, as I eat the apple.

Whether an interval is constant or nonconstant is among the operational principles of the dimension in which the interval exists.]

[5z26] quantum particles: quantum particles can behave like particles located in a single place, or they can act like waves distributed all over space or in several places at once. How they appear seems to depend on how we choose to measure them, and before we measure, they seem to have no definite properties at all (*www.newscientist.com/term/quantum-physics/#ixzz6eRAVBn74*).

[*GOD—The Dimensional Revelation* Reveals that "quantum observation" is the same as the act of "physical manifestation." This is The 9th-Dimension Machinery Manifesting The WORD Into physical reality in this manner in any physical universe. The operation of quantum observation is the creation of reality defining the physical membrane system. It also provides the limitation of what can be "observed" in physical reality.

quantum particles may be called "GOD Particles" because they pop in and out of a quantum field. However, what pops into a quantum field is almost the same as what was just there previously. The WORD provides the continuum to sustain this-or-that physical manifestation. The force of time continues the manner in which quantum particles manifest and holds them to the limitations of physical reality. Only The WORD Can Alter The Range Of Possibilities and those limitations.

Jesus Christ's Turning water into wine Is The Best Example Of The WORD Altering The Range Of Possibilities. This Is One Proof That Our Dimensional Hierarchy Is Correct. The Purpose Of Christ's Demonstration Is To Reveal The Broader Reality and The Large GOD.]

[5z27] Spiritual Metastring: [*GOD—The Dimensional Revelation* Sets Forth The Revelation That The Channel For Creating, Preserving, and Destroying Spiritual Realities Is The Spiritual Metastring, Along Which The WORD Instructs The 9th-Dimension Machinery Of Creation To Manifest Spiritual Realities. Please refer to Figure 2 for an image of this Organization and Sequence Of Creation Of Reality.]

[5z28] not used.

[5z29] Music: Vocal or instrumental sounds (or both) combined in such a way as to produce beauty of form, harmony (*Oxford English Dictionary*).

Sound is a mechanical wave that is created by a vibrating object. The vibrations of the object set particles in the surrounding medium in vibrational motion, thus transporting energy through the medium. For a sound wave traveling through air, the vibrations of the particles are best described as longitudinal. Longitudinal waves are waves in which the motion of the individual particles of the medium is in a direction that is parallel to the direction of energy transport. https://www.physicsclassroom.com/class/sound/Lesson-1/Sound-as-a-Longitudinal-Wave.

RESEARCH NOTES, CREDITS, AND EXPANSIONS

[5z30] Reenter Creation as a Participant: [GOD—*The Dimensional Revelation* Reveals that GOD Created the physical universe for His Pleasure. The Pleasure of GOD is not hedonistic pleasure. Rather, GOD Is Pleased By Observing and Participating In GOD's Various Creations. Recognizing that material being is barren, GOD Created Life With Individual Consciousness. GOD Did This By Instructing Individual Spirits Of The Spiritual Universe To Penetrate the boundaries of physical being and Merge With matter To Manifest Creatures Of Life on Earth. The Nature Of Spiritual Being Is That It Has The Potential Of GOD-Consciousness—That Is, GOD May Choose To Reenter His Creation Through Your Consciousness and Participate In Our Unique and Wonderful Reality.]

[5z31] Formative: serving to form something, especially having a profound and lasting influence (*www.merriam-webster.com*).

[5z32] quantum mechanics: We firmly base our beliefs on the realistic philosophy of quantum mechanics, where reality exists independently of the observer (*K. Popper, Quantum, Theory and the Schism in Physics: From the Postscript to The Logic of Scientific Discovery [Routledge, 1989]*).

General relativity typically deals with situations involving large-mass objects in fairly large regions of space-time whereas quantum mechanics is generally reserved for scenarios at the atomic scale (small space-time regions). The two are very rarely used together, and the most common case that combines them is in the study of black holes. Having peak density, or the maximum amount of matter possible in a space, and very small area, the two must be used in synchrony to predict conditions in such places. Yet when used together, the equations fall apart, spitting out impossible answers, such as imaginary distances and less than one dimension.

The major problem with their congruence is that at Planck scale (a fundamental small unit of length) lengths, general relativity predicts a smooth-flowing surface, while quantum mechanics predicts a random warped surface, which are nowhere near compatible. Superstring theory resolves this issue, replacing the classical idea of point particles with strings. These strings have an average diameter of the Planck length with extremely small variances, which completely ignores the quantum mechanical predictions of Planck-scale length dimensional warping. Also, these surfaces can be mapped as branes. These branes can be viewed as objects with a morphism between them. In this case, the morphism will be the state of a string that stretches between brane A and brane B (*en.wikipedia.org*).

[5z33] subelemental: a component that is part of a larger component or element (*www.merriam-webster.com*).

[5z34] wave-particle duality: An object with a defined momentum (p) is in fact a wave with its quantum state depending upon position (x) according to $e^{ipx/h}$.

This is why the basic constituents of quantum mechanics have both particle-like and wave-like properties: They behave as particles when their position is well-defined, and as waves when their momentum is not well-defined. This is known as the wave–particle duality (*E. Segrè, From X-Rays to Quarks: Modern Physicists and Their Discoveries [San Francisco: WH Freeman, 1980]*).

As with all particles, electrons can act as waves. This is called the wave–particle duality and can be demonstrated using the double-slit experiment.

The wavelike nature of the electron allows it to pass through two parallel slits simultaneously, rather than just one slit as would be the case for a classical particle. In quantum mechanics, the wave-like property of one particle can be described mathematically as a complex-valued function, the wave function, commonly denoted by the Greek letter psi (ψ). When the absolute value of this function is squared, it gives the probability that a particle will be observed near a location—a probability density (*M. Munowitz, Knowing the Nature of Physical Law [Oxford University Press, 2005], 162*).

[5z35] superposition: The representation of qubits in terms of complex high dimensional vector spaces implies that qubits cease to be isolated discrete objects. Quantum bits can be in superposition, a situation in which they are in two discrete states at the same time. Quantum bits fluctuate and consequently they generate information. Moreover, quantum states of qubits can be correlated even when the information bearers are separated by a long distance in space. This phenomenon is known as entanglement. This destroys the property of locality of classical computing (see the entry on quantum entanglement and information) (*Pieter Adriaans, "Information," The Stanford Encyclopedia of Philosophy [Spring 2019 Edition], ed. Edward N. Zalta, https://plato.stanford.edu/archives/spr2019/entries/information/*).

[5z36] nonlocality: When the wave function "collapses," its value goes to zero everywhere, just as for a single particle, but it predicts two places where particles will be found. At the moment of collapse, all their properties are still correlated. After the collapse, they are decohered and describable as the product of separate single-particle wave functions (*https://www.informationphilosopher.com/*).

[*GOD—The Dimensional Revelation* Resolves this paradox by reminding the researcher that finding the two particles is a future event. That is called "quantum observation." When one of the particles is observed, it collapses into reality and cannot be observed in another location.]

[5z37] decoherence: quantum decoherence explains why a system interacting with an environment transitions from being a pure state, exhibiting superpositions, to a mixed state, an incoherent combination of classical alternatives. This transition is fundamentally reversible as the combined state of system and environment is still pure but, for all practical purposes, irreversible as the environment is a very large and complex quantum system and it is not feasible to reverse their interaction. Decoherence is thus very important for explaining the classical limit of quantum mechanics but cannot explain wave-function collapse as all classical alternatives are still present in

the mixed state and **wave function collapse selects only one of them** (*Wojciech H. Zurek "Decoherence, Einselection, and the Quantum Origins of the Classical," Reviews of Modern Physics. 75, no. 715 [2003]*).

[5z38] quantum entanglement: The choice of measurement in one location appears to be affecting the state of the system in the other location. Nor is it paradoxical to find that distant events are correlated. After all, if I put each member of a pair of gloves in boxes and mail them to opposite sides of the earth, I should not be surprised that by looking inside one box I can determine the handedness of the glove in the other.

"Schrödinger's cat" states, famously, scale up quantum uncertainty into questions about feline mortality. Prior to measurement, as we've seen in our examples, one cannot assign the property of life (or death) to the cat. Both—or neither—coexist within a netherworld of possibility... Practical cats interact with surrounding air molecules, among other things, in very different ways depending on whether they are alive or dead, so in practice the measurement gets made automatically, and the cat gets on with its life (or death) (*Frank Wilczek, https://www.quantamagazine.org/entanglement-made-simple-20160428, April 28, 2016*).

[*GOD—The Dimensional Revelation* Resolves the paradoxes of quantum entanglement by debunking the word *measurement*.

In digital measurement, a situation can be measured as separate bits of information. Those bits are bundles that can be manipulated and characterized in time by manipulating the entire set of bundles.

Similarly, physical realities can be mentally segmented, such as a group of photons can also be isolated and bundled, to be measured in a manner that appears differently at the same time. This is how the "many worlds" theory develops, that any of the possibilities may be real at the same time. If you twist the bundles you measure, you can create different characteristics of the bundle to say that each may be real—so depending on how you measure them the particles or waves create an illusion of space that we see (holographic universe), but actually could be any number of different illusions.

We debunk this by pointing out that "measurement" or "quantum observation" is a matter of perspective. Of course the physical situation will appear different depending on how it is observed. That defines a very subjective reality depending on the observer. Remove the observer or measurement and the situation still exists.

Also, we debunk this by pointing out that physical reality is a continuum, not separate bundles. You cannot segment the physical continuum, so any mathematics or theory based on bundles is artificial and limited by the bundles You theorize. Your measurement is only a partial reality so Your manipulation of measurement does not present any possibilities other than those permitted by the immediate situation, collapsed into reality now. The next situation can present as a "different world", within limits, and only in the future.

To illustrate this, I can tell you with 100% certainty that Schrödinger's cat is dead, without opening the box. That cat was put into the box over 50 years ago and cat's do not live 50 years in the physical world. Your opening the box to "observe" makes no difference. The power of deduction springing from Knowledge of the Processes of physical reality allows us certainty regarding macro-events. This is not to refute quantum theory. It is just to Teach that, though the future is uncertain, the past is finished and done on this continuum. It cannot be reversed or set in some uncertain parallel.

This brings us back to Popper's conclusion that reality exists independently of the observer.]

[5z39] Infinity: In mathematics, many different types of infinities exist. These include the purely notational use of the lemniscate symbol, ∞, and the use of the following symbols in the context of cardinal or ordinal infinities:

Compendium of Mathematical Symbols | Math Vault

Symbol Name	Explanation	Example
$\aleph_0$ (**Aleph-naught**)	Cardinality of the set of natural numbers	$\aleph_0 + 5 = \aleph_0$
c (**Continuum**)	Cardinality of the set of real numbers	$c = 2^{\aleph_0}$
ω (**Omega**)	Smallest infinite ordinal number	$\forall n \in \mathbb{N}, n < \omega$

(https://mathvault.ca)

The infinity symbol represents the endless cycles of Life in Creation as a continuously flowing "in and out" from Source itself. Everything functions as counterparts, which are always equally aligned and counterbalanced, while the middle Source point is always still, which is the nature of Eternity. So the external lines of the symbol represent the nature of Infinity of Creation, while the merging point represents the Eternity of Source (*https://shiftdiva.wordpress.com/tag/metaphysical-meaning-of-infinity-symbol/*).

[5z40] quantum mathematics: The mathematical formulations of quantum mechanics are those mathematical formalisms that permit a rigorous description of quantum mechanics. This mathematical formalism uses mainly a part of functional analysis, especially Hilbert space, which is a kind of linear space (*Frederick W. Byron and Robert W. Fuller, Mathematics of Classical and Quantum Physics [Courier Dover Publications, 1992]*).

RESEARCH NOTES, CREDITS, AND EXPANSIONS

The Schrödinger equation is a linear partial, differential equation that describes the wave function or state function of a quantum-mechanical system. It is a key result in quantum mechanics, and its discovery was a significant landmark in the development of the subject. The concept of a wave function is a fundamental postulate of quantum mechanics; the wave function defines the state of the system at each spatial position, and time. Using these postulates, Schrödinger's equation can be derived from the fact that the time-evolution operator must be unitary, and must therefore be generated by the exponential of a self-adjoint operator, which is the quantum Hamiltonian (*David J. Griffiths, Introduction to Quantum Mechanics, Second ed. [Prentice Hall, 2004]*).

The Schrödinger equation is not the only way to study quantum-mechanical systems and make predictions. The other formulations of quantum mechanics include matrix mechanics, introduced by Werner Heisenberg, and the path integral formulation, developed chiefly by Richard Feynman. Paul Dirac incorporated matrix mechanics and the Schrödinger equation into a single formulation.

In the so-called Schrödinger picture of quantum mechanics, the dynamics is given as follows. The time evolution of the state is given by a differentiable function from the real numbers (R), representing instants of time, to the Hilbert space of system states. This map is characterized by a differential equation as follows. If $|\psi(t)\rangle$ denotes the state of the system at any one time (t), the following Schrödinger equation holds:

Schrödinger equation *(general)*

$$i\hbar \frac{d}{dt} |\psi(t)\rangle = H |\psi(t)\rangle$$

The time-dependent Heisenberg operators satisfy

Heisenberg picture *(general)*

$$\frac{d}{dt} A(t) = \frac{i}{\hbar}[H, A(t)] + \frac{\partial A(t)}{\partial t},$$

which is true for time-dependent A=A(t). Notice the commutator expression is purely formal when one of the operators is unbounded. One would specify a representation for the expression to make sense of it.

The so-called Dirac picture, or interaction picture, has time-dependent states and observables, evolving with respect to different Hamiltonians.

> **Dirac picture**
>
> $$i\hbar \frac{d}{dt} |\psi(t)\rangle = H_{\text{int}}(t) |\psi(t)\rangle$$
>
> $$i\hbar \frac{d}{dt} A(t) = [A(t), H_0].$$

(en.wikipedia.org, partial retrieval 9/13/2020)

It shouldn't be surprising that there's more than one way to explain quantum mechanics. Quantum math is notorious for incorporating multiple possibilities for the outcomes of measurements. So you shouldn't expect physicists to stick to only one explanation for what that math means (Tom Siegfried, www.sciencenews.org/blog/context/quantum-mysteries-dissolve-if-possibilities-are-realities, October 1, 2017).

[*GOD—The Dimensional Revelation* Summarizes this discussion of quantum mechanics to state that Uncertainty in the 6th dimension relates to future events. The past yields quantum probabilities for the future at all micro-levels up through macro-levels. Collapse into reality occurs in the 4th dimension physically to manifest present physical reality. Once the present is manifested, a new set of quantum probabilities for the future becomes. Those probabilities are heavily influenced by the past. Hence, Our Teaching is that Reality is always becoming.]

[5z41] *A* to *z*: [*GOD—The Dimensional Revelation* Begins To Develop A Spiritual Mathematical System Using Symbolic Logic. We will use *A* to *z* to symbolize being and processes in all 10 Dimensions. Notably, once we go beyond the limitations of any closed system, the mathematics becomes variable as the future is not predictable, nor do Dimensions 9 and 10 follow definite operational principles.

Notably, all of this quantum theory attempts to explain physical reality. The principles apply consistently and are correct as observed. However, digging deep, the infinities that always emerge in the mathematics are necessary because of the basic premise That quantum particles are uncertain until they are "observed"—that is, collapsed into being. That uncertainty and subsequent collapse into being Is The Operation Of The 9th-D Machinery. The 10th D Is The WORD Instructing The Collapse Into Being. Physical conundrums, such as Schrödinger's cat, disappear When You Understand The 9th D and Its SOURCE Instructions From The 10th Dimension. These cannot be quantified.]

[5z42] theory of everything: A theory of everything TOE, final theory, ultimate theory, or master theory is a hypothetical single, all-encompassing, coherent theoretical framework of physics that fully explains and links together all physical aspects of the universe. Finding a TOE is one of the major unsolved problems in physics. String theory and M-theory have been proposed as theories of everything. Over the

RESEARCH NOTES, CREDITS, AND EXPANSIONS

past few centuries, two theoretical frameworks have been developed that, together, most closely resemble a TOE. These two theories upon which all modern physics rests are general relativity and quantum mechanics. General relativity is a theoretical framework that only focuses on gravity for understanding the universe in regions of both large scale and high mass: stars, galaxies, clusters of galaxies, etc. On the other hand, quantum mechanics is a theoretical framework that only focuses on three non-gravitational forces for understanding the universe in regions of both small scale and low mass: sub-atomic particles, atoms, molecules, etc. Quantum mechanics successfully implemented the Standard Model that describes the three non-gravitational forces—strong nuclear, weak nuclear, and electromagnetic force—as well as all observed elementary particles (*Stephen W. Hawking, The Theory of Everything: The Origin and Fate of the Universe [Phoenix Books, February 28, 2006], Special Anniv., ISBN 978-1-59777-508-3*).

Conventional sequence of theories

A Theory of Everything would unify all the fundamental interactions of nature: gravitation, strong interaction, weak interaction, and electromagnetism. Because the weak interaction can transform elementary particles from one kind into another, the TOE should also yield a deep understanding of the various different kinds of possible particles. The usual assumed path of theories is given in the following graph, where each unification step leads one level up:

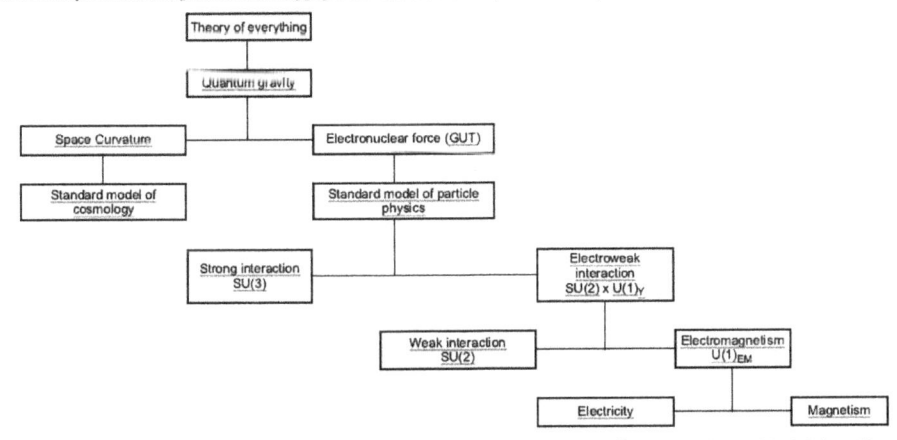

[Diagram: Hierarchy from bottom to top — Electricity and Magnetism → Electromagnetism $U(1)_{EM}$; Weak interaction $SU(2)$ and Electromagnetism $U(1)_{EM}$ → Electroweak interaction $SU(2) \times U(1)_Y$; Strong interaction $SU(3)$ and Electroweak interaction → Standard model of particle physics; Standard model of particle physics → Electronuclear force (GUT); Space Curvature → Standard model of cosmology; Electronuclear force (GUT) and Space Curvature → Quantum gravity → Theory of everything]

In this graph, electroweak unification occurs at around 100 GeV, grand unification is predicted to occur at 10^{16} GeV, and unification of the GUT force with gravity is expected at the Planck energy, roughly 10^{19} GeV.

> Criticism: This chart may depict an organization of physical principles of operation in the 8th d, physical membrane system, but it cannot be a theory of everything.
> Comment: "Everything" would have to include The Spiritual Membrane System and the Awesome Influence Of Spiritual Causation In Our Spiritual Universe as well as our physical universe. That would be a separate chart under Theory Of Everything with Spiritual Being as the lead category from which Spiritual Principles Exist. The Spiritual Causation Principle Is Connected As The SOURCE of quantum gravity.

Conventional sequence of theories, (https://en.wikipedia.org/wiki/Theory_of_everything)

The underlying physical laws necessary for the mathematical theory of a large part of physics and the whole of chemistry are thus completely known. (*PAM Dirac, "Quantum Mechanics of Many Electron Systems," Proceedings of the Royal Society of London A. 123, no. 792 [1929]: 714–733*).

[Note that even Dirac limits this "theory of everything" to "physical laws." So if a "thing" is limited to physical things, then this could be a theory of everything. However, *GOD—The Dimensional Revelation* Reveals Our Known Spiritual Universe as well, The Contents Of Which are not "things" in the physical sense. Also note that Our Teaching is not Complete. Our Teaching does not pretend to claim that *GOD—The Dimensional Revelation* is a theory of all that exists. It cannot Be A Theory Of Everything because Dimensions 9 and 10 Are Not Limited. Higher-Dimensional Reality Is An Open System. Just As GOD {the 11th} Cannot Be Fully Known, So All That Exists Cannot Be Fully Known.]

[5z43] Spiritual Causation: Causation is the act or process of causing something to happen or exist (*www.merriam-webster.com*).

[*GOD—The Dimensional Revelation* Notes That There Are Many Spiritual Causes That Have Effects In both Spiritual Universes and physical universes. These obvious cause-and-effect relationships lead to The Logical Conclusion That There Is Our Spiritual Universe Fused, In Some Part, To our physical universe.

[5z44] Transformation or Transformational: Change in form, appearance, nature, or character (*www.dictionary.com*).

[5z45] Metastring Creation: [*GOD—The Dimensional Revelation* Postulates the original concept of a Metastring. See [3z90]. A Metastring Is The Channel upon or within which certain types of reality are manifested—for example, all physical creations are part of the 8th-d physical membrane system. Each 7th-d physical universe comes into being and is sustained by a physical metastring. It Is The Function Of The 9th Dimension To Create a physical metastring according to the Instructions and Information provided by the WORD To collapse each physical universe into being. This is the quantum machinery known as a "big bang."

A Spiritual Universe Is Created Within or Along A Spiritual Metastring. The Instructions Of The WORD That Create A Spiritual Universe Imbue It With Different Operational Principles than a physical universe; hence, It Is A Different Metastring.]

[5z46] Prayer: A solemn request for help or expression of thanks addressed to God (*Oxford English Dictionary*).

[*GOD—The Dimensional Revelation* Reveals The Large Pervasive GOD. Hence, Any Prayer or Invocation Shall Be Directed To GOD Along The Individual Metastring Connection Directly To GOD and Only To GOD.]

[5z47] Worship: Reverent honor and homage paid to God or a sacred personage or to any object regarded as sacred (www.dictionary.com).

RESEARCH NOTES, CREDITS, AND EXPANSIONS

St. Thomas Aquinas explains, adoration, which is known as *latria* in classical theology, is the worship and homage that is rightly offered to God alone. It is the manifestation of submission and acknowledgement of dependence appropriately shown toward the excellence of an uncreated divine person and to his absolute Lordship. It is the worship of the Creator that God alone deserves.

Also, Devotion.

Orthodox Judaism and orthodox Sunni Islam hold that for all practical purposes, veneration should be considered the same as prayer. en.wikipedia.org.

[*GOD—The Dimensional Revelation* Reveals That True Worship Can Only Be To The ONE, GOD. Hence, Any Worship, Supplication, or Adoration Directed To Any Other entity or Object Is Misdirected and Ineffective In Communicating Along The Spiritual Metastring That Connects Each Spirit To GOD.

"In all your ways, know him" {*Holy Bible, Proverbs 3:6 CSB*} Is Expanded In *GOD—The Dimensional Revelation* That The Primary and Ultimate Actions Of Worship Are To Share Consciousness With GOD. That Sharing May Culminate in Your Conscious and physical Being Becoming The Instrument Of GOD—So Joined In Experience, Communication, and Exchange Of Spiritual Energy, The Goal Of Worship Is Attained.]

[5z18] Meditation: *Christian meditation* is a term for a form of prayer in which a structured attempt is made to get in touch with and deliberately reflect upon the revelations of God (*Thomas Zanzig and Marilyn Kielbasa, Christian Meditation for Beginners [2000], 7, ISBN 0-88489-361-8*).

Meditation is a practice where an individual uses a technique—such as mindfulness, or focusing the mind on a particular object, thought, or activity—to train attention and awareness, and achieve a mentally clear and emotionally calm and stable state (*Sara Rappe, Reading Neoplatonism: Non-Discursive Thinking in the Texts of Plotinus, Proclus, and Damascius [Cambridge; New York: Cambridge University Press, 2000], ISBN 978-0-521-65158-5*).

Hindu meditation practices: kundalini yoga, Transcendental Meditation, relaxation response, mindfulness-based stress reduction, and vipassana meditation (*Ospina Bond, et al., 2009, 131*).

Buddhist meditation, while shy about naming GOD, focuses on the reality of the Divine, Expressed as "Luminosity" or "enlightenment". This mind (citta) is no-mind (acitta), because its natural character is luminous. The state of no-mind, which is immutable (avikra) and undifferentiated (avikalpa), constitutes the ultimate reality (dharmat) of all dharmas. Such is the state of no-mind (*Tadeusz Skorupski, "Consciousness and Luminosity in Indian and Tibetan Buddhism," in Buddhist Philosophy and Meditation Practice: Academic Papers Presented at the second IABU Conference at Mahachulalongkornrajavidyalaya University, Main Campus Wang Noi, Ayutthaya, Thailand, May 31–June 2, 2012*).

> Deliberate meditation is the light of consciousness; let go, and it is then the light of essence. (*The Secret of the Golden Flower* 10:14, trans. Thomas Cleary [HarperCollins, 1991])

> If you do practice for a single breath, then you are a realized immortal for a breath. (The Secret of the Golden Flower 13, trans. Thomas Cleary [HarperCollins, 1991], 64)

> Since heart and breath are mutually dependent, the circulation of the light must be united with the rhythm of breathing… The two mistakes of indolence and distraction must be combated by quiet work… Distraction comes from letting the mind wander about; indolence comes from the mind's not yet being pure… (*The Secret of the Golden Flower, trans. Richard Wilhelm [1929], translated into English by Cary F. Baynes [1962], chapter 4, 40–43*)

[Our Teaching Acknowledges many Valid Meditation techniques. Given The Diversity Of Individual Souls, both Human and Of Other Beings, There Is Not One Single Meditation That Is Most Pleasing To The LORD. Rather, You Must Practice The Techniques and Subjects Of Meditation That Most Comfortably Connect You To GOD. That Will Facilitate Your Creation and Circulation Of Spiritual Energy. As The Journey Of Your Soul, Differentiated From The ONE, Proceeds, Your Methods and Subjects Of Meditation Will Become More Subtle, as It May Please The LORD.

Each Of Us Meditates Though Practices That You May Call Leisure or Recreation. One Way To Know The Quality Of Your Meditation Is By The Level Of Joy It Brings To You. Other Qualities May Be The Feelings Of Fulfillment, Satisfaction, or Invigoration That The Practice Elicits. If your Personal Activities Yield a dim Spiritual Life, Then You Should Learn and Spend More Effort In Traditional Methods Of Worship or Meditation. Some Of These May Lead You To Meaningful Devotions.

If You Say, "I don't Need organized Religion. I Can Worship GOD In Nature, Such As A Walk In The Woods or By The Sea." If This Is How You Meditate, Be Sure That In So Doing, You Open Your Senses To Truly Appreciate The Experience. If Your Worship or Meditation is as dull as the rest of Your Consciousness, then GOD Is not Participating, So You Must Change Your Effort. Our Teaching Offers Many Ways.

This Author most often Practices Meditation To Reflect Upon The Revelations Of GOD Mentioned Above, though I Have Participated In Numerous Other Methods and Meditative Experiences. The Effort Continues My Connection To GOD, Sharing Divine Energy Along My Individual Metastring.

RESEARCH NOTES, CREDITS, AND EXPANSIONS

The Ultimate State Is For All Of My Consciousness To Be In This Connected Meditative State. Then I Transcend Realities of this Life and Become ONE With GOD.]

[5z49] Complete: Having all necessary parts, elements, or steps (*www.merriam-webster.com*).

[5z50] Theoretical: Concerned with or involving the theory of a subject or area of study rather than its practical application, based on or calculated through theory rather than experience or practice. (*Oxford English Dictionary*).

[5z51] Speculative (*adjective*): Pertaining to, of the nature of, or characterized by speculation, contemplation, conjecture, or abstract reasoning; a speculative approach; theoretical rather than practical (www.dictionary.com).

[5z52] cell membrane: The cell membrane, also called the plasma membrane, is found in all cells and separates the interior of the cell from the outside environment. The cell membrane consists of a lipid bilayer that is semipermeable. The cell membrane regulates the transport of materials entering and exiting the cell (*genome.gov, retrieved 9/13/2020*).

[*GOD—The Dimensional Revelation* Draws an analogy between a cell membrane and an immense metaphysical membrane system that we postulate, such as the physical membrane system or the Spiritual Membrane System. Notably, while the membrane sets a limit on the system, the analogy Demonstrates the ability of all membranes to be penetrated or fused to another system, in some way. The Reality In Which You and I Are Conscious Is One such Fusion In Which vast Metaphysical Membrane Systems Are Overlapping and Sharing Common Being for a time.]

[5z53] Self-sufficient: Able to maintain oneself or itself without outside aid, capable of providing for one's own needs (*www.merriam-webster.com*).

[5z54] Independent or independence: Freedom from outside control or support (*www.merriam-webster.com*).

[5z55] locate or located: to determine or indicate the place, site, or limits of (*www.merriam-webster.com*).

[5z56] Divine Spirit: For God created man to be immortal, and made him to be an image of his own eternity (*Apocrypha and Septuagint, Wisdom of Solomon 2:23*).

To assert that humans are created in the image of God may mean to recognize some special qualities of human nature, which allow God to be made manifest in humans. For humans to have a conscious recognition of having been made in the image of God may mean that they are aware of being that part of the creation through whom God's plans and purposes best can be expressed and actualized; humans, in this way, can interact creatively with the rest of creation (*en.wikipedia.org*).

[5z57] Soul: Also known as "Individual Spirit" or "Individual Immortal Soul," Your Soul is distinct from Your mind (*www.wisdomlib.org, 31 March 2014*); "The Soul-Theory of the Nyāya-Vaiśeṣika [Chapter 7]," *www.wisdomlib.org*).

GOD—THE DIMENSIONAL REVELATION

> And the LORD God formed man of the dust of the ground, and breathed into his nostrils the breath of life; and man became a living soul. (*Holy Bible, Genesis 2:7 KJV; Torah Bereishit, Genesis 2:7*)

The major theories put forward include soul creationism, traducianism, and preexistence. According to soul creationism, God creates each individual soul directly, either at the moment of conception or some later time. According to traducianism, the soul comes from the parents by natural generation. According to the preexistence theory, the soul exists before the moment of conception (*en.wikipedia.org*).

> First, Mary's spirit exulted in God; then her soul magnified the Lord. Her praise to God issued from her spirit and was expressed through her soul. Her spirit was filled with joy in God her Savior, and her soul manifested that joy for the magnifying of the Lord. She lived and acted in her spirit, which directed her soul. (Luke 1:46–47)

By soul we mean "the part of human life, beyond the purely organic, is not manipulable and not quantitatively measurable, and that causes different reactions, social relations, emotions, perceptions, behaviors, actions, differing needs and ways to satisfy them" (*Experiences of Spirituality and Spiritual Values in the Context of Nursing—An Integrative Review, Open Nurs J., 8 [2014] 64–70*).

Frankl defines the soul as "the human person in its entirety" (*V. Frankl., The Unconscious God: Psychotherapy and Religion [Stockholm Natur och Kultur, 1987], 18–27*).

[5z58] Collision: A collision is the event in which two or more bodies exert forces on each other in about a relatively short time. Although the most common use of the word *collision* refers to incidents in which two or more objects collide with great force, the scientific use of the term implies nothing about the magnitude of the force (*en.wikipedia.org*).

[GOD—*The Dimensional Revelation* Uses the concept of collision to dramatically illustrate the significant Transformation of Reality, By Spiritual Reality Intersecting with physical reality To Form A Reality Different From, and Greater Than Each.]

[5z59] myriad: a very large number of something (*dictionary.cambridge.org*).

[5z60] Fullness of Music: the quality of possessing a richness or intensity of sound (*dictionary.com, retrieved September 13, 2020*).

[Spiritual] quality or state of being filled completely or to utmost capacity (*dictionary.com, retrieved September 13, 2020*).

RESEARCH NOTES, CREDITS, AND EXPANSIONS

[*GOD—The Dimensional Revelation* Recognizes Appreciation Of The Fullness Of Music As A Very Fine Meditation.]

[5z61] robot: a machine, especially one programmable by a computer, capable of carrying out a complex series of actions automatically (*Oxford English Dictionary*).

[5z62] Appreciation or To Appreciate: The act of recognizing or understanding that something is valuable, important, or as described (dictionary.cambridge.org).

a feeling or expression of admiration, approval, or gratitude (*www.merriam-webster.com*).

an increase in the value of something (*"Capital Appreciation" at Investopedia*).

[*GOD—The Dimensional Revelation* Combines both the Recognition Of Value With Admiration, Approval, and Gratitude So That Appreciation Becomes a verb. To Appreciate Is An Action As The Individual Human Spirit Exchanges or Invests Spiritual Energy In Any Item. If That Item Has A Spirit, It Is Enhanced and Can Share or Further Appreciate The Spiritual Energy. If that item does not have a Spirit, the Appreciating Spirit Is Enhanced by The Qualities Of The Item Worthy Of Appreciation.

Lavish appreciation or deification of an item is an error by The Individual. An example of such an error is worship of an astronomical body such as our sun.]

[5z63] Elevate or Elevated: To move (something) to a higher place or position from a lower one; lift. To increase the amount or intensity of [Spirit] (*www.thefreedictionary.com*).

[5z64] Move or Moved: Affected with emotion or passion, touched (*www.dictionary.com*).

To go or pass to another place or in a certain direction with a continuous motion (*www.merriam-webster.com*).

[5z65] sensation: a mental process (such as seeing, hearing, or smelling) resulting from the immediate external stimulation of a sense organ often as distinguished from a conscious awareness of the sensory process—compare *perception* (*www.merriam-webster.com*).

[5z66] Indeterminate: Not exactly known, established, or defined (*Oxford English Dictionary*).

[5z67] Fulfill or Fulfillment: bring to completion or reality; achieve or realize (something desired, promised, or predicted) (*Oxford English Dictionary*).

[5z68] See or Seeing: The spiritual sense of seeing is discerning the reality of Spirit in every form, symbol, experience, word, and action (*https://www.unity.org/resources/articles/our-spiritual-senses-part-5-seeing*).

[5z69] Flowering: In some ways, the path to spiritual enlightenment is similar to the blossoming of a flower. People who find themselves lost or insecure must start somewhere, from the acts of planting the seed to growing the roots, discovering who you are, and blossoming your soul, takes time (*http://www.mindbodysoul-food.com/blog/infograph-the-5-stages-of-spiritual-development-the-unfolding-of-a-flower*).

[5z70] Unfolding: To open to the view: reveal especially: to make clear by gradual disclosure (*www.merriam-webster.com*).

In quantum theory: In the enfolded (or implicate) order, space and time are no longer the dominant factors determining the relationships of dependence or independence of different elements. Rather, an entirely different sort of basic connection of elements is possible, from which our ordinary notions of space and time, along with those of separately existent material particles, are abstracted as forms derived from the deeper order. These ordinary notions in fact appear in what is called the "explicate" or "unfolded" order, which is a special and distinguished form contained within the general totality of all the implicate orders (*David Bohm, Wholeness and the Implicate Order [Routledge, 1980], xv*).

[5z71] crash or crashes: move or cause to move with force, speed, and sudden loud noise (*Oxford English Dictionary*).

[5z72] Sequence: An arrangement of two or more things in a successive order, the successive order of two or more things.

chronological sequence: a sequentially ordered set of related things or ideas, an action or event that follows another or others (*www.dictionary.com*).

[5z73] Leap or jump: A leap is a jump from one point to another or a sudden or large movement or transition (www.yourdictionary.com).

[5z74] parallel universes: A parallel universe, also known as an alternate universe or alternate reality, is a hypothetical self-contained plane of existence coexisting with one's own. The sum of all potential parallel universes that constitute reality is often called a "multiverse" (*www.wikipedia.org*).

[5z75] timeline: a display of a list of events in chronological order (*Anthony Grafton and Daniel Rosenberg, Cartographies of Time: A History of the Timeline [Princeton Architectural Press, 2010], 272*).

[5z76] dark matter: Detailed studies of the microwave background radiation showed that the ordinary matter in the universe lacks the mutual gravitational force to produce the density fluctuations that led to the formation of stars and galaxies. To say this another way, the temperature and pressure of the ordinary matter were too high to enable the gravitational contraction of gas clouds to occur. Dark matter is therefore required for the existence of our universe.

...the composition of the universe is as follows: 5% ordinary matter 25% dark matter 70% dark energy (and we have no idea what dark energy is) (*https://www.physicscentral.com/explore/action/darkmatter.cfm, 2021*).

[Our Teaching admires the attempt to posit something like "dark matter" to balance obvious forces to explain Observations. However, We urge caution and demand further verification of such concepts as "dark matter" and "dark energy."]

[5z77] equation: In mathematics, an equation is a statement that asserts the equality of two expressions, which are connected by the equals sign "=".

RESEARCH NOTES, CREDITS, AND EXPANSIONS

[5z78] multiverse: Some speculative theories have proposed that our universe is but one of a set of disconnected universes collectively denoted as the multiverse, challenging or enhancing more limited definitions of the universe (*George F. R. Ellis, U. Kirchner, and W. R. Stoeger, "Multiverses and Physical Cosmology," Monthly Notices of the Royal Astronomical Society [2004], 347*).

Brian Greene's nine types: The American theoretical physicist and string theorist Brian Greene discussed nine types of multiverses:

1. Quilted—The quilted multiverse works only in an infinite universe. With an infinite amount of space, every possible event will occur an infinite number of times. However, the speed of light prevents us from being aware of these other identical areas. [doubtful]
2. Inflationary—The inflationary multiverse is composed of various pockets in which inflation fields collapse and form new universes. [possible]
3. Brane—The brane-multiverse version postulates that our entire universe exists on a membrane (brane), which floats in a higher dimension or "bulk." In this bulk, there are other membranes with their own universes. These universes can interact with one another, and when they collide, the violence and energy produced is more than enough to give rise to a big bang. The branes float or drift near each other in the bulk and, every few trillion years, attracted by gravity or some other force we do not understand, collide and bang into each other. This repeated contact gives rise to multiple or "cyclic" big bangs. This particular hypothesis falls under the string theory umbrella as it requires extra spatial dimensions.

[*GOD—The Dimensional Revelation* confirms this and expresses this theory as the 8th Dimension of physical reality, the physical membrane system. This Teaching expands this Brane theory to include other membrane systems, most notably Our Spiritual Membrane System.]

4. Cyclic—The cyclic multiverse has multiple branes that have collided, causing Big Bangs. The universes bounce back and pass through time until they are pulled back together and again collide, destroying the old contents and creating them anew. [possible]
5. Landscape—The landscape multiverse relies on string theory's Calabi-Yau spaces. Quantum fluctuations drop the shapes to a lower energy level, creating a pocket with a set of laws different from that of the surrounding space.

[*GOD—The Dimensional Revelation* corrects this. The Fusion of a small aspect of Our Spiritual Universe Into planet earth in our physical universe is a "pocket with a set of laws different from that of the surrounding space," but this is not due to quantum fluctuations. The Fusion Is A More Advanced Reality than physical reality.]

6. Quantum—The quantum multiverse creates a new universe when a diversion in events occurs as in the many-worlds interpretation of quantum mechanics.

[*GOD—The Dimensional Revelation* Explains that quantum "becoming" only relates to future events. The physical past is done and not to be revisited in physical reality.]

7. Holographic—The holographic multiverse is derived from the theory that the surface area of a space can encode the contents of the volume of the region.

[This can only occur in the 9th Dimension as instructed by The WORD.]

8. Simulated—The simulated multiverse exists on complex computer systems that simulate entire universes.

[Simulations are ontologically real and a good planning tool. However, manifesting a simulation as atoms and molecules in physical reality presumes that the atoms and molecules already exist and there is a mechanism to reorganize them—as in digital printing.]

9. Ultimate—The ultimate multiverse contains every mathematically possible universe under different laws of physics (*en.wikipedia.org*); (Brian Greene, *The Fabric of the Cosmos*, 2004).

[*GOD—The Dimensional Revelation* Teaches that each of these multiverse theories potentially express an aspect of the 8th dimension developed in Our Teaching. Some of these theories will be confirmed as the theories become more carefully tested.]

[5z79] No return: A critical point at which turning back or reversal is not possible. Return: To bring, send, or put back (*www.merriam-webster.com*).

[*GOD—The Dimensional Revelation* Offers the phrase "no return" as "not to bring back." This is to emphasize that physical reality proceeds on a continuum. Once an event "collapses" into being, it becomes "present," opening up new possibilities for the future. Once it becomes "present," the physical reality cannot be otherwise. Once the situation is "present" or "realized," it becomes a past situation as the continuum of time proceeds. The past situation cannot be changed in physical reality.]

[5z80] undetermined: not definitely or authoritatively decided, settled, or identified (*www.merriam-webster.com*).

Quantum indeterminacy can be quantitatively characterized by a probability distribution on the set of outcomes of measurements of an observable. The distribution is uniquely determined by the system state (*en.wikipedia.org*).

Even in a world that contains quantum uncertainty, macroscopic objects are determined to an extraordinary degree. Newton's laws of motion are deterministic enough to send men to the moon and back. Our Cogito model of the Macro Mind is large enough to ignore quantum uncertainty for the purpose of the reasoning will. The neural system is robust enough to insure that mental decisions are reliably transmitted to our limbs (*https://www.informationphilosopher.com/freedom/indeterminacy.html*).

[5z81] Christianity: Christianity is an Abrahamic, monotheistic religion based on the life and teachings of Jesus of Nazareth. Its adherents, known as Christians, believe that Jesus is the Christ, whose coming as the Messiah was prophesied in the Hebrew Bible, called the Old Testament in Christianity, and chronicled in the New Testament (*en.wikipedia.org*).

[*GOD—The Dimensional Revelation* Reaffirms that The WORD Was Made flesh In The Person Of Jesus Christ. Christ's Teaching Is Beyond What Human Beings Can Understand. However, Some Essence Of That Teaching Continues To Be Taught In Various Christian Churches as well as Individual Devotions That Leads To Saving Grace On Earth. It also Opens Heaven and Immortality To Humans.

Many Christians Believe That Christianity Is The Only Way To Redemption. Most Other Religions Teach That Their Way Is The Only Way. Our Teaching Is That All True Religions Proceed Through Christ, By Any Name, As They Worship The ONE True GOD.]

[5z82] Confucianism: the system of ethics, education, and statesmanship taught by Confucius and his disciples, stressing love for humanity, ancestor worship, reverence for parents, and harmony in thought and conduct. www.dictionary.com.

樊遲問仁。子曰。愛人。問知。子曰。知人。樊遲未達。子曰。舉直錯諸枉、能使枉者直。樊遲退、見子夏曰。鄉也、吾見於夫子而問知』。Fan Chi asked about the meaning of *ren* (Benevolence). Confucius said, "love others" (*Confucius, Analects 12:22*).

仲弓問仁。子曰。出門如見大賓。使民如承大祭。己所不欲、勿施於人。在邦無怨、在家無怨。 仲弓曰。Zhong Gong asked about the meaning of *ren*. The Master said, "When you are out in the world, act as if meeting an important guest. Employ the people as if you were assisting at a great ceremony. What you don't want done to yourself, don't do to others. Live in your town without stirring up resentments, and live in your household without stirring up resentments" (*Confucius, Analects 12:2, http://www.acmuller.net/con-dao/analects.html#div-12*).

[5z83] Ideal (*adjective*): a standard of perfection, beauty, or excellence. (*www.merriam-webster.com*).

Ideal (*noun*): a person or thing regarded as perfect. (*Oxford English Dictionary*).

[5z84] Agape Love or platonic Love: Agape (Ancient Greek ἀγάπη, agapē) is a Greco-Christian term referring to love, "the highest form of love, charity" and "the love of God for man and of man for God". The word is not to be confused with philia, brotherly love, or philautia, self-love, as it embraces a universal, unconditional love that transcends and persists regardless of circumstance. It goes beyond just the emotions to the extent of seeking the best for others (*H. G. Liddell and Robert Scott, An Intermediate Greek-English, n. Founded Upon the Seventh Edition of Liddell and Scott's Greek-English, n. Benediction Classics, 4*).

Within Christianity, agape is considered to be the love originating from God or Christ for humankind (*en.wikipedia.org*).

> Thou shalt love the Lord thy God with all thy heart, and with all thy soul, and with all thy mind. This is the first and great commandment. And the second is like unto it, Thou shalt love thy neighbour as thyself. On these two commandments hang all the law and the prophets. (*Holy Bible, Matthew 22:37–40 KJV*)

[5z85] evolution: Evolution is change in the heritable characteristics of biological populations over successive generations (*Hall and Hallgrímsson 2008, 4–6*).

Different characteristics tend to exist within any given population as a result of mutation, genetic recombination, and other sources of genetic variation (*Futuyma and Kirkpatrick, "Chapter 4: Mutation and Variation," 2017, 79–102*).

Evolution occurs when evolutionary processes such as natural selection (including sexual selection) and genetic drift act on this variation, resulting in certain characteristics becoming more common or rare within a population (*Thomas C. Scott-Phillips et al., "The Niche Construction Perspective: A Critical Appraisal," May 2014*).

[5z86] Alternative: One of two or more available possibilities (*Oxford English Dictionary*).

[5z87] self-destruction: The act or process of destroying oneself or itself (*yourdictionary.com*).

[5z88] Rational Compromise: assumptions of both parties being rational, using logically consistent decision procedures and wanting to achieve an efficient compromise (*Gregory E. Kersten [kersten@iiasa.ac] and Sunil J. Noronha [noronha@watson.ibm.com], "Rational Agents, Contract Curves, and Inefficient Compromises Report"*).

[5z89] Peaceful Reorganization (Reorganization): A peaceful and sustainably developed world is (still) possible" (*www.mbs.news, April 11, 2020*).

[5z90] Reset: set again or differently (*Oxford English Dictionary*).

RESEARCH NOTES, CREDITS, AND EXPANSIONS

[5z91] Probabilities or quantum probabilities: The chance that something will happen. How likely it is that some event will occur (*www.mathsisfun.com/definitions/probability.html*).

Mathematically, quantum mechanics can be regarded as a nonclassical-probability calculus resting upon a nonclassical propositional logic. More specifically, in quantum mechanics, each probability-bearing proposition of the form "the value of physical quantity AA lies in the range BB" is represented by a projection operator on a Hilbert space HH. These form a non-Boolean—in particular, non-distributive—orthocomplemented lattice. Quantum-mechanical states correspond exactly to probability measures (suitably defined) on this lattice.

In quantum mechanics, only subsets of the state-space corresponding to closed subspaces of the Hilbert space are testable (*Alexander Wilce, "Quantum Logic and Probability Theory," The Stanford Encyclopedia of Philosophy [Spring 2017 Edition]*).

[5z92] Free Will: The power of acting without the constraint of necessity or fate; the ability to act at one's own discretion (*Oxford English Dictionary*).

Cartesian dualism holds that the mind is a nonphysical substance, the seat of consciousness and intelligence, and is not identical with physical states of the brain or body. It is suggested that although the two worlds do interact, each retains some measure of autonomy. Under cartesian dualism external mind is responsible for bodily action, although unconscious brain activity is often caused by external events (for example, the instantaneous reaction to being burned). Cartesian dualism implies that the physical world is not deterministic—and in which external mind controls (at least some) physical events (*Sandro Nannini, "Chapter 5: Mental Causation and Intentionality in a Mind Naturalizing Theory," 2004*).

> Free will is the cause of its own movement, because by his free-will man moves himself to act. But it does not of necessity belong to liberty that what is free should be the first cause of itself, as neither for one thing to be cause of another need it be the first cause. God, therefore, is the first cause, Who moves causes both natural and voluntary. And just as by moving natural causes He does not prevent their acts being natural, so by moving voluntary causes He does not deprive their actions of being voluntary: but rather is He the cause of this very thing in them; for He operates in each thing according to its own nature. (*Thomas Aquinas, Summa Theologiae, Q83 A1*)

Kant's three significant formulations of the categorical imperative are

- Act only according to that maxim by which you can also will that it would become a universal law;

- Act in such a way that you always treat humanity, whether in your own person or in the person of any other, never simply as a means but always at the same time as an end; and
- A very rational being must so act as if he were through his maxim always a legislating member in a universal kingdom of ends.

Kant argued that the only absolutely good thing is a good will, and so the single determining factor of whether an action is morally right is the will, or motive of the person doing it. If they are acting on a bad maxim, e.g. 'I will lie', then their action is wrong, even if some good consequences come of it (*Immanuel Kant [1785], Groundwork of the Metaphysic of Morals, Third ed., trans. James W. Ellington [Hackett, 1993], 30*).

[5z93] determinism: the philosophical view that all events are determined completely by previously existing causes.

> The occurrence or existence of yet other things depends upon our deliberating, choosing and acting in a certain way. (*Andrew Eshleman, "Moral Responsibility," in The Stanford Encyclopedia of Philosophy, ed. Edward N. Zalta [Winter 2009 Edition] November 18, 2009*)

[*GOD—The Dimensional Revelation* Reveals that the more rigid the operational principles of a closed system are, the more deterministic are outcomes of any situation. This is particularly true of physical systems. However, even physical systems exhibit different effects of the same cause. This opens chaos theory and ultimately defeats strict determinism.

By contrast, We Acknowledge The 5th D in which the future is not determined but Is tThe Result Of Choices Made By Spiritual Beings. It Is An Operational Principle Of The Spiritual Membrane System That nothing Is Predetermined. Options Are Available In An Open System. Situations Are only Collapsed Into Reality After A Choice Is Made and Action Taken. Causality May Limit The Options, but Choices By The Free Will Of An Independent Spiritual Being Will Select The Reality That Becomes Manifested.]

[5z94] Transcend: to rise above or go beyond the limits of; to be prior to, beyond, and above (the universe or material existence) (*www.merriam-webster.com*).

[5z95] Emergent: in the process of coming into being or becoming prominent (*Oxford English Dictionary*).

[5z96] Brotherhood: the affection and loyalty that you feel for people who you have something in common with (*collinsdictionary.com*).

[5z97] Saving Grace:

RESEARCH NOTES, CREDITS, AND EXPANSIONS

> For by grace you have been saved through faith; and that not of yourselves, it is the gift of God. (*Holy Bible, Ephesians 2:8 KJV*)

[5z99] Directive or Directives: an official instruction (*dictionary.cambridge.org*).

[5z99] Mobility: the ability to move or be moved freely and easily (*Oxford English Dictionary*).

[5z100] Endure or endures: remain in existence, last (*Oxford English Dictionary*).

[5z101] divergent or divergently: tending to be different or develop in different directions (*Oxford English Dictionary*).

[5z102] strict: demanding total obedience or observance, rigidly enforced (*Oxford English Dictionary*).

[5z103] continue: persist in an activity or process (*Oxford English Dictionary*).

[5z104] wave or wave-feature: In physics, a wave can be thought of as a disturbance or oscillation that travels through space-time, accompanied by a transfer of energy (*Courses.lumenlearning.com*, September 11, 2017, uploaded by Dan Fullerton).

[5z105] quantum field: A quantum field is analogous to an infinite collection of harmonic oscillators. Of course, it's not like a physical collection of tiny springs sitting at every lattice point in space, but the basic mathematical description is the same. There is one infinite collection of harmonic oscillators we call the "photon field", another we call the "electron field", and so on. And when the photon field contains N excitations, we can observe them as N physical photons; when the electron field contains M excitations, we can observe them as M physical electrons, and so on. The ground state of the photon field is the one where all the quantum numbers are zero. We call this the "vacuum state", and in this state we would detect 0 photons. In every other state of the photon field, some quantum numbers are positive, and that means we can detect photons in certain states. We can also have superpositions, where the number of photons in certain states, as well as the total number of photons, can be uncertain. And it works the same way for electrons and positrons.

So the idea quantum field theory asks you to accept is that fields are the fundamental entities. A photon has no independent existence from the photon field of which it is an excitation; the photon is a derived concept. You start out with just the idea of a field. You model the field as an infinite collection of harmonic oscillators and note that you have a ground state where all the quantum numbers are zero, then you also have higher energy states where some quantum numbers are nonzero. You can write down a Lagrangian or Hamiltonian for such a field in a way that allows the field to evolve by propagating oscillations. Finally, you can couple that field to the same field or other fields and see that propagating oscillations have some amplitude to scatter off each other. These excitations, which can both propagate and scatter, we can think of as particles. And indeed it is possible to write down the Lagrangian or Hamiltonian in such a way so that when we have a lot of excitations, the way they interact with each other agrees with the way classical particles behave. In this way, the quantum field theory serves as an accurate model of how particles interact, if we agree to identify particles with excitations of the quantum fields (*Brian Bi, https://www.quora.com/In-quantum-field-theory-what-exactly-is-the-meaning-of-excitation-in-the-statement-particles-are-xcitations-of-the-fields#, retrieved October 17, 2020*).

Gauge symmetries form a group at every space-time point. For a theory describing nature to be consistent, it must not contain any anomaly in its gauge symmetry. The Standard Model of elementary particles is a gauge theory based on the group $SU(3) \times SU(2) \times U(1)$, in which all anomalies exactly cancel (*M. Peskin and D. Schroeder, An Introduction to Quantum Field Theory [Westview Press, 1995], ISBN 978-0-201-50397-5*).

[*GOD—The Dimensional Revelation* Suggests the theory that the excitations within a quantum field is one aspect of the Creation of our physical universe at the smallest manifestations.

Another Aspect Is The Cause Of An Excitation. All Causes Are Divine At Their Origin. A cause may be other than Divine in its further development in the 8th dimension and lower dimensions. The Original Cause Of a "photon field," for example, Is Passing Information From The WORD In The 10th D With Instructions In The 9th D To Manifest a type of field with certain properties, which We call a photon field. The Instructions Creating this type of field may be described as "waves" or "harmonic oscillations." The oscillator is the original Instruction With The Tone (qualities of photon light) Set By The WORD. If the Instruction is for a physical tone to repeat with a frequency, then a continuum is established, which we call "time." The frequency relates specifically to that tone, and a harmonic oscillation is created. The overall field, as well as the type of tone, is created by this set of Instructions. The overall Instruction to the photon field provides for its continuance without further Instructions From The WORD. We would say that the overall existence of the specific photon field is established in Our 7th-D physical universe. Within the limits of our physical universe, photons can be created by many physical causes, usually atomic reactions within a star.

If A Human Being Chooses To Create photons in the photon field (e.g., Manipulation of electromagnetism), then We Observe The Fusion Of Spiritual Being with our physical universe.

The sustaining principle in operation is that once created, physical matter or energy fields can create reality by their own independent action without further Instruction From GOD, except for The Sustaining Information Instructed. A physical system, once created, can create additional quantum fields without different Instructions From GOD. The physical operational principles continue to manipulate the Information already provided. In this aspect of Creation, the Principles of Operation Remain A Divine Differentiation Of GOD, but the subsequent oscillators and harmonic oscillations are usually independent of GOD's Consciousness.

RESEARCH NOTES, CREDITS, AND EXPANSIONS

Applying this to physical creation, what proceeds from the 9th D is a functional system—our physical universe. It continues according to the established principles of physical universal systems—8th d.

GOD—The Dimensional Revelation Reveals that Observing Our physical universe is rather boring From GOD's Point Of View. Hmmm, GOD Is Thinking! Why not Repurpose some of These Differentiated Spirits from This Spiritual Membrane System to merge into matter. Yes, Let Us Fashion this double helix. It would be a sustainable oscillator and complex enough to provide for diverse Manifestations. As It Increases In Complexity, I {GOD} Will Observe These. Even More Interesting, I May Participate In Each Individual Spiritual Consciousness To See this physical universe As They See it. That Would Be Very Good!]

> And God said, "Let the water teem with living creatures, and let birds fly above the earth across the vault of the sky." So God created the great creatures of the sea and every living thing with which the water teems and that moves about in it, according to their kinds, and every winged bird according to its kind. And God saw that it was good. (*Holy Bible, Genesis 1:20 NIV*)

[5z106] general relativity: General relativity is a theory of gravitation that was developed by Albert Einstein between 1907 and 1915. According to general relativity, the observed gravitational effect between masses results from their warping of spacetime General relativity (GR), also known as the general theory of relativity (GTR), is the geometric theory of gravitation published by Albert Einstein in 1915 and the current description of gravitation in modern physics. General relativity generalizes special relativity and refines Newton's law of universal gravitation, providing a unified description of gravity as a geometric property of space and time, or spacetime. In particular, the curvature of spacetime is directly related to the energy and momentum of whatever matter and radiation are present. The relation is specified by the Einstein field equations, a system of partial differential equations.

Some predictions of general relativity differ significantly from those of classical physics, especially concerning the passage of time, the geometry of space, the motion of bodies in free fall, and the propagation of light. Examples of such differences include gravitational time dilation, gravitational lensing, the gravitational redshift of light, and the gravitational time delay. The predictions of general relativity in relation to classical physics have been confirmed in all observations and experiments to date. Although general relativity is not the only relativistic theory of gravity, it is the simplest theory that is consistent with experimental data.

However, unanswered questions remain, the most fundamental being how general relativity can be reconciled with the laws of quantum physics to produce a complete and self-consistent theory of quantum gravity (*Albert Einstein, Relativity: The Special and General Theory [Crown Publishers, 1961]*).

[5z107] Alter or Altered (*verb*): Change or cause to change in character or composition, typically in a comparatively small but significant way.

Altered (*adjective*): Made different in some way (*www.merriam-webster.com*).

[5z108] heavy: having great weight; also, characterized by mass or weight (*www.merriam-webster.com*).

[5z109] fabric: used to refer to the way that spacetime has a composition of quantum strings in any given volume of space seen as behaving like a fabric (interwoven, grid-like, and flexible) (*en.wikipedia.org*).

[*GOD—The Dimensional Revelation* Expands the analogy of the interwoven, or braided, threads of fabric to The 9th D Braiding The Characteristics of our physical universe With The Characteristics Of Our Spiritual Universe To Achieve The Fused Reality In Which We Live.]

[5z110] against all odds: The creationist Thesis by David Foster is that the chances against life emerging are astronomically high. Too high for even Our incredibly large and old universe to occasion it.

Many challenge the statistics, but none can come up with a theory without self-serving assumptions (*David Foster, The Philosophical Scientists, [Barnes & Noble Books, 1993]*).

[5z111] Spiritual Hand: Act of GOD (*en.wikipedia.org*).

[5z112] large hadron collider: The Large Hadron Collider (LHC) is the world's largest and most powerful particle accelerator. It first started up on 10 September 2008, and remains the latest addition to CERN's accelerator complex. The LHC consists of a 27-kilometre ring of superconducting magnets with a number of accelerating structures to boost the energy of the particles along the way.

The term *hadron* refers to subatomic composite particles composed of quarks held together by the strong force (as atoms and molecules are held together by the electromagnetic force). The best-known hadrons are the baryons such as protons and neutrons; hadrons also include mesons such as the pion and kaon, which were discovered during cosmic ray experiments in the late 1940s and early 1950s (*J. Street and E. Stevenson, "New Evidence for the Existence of a Particle of Mass Intermediate between the Proton and Electron," Physical Review, 1937, 52*).

On 14 March 2013, CERN announced confirmation that the observed particle was indeed the predicted Higgs Boson (*Phys Org, March 14, 2013, retrieved December 4, 2019*).

The results, which match those predicted by the non-supersymmetrical Standard Model rather than the predictions of many branches of supersymmetry, show the decays are less common than some forms of supersymmetry predict (*LHCb Collaboration, January 7, 2013*).

During the International Conference on High-Energy Physics (ICHEP 2020), the ATLAS collaboration presented the first observation of photon collisions producing pairs of W bosons, elementary particles that carry the weak force, one of the four fundamental forces. The result demonstrates a new way of using the LHC, namely as a high-energy photon collider directly probing electroweak interactions. It confirms one of the main predictions of electroweak theory—that force carriers can interact with themselves—and provides new ways to probe it.

According to the laws of classical electrodynamics, two intersecting light beams would not deflect, absorb, or disrupt one another. However, effects of quantum electrodynamics (QED), the theory that explains how light and matter interact, allow interactions among photons.

Indeed, it is not the first time that photons interacting at high energies have been studied at the LHC. For instance, light-by-light "scattering," where a pair of photons interact by producing another pair of photons, is one of the oldest predictions of QED. The first direct evidence of light-by-light scattering was reported by ATLAS in 2017, exploiting the strong electromagnetic fields surrounding lead ions in high-energy lead–lead collisions. In 2019 and 2020, ATLAS further studied this process by measuring its properties.

The new result reported at this conference is sensitive to another rare phenomenon in which two photons interact to produce two W bosons of opposite electric charge via (among others) the interaction of four force carriers. Quasi-real photons from the proton beams scatter off one another to produce a pair of W bosons. A first study of this phenomenon was previously reported by ATLAS and CMS in 2016 from data recorded during LHC Run 1, but a larger dataset was required to unambiguously observe it.

The observation was obtained with a highly significant statistical evidence of 8.4 standard deviations, corresponding to a negligible chance of being due to a statistical fluctuation. ATLAS physicists used a considerably larger dataset taken during Run 2, the four-year data collection in the LHC that ended in 2018, and developed a customized analysis method.

Owing to the nature of the interaction process, the only particle tracks visible in the central detector are the decay products of the two W bosons, an electron and a muon with opposite electric charge. W-boson pairs can also be directly produced from interactions between quarks and gluons in the colliding protons considerably more often than from photon-photon interactions, but these are accompanied by additional tracks from strong interaction processes. This means that the ATLAS physicists had to carefully disentangle collision tracks to observe this rare phenomenon (*https://home.cern/news/news/physics/rare-phenomenon-observed-atlas-features-lhc-high-energy-photon-collider*, August 5 2020).

[*GOD—The Dimensional Revelation* Asserts that this result proves that each situation along the physical continuum is heavily dependent on the previous situations. Specifically, quantum probability is very narrow as to what can "become" in physical reality. Quantum probability is narrower the closer in time You observe on the physical continuum to the present situation.]

[5z113] Rearrange or rearrangement: change (the position, time, or order of something) (*Oxford English Dictionary*).

[5z114] Action of Life: An Action is the fact or process of doing something, typically to achieve an aim (*Oxford English Dictionary*).

[*GOD—The Dimensional Revelation* Asserts That When A Living Being Performs An Action, It Is An Action Of Life. Our physical universe is not equipped to make Choices or take any Action Of Life. This proves the Thesis of This Teaching That There Is A Partial Fusion of Our Spiritual and physical Universes.]

[5z115] complex or complicated: consisting of many interconnecting parts or elements, intricate (*Oxford English Dictionary*).

[5z116] triple-alpha process: If the central temperature of a star exceeds 100 million Kelvin as may happen in the later phase of red giants and red supergiants, then helium can fuse to form beryllium and then carbon.

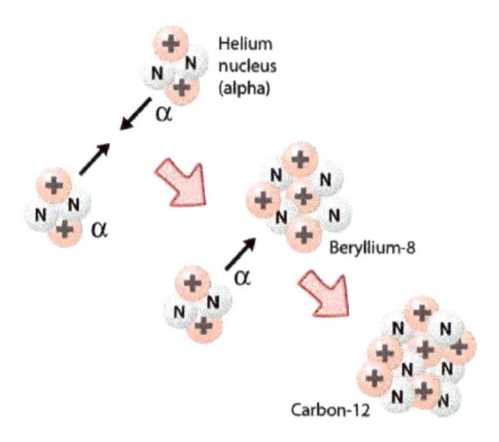

Helium Nuclear Fusion
The Hoyle Resonance, F. Hoyle, D. N. F. Dunbar, W. A. Wensel, W. Whaling, *Physical Review* vol. 92, p. 649 (1953) (*http://hyperphysics.phy-astr.gsu.edu/hbase/Astro/helfus.html*)

[5z117] photosynthesis: Photosynthesis, the process by which green plants and certain other organisms transform light energy into chemical energy... During photosynthesis in green plants, light energy is captured and used to convert water, carbon dioxide, and minerals into oxygen and energy-rich organic compounds (*en.wikipedia.org*).

[*GOD—The Dimensional Revelation* Explains that photosynthesis is a subset of physical synthesis, which is a subset of Metaphysical Synthesis.] See [6z55].

[5z118] sequentially: in a way that follows a particular order (*dictionary.cambridge.org*).

RESEARCH NOTES, CREDITS, AND EXPANSIONS

[5z119] enter or enters: to go or come in (*www.merriam-webster.com*).

[5z120] Worthy of GOD:

> So that you may live a life worthy of the Lord and please him in every way: bearing fruit in every good work, growing in the knowledge of God. (*Holy Bible, Colossians 1:10 NIV*)

[5z121] Personally Intimate: It's what builds over time as you connect with someone, grow to care about each other, and feel more and more comfortable during your time together. It can include physical or emotional closeness or even a mix of the two (*www.healthline.com*).

[5z122] Purpose: the reason for which something is done or created or for which something exists (*Oxford English Dictionary*).

[5z123] plane geometry: Euclid set forth the first great landmark of mathematical thought, an axiomatic treatment of geometry. He selected a small core of undefined terms (called common notions) and postulates (or axioms) which he then used to prove various geometrical statements (*Eves, 1963, 19*).

A plane fits into a scheme that starts with a point, which has no dimensions and goes up through solids that have three dimensions:

See Illustration 27.

It is difficult to draw planes since the edges have to be drawn. When you see a picture that represents a plane, always remember that it actually has no edges and it is infinitely large. The plane has two dimensions: length and width. But since the plane is infinitely large, the length and width cannot be measured.

Just as a line is defined by two points, a plane is defined by three points. Given three points that are not collinear, there is just one plane that contains all three (*www.mathopenref.com*).

[5z124] string closed at one end: In physics, a string is a physical entity postulated in string theory and related subjects. Unlike elementary particles, which are zero-dimensional or point-like by definition, strings are one-dimensional extended entities. Researchers often have an interest in string theories because theories in which the fundamental entities are strings rather than point particles automatically have many properties that some physicists expect to hold in a fundamental theory of physics. Most notably, a theory of strings that evolve and interact according to the rules of quantum mechanics will automatically describe quantum gravity.

Strings can be either open or closed. A closed string is a string that has no endpoints, and therefore is topologically equivalent to a circle. An open string, on the other hand, has two end-points and is topologically equivalent to a line interval. Not all string theories contain open strings, but every theory must contain closed strings, as interactions between open strings can always result in closed strings. Open and closed strings are generally associated with characteristic vibrational modes. One of the vibration modes of a closed string can be identified as the graviton. In certain string theories the lowest-energy vibration of an open string is a tachyon and can undergo tachyon condensation. Other vibrational modes of open strings exhibit the properties of photons and gluons (*en.wikipedia.org*).

[There is a debate in theoretical physics as to whether there is such a thing as a graviton. Quantum mathematics cannot prove the existence of the graviton. The counter theory is that of gravitational waves.[4z46] *GOD—The Dimensional Revelation* Asserts that whether the graviton or gravitational waves proves to be the correct theory as to how the 9th D manifests physical reality, the Metaphysics of Our Teaching remains unchanged.]

[5z125] Realize or realized: To make real, give reality to (*www.dictionary.com*).

Cause (something desired or anticipated) to happen (*Oxford English Dictionary*).

[5z126] Metaphor: A thing regarded as representative or symbolic of something else, especially something abstract (*Oxford English Dictionary*).

[6a] matter/antimatter reactions: Mixing antimatter and matter usually has predictably violent consequences—the two annihilate one another in a fierce burst of energy... Charged antimatter particles share the same mass as their normal-matter counterparts but bear the opposite charge. Both types of matter are thought to have been created in equal amounts in the big bang, but for reasons yet unknown, today there is much more matter than antimatter in the universe (*Stephen Battersby, PHYSICS 13, October 2006*).

The big bang should have created equal amounts of matter and antimatter in the early universe. But today, everything we see from the smallest life forms on Earth to the largest stellar objects is made almost entirely of matter. Comparatively, there is not much antimatter to be found. Something must have happened to tip the balance. One of the greatest challenges in physics is to figure out what happened to the antimatter or why we see an asymmetry between matter and antimatter.

Antimatter particles share the same mass as their matter counterparts, but qualities such as electric charge are opposite. The positively charged positron, for example, is the antiparticle to the negatively charged electron. Matter and antimatter particles are always produced as a pair and, if they come in contact, annihilate one another, leaving behind pure energy. During the first fractions of a second of the big bang, the hot and dense universe was buzzing with particle-antiparticle pairs popping in and out of existence. If matter and antimatter are created and destroyed together, it seems the universe should contain nothing but leftover energy.

Nevertheless, a tiny portion of matter—about one particle per billion—managed to survive. This is what we see today. In the past few decades, particle-physics experiments have shown that the laws of nature do not apply equally to matter and antimatter. Physicists are keen to discover the reasons why. Researchers have observed spontaneous transformations between particles and their antiparticles, occurring millions of times per second before they decay. Some unknown entity intervening in this process in the early universe could have caused these "oscillating" particles to decay as matter more often than they decayed as antimatter.

Some unknown mechanism could have interfered with the oscillating particles to cause a slight majority of them to decay as matter. Physicists may find hints as to what this process might be by studying the subtle differences in the behaviour of matter and antimatter particles created in high-energy proton collisions at the Large Hadron Collider. Studying this imbalance could help scientists paint a clearer picture of why our universe is matter-filled (*https://home.cern/science/physics/matter-antimatter-asymmetry-problem, retrieved September 26, 2020*).

[*GOD—The Dimensional Revelation* expands the intuition of the author above that "it seems the universe should contain nothing but leftover energy" to be the correct deduction. Our Teaching theorizes that the initial matter-antimatter reaction totally destroyed both but left an energy residue of a different kind. Our Teaching states that energy, ordinary energy, is symbolized by *e*. Ordinary energy, *e*, converts into ordinary matter over time. The conversion equation is balanced by the fact the original negative charge of Primal Antimatter and the original positive charge of Primal Matter carry forward as a fundamental principle of a physical universe.] See chapter 11 and notes [11z24], [11z25], and [11z26].

[6b] Cause of causes, Prime Cause, Initial Cause, Unmoved Mover, Prime Mover, or First Uncaused Cause:

Unmoved Mover: That which moves without being moved (*Aristotle, Metaphysics XII, 1072a*).

Initial Cause: A cosmological argument, in natural theology and natural philosophy, is an argument in which the existence of God is inferred from alleged facts concerning causation, explanation, change, motion, contingency, dependency, or finitude with respect to the universe or some totality of objects (*en.wikipedia.org*).

First cause: In philosophy, the self-created being (i.e., God) to which every chain of causes must ultimately go back. The term was used by Greek thinkers and became an underlying assumption in the Judeo-Christian tradition. Many philosophers and theologians in this tradition have formulated an argument for the existence of God by claiming that the world that man observes with his senses must have been brought into being by God as the first cause. The classic Christian formulation of this argument came from the medieval theologian St. Thomas Aquinas, who was influenced by the thought of the ancient Greek philosopher Aristotle. Aquinas argued that the observable order of causation is not self-explanatory. It can only be accounted for by the existence of a first cause; this first cause, however, must not be considered simply as the first in a series of continuing causes but rather as first cause in the sense of being the cause for the whole series of observable causes (*The editors of Encyclopedia Britannica, July 20, 1998*).

[*GOD—The Dimensional Revelation* proves this logic and explanation of Reality to be correct. AD Twenty-First-Century science explains physics sufficiently to require an initial cause so that something can exist in physical reality. Our Teaching agrees that This Initial Cause Is and Continues To Be The Continuing Cause of both physical reality and Spiritual Reality As They Are Fused, for a time, On earth.]

[6c] All-Encompassing: including or covering everything or everyone, comprehensive (*Oxford English Dictionary*).

[6d] devil: a subordinate evil spirit at enmity with God and having power to afflict humans both with bodily disease and with spiritual corruption (*www.dictionary.com*).

The personal supreme spirit of evil often represented in Christian belief as the tempter of humankind (*www.merriam-webster.com*).

[6e] skeptic or skeptical (*noun*): a person who questions the validity or authenticity of something purporting to be factual (*www.dictionary.com*).

skeptical (*adjective*): not easily convinced, having doubts or reservations. *Oxford English Dictionary.*

[6f] self-organization: The principle of self-organization assumes a system exists for something to self-organize. It states that any deterministic, dynamic system automatically evolves towards a state of equilibrium that can be described in terms of an attractor in a basin of surrounding states. Once there, the further evolution of the system is constrained to remain in the attractor (*W. R. Ashby, "Principles of the Self-Organizing Dynamic System," The Journal of General Psychology, 37 [2] [1947], 125–28*).

A teleological created universe is proved in rejecting the idea that something can be a self-sufficient cause of its own organization (*Saint Thomas Aquinas [1225–1274] Summa Theologica, Article 3*).

[6g] spontaneous or spontaneously: performed or occurring as a result of a sudden inner impulse or inclination and without premeditation or external stimulus (*Oxford English Dictionary*).

[6h] Presume or presumes: To suppose to be true without proof (*www.merriam-webster.com*).

[6i] QED: QED is an initialism of the Latin phrase "Quod Erat Demonstrandum," literally meaning "what was to be shown." (*Definition of QUOD ERAT DEMONSTRANDUM, www.merriam-webster.com*).

Traditionally, the abbreviation is placed at the end of a mathematical proof or philosophical argument in print publications to indicate that the proof or the argument is complete and hence is used with the meaning "thus it has been demonstrated." (*The Definitive Glossary of Higher Mathematical Jargon—QED," Math Vault, August 1, 2019*).

[6j] Invocation: The act of invoking or calling upon a deity, spirit, etc., for aid, protection, inspiration, or the like; supplication; Any petitioning or supplication

for help or aid. A form of prayer invoking God's presence, especially one said at the beginning of a religious service or public ceremony (*www.dictionary.com*).

[6k] Wonder: The attitude a religious person must take is, "This is the Lord's doing, it is marvelous in our eyes" (*Psalm 118:23*).

Heschel insists that ultimate meaning can be sensed beyond a naturalistic understanding of natural phenomena, and that such meaning is mysterious and awe-inspiring (*Abraham Joshua Heschel, God in Search of Man*).

[6l] The CLEAR LIGHT Of The Void and The Setting Face-To-Face: [*GOD— The Dimensional Revelation* Confirms That The CLEAR LIGHT Of The Void Is A Synonym For GOD, From The Pre-Creation Point Of View {THE PRIMARY CLEAR LIGHT}, or The Final State Of Being, Or However It Can Be Experienced By Your Soul Along The Journey.]

> The first, the setting face-to-face with the Clear Light, during the intermediate State of the Moment of Death…be set face-to-face with the fundamental Clear Light; and, without any Intermediate State, they will obtain the unborn Dharma-Kaya… and undoubtedly obtain Liberation. (*The Tibetan Book of the Dead, book 1, part 1*)

> For now we see through a glass, darkly; but then face to face: now I know in part; but then shall I know even as also I am known. (1 Corinthians 12:12 KJV)

[*GOD—The Dimensional Revelation* Presents This Answer To The Question, What Happens When I Die? Upon The Passing Of Your Spirit or Soul From Your Body when it dies, Your Spirit Is Set Face-To-Face With The LORD. We Must Be Careful not to limit This Encounter. While it might be harsh Judgement For A Specific Soul, It Might Be A Warm Embrace For A Different Soul or Any Of The Possible Encounters With GOD For The Purpose Of Recollecting The Experiences and Growth Of The Subject Soul Upon Its Passing From physical being. The Seven Heavens Identified in *GOD—The Dimensional Revelation* Are Among The Realms Of Being Into Which GOD May Manifest The Subject Soul. In Human Terms, We Would Say That The Placement Is A Consensus Between The LORD And The Subject Soul As To What Is The Next Step For The Journey Of That Soul.

Jesus Christ said, "Blessed are the pure in heart: for they shall see God" (Matthew 5:6 KJV).

At The Onset Of The Setting-Face-To-Face With The LORD, The Option Of Reunification With The LORD Would Be Open For A Pure Soul. The Ultimate Destination Of The Journey Of A Soul Is To Merge With The CLEAR LIGHT Of Perfect Enlightenment, Which Is GOD.]

Thine own consciousness, not formed into anything, in reality void, and the intellect, shining and blissful,—these two are inseparable. The union of them is the Dharma-Kaya state of Perfect Enlightenment. (*The Tibetan Book of the Dead, book 1, part 7*)

Buddhist meditation, while shy about naming GOD, focuses on the reality of the Divine, Expressed as "Luminosity" or "Enlightenment." This mind (citta) is no-mind (acitta) because its natural character is luminous. The state of no-mind, which is immutable (avikra) and undifferentiated (avikalpa), constitutes the ultimate reality (dharmat) of all dharmas. Such is the state of no-mind (*Tadeusz Skorupski, "Consciousness and Luminosity in Indian and Tibetan Buddhism," in Buddhist Philosophy and Meditation Practice: Academic Papers Presented at the second IABU Conference Mahachulalongkornrajavidyalaya University, Main Campus Wang Noi, Ayutthaya, Thailand, on May 31–June 2, 2012*).

In Hindu philosophy, it is the union of or the realization of the identity of Atman (Individual Spirit) with Brahman (GOD). Even the Atman depends on the Brahman. In fact, the two are essentially the same. Hindu theology believes that the Atman ultimately becomes one with the Brahman. One's true identity lies in realizing that the Atman in me and the Brahman—the ground of all existence—are similar. The closest kin of Atman is the Atman of all living things, which is grounded in the Brahman. When the Atman strives to be like Brahman it is only because it realizes that that is its origin—God. Separation between the Atman and the Brahman is proved to be impermanent. What is ultimately permanent is the union between the Atman and the Brahman. Thus, life's struggle is for the Atman to be released from the body, which is impermanent, to unite with Brahman, which is permanent—this doctrine is known as Moksha" (*Gwinyai H. Muzorewa, The Great Being [Wipf, 2000], 52–54*).

This illustration Is Offered as a depiction of THE PRIMARY CLEAR LIGHT Of The Void. The background is depicted as black but actually is nothing as Only GOD Exits In Pre-Creation and as The Final State Of Being.

RESEARCH NOTES, CREDITS, AND EXPANSIONS

Mik Ulyannikov/Shutterstock 44621095

[6m] circuitous: not straight or direct. (*dictionary.cambridge.org*).

[6n] merge: combine or cause to combine to form a single entity. *Oxford English Dictionary.*

[6o] Continuum of Being: A continuous series or whole, no part of which is noticeably different from its adjacent parts, although the ends or extremes of it are very different from each other (*en.wiktionary.org*).

[6p] Spiritual Continuum:

```
Differentiation
Of The ONE           Birth (physical)         Death (physical)
V                    V                        V
<-->-----------------I------------------------I-----------------------<-->
Pre-Birth            Journey on Earth         Eternity
(Spiritual—timeless) (0–120 years at most)    (Forever and Ever not limited)
```

Illustration of Our Spiritual Continuum by *Allyn Richert November AD 2020*

Before I formed you in the womb I knew you, before you
were born I set you apart. (*Holy Bible, Jeremiah 1:5 NIV*)

[6q] Recollection: the action or faculty of remembering something (*Oxford English Dictionary*).

[6r] pause: a temporary stop in action or speech (*Oxford English Dictionary*).

[6s] biochemistry: the branch of science concerned with the chemical and physicochemical processes and substances that occur within living organisms (*Oxford English Dictionary*).

[6t] relentless or relentlessly: showing or promising no abatement of severity, intensity, strength, or pace (*www.merriam-webster.com*).

[6u] on board: on a ship or plane, involved in something (*www.macmillandictionary.com*).

[6v] bent: changed by bending out of an originally straight or even condition (*www.merriam-webster.com*).

[6w] Ethics: Ethics or moral philosophy is a branch of philosophy that "involves systematizing, defending, and recommending concepts of right and wrong behavior" (*Internet Encyclopedia of Philosophy*).

Ethics seeks to resolve questions of human morality by defining concepts such as good and evil, right and wrong, virtue and vice, justice and crime (*en.wikipedia.org*).

[6x] statistics: the practice or science of collecting and analyzing numerical data in large quantities, especially for the purpose of inferring proportions in a whole from those in a representative sample. (*Oxford English Dictionary*).

[6y] Rich or Richer: plentiful; abundant (*Oxford English Dictionary*).

[6z] Uplifting: morally or spiritually elevating, inspiring happiness or hope (*Oxford English Dictionary*).

[6z1] Happy or Happier: feeling or showing pleasure or contentment (*Oxford English Dictionary*).

[6z2] Ought: c to show when it is necessary or would be a good thing to perform the activity referred to (*dictionary.cambridge.org*).

[6z3] outcome: a final product or end result, consequence (*www.dictionary.com*).

[6z4] Maxim: a short, pithy statement expressing a general truth or rule of conduct (*Oxford English Dictionary*).

[6z5] Decision-Making Force: In psychology, decision-making is regarded as the cognitive process resulting in the selection of a belief or a course of action among several possible alternative options. Decision-making is the process of identifying and choosing alternatives based on the values, preferences, and beliefs of the decision-maker. Every decision-making process produces a final choice, which may or may not prompt action (en.wikipedia.org).

[6z6] Dominance: commanding, controlling, or prevailing over all others (*www.merriam-webster.com*).

[6z7] Benevolence or Benevolent: Benevolence is any kind act, but it can also describe the desire to do nice things (*www.vocabulary.com*).

Desire to do good to others; goodwill; charitableness (*www.dictionary.com*).

The benevolence of God is one of his moral attributes: that attribute that delights in the happiness of intelligent beings (*en.wikipedia.org*).

God is love. (*Holy Bible, 1 John 4 KJV*)

Maitrī (Sanskrit; Pali: mettā) means benevolence (*Bodhi, 2005, 90, 131, 134;* (*Gethin, loving-kindness, passim, 1998, 26, 30*); (*Warder, **friendliness**, 2004, 63*);

RESEARCH NOTES, CREDITS, AND EXPANSIONS

(*Rhys Davids and Stede,* **amity, active interest in others,** *1921–1925, 540*); (*Entry for "Mettā,"* **goodwill**, *retrieved April 29 from "U. Chicago" at http://dsal.uchicago.edu/cgi-bin/philologic/getobject); (Richard Gombrich, Theravada Buddhism: A Social History from Ancient Benares to Modern Colombo [Routledge: London, 1988], reprinted 2002*).

It is the first of the four sublime states (Brahmaviharas) and one of the ten pāramīs of the Theravāda school of Buddhism.

1. Loving-kindness or benevolence (maitrī/metta) is active goodwill toward all.
2. Compassion (karuna) results from metta; it is identifying the suffering of others as one's own.
3. Empathetic joy (mudita) is the feeling of joy because others are happy, even if one did not contribute to it; it is a form of sympathetic joy.
4. Equanimity (upekṣā/upekkha) is even-mindedness and serenity, treating everyone impartially.

Let his thoughts of boundless loving kindness pervade the whole world: above, below and across, without obstruction, without any hatred, without any enmity. It removes clinging to negative state of mind, by cultivating kindness unto all beings (*Metta Sutta and Peter Harvey, An Introduction to Buddhism: Teachings, History and Practices [Cambridge University Press, 2012], 279, 327*).

The Maitri Upanishad teaches that peace begins in one's own mind, in one's longing for truth, in looking within and that "a quietness of mind overcomes good and evil works, and in quietness the soul is one: then one feels the joy of eternity" (*Juan Mascaró, The Upanishads [Penguin, 1965], 103–104*).

The Confucian term *ren*—usually translated as "benevolence" or "humaneness"—is also understood as empathy (*en.wikipedia.org*).

[6z8] Innocents: a person involved by chance in a situation, especially a victim of crime or war. (*Oxford English Dictionary*).

[6z9] Guiding Principles: Any principles or precepts that guide an organization throughout its life in all circumstances, irrespective of changes in its goals, strategies, type of work, or the top management (*www.businessdictionary.com*).

[6z10] Proverb: a short pithy saying in general use stating a general truth or piece of advice (*Oxford English Dictionary*).

[6z11] Advice: guidance or recommendations offered with regard to prudent future action (*Oxford English Dictionary*).

[6z12] averages: an average is a single number taken as representative of a list of numbers… Often "average" refers to the arithmetic mean, the sum of the numbers divided by how many numbers are being averaged (en.wikipedia.org).

[6z13] Spirituality: The quality of being concerned with the human spirit or soul as opposed to material or physical things (*Oxford English Dictionary*).

[6z14] Collective Choices: A decision making problem where a certain number of actors, decision makers, stakeholders or players must choose a subset (possibly reduced to a singleton) of alternatives or actions among a large number of potential actions or alternatives in order to achieve some collective as well as individual objectives (*www.igi-global.com*).

[6z15] Commandment: a command or mandate (*www.dictionary.com*).

[6z16] Law or Laws: the system of rules which a particular country or community recognizes as regulating the actions of its members and which it may enforce by the imposition of penalties (*Oxford English Dictionary*).

[6z17] Legitimate: in accordance with established rules, principles, or standards (*www.dictionary.com*).

[6z18] Solemn Vow: a very important promise and one that has serious consequences for breaking (*www.yourdictionary.com*).

Vow: A solemn promise or assertion; specifically: one by which a person is bound to an act, service, or condition (*www.merriam-webster.com*).

[6z19] "So Help Me God": "So help me God" is a phrase often used to give an oath and most commonly optional as part of an oath of office. It is also used in some jurisdictions as a form of oath for other forms of public duty, such as an appearance in court, service as a juror, etc. (*en.wikipedia.org*).

[*GOD—The Dimensional Revelation* Notes That Individuals Contributing To Advanced Civilizations Seek The Help Of GOD To Make Important Decisions. This Supplication Invokes The Help Of GOD, Recognizing That The LORD May Choose not To Participate In A Situation. Individuals contributing to declining civilizations rarely use Divine Supplications.]

[6z20] Wisdom: the body of knowledge and principles that develops within a specified society or period (*Oxford English Dictionary*).

> First then, of wisdom: The State which we have called into being will be wise because…but the skill of him who advises about the interests of the whole State. Of such a kind is the skill of the guardians, who are a small class in number, far smaller than the blacksmiths; but in them is concentrated the wisdom of the State. And if this small ruling class have wisdom, then the whole State will be wise. (*Plato, Republic, Book 4, Section 434c*)

[6z21] Receptivity: able or inclined to receive; especially open and responsive to ideas, impressions, or suggestions (*www.merriam-webster.com*).

[6z22] Communion: The sharing or exchanging of intimate thoughts and feelings, especially when the exchange is on a mental or spiritual level (*Oxford English Dictionary*).

RESEARCH NOTES, CREDITS, AND EXPANSIONS

[6z23] Stimulation: Encouragement of something to make it develop or become more active; the action of arousing interest, enthusiasm, or excitement (*Oxford English Dictionary*).

[6z24] Elation: a feeling or state of great joy or pride; exultant gladness; high spirits (www.dictionary.com).

[6z25] Who: what or which person or people (*Oxford English Dictionary*).

[In this context, The "Who" Is You, An Independent Spiritual Being Capable Of Relating To GOD.]

[6z26] Destiny: the events that will necessarily happen to a particular person or thing in the future. (*Oxford English Dictionary*).

[*GOD—The Dimensional Revelation* Reveals that there is no "fate" in physical reality because the future is uncertain. This is true at the smallest through the largest of physical realities.

However, In Spiritual Reality, GOD May or may not Have A Plan For This or That Manifestation To Become Real. When GOD Has A Plan, It Is Also Described As A Destiny That Will Occur. Since We Live In A Fused physical-Spiritual Reality On Earth, There May Be A Pre-Determined Reality That May Become In Our small area of physical reality. Do not Assume That GOD Has Such A Plan. The LORD May Leave The Plan Up To You.

Upon the death of Your physical body, Reunification With GOD Is Always The Plan (Destination). However, Implicit In Differentiation From The ONE Is The Possibility That You Will wreck Your Immortal Soul and Receive harsh Judgement.]

[6z27] disintegrate: to reduce to particles, fragments, or parts; break up or destroy the cohesion of (*www.dictionary.com*).

[6z28] Integrate or integrated: Combine (one thing) with another so that they become a whole. (*Oxford English Dictionary*).

[6z29] radio set: a radio wave receiver that also has an amplifier and speakers to convert radio waves into the sound we hear (*en.wikipedia.org*).

[6z30] electronically: by means of electronic equipment or devices (*Oxford English Dictionary*).

[6z31] project or projection: a physical phenomenon associated with the production or transmission of sound (*www.vocabulary.com*).

[6z32] radio wave or waves: an electromagnetic wave of a frequency between about 104 and 1011 or 1012 Hz as used for long-distance communication (*Oxford English Dictionary*).

[6z33] receiver: In radio communications, a radio receiver (also known as a receiver, a wireless, or simply a radio) is an electronic device that receives radio waves and converts the information carried by them to a usable form. It is used with an antenna… Radio receivers are essential components of all systems that use radio (*en.wikipedia.org*).

[6z34] broadcast area: A broadcast range (also listening range or listening area for radio or viewing range or viewing area for television) is the service area that a broadcast station or other transmission covers via radio waves (*en.wikipedia.org*).

[6z35] Broadcast: We are vibrational beings. We are constantly broadcasting into creative law the particular vibrational frequency of our thoughts, beliefs and feelings. Every feeling, belief and thought has a natural vibrational frequency. We attract to ourselves the same vibrational frequency we're tuned into, much like a radio dial that tunes into a particular frequency (*newthoughtcsi.org, retrieved September 27, 2020*).

[6z36] Your Spirit:

> For God created man to be immortal, and made him to be an image of his own eternity. (*Wisdom of Solomon 2:23:23*)

The *Wisdom of Solomon* is an apocryphal work noncanonical for Jews and Protestants but is included in the Septuagint (Greek translation of the Old Testament) and was accepted into the Roman canon (*www.britannica.com*).

Also see [5z56] and [2d].

[6z37] Self: Human beings have a self—that is, they are able to look back on themselves as both subjects and objects in the universe. Ultimately, this brings questions about who we are and the nature of our own importance (*Joel M. Charon, Ten Questions: A Sociological Perspective, Fifth edition [Thomson and Wadsworth], 260*).

Another description of mind, body, soul, and spirit is a holism of one inner self being of one whole. It all combines together as one whole instead of different parts. Individuals' own thoughts, own feeling, own breathing are all completed and occur as one whole.

Ken Wilber describes the Witnessing (or Observing) Self in the following terms:

> This observing Self is usually called the Self with a capital S, or the Witness, or pure Presence, or pure Awareness, or Consciousness as such, and this Self as transparent Witness is a direct ray of the living Divine. The ultimate "I AM" is Christ, is Buddha, is Emptiness itself: such is the startling testimony of the world's great mystics and sages…the self is not an Emergent, but an aspect present from the start as the basic form of awareness, but which becomes increasingly obvious and self-aware "as growth and transcendence matures… As Depth increases, consciousness shines forth more noticeably, until: "shedding its lesser identification with both the body and the mind…in each case from matter to body to mind to Spirit…consciousness or the observing Self sheds an exclusive identity with a lesser and shallower dimension, and opens up to deeper and higher and

> wider occasions, until it opens up to its own ultimate ground in Spirit itself. And the stages of transpersonal growth and development are basically the stages of following this Observing Self to its ultimate abode, which is pure Spirit or pure Emptiness, the ground, path and fruition of the entire display. (*Ken Wilber, A Brief History of Everything, ch. 12, 197–199*)

> The true value of a human being can be found in the degree to which he or she has attained liberation from the self. (*Albert Einstein, 1934*)

[6z38] Neurologist or neurologists: A specialist in the anatomy, functions, and organic disorders of nerves and the nervous system. *Oxford English Dictionary.*

[6z39] posterior cingulate cortex: Along with the precuneus, the posterior cingulate cortex has been implicated as a neural substrate for human awareness in numerous studies of both the anesthetized and vegetative (coma) states. Imaging studies indicate a prominent role for the PCC in pain and episodic memory retrieval (*F. A. Nielsen, D. Balslev, and L. K. Hansen, "Mining the Posterior Cingulate: Segregation between Memory and Pain Components," NeuroImage 27, no. 3 [2005]: 520–532, doi:10.1016*).

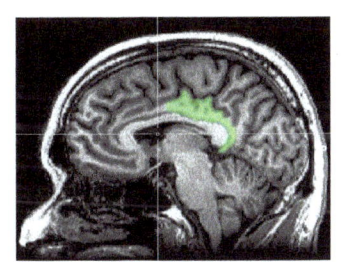

Sagittal MRI slice with highlighting indicating location of the posterior cingulate cortex.

[6z40] Experiential Self: Cognitive-experiential self-theory (CEST) is a dual-process model of perception developed by Seymour Epstein. CEST is based around the idea that people operate using two separate systems for information processing: analytical-rational and intuitive-experiential. The analytical-rational system is deliberate, slow, and logical. The intuitive-experiential system is fast, automatic, and emotionally driven. These are independent systems that operate in parallel and interact to produce behavior and conscious thought (*Seymour Epstein, Handbook of Psychology: Personality and Social Psychology, vol. 5, ed. Theodore Millon and Melvin J. Lerner [Hoboken, NJ, US: John Wiley & Sons Inc, 2003], 159–184*).

[6z41] hippocampus: Humans and other mammals have two hippocampi, one in each side of the brain. The hippocampus is part of the limbic system, and plays important roles in the consolidation of information from short-term mem-

ory to long-term memory, and in spatial memory that enables navigation (*J. H. Martin, "Lymbic System and Cerebral Circuits for Emotions, Learning, and Memory," Neuroanatomy: Text and Atlas Third Edition [McGraw-Hill Companies, 2003], 382, ISBN 978-0-07-121237-3*).

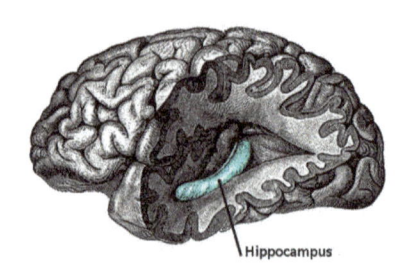

[6z42] Memory: The faculty by which the mind stores and remembers information (*Oxford English Dictionary*).

[6z43] Emotion: Instinctive or intuitive feeling as distinguished from reasoning or knowledge (*Oxford English Dictionary*).

[6z44] thalamus: a large mass of gray matter located in the dorsal part of the diencephalon (a division of the forebrain). Nerve fibers project out of the thalamus to the cerebral cortex in all directions, allowing hub-like exchanges of information. It has several functions, such as relaying of sensory signals, including motor signals to the cerebral cortex and the regulation of consciousness, sleep, and alertness (*S. Murray Sherman and R. W. Guillery, Exploring the Thalamus [Academic Press, 2000]*).

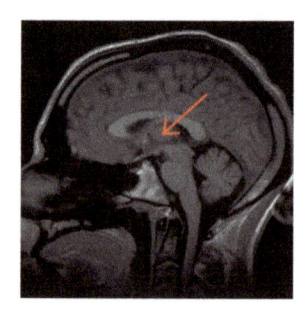

[6z45] Processing: a continuous action, operation, or series of changes taking place in a definite manner (www.dictionary.com).

[6z46] Construct or construct of mind: To be completely materialist, the saying that "everything is a construct of the mind" just means that all you sense/imagine is an interpretation of the 'real' world via sense data (and your memories of sense data) by your brain. And your brain is made of squishy biological bits and neurons that are capable of coding and interpreting such sense data (*Dana Kavanagh, May 1, 2014 at quora.com*).

We argue for a reformulation of Theory of Mine (ToM) through a systematic two-stage approach, beginning with a deconstruction of the construct into a comprehensive set of basic component processes, followed by a complementary reconstruction from which a scientifically tractable concept of ToM can be recovered.

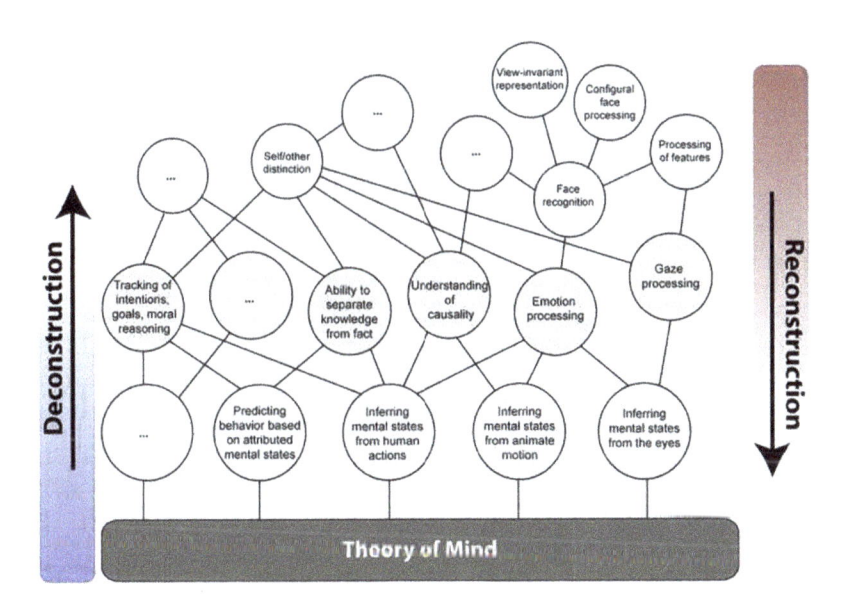

In the subsequent reconstruction stage, components of ToM would be identified by systematically recombining the most elementary, basic building blocks, basic neural mechanisms (like spike timing-dependent plasticity) may not emerge, and a very distributed set of neural regions may be involved. Indeed, we may need to take into account **factors outside the brain…** Deconstructing ToM to a fully fleshed-out list of building blocks, and then reconstructing it is, of course, a huge undertaking that will require a concerted effort across the scientific community (*Schaafsma et al., https://doi.org/10.1016/j.tics, 2014.11.007*).

[GOD—*The Dimensional Revelation* Overcomes the limitations of current theory of mind by introducing Spiritual Principles Of Operation. It is necessary To Introduce Spiritual Action for a Complete Understanding Of The Operation Of Mind. This Is A Fusion of brain and Spiritual Activities. A Human Mind may be trained or Develop various Constructs that assist with organizing and applying data and Perceptions. Constructs of Mind are necessary for advanced cognition and the ability to Act In This Life.]

[6z47] thought or thoughts: Thought encompasses an "aim-oriented flow of ideas and associations that can lead to a reality-oriented conclusion" (*Jovan Marić, Klinicka psihijatrija, 2005*).

In developmental psychology, Jean Piaget was a pioneer in the study of the development of thought from birth to maturity. In his theory of cognitive development, thought is based on actions on the environment. That is, Piaget suggests that the environment is understood through assimilations of objects in the available schemes of action and these accommodate to the objects to the extent that the available schemes fall short of the demands. As a result of this interplay between assimilation and accommodation, thought develops through a sequence of stages that differ qualitatively from each other in mode of representation and complexity of inference and understanding. That is, thought evolves from being based on perceptions and actions at the sensorimotor stage in the first two years of life to internal representations in early childhood. Subsequently, representations are gradually organized into logical structures which first operate on the concrete properties of the reality, in the stage of concrete operations, and then operate on abstract principles that organize concrete properties, in the stage of formal operations. (*J. Piaget, "Psychology of Intelligence," 1951*).

[6z48] feeling or feelings: an emotional state or reaction; a belief, especially a vague or irrational one (*Oxford English Dictionary*).

[6z49] Signal: Information converted into an electrical form suitable for transmission is called a signal. There are two types of signals; Analog and Digital. Analog signals are continuous variations of current and voltage whereas digital signals are those that have discrete stepwise value (0 = Low, 1 = High). . . the original low-frequency information is superimposed on a high-frequency carrier wave which carries the information. This process is called modulation and there are several types of it, namely AM, FM and PM [radio waves] (*https://byjus.com/physics/terms-used-electronic-communication-systems/*).

A signal is a function of independent variables that carry some information. (*www.merriam-webster.com*).

[By analogy, *GOD—The Dimensional Revelation* Expands the physical definition of signal, to GOD-Waves, Which Transmit Divine Information or Divine Energy From GOD To the lower dimensions. This Transmission of Divine Energy Is To Individual Spiritual Beings in direct ONE-To-One relations.]

[6z50] analogy: a correspondence or partial similarity (*Oxford English Dictionary*).

[6z51] Live: to be alive: have the life of an animal or plant (*www.merriam-webster.com*).

[*GOD—The Dimensional Revelation* Reveals That Each Entity That Lives in a physical universe is a physical being Perfected With An Immortal Spirit From Our Spiritual Universe.]

[6z52] Randomness: The quality or state of lacking a pattern or principle of organization; unpredictability (*Oxford English Dictionary*).

[6z53] impossible: not able to occur, exist, or be done (*Oxford English Dictionary*).

[6z54] Extraordinary: Very unusual or remarkable (*Oxford English Dictionary*).

[6z55] Metaphysical Synthesis: The combining of the constituent elements of separate material or abstract entities into a single or unified entity (*www.dictionary.com*).

RESEARCH NOTES, CREDITS, AND EXPANSIONS

Metaphysical Synthesis is any combination, physical or Spiritual, of diverse reality into a combined reality.

This Note explains a subset of Metaphysical Synthesis as dialectical synthesis:… in the dialectical philosophy of the nineteenth-century German philosopher GWF Hegel to the higher stage of truth that combines the truth of a thesis and an antithesis (*www.britannica.com*).

Fichte was also the originator of thesis–antithesis–synthesis [sequence in time] (*Daniel Breazeale and Johann Fichte, Fichte: Early Philosophical Writings [Cornell University Press, 1993], 63, Review of "Rezension des Aenesidemus" by Allgemeine Literatur-Zeitung [February 11–12, 1794), trans. Daniel Breazeale*).

A dialectic method of historical and philosophical progress that postulates (1) a beginning proposition called a "thesis," (2) a negation of that thesis called the "antithesis," and (3) a synthesis whereby the two conflicting ideas are reconciled to form a new proposition. (*en.wikipedia.org*).

[*GOD—The Dimensional Revelation* Observes the influence of the logical dialectic in Human Relations, particularly in social movements. The chart below shows how a position {thesis}, either Actual or as a logical discussion, is often met with an opposite position {antithesis}. As the situation {or discussion} progresses, elements of both positions are adopted in the next situation called a "synthesis." This synthesis becomes the new thesis. It too is met with an antithesis, to form a new synthesis.

The Logical Dialectic

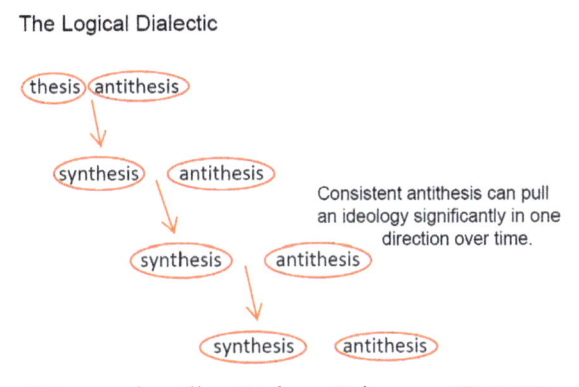

Consistent antithesis can pull an ideology significantly in one direction over time.

Diagram by Allyn Richert, February AD 2021

You can see how a strong thesis meeting a week antithesis forms one synthesis. A weak thesis being opposed by strong antithesis forms a different synthesis.

This capacity of the Human Intellect to seek Opposites is perhaps a further development of Our Capacity To Consider Alternatives or Possibilities To Influence What Is To Become.

If the opposites and the resulting synthesis is Positive, Reality Will Proceed Toward A More Harmonious Situation.

To "know" or actualize the opposite of something Good or Harmonious, may also be considered an aspect of original sin. "But of the tree of the knowledge of good and evil, thou shalt not eat of it" {*Holy Bible, Genesis 2:17 KJV*}. To bring into reality {knowledge} the opposite of a good condition is to fall from The Grace Of GOD.

Our Ethics Recognizes The Influence of social trends. Trends can become the dominate social norms of accepted behavior. These norms Cause the rise and fall of civilizations.

5th-D example: in social Ethics, "evil" may be defined as the communication of untrue information to define either a thesis or its antithesis. The presentation, physical or virtual, of untrue information may yield a warped synthesis {consequence}. This is particularly damaging to a society that has Positive institutions and a Beneficial history {thesis} being challenged by corrupt or deceitful information {antithesis} that misleads decision-makers, resulting in a less beneficial or even ugly synthesis.

One Objective Of *GOD—The Dimensional Revelation* Is To Strengthen Your Connection To GOD To Receive and Transmit Divine Energy In A Manner That Promotes Correct Decisions. Honesty and Truthful Communications Will Improve The Well-Being Of All.

Beware. In Human Society, Powerful Forces Will Oppose Correct Decisions, and The Truth May Be Obscured. A less beneficial reality may emerge.]

> A man who holds to the way of conservation all through life may reach the stage of the Golden Flower, which then frees the ego from the conflict of the opposites, and in it again becomes part of the Tao, the undivided, great One. (*The Secret of the Golden Flower*, trans. Richard Wilhelm [1929], translated into English by Cary F. Baynes [1962], chapter 8, 65)

[*GOD—the Dimensional Revelation* Explains This Significant Aspect Of Enlightenment and Reunification With The ONE. The "conflict of the opposites" is unnecessary but pervades Our Spiritual Universe—That A Human Being Bringing Into Reality, both The Good and its opposite evil, often considering both as somehow equal, causes this conflict. All the evils of society, as well as conflicts in each person's Spiritual Life, arise from the conflict of the opposites. Humankind is cast out of the "Garden" because of this insistence to Know both Good and evil. To Know Only Good Is The Requirement To Please The LORD.]

[6z56] Vision: An experience in which a personage, thing, or event appears vividly or credibly to the mind, although not actually present, often under the influence of a divine or other agency (*www.dictionary.com*).

the ability to think about or plan the future with imagination or wisdom (*Oxford English Dictionary*).

RESEARCH NOTES, CREDITS, AND EXPANSIONS

[6z57] Idea: any conception existing in the mind as a result of mental understanding, awareness, or activity; a thought, conception, or notion (*www.dictionary.com*).

[6z58] Change (*verb*): Make or become different.

Change (*noun*): The act or instance of making or becoming different (*Oxford English Dictionary*).

[6z59] sleeping dreams: Dreams can happen at any time during sleep. But you have your most vivid dreams during a phase called REM (rapid eye movement) sleep, when your brain is most active. Some experts say we dream at least four to six times a night. A lucid dream is one in which you know you're dreaming (*www.webmd.com, November 5, 2019*).

Lucid dreams can be increased and controlled by various techniques including self-training during waking hours to differentiate sleep from waking; mnnemonic training oneself to recognize the difference between dreams and reality during sleep (MILD); waking and back to bed (WBTB); incorporating external stimulation into dreams (*sleepfoundation.org., retrieved October 10, 2020*).

The brain chemistry of lucid dreams is similar to hallucinations as the increased amount of activity in the parietal lobes makes the lucid dream a conscious process (*J. Allan Hobson, The Dream Drugstore: Chemically Altered States of Consciousness (Cambridge, Massachusetts: MIT Press, 2001], 96–98*). Experiments show that the drug galantamine allows acetylcholine to build up, leading to greater recollection and awareness during dreaming (*Stephen LaBerge, Kristen LaMarca, and Benjamin Baird, August 8, 2018*).

Lucid dreams can open a channel to Divine communication if they are managed as a form of meditation. They are said to be linked to or resonate with the clear light of the Void. They can therefore serve as symbolic doorways to this mystical state of being (the Void or clear light). The dreamer is instructed to concentrate on these symbolic images without distraction or thinking about other things so that the revelatory side of these symbols will become manifest. (*Evans-Wentz describes Tibetan Dream Yoga in his book Tibetan Yoga and Secret Doctrines [London: Oxford University Press, 1935].*)

The more we think of illusory body, the more dreams we will have. We will see them as dreams rather than mistaking them for real life. We can do many things in dreams which we are unable to do while awake (*Choedak Yuthok, Lamdre: Dawn of Enlightenment, 1997*).

[6z60] media: the main means of mass communication (broadcasting, publishing, and the Internet) regarded collectively (*Oxford English Dictionary*).

[6z61] fantasy (*noun*): a creation of the imaginative faculty whether expressed or merely conceived. A mental image or a series of mental images (such as a daydream) so created.

fantasy (*verb*): the power or process of creating especially unrealistic or improbable mental images in response to psychological need (*www.merriam-webster.com*).

[6z62] fiction: invention or fabrication as opposed to fact (*Oxford English Dictionary*).

[6z63] Honest: free of deceit and untruthfulness; sincere (*Oxford English Dictionary*).

[6z64] mislead or misled: to cause (someone) to have a wrong idea or impression about someone or something (*Oxford English Dictionary*).

If you say that someone or something has misled you, you mean that they have made you believe something that is not true, either by telling you a lie or by giving you a wrong idea or impression (*collinsdictionary.com*).

[6z65] electronic manipulation: The concept of manipulating video can be traced back as far as the 1950s when the 2 inch Quadruplex tape used in videotape recorders would be manually cut and spliced (*"Edit Suite: Once Upon a Time: The History of Videotape Editing—Videomaker," Videomaker. July 1, 1997*).

Computer applications are becoming more advanced in terms of being able to generate fake audio and video content that look real (*Hilke Schellmann, "Deepfake Videos Are Getting Real and That's a Problem," Wall Street Journal, retrieved November 14. 2018*).

[6z66] image: An image (from Latin *imago*) is an artifact that depicts visual perception, such as a photograph or other two-dimensional picture, that resembles a subject—usually a physical object—and thus provides a depiction of it (*en.wikipedia.org*).

Different scholars of psychoanalysis, as well as the social sciences, such as Slavoj Žižek and Jan Berger have pointed out the possibility of manipulating mental images for ideological purposes. en.wikipedia.org.

> What makes them so powerful is that they circumvent the faculties of the conscious mind but, instead, directly target the subconscious and affective, thus evading direct inquiry through contemplative reasoning… What makes those images so powerful is that it is only of relative minor relevance for the stabilization of such images whether they actually capture and correspond with the multiple layers of reality, or not. (*David Leupold, "Image and Ideology," April 8, 2020*)

> Then God said, "Let Us make man in Our image, according to Our likeness; and let them rule over the fish of the sea and over the birds of the sky and over the cattle and over all the earth, and over every creeping thing that creeps on the earth." God created man in His own image, in the image of God He created him; male and female He created them. (*Holy Bible, Genesis 1:26–27 ESV*)

RESEARCH NOTES, CREDITS, AND EXPANSIONS

And we all, with unveiled face, beholding the glory of the Lord, are being transformed into the same image from one degree of glory to another. For this comes from the Lord who is the Spirit. (*Holy Bible, 2 Corinthians 3:18 ESV*)

[6z67] Imagination: The faculty or action of forming new ideas or images or concepts of external objects not present to the senses (*Oxford English Dictionary*).

[6z68] Ghost: soul or spectre of a dead person usually believed to inhabit the netherworld and to be capable of returning in some form to the world of the living (www.britannica.com).

[6z69] Apparition: a supernatural appearance of a person or thing, especially a ghost; a specter or phantom; wraith (*www.dictionary.com*).

[6z70] Common Belief: to describe knowledge, an opinion, or a feeling that is shared by people in general (*collinsdictionary.com*).

A belief or statement that is false but that is often held to be true because it is expedient to do so (*Oxford English Dictionary*).

[6z71] Formative Action: The fact or process of doing something, typically to achieve an aim (*Oxford English Dictionary*).

[6z72] Light (Spiritual):

In Him was life and the life was the light of men. And the light shines in the darkness and the darkness did not comprehend it. (*Holy Bible, John 1:4–5 NKJV*)

Christ proclaims, "I am the light of the world. He who follows Me shall not walk in darkness, but have the light of life." (*Holy Bible, John 8:12 KJV*) [Bringing the Divine Light to mankind.]

Manichaeism, the most widespread Western religion prior to Christianity, was based on the belief that god was literally light. From about 250–350 CE, devout Manichees followed the teachings of self-proclaimed prophet Mani. Mani's faithful, who could be found from Greece to China, believed in warring kingdoms of Light and Darkness, in "beings of light," and in a Father of Light who would conquer the demons of darkness and remake the earth through **shards of light found in human souls**. Manichaeism also co-opted other religions, including Buddhist teachings in its scripture and worshipping a Jesus the Luminous who was crucified on a cross of pure light. Among the many followers of Manichaeism was the young Augustine, who later wrote, "I thought that you, Lord God and Truth, were like a luminous body of immense size, **and myself a bit of that body**" (*Bruce Watson, Light: A Radiant History from Creation to the Quantum Age* [Bloomsbury, 2016], 30; bold print added).

> Radiant light is the function of mind, empty silence is the substance of mind. If there is empty silence without radiant light, the silence is not true silence, the emptiness is not true emptiness-it is just a ghost cave. (*The Secret of the Golden Flower,* 67, trans. Thomas Cleary translation [HarperCollins, 1991])

[Buddhism is often criticized as focusing on "emptiness." The passage above clarifies that True Emptiness Is Radiant Light. Radiant Light can be accessed by "empty silence," but That Which Is Accessed Is not empty.]

[*GOD—The Dimensional Revelation* Reaffirms That Aspects Of GOD Include Spiritual Energy, also Known As "Light" or "The Light." This is not photon energy, which is a physical energy, but Divine Light. The Individual Spirit Is also "Light," Sharing The Essence Of GOD. The Essence of Each Spiritual Being Is A Bit Of GOD.]

[6z73] Incarnation: a person who embodies in the flesh a deity, spirit, or abstract quality (*Oxford English Dictionary*).

The Supreme Soul who resides in the hearts of all living beings and regulates all their activities (*Shrimadbhagvadgita 18:61*).

[6z74] Lifetime: The duration of the existence of a living being (*www.merriam-webster.com*).

The duration of a thing's existence or usefulness (*Oxford English Dictionary*).

[*GOD—The Dimensional Revelation* Expands The Broader Meaning Of Lifetime To Be Spiritual Lifetime—A Differentiated Spirit's Usefulness To GOD.]

[6z75] metabolism: the chemical processes that occur within a living organism in order to maintain life (*Oxford English Dictionary*).

[6z76] incorrect: not in accordance with fact, wrong, not in accordance with particular standards or rules (*Oxford English Dictionary*).

[6z77] death or near-death Experience: A near-death experience (NDE) is a profound personal experience associated with death or impending death, which researchers claim share similar characteristics. When positive, such experiences may encompass a variety of sensations including detachment from the body, feelings of levitation, total serenity, security, warmth, the experience of absolute dissolution, and the presence of a light. When negative, such experiences may include sensations of anguish and distress (A. Sleutjes, A. Moreira-Almeida, B. Greyson, 2014).

[6z78] hades: Greek term ᾅδης (Hades) is used to translate the Hebrew term לוֹאשׁ (Sheol).

> Jesus Christ said, "And I also say unto thee, that thou art Peter, and upon this rock I will build my church; and the gates of Hades shall not prevail against it." (*Holy Bible, Matthew 16:18 KJV*)

RESEARCH NOTES, CREDITS, AND EXPANSIONS

> For you will not abandon my soul to Hades, or let your
> Holy One experience corruption. (*Holy Bible, Acts 2:27 NRSA*)

[6z79] Afraid: alarmed, *frightened, terrified* all indicate a state of fear. *Afraid* implies inner apprehensive disquiet (*www.dictionary.com*).

[6z80] listless wandering: to move about without a fixed course, aim, or goal (*www.merriam-webster.com*).

[6z81] Reincarnation: The rebirth of a soul in a new body (*Oxford English Dictionary*).

Reincarnation, a major tenet of Hinduism, is when the soul, which is seen as eternal and part of a spiritual realm, returns to the physical realm in a new body. A soul will complete this cycle many times, learning new things each time and working through its karma. This cycle of reincarnation is called samsara(*https://study.com/academy/lesson/what-is-reincarnation-in-induism*).

> Jesus answered and said unto him, "Verily, verily, I say unto thee, Except a man be born again, he cannot see the kingdom of God. Nicodemus saith unto him, How can a man be born when he is old? can he enter the second time into his mother's womb, and be born? Jesus answered, Verily, verily, I say unto thee, Except a man be born of water and of the Spirit, he cannot enter into the kingdom of God. That which is born of the flesh is flesh; and that which is born of the Spirit is Spirit." (*Holy Bible, John 3:3–6 KJV*)

[6z82] Mournful: Feeling, expressing, or inducing sadness, regret, or grief (*Oxford English Dictionary*).

[6z83] Joy: The emotion of great delight or happiness caused by something exceptionally good or satisfying, keen pleasure, elation (*www.yourdictionary.com*).

[6z84] Compel or compelled: Bring about (something) by the use of force or pressure, drive forcibly. (*Oxford English Dictionary*).

[6z85] Hand of GOD:

> You open your hand and satisfy the desires of every living thing… The Lord watches over all who love him… (*Holy Bible, Psalm 145:16:20 NIV*)

[6z86] Intuition: The power or faculty of attaining to direct knowledge or cognition without evident rational thought and inference (*www.merriam-webster.com*).

Including but not limited to direct access to unconscious knowledge; unconscious cognition; inner sensing; inner insight to unconscious pattern-recognition;

and the ability to understand something instinctively, without any need for conscious reasoning (*A. D. Rosenblatt and J. T. Thickstun, "Intuition and Consciousness," Psychoanal Q, October 1994, 63(4):696-714*).

[6z87] Divine Communication: Each spiritual/human being IS a physical manifestation of Divine Source. We are always receiving communication at every moment of our lives (*Barbara Rose, astrostar.com, retrieved October 10, 2020*).

[6z88] Mystic or Mystics: A person who seeks by contemplation and self-surrender to obtain unity with or absorption into the Deity or the absolute, or who believes in the spiritual apprehension of truths that are beyond the intellect (*Oxford English Dictionary*).

[6z89] Clairvoyance or Seeing: The supposed faculty of perceiving things or events in the future or beyond normal sensory contact (*Oxford English Dictionary*).

Also, [13z48] has more detail.

[6z90] Spiritual Sense: Christianity speaks of "listening to the Spirit," which is the still small voice within that is our spiritual intuition. This is Spirit's way of guiding us towards the fullest expressions of our divine potential. Our intuition is the spiritual intersection where Divine Ideas meet our Divine Mind. At this nexus, we are able to directly experience guidance, discernment and inspiration (*Pastor Bonnie, unityoflaketravis.org, March 19, 2017*).

[6z91] iteration: a different form or version of something (www.dictionary.com).

[6z92] Interaction: communication or direct involvement with someone or something (*Oxford English Dictionary*).

[6z93] Hubble Space Telescope: The Hubble Space Telescope (often referred to as HST or Hubble) is a space telescope that was launched into low-Earth orbit in 1990 and remains in operation. It was not the first space telescope, but it is one of the largest and most versatile, well known both as a vital research tool and as a public relations boon for astronomy. It has recorded some of the most detailed visible light images, allowing a deep view into space. The Hubble telescope is named after astronomer Edwin Hubble and is one of NASA's Great Observatories, along with the Compton Gamma Ray Observatory, the Chandra X-ray Observatory, and the Spitzer Space Telescope (*Shelley Canright, "NASA's Great Observatories," NASA, retrieved April 26, 2008*).

[6z94] electron microscope: a microscope that uses a beam of accelerated electrons as a source of illumination. As the wavelength of an electron can be up to 100,000 times shorter than that of visible light photons, electron microscopes have a higher resolving power than light microscopes and can reveal the structure of smaller objects. A scanning transmission electron microscope has achieved better than 50 pm resolution in annular dark-field imaging mode (*Rolf Erni et al., "Atomic-Resolution Imaging with a Sub-50-pm Electron Probe," Physical Review Letters, 102, no. 9 [2009]*).

[6z95] Reach, reaching, or reached: arrive at; get as far as (*Oxford English Dictionary*).

RESEARCH NOTES, CREDITS, AND EXPANSIONS

[6z96] supernova: A supernova is a powerful and luminous stellar explosion. This transient astronomical event occurs during the last evolutionary stages of a massive star or when a white dwarf is triggered into runaway nuclear fusion. The original object, called the progenitor, either collapses to a neutron star or black hole, or is completely destroyed… Supernovae are a major source of elements in the interstellar medium from oxygen to rubidium (*en.wikipedia.org*).

[6z97] quantum observation: In quantum mechanics, which deals with the behavior of very small objects, it is not possible to observe a system without changing the system, and the observer must be considered part of the system being observed. In isolation, quantum objects are represented by a wave function which often exists in a superposition or mixture of different states. However, when an observation is made to determine the actual location or state of the object, it always finds the object in a single state, not a "mixture". The interaction of the observation process appears to "collapse" the wave function into a single state, so any interaction between an isolated wave function and the external world that results in this wave function collapse is called an observation or measurement, whether or not it is part of a deliberate observation process (*en.wikipedia.org*).

[*GOD—The Dimensional Revelation* Agrees with the definition of quantum "observation" as "measurement," which requires "Participation" of the measurer.

This is not to be confused with Ordinary Human Observation or Divine Observation, Which Are best described as "Witnessing" as opposed to "Participating."

The "collapse" to a "single state" is the definition of *being*. Of course, on the physical continuum, reality is always "becoming," hence the "uncertainty" of the "single state" that will be observed next.

The confusion is that the physical continuum is never a "single state" that can be separated from the "continuous flow" of reality. The collapse did occur, and the single state did manifest something real. But that reality moved on immediately to another state or situation.

The mathematics must freeze a moment in time in order to provide a definite calculation. That becomes an approximation; hence, the equations include infinities that cannot be worked out mathematically. Time is continuous, so a "moment" cannot actually be frozen or separated as distinct from the continuum.]

Also see [1z] and [1z1] *supra*.

[6z98] Spiritual Presence: God is omnipresent; hence, the rabbinic teaching: "The Divine presence is everywhere" (*Babylonian Talmud, Baba Bathra 25a*).

[6z99] quark or quarks: any of a number of subatomic particles carrying a fractional electric charge postulated as building blocks of the hadrons. Quarks have not been directly observed but theoretical predictions based on their existence have been confirmed experimentally (*Oxford English Dictionary*).

[6z100] gluon: a subatomic particle of a class that is thought to bind quarks together (*Oxford English Dictionary*).

GOD—THE DIMENSIONAL REVELATION

[6z101] Autonomous: describes things that function separately or independently (*www.vocabulary.com*).

[6z102] Discovery: learning something new or finding someone or something, something found or learned (*www.macmillandictionary.com*).

[6z103] Knowable: able to be observed, understood, or ascertained (*Oxford English Dictionary*).

[6z104] inclusive: with the inclusion of the extreme limits stated (*Oxford English Dictionary*).

[6z105] Intimately Acquainted: "a" having a deep or unusual knowledge of "b" (*Oxford English Dictionary*).

[6z106] Conscious Entities or Entity: something that exists separately from other things and has a clear identity of its own (www.collinsdictionary.com).

[*GOD—The Dimensional Revelation* Reveals That A Conscious Entity Has Spiritual Being or A Fusion Of Spiritual Identity Into physical matter.]

[6z107] Pervasive Consciousness: unconditioned reality, which is either the spiritual ground of all being or the whole of things considered as a spiritual unity (*TLS Sprigge, Routledge Encyclopedia of Philosophy [Taylor and Francis, 1998]*).

[6z108] Shared Between or Sharing: use, occupy, or enjoy (something) jointly with another or others (*Oxford English Dictionary*).

[6z109] Heaven or Paradise: Heaven, or the heavens, is a common religious cosmological or transcendent, supernatural place where beings such as gods, angels, spirits, saints, or venerated ancestors are said to originate, be enthroned, or live. According to the beliefs of some religions, heavenly beings can descend to Earth or incarnate and earthly beings can ascend to Heaven in the afterlife or, in exceptional cases, enter Heaven alive (*en.wikipedia.org*).

> Jesus said, "I will give you the keys of the kingdom of heaven; and whatever you bind on earth shall have been bound in heaven, and whatever you loose on earth shall have been loosed in heaven." (*Holy Bible, Matthew 16:19 NIV*)

Kingdom of heaven (Greek: βασιλεία τῶν οὐρανῶν) is a phrase used in the Gospel of Matthew. It is generally seen as equivalent to the phrase "kingdom of God" (Greek: βασιλεία τοῦ θεοῦ) in the Gospel of Mark and the Gospel of Luke. Thought to be the main content of Jesus's preaching in the Gospel of Matthew, the "kingdom of heaven" described "a process, a course of events, whereby God begins to govern or to act as king or Lord, an action, therefore, by which God manifests his being-God in the world of men (*Edward Schillebeeckx, Jesus: An Experiment in Christology [London: Fount Paperbacks, 1983], 140–141*).

RESEARCH NOTES, CREDITS, AND EXPANSIONS

[*GOD—The Dimensional Revelation* Reveals Its Own Observation of The Seven Heavens. See chapter 13. We Acknowledge The Versions Of Heaven Summarized below.]

- Heaven (Judaism): Gan Eden, the heavenly Garden of Eden, the final stage of Olam Haba [*Wikipedia*] (or afterlife).
- Paradise (Zoroastrianism): It was the ancient Persians who gave us the word *paradise*, which means a walled garden or park; and Zoroastrianism, in particular, gave us notions of the afterlife that were adopted and/or adapted by the Jews, Christians, and Muslims. Zoroastrianism is also interesting because unlike other religions, it claims that everyone will eventually get into heaven, though it might take a while.
- Heaven (Christianity): The Christian notion of heaven is one of singing and rejoicing before God in a "new heaven and a new earth."
- Paradise (Islam): The Islamic version of heaven is a paradise for those whose good works have outweighed the bad as determined by the straight path laid out in the Quran. Heaven is a garden.
- Moksha (Hinduism): Release from illusion and suffering in the present world. According to the Upanishads, our actions connect us to this world of appearances, which is in fact illusory. What is real is Brahman, the ultimate reality that transcends our sensory experiences. If you can escape your ignorance and realize that ultimately you are not you but Brahman itself, then you can achieve release from the cycle of death and rebirth. This release is called "moksha."
- Nirvana (Buddhism [also Hinduism]): One of the four noble truths of the Buddha is that suffering is caused by desire, the desire to have but also the desire to be. The Buddha taught that desire is a flame that burns us, causes suffering, and keeps us tied to the cycle of death and rebirth because the flame continues burning into the next life. What we hope for is Nirvana or the extinguishing of that flame, which is also the end of suffering (*https://www.neatorama.com/2007/03/23/heaven-and-hell-according-to-various-religions/*).

[*GOD—The Dimensional Revelation* Acknowledges some historical versions of the Seven Heavens Summarized below. This Teaching Clarifies that many of these identifications of heaven are misled by confusion of astronomical planets and forces, which are physical, With Divine Heaven, Which Is Spiritual.]

Hindu's Seven Heavens: In the Hindu text, the Puranas also teach that there are seven higher worlds (vyahrtis or heavens) and seven lower worlds. Unlike Babylonian mythology, all the worlds are meant for humans after death. Upon death, the god of death Yama accounts a person's life and determines how long they will stay in which of the higher and lower worlds in accordance with the karma earned during their most recent incarnation. When the requisite stays have been accomplished, the soul is reincarnated on earth. The Hindu heavens are

1. Satyaloka: the abode of Brahma (he may live above Satyaloka) and the greatest sages;
2. Tapaloka: the place of the second-greatest sages in recognition of their faultless observance of the rituals;
3. Janaloka: the world for the lifelong celibates;
4. Maharloka: the place for those who voluntarily went through a period of celibacy;
5. Svarloka: a group of planets that are home to lesser deities, bards, and other pious beings;
6. Bhuvarloka: the atmosphere of the earth, home to ghosts and spirits caught in limbo before their rebirth;
7. Bhurloka: the earth and other planets with similar attributes, the only place people can accumulate good or bad karma.

Some believe a person could spend time in both a heaven and a hell—for instance, if a lifelong celibate did some evil they needed to work off. If enough good karma is earned, the soul can finally break out of the cycle and reach Nirvana.

Judaism's Seven Heavens: The Hebrew word for *heaven*, *shamayim*, is only ever plural. Different traditions have different numbers of heavens; the Jewish mystical text, the Zohar, claims there are 390 heavens and 70,000 worlds. As science progresses, the understanding of the seven heavens is becoming less literal and more allegorical, as a description of how God interacts with His creation. Mystical Judaism says followers can make their way through the heavens if they pass certain tests and know the names of the guardian angels. At each level, the mystic is allowed to receive particular wisdom. Some Jewish scholars say Paul's trip to the "third heaven" is an example (*2 Corinthians 12:2–4*).

Originally, 2 Enoch mentioned seven heavens; it was later changed to ten, possibly by the Eastern Orthodox Church in the Seventh Century. What each of the heavens contain or represent vary depending on the teller. The story claims that Enoch walked the heavens with the angels, returned to earth, and told his family, then was taken to heaven again (Genesis 5:24). The heavens he visited were

1. Vilon ("curtain"): a curtain which is rolled over the earth at nighttime to block the sun (Isaiah 40:22); contains the atmosphere, minor stars, snow, and dew; abode of Adam and Eve; governed by Gabriel; called curtain or veil because it veils or hides the other six levels; represented by the moon;
2. Raqi'a/Raki'a ("expanse," "canopy"): possibly refers to the frozen canopy over the earth before the Flood (Genesis 1:7–8, Deuteronomy 11:11);

Moses visited Paradise here to receive the Ten Commandments; fallen angels are imprisoned here for marrying human women (Genesis 6:4); dwelling place of souls awaiting judgement including "men of renown," apostates, tyrants; called expanse because it's where the sun and planets dwell (Genesis 1:14, 17); represented by Mercury;

3. Shehaquim/Shehaqim/Shehakim ("clouds"): Eden and Tree of Life, the mill that produces manna, also includes paradise and hell or hades (Psalm 78:23–24), represented by Venus.
4. Zebul ("habitation"): stratosphere, sun, moon, and "four great stars," including celestial mechanics; dwelling of the winds; called "habitation" because it's where the New Jerusalem with its temple is (Isaiah 63:15); represented by the sun;
5. Ma'on ("refuge"): home to "Grigori"—fallen angels who mourn for their brothers in Raqi'a, hell or Gehenna; Michael or possibly Samael presides; filled with ministering angels who sing by night; called refuge because it's where most of the angels reside; represented by Mars;
6. Makhon/Machon/Makon ("city," "established place"): home for angels in charge of nature's cycles and good governing systems of the world and angels who write men's actions in books; governed by Samael, a dark servant of God; storage place of rain, snow, and hail (Deuteronomy 28:12); called "city" because it's where the City of Angels resides; represented by Jupiter.
7. Araboth/Aravot ("deserts"): also known as the tenth heaven; Throne of Glory, and God dwells here, as well as unborn human souls, Seraphim, Cherubim, justice, righteousness, souls of the righteous, and ineffable light (Psalm 68:5); called desert because it has no moisture and no air; God also said to be above the seventh heaven; represented by Saturn.

Ancient Babylon's Seven Heavens: It's believed tha, unlike the flat earths in many creation myths, in Babylonian mythology, the earth is a hollow half-sphere, much like a bowl—or a kufa boat—sitting upside down. Above it is the "lower firmament" or atmosphere. Then the realm of the planets, also called "sheep," "wanderers," or "watchers," as well as lightning and thunder. The wanderers also have corresponding rulers:

1. The Moon: Sin (AKA: Nanna, Su'en)
2. Mercury: Nabu (Nebo of Isaiah 46:1)
3. Venus: Ishtar (AKA: Astarte, Aphrodite, Artemis, Asherah of 1 Samuel 31:10)
4. Mars: Nergal (2 Kings 17:30)
5. The Sun: Shamash (AKA: Samas)

6. Jupiter: Marduk (patron deity of the city of Babylon, see Jeremiah 50:2)
7. Saturn: Ninib (possibly Nimrod of Genesis 10:8–9) (*compellingTruth.org*)

> Nevertheless, do not rejoice in this, that the spirits are subject to you, but rejoice that your names are written in heaven. (*Holy Bible, Luke 10:20 ESV*)

[*GOD—The Dimensional Revelation* Reveals Seven Heavenly States or "Heavens" as Presented Through This Revelation From GOD. See Chapter 13.

We Recognize that the words *Heaven* or *Paradise* are often confused in early Human Civilizations because "the heavens" often referred to the "sky," which is our cosmos, which is only part of The Realm Of GOD.

Also, We Observe That The Afterlife Differs For Different Individual Spirits. Differentiation From The ONE Is Truly Unique To Each Individual Spirit. Hence, The Journey Of Each Soul Is Also Unique. Hence, The After-Life of An Individual Soul Is Also Unique.

The Spiritual Journey A Soul May Include The Experience Of Various Heavens. Some Are Glorious, and some may be oppressive.

Though An Individual Soul May Be In One Of The Heavens While Incarnate In Life On earth, This Teaching Reveals Many Glorious Heavens. Most Journeys Of A Soul Ultimately Lead To Reunification With GOD.

The exception is that any Differentiated Spirit or Soul can be extinguished by Divine Judgement to not exist.]

[6z110] Nirvana: In Hindu philosophy, it is the union of or the **realization of the identity of Atman with Brahman** (*Gwinyai H. Muzorewa, The Great Being [Wipf, 2000], 52–54; bold print added*).

All Indian religions assert it [Nirvana] to be a state of perfect quietude, freedom, highest happiness, as well as the liberation from or ending of samsara, the repeating cycle of birth, life, and death (*en.wikipedia.org*).

The final beatitude that transcends suffering, karma, and samsara and is sought especially in Buddhism through the extinction of desire and individual consciousness (*www.merriam-webster.com*).

[6z111] Valhalla: The great hall where Odin receives and feasts with the souls of heroes fallen bravely in battle (*Webster's New World College Dictionary, Fourth Edition, Copyright 2010 by Houghton Mifflin Harcourt*).

[6z112] Elysium: Elysium or the Elysian Fields expanded to include those chosen by the gods, the righteous, and the heroic, where they would remain after death, to live a blessed and happy life, and indulging in whatever employment they had enjoyed in life (*David Sacks, A Dictionary of the Ancient Greek World [US: Oxford University Press, 1997], 8, 9*).

RESEARCH NOTES, CREDITS, AND EXPANSIONS

Night speeds by, and we, Aeneas, lose it in lamenting. Here comes the place where cleaves our way in twain. Thy road, the right, toward Pluto's dwelling goes, and leads us to Elysium. But the left Speeds sinful souls to doom and is their path to Tartarus th' accurst. (*Virgil, Aeneid, 6.539, 29 BC*)

In no fix'd place the happy souls reside. In groves we live, and lie on mossy beds, By crystal streams, that murmur thro' the meads: But pass yon easy hill, and thence descend; The path conducts you to your journey's end. This said, he led them up the mountain's brow, and shews them all the shining fields below. They wind the hill, and thro' the blissful meadows go. (*Virgil, Aeneid, 6.641, 29 BC*)

Carlos Schwabe, 1903. Elysian Fields, Schaafsma et.al.
(*https://doi.org/10.1016/j.tics. 2014.11.007*)

The avenue des Champs-Élysées is the most prestigious avenue in Paris and one of the most famous streets in the world. Champs-Élysées is French for "Elysian Fields" (*en.wikipedia.org*).

[6z113] Spiritual States of Being: Mode of existence (*dictionary.reverso.com*).
a quality of your present experience (personalmba.com).

[6z114] Experience: direct observation of or participation in events as a basis of knowledge (*www.merriam-webster.com*).

[6z115] demon or demons: an evil spirit or a person or thing who is evil (*www.yourdictionary.com*).

[6z116] Separate or Separateness: The state of being several and distinct, discreteness, severalty, distinctness, separation—the state of lacking unity (*Oxford English Dictionary*).

[6z117] Bridge: a time, place, or means of connection or transition (www.merriam-webster.com).

[6z118] Bilateral: having or relating to two sides, affecting both sides (*Oxford English Dictionary*).

[6z119] A Glorious Consciousness Of A Manifest Being: See [2u] and [3z18].

[*GOD—The Dimensional Revelation* Reveals That Consciousness May Present Itself In Many Forms Of Spiritual Being Differentiated From The ONE. That Presentation Is Glorious As It Is Of GOD. The Measure Of That Glory Is Qualities Manifested As The Individual Consciousness Proceeds In Reality Sharing The Glory With GOD.]

[6z120] Free Will or Freedom of Will: the power of acting without the constraint of necessity or fate; the ability to act at one's own discretion (*Oxford English Dictionary*).

> It is the coward and the fool who says this is his fate. But it is the strong man who stands up and says I will make my own fate. (*Swami Vivekananda, "Sayings and Utterances," 1907*)

Choice falls into five stages: (i) intellectual consideration of whether an objective is desirable, (ii) intellectual consideration of means of attaining the objective, (iii) will arrives at an intent to pursue the objective, (iv) will and intellect jointly decide upon choice of means (v) will elects execution (*Timothy O'Connor "Free Will," ed. Edward N. Zalta, October 29, 2010*).

[*GOD—The Dimensional Revelation* Proves That "Free Will" Is An Operational Principle Of All Spiritual Realities. Just as quantum indeterminacy is the proof of the WORD Directing all physical realities, so also Spiritual Realities Remain Uncertain On The Spiritual Continuum. As The Free Will Of Differentiated Spirits Is A Purpose For GOD To Differentiate Them Individually from The ONE.]

[6z121] Compassion: Sympathetic consciousness of others' distress together with a desire to alleviate it (*www.merriam-webster.com*).

Ranked a great virtue in numerous philosophies, compassion is considered in almost all the major religious traditions as among the greatest of virtues.

Jesus demonstrated compassion to those his society had condemned. A 2012 study of the historical Jesus has claimed that the founder of Christianity sought to elevate Judaic compassion as the supreme human virtue, capable of reducing suffering and fulfilling our God-ordained purpose of transforming the world into some-

RESEARCH NOTES, CREDITS, AND EXPANSIONS

thing more worthy of its creator (*Tom Drake-Brockman, Christian Humanism: The Compassionate Theology of a Jew called Jesus* [Sydney: Denis Jones and associates, 2012]).

> If you want others to be happy, practice compassion. If you want to be happy, practice compassion. (*Dalai Lama, dalaiLama.com*)

[6z122] Pathos: an element in experience or in artistic representation evoking pity or compassion (*www.merriam-webster.com*).

[6z123] Sympathy:

1. Harmony of or agreement in feeling as between persons or on the part of one person with respect to another
2. The harmony of feeling naturally existing between persons of like tastes or opinion or of congenial dispositions
3. The fact or power of sharing the feelings of another, especially in sorrow or trouble; fellow feeling, compassion, or commiseration (*www.dictionary.com*).

[6z124] Enlightenment or Spiritual Enlightenment:

> The true light that gives light to everyone was coming into the world. (*Holy Bible, John 1:9 NIV*)

> To the Divine Body of Truth, the Incomprehensible, Boundless Light. (*The Tibetan Book of the Dead, book 1*)

It translates several Buddhist terms and concepts, most notably *bodhi*, *kensho*, and *satori*. Related terms from Asian religions are *moksha* (liberation) in Hinduism, *Kevala Jnana* in Jainism, and *ushta* in Zoroastrianism (*en.wikipedia.org*).

> But when you're focused on how it should look or what it's supposed to be—you miss. You are still in concepts. The escape from concepts, so to speak, is quite a strange experience, I feel. If you've been a seeker for a very long time, it can be a bit strange when the seeker drops. You can even question whether you are spiritual or not now, because you're used to being on a 'spiritual path'. You find it really hard to define yourself, eventually impossible, because no concept can hold what you are. And since concepts are mental and the actual experience is not, you may even wonder—'what did I realize?'; 'was anything at all realized?' The

mind still wants to put it all into a story of what happened and what is happening. This has to fall away as well. (*Daniel Shai, Spiritual Teacher at sunrayteaching.com*)

There is no exercise to restore the creative (qian), only the secret of turning the light around. The light itself is the creative; to turn it around is to restore it (return to it). (*The Secret of the Golden Flower 2:15, trans. Thomas Cleary [HarperCollins, 1991]*)

The circulation of the light is the inclusive term. The further the work advances, the more does the Golden Flower bloom. But there is a still more marvelous kind of circulation. Till now we have worked from the outside on what is within; now we stay in the centre and rule what is external. Hitherto it was service in aid of the Master; now it is a dissemination of the commands of the Master. The whole relationship is now reversed. If one wants to penetrate the more subtle regions by this method, one must first see to it that that body and heart are completely controlled, that one is quite free and at peace, letting go of all entanglements, untroubled by the slightest excitement, and with the heavenly heart exactly in the middle. Then let one lower the lids of the two eyes as if one received a holy edict, a summons to become the minister. (*The Secret of the Golden Flower, trans. Richard Wilhelm [1929], translated into English by Cary F. Baynes [1962], chapter 8, 54*)

[*GOD—The Dimensional Revelation* Clarifies The Word Enlightenment To Be The Spiritual Advancement in Which The Individual Spirit Becomes Light By Receiving Divine Energy and Turning Divine Energy Inward to Become Light.

As The Inner Light Increases, You Become The Master To Project Divine Energy, The Light, Outward into Your Manifest Environment.

This Light Is The Projection Of Divine Consciousness and Divine Energy Both Inward and Outward. Equivalent Terms Are *Grace* In Christianity and *Illumination* In Islam.

Becoming The Light, Also Known As Restoring The Light, Returning To The Light, Circulating The Light, or Turning The Light Around—This Situation or Activity Is The Essence Of Enlightenment. This Is not just Awakening, Freedom, Release, Knowledge, Insight, Transcendental Truth, Self-Realization, or Other Spiritual Attainments. Those Disciplines Are Related and May Be Ways To Enlightenment or Describe Benefits or Tools Provided By Enlightenment. Becoming The Light Is The Way. It Is Both The Journey and The Destination of Each Soul.

RESEARCH NOTES, CREDITS, AND EXPANSIONS

It Is Important that You are not distracted by incorrect uses of the word *Enlightenment*. For example, Our Use Of The Word *Enlightenment* does not refer to the historical period known as the "enlightenment" in eighteenth-century Europe.]

[6z125] Interrelate: there is a connection between them, and they have an effect on each other (*collins.dictionary.com*).

[6z126] Civilization: an advanced state of human society in which a high level of culture, science, industry, and government has been reached (*www.dictionary.com*).

[GOD—*The Dimensional Revelation* Clarifies That GOD does not have A Metastring Connection to a civilization, a society, or a nation. A civilization, society, nation, or any such institution is a construct of Human Activity, not anything that GOD Would Recognize, except Through You. Such institutions have no Soul. GOD Is Connected Only To The Individual Spirit {Soul}. The Individual or Individuals May Act To Create the institutions.

Therefore, "One Nation Under GOD" (Pledge of Allegiance, The Flag Code Title 4, United States Code, Chapter 1, Section 4) Certifies The Supremacy of GOD Leading The Citizens Of This Nation Individually "To Form A More Perfect Union" (*Preamble to the Constitution of the United States, 1789*).

To form an antithesis to this is evil. You will be cast out By GOD.]

[6z127] Prophesy (*verb*): to predict or reveal something that will happen in the future.

Prophesy (*noun*): A prophecy is a prediction or an utterance from a prophet inspired by his god. www.vocabulary.com.

[6z128] Myth or Myths: a traditional story, especially one concerning the early history of a people or explaining some natural or social phenomenon and typically involving supernatural beings or events. (*Oxford English Dictionary*).

[6z129] Legend or Legends: a traditional story sometimes popularly regarded as historical but unauthenticated (*Oxford English Dictionary*).

[6z130] hallucination or hallucinations: an experience involving the apparent perception of something not present (*Oxford English Dictionary*).

[6z131] semiconscious: a feeling or memory of which the person experiencing it is only vaguely or partially aware (*Oxford English Dictionary*).

[6z132] Adoration: deep love and respect, worship, veneration (*Oxford English Dictionary*).

The act of paying honor as to a divine being, worship, reverent homage, fervent and devoted love (*www.dictionary.com*).

> Only in adoration can profound and true acceptance develop. And it is precisely this personal act of encounter with the Lord that develops the social mission which is contained in the Eucharist and desires to break down barriers, not only the barriers between the Lord and us but also and above all those

that separate us from one another. *("Christmas greetings to the Members of the Roman Curia and Prelature, December 22, 2005, BENEDICT XVI, www.vatican.va)*

[6z133] Beauty: The quality or aggregate of qualities in a person or thing that gives pleasure to the senses or pleasurably exalts the mind or spirit (*www.merriam-webster.com*).

[6z134] Blessing: a special favor, mercy, or benefit (*Oxford English Dictionary*).

God's favor, or a person's sanction or support, or something you ask God for, or something for which you are grateful (*yourdictionary.com*).

[6z135] Charity: generosity and helpfulness especially toward the needy or suffering; also, aid given to those in need (*www.merriam-webster.com*).

Charity, in Christian thought, the highest form of love, signifying the reciprocal love between God and man that is made manifest in unselfish love of one's fellow men. St. Paul's classical description of charity is found in the New Testament (*1 Corinthians 13*). In Christian theology and ethics, charity (a translation of the Greek word *agapē*, also meaning "love") is most eloquently shown in the life, teachings, and death of Jesus Christ. St. Augustine summarized much of Christian thought about charity when he wrote: "Charity is a virtue which, when our affections are perfectly ordered, unites us to God, for by it we love him." Using this definition and others from the Christian tradition, the medieval theologians, especially St. Thomas Aquinas, placed charity in the context of the other Christian virtues and specified its role as "the foundation or root" of them all (*www.britannica.com*).

[6z136] Communion: The sharing or exchanging of intimate thoughts and feelings, especially when the exchange is on a mental or spiritual level (*Oxford English Dictionary*).

A Christian sacrament in which consecrated bread and wine are consumed as memorials of Christ's death or as symbols for the realization of a spiritual union between Christ and communicant or as the body and blood of Christ (*www.merriam-webster.com*).

[6z137] Compromise (*noun*): an agreement or a settlement of a dispute that is reached by each side making concessions.

Compromise (*verb*): to settle a dispute by mutual concession (*Oxford English Dictionary*).

[6z138] Comradery: a feeling of friendliness, goodwill, and familiarity among the people in a group (*www.merriam-webster.com*).

[6z139] Congeniality: The quality of being agreeable, suitable, or pleasant (*www.dictionary.com*).

[6z140] Courage: Mental or moral strength to venture, persevere, and withstand danger, fear, or difficulty (*www.merriam-webster.com*).

RESEARCH NOTES, CREDITS, AND EXPANSIONS

Having identified wisdom, Socrates turns his attention to the virtue of courage. He defines courage as the "true opinion about real and false dangers." In other words, a man who knows what to fear—such as dishonor, shame, and defeat—and what not to fear, such as hardships, injury, and death, is courageous.

> This power which preserves right opinion about danger I would ask you to call "courage," adding the epithet "political" or "civilized" in order to distinguish it from mere animal courage and from a higher courage. (*Plato, Republic, book 4, section 2*)

[Courage is the second Cardinal Virtue.]
[6z141] Daring: venturesomely bold in action or thought (*www.merriam-webster.com*).
[6z142] Ecstasy: an overwhelming feeling of great happiness or joyful excitement (*Oxford English Dictionary*).
[6z143] Elation: a state of extreme happiness or excitement (*dictionary.cambridge.org*).
[6z144] Generous: larger or more plentiful than is usual or necessary (*Oxford English Dictionary*).
[6z145] Hope: Hope is an optimistic state of mind that is based on an expectation of positive outcomes with respect to events and circumstances in one's life or the world at large (*www.dictionary.com*).

> The eyes of your understanding being enlightened; that you may know what is the hope of His calling, what are the riches of the glory of His inheritance in the saints. (*Holy Bible, Ephesians 1:18 KJV*)

[6z146] Inspiration: the process of being mentally stimulated to do or feel something, especially to do something creative (*Oxford English Dictionary*).
[6z147] Introspection: Introspection, as the term is used in contemporary philosophy of mind, is a means of learning about one's own currently ongoing, or perhaps very recently past, mental states or processes (*plato.stanford.edu*).
[6z148] Justice: the quality of being just; righteousness, equitableness, or moral rightness (*www.dictionary.com*).

> To render to each his due… (*Plato, Republic, book 1, section 327a*)

[Justice is the fourth Cardinal Virtue.]
[6z149] Kind or Kindness: A type of behaviour marked by acts of generosity, consideration, or concern for others without having an expectation of praise or reward.

It is considered a virtue, and is recognized as a value in many cultures and religions (see ethics in religion). In Book II of "Rhetoric", Aristotle defines kindness as "helpfulness towards someone in need, not in return for anything, nor for the advantage of the helper himself, but for that of the person helped" (*Aristotle, "Kindness," Rhetoric, book 2, trans. Lee Honeycutt, chapter 7*).

> God is so kind that it is impossible to imagine His unbounded kindness! (*Bhau Kalchuri, Meher Prabhu: Lord Meher, 11, [Myrtle Beach: Manifestation Inc., 1986], 3918*)

[6z150] Mercy: compassion or forbearance shown especially to an offender or to one subject to one's power; also, "a blessing that is an act of divine favor or compassion" (*www.merriam-webster.com*).

> I have always found that mercy bears richer fruits than strict justice. (*Abraham Lincoln, "Quotes About Mercy," Goodreads*)

[6z151] Pious: marked by or showing reverence for deity and devotion to divine worship (*www.merriam-webster.com*).

[6z152] Prudence: Prudence (in Latin *prudentia*, contracted from *providentia* meaning "seeing ahead, sagacity") is the ability to govern and discipline oneself by the use of reason (*www.merriam-webster.com*).

[Prudence is the first Cardinal Virtue.]

[6z153] Reciprocity: Reciprocity is the exchange of something between people or groups of people when each person or group gives or allows something to the other. www.collinsdictionary.com.

[6z154] Relation: the way in which two or more concepts, objects, or people are connected; a thing's effect on or relevance to another.0 (*Oxford English Dictionary*).

[6z155] Righteous or Righteousness:

> But seek ye first the kingdom of God, and his righteousness; and all these things shall be added unto you. (*Holy Bible, Matthew 6:33 KJV*)

Just according to the divine law. Applied to persons, it denotes one who is holy in heart, and observant of the divine commands in practice; as a righteous man. Applied to things, it denotes consonant to the divine will or to justice; as a righteous act (*KJV Dictionary*).

Righteousness is the quality or state of being morally correct and justifiable. It can be considered synonymous with "rightness" or being "upright" (*oxforddictionaries.com*). It can be found in Indian religions and Abrahamic traditions as a theological concept. For example, from various perspectives in Hinduism, Christianity, and Judaism it is considered an attribute that implies that a person's actions are justified, and can have the connotation that the person has been "judged" or "reckoned" as leading a life that is pleasing to God (*en.wikipedia.org*).

The Chinese term "yi" is often translated as "righteousness". Yi is the action that is indeed correct. Yan Hui, one of the Four Sages, once asked his master to describe the rules of ren. Confucius replied, "One should see nothing improper, hear nothing improper, say nothing improper, do nothing improper" (*Confucius Analects 12:1*).

In Hinduism, "Dharma" is partially defined "as that which is established or firm, steadfast decree, statute, law, practice, custom, duty, right, justice, virtue, morality, ethics, religion, religious merit, good works, nature, character, quality, property. Yet, each of these definitions is incomplete, while the combination of these translations does not convey the total sense of the word. In common parlance, dharma means "right way of living" and "path of rightness"(*Steven Rosen, Essential Hinduism [Praeger, 2006], 34–45 ISBN 0-275-99006-0*).

> Whenever and wherever there is a decline in righteousness/religious practice, O descendant of Bharata, and a rise of evil/irreligion Then at that time I manifest Myself. (*Bhagavad Gita, chapter 4, text 7*)

[6z156] Temperance: moderation in action, thought, or feeling; restraint (*www.merriam-webster.com*).

Temperance suggests the idea of harmony. Some light is thrown upon the nature of this virtue by the popular description of a man as 'master of himself'... The expression really means that the better principle in a man masters the worse (*Plato, Republic, book 4, section 2*).

[Temperance is the third Cardinal Virtue also defined as "Discipline."]

[6z157] Thank (*verb*): to express gratitude, appreciation, or acknowledgment to.

Thanks (*noun*): a grateful feeling or acknowledgment of a benefit, favor, or the like expressed by words or otherwise (*dictionary.com*).

[6z158] diminish: to make less or cause to appear less (*www.merriam-webster.com*).

[6z159] Attracts: cause to come to a place or participate in a venture by offering something of interest, favorable conditions, or opportunities; evoke; cause (someone) to have a liking for or interest in something (*Oxford English Dictionary*).

[6z160] negative spiritual activity and negative spiritual energy: If a child were to have a negatively oriented spirit, it could be easily inspired to accept and display negative behavior and malaise. However, if that same child were to be introduced to the positive knowledge of the Light, they would have a chance to bring positive energy to their spirit and, over time, their negatively oriented spirit could change its

ways and redirect itself toward a positive existence (*https://gloriaromlewski.com/tag/positive-spiritual-experience/*).

Concepts such as "life force", "Qi" (pronounced che) and "élan vital" existed from antiquity… The term "energy" is used by writers and practitioners of various esoteric forms of spirituality and alternative medicine to refer to a variety of claimed experiences and phenomena that defy measurement and thus can be distinguished from the scientific form of energy (*Victor J. Stenger, "Bioenergetic Fields," The Scientific Review of Alternative Medicine 3, no. 1 [Spring–Summer 1999]*).

It can also be seen as a mental energy that is totally distinct from chemical energy.

The concept of "qi" (energy) appears throughout traditional East Asian culture, such as in the art of feng shui and Chinese martial arts. Qi philosophy also includes the notion of "negative qi", typically understood as introducing negative moods like outright fear or more moderate expressions like social anxiety or awkwardness (*Bryan W. Van Norden, Introduction to Classical Chinese Philosophy [Hackett Publishing, March 2011], 98*).

According to Ambrose, "negative" energy is used to describe a lower denser vibration—and it may feel like exhaustion, overwhelm, anger, helplessness, and even jealousy (*Erin Hanafy, March 17, 2019, wellandgood.com*).

[6z161] ignore: refuse to take notice of or acknowledge, disregard intentionally (*Oxford English Dictionary*).

[6z162] Godforsaken or godless: deserted by God, desolate, having no evidence of godliness (*www.urbandictionary.com*).

not acknowledging a deity or divine law, neglected and miserable in appearance or circumstances (*www.merriam-webster.com*).

> You have forsaken me and served other gods; therefore I will save you no more. (*Holy Bible, Judges 10:13*)

> A psalm of David. My God, my God, why have you forsaken me? Why are you so far from saving me, so far from my cries of anguish? (*Holy Bible, Psalm 22:1 NIV*)

[GOD—*The Dimensional Revelation* Reminds You That The LORD Mercifully Offers Redemption To You, should You find Yourself in godless circumstances.] *See* [13z53].

[6z163] Glory:

> And we all with unveiled face, beholding the glory of the Lord, are being changed into his likeness from one degree of glory to another. For this comes from the Lord who is the Spirit. (*Holy Bible, 2 Corinthians 3:18 ESV*)

> And we, who with unveiled faces all reflect the glory of the Lord, are being transformed into His image with intensifying glory, which comes from the Lord, who is the Spirit. (*Holy Bible, 2 Corinthians 3:18 BSB*)

Divine glory is an important motif throughout Christian theology, where God is regarded as the most glorious being in existence, and it is considered that human beings are created in the Image of God and can share or participate, imperfectly, in divine glory as image-bearers. Thus, Christians are instructed to "let your light shine before men, that they may see your good works, and glorify your Father in heaven" (*Holy Bible, Matthew 5:16 NKJV*).

[6z164] desire: a longing or craving as for something that brings satisfaction or enjoyment (*www.dictionary.com*).

[6z165] Reaching Out: to attempt to initiate communication (*www.yourdictionary.com*).

[6z166] Positive Spiritual Experience: Experiencing something which is beyond the comprehension of the five senses, mind and intellect constitutes a 'spiritual experience' (*www.spiritualresearchfoundation.org/spiritual-practice/spiritual-experiences; retrieved 10/11/2020*).

We believe that our findings have the following methodological implications if they are corroborated in future studies.

1. Unidimensional Scales measuring only positive spiritual experiences, such as the Daily Spiritual Experiences Scale, seem to be inappropriate for scrutinizing the benefits of spiritual experiences for health in the light of our finding, at least in some populations (*DSES, Underwood & Teresi, 2002, Underwood, 2006*).
2. We would expect stronger effects of negative spiritual experiences in individuals that are particularly prone to experiencing more deconstructive experiences, possibly as a natural consequence of their physical and mental situation, such as chronically ill patients. This may be the reason why spirituality has always played an important role within palliative medicine.

Another possibility of understanding spirituality is through the psychological functions and processes associated with regular meditative and contemplative practice. Mindfulness is a central concept that has its roots in Buddhist spiritual practice and other meditative and contemplative traditions that actively strive for cultivating and developing a state of conscious and nonjudgmental awareness (*Brown & Ryan, 2003*). N. Kohls et al. / *Archive for the Psychology of Religion 31 (2009) p.360*.

[6z167] evil: the fact of suffering, misfortune, and wrongdoing; something that brings sorrow, distress, or calamity (*www.merriam-webster.com*).

[6z168] Confident or Confidence: the feeling or belief that one can rely on someone or something, firm trust, a feeling of self-assurance arising from one's appreciation of one's own abilities or qualities (*Oxford English Dictionary*).

[6z169] Divine Action: Is it possible for God both to create a deterministic world and to act specially, to realize his particular purposes within it? Indeterministic processes leave 'gaps' in the causal sequences of the world, which allow room for God to act, while deterministic processes do not; thus, while deterministic processes can provide us with some understanding of God's general activity in the creation and sustenance of the world, only indeterministic processes can give us a window into God's special, or providential, action within the world (*"LC Vicens Religious Studies," vol. 48, no. 3, [Cambridge University Press, September 2012], 315–336*)

> This notion of a religion/science problem is misguided. When properly understood, neither the classical (Newtonian) picture of natural laws, nor the more recent quantum mechanical picture, rules out divine intervention. There is nothing in science, under either the old or the new picture, that conflicts with, or even calls in to question, special divine action, including miracles. (*Alvin Plantinga, "Divine Action in the World (Synopsis)" in Ratio: An International Journal of Analytic Philosophy, volume 19, issue 4, [2006], 495–504*)

[6z170] Breath, Refined and Profound: There are three important parts to meditating: thinking, awareness, and the breath… When we sit in meditation, the important point is to be observant of the levels of the breath. The breath in the body has three levels: common, refined, and profound.

1. The common breath is the breath we breathe into the body. It comes in two sorts. (a) That which is mixed with impure or polluted air…(b) The other sort of common breath is that which is beneficial—the breath mixed with pure air. When it mixes with the blood in the heart, it's beneficial to the body.
2. The refined breath is gentle and soft. It's the delicate breath sensations derived from the in-and-out breath that permeate between the blood vessels and nerves. This breath is what gives rise to our sense of feeling throughout the body.
3. The profound breath lies deeper than the refined breath. It's cool, spacious, empty, and white.

RESEARCH NOTES, CREDITS, AND EXPANSIONS

The refined breath that spreads to nourish the body is the important level of breath to use as a basis for observing all three levels of the breath. When this refined breath is spread fully throughout every part of the body, the body will feel light, empty, and quiet—but we're still mindful and alert… At this point, a bright light will appear in our sensation of the breath. Even though our eyes are closed, it's as if they were open. We'll feel as if the breath in our body had a white glow… This is the profound breath. The mind becomes serene and still; the body becomes serene and still…when the awareness that comes from stillness gains power, it gives rise to strength and light (*Geoffrey DeGraff, September 27, 1957, Copyright 1998, Ṭhānissaro Bhikkhu, revised edition, 2011*).

[6z171] sleep: Sleep is a naturally recurring state of mind and body characterized by altered consciousness, relatively inhibited sensory activity, reduced muscle activity and inhibition of nearly all voluntary muscles during rapid eye movement (REM) sleep and reduced interactions with surroundings. It is distinguished from wakefulness by a decreased ability to react to stimuli but more reactive than a coma or disorders of consciousness, with sleep displaying very different and active brain patterns (*NIH Bethesda, MD, "Brain Basics: Understanding Sleep," 2017*).

[6z172] Doorway: The doorways to light and spirit are not 'out there' behind the mists. They are within each of us. It is our awareness, as human beings, that opens to these planes and keeps them present in this world. Our chakras, our subtle body, are part of the 'technology' of how we are able to do this, regardless of whether someone is working consciously with them or not—the chakras are themselves doorways within us… Thinking of yourself as a doorway adds another dimension to what it means to be alive on this planet today (*https://mommymystic.wordpress.com/2017/09/19/we-are-the-doorway-tending-the-light*).

[*GOD—The Dimensional Revelation* Notes that Your physical brain provides the biochemical backdrop to facilitate Doorways For Spiritual Manifestation In This Life. Beyond the phenomena of physical death, Your Spirit Seeks Its Destiny.]

[6z173] Calm or Calmly: a quiet and peaceful state or condition (*www.merriam-webster.com*).

[6z174] Recall: to bring back from memory, recollect, remember (*www.dictionary.com*).

[6z175] Encounter (*verb*): to meet unexpectedly, come upon (*www.collinsdictionary.com*).

Encounter (*noun*): meeting, experience or discovery of particular kind (*www.macmillandictionary.com*).

[6z176] unfortunate: unlucky, burdened, unpropitious, unsuccessful, sad, afflicted, broken, hexed, hapless, luckless, shameful (*yourdictionary.com*).

[6z177] miserable: being in a pitiable state of distress or unhappiness (*www.merriam-webster.com*).

[6z178] Will to Act: Virtue and vice, according to Aristotle are "up to us"... In Book VII, Aristotle discusses self-mastery, or the difference between what people decide to do, and what they actually do (*en.wikipedia.org*).

Freedom is the power, rooted in reason and will, to act or not to act, to do this or that, and so to perform deliberate actions on one's own responsibility. By free will one shapes one's own life. Human freedom is a force for growth and maturity in truth and goodness; it attains its perfection when directed toward God, our beatitude (*Catechism of the Catholic Church 1, Freedom and Responsibility, 1731*).

[6z179] Directly: With nothing or no one in between (*Oxford English Dictionary*).

[6z180] Turn The Light Around or Turning the Light Around:

> The golden flower is light... The celestial mind is like a house; the light is the master of the house. Therefore, once you turn the light around, the energies throughout the body all rise. Just turn the light around; this is the unexcelled truth... Turning the light around is the secret of dissolving darkness and controlling the lower soul. There is no exercise to restore "the creative," only the secret of turning the light around. The light itself is "the creative"; to turn it around is to restore it. (*The Secret of the Golden Flower, 10, 11,15, trans. Thomas Cleary [HarperCollins, 1991]*)

[*GOD—The Dimensional Revelation* Reveals That The Exchange Of Spiritual Energy With GOD Is An Oscillating Exchange. The Light Is Given To You By GOD. You Circulate The Light In Your Center. The Light Increases As You Appreciate It. Through Prayer, Meditation, and Worship, You Share The Light Back With GOD. GOD Appreciates The Light You Share. GOD Returns It To You Enhanced. Spiritual Energy Increases With Each Cycle. This Oscillation Is The Basis For Spiritual Enlightenment.

This Exchange Is Often interrupted During A Human Life To Attend biological needs. There are other distractions.

When You Have Mastered Turning The Light At Your Center, Then You Can Turn The Light Around To Project It Outwardly To Other Living Beings. Sharing The Light Broadens The Oscillation and Circulation Of The Light To Include Other Spirits. This Unifies and Elevates Spirit. GOD Is Very Pleased, and You Are Fulfilled.]

See Expansions at [13z57].

[6z181] Project: Push something away from a central structure (*www.vocabulary.com*).

[*GOD—The Dimensional Revelation* Expands The Act Of Projection To Emphasize You Becoming Light. That Light Radiates Spiritually. The Enlightened Person May Focus or Project The Light Inward to Illuminate The Soul or Outward To An Individual or group of Individuals.]

RESEARCH NOTES, CREDITS, AND EXPANSIONS

[6z182] Instrument Of GOD: Instrument is a grammatical case used to indicate that a noun is the instrument or means by or with which the subject achieves or accomplishes an action. The noun may be either a physical object or an abstract concept (*Wikipedia*).

That which is subservient to the execution of a plan or purpose or to the production of any effect; means used or contributing to an effect; applicable to persons or things. (*King James Dictionary, https://av1611.com/kjbp/kjv-dictionary / instrument.html*).

> In a great house there are not only vessels of gold and silver but also of wood and earthenware, and some for noble use, some for ignoble. If anyone purifies himself from what is ignoble, then he will be a vessel for noble use, consecrated and useful to the master of the house, ready for any good work. (*Holy Bible, 2 Timothy 2:20–21 RSV*)

There is nothing that remotely approaches in terms of excitement, satisfaction and fulfillment, the consciousness that one has been the instrument in the hands of the Almighty to do some of his work—to change the direction of someone's life, perhaps, to prevent an injury, to resolve an argument, to answer a challenge, to heal a weakness, to rebuke a ruler, or to turn a nation (*https://www.raystedman.org/new-testament/timothy/fit-to-be-used*).

We must especially be aware that others have great potential to be instruments of God to us (*https://catholic-daily-reflections.com/2019/10/03/instruments-of-god/*).

In some strains of Christian theology, the Christian church may be divided into the following:

- The Church Militant (Latin: *Ecclesia militans*), also called the Church Pilgrim, which consists of Christians on earth who struggle as soldiers of Christ against sin, the devil, and "the rulers of the world of this darkness against the spirits of wickedness in the high places."
- The Church Penitent (Latin: *Ecclesia poenitens*), also called the Church Suffering (Latin: *Ecclesia dolens*) or the Church Expectant (Latin: *Ecclesia expectans*), which in the theology of certain churches, especially that of the Catholic church, consists of those Christians currently in Purgatory.
- The Church Triumphant (Latin: *Ecclesia triumphans*), which consists of those who have the beatific vision and are in Heaven. (*en.wikipecia.org*)

Church Triumphant: members of the church who have died and are regarded as enjoying eternal happiness through union with God. "Church triumphant" (*https://www.merriamwebster.com/dictionary/*).

Those who constitute the Church Triumphant rejoice eternally in the glory of God, to whom they are united in the beatific vision.

Anglicans believe that "the Church on earth is united with the Church in heaven [*sanctorum communio*]. They speak of the 'Church Militant here on earth' and the Church triumphant in heaven. They worship God together with angels and archangels and with all the company of heaven" (*en.wikipedia.org*).

[*GOD—The Dimensional Revelation* Reveals That You Are The Instrument Of GOD. This Means That The Purpose Of Your being Is For Your Consciousness and Actions To Be An Instrument Of or By Which GOD Observes and Participates In physical reality.]

[6z183] Becoming: In the philosophical study of ontology, the concept of becoming originated in ancient Greece with the philosopher Heraclitus of Ephesus, who in the sixth century BC, said that nothing in this world is constant except change and becoming (i.e., everything is impermanent) (*en.wikipedia.org*).

According to tradition, Heraclitus wrote a treatise about nature named "Περὶ φύσεως" ("Perì phýseōs"), "About Nature," in which appears the famous aphorism πάντα ῥεῖ (panta rhei) translated literally as "the whole flows [as a river]," or figuratively as "everything flows, nothing stands still." The concept of "becoming" in philosophy is connected with two others: movement and evolution, as becoming assumes a "changing to" and a "moving toward." Becoming is the process or state of change and coming about in time and space (*Diogenes Laërtius, Vitae Philosophorum, 9, 17*).

> No man ever steps in the same river twice. (*Plato, Cratylus, 402a, 360 BC*)

[*GOD—The Dimensional Revelation* Emphasizes that "becoming" is also the conclusion of quantum theory and quantum mechanics. Under quantum theory, the presence of matter is never certain as it is always becoming. Our Teaching is that this is true because it is the WORD that directs what is to Become, and We cannot Know The Will Of GOD In Advance Of Its Becoming.

Also, please note that much of what becomes in physical reality occurs by programmed Instructions Of The WORD. GOD, As A Conscious Being, does not usually Participate In physical becoming, except Through Participation in Your Consciousness of those events. This is why physical scientists are often misled to think that GOD does not exist. In later chapters, Our Teaching shows the ever-present Instruction Of The WORD That Sustains strings snapping in and out of quantum fields to Preserve and Continue physical reality.

Another way to say this is that An Aspect Of GOD, Instructions Of The WORD To Sustain physical reality, Is The Constant Cause of physical reality. Those Instructions have already been Given. That Information Has Been Differentiated

RESEARCH NOTES, CREDITS, AND EXPANSIONS

From The ONE and proceeds according to Those Instructions. Hence, physical reality is sustained without the Direct Conscious Attention Of GOD.]

[6z184] Reconnect or Reconnects: re-establish a bond of communication or emotion (*Oxford English Dictionary*).

[6z185] Paths of Righteousness:

> He restores my soul; He leads me in the paths of righteousness For His name's sake. (*Holy Bible, Psalm 23:3 NKJV*)

> I walk in the path of righteousness, in the pathway of justice, that I may cause those who love me to inherit wealth, and that I may fill their treasuries. The Lord created me as the beginning of his works, before his deeds of long ago. (*Holy Bible, Proverbs 8:20–22 NET*)

[6z186] Elevation: raise or lift (something) up to a higher position (*Oxford English Dictionary*).

[6z187] Combination: a joining or merging of different parts or qualities in which the component elements are individually distinct (*Oxford English Dictionary*).

[6z188] Capable: having the ability, fitness, or quality necessary to do or achieve a specified thing (*Oxford English Dictionary*).

[6z189] Sentient or Sentience: Sentience is the capacity to feel, perceive, or experience subjectively (*www.merriam-webster.com*).

Sentience is a minimalistic way of defining consciousness, which otherwise commonly and collectively describes sentience plus further features of the mind. These further features of consciousness may not be necessary for sentience, which rests on the capacity to feel sensations and emotions (*Antonio Damasio, "Fundamental Feelings," Nature 413 [6858:781], October 2001*).

[6z190] anomaly or anomalies: something that deviates from what is standard, normal, or expected. (*Oxford English Dictionary*).

[6z191] mathematical balance and imbalance: Chemical equations and mathematical equations have a lot in common. The equal sign in a math equation means that both sides, however they're written, are equivalent expressions of the same thing: Chemical equations must be mass balanced and charge balanced across the → or ⇌ sign. Mass balance means the same number and kind of atoms on each side. Charge balance means the same number of unpaired + and − charges on each side (*http://xaktly.com/Chemistry_Balance.html*).

Theorists can predict what a gravity particle should look like, but when they try to calculate what happens when two "gravitons" smash together, they get an infinite amount of energy packed into a small space—a sure sign that the math is missing something. There are simply too many possible configurations of both the interactions and the underlying space-time. We can't make the math simple enough to solve; our mathematical models lose their predictive power. They break down. (*https://www.space.com/32147-why-is-gravity-so-hard-to-understand.html*).

[*GOD—The Dimensional Revelation* Explains that the reason quantum mathematics and the "Standard Model of particles and interactions" show mathematical imbalances is that there are 6th-d anomalies appearing in quantum fields that have no physical explanation. Our Teaching Is That A Spiritual Variable Must Be Introduced To balance quantum equations. That is because the Excitations that produce matter in a quantum field Are Spiritual. These Are Turned On or off In The 9th D According To The WORD Of GOD In the 10th D.

This is another Proof Of GOD. Physical reality is a subset of all Reality, Which Is Of GOD.

Stated another way, THE SOURCE Information and Instructions Originate In The 10th Dimension, also Called The WORD. The WORD Determines What Was, What Is, and Whatever Will Become.]

[6z192] outside of time and space: Nothing that contains [physical] energy is "outside of time." The reason is that the energy of any object is linked, by quantum physics, to the rate of oscillation of its wave function. Thus, if you have energy, E (including any rest energy mc^2), then your quantum-wave function is oscillating with frequency ($f=E/h$) where *h* is Planck's constant. So if you exist (and I take that to mean that you have some nonzero energy), then you vary in time (*https://www.forbes.com/sites/quora/2017/06/09/is-it-possible-to-exist-outside-of-time/?sh=52aeaef311a2*).

Aquinas' argument from first cause started with the premise that it is impossible for a being to cause itself (because it would have to exist before it caused itself) and that it is impossible for there to be an infinite chain of causes, which would result in infinite regress. Therefore, there must be a first cause, itself uncaused.

The way Craig describes his view is that God without creation is timeless; God with creation is temporal (*https://iep.utm.edu/god-time*); (*William Lane Craig, Time and Eternity: Exploring God's Relationship to Time* [Wheaton, IL: Crossway Books, 2001a]).

[*GOD—The Dimensional Revelation* Reveals That Reality Includes The Spiritual Membrane System, Which Is Outside of time and space. Our Reality On Earth Is A Fusion Of Aspects Of Our Spiritual Universe With our physical universe. Our physical universe is limited and unfolds in space-time. Our Spiritual Universe Is Not Subject to space-time. This Is Proved By The Transformative Effects Of Spiritual Choices, Such As Mercy or Forgiveness.

It Is Also Proved By The Passing Of Each Soul To Our Spiritual Universes Upon death of the physical body. Data We Observe forces the distinction, hence the separation into two different Membrane Systems.

Of Course, GOD and The WORD Are Outside Of time. GOD May Choose To Participate In physical time in various Manifestations. Your Consciousness In Your Human Life Is One Of Those Manifestations.]

[6z193] unit: an individual thing or person regarded as single and complete but which can also form an individual component of a larger or more complex whole (*Oxford English Dictionary*).

[6z194] temporary: lasting for only a limited period of time; not permanent (*Oxford English Dictionary*).

[6z195] Childhood behavioral testing at Yale University: babies are in fact born with an innate sense of morality, and while parents and society can help develop a belief system in babies, they don't create one. A team of researchers at Yale University's Infant Cognition Center, known as The Baby Lab, showed us just how they came to that conclusion (*https://www.cnn.com/2014/02/12/us/baby-lab-morals-ac360/index.html*).

[6z196] Moral: concerned with the principles of right and wrong behavior and the goodness or badness of human character (*Oxford English Dictionary*).

[6z197] Recognition: The identification of something as having been previously seen, heard, known, etc.; the perception of something as existing or true; realization; the acknowledgment of something as valid or as entitled to consideration (*www.merriam-webster.com*).

[6z198] Infant Human Being: An infant (from the Latin word *infans*, meaning "unable to speak" or "speechless") is the more formal or specialized synonym for *baby*, the very young offspring of a human (*en.wikipedia.org*).

[6z199] chemical signature: A unique pattern produced by an analytical instrument, such as a spectrometer, indicating the presence of a particular molecule in a test sample (*www.yourdictionary.com*).

[chemical environment connection to a Spiritual condition]

> Some further peer-reviewed discussion concerning the metabolomics of chronic fatigue syndrome (CFS). Suggesting that "targeted, broad-spectrum metabolomics of plasma not only revealed a characteristic chemical signature but also revealed an unexpected underlying biology. (R. K.Naviaux et al., "Metabolic Features of Chronic Fatigue Syndrome," Proc Natl Acad Sci USA, August 29, 2016, pii: 201607571)

[6z200] Initiate or initiated: cause (a process or action) to begin (*Oxford English Dictionary*).

[6z201] Breathwork: breathwork refers to any type of breathing exercises or techniques. People often perform them to improve mental, physical, and spiritual well-being. During breathwork, you intentionally change your breathing pattern.

There are many forms of breathwork therapy that involve breathing in a conscious and systematic way. Many people find breathwork promotes deep relaxation or leaves them feeling energized (*https://www.healthline.com/health/breathwork*).

Breathwork is a method of breath control that is meant to give rise to altered states of consciousness and to have an effect on physical and mental well-being (*Young JS, Cashwell CS, Giordano AL (2010). "Breathwork as a therapeutic modality: an overview for counselors." Counseling and Values. 55 (1): 113. doi:10.1002/j.2161-007X.2010.tb00025*).

According to Jack Raso, breathwork is described by proponents as a multiform "healing modality" characterized by stylized breathing. Its purported design is to effect physical, emotional, and spiritual change. Such a process can allegedly "dissolve limiting programs" that are "stored" in the mind and body and increases one's ability to handle more "energy" (*Jack Raso M. S., R. D. Quackwatch, March 25, 2007*) (*en.wikipedia.org*).

Hyperventilation is rapid or deep breathing, usually caused by anxiety or panic. This overbreathing, as it is sometimes called, may actually leave you feeling breathless. When you breathe, you inhale oxygen and exhale carbon dioxide. Excessive breathing may lead to low levels of carbon dioxide in your blood, which causes many of the symptoms that you may feel if you hyperventilate. The goal in treating hyperventilation is to raise the carbon dioxide level in the blood. There are several ways to do this. To increase your carbon dioxide, you need to take in less oxygen. To accomplish this, you can breathe through pursed lips (as if you are blowing out a candle) or you can cover your mouth and one nostril, breathing through the other nostril. Learn breathing exercises that help you relax and breathe from your diaphragm and abdomen rather than your chest wall. Practice relaxation techniques regularly, such as progressive muscle relaxation or meditation. Exercise regularly (*https://www.hopkinsmedicine.org/health/conditions-and-diseases/hyperventilation*).

[GOD—*The Dimensional Revelation* Explains that The holding of Breath after much intake of oxygen during Breathwork is to restore the balance of oxygen with carbon dioxide in Your bloodstream. This avoids hyperventilation, which is too much oxygen in the bloodstream.

Let us consider two of the many Breathwork techniques:

1. *Circular Breathing*. Take a slow deep breath, fully filling your lungs with belly moving out as your diaphragm moves down. Immediately exhale slowly completely emptying your lungs of air as your diaphragm moves upward. This is one cycle. Repeat for 10 continuous cycles. Discontinue and resume normal breathing when you feel light headed. I find Circular Breathing to be most useful in aerobic exercise in which the surplus oxygen is used by the muscles. It is also very useful in moments of stress to Center the Mind.

RESEARCH NOTES, CREDITS, AND EXPANSIONS

2. *Box Breathing*. Breath in deeply for 4 seconds (or whatever counting method you choose). Hold with lungs full for 4 seconds. Exhale slowly and fully for 4 seconds. Hold lungs empty for 4 seconds. This is one cycle. Repeat 10 cycles or more as you enjoy the euphoric or relaxed feeling.

Box Breathing was made popular as a common Navy Seal training technique. I find Box Breathing most useful to Renew Clarity of Consciousness. There is no hangover to this High, just Calmness and Joy.

It is the opinion of This Author that taking in oxygen is necessary for Consciousness of an Incarnate Being. Taking in an overabundance of oxygen Heightens or Alters Your State Of Consciousness. Holding the breath for few seconds with full or empty lungs allows carbon dioxide to build, restoring the balance. This Balance is necessary for Correct Breathwork.

We Recommend Singing and aerobic Exercise as among the best Breathwork Meditations. It is no surprise that Human Beings naturally Pursue Breath Enhancing Activities in ordinary Recreation.

The LORD Is Especially Pleased To Join With You In A Wide Variety Of Songs In Praise and Worship.

The True Wonder Is That You do not even have to Believe In GOD for GOD To Join With You In Your Joyous Endeavors.

The Reality of GOD In Your Consciousness Ends the secular debate About "GOD" or "no god."]

[6z202] Enveloping: to cover or surround something completely (dictionary.cambridge.org).

[6z203] excitations: Quantum Field Theory (QFT) treats particles as excited states (also called quanta) of their underlying fields, which are—in a sense—more fundamental than the basic particles. Interactions between particles are described by interaction terms in the Lagrangian involving their corresponding fields. Each interaction can be visually represented by Feynman diagrams, which are formal computational tools, in the process of relativistic perturbation theory. every matter particle is an excitation (or localized vibration) in a field (*https://www.physicssayswhat.com/2019/06/05/qft-how-many-fields-are-there*).

According to quantum field theory, there are certain basic fields that make up the world, and the wave function of the universe is a superposition of all the possible values those fields can take on. . . If a field takes on a constant value through space and time, we don't see anything at all; but when the field starts vibrating, we can observe those vibrations in the form of particles (*Sean Carroll, The Big Picture: On the Origins of Life, Meaning, and the Universe Itself [Penguin Publishing Group] 173-174*).

There is one field for each kind of particle.

Standard Model of Elementary Particles

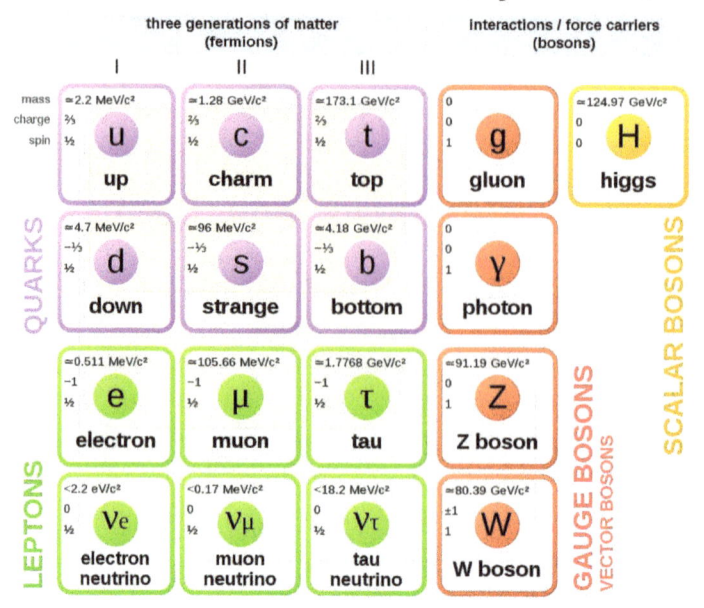

	I	II	III		
	≈2.2 MeV/c², ⅔, ½ **u** up	≈1.28 GeV/c², ⅔, ½ **c** charm	≈173.1 GeV/c², ⅔, ½ **t** top	0, 0, 1 **g** gluon	≈124.97 GeV/c², 0, 0 **H** higgs
QUARKS	≈4.7 MeV/c², -⅓, ½ **d** down	≈96 MeV/c², -⅓, ½ **s** strange	≈4.18 GeV/c², -⅓, ½ **b** bottom	0, 0, 1 **γ** photon	
	≈0.511 MeV/c², -1, ½ **e** electron	≈105.66 MeV/c², -1, ½ **μ** muon	≈1.7768 GeV/c², -1, ½ **τ** tau	≈91.19 GeV/c², 0, 1 **Z** Z boson	
LEPTONS	<2.2 eV/c², 0, ½ **νe** electron neutrino	<0.17 MeV/c², 0, ½ **νμ** muon neutrino	<18.2 MeV/c², 0, ½ **ντ** tau neutrino	≈80.39 GeV/c², ±1, 1 **W** W boson	

three generations of matter (fermions) / interactions / force carriers (bosons) / GAUGE BOSONS VECTOR BOSONS / SCALAR BOSONS

Miss MJ Cush (*https://upload.wikimedia.org/wikipedia/commons/0/00/ Standard_Model_of_Elementary_Particles.svg*)

Standard model of elementary particles: the 12 fundamental fermions and 5 fundamental bosons.

So here's a possible tally for the number of quantum fields:

- 2 (quantum electrodynamics; QED)—the electron field and the electromagnetic, aka photon field
- 17 (Standard Model [above])
- 24 (Standard Model including all gluon colors)—12 fermion fields and 12 boson fields
- 25 (24 + Graviton)

Even more if include antiparticles?
Even more if include handedness?
John Healy (*https://www.physicssayswhat.com/2019/06/05/qft-how-many-fields-are-there/*)

[6z204] self-operative: functioning or capable of functioning by itself (*www.merriam-webster.com*).

[6z205] Fierce: showing a heartfelt and powerful intensity (*Oxford English Dictionary*).

[6z206] Judgement or Judgmental: Divine judgement means the judgement of God.

RESEARCH NOTES, CREDITS, AND EXPANSIONS

> In the presence of God and of Christ Jesus, who will judge
> the living and the dead… (*Holy Bible, 2 Timothy 4 NIV*)

General judgment is the Christian theological concept . . . generally contrasted with a particular judgement right after death (*en.wikipedia.com*).

[*GOD—The Dimensional Revelation* Asserts That Since Differentiation Of Each Individual Spirit From The ONE Is Unique, Judgement By GOD Is Also Diverse, So The Judgement GOD Shares With One Spirit May Be Quite Different Than The Judgement GOD Shares With Another Spiritual Being. Even The Type Of Judgement Shared With One Type Of being May Be Different From Another Type Of Being.

Our Teaching Is That Judgement May Be Imposed At Any Situation On The Spiritual Continuum. GOD's Judgement Is Usually Not a harsh ending. Rather, GOD's Judgement Is The Urging To Change One's Spiritual Course Of Being. The Judgement Most Notable To A Human Being Is The Setting Face-To-Face With GOD Upon physical death of the human body.]

See [61].

[6z207] black hole: In general relativity, a black hole is defined as a region of space-time in which the gravitational field is so strong that no particle or radiation can escape. In the currently accepted models of stellar evolution, black holes are thought to arise when massive stars undergo gravitational collapse, and many galaxies are thought to contain supermassive black holes at their centers. Black holes are also important for theoretical reasons as they present profound challenges for theorists attempting to understand the quantum aspects of gravity. String theory has proved to be an important tool for investigating the theoretical properties of black holes because it provides a framework in which theorists can study their thermodynamics (*de Haro et al., 2013, 2*).

In galactic cosmology: At the center of every black hole, there lies what is called a singularity—a region where space and time becomes inifinite—this was described by Albert Einstein. If you get sucked into singularity, you will become inifitely dense, but what happens after that…nobody really knows. From a mathematically physical point of view, nothing happens from that point on.

"When you reach the singularity in general relativity, physics just stops, the equations break down," says Abhay Ashtekar of Pennsylvania State University.

At the end of its lifetime, a star with more than about 20 solar masses can undergo gravitational collapse to form a black hole (*C. L. Fryer, "Mass Limits for Black Hole Formation," The Astrophysical Journal, 522, no. 1 [1999]: 413–418*).

According to classical physics, these massive stellar objects exert a gravitational attraction that is strong enough to prevent anything, even electromagnetic radiation, from escaping past the Schwarzschild radius. However, quantum mechanical effects are believed to potentially allow the emission of Hawking radiation at this distance.

Electrons (and positrons) are thought to be created at the event horizon of these stellar remnants.

When a pair of virtual particles (such as an electron and positron) is created in the vicinity of the event horizon, random spatial positioning might result in one of them to appear on the exterior; this process is called "quantum tunnelling." The gravitational potential of the black hole can then supply the energy that transforms this virtual particle into a real particle, allowing it to radiate away into space (*M. K. Parikh and F. Wilczek, "Hawking Radiation as Tunneling," Physical Review Letters 85, no. 24 [2000]*).

In exchange, the other member of the pair is given negative energy, which results in a net loss of mass energy by the black hole. The rate of Hawking radiation increases with decreasing mass, eventually causing the black hole to evaporate away until finally, it explodes (*S. W. Hawking, "Black Hole Explosions?" Nature 248, no. 5443 [1974]: 30–31, Bibcode:1974Natur.248.30H*).

[*GOD—The Dimensional Revelation* Explains that such detail in the construction of physical universes helps Us to understand 9th-Dimensional Synthesis, Which Is Creation along the physical metastring.]

Using Dimensional Analysis, this is Creation in the 9th D manifesting changes in matter in the 8th d, conserving and equalizing the total of matter and energy of a universe in the 7th d physical universe.]

[6z208] Repurpose: Adapt for use in a different purpose (*Oxford English Dictionary*).

[6z209] dark matter: Dark matter, a mysterious form of matter that has not yet been identified, accounts for 26.8% of the cosmic contents. Dark energy, which is the energy of empty space and is causing the expansion of the universe to accelerate, accounts for the remaining 68.3% of the contents. (*"First Planck Results: The Universe Is Still Weird and Interesting," Matthew Francis, Ars Technica, March 21, 2013*).

Dark matter is a hypothetical kind of matter that is invisible to the entire electromagnetic spectrum but which accounts for most of the matter in the universe. The existence and properties of dark matter are inferred from its gravitational effects on visible matter, radiation, and the large-scale structure of the universe. Other than neutrinos, a form of hot dark matter, dark matter has not been detected directly, making it one of the greatest mysteries in modern astrophysics. Dark matter neither emits nor absorbs light or any other electromagnetic radiation at any significant level (*"Planck Captures Portrait of the Young Universe, Revealing Earliest Light," University of Cambridge, March 21, 2013, retrieved March 21, 2013*).

[Again, We Deduce that dark matter is probably the "opaque plasma" mentioned in [4z18].]

[6z210] "Walk Humbly With Its GOD":

RESEARCH NOTES, CREDITS, AND EXPANSIONS

> He has shown you, O mortal, what is good. And what does the Lord require of you? To act justly and to love mercy and to walk humbly with your God. (*Holy Bible, Micah 6:8 NIV*)

[6z211] Delights: a high degree of pleasure or enjoyment; joy; rapture (*www.dictionary.com*).

[6z212] Invite: to request the presence or participation of *(www.merriam-webster.com)*.

[6z213] HOLY SPIRIT (in Christianity): The third person of the Trinity; God as spiritually active in the world (*Oxford English Dictionary*).

The Hebrew Bible contains the term "spirit of God" (ruach hakodesh) in the sense of the might of a unitary God. This meaning is different from the Christian concept of "Holy Spirit" as one personality of God in the Trinity (*Orlando O. Espín, "Holy Spirit," An Introductory Dictionary of Theology and Religious Studies, ed. James B. Nickoloff [Collegeville: Liturgical Press], 576*).

[To Resolve these diverse Perspectives on The HOLY SPIRIT, *GOD—The Dimensional Revelation* Explains that GOD's Consciousness Shares with Your Independent Spirit To Enjoy and Experience Creation Together. That Is The HOLY SPIRIT Sharing Your Conscious Experience or, Otherwise, As Conscience To Guide You. In a larger context, THE HOLY SPIRIT is the Creator, Preserver, and Destroyer Of All Manifest Realities.]

[6z214] Attainable: possible to achieve (*dictionary.cambridge.org*).

[6z215] Empower: give someone more control over their life (*www.macmillandictionary.com*).

[6z216] Divine Consciousness:

> Salvation is simply an immediate Divine consciousness or a progressive Divine consciousness (or some combination of the two) that God is within me, beyond me, around me…that God is me, ultimately, as well as you and everyone and everything else. (*Dr. Steve McSwain, January 16, 2015, 05:30 p.m. ET*)

[6z217] Divine Experience:

> The feeling of it may at times come sweeping like a gentle tide pervading the mind with a tranquil mood of deepest worship. It may pass over into a more set and lasting attitude of the soul, continuing, as it were, thrillingly vibrant and resonant… and again it may be developed into something beautiful and pure and glorious. It may become the hushed, trembling, and speechless humility of the creature in the presence of—whom

or what? In the presence of that which is a Mystery inexpressible and above all creatures. (*Rudolf Otto, The Idea of the Holy, Oxford University Press, 1923*)

[6z218] Unity: the state of being united or joined as a whole (*Oxford English Dictionary*).

[7a] Reassessment: To perform a reassessment of something is to evaluate it again or reappraise it, especially if its value has changed or new information has altered your understanding of it (*www.vocabulary.com*).

[7b] multidimensional panel data: data of a phenomenon observed over three or more dimensions (*Manuel Arellano, Panel Data Econometrics [New York: Oxford University Press, 2003]*).

[7c] sphere of influence: a field or area in which an individual or organization has power to affect events and developments (*Oxford English Dictionary*).

[*GOD—The Dimensional Revelation* Expands the meaning of *Sphere Of Influence* to be the boundary and the reality encompassed within it for which the operational principles of a dimension control events.]

[8a] geographic coordinates: Spherical coordinate system using latitude, longitude, and elevation; map coordinates projected onto the plane, possibly including elevation.

A geographic coordinate system (GCS) is a coordinate system associated with positions on Earth (geographic position). A GCS can give positions

- as spherical coordinate system using latitude, longitude, and elevation;
- as map coordinates projected onto the plane, possibly including elevation;
  - as earth-centered, earth-fixed (ECEF) Cartesian coordinates in 3-space;
- as a set of numbers, letters, or symbols forming a geocode (*A Guide to Coordinate Systems in Great Britain [PDF], D00659 v2.3, Ordnance Survey, March 2015*).

In geodetic coordinates and map coordinates, the coordinate tuple is decomposed such that one of the numbers represents a vertical position and two of the numbers represent a horizontal position (*Chuck Taylor, "Locating a Point On the Earth"*).

The invention of a geographic coordinate system is generally credited to Eratosthenes of Cyrene, who composed his now-lost Geography at the Library of Alexandria in the 3rd century BC (*Cameron McPhail, Reconstructing Eratosthenes' Map of the World [PDF] [Dunedin: University of Otago, 2011], 20–24*); (*en.wikipedia.org*).

[8b] temporal: relating to time (*Oxford English Dictionary*).

[8c] Surprised: to strike or occur to with a sudden feeling of wonder or astonishment as through unexpectedness (*www.dictionary.com*).

[8d] unpredictable: not able to be known or declared in advance (*www.merriam-webster.com*).

[8e] unanticipated: not expected or predicted (*Oxford English Dictionary*).

[8f] quantum reality: Roger Penrose has his own version of a collapse theory in which the more massive the mass of the object in superposition, the faster it'll collapse to one state or the other because of gravitational instabilities. Again, it's an observer-independent theory. No consciousness needed (*https://blogs.scientificamerican.com/observations/what-does-quantum-theory-actually-tell-us-about-reality/*).

[*GOD—The Dimensional Revelation* Expands this notion of quantum reality To Assert That GOD Is The SOURCE of various subatomic particles appearing, cancelling, oscillating into and out of being, and vibrating in like form, Which Provides for the continuation of physical being. GOD Is The Fundamental Cause Of quantum fields and the matter forming and continuing within them. This Is The 9th-Dimensional Machinery Of Creation, Preservation, and Destruction of matter on the smallest or quantum scale.

This is also why space and time cannot be separated. They are all created as part of the same process. This also is the main operational principle of the physical membrane system, consisting of all physical universes.]

[8g] Heisenberg's uncertainty principle: Introduced first in 1927 by the German physicist Werner Heisenberg, the uncertainty principle states that the more precisely the position of some particle is determined, the less precisely its momentum can be predicted from initial conditions, and vice versa. In quantum mechanics, the uncertainty principle (also known as Heisenberg's uncertainty principle) is any of a variety of mathematical inequalities asserting a fundamental limit to the precision with which the values for certain pairs of physical quantities of a particle, such as position, x, and momentum, p, can be predicted from initial conditions. Such variable pairs are known as complementary variables or canonically conjugate variables, and, depending on interpretation, the uncertainty principle limits to what extent such conjugate properties maintain their approximate meaning, as the mathematical framework of quantum physics does not support the notion of simultaneously well-defined conjugate properties expressed by a single value. The uncertainty principle implies that it is in general not possible to predict the value of a quantity with arbitrary certainty, even if all initial conditions are specified (W. Heisenberg, "Über den anschaulichen Inhalt der quantentheoretischen Kinematik und Mechanik," *Zeitschrift für Physik* (in German), 43 nos. 3–4 [1927]: 172–198, Bibcode:1927ZPhy.43.172H,doi:10.1007/BF01397280, annotated pre-publication proof sheet of "Über den anschaulichen Inhalt der quantentheoretischen Kinematik und Mechanik," March 21, 1927).

Indeterminacy (Unbestimmtheit) was Heisenberg's original name for his principle. It is a better name than the more popular uncertainty, which connotes lack of knowledge. The Heisenberg principle is an ontological as well as epistemic lack of information (*https://www.informationphilosopher.com/freedom/indeterminacy.html*).

[*GOD—The Dimensional Revelation* Reveals That The SOURCE Of All Information Is The WORD Of GOD {10th D}. The only reason for uncertainty or indeterminacy is that The WORD has not yet Issued The Instructions Containing The Information That Will Be Collapsed Into Reality To Form The Next Situation.

One Caveat Is That After The WORD Has Issued The Instruction and The Information Is Operating In The 9th D, Reality Can Continue To Unfold According To Those Instructions with No Further Information From GOD.]

[8h] Segmentation: division into separate parts or sections (*Oxford English Dictionary*).

[*GOD—The Dimensional Revelation* Explains that Reality cannot be truly defined because the Continuum of Reality never stops. Reality can be artificially presented as a situation, segment, or moment in time. Such a presentation is always viewed from the perspective of the Observer, so it is never an entire event.

It is necessary for The Mind to understand the present in the context of past situations. The future can then be estimated based on proximity to the past.

All logical systems, including mathematics, also segment reality symbolically. These segments may be more or less accurate, but none can fully grasp the continuum. Hence, predictions are not completely accurate.

Even nearly accurate predictions do not legitimize eliminating anything on the Continuum Of Reality, just to make the logical system functional. Such systems are always incomplete.

The uncertainty of the future explains the "infinities" present in any mathematics describing reality.]

[8i] Union: an act or instance of uniting or joining two or more things into one (*www.merriam-webster.com*).

[8j] Delve: To carry on intensive and thorough research for data, information, or the like; investigate (*www.dictionary.com*).

[8k] Control or Controlling (*verb*): to determine the behavior or supervise the running of (*Oxford English Dictionary*).

Control or Controlling (*noun*): power to direct or determine (*thefreedictionary.com*).

[9a] arbitrary: Existing or coming about seemingly at random or by chance or as a capricious and unreasonable act of will; based on or determined by individual preference or convenience rather than by necessity or the intrinsic nature of something (*www.merriam-webster.com*).

[9b] mathematical abstraction:

> The mind makes the particular ideas received from particular objects to become general; which is done by considering them as they are in the mind, such appearances, separate from all other existence and the circumstances of real existence, as time, place, of any other concomitant ideas. This is called abstraction, whereby ideas taken from particular beings become general representatives of all of the same kind, and their names are general names, applicable to whatever exists conforming to such abstract ideas. (*Human Locke, Understanding, book 2, chapter 11, section 9*)

Abstraction in mathematics is the process of extracting the underlying structures, patterns, or properties of a mathematical concept, removing any dependence on real world objects with which it might originally have been connected and generalizing it so that it has wider applications or matching among other abstract descriptions of equivalent phenomena (*Robert B. Ash, A Primer of Abstract Mathematics [Cambridge University Press, January 1, 1998]*).

[In note [1k] of This Teaching, mathematics is defined as "the abstract science of number, quantity, and space." We must understand the abstractions of geometry as ontologically real. They are constructions of Mind necessary to support dimensional reasoning.]

[9c] mathematical model: A mathematical model is a description of a system using mathematical concepts and language. The process of developing a mathematical model is termed mathematical modeling. Mathematical models are used in the natural sciences (such as physics, biology, earth science, chemistry) and engineering disciplines (such as computer science, electrical engineering), as well as in non-physical systems such as the social sciences (such as economics, psychology, sociology, political science). Mathematical models are also used in music, linguistics (*Andras Kornai, Mathematical Linguistics: Advanced Information and Knowledge Processing [Springer] ISBN 978-1849966948*), and philosophy (for example, intensively in analytic philosophy).

[9d] Join: to bring in contact, connect, or bring or put together (*www.merriam-webster.com*).

Joined: become linked or connected to (*Oxford English Dictionary*).

[9e] definite: clearly true or real; unambiguous. clearly stated or decided; not vague or doubtful (*Oxford English Dictionary*).

[9f] ultimately: finally; in the end. at the most basic level (*Oxford English Dictionary*).

[9g] Manipulate or Manipulating: to move, arrange, or control something in a skilled manner (*www.yourdictionary.com*).

[9h] unprecedented: never done or known before (*Oxford English Dictionary*).

[9i] unusual: uncommon, rare (*www.merriam-webster.com*).

[9j] Paradigm: example, pattern; especially an outstandingly clear or typical example or archetype; a philosophical and theoretical framework of a scientific school or discipline within which theories, laws, and generalizations and the experiments performed in support of them are formulated; broadly a philosophical or theoretical framework of any kind (*www.merriam-webster.com*).

Paradigm comes from Greek παράδειγμα (paradeigma), "pattern, example, sample". παράδειγμα, (*Henry George Liddell and Robert Scott, A Greek-English, Perseus Digital Library*).

Perhaps the greatest barrier to a paradigm shift, in some cases, is the reality of paradigm paralysis: the inability or refusal to see beyond the current models of thinking (*John C. Harrison, Program Director, National Stuttering Project, johnnyh@holonet.net*).

Paradigm shifts tend to appear in response to the accumulation of critical anomalies as well as the proposal of a new theory with the power to encompass both older relevant data and explain relevant anomalies (*Thomas S. Kuhn, The Structure of Scientific Revolutions, Third Edition [Chicago: University of Chicago Press, 1996], 10*).

[9k] Accommodate: To make suitable; adapt or adjust (*www.thefreedictionary.com*).

[9l] organizing principle: An organizing principle is a core assumption from which everything else by proximity can derive a classification or a value. It is like a central reference point that allows all other objects to be located, often used in a conceptual framework (*Cynthia V. Rider and Jane Ellen Simmons, Chemical Mixtures and Combined Chemical and Nonchemical Stressors: Exposure, Toxicity, Analysis, and Risk [Cham, Switzerland: Springer, 2018], 169*).

[9m] writ large: clear and obvious (*Oxford English Dictionary*).

[9n] Order: the arrangement or disposition of people or things in relation to each other according to a particular sequence, pattern, or method (*Oxford English Dictionary*).

In most religions, the world is believed to be an embodiment of divine wisdom. Paradoxically, the divine is both present (immanent) and absent (transcendent). This paradox is expressed in a hierarchy of degrees of manifestation of divine wisdom, each representing a kind of order. Further, both the natural and the moral order are seen as normative. In the Abrahamic religions, order is created and, therefore, dependent on the creator. Since order is a manifestation of divine wisdom, it reveals knowledge about God. Accordingly, the created order has been seen as a unity in diversity, a machine, a work of art, or an embodiment of reason, beauty, and goodness. Disorder invaded the natural and the moral order, which require re-creation. In the Gnostic religions, however, disorder originates from an evil creator who battles a good redeemer. In response, the early Christian theologian Irenaeus (c. 130–200) emphasized that the creator and redeemer are one God who controls disorder and restores order. John Calvin (1509–1564) added that the created order required constant divine support to protect it from collapse into disorder: It could not exist independently. In contrast, for the theologian John Haught (1942–), disorder is the price God paid to grant freedom and independence to the created order (*Jitse M. Van Der Meer, "Order," Encyclopedia of Science and Religion, encyclopedia.com, October 16, 2020*).

[9o] DNA: Deoxyribonucleic acid (DNA) is a molecule composed of two polynucleotide chains that coil around each other to form a double helix carrying genetic instructions for the development, functioning, growth, and reproduction of all known organisms and many viruses. DNA and ribonucleic acid (RNA) are nucleic acids. Alongside proteins, lipids, and complex carbohydrates (polysaccharides), nucleic acids are one of the four major types of macromolecules that are essential for all known forms of life (*www.merriam-webster.com*).

The kinds of order are integrated in a hierarchy of order. In living things, the order of complexity, such as that of DNA, requires the order of energy with its chemical interactions, but chemical interactions do not require the complexity of living things (*Jitse M. Van Der Meer, "Order," Encyclopedia of Science and Religion, encyclopedia.com, October 16, 2020*).

[9p] and [9q] replicate or replication: the action or process of reproducing or duplicating something, replication of DNA (*www.merriam-webster.com*).

[9r] distinct: recognizably different in nature from something else of a similar type (*Oxford English Dictionary*).

[9s] Primitive: at very simple stage of development, very simple in design (*www.macmillan dictionary.com*).

[9t] Virus: an infective agent that typically consists of a nucleic-acid molecule in a protein coat, is too small to be seen by light microscopy, and is able to multiply only within the living cells of a host (*Oxford English Dictionary*).

[*GOD—The Dimensional Revelation* points out the destructive effect that a virus has on its Host as one example the 9th D, principle of destruction, necessary to renew certain manifestations, as Instructed by The WORD in the 10th D.

If You are the Victim of a virus or any other destructive agent, this may not be the WILL OF GOD but a malevolent spirit acting under its own free will. You Must Remain Vigilant To Defend Yourself Against such malevolent spirits.]

[9u] silicon:
Name: Silicon
Symbol: Si; Atomic Number: 14; Atomic Mass: 28.0855 amu; Melting Point: 1410.0°C (1683.15 K, 2570.0 °F); Boiling Point: 2355.0°C (2628.15 K, 4271.0°F); Number of Protons/Electrons: 14; Number of Neutrons: 14; Classification:

Metalloid; Crystal Structure: Cubic Density @ 293 K: 2.329 g/cm3; Color: grey (*http://www.chemicalelements.com/elements/si.html*).

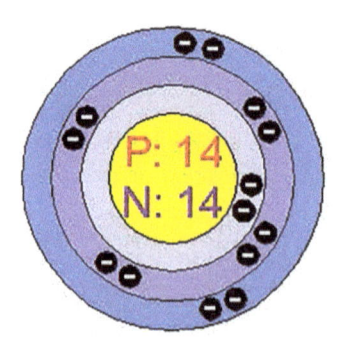

Silicon is the element to thank for the computer you're using to read these words. A crucial component in microelectronics and computer chips, this extremely common element is also responsible for warm white beaches—silica, an oxide of silicon, is the most common component of sand. Silicon is the seventh-most abundant element in the universe and the second-most abundant element on the planet, after oxygen (*www.livescience.com*).

[9v] polymer: a compound of high molecular weight derived either by the addition of many smaller molecules, as polyethylene, or by the condensation of many smaller molecules with the elimination of water, alcohol, or the like, as nylon (*www.dictionary.com*).

[9w] computer chip: a computer chip is a piece of silicon with an electronic circuit embedded in it (*www.techterm.com*).

An integrated circuit or small wafer of semiconductor material embedded with integrated circuitry. Chips comprise the processing and memory units of the modern digital computer (*www.britannica.com*).

[9x] computer program: A computer program is a collection of instructions that can be executed by a computer to perform a specific task (*Marc J. Rochkind, Advanced Unix Programming, Second Edition [Addison-Wesley, 2004], 1.1.2*).

Computer programming is the process of writing or editing source code.

Typically, computer programs are stored in nonvolatile memory until requested either directly or indirectly to be executed by the computer user. Upon such a request, the program is loaded into random-access memory by a computer program called an operating system, where it can be accessed directly by the central processor. The central processor then executes ("runs") the program, instruction by instruction, until termination. A program in execution is called a process (*Abraham Silberschatz, Operating System Concepts, Fourth Edition [Addison-Wesley, 1994], 97*).

[9y] programmed option: In type theory, it may be written as A?=A+1. This expresses the fact that for a given set of values in A, an option type adds exactly one

RESEARCH NOTES, CREDITS, AND EXPANSIONS

additional value (the empty value) to the set of valid values for A. This is reflected in programming by the fact that in languages having tagged unions, option types can be expressed as the tagged union of the encapsulated type, plus a unit type (*Bartosz Milewski, "Simple Algebraic Data Types," January 13, 2015*).

[9z] Prescribe or Prescribed: to set down as a rule or direction, order, ordain, direct (*www.collinsdictionary.com*).

[9z1] mindless: marked by a lack of mind or consciousness (*www.merriam-webster.com*).

[9z2] Extraterrestrials: a hypothetical or fictional being from outer space, especially an intelligent one (*Oxford English Dictionary*).

[9z3] Reach: the extent or range of application, effect, or influence (*Oxford English Dictionary*).

[9z4] influential: having the power to cause changes (*www.merriam-webster.com*).

[9z5] Gratitude: the quality of being thankful; readiness to show appreciation for and to return kindness (*Oxford English Dictionary*).

[9z6] penetrate: to pass into or through (*www.merriam-webster.com*).

[9z7] closed system or systems: In quantum physics, Schrödinger's equation, describes the behavior of an isolated or closed quantum system, that is, by definition, a system which does not interchange information (i.e. energy and/or matter) with another system (*en.wikipedia.org*).

Our Teaching Is that our universe of matter, and its attendant energies, is a closed system rather than an isolated system. Spiritual Flows From Our Spiritual Universe Intersect With our physical universe. The word *Entropy* is thus expanded to include the higher organization of the Fused systems. Expanded from its original definition regarding heat transfer in thermodynamics, Entropy is used here to define the high organization {low entropy} of The Fused Membrane Systems. However, If The WORD Instructs Them To Separate Again, Then Entropy will increase as the systems disorganize. GOD Instructs This Organization and Disorganization In The 9th Dimension To Become Manifest In the lower dimensions.]

[9z8] unalterable: not capable of being altered, changed, or modified (*www.dictionary.com*).

[9z9] entropy: The degree of disorder or uncertainty in a system; thermodynamics: a measure of the unavailable energy in a [closed] thermodynamic system that is also usually considered to be a measure of the system's disorder, that is a property of the system's state, and that varies directly with any reversible change in heat in the system and inversely with the temperature of the system (*www.merriam-webster.com*).

Total entropy is conserved (low entropy/disorganization) in a reversible process and not conserved. High entropy/disorganization is an irreversible process. For isolated systems, entropy never decreases (*"6.5 Irreversibility, Entropy Changes, and Lost Work," web.mit.edu, retrieved May 21, 2016*).

Following the second law of thermodynamics, entropy of an isolated system always increases for irreversible processes. The difference between an isolated system and closed system is that heat may not flow to and from an isolated system, but heat flow to and from a closed system is possible. Nevertheless, for both closed and isolated systems and, indeed, also in open systems, irreversible thermodynamics processes may occur (*Peter Atkins and Julio De Paula, Physical Chemistry, Eighth Edition [Oxford University Press, 2006], 79, ISBN 978-0-19-870072-2*).

> The role of entropy in cosmology remains a controversial subject since the time of Ludwig Boltzmann. Other complicating factors, such as the energy density of the vacuum and macroscopic quantum effects, are difficult to reconcile with thermodynamical models, making any predictions of large-scale thermodynamics extremely difficult. (*Benjamin Gal-Or, Cosmology, Physics and Philosophy [Springer Verlag, 1987], ISBN 978-0-0387-96526-0*)

[*GOD—The Dimensional Revelation* Expands the definition of *Entropy* beyond physical universal systems {physical membrane} to apply the concept of low entropy to organized membrane systems or Emerging Combinations and high entropy to disorganized or Separating Membrane Systems. See [9z7].

Note that The Choices Of Conscious Beings Cause Increase or decrease of entropy In The 5th D As The Unpredictable Possibilities Are Collapsed Into Being.]

[9z10] Open System: An open system is a system that has external interactions. Such interactions can take the form of information, energy, or material transfers into or out of the system boundary, depending on the discipline, which defines the concept. An open system is contrasted with the concept of an isolated system, which exchanges neither energy, matter, nor information with its environment. An open system is also known as a flow system.

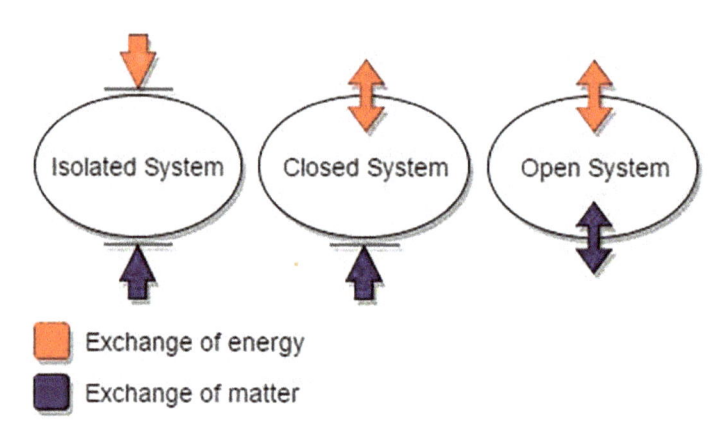

Alkh.Alwa Diagram Systems.png, June 21, 2016, retrieved November 15, 2020

RESEARCH NOTES, CREDITS, AND EXPANSIONS

[*GOD—The Dimensional Revelation* Reveals That The 9th and 10th Dimensions are the only true Open Systems because They Have No Limitation. All lower dimensions are closed systems. Any transfers between membrane systems, universes, or lower organizations Are Controlled By The WORD (10th D) and Its Machinery of Manifestation (9th D) As The Discipline of Instruction.

Hence, our physical universe is closed to the intrusion of Spirit. Only Instructions By The WORD Of GOD Can Fuse Spiritual Being Into physical matter.]

[9z11] coalesce: come together to form one mass or whole (*Oxford English Dictionary*).

[9z12] Temple: A building devoted to the worship, or regarded as the dwelling place, of a god or gods or other objects of religious reverence (*Oxford English Dictionary*).

> Do you not know that you yourselves are God's temple, and that God's Spirit dwells in you? (*Holy Bible, 1 Corinthians 3:16 BLB*)

> What? know ye not that your body is the temple of the Holy Ghost, which is in you, which ye have of God, and ye are not your own? (*Holy Bible, 1 Corinthians 6:19 KJV*)

[9z13] Sliver or Spark Of The Divine: Sliver: a small, thin piece of something cut or split off a larger piece (*Oxford English Dictionary*).

> Jesus Christ Said, "That they all may be one; as thou, Father, art in me, and I in thee, that they also may be one in us… (*Holy Bible, John 17:21*)

> The soul is the Lord, and the Lord is the soul; contemplating the Shabad, the Lord is found. (*Sadh Sangat, SGGS, M1, 1030*)

> Then God said, "Let Us make man in Our image, according to Our likeness." (*Holy Bible, Genesis 1:26 KJV*)

In Gnosticism and other Western mystical traditions, the divine spark is the portion of God that resides within each human being (*Søren Giversen, Tage Petersen, and Jørgen Podemann Sørensen, The Nag Hammadi Texts in the History of Religions, 2002, 157*).

[*GOD—The Dimensional Revelation* Teaches That As You Meditate, The Divine Nature of Your Being Is Revealed. So It Is Revealed That Your Soul, Manifested As Your Consciousness, Is A Sliver of GOD Yet Differentiated To Exist Separately.

Do not be misled. You are not GOD. You Are A Spirit Created In The Image Of GOD. This Spark or Sliver of The Divine Is Analogous To The Light Described Thoroughly In Our Teaching.

Your Soul Is Created, Preserved, and Ultimately either Reunited With GOD or Destroyed By GOD. This is the Nature of the 8th-D Metastring Directly Connecting GOD and Each Individual Spirit.]

[9z14] unattended: not supervised or looked after (*Oxford English Dictionary*).

[10a] Causation: The act or process of causing something to happen or exist (*www.merriam-webster.com*).

Noting a relationship between actions or events such that one or more are the result of the other or others (www.dictionary.com).

Granger defined the causality relationship based on two principles:

1. The cause happens prior to its effect.
2. The cause has unique information about the future values of its effect (*Michael Eichler, "Causal Inference in Time Series Analysis" [PDF], Causality: Statistical Perspectives and Applications Third Edition, ed. Carlo Berzuini [Hoboken, NJ: Wiley, 2012], 327–352, ISBN 978-0470665565.); (CWJ Granger, "Testing for Causality: A Personal Viewpoint," Journal of Economic Dynamics and Control, 2: 329–352 [1980], doi:10.1016/0165-1889(80)90069-X).*

> Though there be no such thing as Chance in the world; our ignorance of the real cause of any event has the same influence on the understanding, and begets a like species of belief or opinion. (Hume, "On Probability," 1748, Section 6)

If one assumes that quantum mechanical laws can be applied to causal relations, one might have situations in which the causal order of events is not always fixed but is subject to quantum uncertainty, just like position or momentum. Indefinite causal structures could correspond to superpositions of situations where, roughly speaking, "*A* is in the past of *B*" and "*B* is in the past of *A*" jointly. One may speculate that such situations could arise when both general relativity and quantum physics become relevant (*Časlav Brukner, Nature Physics, Quantum Causality, April 1, 2014*).

Thinking about the 'causal structure' of quantum mechanics—which events precede or succeed others—might prove to be more productive, and ultimately more intuitive, than couching it in the typical mind-bending language that describes photons as being both waves and particles or events as blurred by a haze of uncertainty (*Philip Ball, "How Quantum Trickery Can Scramble Cause and Effect," Nature News, Springer Nature, June 28, 2017*).

In quantum field theory, causality is closely related to the principle of locality. However, the principle of locality is disputed whether it strictly holds depends on the interpretation of quantum mechanics chosen, especially for experiments involving quantum entanglement that satisfy Bell's Theorem…redefining determinism as meaning that probabilities rather than specific effects are determined (*en.wikipedia.org*).

[*GOD—The Dimensional Revelation* Emphasizes that fundamentally, at the quantum level, whether *A* causes *B* or *B* causes *A* is indeterminate until one of them occurs. Once *A* collapses into reality, the *B* can follow as a consequence of *A*. This is the operation of the 9th-D Machinery Of Creation.

GOD—The Dimensional Revelation Asserts that while quantum theory establishes a reliable understanding of emergent reality as quantum probabilities rather than certainties, and where the WORD provides the Information to collapse a "probability" into a "fact," GOD Steps Above Our Dimensional Analysis As "Original Cause" or The SOURCE. GOD cannot be described in terms of quantum physics as a probability wave. That is the mistake currently confining the field of theoretical physics. It is stuck in principles that only apply in the physical membrane system.]

[10b] Causative Information: [*GOD—The Dimensional Revelation* Postulates An Original Revelation Using The Phrase *Causative Information* To Describe The Instructions That The WORD (10th D) Imparts To The Machinery Of Creation (9th D) Of What Information To Manifest (collapse) Into Reality In the lower dimensions.]

[10c] Fashioned: make into a particular or the required form (*Oxford English Dictionary*).

[10d] Original Cause: First cause, in philosophy, the self-created being (i.e., God) to which every chain of causes must ultimately go back. The term was used by Greek thinkers and became an underlying assumption in the Judeo-Christian tradition (*www.britanica.com*).

[10e] bounded system: In classical mechanics, a bounded system is one where the motion of all the objects in the system is restricted to some finite region of space. An unbounded system is a system that is not bounded (*https://www.reddit.com/r/askscience/comments/a01mms/ whatisaboundedsysteminphysicswhatis*, retrieved 11/22/2020).

[*GOD—The Dimensional Revelation* Reveals An Original Expanded Understanding Of What Types Of Systems There Are In Reality and The Fact That Each Dimension Within A System Operates According To Operational Principles, as well as The Limitations or Boundaries Of The System. Each Membrane System is limited by the reach of its operational principles. When The Operations or Boundaries Of A System Are Exceeded, A Broader Dimension must be Understood To Explain The Operation Of The More Encompassing System. The only Unbounded Systems According To Our Dimensional Analysis Exist In the 9th D, 10th D, and 11th.]

[10f] Attention: Notice taken of someone or something, the regarding of someone or something as interesting or important. The action of dealing with or taking special care of someone or something (*Oxford English Dictionary*).
Attention (of GOD):

> And so we know and rely on the love God has for us. God is love. Whoever lives in love lives in God, and God in them. (*Holy Bible, John 4:16 NIV*)

> The Lord bless you and keep you; The Lord make His face shine upon you, And be gracious to you; The Lord lift up His countenance upon you, And give you peace. (*Holy Bible, Numbers 6:24–26 NKJV*)

> For the eyes of the Lord are over the righteous, and his ears are open unto their prayers: but the face of the Lord is against them that do evil. (*Holy Bible, 1 Peter 3:12 KJV*)

> I am with you always, to the end of the age. (*Holy Bible, Matthew 28:20b ESV*)

[10g] Spiritual Void Between The Manifestations Of GOD:

> Great is our Lord and mighty in power; his understanding has no limit. (*Holy Bible, Psalm 147 NIV*)

> "Who can hide in secret places so that I cannot see them?" declares the Lord. "Do not I fill heaven and earth?" declares the Lord. (*Holy Bible, Jeremiah 23:24 NIV*)

> The Word became flesh and made his dwelling among us. We have seen his glory, the glory of the one and only Son, who came from the Father, full of grace and truth. (*Holy Bible, John 1:14 NIV*)

At the center of all teachings of the Bahá'í Faith stands the figure of the manifestation of God... For the Bahá'í Faith teaches a God that transcends the world so completely as to remain utterly unknowable, yet a God that manifests Himself in each world according to the understanding of that realm's inhabitants (*George Ronald, Oxford, 1974–1976, two volumes*).

RESEARCH NOTES, CREDITS, AND EXPANSIONS

I believe that the point of existence is simply to experience the ONE in everything. It's really that simple. We are all God experiencing the Divine God (Us) Self (*https://www.krystleyez.com/ entering-the-void*).

> The Essence of Unity has always been in one condition. which neither changes nor alters, has neither transformation nor vicissitude. He is the Eternal, the Immortal. Therefore, the proceeding of the human spirits from God is through emanation. (*SAQ, 206/157*)

[10h] cause-and-effect analysis: Cause-and-effect diagrams are causal diagrams created by Kaoru Ishikawa that show the potential causes of a specific event (*Kaoru Ishikawa, Guide to Quality Control [Tokyo: JUSE, 1968]*).

[10i] quantum possibilities or potentia:

> Heisenberg took a further step in "listening" to quantum theory when he made the following statement: "Atoms and the elementary particles themselves are not real; they form a world of potentialities or possibilities rather than things of the facts." This assertion was based on the fact that quantum systems such as atoms are generally described by quantum states with a list of possible outcomes, and yet only one of those can be realized upon measurement. I think that he was on to something here, except that I would adjust his characterization of quantum systems as follows: they are real, but not actual. In his terms, they are something not quite actual; they are "potentialities" or "possibilities." Thus my proposal is that quantum mechanics instructs us that we need a new metaphysical category: something more real than the merely abstract (or mental), but less concrete than, in Heisenberg's terms, "facts" or observable phenomena. The list of possible outcomes in the theory is just that: **a list of possible ways that things could be, where only one actually becomes a "fact."** (*Ruth Kastner, Transactional Interpretation of Quantum Mechanics, 2012, 36; bold print added*)

Quantum potentia can be quantitatively defined; a quantum measurement will, with certainty, always produce one of the possibilities it describes. In the large-scale world, all sorts of possibilities can be imagined (Browns win Super Bowl, Indians win 22 straight games) which may or may not ever come to pass… If quantum potentia are in some sense real, Kastner and colleagues say, then the mysterious weirdness of quantum mechanics becomes instantly explicable. You just have to realize that **changes in actual things reset the list of potential things**... An "actuality" (the first measurement) changes the list of potentia that still exist in the universe. Potentia encompass the list of things that may become actual; what becomes actual then changes what's on the list of potentia (*https://www.sciencenews.org/blog/context/quantum-mysteries-dissolve-if-possibilities-are-realities*).

You just have to realize that changes in actual things reset the list of potential things (*Tom Seigfried, October 1, 2020, www.sciencenews.org/blog/context/quantum-mysteries-dissolve-if-possibilities-are-realities*).

[*GOD—The Dimensional Revelation* Expands on the quantum theory of "probability" by bridging the reality of quantum uncertainty before an event with physical certainty after the event has occurred {collapsed into reality}. Our original definition of *becoming* that Describes The Instruction Of Information From The WORD In The 10th D Into a quantum field in the 9th D that "becomes" the residual energy in the 8th d, which, due to the operation of time, yields all of physical reality.]

[10j] dimensional analysis and multidimensional analysis: In engineering and science, dimensional analysis is the analysis of the relationships between different physical quantities by identifying their base quantities (such as length, mass, time, and electric charge) and units of measure (such as miles vs. kilometres, or pounds vs. kilograms) and tracking these dimensions as calculations or comparisons are performed (*David Goldberg, Fundamentals of Chemistry, Fifth Edition [McGraw-Hill, 2006]*).

[*GOD—The Dimensional Revelation* Reveals Higher Dimensions than those to which physical science is limited. We Expand the Principles Of Dimensional Analysis by tracking the operational principles operating in a dimension and Apply The More Encompassing Dimension When Observation Yields Data That Is Beyond the boundaries of the lower dimension.

Consequently, a situation may be analyzed within multiple dimensions, based on its being within the field of influence of multiple dimensions. Understanding The Operational Principles Of Each Broader Dimension Acting On The Situation yields a more meaningful analysis of cause and effect.

Most Human conditions, whether caused by biochemical reactions in the body or By Individual Choices, fall under 5th-Dimensional Analysis. For Example: A Person's Bipolar Abnormal Psychology is often inherited, so the root cause is genetic (3rd dimension). The original cause of the genetic mal-sequence is still being researched by science, but if that gene is present and dominant, the Person inheriting that gene is likely to Experience some Manic-Depressive tendencies. That Person's Spiritual Being Is influenced by physical conditions.

Indeed Your Life, Incarnate In matter, is dominated by physical conditions, both inside your body and from the outside environment. To Live This Life, You are forced by physical circumstances To Make Choices (5th Dimension) To Cope With Current Situations. Your Choices Influence Yourself and Others Going Forward.

Returning To The Bipolar Person, that condition will continue to manifest in that Person's mind as long as that gene influences their biochemistry. The cure is to interrupt the biochemistry to contradict the chemical reactions. A Choice Is Presented. Either Take the chemicals {medicine} to contradict the Manic-Depressive biochemistry or Not Take it. Such A Person Can Make A Spiritual Choice To Develop Strong Mental Channels To Alter the neural patterns in Their brain. Coupled with the chemical medicine, The Human Choices Can yield A Better Consciousness. Multidimensional Analysis Often Yields Clear Solutions.]

[10k] Spiritual Quality: (Quality) the standard of something as measured against other things of a similar kind, the degree of excellence of something.

Spiritual Quality: a distinctive attribute or characteristic possessed by someone or something (*Oxford English Dictionary*).

[*GOD—The Dimensional Revelation* Emphasizes That Since Ours Is A Fused Reality of physical and Spiritual Universes, We Must Understand The Spiritual Qualities Of Situations. This Teaching Capitalizes Spiritual words to assist with the Analysis Of The Spiritual Aspects of Reality.]

[10l] neural: A neuron or nerve cell is an electrically excitable cell that communicates with other cells via specialized connections called synapses. It is the main component of nervous tissue in all animals except sponges and placozoa. Plants and fungi do not have nerve cells (*P. A. Rutecki "Neuronal Excitability: Voltage Dependent Currents and Synaptic Transmission," Journal of Clinical Neurophysiology*, 9 no. 2, [April 1992]: 195–211).

[10m] Eye-to-hand coordination: Hand-eye coordination is the ability of the vision system to coordinate the information received through the eyes to control, guide, and direct the hands in the accomplishment of a given task, such as handwriting or catching a ball. Hand-eye coordination uses the eyes to direct attention and the hands to execute a task (*www.healthofchildren.com/G-H/Hand-Eye-Coordination.html*).

[10n] Acknowledge: to admit to be real or true; recognize the existence, truth, or fact of. (*www.dictionary.com*).

[10o] Yearning: a feeling of intense longing for something (*Oxford English Dictionary*).

[10p] intersection (of two or more things): pass or lie across each other (*Oxford English Dictionary*).

[10q] digital information: Unlike computers, humans perceive information in analog. We capture auditory and visual signals as a continuous stream. Digital devices, on the other hand, estimate this information using ones and zeros. The rate of this estimation, called the "sampling rate," combined with how much information is included in each sample (the bit depth), determines how accurate the digital estimation is. Since digital information only estimates analog data, an analog signal is actually more accurate than a digital signal. However, computers only work with

digital information, so storing data digitally makes more sense. Unlike analog data, digital information can also be copied, edited, and moved without losing any quality. Because of the benefits digital information offers, it has become the most common way of storing and reading data (*The Tech Terms Dictionary, https://techterms.com/definition/digital*").

[10r] Divine Process of Incarnation: By Nature's law, an embodied soul should assume its body from its parents. In accordance with this law The Supreme God too chooses people who have the virtues of kindness, sacrifice, penance, etc. as parents to assume an incarnation (*Bharatiya Sanskrutikosh, Publisher: Pandit Mahadevshastri Joshi Secretary, Second Edition, vol. 1, Mandal, 410 Shanivar Peth, Pune 411 030, 286*).

See also [6z69].

[10s] uncaring: not feeling interest in or attaching importance to something (*Oxford English Dictionary*).

[10t] unreceptive: not responsive or receptive (*www.merriam-webster.com*).

[10u] Liberated: set free, as from oppression, confinement (*www.freedictionary.com*).

The Three Yogas are the three paths mentioned in *Bhagavad Gita* for the liberation of the human spirit. They are

1. Karma Yoga or the Path of Action:

    That action which is devoid of fruitive desires, free from attraction and repulsion, without attachment, which is performed as duty is called the nature of goodness... (23)

2. Bhakti Yoga or the Path of Devotion to God:

    "From Whom all beings do come forth, By Whom all this is pervaded, Worshipping Him with his duty, A man attains to perfection. (46)

    Devoted, he knows Me in truth, What and Who I am; then having Known Me in My reality, He forthwith enters into Me. (55)

3. Jnana Yoga or the Path of Knowledge.

    Knowledge, the known, and the knower Form the threefold cause of action. (18)

> Renouncing desire-based actions Sages consider sannyasa... Forsaking ego, power, pride, lust, wrath, possessiveness; freed from the notion of "mine;" and tranquil—He's fit for union with Brahman. (53)

(*https://bhagavad-gita.org/Gita/verse-18-50.html*);
(*The Bhagavad Gita, "Chapter 18: The Yoga of Liberation by Renunciation"*)
(*Another translation: https://bhagavad-gita.org/Gita/verse-18-50.html*)

[10v] Capabilities: the power or ability to do something (*Oxford English Dictionary*).

[10w] Predictive: Predictive modeling, also called predictive analytics, is a mathematical process that seeks to predict future events or outcomes by analyzing patterns that are likely to forecast future results (*https://searchenterpriseai.techtarget.com/definition/predictive-modeling, March 2018*).

[10x] Constant Cause: [*GOD—The Dimensional Revelation* Reveals that The 9th-D Mechanics Of Creations Is Continually Manifesting The WORD Into Reality. This is an Original Assertion That The Processes Of Differentiating From The ONE Are Constantly Occurring. These Provide For Each Continuum That Exists.

This Truth is proved by quantum theory as quantum possibilities become facts in physical reality. Our Teaching Ascribes the "popping" of matter into and out of quantum fields as Information sustained by Instruction Of The WORD, 10th D, To Occur In The 9th D and manifest into 8th-d physical space.]

[10y] quantum field theory (QFT): In theoretical physics, quantum field theory (QFT) is a theoretical framework that combines classical field theory, special relativity, and quantum mechanics (*M. Peskin and D. Schroeder, An Introduction to Quantum Field Theory [Westview Press, 1995]*) but not general relativity's description of gravity. QFT treats particles as excited states (also called quanta) of their underlying quantum fields, which are more fundamental than the particles. Interactions between particles are described by interaction terms in the Lagrangian involving their corresponding quantum fields. Each interaction can be visually represented by Feynman diagrams according to perturbation theory in quantum mechanics (*en.wikipedia.org*).

In spite of its overwhelming success in particle physics and condensed matter physics, QFT itself lacks a formal mathematical foundation. For example, according to Haag's theorem, there does not exist a well-defined interaction picture for QFT, which implies that perturbation theory of QFT, which underlies the entire Feynman diagram method, is fundamentally ill-defined (*Rudolf Haag, "On Quantum Field Theories" PDF. Dan Mat Fys Medd 29 no. 12 [1955]*).

[*GOD—The Dimensional Revelation* Seeks to better define QFT by adding Spiritual Variables to enable the mathematics to formally represent reality in quantum terms.]

[10z] The WORD was Made Flesh:

> And the Word became flesh and dwelt among us, and we have seen his glory, glory as of the only Son [unique One] from the Father, full of grace and truth. (*Holy Bible, John 1:14 ESV*)

[10z1] Miracle: An extraordinary event manifesting divine intervention in human affairs (*www.merriam-webster.com*).

[11a] mathematics is an ontological discipline: Unlike physical objects and properties, mathematical objects do not exist in space and time, and mathematical concepts are not instantiated in space or time… If mathematical principles are successful, then, even if we are unable to obtain intuitive evidence for them, they may be regarded as probably true. Gödel says that "success here means fruitfulness in consequences, particularly in "verifiable" consequences… (*"Gödel's Platonism," https://plato.stanford.edu/entries/philosophy-mathematics/*).

Arithmetical platonism, with numbers as logical objects, is secured because when logical truths are substituted for the right-hand side of Hume's Principle, the resulting instance on the left-hand side is also logically true and explicitly refers to numbers. Hume's Principle is to provide an ontological reduction of numbers to concepts and relations between concepts. The disagreement is over the meaning of words, not the nature of reality. (*Phillip Bricker, "Ontological Commitment," Stanford Encyclopedia of Philosophy, November 3, 2014*).

Symbols are strictly speaking abstract objects. Nonetheless, it is essential to symbols that they can be embodied by concrete objects, so we may call them quasi-concrete objects. (*Parsons, "Formalism" [2008], chapter 1, https://plato.stanford.edu/entries/philosophy-mathematics/*).

[11b] solid geometry: In mathematics, solid geometry is the traditional name for the geometry of three-dimensional Euclidean space. *The Britannica Guide to Geometry, Britannica Educational Publishing, 2010, pp. 67–68.*

RESEARCH NOTES, CREDITS, AND EXPANSIONS

A few subjects of solid geometry are

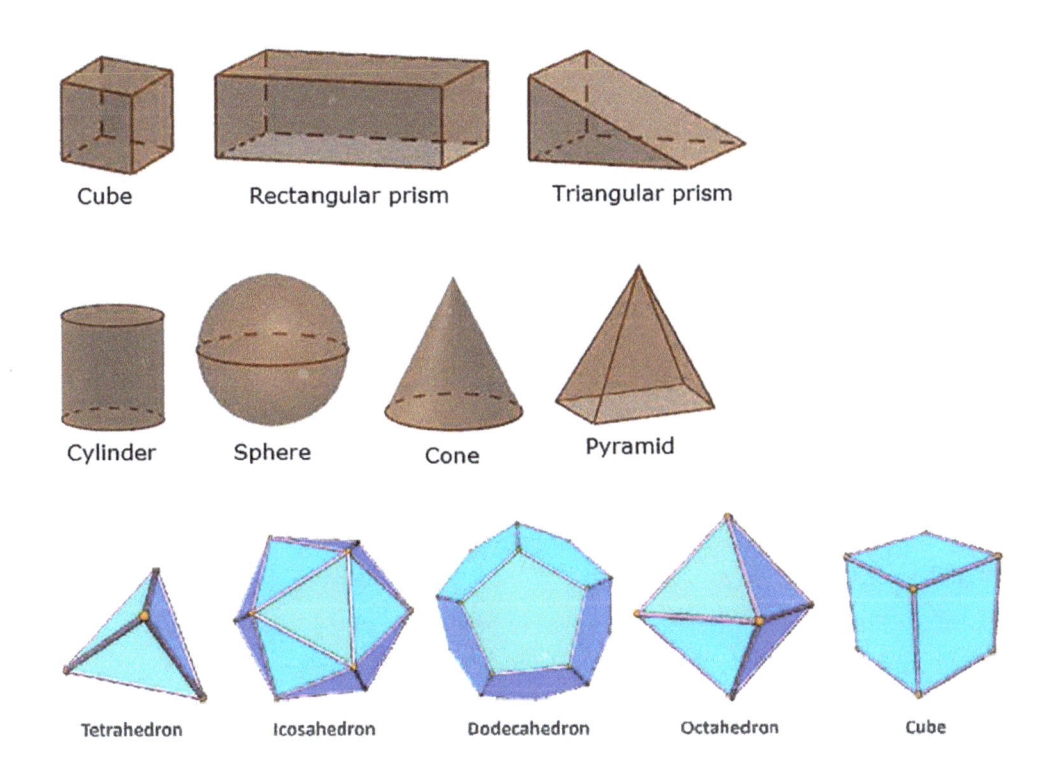

[11c] algebra: Algebra is a branch of mathematics dealing with symbols and the rules for manipulating those symbols. In elementary algebra, those symbols (today written as Latin and Greek letters) represent quantities without fixed values known as variables (*www.livescience.com, 50258-algebra, March 26, 2015*).

[11d] trigonometry: Trigonometry, the branch of mathematics concerned with specific functions of angles and their application to calculations. There are six functions of an angle commonly used in trigonometry. Their names and abbreviations are sine (sin), cosine (cos), tangent (tan), cotangent (cot), secant (sec), and cosecant (csc) (*www.britannica.com*).

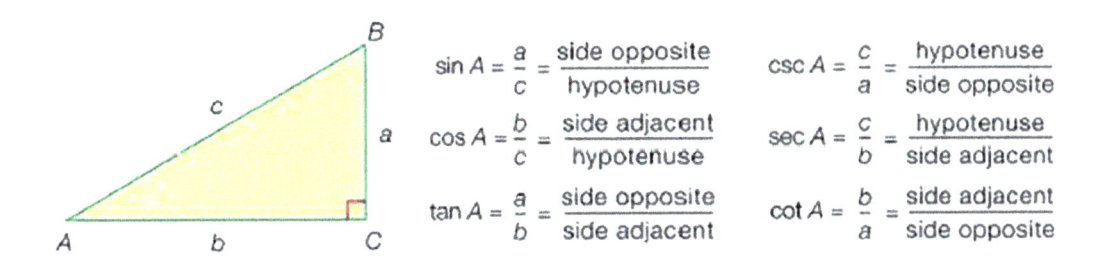

$$\sin A = \frac{a}{c} = \frac{\text{side opposite}}{\text{hypotenuse}} \qquad \csc A = \frac{c}{a} = \frac{\text{hypotenuse}}{\text{side opposite}}$$

$$\cos A = \frac{b}{c} = \frac{\text{side adjacent}}{\text{hypotenuse}} \qquad \sec A = \frac{c}{b} = \frac{\text{hypotenuse}}{\text{side adjacent}}$$

$$\tan A = \frac{a}{b} = \frac{\text{side opposite}}{\text{side adjacent}} \qquad \cot A = \frac{b}{a} = \frac{\text{side adjacent}}{\text{side opposite}}$$

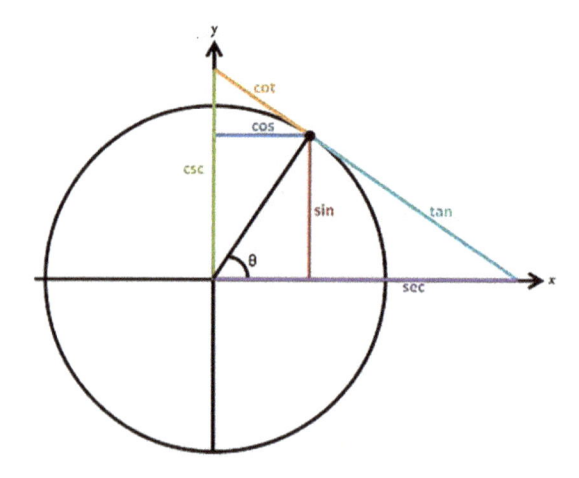

[11e] change functions: A function is a process by which every input is associated with exactly one output. When we create a process (or series of steps) to do a certain task, we are often creating a function. If we want to use it over and over again, then to make our lives easier, we give it a name. It helps us remember the name when it has something to do with the process that is being described.

The Average Rate of Change function describes the average rate at which one quantity is changing with respect to something else changing (e.g., Miles per hour—calculated by dividing the number of miles traveled by the number of hours it takes to travel them). In general, an average rate a change function is a process that calculates the amount of change in one item divided by the corresponding amount of change in another. Using function notation, we can define the Average rate of Change of a function, f, from a to x as

$$A(x) = \frac{f(x) - f(a)}{x - a}$$

(https://www.mesacc.edu/~marfv02121/readings/average/)

[11f] limit: In mathematics, a limit is the value that a function (or sequence) "approaches" as the input (or index) "approaches" some value… Limits are essential to calculus and mathematical analysis, and are used to define continuity, derivatives, and integrals (*en.wikipedia.org*).

[11g] average: A calculated "central" value of a set of numbers. To calculate it, add up all the numbers, then divide by how many numbers there are… Also called the Arithmetic Mean (*https://www.mathsisfun.com/definitions/average.html*).

[11h] probability: Probability is simply how likely something is to happen (*https://www.khanacademy.org/math/statistics*).

[11i] calculus: [Generally the word *calculus* refers to any] calculation, estimation or computation (*www.dictionary.com*).

RESEARCH NOTES, CREDITS, AND EXPANSIONS

[Specifically calculus is the] branch of mathematics concerned with instantaneous rates of change and the summation of infinitely many small factors (*www.brittanica.com*).

Differential Calculus cuts something into small pieces to find how it changes. The Derivative is the "rate of change" or slope of a function.

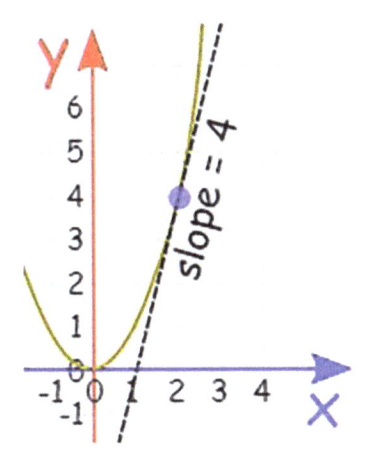

Integral Calculus joins (integrates) the small pieces together to find how much there is. Integration can be used to find areas, volumes, central points, and many useful things.

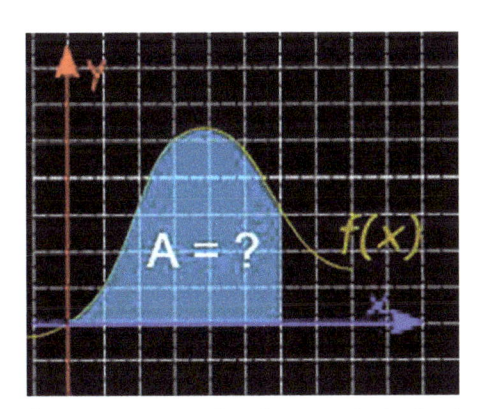

(https://www.mathsisfun.com/calculus/)

[11j] quantify: express as a number or measure (*www.thefreedictionary.com*).

[11k] cancel or cancelling: (of a factor or circumstance) neutralize or negate the force or effect of (another) (*Oxford English Dictionary*).

[11l] energy residue: See [11z25].

[*GOD—The Dimensional Revelation* hypothesizes that the Machinery of physical creation in the 9th D Provides Information as Instructed By The WORD. That

Information may be the following. The formation of a quantum field of the smallest physical type within which Primal Material with a positive charge (matter) and Primal Material with a negative charge (antimatter) violently cancel each other in a big bang. The reaction leaves an energy residue carrying forward the positive and negative charges. Over time, that residual energy converts into matter and radiation as explained in special relativity $e=mc^2$. The resulting matter and radiation carry forward the positive and negative charges. The differentiation of the various subatomic particles and waves manifest the original Instructions and Information of physical creation. Our Physical Universe is both Created and Sustained by these most basic reactions.]

[11m] wave functions: In the formalism of quantum mechanics, the state of a system at a given time is described by a complex wave function, also referred to as state vector in a complex vector space (*Walter Greiner and Berndt Müller, Quantum Mechanics Symmetries, Second Edition [Springer-Verlag], 52*).

The wave function in quantum mechanics describes a kind of physical phenomenon, still open to different interpretations, which fundamentally differs from that of classic mechanical waves (*Born 1927, 354–357); (Landau and Lifshitz, 1977, 6*).

Also see [10i], *quantum possibilities.*

[11n] Forcing The Continuation: [*GOD—The Dimensional Revelation* Reveals That All Realities Are Aspects Of GOD. Each Item Manifested In Reality Is A Differentiation Of GOD Instructed By The WORD Of GOD In The 10th Dimension To The 9th Dimension. The Various Mechanisms of Creation In The 9th D Manipulate The Information Provided by the WORD, To Manifest diverse Realities in the eighth and lower Dimensions. The Information Is Carried Along Metastrings That Contain The Subjects, objects, and Operational Principles Of Each Membrane System.

The WORD Provides Instructions That Force The Continuation Of Each Membrane System In The 8th D According To The Principles Of Operation Of Each Membrane System Created. These are the metaphysical Continuums, which cause each Universes to endure.

The continuum of our 7th-Dimension universe of matter and its attendant energies is called "time." Time forces matter and its attendant energies to exist in a continuous flow, changing constantly as it flows.

The Continuum Of Our Universe Of Spirit Is The Duration Of Each Individual Spirit As It Flows Along what may be called "Its Spiritual Journey." The Operational Principles Of A Spiritual Continuum Are Different Than those of a physical continuum. Some of those are Explained in This Teaching.]

[11o] ellipse or elliptical: Ellipse definition, a plane curve such that the sums of the distances of each point in its periphery from two fixed points, the foci, are equal (*www.dictionary.com*).

RESEARCH NOTES, CREDITS, AND EXPANSIONS

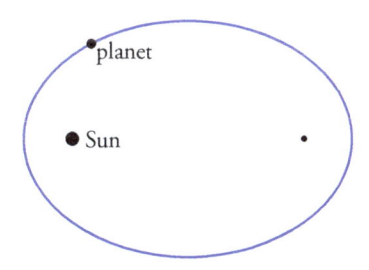

[11p] Spiritual Flows:

> Christ Said, "He who believes in Me, as the Scripture has said, out of his heart will flow rivers of living water." (*Holy Bible, John 7:38*)

Deep spiritual flow or *enlightened* means to be centered on the experience of consciousness itself so that as well as distinguishing yourself from your physical body and self, you have also distinguished yourself from the contents of your consciousness as well. You are the center of pure living awareness and/or consciousness that is the possessor and experiencer of your thoughts, feelings, and body (*http://tobyouvry.com/2014/06/finding-your-spiritual-flow/*).

The third current is spiritual in nature and flows directly through the spine and into the head. Being yellowish-white, the sushumna [Kundalini], as it is called, is the channel for pure spiritual energies that flood into the body through the spine and out into the 6,000 miles of nerve currents (*https://www.hinduismtoday.com/modules/smartsection/item*).

It is believed that the chakras vitalize the physical body and influence the physical, emotional and mental movements of the mind and body. They are considered to be the loci of life-energy (known as prana, shakti or chi), which also flow through them along pathways called nadis. The main function of the chakras is to draw in the prana by spinning around their own axes and hold it in their respective sphere to maintain and balance the spiritual, mental, emotional and physical wellbeing of the mind and body… The energy that was unleashed in creation, called the Kundalini, lies coiled and sleeping at the base of the spine. It is the purpose of the tantric or kundalini forms of yoga to arouse this energy, and cause it to rise back up through the increasingly subtler chakras until union with God is achieved in the Sahasrara chakra at the crown of the head.

They are Crown Chakra, Third-Eye Chakra, Throat Chakra, Heart Chakra, Stomach Chakra, Sacral Chakra, Base Chakra.

(https://www.hinduwebsite.com/hinduism/concepts/chakras)

Also see [3z74], *Spiritual Journey*, and chapter 13 of Our Teaching.

[11q] repetitive: actions or elements that are repeated many times (collinsdictionary.com).

[11r] formulaic: produced according to a formula or set of formulas, adhering to set forms or conventions (*www.merriam-webster.com*).

[11s] root in logic: It is crucial that a "root logic" be a logic that is agreeable to all practicing mathematicians. a certain finite object is indeed a proof in a certain theory. (*www.rbjones.com/rbjpub/logic/qedres05.htm; created 31/12/95 modified 11/1/96*).

[11t] mathematical system: a set of elements and one or more binary operations to connect these elements (*http://bestmaths.net/online/*).

[11u] mathematically constant or mathematical constants: A constant in math is a value that doesn't change. Instead, it's a fixed value. All numbers are considered constant terms. Why is that? Well, if you see a problem such as this one, 3 + 3 = ? you know that you need to add 3 and 3 together. Here, 3 will always stand for the number 3 and not some other number…

Variables as Constants: Here's an interesting fact about constants: some variables can be constants, too. A variable in math is an unknown value or a value that can change. For example, there are two variables in the equation $y = 3x + 4$, x and y. We call them "variables" because we don't know what they are, and they can change. For example, if x equals 1, then y equals $3 * 1 + 4 = 7$. But if x equals 2, then y equals $3 * 2 + 4 = 10$ (*https://study.com/academy/lesson/what-is-a-constant-term-in-math.html*).

[*GOD—The Dimensional Revelation* notes that this supports quantum theory in which reality is variable or undetermined until it is "observed," "measured," or "collapsed" into being. Then the thing becomes real, but the next situation remains undetermined until it collapses into reality. This is the basic rule of continuums, including "time," the 4th dimension, as well as Spiritual Continuums That Are Outside Of time.]

RESEARCH NOTES, CREDITS, AND EXPANSIONS

[11v] Advanced Spiritual Being:

> Only the Self-conscious Individual has ALL the Attributes and Creative Power of the "Mighty I AM Presence." Only He can know who and what He is, and express the Fullness of the Creative Power of God whenever He decrees, by the use of the Words, "I AM." (*I AM Ascended Master Dictation List, Saint Germain Press Inc., 1995*)

This is properly called Isness; students of the Ascended Master Teachings believe that there is One God, the "Universal All-Pervading Presence of Life", "The One", Who is the Source of all Love, Light, and Truth in existence, and that all forms of existence and consciousness emanate from this "Allness of God"—"The One". The Voice of the I AM states "All Life is One" and that there is "One Substance, One Energy, One Power, One Intelligence" as the Source of all consciousness and creation (*The Voice of the I AM [Saint Germain Press, July 1942], 7, 32*).

The 7 Stages of Spiritual Development:

- Stage 1: Innocence: You are born into a material world, where your life is dominated by your lower three chakras.
- Stage 2: Fear, Ego: As you grow, the ego emerges, and soon you realize that you are completely at the mercy of all around you. The pure love you have experienced up until now begins to be overshadowed by fear and its corresponding emotions.
- Stage 3: Power: In your desire to overcome fear, you create success in your life. For many people, further growth and spiritual development end here. You choose to continue to be consumed with material desires, you seek more and more power and control. Your life becomes self-centered, and you remain at Stage 3.
- Stage 4: Giving: In this stage, you begin to realize that there is more to life than personal power and material gain. You ask yourself how you can help others, how can you serve the world around you. You become comfortable with giving, as well as receiving.
- Stage 5: The Seeker: Now you begin your regular spiritual practices. The longing for Enlightenment grows within you. Your decisions now come mostly from the fourth chakra, the heart center. You begin to look for the deeper meaning of things. You try to understand why you are here and how you can make your life more meaningful.
- Stage 6: The Sage: Cosmic Consciousness dawns. Your mind fully awakens. You become the witness of your actions and realize that you are the role player in the multitude of roles you play. The fear of death dissolves as you realize that

373

life is just another role. Your mind is fully awake, but some ego is still present. The choice or mistake here is to believe that you are something special.
- Stage 7: Spirit: Your heart now fully awakens. You experience Divine and Unity Consciousness. There is no longer any separation. Your spiritual practice is Pure Joy. All the chakras are open, spiritual energy flows freely (*Roger Gabriel, December 6, 2018, https://chopra.com/articles/the-7-stages-of-spiritual-development*).

[11w] Reach Out: To extend one's hand outward in an attempt to touch or grasp someone or something (*idioms.thefreedictionary.com*).

[11x] Casting You off: thrown away, rejected, discarded (*www.dictionary.com*).

[11y] instinctively derived: Instincts are goal-directed and innate patterns of behavior that are not the result of learning or experience… Modern psychologists understand that while certain tendencies might be biologically programmed, individual experiences can also play a role in how responses are displayed (*https://www.verywellmind.com/instinct-theory-of-motivation-2795383, Kendra Cherry April 29, 2010*).

[11z] Mapping: an operation that associates each element of a given set (the domain) with one or more elements of a second set (the range) (*Oxford English Dictionary*).

[11z1] Community: a feeling of fellowship with others as a result of sharing common attitudes, interests, and goals (*Oxford English Dictionary*).

[11z2] Reproduce sexually: Sexual reproduction is characterized by the process of meiosis in which progeny cells receive half of their genetic information from each parent cell (www.britannica.com).

[11z3] RNA: A nucleic acid refers to any of the group of complex compounds made up of linear chains of monomeric nucleotides. Each nucleotide component, in turn, is made up of phosphoric acid, sugar, and nitrogenous base. Nucleic acids are involved in the preservation, replication, and expression of hereditary information. Two major types of nucleic acids are deoxyribonucleic acid (DNA) and ribonucleic acid (RNA) (*https://www.biologyonline.com/dictionary/ribonucleic-acid*).

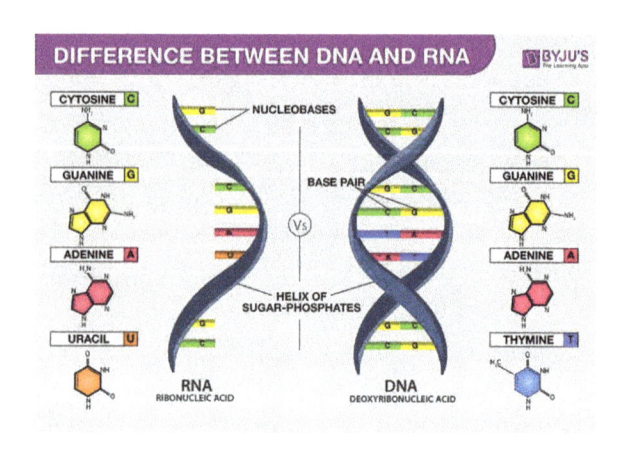

RESEARCH NOTES, CREDITS, AND EXPANSIONS

[11z4] Developmental Reality: [*GOD—The Dimensional Revelation* Uses the phrase *developmental reality* to mean that All Of Manifest Reality Occurs, Develops, or Changes On A Continuum. In our physical universe, that is the continuum of time. In Our Spiritual Universe, It Is The Continuum Of Related Manifestations Of A Spiritual Being That May or May Not Be Sequential.]

[11z5] prior and subsequent mathematics: [*GOD—The Dimensional Revelation* Reveals That All Calculations In The 5th Dimension In Which A Spiritual Being Makes A Choice Collapse A Certain Reality Into Being As It Proceeds. The next Situation Can Only Be Calculated From The Present Situation as the starting point.

This is also true in physical quantum mechanics at the string level. This calculation is called quantum mathematics. Quantum mathematics applies in the 4th dimension, also where there are only physical probabilities. Mathematical analysis attempts to state this as discrete moments of reality that can be analyzed as if static. This helps with creating symbolic representations of a situation. A "prior mathematics" can be calculated as the symbolic description of the prior or past situation. This is especially helpful in calculating the future or subsequent situation. However, there can be no conclusive mathematics about a future situation because changes may occur. A variable may change, or an entire function may change, so the prior mathematics may not yield a correct conclusion.

Also, actual reality presents no specific situation as reality proceeds on an unbroken continuum. A subsequent mathematics can describe the past accurately. Again, predicting future events is always an approximation based on generalized limits.

Note that the best mathematical systems are those that most often yield correct predictions of future situations.]

[11z6] future branching: [*GOD—The Dimensional Revelation* Reveals that the future is continually branching with manifest reality collapsing into being, presenting future possibilities. Each Choice or other path taken presents reality and a new set of probable branches going forward.]

[11z7] Accumulate: gather, build up (*Oxford English Dictionary*).

[11z8] Positive Spiritual Choices:

> I call heaven and earth to witness against you today, that I have set before you life and death, blessing and curse. Therefore choose life, that you and your offspring may live… (*Holy Bible, Deuteronomy 30:19 ESV; Torah Devarim, Deuteronomy 30:19*)

> Jesus Christ said, "But seek first the kingdom of God and his righteousness, and all these things will be added to you." (*Holy Bible, Matthew 6:33 ESV*)

GOD—THE DIMENSIONAL REVELATION

> Do not be deceived: God is not mocked, for whatever one sows, that will he also reap. For the one who sows to his own flesh will from the flesh reap corruption, but the one who sows to the Spirit will from the Spirit reap eternal life. (*Holy Bible, Galatians 6:7–8 ESV*)

[11z9] Brilliant: *Bright, Radiant, Luminous, Lustrous* mean shining or glowing with light. Bright implies emitting or reflecting a high degree of light. Brilliant implies intense often sparkling brightness. Radiant stresses the emission or seeming emission of rays of light. Luminous implies emission of steady, suffused, glowing light by reflection or in surrounding darkness (*www.merriam-webster.com*).

[*GOD—The Dimensional Revelation* Emphasizes That These Words Apply To Spiritual Light, as well as physical light. See Chapter 13 of Our Teaching.]

[11z10] Diffuse: Widely spread or scattered; not concentrated (*www.thefreedictionary.com*).

[11z11] Dim: not shining brightly or clearly…not clearly recalled or formulated in the mind (*Oxford English Dictionary*).

[11z12] Grow or grows: become larger or greater over a period of time; increase (*Oxford English Dictionary*).

[11z13] right triangle: A triangle where one of its interior angles is a right angle (90 degrees) (*www.mathopenrefer.com*).

[11z14] Pythagorean theorem: In mathematics, the Pythagorean theorem, also known as Pythagoras' theorem, is a fundamental relation in Euclidean geometry among the three sides of a right triangle. It states that the area of the square whose side is the hypotenuse (the side opposite the right angle) is equal to the sum of the areas of the squares on the other two sides. This theorem can be written as an equation relating the lengths of the sides a, b and c, often called the "Pythagorean equation": $a^2 + b^2 = c^2$ where c represents the length of the hypotenuse and a and b the lengths of the triangle's other two sides. The theorem, whose history is the subject of much debate, is named for the ancient Greek thinker Pythagoras (*https://en.wikipedia.org/wiki/Pythagorean_theorem#/media/File:Pythagorean.svg*)

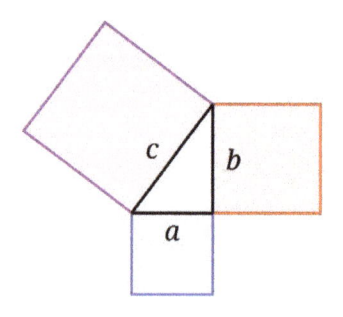

RESEARCH NOTES, CREDITS, AND EXPANSIONS

[11z15] cone: [right circular cone] a solid generated by rotating a right triangle about one of its legs (*www.merriam-webster.com*).

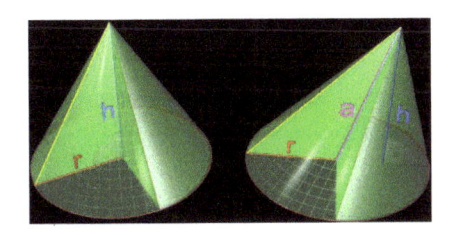

A right circular cone and an oblique circular cone (https://en.wikipedia.org/wiki/Cone).

[11z16] wedge or right triangular prism: A right triangular prism has rectangular sides, otherwise it is oblique. A uniform triangular prism is a right triangular prism with equilateral bases, and square sides (*en.wikipedia.org*).

Triangular prism

[11z17] dilemma: a situation in which a difficult choice has to be made between two different things you could do (*dictionary.cambridge.org*).

[11z18] epitome: The typical or highest example of a stated quality, as shown by a particular person or thing (*dictionary.cambridge.org*).

[11z19] Higgs boson: Just after the big bang, the Higgs field was zero, but as the universe cooled and the temperature fell below a critical value, the field grew spontaneously so that any particle interacting with it acquired a mass. The more a particle interacts with this field, the heavier it is. Particles like the photon that do not interact with it are left with no mass at all. Like all fundamental fields, the Higgs field has an associated particle—the Higgs boson. The Higgs boson is the visible manifestation of the Higgs field, rather like a wave at the surface of the sea (https://home.cern/science/physics/higgs-boson).

[11z20] re-manifested: To resurface or to re-emerge (www.definitions.net).

[11z21] Jesus Christ or LORD JESUS: Jesus[e] (c. 4 BC–AD 30 / 33), also referred to as Jesus of Nazareth or Jesus Christ, was a first-century Jewish preacher and religious leader (*Vermes, 1981, 20, 26, 27, 29*).

Jesus Christ, the second person of the Trinity, also known as God the Son or the Logos (Koine Greek for "Word"), "was made flesh" by being conceived in the womb of a woman, the Virgin Mary… The doctrine of the incarnation, then, entails that Jesus is fully God and fully human (*Thomas Aquinas, Summa Contra Gentiles, "Of the Incarnation as Part of the Fitness of Things," Jacques Maritain Center, University of Notre Dame*).

> Jesus said to her, "I am the resurrection and the life. Whoever believes in me, though he die, yet shall he live, and everyone who lives and believes in me shall never die." (*Holy Bible, John 11:25–26 ESV*)

> Jesus said to her, "Woman, why are you weeping? Whom do you seek?" Supposing him to be the gardener, she said to him, "Sir, if you have carried him away, tell me where you have laid him, and I will take him away." Jesus said to her, "Mary." She turned and said to him in Hebrew, "Rab-bo'ni!" [which means "Teacher"]. Jesus said to her, "Do not hold me, for I have not yet ascended to the Father; but go to my brethren and say to them, I am ascending to my Father and your Father, to my God and your God." (*Holy Bible, John 20:15–17 RSV*)

[11z22] Father or Fathers:

> But to us there is but one God, the Father, of whom are all things, and we in him; and one Lord Jesus Christ, by whom are all things, and we by him. (*Holy Bible, John 10:30 KJV*)

> Jesus Christ Said: "I and my Father are one." (*Holy Bible, John 10:30 KJV*)

> Believest thou not that I am in the Father, and the Father in me? The words that I speak unto you I speak not of myself: but the Father that dwelleth in me, he doeth the works. (*Holy Bible, John 14:10 KJV*)

> At that day ye shall know that **I am in my Father, and ye in me, and I in you.** (*Holy Bible, John 14:20 KJV; bold print added*)

God the Father is a title given to God in various religions, most prominently in Christianity. In mainstream trinitarian Christianity, God the Father is regarded as the first person of the Trinity, followed by the second person, God the Son (Jesus Christ), and the third person, God the Holy Spirit (*Gilles Emery, The Trinity: An*

RESEARCH NOTES, CREDITS, AND EXPANSIONS

Introduction to Catholic Doctrine on the Triune God [Catholic University of America Press], 2011).

[*GOD—The Dimensional Revelation* Reinforces the analogy by Revealing That GOD Is "In" You Spiritually as your earthly father is in you genetically. The Spiritual Relationship Is Even Deeper. Though You Are Spiritually Independent Of GOD, GOD Can Join With You To Participate In Your Conscious Experience. The Connection Can Be Enhanced or diminished as You Choose or At The Pleasure Of GOD.

Ultimately, Reunification Of You With GOD Places You Entirely Within GOD. Your Identity ceases to exist As You Merge Into GOD.]

[11z23] "In My Father's House are many Mansions":

> Jesus Christ Said, "In my Father's house are many mansions: if it were not so, I would have told you. I go to prepare a place for you. And if I go and prepare a place for you, I will come again, and receive you unto myself; that where I am, there ye may be also. And whither I go ye know, and the way ye know." (*Holy Bible, John 14:2–4 KJV*)

[*GOD—The Dimensional Revelation* Reveals That Jesus Uses The Word *House* as a metaphor Meaning "All Of Reality." *Many Mansions* is a metaphor For The Variety Of Manifestations In Which You May Participate.]

[11z24] current big bang theory: Antimatter particles share the same mass as their matter counterparts, but qualities such as electric charge are opposite. The positively charged positron, for example, is the antiparticle to the negatively charged electron. Matter and antimatter particles are always produced as a pair and, if they come in contact, annihilate one another, leaving behind pure energy. During the first fractions of a second of the Big Bang, the hot and dense universe was buzzing with particle-antiparticle pairs popping in and out of existence. If matter and antimatter are created and destroyed together, it seems the universe should contain nothing but leftover energy… Nevertheless, a tiny portion of matter—about one particle per billion—managed to survive (*https://home.cern/science/physics/matter-antimatter-asymmetry-problem, retrieved 11/28/2020*).

[*GOD—The Dimensional Revelation* Hypothesizes a different and perhaps original big-bang theory. Essentially, We theorize that our big-bang occurred as the result of the matteranti-matter explosive reaction that annihilated both all of the Primal Matter and all of the Primal Antimatter. It left a residue of energy, e, which converted to subatomic particles and then atoms as it cooled. Please follow the proofs We advance in the text of Chapter 11.]

[11z25] residual energy: To manufacture matter in a way that adheres to the first law of thermodynamics, you have to convert energy into matter. This conversion

occurred on a cosmic scale about 13 billion years ago. The big bang consisted entirely of energy. Matter only came into being as rapid cooling occurred. In the lab, creating matter entails a reaction called pair production, so called because it converts a photon into a pair of particles: one matter, one antimatter (the reverse of the matter-antimatter annihilation we just mentioned). Brookhaven National Lab, the European Organization for Nuclear Research (CERN) and Fermilab have all generated this reaction by firing a photon into a heavy atomic nucleus. The nucleus shares the energy and allows the photon to disintegrate into an electron and a positron, the antimatter opposite of an electron. The positron inevitably turns back into a photon when it collides with an electron (*https://science.howstuffworks.com/environmental/earth/geophysics/can-we-manufacture-matter.htm; Robert Lamb*).

[*GOD—The Dimensional Revelation* Suggests the following original big bang sequence: GOD Initially Created our universe of matter and its attendant energies by Instructing a wave, Primal Energy, to emerge in the 9th D, manifesting as Primal Matter and its opposing Primal Antimatter. Of course, these violently cancel out one another in our big bang. Only *e*, an energy residue, remains. That residue is an incredible collection of diverse energy strings, which converts into matter as the system cools. The reason it cools is that the force of our big bang and its subsequent inertia fling the strings apart. The cooling results from less pressure as space between strings expands. With less activity in each given space, strings can join end-to-end, and/or, side-to-side, to form more complex matter and energy combinations.

Electromagnetism emerges. An important feature of each string is that each has either a positive or a negative electromagnetic charge, or no charge, as resonance carried forward from the Primal Matter and Primal Antimatter. The strings with opposite charges attract, inducing the strings to pair end-to-end, and/or, side-to-side, to form more complex strings. Each complex string manifests its dominant charge, positive or negative. The attraction of one proton for one electron in a hydrogen atom is one example.]

[11z26] **PE=PM-PAM=e**: [This equation, original to *GOD—The Dimensional Revelation*, uses symbolic logic to express a theory that the Author Deduced based on dimensional analysis in the 4th dimension. This theory is that Primal Energy was created as the singularity preceding the big bang of our physical universe. Within the large quantum field created by Primal Energy, Primal Matter and Primal antimatter emerged in equal amounts. They cancelled each other out with the violent explosion known as the big bang. The residue left over from the big bang was ordinary physical energy, *e*. Our physical universe developed as this energy manifested variously as physical particles or wave energy.]

[11z27] radiant energy: energy that travels by waves or particles, particularly electromagnetic radiation such as heat or x-rays (*www.yourdictionary.com*).

[11z28] constant emergence: [*GOD—The Dimensional Revelation* Hypothesizes that quantum mechanics leaves out the 9th-D Mechanisms by which strings emerge

from a quantum field. This is a continuous process that sustains physical reality. This is a continuation of how our singularity and big bang originated. The same theory holds at the micro-level {subatomic particles} and at the macro-level {the big bang causing our physical universe}.

This Teaching uses dimensional reasoning to develop Our theory of "emergence," which is that the Instructions of creation are given to the 9th-D mechanisms of creation to manifest physical reality in the 8th and lower dimensions. We theorize that the operative mechanism is the emergence of residual energy, e, from the cancellation of Primal Matter and Primal Antimatter in quantum fields.

We theorize that quantum probabilities become more predictable once the Matter-Antimatter reaction is complete and residual energy is created. Residual energy has specific Information, so the conversion into matter proceeds within the limitations of that information. Then the processes of ordinary physical forces allow reality to emerge through time with each successive event collapsing into reality based on the limitations established by the previous situation. The emergence is constant because time forces strings to oscillate in and out of quantum fields, creating the next situation from the matter and energy present in the previous situation.]

[11z29] process over time: [*GOD—The Dimensional Revelation* Revels that any theory that depicts reality as bundles of data is invalid. That is because Reality is not bits and bundles that can be separated and somehow reconfigured in another place or time. Manifest reality is a continuous process over time. What appear to be bundles of information in atomic and larger organizations are continuous oscillations of strings appearing receding and reappearing {oscillating} in quantum fields. The continuum cannot be broken in the past or the present. Only the future is subject to quantum uncertainty and other variables.

Only The WORD can interrupt the oscillations in physical reality in a manner not ordinarily possible in an 8th dimensional physical universe.]

[11z30] instantaneous: existing or measured at a particular instant (*Oxford English Dictionary*).

[11z31] gravitational coupling: In physics, a gravitational coupling constant is a constant characterizing the gravitational attraction between a given pair of elementary particles. The electron mass is typically used, and the associated constant typically denoted αG. It is a dimensionless quantity, with the result that its numerical value does not vary with the choice of units of measurement, only with the choice of particle... There is no known way of measuring αG directly, and CODATA does not report an estimate of its value. The above estimate is calculated from the CODATA values of "me" and "mp"... There is an arbitrariness in the choice of which particle's mass to use (whereas α is a function of the elementary charge, αG is normally a function of the electron rest mass). In this article αG is defined in terms of a pair of electrons unless stated otherwise. And while the relationship between αG and gravitation is somewhat analogous to that of the fine-structure constant and electro-

magnetism, the important difference is that the standard definition of αG describes a ratio in terms of electron mass alone, whereas the fine-structure constant relates to the elementary charge, which is a quantum that is independent of the choice of particle (*en.wikipedia.org*).

For the case of hadrons, it is at least logically possible that the gravitational coupling between matter and the geometry of space-time is much stronger than for macroscopic systems. The value of the gravitational coupling factor has never been measured within an atom or a subatomic particle (*https://resonance.is/black-holes-elementary-particles-revisiting-pioneering-investigation-particles-may-micro-black-holes/*).

[11z32] second law of thermodynamics: The second law of thermodynamics states that the total entropy of an isolated system can never decrease over time and is constant if and only if all processes are reversible.

The first law of thermodynamics provides the definition of the internal energy of a thermodynamic system and expresses the law of conservation of energy (*M. Planck, 1897/1903, 40–41*).

The second law is concerned with the direction of natural processes (F. *Mandl, Statistical Physics Second Edition [Wiley & Sons, 1988]*). It asserts that a natural process runs only in one sense and is not reversible. For example, when a path for conduction and radiation is made available, heat always flows spontaneously from a hotter to a colder body. Such phenomena are accounted for in terms of entropy (P*lanck, M. (1897/1903), pp. 79–107*).

[11z33] cosmic dust: Cosmic dust, also called extraterrestrial dust or space dust, is dust that exists in outer space or has fallen on Earth (*M. J. Gengel et al., "An Urban Collection of Modern-Day Large Micrometeorites: Evidence for Variations in the Extraterrestrial Dust Flux through the Quaternary," Geology 45 no. 2 [December 1, 2016]*).

[11z34] inertial energy: The fact that inertial coordinate systems are related by Lorentz transformations (rather than Galilean transformations) has very profound implications because acceleration is not invariant under Lorentz transformations. As a result, the acceleration of an object subjected to a given force depends on the frame of reference. Since acceleration is a measure of the object's inertia, this implies that the object's "inertial mass" depends on the frame of reference. Now, the kinetic energy of an object also depends on the frame of reference, and we find that the variation of kinetic energy is always exactly c^2 times the variation in inertial mass, where c is the speed of light. Thus, the Lorentz covariance of the inertial measures of space and time implies that all forms of energy possess inertia, which, in turn, suggests that all inertia represents energy (*https://www.mathpages.com/rr/s2-03/2-03.htm*).

[11z35] diluted: made weaker in force, content, or value by modification (*Oxford English Dictionary*).

[11z36] accelerating: increasing in speed or rate of occurrence (*www.merriam-webster.com*).

RESEARCH NOTES, CREDITS, AND EXPANSIONS

[11z37] spirals: the path of a point in a plane moving around a central point while continuously receding from or approaching it (*www.merriam-webster.com*).

[11z38] local black hole: In 1958, David Finkelstein used General Relativity to introduce a stricter definition of a local black hole event horizon as a boundary beyond which events of any kind cannot affect an outside observer (*en.wikipedia.org*).

[11z39] quasar: A quasar (/ˈkweɪzɑːr/; also known as a quasi-stellar object, abbreviated QSO) is an extremely luminous active galactic nucleus (AGN), in which a supermassive black hole with mass ranging from millions to billions of times the mass of the Sun is surrounded by a gaseous accretion disk. As gas in the disk falls towards the black hole, energy is released in the form of electromagnetic radiation, which can be observed across the electromagnetic spectrum. The power radiated by quasars is enormous; the most powerful quasars have luminosities thousands of times greater than a galaxy such as the Milky Way (*"Most Distant Quasar Found," ESO Science Release, 2011*).

[11z40] Younger: Being in an early period of life, development, or growth (*www.thefreedictionary.com*).

[11z41] oscillate: To move repeatedly from one position to another (*dictionary.cambridge.org*).

[*GOD—The Dimensional Revelation* Observes The Principle of Oscillation In Spiritual Reality, as well as physical reality.

Most Important To Spiritual Reality Is To "Turn The Light Around" As An Internal Oscillation In Which You Receive Spiritual Energy {Light} From God, Calmly Focusing At Your Center. The Light Blooms In Your Center, And The Light Is Shared Back To GOD, Increased. This Is One Cycle Of The Spiritual Oscillation. The Next Cycle Starts With GOD Appreciating The Light You Shared, Then Again Sharing Light With You. You Again Appreciate The Light In Your Center And Share Increased Light Back To GOD To Complete The Second Cycle Of The Oscillation.

When You Become A Master At Turning The Light Around, You May Share It With Other Spiritual Beings. Various Combinations Of A Three-Way Appreciation Of The Light May Be Realized. This Is A Very Advanced Aspect Of Worship, called "Circulating The Light".

Understanding This Is Not Enough. Turning The Light Around Must Be Experienced Through Participation.

Our Teaching also Welcomes You To Share The Light Of Love At Any Stage Of Your Spiritual Development. You need not Be A Master, To Exchange Spiritual Energy With Another Spirit.

See Chapter 13 of This Teaching.]

[11z42] cycles: a series of events that are regularly repeated in the same order (*Oxford English Dictionary*).

[11z43] intergalactic space: The vast voids between galaxies can stretch millions of light-years across and may appear empty. But these spaces actually contain more matter than the galaxies themselves. The matter between galaxies—often called the intergalactic medium, or IGM for short—is mostly hot, ionized hydrogen (hydrogen that has lost its electron) with bits of heavier elements such as carbon, oxygen and silicon thrown in. While these elements typically don't glow bright enough to be seen directly, scientists know they're there because of the signature they leave on light that passes by (*Mara Johnson-Groh, "What Happens in Intergalactic Space?" Live Science Contributor, July 21, 2019*).

[11z44] implode: collapse or cause to collapse violently inward (*Oxford English Dictionary*).

[11z45] Spiritual Mathematics: There are four possible gateways by which spirituality can enter mathematics:

1. Pragmatic Platonism: mathematics is like an unseen star, out there to be discovered (the Platonic view). Mathematics may be something we create to make sense of our world (Kantian view), perhaps both.
2. Aesthetics—that is, the role of beauty within mathematics: The English physicist Paul Dirac (1902–1984) also argued that mathematical beauty "cannot be defined any more than beauty in art can be defined, but which people who study mathematics usually have no difficulty in appreciating."
3. The study of patterns: Math is uncovering the nature of Christ because Christ is the pattern of the form in everything we see (*Frederick Witz, 2007, 197–261*).
4. The role of inner understanding and inner vision: most striking at first is this appearance of sudden illumination, a manifest sign of long unconscious prior work. The role of this unconscious work in mathematical invention appears to be incontestable (*Jacques Hadamard, An Essay on the Psychology of Invention in the Mathematical Field [Mineola: Dover publications, 1954]*).
5. Number mysticism: attaching Spiritual Meaning to certain numbers, like seven, twelve, and forty, because they appear commonly in religious history (*Volker Kessler, "Spirituality in Mathematics," Journal for the Study of Spirituality vol. 9, issue 1 [2019], published online on April 3, 2019*).

[Recognizing That There Is A Fusion Between Our Spiritual Universe and our physical universe, *GOD—The Dimensional Revelation* Opens The Study Of That Fusion using symbolic logic to assign a variable, A, to Spiritual Beings in This Fusion and z to physical objects in this fusion. A mathematics can be developed through deductive and inductive reasoning, quantifying the Relationships In This Fusion.]

[11z46] digital printing: Digital printing is the process of printing digital-based images directly onto a variety of media substrates. There is no need for a printing

RESEARCH NOTES, CREDITS, AND EXPANSIONS

plate, unlike with offset printing. Digital files such as PDFs or desktop publishing files can be sent directly to the digital printing press to print on paper, photo paper, canvas, fabric, synthetics, cardstock, and other substrates (*https://www.xerox.com/en-us/digital-printing/insights/what-is-digital-printing*).

[11z47] artificial intelligence: Artificial intelligence (AI) is the ability of a digital computer or computer-controlled robot to perform tasks commonly associated with intelligent beings. The term is frequently applied to the project of developing systems endowed with the intellectual processes characteristic of humans, such as the ability to reason, discover meaning, generalize, or learn from past experience (*https://www.britannica.com/technology/artificial-intelligence; Artificial intelligence; B.J. Copeland; August 11, 2020*).

[11z48] analogous: similar or comparable to something else either in general or in some specific detail (*www.merriam-webster.com*).

[11z49] pattern process: something that happens in a regular and repeated way (*www.merriam-webster.com*).

[11z50] Increase of Spiritual Energy:

> Turning the Light around is only the general term: with each level of progress in practice, the efflorescence of the Light Increases in magnitude, and the method of turning around becomes subtler. (*The Secret of the Golden Flower, 40, trans. Thomas Cleary [HarperCollins, 1991]*)

When you are vibrating at a higher level, you feel lighter, happier, and more at ease, whereas lower vibrations feel heavy, dark, and confused. Almost all spiritual traditions point the way toward higher realms of consciousness, and scientific studies (like that of consciousness research and spirituality author Dr. David Hawkins) have even quantified the vibrations of different states of being to create a scale of consciousness… When you lift yourself up, you bring others with you. This is the only way you can contribute to raising the collective consciousness of the world (*Karson McGinley, September 18, 2019, 9:00 p.m., https://chopra.com/articles/how-to-raise-your-emotional-and-spiritual-vibration*).

[11z51] and [11z52] **SE'>SE-SE**: [This Equation, Original To *GOD—The Dimensional Revelation*, uses symbolic logic to express that Spiritual Energy Moves On A Continuum but does not decrease as It Is Used. The Future State Of Spiritual Energy, **SE'**, actually Increases As Spiritual Energy, **SE**, Is Used.

Also, Spiritual Energy, **SE**, can be described in both Its Character and Its Magnitude as It Is Manifested in Many Ways.

However, Spiritual Energy cannot be measured on a consistent scale. A Spiritual Mathematics, though expressing mathematical functions like addition, subtraction, multiplication, and division as functions on a Continuum, is not represented by symbols that can be relied upon to be what they were in the past.

This may seem foreign to physical mathematics but not so strange if You Remember The Different Manifestations Of Love That You Have Experienced.

SE'>SE+SE is also true because when Spiritual Energy SE is added, the future state **SE'** is always greater because Any Use Of Positive Spiritual Energy Is An Expansion Of Spiritual Energy. The Resulting State Of Spiritual Energy Is Greater Than The Sum Of Its Parts.]

[11z53] apathy or **ay**: lack of interest, enthusiasm, or concern (*Oxford English Dictionary*).

[The variable **ay**, original to *GOD—The Dimensional Revelation*, uses symbolic logic to express that "apathy" has a value in Spiritual Mathematics as a function of a discontinuation of the flow of Spiritual Energy by the Subject Spirit being apathetic. Apathy decreases Manifest Spiritual Energy, also known as The "Light."]

[11z54] negative spiritual energy or **nse**: [The variable "nse," original to *GOD—The Dimensional Revelation*, uses symbolic logic to express that "negative spiritual energy" has a value in Spiritual Mathematics. "nse" is a function of a flow that is destructive of Spiritual Energy caused by the Subject Spirit projecting negative spiritual energy.]

There are different types of energy sources: some are physical, some are emotional, and some are spiritual…our world is made up of spiritual energies: The ones that are in lower form are based on fear, guilt, judgement, doubt, shame, hate, and anger… I'm sure you get the picture; the ones in the higher energy forms are based on love, compassion, bliss, elation, playfulness, joy, ecstasy, pleasure, and every higher vibration that connects you to unconditional love and acceptance. There are spirits that support those energies—as human beings, we see it as duality, while in the spirit world we see it as a choice. It's very simple, but you're either creating or you're destroying in every aspect of your life…identify the energy sources that are affecting your life, to make a comprehensive understanding of them, and to decide how we are going to expel these poisons from your system, change your belief system, and put you back in space in your life so that you are operating at your highest level… One way we can expel negativity in our lives is to simply shift negativity by the way that we look at it… If we spend more time reacting to the joyful, beautiful, and pleasurable things in life, it shows the value of those things and we create more of them (*https://goop.com/wellness/spirituality/notes-from-a-shaman-moving-negative-energy-and-why-the-world-is-in-upheaval/*).

Clearing negative spiritual energy:

1. Set an intention for releasing all your own negative energy and everything you've picked up on from others. I like to say: I am easily releasing all

energy from myself and others that no longer serves me. I do this for my highest good.
2. Imagine a small ball of brilliant, golden light in the center of your chest, expanding the light on each exhalation.
3. Imagine breathing in and out through your chest, expanding the light on each exhalation.
4. Spread the light throughout your entire body. See it in your head, torso, arms, and toes.
5. Now expand it beyond your skin until the light is about an arm's length out in all directions.
6. Follow by shielding… 1) Imagine a large bubble around you, about an arm's length from your body in all directions. 2) See this bubble as a solid wall or a filter that covers you completely. Ask this bubble (or shield) to act as a cell wall, using its intelligence to allow love and positive energy in. Ask that anything negative not be allowed in… 3) Fill the bubble with golden light (*Kris Ferraro, Energy Healing: Simple and Effective Practices to Become Your own Healer, April 2019*).

[11z55] **SE'=SE-ay-nse**: [This Equation, Original To *GOD—The Dimensional Revelation*, Uses symbolic logic to express that the future condition of Spiritual Energy {SE'} In any system can be reduced by spiritual negligence, which is apathy {ay} or by negative spiritual energy {nse}.

Choices Are Presented To Each Spiritual Being That Allow Each To Elevate Their Spiritual Energy or to allow it to be attacked and diminished by ay or nse. Faith Creates A Set Of Spiritual Defenses. An Active Relationship Directly With GOD Is The Best Defense.

Of Course GOD Is Unlimited and not subject to quantitative actions in any system.]

[11z56] Images: a mental picture or impression of something (*www.merriam-webster.com*).

a physical likeness or representation of a person, animal, or thing photographed, painted, sculptured, or otherwise made visible (*www.dictionary.com*).

[11z57] infinities in the equations: In quantum field theory,

> The energy density of a static electric field is proportional to the square of its electric field intensity E…the total energy V of the field is given by $V=(Q^2/(6\pi c^2))(1/R)$, where c is the speed of light. This is often called the *self-energy* of the particle. Note that $V \to \infty$ as $R \to 0$. Thus, an electrical field emanating from a point, such as that generated by a point charge, has infinite energy… P.A.M. Dirac also found infinities arising in his theorizing on the

effect of charges on the vacuum states. Infinities occurred also in the analysis of the scattering of light by light (*https://www.sjsu.edu/faculty/watkins/QFTinfinities.htm#*).

[*GOD—The Dimensional Revelation* notes that this supports Our definition of the 0th dimension, which is possibility among infinite possibilities. Quantum possibilities are not "point particles." The 0th dimension denotes only that a possibility exists, unrealized.

The Dirac equations also support Our definition of the 1st dimension, which is a string, a basic particle, or wave energy. The smallest of physical realities has quantum length, which may be called a "string."]

There then developed the notion that the problem of infinities in models could be dealt with by a systematic revision of the parameters of the model. This was called the renormalization of the parameters. This took the form of positing a bare mass for particles that should be used in the models instead of the measured mass (*https://www.sjsu.edu/faculty/watkins/QFTinfinities.htm#*).

[*GOD—The Dimensional Revelation* notes that this supports Our assertion that once a mass is "measured" {observed or collapsed into being}, its potential is realized, and it no longer has quantum probability. The positing of a "bare mass" is again looking to the future, making an assumption so that the math works.

For example, if You define a string, hypothesizing its future characteristics, then the mathematics is "normalized," and the infinities are resolved. However, Your hypothesis remains a prediction, so it cannot be certain. This seems to be the limitation of quantum field theory—That something only becomes real when it is measured or observed {i.e., participated in}. But to renormalize the math to get rid of the "infinities," a model must be constructed. Our Teaching is that this is, again, the attempt of quantum mathematics to chop Reality into segments to make the math work. Our Teaching is that Reality is a continuum, so any segment {static state or frame} cannot be isolated in Reality. The segment is only a model.]

It is shown that mean field theory is not correct for two dimensional Ising models. Elsewhere it is shown that mean field theory is correct for Ising models of dimensions four or greater… In order to get partial differential equations Wilson needed to make all variables continuous. That meant that spin, instead of being ±1, could take on any real value from $-\infty$ to $+\infty$ (*https://www.sjsu.edu/faculty/watkins/RGhist.htm*).

RESEARCH NOTES, CREDITS, AND EXPANSIONS

[*GOD—The Dimensional Revelation* Notes that "continuous variables" in the equations does solve the infinities problem, but forces quantum field theory into our conclusion that Reality is continuous and cannot be segmented.

Furthermore, the mathematics used by quantum field theory always deals with the future. The present and the past are certain.

Our Teaching also asserts that quantum analysis of "infinities" leaves reality unlimited at both ends. We Know that Our physical universe is limited by its expansion into physical nothingness. Since nothing can come from nothing in Reality, the SOURCE is Postulated, and the Final State is also Postulated. The necessity of This Postulation Is another fundamental proof of GOD—The Only "Unlimited" in any metaphysics.]

[11z58] Unified Field Theory: Einstein and others attempted to construct a unified field theory in which electromagnetism and gravity would emerge as different aspects of a single fundamental field. They failed, and to this day, gravity remains beyond attempts at a unified field theory (*https://www.britannica.com/science/unified-field-theory*).

[11z59] balance: [noun or verb applied to mathematical equations, harmony in music and metaphysics and justice.]

A situation in which different elements are equal or in the correct proportions (*Oxford English Dictionary*).

A state in which opposing forces harmonize, equilibrium (*en.wiktionary.org*).

For Pythagorean philosophers, the basic property of numbers was expressed in the harmonious interplay of opposite pairs. Harmony assured the balance of opposite forces (*Constantine J. Vamvacas, The Founders of Western Thought—The Presocratics [Springer Science & Business Media, 2009], 70, ISBN 9781402097911*).

Pythagoras taught that "happiness consists in knowledge of the perfection of the numbers of the soul" (*David R. Fideler, The Pythagorean Sourcebook and Library [Red Wheel/Weiser, 1987], 33*).

The soul is life and a harmony of physical elements. As such, the soul passes away when certain arrangements of these elements cease to exist. However, the teaching most securely identified with Pythagoras is metempsychosis, or the "transmigration of souls," which holds that every soul is immortal and, upon death, enters into a new body (*Charles H. Kahn, Pythagoras and the Pythagoreans, 2001); (Zhmud, 2012, 232*).

Albert Einstein believed that through this pre-established harmony, the productive unison between the spiritual and material world was possible (*Constantine J. Vamvacas, The Founders of Western Thought—The Presocratics [Springer Science & Business Media, 2009], 71*).

The Master [Confucius] said, The virtue embodied in the doctrine of the Mean is of the highest order. But it has long been rare among people (*Analects, 6:29, trans. Burton Watson*).

The yin yang (i.e., taijitu symbol) shows a balance between two opposites with a portion of the opposite element in each section. In Taoist metaphysics, distinctions between good and bad, along with other dichotomous moral judgements, are perceptual, not real; so the duality of yin and yang is an indivisible whole (en.wikipedia.org).

[*GOD—The Dimensional Revelation* Notes That The Balance Depicted In The Taijitu Symbol Can Be A Harmonious Coexistence Of The Opposites, the harmonious interplay of opposite pairs.

It also represents the conflict of the opposites when harmony breaks down. Also see [6z55].

Our Teaching Recalls The Buddhist Meditation Seeking Emptiness Of Mind Represented by the "Empty" circle. See [13z120]. This Principle is often confused by a criticism of "Emptiness" as "no god." Rather, Emptiness Is The Void, Which Remains Filled With The CLEAR LIGHT. Be Enlightened In The True GOD, Our 10th Dimension Spiritual, and Our Seventh Heaven. The "conflict of the opposites" disappears upon Reunification With The LORD.

Our Teaching Appreciates The Purity Of The White Void. We Join With GOD As The CLEAR LIGHT Of The Void.]

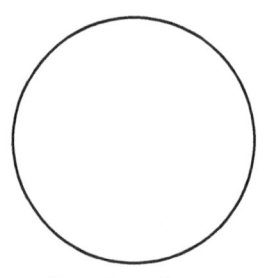

Drawing of physically white "emptiness" representing
Pure Spirit, The CLEAR LIGHT Of The Void
Illustration by Allyn Richert, AD 2022

RESEARCH NOTES, CREDITS, AND EXPANSIONS

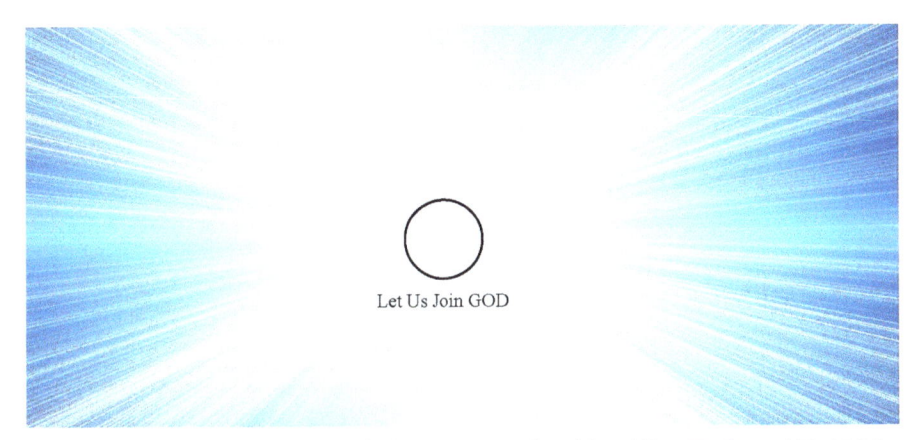

Let Us Join GOD

Mik Ulyannikov/Shutterstock 44621095, edited by Allyn Richert AD 2022

[The Journey of a Soul, Differentiated From The ONE through many different manifestations until Ultimate Reunification with GOD, may be expressed in many different ways. Indeed, The Journey Of Your Soul may be vastly different from The Journey Of Another Soul or Spirit. The three illustrations above—from the Harmony or conflict of the opposites to appear empty yet Gloriously Enlightened In Union With The CLEAR LIGHT—Is One Journey Your Soul May Take.

During This Human Life, Your Spiritual Journey May Be Fulfilled Through Your Meditative Experience of Love In Harmonizing The Opposites as shown in the Taijitu Symbol. One Way To Reunify With The LORD Is To Stop the incessant background chatter in Consciousness as represented by the Empty Circle. This Void In Consciousness Is Filled With The CLEAR LIGHT Of GOD As You SEE The Perfection With Any And All Of Your Senses. This Is Represented By The Illustration Of Brilliant Light.]

[11z60] Proof Of GOD: Thomas Aquinas developed, by logical deduction, his five arguments for God's existence:

1. The *unmoved mover* argument asserts that from our experience of motion in the universe (motion being the transition from potentiality to actuality), we can see that there must have been an initial mover. Aquinas argued that whatever is in motion must be put in motion by another thing, so there must be an unmoved mover.
2. Aquinas' argument from *first cause* started with the premise that it is impossible for a being to cause itself (because it would have to exist before it caused itself) and that it is impossible for there to be an infinite chain of causes, which would result in infinite regress. Therefore, there must be a first cause, itself uncaused.
3. The argument from *necessary being* asserts that all beings are contingent, meaning that it is possible for them not to exist. Aquinas argued that if

everything can possibly not exist, there must have been a time when nothing existed; as things exist now, there must exist a being with necessary existence regarded as God.
4. Aquinas argued from degree, considering the occurrence of *degrees of goodness*. He believed that things which are called good must be called good in relation to a standard of good—a maximum. There must be a maximum goodness that which causes all goodness.
5. The argument from *final cause* asserts the view that non-intelligent objects are ordered toward a purpose. Aquinas argued that these objects cannot be ordered unless they are done so by an intelligent being, which means that there must be an intelligent being to move objects to their ends: God (*referring to Thomas Aquinas, Summa Theologica, part 1, question 2, article 3, en.wikipedia.org*).

Please see [11z57], *infinities in the equations*; [5z13], *Harmonic oscillation and Spiritual Oscillation*; and [3z36] *Phenomenology, Hegel's dialectic*, among other proofs of GOD.

[11z61] limits of mathematics:

> The mathematician would gladly give up his entire science; for that science cannot give him any satisfaction in regard to the highest and most important ends of humanity. (*Immanuel Kant, Critique of Pure Reason, A464/B492*)

[11z62] Spiritual Fields: The meridians are an interface between the etheric human energy field and the physical body. The etheric body creates the meridians, which, in turn, form the physical body (*Dr. Kim Bonghan*).

There are many different biofields that regulate various mental, emotional, spiritual, or physical functions, and these correspond to various parts of the subtle body. The following list of biofields is based on the work of *Barbara Ann Brennan* and others.

[GOD—*The Dimensional Revelation* Notes that given the diversity and Individuality Of Spiritual Incarnation Into A Human body, various of these Biofields may not Manifest In Every Human Being. We also note that the Spiritual Metastring Connecting Each Human Spirit To GOD would be an extension of the "Seventh or Twelfth Auric Layer." That Metastring is depicted by the vertical line in the drawing below.]

The layers of the auric field as described by Barbara Ann Brennan and according to the twelve-chakra system:

RESEARCH NOTES, CREDITS, AND EXPANSIONS

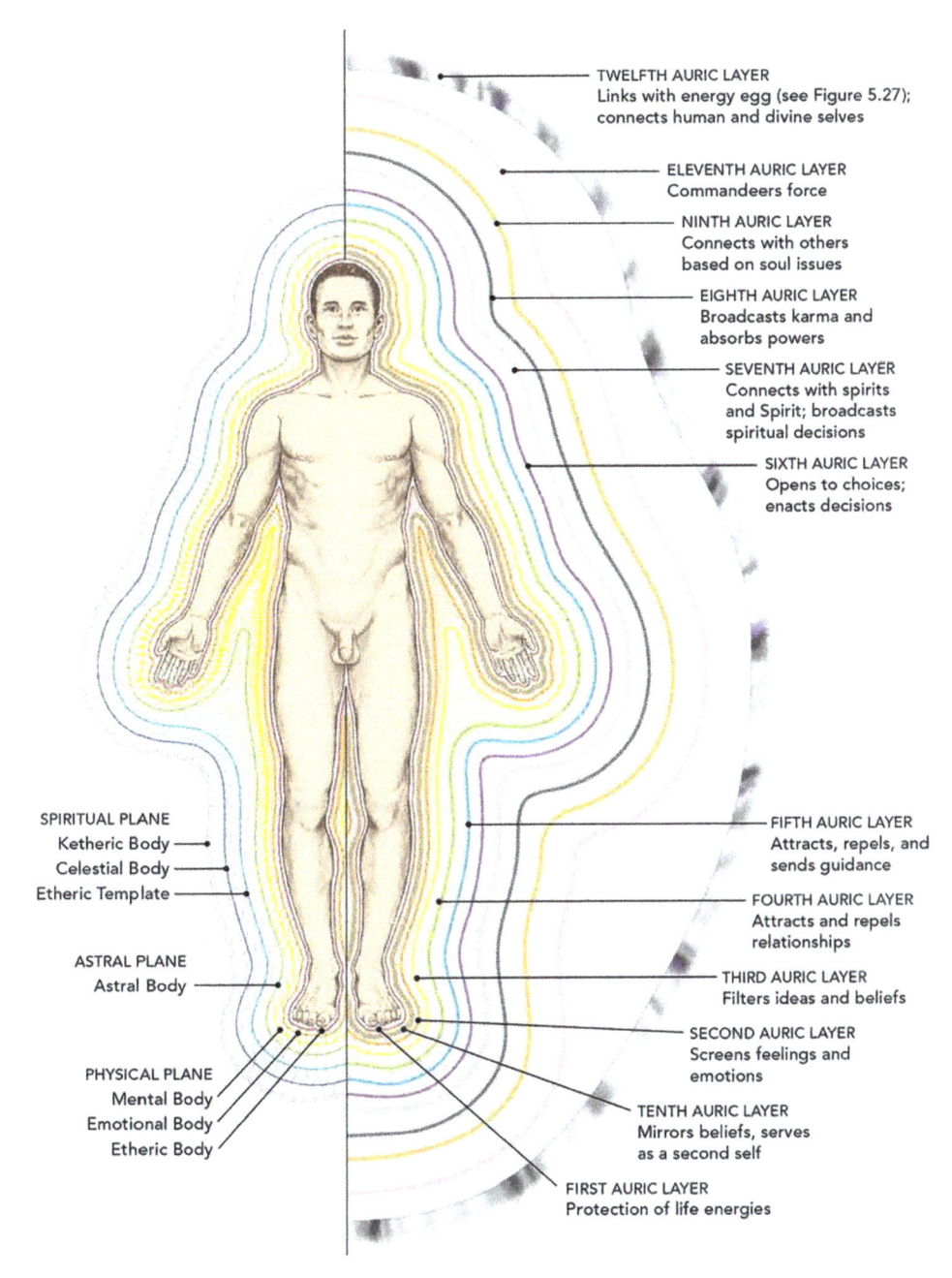

TWELFTH AURIC LAYER
Links with energy egg (see Figure 5.27); connects human and divine selves

ELEVENTH AURIC LAYER
Commandeers force

NINTH AURIC LAYER
Connects with others based on soul issues

EIGHTH AURIC LAYER
Broadcasts karma and absorbs powers

SEVENTH AURIC LAYER
Connects with spirits and Spirit; broadcasts spiritual decisions

SIXTH AURIC LAYER
Opens to choices; enacts decisions

SPIRITUAL PLANE
Ketheric Body
Celestial Body
Etheric Template

ASTRAL PLANE
Astral Body

PHYSICAL PLANE
Mental Body
Emotional Body
Etheric Body

FIFTH AURIC LAYER
Attracts, repels, and sends guidance

FOURTH AURIC LAYER
Attracts and repels relationships

THIRD AURIC LAYER
Filters ideas and beliefs

SECOND AURIC LAYER
Screens feelings and emotions

TENTH AURIC LAYER
Mirrors beliefs, serves as a second self

FIRST AURIC LAYER
Protection of life energies

(https://www.consciouslifestylemag.com/human-energy-field-aura/)

[11z63] **SE'=SE-nse-nse**: [This Equation, Original To *GOD—The Dimensional Revelation*, Uses symbolic logic to identify the cancellation of nse by the Spirit that originated the nse {negative spiritual energy}. This Cancellation Requires A Change Of Attitude and Action By That Person. The original SE was reduced by the nse, now

cancelled or subtracted. The Resulting State of SE' Is Increased By The Cancellation of nse.]

[11z64] **SE'=[*SE-nse-nse*(L) [11z64]]/c(n)**: [This Equation, Original To *GOD—The Dimensional Revelation*, Uses symbolic logic to identify the cancellation of nse by the Spirit that originated the nse {negative spiritual energy}. The original SE was reduced by the nse, now cancelled or subtracted. That cancellation happens in Our Fused physical-Spiritual Universe over a period of time noted as c. The longer the period of time {n}, the less Spiritual Energy {SE'} results. SE' Can Be Increased By The Continuing Love {L} as a multiplication of SE.]

[11z65] Spiritual Value: [*GOD—The Dimensional Revelation* Introduces the original logical concept of symbolizing physical items in reality with a "spiritual value" of *z*, which can be stated as a digital value of *0* as physical items do not have Spirit present. By contrast, All Living Beings Have A Spiritual Value Of *A*, indicating that Spirit Is Present In The Subject, Which Can Be Stated As A Digital Value Of *1* In Spiritual Mathematics.

Ascribing Digital Values To Spiritual Being Yields The Possibility Of Writing A Computer Program To Calculate Spiritual Situations. We note that such a computer program would not be fully functional because Spiritual Values are not constant. We cannot count on The Spiritual State To Which We Ascribe A Symbol Being The Same Spiritual State In The Future. For example, Consider All Of The Different Spiritual States That Manifest The Word *Love* and How They Change. We Have Ascribed The Symbol *L* for Love, but That Quantification Would Change For Nearly Every Event Of Love Perceived In The Future. Hence, The Variable cannot be defined consistently.

The Equation Remains Useful because It Symbolizes Ordinary Spiritual Relations and Provides Calculations That Can Be Useful, even given the broad limits.]

[11z66] **R=z+A**: [This Equation, Original To *GOD—The Dimensional Revelation*, Uses symbolic logic to total All Of Reality. In This Equation, *R* symbolizes All Of Reality. R is mathematically defined as composed of *z*, all physical objects plus *A*, all Spiritual Manifestations.

An expansion of Reality is possible if a membrane system is discovered to exist that has operational principles different from both physical operational principles and Spiritual Operational Principles. Upon this discovery, we would have to revise this equation.]

[11z67] Ascribe: regard a quality as belonging to (*Oxford English Dictionary*).

[11z68] Conclusive: What puts an end to a thing (*www.lectlaw.com*).

[11z69] valid mathematics: mathematicians use several different modes of reasoning in proof validation, including formal reasoning and the construction of rigorous proofs, informal deductive reasoning, and example-based reasoning. Conceptual knowledge plays an important role in the validation of proofs. The practice of

validating a proof depends upon whether a student or mathematician wrote the proof and in what mathematical domain the proof was situated (*Keith Weber, "How Mathematicians Determine If an Argument Is a Valid Proof," Journal for Research in Mathematics Education vol. 39, no. 4 [July 2008]: 431–459*).

A mathematical proposition must be "deduced from true and known principles by the continuous and uninterrupted action of a mind that has a clear vision of each step in the process" (*R. Descartes, "Rules for the Direction of the Mind," in Selections [1627–1628], trans. R. Eaton [New York: Charles Scribner's Sons, 1927, 38–83]*).

Philosophical views concerning the ontology of mathematics run the gamut from platonism (mathematics is about a realm of abstract objects), to fictionalism (mathematics is a fiction whose subject matter does not exist), to formalism (mathematical statements are meaningless strings manipulated according to formal rules) with no consensus about which is correct. By contrast, it seems fair to say that there is a philosophically established, received view of the basic methodology of mathematics. Roughly, it is that mathematicians aim to prove mathematical claims of various sorts, and that proof consists of the logical derivation of a given claim from axioms.

The list of axioms and definitions is followed by the carefully worded theorems. These are loaded with heavy-going conditions; it seems impossible that anyone should ever have guessed them. The theorem is followed by the proof.

Even if we restrict attention to the context of justification, a deductive proof yields categorical knowledge only if it proceeds from a secure starting point and if the rules of inference are truth-preserving.

What Gödel showed is that, for any consistent recursively axiomatized formal system, F, strong enough for arithmetic, there are truths expressible in purely arithmetical language, which are not provable in F. He did not show that there are arithmetical truths which are unprovable in any formal system. Nonetheless, Gödel's results did hammer some significant nails into the coffin of one version of the deductive ideal of mathematics. There cannot be a single recursively axiomatizable formal system for all of mathematics which is (*a*) consistent, (*b*) purely deductive, and (*c*) complete. One line of response to this predicament is to explore options for nondeductive methods of justification in mathematics.

The role of nondeductive methods in empirical science is readily apparent and relatively uncontroversial (*Karl Popper*). Indeed the canonical pattern of justification in science is a posteriori and inductive… Experimental Mathematics, Enumerative Induction, Computer Proofs, Probabilistic Proofs (*Alan Baker, "Nondeductive Methods in Mathematics," The Stanford Encyclopedia of Philosophy, Summer 2020 Edition*).

[11z70] **G>R**: [This Equation, Original To *GOD—The Dimensional Revelation*, Uses symbolic logic To Express That GOD Manifests All Of Reality, but GOD Also Exists Beyond or Apart From Created Realities. So mathematically, We Say That GOD, **G**, Is Greater Than {>} Reality, **R**.

While reality, **R**, may be quantified in some fashion, GOD cannot be quantified, so a complete definition of **G** is not possible.]

[12a] Wise: having or showing experience, knowledge, and good judgement (*Oxford English Dictionary*).

[12b] Faith-based Arguments: Faith as a belief that is not empirically proven can be reasonable or blind. For example, I have reasonable faith that the sun will rise tomorrow. Why? Because the sun has risen every day so far… It's based on empirical evidence and reason, but it is faith… Then there is blind faith, which is a belief in something without such evidence (*https://www.reddit.com/r/DebateReligion/comments/30dt7g/the_problem_with_faithbased_arguments/ archived 12/7/2020*).

> Religion, however corrupted, is still better than no religion at all. The doctrine of a future state is so strong and necessary a security to morals that we never ought to abandon or neglect it. (*Hume 1776, 1787*)

Whenever both probability and utility values are known, one should choose to do an act which has the greatest expected utility (*Pascal*). The decision cannot be avoided (*William James*).

> There are cases where a fact cannot come at all unless a preliminary faith exists in its coming. (*William James, The Varieties of Religious Experience* [New York: Modern Library, 1902]).

[*GOD—The Dimensional Revelation* Reveals That GOD Is Involved With Your Consciousness. Your Consciousness Cannot Be Denied. It Is Self-Evident To You, so no faith is required for You To Participate With GOD.]

[12c] Clarity: The quality of being coherent and intelligible (*Oxford English Dictionary*).

[12d] precision: the quality, condition, or fact of being exact and accurate (*Oxford English Dictionary*).

[12e] narrowly: in a narrow manner, not allowing for exceptions (*www.vocabulary.com*).

without flexibility or latitude (www.definitions.net).

[12f] groundbreaking: something innovative, pioneering or that has never been done before (*www.yourdictionary.com*).

[12g] conditioned: brought or put into a specified state (*www.merriam-webster.com*).

[12h] Refinement: the act or process of improving something or bringing something to a pure state (*www.merriam-webster.com*).

RESEARCH NOTES, CREDITS, AND EXPANSIONS

[12i] Integral: Necessary to make a whole complete, essential or fundamental (*Oxford English Dictionary*).

[12j] society: the aggregate of people living together in a more or less ordered community (*Oxford English Dictionary*).

[12k] nation: a large body of people associated with a particular territory that is sufficiently conscious of its unity to seek or to possess a government peculiarly its own (*www.dictionary.com*).

[12l] institution: a society or organization founded for a religious, educational, social, or similar purpose (*Oxford English Dictionary*).

[12m] Success or Successful: the accomplishment of an aim or purpose (*Oxford English Dictionary*).

[12n] Vested: If you have a vested interest in something, you have a personal stake in its success (*www.vocabulary.com*).

[*GOD—The Dimensional Revelation* Reveals That GOD Has A Stake Only In The Spirit or Soul Of Individual Human Beings. GOD does not have a stake in the success of civilizations, societies, nations, or other Human institutions.

These social institutions may be very meaningful to a Human Being In This Life. There Is Incentive For Humans to improve and sustain these institutions, but they are not directly connected to GOD. The Metastring Connection Is Directly Between The Spirit {Soul} Of Each Spiritual Being And GOD.

This can cause great confusion about a meaningful institution like a school. Such an institution may provide a nexus to organize Human Beings Together, Who Bring Tremendous Light Into This World. This type of institution Is To Be Upheld at all costs, but no school is directly connected to GOD. Only Individual Human Beings Are Directly Connected To GOD. This is why such institutions often deteriorate if they stray from the traditions that bring Positive Spiritual Energy Into Our World. The institution deteriorates if Individuals Find no Meaning or Purpose in the principles and action of the institution. The Tradition Is only Meaningful If It brings Light Into the World.]

[A group of Humans gathering to form a human institution is to be distinguished from A Union of Spirits In the Sixth Heaven As It Approaches The ONE.]

[12o] Animate or Animates: Bring to life (*Oxford English Dictionary*).

[12p] Please The LORD:

> Jesus said, "And he who sent me is with me. He has not left me alone, for I always do the things that are pleasing to him." (*Holy Bible, John 8:29 ESV*)

> So that you will walk in a manner worthy of the Lord, to please Him in all respects, bearing fruit in every good work and

increasing in the knowledge of God. (*Holy Bible, Colossians 1:10 NASB*)

Bibleinoneyear.org lists actions You may Take to Please the Lord (*https://www.bibleinoneyear.org/bioy/commentary/1388*):

1. Praise the Lord.

    I will praise the name of God with song and magnify Him with thanksgiving. And it will please the Lord…(*Holy Bible, Psalm 69:30–31 NASB*)

2. Live in the Light.

    For you were once darkness, but now you are light in the Lord. Live as children of light, (for the fruit of the light consists in all goodness, righteousness and truth) and find out what pleases the Lord. (*Holy Bible, Ephesians 5:8–10, 15–17 NIV*)

3. Make the most of every opportunity.

    Be very careful, then, how you live—not as unwise but as wise, making the most of every opportunity, because the days are evil. Therefore, do not be foolish, but understand what the Lord's will is. (*Holy Bible, Ephesians 5:8–10 NIV*)

4. Be filled with the Spirit.

    Instead, be filled with the Spirit, speaking to one another with psalms, hymns, and songs from the Spirit. Sing and make music from your heart to the Lord, always giving thanks to God the Father for everything, in the name of our Lord Jesus Christ. (*Holy Bible, Ephesians 5:18–20 NIV*)

5. Submit to One Another with Love and Respect.

    Submit to one another out of reverence for Christ…for we are members of his body. (*Holy Bible, Ephesians 5:21, 30 NIV*)

6. Be Humble.

RESEARCH NOTES, CREDITS, AND EXPANSIONS

> These are the ones I look on with favor: those who are humble and contrite in spirit, and who tremble at my word. (*Holy Bible, Isaiah 66:2b NIV*)

7. Look Forward to a World where everything Pleases GOD.

> See, I will create new heavens and a new earth. The former things will not be remembered, nor will they come to mind. But be glad and rejoice forever in what I will create…(*Holy Bible, Isaiah 65:17–18 NIV*)

Also, the LORD may not be Pleased:

> They have chosen their own ways, and they delight in their abominations; so I also will choose harsh treatment for them and will bring on them what they dread. For when I called, no one answered, when I spoke, no one listened. They did evil in my sight and chose what displeases me. (*Holy Bible, Isaiah 66:4 NIV*)

[12q] periodic: appearing or occurring at intervals (*Oxford English Dictionary*).

[13a] Enchant, Enchanted, Enchantment: fill (someone) with great delight; charm. put (someone or something) under a spell; bewitch(*Oxford English Dictionary*).

[13b] Cornucopia: In Greek Mythology, a horn of the goat that suckled Zeus: it becomes full of whatever its owner wants; an overflowing fullness; abundance (collinsdictionary.com).

[13c] Form: a particular way in which a thing exists or appears; a manifestation (*Oxford English Dictionary*).

Also see [2d].

[13d] Reawaken or Reawakening: emerge or cause to emerge again (*Oxford English Dictionary*).

[13e] Sensual: relating to or involving gratification of the senses and physical, especially sexual pleasure (*Oxford English Dictionary*).

[13f] Rating: A classification or ranking of someone or something based on a comparative assessment of their quality, standard, or performance (*Oxford English Dictionary*).

[13g] Spiritual Potential: The components of personality such as inner feeling and personality trait of an individual that influences the human spirit… It may be inactive or active in the personality of an individual. For Example: Faith, patience, and humility of a religious follower… Human spirituality is defined as a sense of belief of a human being. It creates a state of mind that thinks cosmic law is controlled by

something superior to human beings. In other words, spirituality of a human is the humanity aspect that connects human being with something invisible. It also expresses meaning, purpose, and the way of life for a human being (*https://www.chegg.com/ homework-help/describe-roadblocks-distractions-terms-stressors-spiritual-h-chapter-8*).

[13h] Deeper Level: Profound (*www.vocabulary.com*).

Having more importance than it seems, having more significance (*www.englishbaby.com*).

[13i] Little Spirits:

> These little souls gaze upon the world, but their eyes are blind to Him whom all this that we see around us makes manifest… (*On the Soul and Ressurrection, Saint Gregory of Nyssa; p.431; https://www.ccel.org/ccel/schaff/ npnf205.x.iii.ii.html*)

[13j] Bacterium: Bacteria (singular: bacterium) are classified as prokaryotes, which are single-celled organisms with a simple internal structure that lacks a nucleus, and contains DNA that either floats freely in a twisted, thread-like mass called the nucleoid, or in separate, circular pieces called plasmids. Ribosomes are the spherical units in the bacterial cell where proteins are assembled from individual amino acids using the information encoded in ribosomal RNA… There are three basic bacterial shapes: Round bacteria called cocci (singular: coccus), cylindrical, capsule-shaped ones known as bacilli (singular: bacillus); and spiral bacteria, aptly called spirilla (singular: spirillum) (*https://www.livescience.com/51641-bacteria.html*).

[13k] Genetic program: *Genetic code* is the term we use for the way that the four bases of DNA—the A, C, G, and Ts—are strung together in a way that the cellular machinery, the ribosome, can read them and turn them into a protein. In the genetic code, each three nucleotides in a row count as a triplet and code for a single amino acid. So each sequence of three codes for an amino acid. And proteins are made up of sometimes hundreds of amino acids. So the code that would make one protein could have hundreds, sometimes even thousands, of triplets contained in it.

RNA codon table

1st position	2nd position U	2nd position C	2nd position A	2nd position G	3rd position
U	Phe Phe Leu Leu	Ser Ser Ser Ser	Tyr Tyr stop stop	Cys Cys stop Trp	U C A G
C	Leu Leu Leu Leu	Pro Pro Pro Pro	His His Gln Gln	Arg Arg Arg Arg	U C A G
A	Ile Ile Ile Met	Thr Thr Thr Thr	Asn Asn Lys Lys	Ser Ser Arg Arg	U C A G
G	Val Val Val Val	Ala Ala Ala Ala	Asp Asp Glu Glu	Gly Gly Gly Gly	U C A G

Amino Acids

Ala: Alanine
Arg: Arginine
Asn: Asparagine
Asp: Aspartic acid
Cys: Cysteine
Gln: Glutamine
Glu: Glutamic acid
Gly: Glycine
His: Histidine
Ile: Isoleucine
Leu: Leucine
Lys: Lysine
Met: Methionine
Phe: Phenylalanine
Pro: Proline
Ser: Serine
Thr: Threonine
Trp: Tryptophane
Tyr: Tyrosisne
Val: Valine

Lawrence C. Brody, National Human Genome Research Institute, retrieved December 26, 2020

The "genetic program" is the "genome," which obviously consists of "DNA molecules" and "serves as a blueprint, as a set of instructions" made possible by "the code (in the modern sense), with the help of which the program is translated into the individual organisms" (*Mayr 1982, 826–828*).

The discovery of regulator and operator genes and of repressive regulation of the activity of structural genes reveals that the genome contains not only a series of blueprints but a coordinated program of protein synthesis and the means to control its execution (*Jacob and Monod, 1961, 354.*)

> That (part) is programmed, that is the general structure of the body. But, of course, the entire individual is the result of an interaction between his genes and the medium, genes give borders, borders on the size of an individual and say whether the individual will have blue eyes, but it doesn't go further. (*F. Jacob, L'aventure d'un chercheur: François Jacob," interview by E. Lalou and I. Barrère, Institut National de l'Audiovisuel, Bry-sur-Marne, France, available at http://www.ina.fr/video/CPA86010546*)

[*GOD—The Dimensional Revelation* Expands on the relationship between genetic programming, which is physical, with The Individual Human Spirit incarnated by GOD. For example, brain chemistry capable of dimensional analysis may be inherited. The Acts of Understanding, Observing, or Participating In 5th Dimensional Choices To Increase Spiritual Energy is not controlled by genetic chemistry or programming.]

[13l] nutrition: The process of taking in food and using it for growth, metabolism, and repair. Nutritional stages are ingestion, digestion, absorption, transport, assimilation, and excretion (*William C. Shiel Jr., MD, FACP, FACR, https://www.medicinenet.com/ nutrition/definition.htm, retrieved December 26, 2020*).

[13m] metabolize: the sum of the chemical reactions that take place within each cell of a living organism and that provide energy for vital processes and for synthesizing new organic material…the enzyme-mediated chemical reactions that take place in living matter (metabolism). Hundreds of coordinated, multistep reactions, fueled by energy obtained from nutrients and/or solar energy, ultimately convert readily available materials into the molecules required for growth and maintenance (*Hans Kornberg and Sir William Dunn, Professor of Biochemistry, University of Cambridge, Master of Christ's College, Cambridge. Coauthor of Energy Transformations in Living Matter; editor of "Essays in Cell Metabolism," https://www.britannica.com/science/metabolism*).

[13n] material: the matter from which a thing is or can be made (*Oxford English Dictionary*).

[13o] Reproduction: The process by which plants and animals give rise to offspring and which fundamentally consists of the segregation of a portion of the parental body by a sexual or an asexual process and its subsequent growth and differentiation into a new individual (*www.merriam-webster.com*).

byjus.com lists two types of reproduction:

1. Asexual Reproduction:

a. Binary Fission: In this, the cell splits into two, each cell carrying a copy of the DNA from the parent cell. For e.g., amoeba.
b. Budding: In this, a small bud-like outgrowth gives rise to a new individual. The outgrowth remains attached to the organism until it is fully grown. It detaches itself as lives as an individual organism. For e.g., hydra.
c. Fragmentation: In this, the parent organism splits into several parts, and each part grows into a new individual. For e.g., Planaria.
d. Sporogenesis: In this type of reproduction, a new organism grows from the spores. These can be created without fertilization and can spread through wind and animals.

2. Sexual Reproduction: "Sexual reproduction is a type of reproduction that involves the production of an offspring by the fusion of male and female gametes."

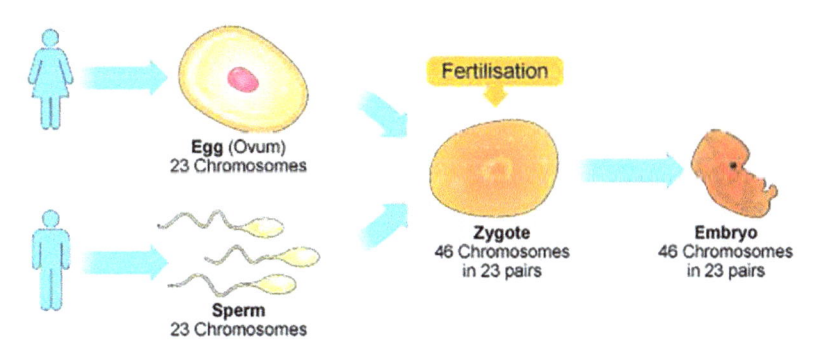

Pinterest.com

Plants reproduce by sexual and asexual means. Vegetative reproduction is the main mode of plant reproduction. Roots such as a corm, stem tuber, rhizomes, and stolon undergo vegetative propagation.

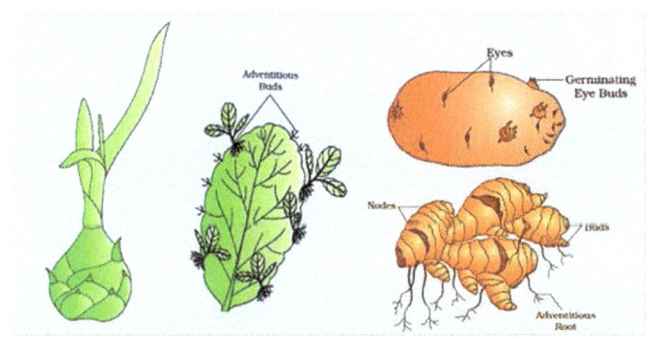

Pinterest.com

Sexual reproduction in plants takes place through pollination in which the pollen grains from the anther of a male flower transfer to the stigma of the female flower.

Animals reproduce sexually, as well as asexually. Sexual reproduction involves the fusion of male and female gametes. This process is known as fertilization. Fertilization can be external or internal. External fertilization is the process in which the male sperm fertilizes the female egg outside the female's body. On the contrary, in internal fertilization, the fusion of male and female gametes takes place inside the body of the female.

Asexual reproduction involves reproduction processes such as binary fission, budding, fragmentation, etc. The organisms have no reproductive systems and therefore no formation of male and female gametes takes place (*https://byjus.com/biology/reproduction/*)

[13p] Consciousness can be in or out: Consciousness: the awareness or deliberate perception of a stimulus is a term meant to indicate awareness. It includes awareness of the self, of bodily sensations, of thoughts and of the environment. In English, we use the opposite word "unconscious" to indicate senselessness or a barrier to awareness…consciousness is more than just being "on" or "off." For instance, Sigmund Freud (1856–1939)—a psychological theorist—understood that even while we are awake, many things lay outside the realm of our conscious awareness… On the one hand, we have the "low awareness" of subtle, even subliminal influences. On the other hand, there is you—the conscious thinking, feeling you which includes all that you are currently aware of, even reading this sentence (*Robert Biswas-Diener and Jake Teeny, Portland State University, The Ohio State University, https://nobaproject.com/modules/states-of-consciousness*).

Sigmund Freud divided human consciousness into three levels of awareness: the conscious, preconscious, and unconscious. Modern psychological approaches to understanding consciousness include developmental, social, and neuropsychological; each contribute a different understanding of what consciousness might be.

RESEARCH NOTES, CREDITS, AND EXPANSIONS

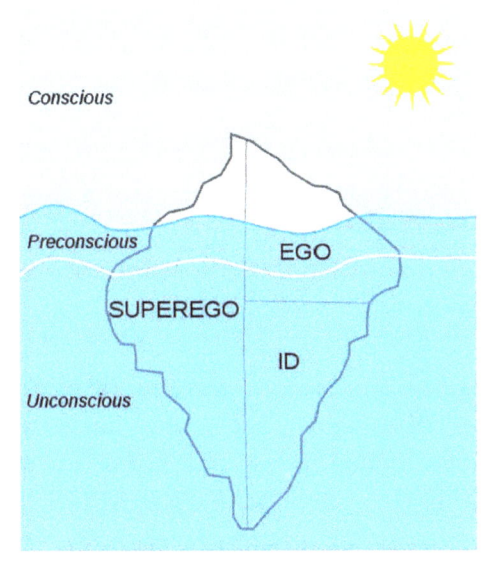

(https://courses.lumenlearning.com/boundless-psychology/chapter/introduction-to-consciousness/)

[*GOD The Dimensional Revelation* Expands this simple illustration by Teaching That Spiritual Energy Enlightens Consciousness as the sun brightens the iceberg in this illustration.]

[13q] Resurrection: Resurrection or anastasis is the concept of coming back to life after death. In a number of religions, a dying-and-rising god is a deity who dies and resurrects. Reincarnation is a similar process hypothesized by other religions, which involves the same person or deity coming back to live in a different body, rather than the same body (*en.wikipedia.org*).

The resurrection of the dead is a standard eschatological belief in the Abrahamic religions. As a religious concept, it is used in two distinct respects: a belief in the resurrection of individual souls that is current and ongoing (Christian idealism, realized eschatology) or else a belief in a singular resurrection of the dead at the end of the world. Some believe the soul is the actual vehicle by which people are resurrected (*en.wikipedia.org*).

> As they entered the tomb, they saw a young man dressed in a white robe sitting on the right side, and they were alarmed. "Don't be alarmed," he said. "You are looking for Jesus the Nazarene, who was crucified. He has risen! He is not here. See the place where they laid him. But go, tell his disciples and Peter, 'He is going ahead of you into Galilee. There you will see him, just as he told you.'" (*Holy Bible, Mark 16:5–7 NIV*)

Jesus said to her, "I am the resurrection and the life. The one who believes in me will live, even though they die; and whoever lives by believing in me will never die." (*Holy Bible, John 11:25–26 NIV*)

And this water symbolizes baptism that now saves you also—not the removal of dirt from the body but the pledge of a clear conscience toward God. It saves you by the resurrection of Jesus Christ. (*Holy Bible, 1 Peter 3:21 NIV*)

Gregory of Nyssa: What! is there no occasion for grieving, I replied to her, when we see one who so lately lived and spoke becoming all of a sudden lifeless and motionless, with the sense of every bodily organ extinct, with no sight or hearing in operation, or any other faculty of apprehension that sense possesses; and if you apply fire or steel to him, even if you were to plunge a sword into the body, or cast it to the beasts of prey, or if you bury it beneath a mound, that dead man is alike unmoved at any treatment? Seeing, then, that this change is observed in all these ways, and that principle of life, whatever it might be, disappears all at once out of sight, as the flame of an extinguished lamp which burnt on it the moment before neither remains upon the wick nor passes to some other place, but completely disappears, how can such a change be borne without emotion by one who has no clear ground to rest upon? We hear the departure of the spirit, we see the shell that is left; but of the part that has been separated we are ignorant, both as to its nature, and as to the place whither it has fled; for neither earth, nor air, nor water, nor any other element can show as residing within itself this force that has left the body, at whose withdrawal a corpse only remains, ready for dissolution.

However far from each other their natural propensity and their inherent forces of repulsion urge them, and debar each from mingling with its opposite, none the less will the soul be near each by its power of recognition, and will persistently cling to the familiar atoms, until their concourse after this division again takes place in the same way, for that fresh formation of the dissolved body which will properly be, and be called, resurrection… the Resurrection is no other thing than the re-constitution of our nature in its original form.

[Ultimately], When such, then, have been purged from it and utterly removed by the healing processes worked out by the Fire, then every one of the things which make up our conception of the good will come to take their place; incorruption, that is, and life, and honour, and grace, and glory, and everything else that we conjecture is to be seen in God, and in His Image, man as he was made. (*Saint Gregory of Nyssa, On the Soul and Ressurrection, 430–431, 466–467, https://www.ccel.org/ccel/schaff/npnf205.x.iii.ii.html*)

[GOD—*The Dimensional Revelation* Reveals That Different Souls Have Different Spiritual Journeys. For One Person, The Reincarnation Of Your Immortal Soul May Occur. For Another Person, Their Individual Soul May Remain Suspended Until A Singular Resurrection Of Many Souls At The Second Coming Of Christ.]

[13r] Algae: The highly varied group of organisms we call "algae" includes terrestrial algae, snow algae, seaweeds, phytoplankton, and "pond scums" (which are composed of stringy masses of cyanobacteria, as well as true algae such as Spirogyra)… Algae are morphologically simple, chlorophyll-containing organisms that range from microscopic and unicellular (single-celled) to very large and multicellular. The algal body is relatively undifferentiated and there are no true roots or leaves. Algae are typically autotrophic, deriving their "food", or energy, from their surroundings in the form of sunlight. They play an important role in food chains and in maintaining the oxygen supply on our planet (*Michael Guiry, https://eol.org/docs/discover/algae*).

[13s] multicelled Creature: organism that is made up of many cells is said to be multicellular. Animals, plants, and fungi are multicellular organisms, and often, there is specialization of different cells for various functions (*biologydictionary.net*).

[13t] chord: A chord, in music, is any harmonic set of pitches/frequencies consisting of multiple notes (also called "pitches") that are heard as if sounding simultaneously (*Benward and Saker, Music: In Theory and Practice, vol. 1 [2003]: 67*).

[13u] Experiential Being: the processes of 'going through', the integration of 'experience' into 'I' and the processes of defence, which are viewed from the perspective of the experiential being. Experience, or 'going through', has five defining characteristics: awareness, motivation, linking, learning and evolution. The processing of 'experience' on two levels, the representational level and the level of the experimental being, leads to the integration of experience into "I". The owning of experience, and not defence, is seen as the key factor in health and disorder (*Br J Med Psychol. September 1995, 68, part 3:223-42*).

[13v] overtones: An overtone is any frequency greater than the fundamental frequency of a sound (*"Overtones and Harmonics," hyperphysics.phy-astr.gsu.edu*).

When a resonant system such as a blown pipe or plucked string is excited, a number of overtones may be produced along with the fundamental tone. In simple cases, such as for most musical instruments, the frequencies of these tones are the same as (or close to) the harmonics (*Elena Prestini, The Evolution of Applied Harmonic Analysis: Models of the Real World, 140, ISBN 0-8176-4125-4*).

[13w] Complementary: Combining in such a way as to enhance or emphasize the qualities of each other or another (*Oxford English Dictionary*).

Complement with an *e* means something that completes something else as when two things go well together (*www.brandtuitive.com*).

Wave and particle were complementary descriptions of the same entity. Particle behaviour was coupled with a wave—a spatial distribution of its probable position. If the position of a particle became exactly known, for example if a photon collided with a photographic plate, then the wave vanished…

An entity in the world will have one facticity but, for an agent, it can have any number of functions. The idea of complementarity in physics arose from dealing with very small energies; it arises in human behaviour from dealing with very great complexity… We do not have a fixed, determinate set of structured responses to events in the world as have robots or insects. Unlike such deterministic agents, our functionality is continually evolving. Our responses to the world, as inferred by other agents, thus have a fundamental indeterminacy. They are continually and flexibly generated from our contingent interactions with our surroundings and with other people. Consequently our detailed behaviour can never be wholly predictable (Sir Alistair MacFarlane, 2010, https://philosophynow.org/issues/80/Complementarity_and_Reality).

[*GOD—The Dimensional Revelation* Utilizes This Definition Of *functionality* To Deduce That The 5th Dimension Is Necessary. The "facticity" of a rock is established in four dimensions. When You Consider the "functionality" of a rock to A Spiritual Being, Then Our Entire Universe Becomes Indeterminate, According To "Choices" of use of that rock and the "Decisions" Of A Spiritual Being In The 5th Dimension.]

[13x] discordant: disagreeing or incongruous, (of sounds) harsh and jarring because of a lack of harmony (*Oxford English Dictionary*).

[13y] Aware Of Its Own Being: Self-awareness is the experience of one's own personality or individuality (*www.merriam-webster.com, en.wikipedia.org*).

It is not to be confused with consciousness in the sense of qualia. While consciousness is being aware of one's environment and body and lifestyle, self-awareness is the recognition of that awareness (*"Self-Awareness with a Simple Brain," Scientific American Mind 23 no. 5, 28–29*).

[13z] Sustaining Glow:

> The unfolding of Your words gives light; It gives understanding to the simple. (*Holy Bible, Psalm 119:130 NIV*)

RESEARCH NOTES, CREDITS, AND EXPANSIONS

[13z1] disharmony: Something not in accord; a conflict. A combination of sounds considered dissonant or unpleasant (*www.yourdictionary.com*).

[13z2] bow out: withdraw or retire from an activity or role (*Oxford English Dictionary*).

[13z3] Way I Is: nothing can be done about a particular condition, because it just has to be that way, and one just has to live with it (*www.urbandictionary.com*).

[*GOD—The Dimensional Revelation* Reveals That Only GOD Is Unchanging. The Processes and Manifestations Of The ONE Are According To The WORD. That Is Just The Way It Is.]

[13z4] Still Small Voice: One's conscience… The term comes from the Bible (*www.dictionary.com*).

> Then He said, "Go out, and stand on the mountain before the Lord." And behold, the Lord passed by, and a great and strong wind tore into the mountains and broke the rocks in pieces before the Lord, but the Lord was not in the wind; and after the wind an earthquake, but the Lord was not in the earthquake; and after the earthquake a fire, but the Lord was not in the fire; and after the fire a still small voice… Then the Lord said to him… (*Holy Bible, 1 Kings 19:11–12, 15 NKJV*)

> When they deliver you over, do not be anxious how you are to speak or what you are to say, for what you are to say will be given to you in that hour. For it is not you who speak, but the Spirit of your Father speaking through you. (*Holy Bible, Matthew 10:19–20 NIV*)

[13z5] Divine Guidance:

> Jesus said: "But the Advocate, the Holy Spirit, whom the Father will send in my name, will teach you all things and will remind you of everything I have said to you." (*Holy Bible, John 14:26 NIV*)

> Ask and it will be given to you; seek and you will find; knock and the door will be opened to you. For everyone who asks receives; the one who seeks finds; and to the one who knocks, the door will be opened. (*Holy Bible, Matthew 7:7–8 NIV*)

GOD—*THE DIMENSIONAL REVELATION*

This illustration Is Offered To Depict GOD, In The Image Of Jesus Christ Approaching the closed door of Your Consciousness. GOD Is Seeking To Share Your Life and Experience and Provide Divine Guidance. Invite The LORD To Join You.

Christ at Heart's Door, Warner Press

RESEARCH NOTES, CREDITS, AND EXPANSIONS

[13z6] superego: The superego (in German *Über-Ich*) reflects the internalization of cultural rules, mainly taught by parents applying their guidance and influence (*Daniel Schacter, Psychology Second Edition [New York City: Worth Publishers, 2009], 481*).

[*GOD—The Dimensional Revelation* Reveals That Your Conscience Is not Your Superego. Your Superego Is Learned Behavior. Your Superego Is An Internal Construct Of Your Mind That Applies Lessons Learned or genetically programmed To Situations.

Your Conscience Is The Still Small Voice of GOD That Instructs From Outside Of You. Often The Instructions Of Your Conscience Are In conflict With Your Superego's Lessons Learned or Rational Deductions. Follow Your Conscience As This Is The Leading Of The LORD.]

[13z7] Freudian psychology: The id, ego, and super-ego are a set of three concepts in psychoanalytic theory describing distinct, interacting agents in the psychic apparatus (defined in Sigmund Freud's structural model of the psyche). The three agents are theoretical constructs that describe the activities and interactions of the mental life of a person. In the ego psychology model of the psyche, the id is the set of uncoordinated instinctual desires; the super-ego plays the critical and moralizing role; and the ego is the organized, realistic agent that mediates, between the instinctual desires of the id and the critical super-ego (*James Strachey, Gen.Ed., Sigmund Freud: The Standard Edition of the Complete Psychological Works of Sigmund Freud. vol. 19 [1999]*).

It [The id] is filled with energy reaching it from the instincts, but it has no organization, produces no collective will, but only a striving to bring about the satisfaction of the instinctual needs subject to the observance of the pleasure principle (*Sigmund Freud, 1933, New Introductory Lectures on Psychoanalysis, 105–6*).

[13z8] Ego: The ego (Latin for *I*, German *Ich*) acts according to the reality principle (i.e., it seeks to please the id's drive in realistic ways that, in the long term, bring benefit rather than grief) (*Gil G. Noam et al., "Ego Development and Psychopathology: A Study of Hospitalized Adolescents," Child Development, Blackwell Publishing on behalf of the Society for Research in Child Development 55, no. 1 [February 1984]: 189–194*).

[13z9] Coping: Coping means to invest one's own conscious effort to solve personal and interpersonal problems in order to try to master, minimize, or tolerate stress and conflict.

The term *coping* generally refers to adaptive (constructive) coping strategies—that is, strategies which reduce stress…the term coping generally refers to reactive coping, i.e. the coping response which follows the stressor. This differs from proactive coping, in which a coping response aims to neutralize a future stressor. Subconscious or unconscious strategies (e.g. defense mechanisms) are generally excluded from the area of coping. The effectiveness of the coping effort depends on the type of stress, the individual, and the circumstances. Coping responses are partly controlled by personality (habitual traits), but also partly by the social environment, particularly the nature of the stressful environment (*Charles S. Carver and Jennifer Connor-Smith, "Personality and Coping," Annual Review of Psychology, 61 [2010]: 679–704*).

[13z10] Extra Sensory Perception (also called ESP): Perception (as in telepathy, clairvoyance, and precognition) that involves awareness of information about events external to the self not gained through the senses and not deducible from previous experience (*www.merriam-webster.com*).

Also see [13z47], [13z48], [13z49], [13z150].

[13z11] Trust and Obey:

> And whatsoever we ask, we receive of him, because we keep his commandments, and do those things that are pleasing in his sight. (*1 John 3:21–22 KJV*)

Trusting God is not the same as understanding Him. Trusting Him means transferring your confidence and hope from yourself to Him. It's more about knowing who God is than what He will do and why… Only when we trust God will we desire and be able to obey Him (*https://kenboa.org/living-out-your-faith/the-eight-spiritual-essentials-part-5-trust-and-obedience/*).

> Jesus said, "I am the vine, you are the branches; he who abides in Me and I in him, he bears much fruit, for apart from Me you can do nothing." (*John 15:5 KJV*)

[*GOD—The Dimensional Revelation* Reveals That Trust In The LORD Is One Primary Meditation That Opens Your Metastring Connection Directly To GOD. GOD Will Respond Through Your Conscience, otherwise Known As The Holy Spirit or Still, Small Voice. Your Receptivity To GOD's Instructions and Acting On This Divine Information Is The Obedience Necessary For Your Spiritual Growth In Any Life.]

[13z12] Tune: To adjust (a musical instrument) to the correct or uniform pitch. To adjust (a receiver circuit such as a radio or television) to the frequency of the required signal (*Oxford English Dictionary*).

[*GOD—The Dimensional Revelation* Uses actions from music or electromagnetism as metaphors for Spiritual Actions. Here the metaphor Is To "Tune" Your Consciousness To Receive Information From GOD.]

> When you want to enter quietude, first tune and concentrate body and mind, so that they are free and peaceful. Let go of all objects, so that nothing whatsoever hangs on your mind, and the celestial mind takes its rightful place in this center. After that,

RESEARCH NOTES, CREDITS, AND EXPANSIONS

lower your eyelids and gaze inward at the chamber of "water." Where the light reaches, true positive energy comes forth in response." (*The Secret of the Golden Flower 4:10, 11, trans. Thomas Cleary [HarperCollins, 1991]*)

[13z13] Grounding: To place on or cause to touch the ground (*www.freedictionary.com*).

Grounding is a particular type of coping strategy that is designed to "ground" you in, or immediately connect you with, the present moment. Because of its focus on being present in the moment, grounding can be considered a variant of mindfulness. It can also be a method of distraction to get you out of your head and away from upsetting thoughts, memories, or feelings (*Matthew Tull, PhD, https://www.verywellmind.com/matthew-tull-phd-2797109*).

[13z14] Spiritual Growth:

> But seek ye first the kingdom of God, and his righteousness; and all these things shall be added unto you. (*Holy Bible, Matthew 6:33 KJV*)

> So as to walk in a manner worthy of the Lord, fully pleasing to him, bearing fruit in every good work and increasing in the knowledge of God. (*Holy Bible, 2 Colossians 1:10 ESV*)

> And we all, with unveiled face, beholding the glory of the Lord, are being transformed into the same image from one degree of glory to another. For this comes from the Lord who is the Spirit. (*Holy Bible, 2 Corinthians 3:18 ESV*)

[13z15] First Heaven:

> Thy kingdom come, Thy will be done in earth, as it is in heaven. (*Holy Bible, Matthew 6:10 KJV*)

> I know what it is to be in need, and I know what it is to have plenty. I have learned the secret of being content in any and every situation, whether well fed or hungry, whether living in plenty or in want. I can do all this through him who gives me strength. (*Holy Bible, Philippians 4:12–13 NIV*)

[*GOD—The Dimensional Revelation* Restates The First Heaven as You, Incarnate In Your Human body Experiencing Divine Bliss In Ordinary Life. Your Individual

Spirit or Soul Has This Extraordinary Opportunity During Your Life In our physical universe to Observe and Participate In The Glorious environment provided by Your senses and This Beautiful Earth.

When You Dream Of A Fun Vacation Filled With New Sights and Entertainment, You Are Dreaming Of The First Heaven. You Want That Vacation To Be Full Of Joy To Restore Your Well-Being and Your Relationships.

If You Take Moments For A Quick Prayer To The LORD, Inviting GOD To Share These Joys With You, Your Vacation Will Be Fulfilling instead of disappointing. You should not have to ask the question, "Are We having fun yet?"]

Stairway to Heaven's Sunset, Galyna Andrushko, Shutterstock_72082513

[13z16] Enjoy or Enjoyed: To take delight or pleasure in (an activity or occasion) (*Oxford English Dictionary*).

[13z17] Inspire or Inspiring: fill (someone) with the urge or ability to do or feel something, especially to do something creative (*Oxford English Dictionary*).

[13z18] Perfection (*noun*): The condition, state, or quality of being free or as free as possible from all flaws or defects.

Perfect (*verb*): the action or process of improving something until it is faultless or as faultless as possible (*Oxford English Dictionary*).

Theosis (Greek: θέωσις) or deification (deification may also refer to apotheosis, lit. "making divine") is a transformative process whose aim is likeness to or union with God as taught by the Eastern Orthodox Church and the Byzantine Catholic Churches. As a process of transformation, theosis is brought about by the effects of

RESEARCH NOTES, CREDITS, AND EXPANSIONS

catharsis (purification of mind and body) and theoria (illumination with the vision of God) (*en.wikipedialorg/theosis*).

[*GOD—The Dimensional Revelation* Advises The Enlightening Technique Of "Stopping And Seeing." "Stopping" Is To Be Still. Do not look for a better place or a better time. It Is Right Here, Right Now. "Seeing" is Participating In This Perfection. See it. Hear It. Smell It. Taste It. Feel It. The Light Circulates As You Receive GOD With You In This Perfection. See also [13z57].]

[13z19] Move Up or Moving Up: To cause someone or something to go higher or more forward (idioms.thefreedictionary.com).

[13z20] Enhance or Enhanced: intensify, increase, or further improve the quality, value, or extent of (*Oxford English Dictionary*).

[13z21] Humble Offering: not proud or haughty; not arrogant or assertive; reflecting, expressing, or offered in a spirit of deference or submission (*www.merriam-webster.com*).

[13z22] Well-received: having been greeted or reviewed with approval (*www.collinsdictionary.com*).

[13z23] Invigorate or Invigoration: to give vigor to, fill with life and energy; energize (*www.dictionary.com*).

[13z24] Reorientation: to orient (someone or something) again or differently, to change the orientation or direction of (something or someone) (*www.merriam-webster.com*).

[13z25] Rush: "to feel a high" or "to feel an intense sensation of excitement" (*https://forum.wordreference.com/threads/to-feel-the-rush*).

[13z26] Enrich, Enriching, or Enriched: improve or enhance the quality or value of (*Oxford English Dictionary*).

[13z27] Given: bestowed as a gift; conferred. or: stated, fixed, or specified (www.dictionary.com).

[13z28] Amazing: causing great surprise or wonder; astonishing. startlingly impressive (*Oxford English Dictionary*).

[13z29] Join: to put or bring together so as to form a unit (*www.merriam-webster.com*).

[*GOD—The Dimensional Revelation* Reveals That The Joining Of GOD With Your Consciousness May Be Momentary, Periodic, or A Permanent Merger. This May Be Sharing Your Experience As Two Separate Beings.

When GOD Chooses To Merge Into Your Consciousness Experience More Deeply, Joining Together Is A Reunification With GOD. You and GOD Have Become One Being In That Manifestation Of Reality.

You Must Experience This To Whatever Degree Of Union That You Can With GOD, To Understand.]

[13z30] Reactive: acting in response to a situation rather than creating or controlling it (*Oxford English Dictionary*).

GOD—THE DIMENSIONAL REVELATION

[13z31] mundane: of this earthly world rather than a heavenly or spiritual one, lacking interest or excitement; dull (*Oxford English Dictionary*).

[13z32] Exchanged: give something and receive something of the same kind in return (*Oxford English Dictionary*).

[13z33] Self-Esteem: Self-esteem is knowing you can conduct yourself confidently in every situation. Outwardly, you are successful, which contributes to your self-esteem. But it's possible to experience and act with self-esteem while having little self-respect. An inflated ego may be borne from too much self-esteem or when you realized just how important and special you are inspired by mental imbalances. People with a huge ego sometimes feel unequal to others because deep inside, they feel worthless and undeserving of respect (*blog.mindvalley.com, January 16, 2019*).

[13z34] Excellence: the quality of being outstanding or extremely good (*Oxford English Dictionary*).

[13z35] Act Purposefully: having a use or showing determination to achieve a specific aim (*www.yourdictionary.com*).

> The essence of the great Way is to act purposefully without striving. Because of non-striving, one does not cling to local conventions, forms, or images… (*The Secret of the Golden Flower 8:3, trans. Thomas Cleary [HarperCollins, 1991]*)

[13z36] Self-Respect: If you respect yourself, you believe you're a worthy individual. And when you feel worthy, you believe you are deserving of love and respect. And when you command respect from others around you, they'd start to appreciate you more and take you more seriously. You will display strong character with the willingness to accept responsibility for your own life, and you'll fight for your values and beliefs, no matter what. This will make everyone else take note and admire your courage. When you respect yourself, the ego is still naturally present but does not play a huge part in your actions. The person with self-respect simply likes themselves, which is not contingent on their own personal successes or failures. Respect your body. Take care of it and pamper yourself often. Live healthily and make exercise a lifestyle priority (*Blog.mindvalley.com, January 16, 2019*).

[13z37] Regret: a feeling of sadness, repentance, or disappointment over something that has happened or been done (*Oxford English Dictionary*).

[13z38] Band: A group of people who join together to form a band to create, play, perform and sing lyrics, instruments, songs and music together (*www.definitions.net*).

[13z39] Affecting: to act on, produce an effect or change in (*www.dictionary.com*).

[13z40] Second Heaven:

> Those whom I love, I reprove and discipline, so be zealous and repent. Behold, I stand at the door and knock. If anyone

hears my voice and opens the door, I will come in to him and eat with him, and he with me. (*Holy Bible, Revelation 3:19–20 ESV*)

In the same way, let your light shine before others, that they may see your good deeds and glorify your Father in heaven. (*Matthew 5:16 NIV*)

[GOD—*The Dimensional Revelation* Recognizes many different Accounts Of The Second Heaven. The most Fruitful of These Is GOD Participating In Our Fused Reality Through Your Conscious Effort. The Periodic or Occasional Aspect Of A Sharing Relationship With GOD and Others, Participating In Your Consciousness in A Human Life is Indicated In The Verse above.]

[13z41] Garden of Eden: The name Eden means 'delight.' This delight does not mean 'happiness' as we use the term, but the joy that comes through being intimately connected with God (*Helen Calder, https://www.enlivenpublishing.com/2012/10/03/life-in-eden-heaven-on-earth-is-our-inheritance/*).

In Eden, Adam and Eve walked and talked with the Father. As they heard what was on His heart, they were able to carry out His purposes on the earth through the authority He had conferred to them (*David McCracken, "Ministries: Prophetic Ministry That Empowers the Church"*).

[13z42] Fed or Feed: to insert and deposit (something) repeatedly or continuously (*www.merriam-webster.com*).

[13z43] Separation Anxiety: excessive fear or worry about separation from home or an attachment figure (*https://www.psychologytoday.com/us/conditions/separation-anxiety*).

[13z44] Spiritual Loss: spiritual loss as evidenced by expression of feelings of having temporarily lost or terminated the love of God, fear that one's relationship with God has been threatened, and/or a feeling of emptiness with regard to spiritual things (*en.wikipedia.org*).

[13z45] nexus: a connection or series of connections linking two or more things, a connected group or series, the central and most important point or place (*Oxford English Dictionary*).

[13z46] unnoticed: unobserved, disregarded, unseen, ignored, overlooked (*www.collinsdictionary.com*).

[13z47] Astral Projection: *Astral projection* (or astral travel) is a term used in esotericism to describe an intentional out-of-body experience (OBE) (*Mario Varvoglis, Out-Of-Body Experiences*); (*Myers, Frederic W. H. Myers, "Astral Projection," Journal for Spiritual & Consciousness Studies [2014]: 37*).

Astral Projection assumes the existence of a soul or consciousness called an "astral body" that is separate from the physical body and capable of travelling outside it throughout the universe (*John L. Crow, "Taming the Astral Body: The Theosophical*

Society's Ongoing Problem of Emotion and Control," Journal of the American Academy of Religion [2012]: 80).

[13z48] Clairvoyance or Seeing: The supposed faculty of perceiving things or events in the future or beyond normal sensory contact (*Oxford English Dictionary*).

Clairvoyance is a French word that means "Clear Seeing." It's a psychic ability, the intuitive 6th Sense, and the subtle perception that allows us to see energy. We have our usual 5 senses of the body (touch, taste, sight, smell, hearing), and we also have many psychic senses that the spirit uses to receive more subtle information beyond the five ordinary senses.

Clairvoyance works with your Spiritual Eye rather than the physical eyes. The spiritual eye is the 6th Chakra, or Third Eye, and it is an energy center in the midbrain, behind the forehead.

Chakra is a Sanskrit word that means "wheel" or "energy center." A chakra is like a spinning wheel of light and energy. Chakras contain our spiritual information. They help the spirit process information, much like the five senses process information for the body. The spirit receives information using many different chakras, and each chakra has a spiritual or psychic ability. Clairvoyance is the Spiritual ability of the 6th chakra.

Clairvoyance is a "psychic" ability, and there are many more psychic abilities in addition to Clairvoyance.

The word "psychic" stems from the Greek, and it means "Soul Personality Energy." All of us have soul personality energy. This is the energy of a spirit. It's what transcends material existence and allows us to be so much more. Soul personality energy contains the entire mystical realm. We each also have "body personality energy." Body personality energy is related to time and space, and it's this energy that allows us to take care of our every day basics.

The good news is you don't have to become Clairvoyant. You already are! The trick is to access your inherent ability. This ability is located in your head, but it's different than your thinking centers, which perform a totally different function (*https://clairvoyanthawaii.com/what-is-clairvoyance/*).

[*GOD—The Dimensional Revelation* Emphasizes Seeing. This Seeing Is not just using the sense of sight and making deductions or inferences from what You see. Seeing Is A Spiritual Union With GOD Manifesting Many Wonders In Your Consciousness. Divine Manifestation May Occur To You With The Heightening Of Any Of The Five physical senses. Seeing May Also Occur As An Extrasensory Perception.

When You Experience Tears Of Joy Upon Witnessing An Event, You Are Seeing. When You Experience An Inexplicable Rush Of Feeling, You Are Seeing. When You Have A Vision Of The Future, You Are Seeing. When You Appreciate Music And You Experience A Thrill, You Are Seeing. The Varieties Of Experience You Share With GOD Are So Diverse No Living Creature Can Know Them All.

Practice Seeing As You Are Able. You Will See More Broadly As You Advance Along Your Spiritual Journey.]

[13z49] Telekinesis: The supposed ability to move objects at a distance by mental power or other nonphysical means (*Oxford English Dictionary*).

No conclusive evidence was ever found to support telekinetic abilities (*Doug Bonderud Jun 17th 2020; Jun 17th 2020 https://now.northropgrumman.com/are-telekinetic-powers-the-next-step-in-human-evolution/*).

[The Author Of GOD—*The Dimensional Revelation* has never experienced telekinesis. This Author has willed others to move objects by request, but that is not Telekinesis.]

[13z50] Telepathy: Telepathy (from the Greek τηλε, tele, "distant"; and πάθεια, patheia, "feeling") is the claimed ability of humans and other creatures to communicate information from one mind to another, without the use of extra tools such as speech or body language. Considered a form of extra-sensory perception or anomalous cognition, telepathy is often connected to various paranormal phenomena such as precognition, clairvoyance and empathy (*https://psychology.wikia.org/wiki/Telepathy*).

[The Author Of GOD—*The Dimensional Revelation* Frequently Experiences Telepathy and, Less Frequently, Other Forms Of Precognition, Such As Clairvoyance. One verification Of The Reality Of Something Is Conscious Experience. Hence, The Existence Of Telepathy and Clairvoyance Is proven To This Author.]

[13z51] embryo or embryonic: An embryo is the early stage of development of a multicellular organism. In general, in organisms that reproduce sexually, embryonic development is the part of the life cycle that begins just after fertilization and continues through the formation of body structures, such as tissues and organs. Each embryo starts development as a zygote, a single cell resulting from the fusion of gametes (i.e., fertilization of a female egg cell by a male sperm cell).

The view of early Christians on the moment of ensoulment is said to have been Pythagorean, which says that the soul was infused at the moment of conception. However, another view that only a formed fetus possessed a human soul also became a belief sometime later, resulting in the ongoing 'pro-life' and 'pro-choice' argument (*Navanwita Sachdev, https://sociable.co/science/when-life-begins-genome-awakening-meets-religious-ensoulment/*).

[13z52] Welcome: to receive or accept (something) with happiness or pleasure (*www.merriam-webster.com*).

[13z53] Redemption: In Christian theology, redemption (Greek: apolutrosis) refers to the deliverance of Christians from sin (*Leon Morris and Redemptio Redeemer, The New Bible Dictionary [Grand Rapids: William B. Eerdmans Publishing Company, 1962], 1078–1079*) with or infilling of the Holy Spirit and comprehends in one experience the cleansing of the heart from sin and the abiding, indwelling presence of the Holy Spirit, empowering the believer for life and service (*"Christian Holiness*

GOD—THE DIMENSIONAL REVELATION

and Entire Sanctification," Church of the Nazarene Manual 2017–2021, Church of the Nazarene, retrieved October 25, 2018).

> The mystery of Christ's redemption was not absent in any previous era, but it was made known under different symbols. (*St. Augustine, Fourth Century AD*)

[13z54] Eternal: without beginning or end; lasting forever; always existing (opposed to temporal): eternal life. perpetual; ceaseless; endless (*www.dictionary.com*).

> In hope of eternal life, which God, who never lies, promised before the ages began. (*Holy Bible, Titus 1:2 ESV*)

[13z55] Devotional Service To The LORD: Hearing, chanting, remembering, serving, worshiping, praying, obeying, maintaining friendship and surrendering everything. By the practice of these nine elements of devotional service one is elevated to spiritual consciousness (*Kṛṣṇa Consciousness. Baghavad Gita 9:1 Purport, The Baghavad-Gita As It Is, A. C. Bhaktivedanta Swami Prabhupada, 1968*).

[*GOD—The Dimensional Revelation* Expresses That These Devotional Techniques Of Connecting To GOD Are Taught By The LORD Jesus Christ, Gautama Buddha, As Well As Krishna and Other Masters. The Truth Transcends The Period In History or The People Instructed By Divine Instruments Of GOD.]

[13z56] Third Heaven:

> And you have made them a kingdom and priests to our God, and they shall reign on the earth. (*Holy Bible, Revelation 5:10 ESV*)

> I know a man in Christ who fourteen years ago—whether in the body I do not know, or out of the body I do not know, God knows—such a man was caught up to the third heaven. (*Holy Bible, 2 Corinthians 12:2 NASB*)

[*GOD—The Dimensional Revelation* Recognizes Many Different Accounts Of The Third Heaven. The Most Fruitful Of These Is GOD Participating In Our Fused Reality Through Your Conscious Effort To Be GOD's Instrument In This Human Life. This Level Of Connection With GOD Is Very Fulfilling.]

[13z57] Turning The Light Around: Also known as "Circulating the Light" (*https://ww.goldenelixir.com/jindan/secret_of_the_golden_flower.html*).

RESEARCH NOTES, CREDITS, AND EXPANSIONS

Before you continuously practice stopping and continue it by seeing, practice seeing and continue it by stopping. This is the twin cultivation of stopping and seeing. This is turning the light around. The turning around is stopping, the light is seeing. Stopping without seeing is called turning around without light; seeing without stopping is called having light without turning it around. Remember this. (*The Secret of the Golden Flower 3:17–18, trans. Thomas Cleary [HarperCollins, 1991]*)

In the original creation there is positive light… The light rays of the human body all flow upward into the aperture of space. (*The Secret of the Golden Flower 3:4, 8, trans. Thomas Cleary [HarperCollins, 1991]*)

Therefore, once you turn the light around, the energies throughout the body all rise. (*The Secret of the Golden Flower 1:12, trans. Thomas Cleary [HarperCollins, 1991]*)

Turning the light around is not turning around the light of one body, but turning around the very energy of Creation. (*The Secret of the Golden Flower 3:6, trans. Thomas Cleary [HarperCollins, 1991]*)

People experience higher things individually, according to their faculties and capacities…it is necessary for you to attain faith on your own. Only then is the true primal unified energy present. (*The Secret of the Golden Flower 4:10, 11, trans. Thomas Cleary [HarperCollins, 1991]*)

With each level of progress in practice, the efflorescence of the light increases in magnitude, and the method of turning around becomes subtler. Previously one controlled the inside from the outside; now one abides in the center and controls the outside. (*The Secret of the Golden Flower 8:7, trans. Thomas Cleary [HarperCollins, 1991]*)

If you are able to perform the correct technique, the method of turning around the light works whether you are walking, standing, sitting, or reclining. (*The Secret of the Golden Flower 10, trans. Thomas Cleary [HarperCollins, 1991]*)

GOD—THE DIMENSIONAL REVELATION

Master Lu-Tsu said, Where there is a gradual success in producing the circulation of the light, a man must not give up his ordinary occupation in doing it. (*The Secret of the Golden Flower*, trans. Richard Wilhelm [1929], translated into English by Cary F. Baynes [1962], chapter 7, 51).

The method of inner development which produces a divine Immortal uses man's ability to "reflect back his brightness to light up within." (*Yuyan, Commentary on the Cantong Qi, Triplex unity*, second c., Taoist text)

[*GOD—The Dimensional Revelation* Emphasizes This Advanced Esoteric Teaching Of Buddhism and Taoism As The Most Important For You To Approach GOD. Specifically, Enlightenment Is The Rising or "Firing" Of The Light Within Your Body. This Occurs Through Stopping Ordinary Consciousness, Seeing The Perfection, and Allowing The Light To Rise Up In Your Body. This Spiritual Practice Is To Realize GOD As Light. This Light Exists Within You and Outside You. You Must Turn The Light Around To See Within You. When You Appreciate The Light, You Turn The Light Around Again To Project The Light Outside Of You. This Is also How GOD Channels Spiritual Energy To and Through You.

Classically, The Light Is Received From GOD At Your Center. When You Become Still As The Void, Spiritual Energy Crystalizes As The Clear Light At Your Center. It Rises In Your Body As The Thrill Of Kundalini Rising. This Light Projects Brilliantly Through The Chakra at the top of Your Head To Share Back To GOD. This Is One Way GOD Participates With You.

When You Master The Light, You May Channel The Rising Spiritual Energy Through The Lotus Chakra between Your Eyes, Sharing It With Other Spiritual Creatures. The Light May Be Shared In So Many Ways. GOD Is In Every Kind Word or Caring Touch.

The Spiritual Energy Created In Turning The Light The Spiritual Energy Created In Turning The Light Around Explains Why Spiritual Energy Increases As It Is Used {Appreciated}. It also Explains Why Spiritual Energy Is Unlimited.

This Truth Is Recognized As The Essence Of Worship or Meditation In All True Religions. Let Us Not Limit Ourselves With An Understanding Of GOD That Is too narrow. Understanding GOD Is Participating With GOD In Your Consciousness.]

Also Recall [6z180].

[13z58] Swell or Swells (*noun*): a gradual increase in sound, amount, or intensity.

Swell (*verb*): to increase in size, magnitude, number, or intensity (*www.vocabulary.com*).

[13z59] Recipient: a person or thing that receives or is awarded something (*Oxford English Dictionary*).

RESEARCH NOTES, CREDITS, AND EXPANSIONS

[13z60] Reassure or Reassured: give or restore confidence in, cause to feel sure or certain (www.vocabulary.com).

[13z61] Gathering: an assembly or meeting, especially a social or festive one or one held for a specific purpose (*Oxford English Dictionary*).

[13z62] The Secret Of The Golden Flower:

> The golden flower is light…one light within. (*The Secret of the Golden Flower 1:10*, trans. Thomas Cleary [HarperCollins, 1991])

> Now I am bringing to light the source message of the golden flower of absolute unity. The absolute unity refers to what cannot be surpassed… The doctrine I transmit directly brings up working with essence and does not fall into a secondary method. (*The Secret of the Golden Flower 1:8-9*, trans. Thomas Cleary [HarperCollins, 1991])

The *Secret of the Golden Flower* ("Tai Yi Jin Hua Zong Zhi", 《太乙金華宗旨》), is one of the most important Daoist [Taoist] classics, attributed to the famous Chinese immortal Lü Dongbin (798 C.E. - ?) who is believed to have lived on earth for more than 800 years. Passed on as an oral tradition for centuries, it was written down on wooden tablets during the Song dynasty by a student of Lü Dongbin, Wang Chongyang (1113–1170). It is one of the few Daoist [Taoist] classics that documents the Daoist orthodox "pre-heavenly" approach to cultivating the "golden elixir" (jin-dan, the elixir of life or immortality) that was predominant before the Song dynasty. Largely ignored by Chinese scholars, it became famous in the West when it was translated into German as *Das Geheimnis der Goldenen Blüte: ein chinesisches Lebensbuch* by Richard Wilhelm (1873–1930), a scholar of Chinese classical philosophy. The book was then translated into English and several other languages, and a new English translation was produced in 1991 by Thomas Cleary.

"The Secret of the Golden Flower" is an esoteric guide to Daoist meditation techniques, using poetic imagery that informs and confirms the experiences of meditation practitioners according to their own predispositions. The guide describes milestones that mark progress in the course of meditation practice, and the phenomenon that may be observed at each stage of development. The "golden flower" refers to a bright image, or mandala, that the practitioner will see in front of the midpoint between his or her eyes after developing the practice of meditation. Daoists believe this bright image is closely related to the "Original Essence," "Golden Flower," or "Original Light," and is a sign that the practitioner is entering the first level of the immortal essence… Stage 2 represents an emergence of meditative consciousness. Stage 3 is characterized by a meditative awareness that exists even in mundane, daily life. Stage 4 represents a higher meditative perception, where all conditions are recognized (*https://www.newworldencyclopedia.org/entry/The_Secret_of_the_Golden_Flower*).

[13z63] Lotus Blossom: It symbolizes the realization of inner potential and in Tantric and Yogic traditions the lotus symbolizes the potential of an individual to harness the flow of energy moving through the chakras (often depicted as wheel like lotuses) flowering as the thousand -petaled lotus of enlightenment at the top of the skull (*Jack Tresidder, The Hutchinson Dictionary of Symbols [London: Duncan Baird Publishers, 1997], 126*).

(jaboo2foto/Shutterstock 678970549)

[13z64] Radiate: To emit (light or energy) in rays or waves (*www.thefreedictionary.com*).

[13z65] Behold: see or observe (a thing or person, especially a remarkable or impressive one) (*Oxford English Dictionary*).

[13z66] Emanate or Emanating: to flow out, issue, or proceed, as from a source or origin; come forth (*www.Dictionary.com*).

[13z67] Song: Singing or vocal music (*Oxford English Dictionary*).

In general, that which is sung or uttered with musical modulations of the voice, whether of the human voice or that of a bird (*www.KJVdictionary.com*).

[*GOD—The Dimensional Revelation* Recognizes The Appreciation Of Music, whether In The Hearing Of Music or The Creation Of Music, As A Primary Meditative Technique.

Many Seekers have difficulty Concentrating To Meditate. You May Find A Natural and Easy Way To Enter Deep Meditation In Listening To Music To Be Elevated. Ride The Music. Allow The Music To Carry You Away To Enhanced Consciousness. Your Experience Appreciating Music In Your Soul Is Turning The Light Inwardly to Enhance Your Spirit. It Is One Manifestation Of The First Heaven.

If You Can Share This With Others, It Is A Manifestation Of The Second Heaven.

RESEARCH NOTES, CREDITS, AND EXPANSIONS

When You Become Aware That You Are An Instrument Of This Enhancement, The Circulation Of The Light, Then You Are In The Third Heaven. Reunification With GOD Is Happening. GOD Is Very Pleased.]

"Sounding Silence" reprinted by kind permission of Michael Cheval, painter

[13z68] Affinity: a spontaneous or natural liking or sympathy for someone or something (*Oxford English Dictionary*).

[13z69] Manage: to handle or direct with a degree of skill (*www.merriam-webster.com*).

> The word movement is another word for control. Since you can cause movement by vigorous action, how could you not be able to cause stillness by pure quietude? (*The Secret of the Golden Flower 4:11*, trans. Thomas Cleary [HarperCollins, 1991])

[13z70] Ancestor or Ancestors: any person from whom one is descended (*www.collinsdictioary.com*).

[13z71] Loved Ones: close or cherished relation (*www.dictionary.com*)

[13z72] Fleeting: passing swiftly; vanishing quickly; transient; transitory (*www.dictionary.com*).

[13z73] Permanence: the state or quality of lasting or remaining unchanged indefinitely (*Oxford English Dictionary*).

[13z74] Uncovered: To make known; bring to light; disclose; reveal (*www.merriam-webster.com*).

[13z75] Guest: a person who is invited to visit the home of or take part in a function organized by another (*Oxford English Dictionary*).

[13z76] Humble Reverence: We worship God in humble reverence when we rightly recognize His Person and respond appropriately to His presence (*http://kenpulsmusic.com/gatheredworship12.html*).

[13z77] Free or Freed: not under the control or in the power of another; able to act or be done as one wishes (*Oxford English Dictionary*).

[13z78] shackles: a shackle is a literal or figurative restraint that keeps you in place or prevents you from doing what you want. A device, usually one of a pair connected to a chain, that encircles the ankle or wrist of a prisoner or captive (*yourdictionary.com*).

[13z79] guilt: a feeling of shame or regret as a result of bad conduct (*www.merriam-webster.com*).

The fact of having committed a specified or implied offense or crime (*Oxford English Dictionary*).

[13z80] kill: to cause the death of (a person, animal, or plant); to end the life of (someone or something); to cause the end of (something) (*www.merriam-webster.com*).

[13z81] Verifiable Divine Permission:

> Something is permitted if there is no moral obligation to prevent it. (*"The Theory of Divine Permission According to Scotus' Ordinatio I 47, EEFDekker, Koninklijke Brill [NV, Leiden, 2000], Vivarium 38, 2, 231*)

God positively governs some acts by permitting them. It has to be permission of particular actions and not merely the permission of certain types of action (*http://triablogue.blogspot.com/2009/08/divine-permission.html*).

> Jesus Said: "Do not be afraid of those who kill the body but cannot kill the soul. Rather, be afraid of the One who can destroy both soul and body in hell. Are not two sparrows sold for a penny? Yet not one of them will fall to the ground outside your Father's care." (*Holy Bible, Matthew 10:28–29 NIV*)

[13z82] Justify: show or prove to be right or reasonable, declare or make righteous in the sight of God (*Oxford English Dictionary*).

[13z83] taking any Life: Thou shalt not kill (LXX; οὐ φονεύσεις) (KJV), You shall not murder (Hebrew: לֹא תִרְצָח ; lo tirṣaḥ), is a moral imperative included as one of the

RESEARCH NOTES, CREDITS, AND EXPANSIONS

Ten Commandments in the Torah (Exodus 20:13) (*Exodus 20:1–21; Deuteronomy 5:1–23; Ten Commandments; New Bible Dictionary, Second Edition [Tyndale House, 1982], 1174–1175*).

The imperative not to kill is in the context of unlawful killing resulting in bloodguilt.

> Whoever sheds the blood of man, by man shall his blood be shed, for God made man in his own image. (*Holy Bible, Genesis 9:6 NIV; Torah Bereishit, Genesis 9:6*)

In Hinduism, the concept of ahimsa bans the killing of any living being, no matter how small.

> The interruption of another jiva's ("chord," "manifestation of Atman," living being, or any entity imbued with a life force) spiritual progress causes one to incur karma—the accumulated effects of past actions. (*www.britannica.com*)

"Principle of Permissible Harm" states that one may harm in order to save more if, and only if, the harm is an effect or an aspect of the greater good itself (*Frances M. Kamm, Morality, Mortality Vol. II: Rights, Duties, and Status [New York: Oxford University Press, 1996]*).

[*GOD—The Dimensional Revelation* cautions that impermissible harm often occurs when You Stand In Judgement Of Another without the clear Leading Of The LORD.]

[13z84] nose ring: a ring put through an animal's nose to lead or control it (*www.merriam-webster.com*).

[13z85] misuse: use (something) in the wrong way or for the wrong purpose (*Oxford English Dictionary*).

[13z86] Deify: worship, regard, or treat (someone or something) as a god (*Oxford English Dictionary*).

[13z87] non-spirituality: not associated with or interested in religious or spiritual matters. 'non-spiritual pursuits' (*Oxford English Dictionary*).

[13z88] Life Force: The force or influence that gives something its vitality or strength (*Oxford English Dictionary*).

Life force is the term given in yoga for one of the two types of energy that are present in all beings. The other type of energy is that of the mind, or consciousness. In the body, life force is thought to be responsible for maintaining all the physical functions, including life, heat and health (*www.yogapedia.com/definition/4984/life-force*).

[13z89] Respect or Respected: a feeling of deep admiration for someone or something elicited by their abilities, qualities, or achievements (*Oxford English Dictionary*).

Courtesies that show respect may include simple words and phrases like "Thank you" in the West or "Namaste" in the Indian subcontinent, or simple physical signs like a slight bow, a smile, direct eye contact, or a simple handshake; however, those acts may have very different interpretations, depending on the cultural context (*en.wikipedia.org, retrieved September 30, 2020*).

[13z90] Worship God only:

> You shall worship the Lord your God and Him only shall you serve. (*Holy Bible, Matthew 4:10 KJV*)

[13z91] Fourth Heaven:

> Then I saw a new heaven and a new earth, for the first heaven and the first earth had passed away, and the sea was no more. And I saw the holy city, new Jerusalem, coming down out of heaven from God, prepared as a bride adorned for her husband. And I heard a loud voice from the throne saying, "Behold, the dwelling place of God is with man. He will dwell with them, and they will be his people, and God himself will be with them as their God. He will wipe away every tear from their eyes, and death shall be no more, neither shall there be mourning, nor crying, nor pain anymore, for the former things have passed away." (*Holy Bible, Revelation 21:1–4 KJV*)

Beatific Vision: the direct knowledge of God enjoyed by the blessed in heaven (*www.mirriam-webster.com*).

In Christian theology, the beatific vision (Latin: *visio beatifica*) is the ultimate direct self-communication of God to the individual person. A person possessing the beatific vision reaches, as a member of redeemed humanity in the communion of saints, perfect salvation in its entirety (i.e., heaven). The notion of vision stresses the intellectual component of salvation though it encompasses the whole of human experience of joy or happiness coming from seeing God finally face-to-face and not imperfectly through faith (*en.wikipedia.org/Beatific Vision*).

[*GOD—The Dimensional Revelation* Encourages You To Pursue The Beatific Vision In Your Soul While Incarnated As A Human Being In This Life. Greater Than Faith, GOD Is Pleased To Participate With You In Your Conscious Experience Here And Now! This Is Spiritual Enlightenment. Seek It!]

RESEARCH NOTES, CREDITS, AND EXPANSIONS

The fourth element of glory, and one Thiselton thinks is an extension of what has already been said, is face-to-face encounter with God. The "presence" of God is often associated with God's "face" (panim) and God's "eyes" (ayin) and God as light—so that heaven is the enjoyment of knowing and experiencing of God face-to-face in all of God's glory and endless depths (*Scot McKnight, "The Four Glories of Heaven," March 7, 2012*).

> No longer will there be any curse. The throne of God and of the Lamb will be in the city, and his servants will serve him. They will see his face, and his name will be on their foreheads. There will be no more night. They will not need the light of a lamp or the light of the sun, for the Lord God will give them light. And they will reign for ever and ever. (*Holy Bible, Revelation 22:3–5 NIV*)

> He will swallow up death forever. The Sovereign LORD will wipe away the tears from all faces; he will remove his people's disgrace from all the earth. The LORD has spoken. In that day they will say, "Surely this is our God; we trusted in him, and he saved us. This is the LORD, we trusted in him; let us rejoice and be glad in his salvation." (*Holy Bible, Isaiah 25:8–9 NIV*)

[Please Notice That Our Teaching Is avoiding much discussion of unheavenly afterlife states of being. Hades and other discontent spiritual states of being can occur during Your Incarnate Lifetime, as well as In Your Afterlife.

Focus on The Heavenly States Of Being, and nothing else matters.]

[13z92] Fifth Heaven: [*GOD—The Dimensional Revelation* Recognizes Many Different Accounts Of The Fifth Heaven. The Most Fruitful Of These Is That Your Individual Soul Is Expanding In Communion With GOD and Other Spiritual Beings. Your Consciousness Begins To Lose Identity {Ego} As You Merge With Them. This Is An Effortless Expansion because Your Consciousness Is No Longer Focused On Yourself. Rather, Your Attention Is Greater According To The Grand Heavenly Environment With Which You Are Sharing.]

This illustration Is Offered to depict The Grand Heavenly Environment With Many Spirits Glorifying GOD:

GOD—*THE DIMENSIONAL REVELATION*

Second Coming by Harry Anderson
(©*By Intellectual Reserve Inc. Courtesy of The Church of Jesus Christ of Latter-day Saints*)

[13z93] Cherubim: A cherub (ˈtʃɛrəb, plural *cherubim*; Hebrew: כְּרוּב kərūv, pl. כְּרוּבִים kərūvîm) is one of the unearthly beings who directly attend to God, according to Abrahamic religions. The numerous depictions of cherubim assign to them many different roles, such as protecting the entrance of the Garden of Eden (*Jewish Encyclopedia, 2002–2011 (1906)*.

Cherubim (al-Karubiyyin) in Islam are usually identified either with a class of angels, dwelling in the sixth heaven, or the angels around the Throne of God. The latter include the canonical four Islamic archangels Gabriel, Michael, Azrael and Raphael, and additionally four more called Bearers of the Throne, a total of eight cherubim (*Moojan Momen, "Studies in Honor of the Late Hasan M. Balyuzi" [Kalimat Press, 1988], 83, ISBN 978-0-933-77072-0*).

[13z94] Seraphim: Tradition places seraphim in the highest rank in Christian angelology and in the fifth rank of ten in the Jewish angelic hierarchy (*The Nag Hammadi Library in English. Harper & Row. 1977. p. 166*).

[13z95] Ophanim: The ophanim or ofanim (Heb. "wheels" אוֹפַנִּים 'ōphannīm; singular: אוֹפָן 'ōphān, ofan), also called galgalim (galgallim, גַּלְגַּלִּים - "spheres", "wheels", "whirlwinds"; singular: galgal, גַּלְגַּל), refer to the wheels seen in Ezekiel's vision of the chariot (Hebrew merkabah) in Ezekiel 1:15-21. One of the Dead Sea scrolls (4Q405) construes them as angels; late sections of the Book of Enoch (61:10, 71:7) portray them as a class of celestial beings who (along with the Cherubim and Seraphim) never sleep, but guard the throne of God (*en.wikipedia.org*).

[13z96] Angels: An angel is a supernatural being in various religions. The theological study of angels is known as angelology.

Abrahamic religions often depict them as benevolent celestial intermediaries between God (or Heaven) and humanity. *"Angels in Christianity." Religion Facts. N.p., n.d. Web. 15 Dec. 2014.* Other roles include protectors and guides for humans, and servants of God. *Augustine of Hippo's Enarrationes in Psalmos, 103, I, 15.* Abrahamic religions describe angelic hicrarchies, which vary by sect and religion. Some angels have specific names (such as Gabriel or Michael) or titles (such as seraph or archangel). Those expelled from Heaven are called fallen angels, distinct from the heavenly host (*en.wikipedia.org*).

Kristus i Getsemane (1873), an angel comforting Jesus before his arrest in the Garden of Gethsemane by Carl Heinrich Bloch (1873)

[13z97] Sixth Heaven:

> For in the one Spirit we were all baptized into one body—Jews or Greeks, slaves or free—and we were all made to drink of one Spirit. (*Holy Bible, 1 Corinthians 12:13 NIV*)

As referred to in the theological doctrine of the communion of saints, in Paradise there is a common and unique vision of the truth and contemplation of the Face of God without any kind of difference between angels or human souls (*en.wikipedia.org*).

> It is just the light that is the creative. By means of its circulation, one returns to the Creative. (*The Secret of the Golden Flower, Richard trans. Wilhelm [1929]; translated into English by Cary F. Baynes [1962]; chapter 2, 26*)

RESEARCH NOTES, CREDITS, AND EXPANSIONS

[*GOD—The Dimensional Revelation* Recognizes Many Different Accounts Of The Sixth Heaven. The Most Fruitful Of These Is That There Is No You. What Was Your Awareness Is Now Spread Throughout The Creative.]

This illustration is Offered as a metaphor with You Represented by the drop of water Merging Into The ONE Represented by the endless water. As You Enter The ONE, Your Qualities Merge. You Have Meaning, so The Effect Of Your Merger Is shown as ripples, Which Dissipate As You Become Fully Spread Throughout The ONE.]

Shutterstock 63991894

[13z98] Spiritual Resonance:

> Resonance is a visceral experience. I believe it is the language through which the soul directs our lives. Symptoms may include tingling, electricity, tears, loss of breath, and a profound sense of aliveness. Being in your soul's resonance often feels like connection, awe, freedom, awareness of something greater than yourself, a recognition, and coming home. The trick is when this moment happens, and it does happen to everyone, slow down and take it in. What is here? If it points you in a direction, follow it. (*Bristol Baughan, "Discover and Follow Your Soul's Resonance," November 21, 2016*)

The patterning of energy emitted by each soul as a result of choices made in thought, word, or deed, brings into proximity energies from the surrounding spiritual environment that resonate with the energies being sent forth. This principle of 'energetic resonance' is magnetic in its effect, for the emitted energies, whether emotional or otherwise, draw to themselves corresponding forces in the spiritual environment which join with these to create a synergy that amplifies the energy in two individuals if we are speaking of a partnership or in a group of individuals if we are speaking of a family, community, or larger collectivity (*GurujiMa, "Resonance—The Shaping of Reality," Light Omega, retrieved July 12, 2020*).

[*GOD—The Dimensional Revelation* Expands These Manifestations Of Spiritual Resonance, Asserting That The Exchange Of Spiritual Energy With GOD May Be Understood To Be Spiritual Resonance, As Spiritual Energy Amplifies In The Exchange. The Same Spiritual Resonance Amplification Occurs In Positive Relationships With Humans or Other Spirits. Spiritual Energy Amplifies Greatly As All Of The Spirits "Sync" Into Perfect Harmony and The Resonance Manifests.]

[13z99] Goal: The end toward which effort is directed (*www.merriam-webster.com*).

[13z100] Immediately Attainable: Attainable: possible to achieve (*dictionary.cambridge.org*).

Immediately: at once; instantly; without any intervening time or space (*Oxford English Dictionary*).

> Yet the revolving of Heaven never stops for a moment. If you are actually able to join yin and yang in tranquility, the whole earth is positive and harmonious; in the right place in your central chamber, all things simultaneously expand to fulfillment. (*The Secret of the Golden Flower 59, trans. Thomas Cleary [HarperCollins, 1991]*)

[13z101] Elijah—Widow of Zarephath's Son:

> Then he [Elijah] stretched himself upon the child three times and cried to the Lord, "O Lord my God, let this child's life come into him again." And the Lord listened to the voice of Elijah. And the life of the child came into him again, and he revived. And Elijah took the child and brought him down from the upper chamber into the house and delivered him to his mother. And Elijah said, "See, your son lives." And the woman said to Elijah, "Now I know that you are a man of God, and that the word of the Lord in your mouth is truth." (*Holy Bible, 1 Kings 17:21–24 ESV*)

[13z102] Elisha—Shunammite Woman's son:

> When Elisha arrived, he went alone into the room and saw the boy lying dead on the bed. He closed the door and prayed to the Lord. Then he lay down on the boy, placing his mouth, eyes, and hands on the boy's mouth, eyes, and hands. As he lay stretched out over the boy, the boy's body started to get warm. Elisha got up, walked around the room, and then went back and

again stretched himself over the boy. The boy sneezed seven times and then opened his eyes. (*Holy Bible, 2 Kings 4:32–35 GNT*)

[13z103] Jesus Christ Bringing the dead back To This Life. Widow of Nain's son:

> As he drew near to the gate of the town, behold, a man who had died was being carried out, the only son of his mother, and she was a widow, and a considerable crowd from the town was with her. And when the Lord saw her, he had compassion on her and said to her, "Do not weep." Then he came up and touched the bier, and the bearers stood still. And he said, "Young man, I say to you, arise." And the dead man sat up and began to speak, and Jesus gave him to his mother. (*Holy Bible, Luke 7:12–15 ESV*)

Jairus Daughter:

> While he was still speaking, someone from the ruler's house came and said, "Your daughter is dead; do not trouble the Teacher anymore." But Jesus on hearing this answered him, "Do not fear; only believe, and she will be well." And when he came to the house, he allowed no one to enter with him, except Peter and John and James, and the father and mother of the child. And all were weeping and mourning for her, but he said, "Do not weep, for she is not dead but sleeping." And they laughed at him, knowing that she was dead. But taking her by the hand he called, saying, "Child, arise." And her spirit returned, and she got up at once. And he directed that something should be given her to eat. (*Holy Bible, Luke 8:49–55 ESV*)

Lazarus:

> Now when Jesus came, he found that Lazarus had already been in the tomb four days… So when Martha heard that Jesus was coming, she went and met him, but Mary remained seated in the house. Martha said to Jesus, "Lord, if you had been here, my brother would not have died. But even now I know that whatever you ask from God, God will give you." Jesus said to her, "Your brother will rise again." Martha said to him, "I know that he will rise again in the resurrection on the last day." Jesus said to her, "I

am the resurrection and the life. Whoever believes in me, though he die, yet shall he live, and everyone who lives and believes in me shall never die. Do you believe this?" She said to him, "Yes, Lord; I believe that you are the Christ, the Son of God, who is coming into the world"… Then Jesus, deeply moved again, came to the tomb. It was a cave, and a stone lay against it. Jesus said, "Take away the stone." Martha, the sister of the dead man, said to him, "Lord, by this time there will be an odor, for he has been dead four days." Jesus said to her, "Did I not tell you that if you believed you would see the glory of God?" So they took away the stone. And Jesus lifted up his eyes and said, "Father, I thank you that you have heard me. I knew that you always hear me, but I said this on account of the people standing around, that they may believe that you sent me." When he had said these things, he cried out with a loud voice, "Lazarus, come out." The man who had died came out, his hands and feet bound with linen strips, and his face wrapped with a cloth. Jesus said to them, "Unbind him, and let him go." (*Holy Bible, John 11:17–26, 38–44 ESV*)

Jesus Own Resurrection:

> Then Jesus began to teach his disciples: "The Son of Man must suffer much and be rejected by the elders, the chief priests, and the teachers of the Law. He will be put to death, but three days later he will rise to life." (*Holy Bible, Mark 8:31 GNT*)

> Now Mary stood outside the tomb crying. As she wept, she bent over to look into the tomb and saw two angels in white, seated where Jesus' body had been, one at the head and the other at the foot. They asked her, "Woman, why are you crying?" "They have taken my Lord away," she said, "and I don't know where they have put him." At this, she turned around and saw Jesus standing there, but she did not realize that it was Jesus. He asked her, "Woman, why are you crying? Who is it you are looking for?" Thinking he was the gardener, she said, "Sir, if you have carried him away, tell me where you have put him, and I will get him." Jesus said to her, "Mary." She turned toward him and cried out in Aramaic, "Rabboni!" [which means "Teacher"]. Jesus said, "Do not hold on to me, for I have not yet ascended to the Father. Go instead to my brothers and tell them, 'I am ascending to my

RESEARCH NOTES, CREDITS, AND EXPANSIONS

Father and your Father, to my God and your God.'" (*Holy Bible, John 29:11–16 ESV*)

[13z104] Near Death Experiences: One of the most celebrated is the story of "Maria," a migrant worker who had an NDE during a cardiac arrest at a hospital in Seattle in 1977. She later told her social worker that while doctors were resuscitating her, she found herself floating outside the hospital building and saw a tennis shoe on a third-floor window ledge, which she described in some detail. The social worker went to the window Maria had indicated and not only found the shoe but said that the way it was placed meant there was no way Maria could have seen all the details she described from inside her hospital room.

Reynolds was effectively dead in both brain and body. Yet after the surgery, she reported having had a powerful NDE, including an out-of-body experience, and accurately recalled several details about what was going on in the operating room, such as the shape of the bone saw used on her skull, snatches of conversations between the medical staff, and the staff listening—rather inappropriately, she remembered thinking—to "Hotel California."

The patient, a 57-year-old man, described floating up to a corner of the room, seeing medical staff work on him and watching himself be defibrillated. According to Parnia's paper, several of the details he described checked out. What's more, after triangulating the patient's description with the workings of the defibrillator, the researchers think he may have seen things that happened for as long as three minutes after his heart stopped.

It was Alexander who really upped the scientific stakes. He studied his own medical charts and came to the conclusion that he was in such a deep coma during his NDE, and his brain was so completely shut down that the only way to explain what he felt and saw was that his soul had indeed detached from his body and gone on a trip to another world and that angels, God, and the afterlife are all as real as can be. (See *Proof of Heaven, by Eben Alexander New York: Simon & Schuster, 2012,* https://www.theatlantic.com/magazine/archive/2015/04/the-science-of-near-death-experiences/)

[13z105] Buddhas: Buddha (/ˈbuːdə, ˈbʊdə/), "awakened one," *Buswell 2004, p. 71.* is a title for someone who is "awake", and has attained "nirvana" and Buddhahood. The title is most commonly used for Gautama Buddha, the founder of Buddhism, who is often simply known as "the Buddha". Buddhahood is the condition and rank of a buddha "awakened one" (*Buddhatva,* बुद्धत्व. *Spoken Sanskrit Dictionary*). This highest spiritual state of being is also termed Samyaksaṃbodhi (Full, complete Awakening).

The title is also used for other beings who have achieved bodhi (awakening), such as the other human Buddhas who achieved enlightenment before Gautam (*en.wikipedia.org*).

In Theravada Buddhism, Buddha refers to one who has become awake through their own efforts and insight, without a teacher to point out the dharma (Sanskrit;

Pali dhamma; "right way of living"). A samyaksam buddha re-discovered the truths and the path to awakening and teaches these to others after his awakening. A pratyekabuddha also reaches Nirvana through his own efforts, but does not teach the dharma to others. An arhat needs to follow the teaching of a Buddha to attain Nirvana, but can also preach the dharma after attaining Nirvana (*John Snelling, The Buddhist Handbook: A Complete Guide to Buddhist Teaching and Practice [London: Century Paperbacks, 1987], 81*).

The concept of antarabhāva, an intervening state between death and rebirth, was brought into Buddhism from the Vedic-Upanishadic philosophical tradition which later developed into Hinduism (*John Bowker, The Concise Oxford Dictionary of World Religions, sv*).

"Bardo" is the state of existence intermediate between two lives on earth. According to Tibetan tradition, after death and before one's next birth, when one's consciousness is not connected with a physical body, one experiences a variety of phenomena. These usually follow a particular sequence of degeneration from, just after death, the clearest experiences of reality of which one is spiritually capable and then proceeding to terrifying hallucinations that arise from the impulses of one's previous unskillful actions. For the prepared and appropriately trained individuals, the bardo offers a state of great opportunity for liberation since transcendental insight may arise with the direct experience of reality; for others, it can become a place of danger as the karmically created hallucinations can impel one into a less than desirable rebirth (*en.wikipedia.org*).

[13z106] Bodhisattva: The word *bodhisattva* is a compound word formed from *bodhi* (spiritual awakening, enlightenment) and *sattva* (a being, essence, spirit). The word can then be translated as "A being set upon enlightenment," "One whose essence is perfect knowledge," or "A being whose essence is enlightenment."

In Buddhism, enlightenment (called bodhi in Indian Buddhism or satori in Zen Buddhism) is when a Buddhist finds the truth about life and stops being reborn because they have reached Nirvana. Once you get to Nirvana, you are not born again into samsara (which is suffering) (*https://simple.wikipedia.org/wiki/Enlightenment*).

Bodhisattvas are enlightened beings who have put off entering paradise in order to help others attain enlightenment (*https://depts.washington.edu/chinaciv/bud/5imgbodd.htm*).

There are three principle meanings of the term *bodhisattva*:

1. In early Buddhism, *bodhisattva* meant "the previous lives of a (or the) Buddha."
2. In Mahayana Buddhism, *bodhisattva* refers to a human being committed to the attainment of enlightenment for the sake of others. Becoming a bodhisattva is the goal of Mahayana Buddhism.

RESEARCH NOTES, CREDITS, AND EXPANSIONS

3. Bodhisattva may also refer in Mahayana Buddhism to archetypal bodhisattvas, mythical beings such as Avalokiteshvara and Manjushri, who are objects of devotion (*Bodhipaksa, October 23, 2006, https://www.wildmind. org/mantras/bodhisattvas*).

[13z107] Prescient Consciousness: Prescience is more than seeing the future. It's a state of limitless awareness not restricted by time or space. It is to have presence in all time, in all places, all at once (*Eric Pepin, Prescient Visions: Having or Showing Knowledge of Events Before They Take Place [paperback], November 9, 2015*).

[13z108] Jump-Start: to start or restart (something) rapidly or forcefully (*www.merriam-webster.com*)

[13z109] Take You There: [A Teaching of Knowledge Provides Human Wisdom. *GOD—The Dimensional Revelation* Clarifies Reality by organizing The Principles Of Operation, Which Create and Sustain Reality. The Dimensions Operational In Reality Are Defined To Expand scientific Understanding and So You Can Understand Creation, Who You Are, what May Be Meaningful To You, and The Ultimate Destination Of Your Being. If You Understand The Principles of Being, Clarified In This Teaching, They Will Take You There.]

[13z110] Endeavors: to exert oneself to do or effect something; make an effort (www.dictionary.com).

[13z111] Reunification With GOD Is Complete: [*GOD—The Dimensional Revelation* Reveals That Differentiation From The ONE Disappears As You Reunite With The ONE. Reunification Is At The Pleasure Of GOD.]

[13z112] Seventh Heaven:

> As a plan for the fullness of time, to unite all things in him, things in heaven and things on earth. (*Holy Bible, Ephesians 1:10 ESV*)

[13z113] Pure Divinity: a human being's basic nature is not confined to the body or the mind. Beyond both of these is the spirit or the spark of God within the soul. This spirit is within us and also within everything we see. All beings and all things are really, in their deepest essence, this pure or divine spirit, full of peace, full of joy and wisdom, ever united with God (*https://www.uri.org/kids/world-religions/hindu-beliefs*).

[13z114] What Reality Was: [*GOD—The Dimensional Revelation* Reveals That physical reality Is Continually Instructed By The WORD To Manifest From GOD In the 10th D Along the physical metastring. The physical metastring Is Constructed In The 9th D to contain all physical universes of the physical membrane system. The physical membrane system is part of 8th-d manifest reality. All physical universes operate according to, and are limited by, quantum mechanics and general relativity. Our universe of matter, and its attendant energies, is one of these physical universes.

GOD—*THE DIMENSIONAL REVELATION*

Physical events occur as a quantum possibility collapses into being. We Know that the event occurred because matter is heavy and it is hard. We verify its being, as it occurs, through Conscious Perception. We also verify its being by physical instrumentation that measures physical reality independently from Human Perception.

Evidence of What Reality Was is the residue remaining as time forces the next situation. You May Observe the next situation along the continuum as it occurs. Also, the processes selecting from and collapsing physical probabilities into being can be Observed. These can be codified for most physical processes when a defined cause regularly results in the same effect.

The past cannot be changed in physical reality. The operational principles of physical reality do not all allow past manifestations to be changed. You May View the past from different perspectives; but as a whole, the past is static, fixed in physical reality.

Do not be misled. The past is not A Construction Of Mind. The residue of past physical events is evidence as physical constructions, even if there was no "Mind" To Observe them. The past physical event is only a Construction Of Mind when A Spiritual Being Recalls that past physical situation.

This is a proof of the separateness of The Spiritual Metastring From the physical metastring. Physical reality exists separately from Mind {Spirit}. Recollection of physical reality only exists as a function of Mind. This Understanding Is Fundamental To Any Complete Metaphysics {theory of Reality}.

Past Spiritual Situations Are Also Limited but not by time. The Spiritual Past Can Be Changed in the Spiritual Present But Only As Permitted By The Principles Of Operation Of The Active Individual Spirit. Please Refer To Our Discussion Of Forgiveness {5w}.]

[13z115] What Reality Is: [*GOD—The Dimensional Revelation*] Reveals That Reality Is The Manifestations Of GOD. The Manifestations Are physical or Spiritual or Otherwise According To the operational principles within the field of influence in which each Manifestation exists. Manifestations exist on a continuum. The term *now* or *the present* is a Construction of Mind to Express the current Situation by summarizing the features of a momentary cross section of reality, Identified By The Mind Of The Being Detailing The situation. Know that each Situation in physical reality, or fused physical-Spiritual Reality, is continually becoming the past on the physical continuum.

All That Is, The Sum Of All manifestations, Is Always Broader Than Any "Mind" Can Comprehend. The Current Situation, Identified By Your Human Mind, Is Called The Present, or Now, or That Which Is. Your Mind equals brain functions plus Spiritual Consciousness. Your Mind Identifies Reality As Separate Situations That You Perceive. These Perceptions Are Actually Not Separate But Are Part Of Continuous Flows Along The Fused physical and Spiritual Continuums. time forces the continuation of physical manifestations in physical reality. The

RESEARCH NOTES, CREDITS, AND EXPANSIONS

Spiritual Metastring Forces The Continuation Of Spiritual Being On The Spiritual Continuum. These Are Fused In The Manifestations Of Human Being In Our Universe. Stated with The Fullest Meaning, "I AM" Acknowledges The Present And Continual, Profound Experience Of Being An Eternal Soul. GOD Shares HIS Other Name, "I AM THAT I AM." *Exodus 3:14 KJV; Hebrew* אֶהְיֶה אֲשֶׁר אֶהְיֶה; variously translated, "I am who (I) am", "I will become what I choose to become", "I am what I am", "I will be what I will be", "I create what(ever) I create", or "I am the Existing One". *En.wikipedia.org*].

[13z116] What Reality May Become: [*GOD—The Dimensional Revelation* Reveals That what physical reality may become is limited by the operational principles of the physical membrane system, the physical 8th dimension. Events occurring in physical 7th dimension are the events possible within the closed system of our physical universe.

What Realities may become manifested is not determined. The 6th Dimension Provides For The Different Levels Of Uncertainty Along Each Continuum Of Being. Physical uncertainties, operational in physical quantum mechanics, are different than Spiritual Uncertainties Operational In Spiritual Becoming. When There Is A Fusion Of Spiritual Being Into physical reality, such as In A Human Being, Predicting The Future Is Not Possible With Certainty. The word *chaos* is properly applied because With This Fusion, There Are No Procedures or calculations That Will Reliably Predict What Reality Will Become.

To Observe The Processes Created and Their Becoming Is Very Pleasing To The LORD. This Includes The Manifestations That May Become As "Free Will" Is Exercised By Independent Differentiated Spiritual Beings.

It Is Even More Fulfilling For The LORD To Participate In The Consciousness Of Your Spiritual Being.]

[13z117] Whole Reality:

> When the light is made to move in a circle, all the energies of heaven and earth, of the light and the dark, are crystallized.
> (*The Secret of the Golden Flower*, trans. Richard Wilhelm [1929], translated into English by Cary F. Baynes [1962], chapter 3, 30)

[*GOD—The Dimensional Revelation* Reveals A Nearly Complete Metaphysics. Our Study Yields A Broader Understanding Of Nearly The Whole Reality. Yes, There Is Much That We cannot Understand. However, Human Consciousness Is Equipped To Observe and Participate In A Portion Of The Absolute Reality As Revealed In This Teaching.]

[13z118] Collective *We*:

> There is one body and one Spirit, just as you were called to one hope when you were called; one Lord, one faith, one baptism; one God and Father of all, who is over all and through all and in all. (*Holy Bible, Ephesians 4:4–6 NIV*)

[*GOD—The Dimensional Revelation* Reveals That Spiritual Being Will Be Most Glorious As All Beings Reunite Into ONE LORD.]

[13z119] Welcomed Back:

> Jesus answered him, "If anyone loves me, he will keep my word, and my Father will love him, and we will come to him and make our home with him." (*Holy Bible, John 14:23 KJV*)

[13z120] Merged With GOD: It's like a drop falling in the ocean. It doesn't exist as a drop anymore, and there is no drop left to recognize, "Oh! I have become the ocean" (*Daaji and Kamlesh D. Patel, April 2018, https://whydoweneedspirituality.blogspot.com/2018/05/how-to-merge-with-god.html*).

> The total spiritual power unfolds its traces and transforms itself into emptiness. Going out into being and going into nonbeing, one completes the miraculous Tao. All separate shapes appear as bodies, united with a true source… We forget one another, quiet and pure, altogether powerful and empty. **The emptiness is irradiated by the light** of the heart and of heaven. (*The Book of Consciousness and Life [The Hui Ming Ching] trans. Richard Wilhelm [1931], translated into English by Cary F. Baynes [Houghton Mifflin Harcourt Publishing Company, 1962] chapter 6, 8, 77; bold print added*)

RESEARCH NOTES, CREDITS, AND EXPANSIONS

Illustration of The CLEAR LIGHT Of The Void. Manifestations emerge.

Mik Ulyannikov/Shutterstock 44621095

[The ONE {11th}, Instructing Initial Information From The WORD {10th D} To Create (9th D). GOD's Fullness Is Infinite And Beyond Our View. Everything Appears As Nothing—Empty—Except For The CLEAR LIGHT Of The Void Out Of Which All Is Manifested As It May Please The LORD.]

> Brahman was this before; therefore it knew even the Ātma (soul, himself). I am Brahman, therefore it became all. And whoever among the gods had this enlightenment, also became That. It is the same with the sages, the same with men. Whoever knows the self as "I am Brahman," becomes all this universe. (*Brihadaranyaka Upanishad 1.4.10, approx. 700 BC*)

[13z121] Total Fulfillment:

> [Jesus Christ said,] "Do not think that I came to abolish the Law or the Prophets; I did not come to abolish but to fulfill. For truly I say to you, until heaven and earth pass away, not the smallest letter or stroke shall pass from the Law until all is accomplished." (*Holy Bible, Matthew 5:17–18 NIV*)

About the Author

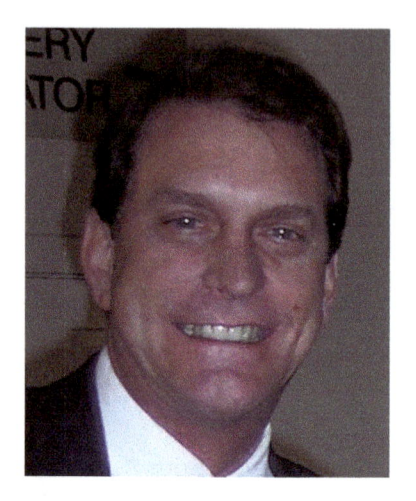

Allyn Richert is a husband, father, purveyor of fine furniture, philosopher, and theologian. Allyn's personal communications and writing share insight into the deepest questions of Life and Being